Global Problems and the Culture of Capitalism

Sixth Edition

Global Problems and the Culture of Capitalism

Richard H. Robbins

State University of New York at Plattsburgh

Boston   Columbus   Indianapolis   New York   San Francisco   Upper Saddle River
Amsterdam   Cape Town   Dubai   London   Madrid   Milan   Munich   Paris   Montréal   Toronto
Delhi   Mexico City   São Paulo   Sydney   Hong Kong   Seoul   Singapore   Taipei   Tokyo

Editor in Chief: Ashley Dodge
Publisher: Nancy Roberts
Editorial Assistant: Molly White
Director of Marketing: Brandy Dawson
Executive Marketing Manager: Kelly May
Marketing Coordinator: Jessica Warren
Managing Editor: Denise Forlow
Program Manager: Mayda Bosco
Production Project Manager: Liz Napolitano
Manager, Central Design: Jayne Conte
Cover Designer: Bruce Kenselaar

Cover Montage Images: top left: ©David Norton
Photography/Alamy; **top center:** ©Jules Glazier/Alamy;
top right: ©David W. Hamilton/Alamy; **center left:**
©dbimages/Alamy; **center right:** ©tony french/Alamy
Director, Digital Media: Brian Hyland
Digital Media Project Manager: Tina Gagliostro
Full-Service Project Management: Shiny Rajesh/Integra
Software Services Pvt. Ltd
Printer/Binder: Edwards Brothers / Malloy—Jackson Road
Cover Printer: Lehigh / Phoenix Color
Text Font: 10/12, Times

Credits and acknowledgments borrowed from other sources and reproduced, with permission, in this textbook appear on appropriate page within text.

Library of Congress Cataloging-in-Publication Data
Robbins, Richard H. (Richard Howard)
  Global problems and the culture of capitalism / Richard H. Robbins.—6th ed.
    p. cm.
  ISBN-13: 978-0-205-91765-5 (alk. paper)
  ISBN-10: 0-205-91765-8 (alk. paper)
  1. Economic history—1990–   2. Social problems.   3. Capitalism.   4. Consumption (Economics)
5. Poverty.   6. Financial crises.   I. Title.
HC59.15.R63 2014
330.12'2—dc22

                                                                    2010010395

10 9 8 7 6 5 4 3 2

ISBN 10:   0-205-91765-8
ISBN 13: 978-0-205-91765-5

BRIEF CONTENTS

CONTENTS

PREFACE

Over the past 400 to 600 years, a culture and society, originating for the most part in Europe and dedicated to the idea of trade and consumption as the ultimate source of well-being, began to expand to all parts of the globe. In many ways it is the most successful culture and society the world has ever seen, and its technology, wealth, and power stand as monuments to its success; however, accompanying its expansion have been problems—growing social and economic inequality, environmental destruction, mass starvation, and social unrest. Most members of this society and culture perceive these problems as distant from themselves or as challenges for them to meet. However, there is the possibility that these problems, which threaten to negate everything this culture has accomplished, are intrinsic to the culture itself. That is the possibility to be explored in this book.

The outline of this book emerged when, a few years ago, my colleagues at the State University of New York at Plattsburgh, James Armstrong and Mark Cohen, and I began developing a course on global problems. We wanted to create a course that would help students understand the major global issues that they confront in the mass media—problems such as the so-called population explosion, famine and hunger, global environmental destruction, the emergence and spread of new diseases, so-called ethnic conflict and genocides, terrorism, and social protest. We learned quickly that to make the course successful, we had to overcome the often-ethnocentric perspectives of the students, perspectives that were often reinforced by media coverage of global affairs. We needed also to compensate for the students' lack of backgrounds in anthropology, history, and economics, all crucial for understanding the roots of the problems we were to examine. Finally, we needed to illustrate that the problems we examined were relevant to them, that the problems would affect them either directly or indirectly, and that their actions now or in the future would determine the extent to which the origins of these problems could be acknowledged, let alone ever addressed. The form of this book emerged from our efforts at dealing with these pedagogical issues and the classroom interactions that these efforts stimulated.

THE FOCUS OF THIS BOOK

We can summarize our approach in this book as follows: There has emerged over the past five to six centuries a distinctive culture or way of life dominated by a belief in trade and commodity consumption as the source of well-being. This culture flowered in Western Europe, reached fruition in the United States, and spread to much of the rest of the world, creating what some anthropologists, sociologists, and historians call the world system. People disagree on the critical factors in the development of this system and even whether it was unique historically, although most agree on certain basic ideas. Among the most important are the assumptions that the driving force behind the spread of the contemporary world system was industrial and corporate capitalism, and that the spread of the world system is related in some way to the resulting division of the world into wealthy nations and poor nations or into wealthy core, developed, or industrialized areas and dependent peripheral, undeveloped, or nonindustrialized areas.

The spread of the capitalist world system has been accompanied by the creation of distinctive patterns of social relations, ways of viewing the world, methods of food production, distinctive diets, patterns of health and disease, relationships to the environment, and so on. However, the spread of this culture has not gone uncontested; there has been resistance in the form of direct and indirect actions—political, religious, and social protest and revolution. How and why capitalist culture developed and the reasons why some groups resisted and continue to resist its development are among the questions posed in this book.

The answers to these questions are based on specific assumptions. First, a central tenet of anthropology is that personal, social, cultural, and historical factors determine the point of view any person might have regarding a certain phenomenon. No less is true of those participating in the culture of capitalism who have created a view of global events that we share. Consequently, these views tend to be, to one extent or another, ethnocentric; that is, they describe, evaluate, and judge events solely from a specific cultural perspective. Among the major purposes of anthropology is to teach ways to avoid ethnocentrism and appreciate the importance of understanding the beliefs and behaviors of others from their perspectives rather than from our own, a view anthropologists refer to as *cultural relativism*. To some extent ethnocentrism is unavoidable, and the job of the person who interprets global events—whether a journalist, economist, sociologist, or anthropologist—is to make the event comprehensible to those people for whom that person is writing. Our assumption is that to minimize cultural bias we must recognize that our views of events are partially influenced by our culture and, for that reason, we must make our own culture an object of analysis.

Second, we assume that an understanding of global events requires us to recognize that no contemporary culture or society exists independent of what anthropologists refer to as the world system, and that each falls within either the core or the periphery of that system. Using this terminology to refer to different parts of the world permits us to avoid the more value-laden distinctions implicit in the use of terms such as *developed* or *undeveloped, modern* or *traditional*, and *First, Second*, or *Third World*. World system theorists often include a third category, semi-periphery, to denote those nation-states or regions that are moving toward the core or that have moved out of the core. These distinctions recognize that countries can move from one category to another. For example, the three nation-states that world system theorists consider to have been dominant in the past four centuries—the Netherlands, the United Kingdom, and the United States—all began as semiperipheral to the world system.

Third, we assume that global events and actions cannot be adequately understood without considering the events that preceded them; we must develop a historical perspective. For example, we live in a period of human history largely defined by a sequence of events that began some four to five hundred years ago, loosely termed the *Industrial Revolution*. Because each of us has lived during only a particular phase of that history, we tend to take it for granted that the world has always been as it is today. Yet the modern industrial world order is, in historical terms, a very recent event. We are deceived by our biology, by our limited life span, into thinking of sixty, seventy, or eighty years as a long time, but in the perspective of human history it is a fleeting moment. Human beings have for most of their existence lived as bands of gatherers and hunters, for a shorter time as agriculturists and farmers, and only recently as industrialists and wage laborers. Yet the Industrial Revolution has transformed the world and human societies as has no other event in history. We cannot understand the events, issues, and problems of today's world without understanding the how's and why's of the Industrial Revolution.

It will be clear that the emergence of capitalism represents a culture that is in many ways the most successful that has ever been developed in terms of accommodating large numbers of individuals in relative and absolute comfort and luxury. It has not been as successful, however, in integrating all in equal measure, and its failure here remains one of its major problems. It has solved the problems of feeding large numbers of people (although certainly not all), and it has provided unprecedented advances in health and medicine (but, again, not for all). It has promoted the development of amazingly complex technological instruments and fostered a level of global communication without precedent. It has united people in common pursuits as no other culture has. Yet it remains to be seen when the balance sheet is tallied whether capitalism represents the epitome of "progress" that some claim.

NEW TO THE SIXTH EDITION

Since the publication of the fifth edition of *Global Problems and the Culture of Capitalism*, we have experienced significant global upheaval as well as heightened concerns over global immigration, urbanization, climate change, and regional conflict, as well as levels of protest, all of which are addressed in this, the sixth, edition of the book. Specific changes include the following:

- Additional discussion of money as debt, the movement of money, and the consequences and the importance of perpetual growth.
- Material on advertising targeted to children and the scope of the practice.
- Coverage of immigration, its history, and its social, political, and economic impact.
- Coverage of urbanization and its impacts
- Discussion of climate change and its impact on the economy and society as a whole.
- Timely information on Occupy Wall Street and the philosophy and techniques of Direct Action.
- A new, comprehensive Chapter 13 discussing how to address many of the issues raised in the book.

Throughout this edition, I have tried to make the nature and origin of complex problems accessible to general readers and undergraduates without oversimplifying the gravity of the problems.

As always, I welcome comments and communications from readers and can be reached by email at richard.robbins@plattsburgh.edu. In addition, readers are encouraged to use the Web resources, including readings, online videos, and references created especially for the book, at http://www.plattsburgh.edu/legacy.

This text is available in a variety of formats—digital and print. To learn more about our programs, pricing options, and customization, visit www.pearsonhighered.com.

ACKNOWLEDGMENTS

Many people have contributed to the writing of this book. I have already mentioned my colleagues James Armstrong and Mark Cohen. Others include Alfred Robbins, Michael Robbins, Rachel Dowty, Tom Moran, Philip Devita, Gloria Bobbie, Douglas Skopp, Edward Champagne, Vincent Carey, Larry Soroka, Ellen Fitzpatrick, Ann Kimmage, Michael Miranda, John Hess, Jan Rinaldi, Tina Charland, Tim Harnett, Daphne Kutzer, Monica van Beusekom, Russell Kleinbach, Peggy Lindsey, Dan and Mary Abel, Amy Weisz Predmore, Mark White, Barbara Harris, Art Orme, Sam Baldwin, and Mary Turner, along with the many students who helped me better articulate important issues. I also thank members of the email list H-World, particularly its moderator Patrick Manning; Richard Winkel, moderator of the email list Activ-L (aml@webmap.missouri.edu), and its many contributors; and many of the students who used one or another version of this book and who provided invaluable feedback. I would also like to thank the book's reviewers.

Reviewers of the first edition were John L. Aguilar, Charles O. Ellenbaum, Cynthia Mahmood, Richard Moore, Jon Olson, and Dave Winther. Reviewers of the second edition were Elliot Fratkin, Smith College; James Loucky, Western Washington University; Luis A. Vivanco, University of Vermont; and Vaughn Bryant, Texas A&M University. Reviewers of the third edition were Eric Mielants, Fairfield University; William Leggett, Middle Tennessee; Nancy McDowell, Beloit College; and Benjamin Brewer, James Madison University. Reviewers of the fifth edition were George Esber, Miami University, Middletown; Suzanne Scheld, California State University, Northridge; James Sewastynowicz, Jacksonville State University; and Miguel Vasquez, Northern Arizona University.

I owe a special debt of gratitude to Sylvia Shephard for her initial support of the project; to Sarah Kelbaugh, Dave Repetto, Nancy Roberts, and Barbara Reiley of Pearson and Jennifer Jacobson and Dan Vest of Ohlinger Publishing Services for guiding the project through to its present edition; as well as to Shiny Rajesh, who managed the latest edition, and Sayed Zakaullah, whose copyediting will make reading the book far easier than it would have been otherwise. And special thanks go to Amy, Rebecca, and Zoey, who tolerated with unusual understanding my periods of self-imposed isolation. Needless to say, the final form of the book, for better or worse, is the result of my own decisions.

PART ONE

Introduction: The Consumer, the Laborer, the Capitalist, and the Nation-State in the Society of Perpetual Growth

[W]hat difference it would make to our understanding if we looked at the world as a whole, a totality, a system, instead of as a sum of self-contained societies and cultures; if we understood better how this totality developed over time; if we took seriously the admonition to think of human aggregates as "inextricably involved with other aggregates, near and far, in weblike, netlike, connections."

—ERIC WOLF, *Europe and the People without History*

On or about December 1910, wrote novelist Virginia Woolf, human character changed.[1] On his repeated visits to the United States, Frenchman André Siegfried (1928; see also Leach 1993:266) noted much the same thing: "A new society has come to life in America," he said. "It was not clear in 1901 or 1904; it was noticeable in 1914, and patent in 1919 and 1925." Samuel Strauss (1924, 1927; see also Leach 1993:266), a journalist and philosopher writing in the 1920s, suggested the term *consumptionism* to characterize this new way of life that, he said, created a person with

> a philosophy of life that committed human beings to the production of more and more things—"more this year than last year, more next year than this"— and that emphasized the "standard of living" above all other values.

It is obvious, he continued,

> that Americans have come to consider their standard of living as a somewhat sacred acquisition, which they will defend at any price. This means that they would be ready to make many an intellectual or even moral concession in order to maintain that standard.

---

[1] The quote, which has been widely used (see, e.g., Fjellman 1992:5; Lears 1983), appeared in an essay, "Mr. Bennett and Mrs. Brown," in *The Captain's Death Bed and Other Essays,* but was originally part of a paper Woolf read to the Heretics, Cambridge, on May 18, 1924. "On or about December 1910 human character changed...The change was not sudden and definite...But a change there was nevertheless, and since one must be arbitrary, let us date it about the year 1910" (Woolf 1950).

There is no question that in America, the half-century from 1880 to 1930 marked a major transition in the rate and level of commodity consumption—the purchase, use, and waste of what comedian George Carlin called "stuff." Food production grew by almost 40 percent from 1899 to 1905; the production of men's and women's ready-made clothing, along with the production of costume jewelry, doubled between 1890 and 1900; and glassware and lamp production went from 84,000 tons in 1890 to 250,563 tons in 1914. In 1890, 32,000 pianos were sold in the United States; by 1904, the number sold increased to 374,000 (Leach 1993:16).

During this period, the perfume industry became the country's tenth largest; at one department store, sale of toiletries rose from $84,000 to $522,000 between 1914 and 1926. The manufacture of clocks and watches went from 34 million to 82 million in ten years. By the late 1920s, one of every six Americans owned an automobile.

Of course, these figures are dwarfed by what Americans and others around the world consume today. World and national consumption expanded at an unprecedented pace during the twentieth century, with household consumption expenditures reaching $37 trillion in 2010, three times the level of 1975 and six times that of 1950. In 1900, real consumption expenditure was barely $1.5 trillion (United Nations Development Programme 1997). Today there are as many cars in the United States as the number of people with drivers' licenses, and the rest of the world is doing everything that it can to catch up. China and India, alone, have added at least half-a-billion middle-class consumers in the new century demanding everything that consumers in the West desire.

However, although consumption rates were not nearly as high as they are today, the early twentieth century is notable because it marked the early phase of what Ernest Gellner (1983:24) called *the society of perpetual growth* and the creation of a new type of culture: consumer capitalism.

The emergence of the society of perpetual growth and the culture of capitalism marked a new stage in an ongoing global historical process that began (to the extent that it can be said to have a beginning) anytime from the fifteenth to the early nineteenth centuries. The creation of the human type that characterizes this stage, *the consumer,* followed soon after the emergence of two other historically unique categories of human types: *the capitalist* and *the laborer.* Merchants had existed, of course, for thousands of years, and people had always labored to produce goods and liked to consume what they'd produced. But never before in history has there existed a society founded on three categories of people: the capitalist, whose sole purpose is to invest money to earn more; the laborer, whose sole means of support comes from the sale of his or her labor; and the consumer, whose sole purpose is to purchase and consume ever-increasing quantities of goods and services.

At some point in their lives, virtually everyone plays the roles of consumer, laborer, or capitalist: as consumers, they buy goods and services; as laborers, they work for wages; and as capitalists, they invest money in banks, insurance policies, pension plans, stocks (slightly more than half of American families participate in the stock market, either directly or through investment accounts), education, or other enterprises from which they expect to profit. What ties together these roles, and indeed the entire culture, is money.

Thus, we can perhaps best conceptualize the working of the culture of capitalism as sets of relations between capitalists, laborers, and consumers, tied together by the pursuit of money, each depending on the other, yet each placing demands on, and often conflicting with, the others. Regulating these relationships is the fourth element in our scheme, the nation-state. In this cultural scheme, the *nation-state* serves as, among its other functions, a mediator, controlling the creation and flow of money and setting and enforcing the rules of interaction. (Figure I.1 is a highly simplified model, but it serves to underline the key features and unique style of the culture of capitalism.)

FIGURE I.1

Patterns of Relations in the Culture of Capitalism

However, money is, obviously, the key to understanding this culture. Jacob Needleman (1991:40–41) wrote that, in another time and place, not everyone has wanted money above all else. People, he said,

> have desired salvation, beauty, power, strength, pleasure, prosperity, explanations, food, adventure, conquest, comfort. But now and here, money—not necessarily even the things money can buy, but money—is what everyone wants…. Therefore, if one wished to understand life, one must understand money in this present phase of history and civilization.

People require money as a means of exchange and, for the modern capitalist system to function, money must constantly increase in supply—that is, it must perpetually grow. Why this is so is not immediately apparent, even to many economists, but should the money supply fail to expand, the whole system could collapse in economic, political, and social ruin. Thus, virtually all of the issues discussed in this book relate in one way or the other to money and people's efforts to acquire it or compensate for the lack of it.

Part I of the book describes the emergence of the consumer, the capitalist, the laborer, and the nation-state and outlines how each must function for our society to work. In Part II, we examine what economists call *market externalities*—that is, some of the mostly unintended consequences that follow from the interaction between the consumer, the laborer, the capitalist, and the nation-state. Finally, in Part III we explore the range of resistance to these externalities.

But first, given its central role in the working of the entire society, let's begin with a brief primer on the nature of money and an exploration of how money has assumed its importance and how it determines how we live our lives.

A PRIMER ON MONEY: THE PHILOSOPHER'S STONE

Commonly we consider money simply as a standardized means of exchange—that is, as a substance with which the value of goods and services can be compared and traded, a tool, so to speak. But to view money only in that way is to misunderstand its true importance. To better explain, think, instead, of the philosopher's stone. Magicians or alchemists sought the philosopher's stone because it was thought to have the magical power to transmute base metals into gold, which implies taking something that was considered worthless and converting it into something of value. Money is the modern-day equivalent of the philosopher's stone.

To appreciate the magic of money, the most important thing to consider is that *the prime directive of the culture of capitalism is that it must maintain economic growth.* People must buy, produce, invest, and profit more this year than the last and more next year than this in perpetuity. Failure to maintain growth would threaten the economic, social, and political foundations and stability of our entire society. People would be unable to repay debts, banks would fail, millions would lose their jobs, and millions of businesses would go bankrupt, to name only a few of the obvious consequences. Aside from a few notable periods of economic contraction, such as the periodic depressions

Alchemists believed that the philosopher's stone could convert something worthless into something of value, namely, worthless metal into gold. By adopting paper money as a medium of exchange, the culture of capitalism has invented a new philosopher's stone—one every bit as powerful as that sought by magicians of another time. (Mary Evans Picture Library/ Alamy.)

TABLE I.1   Level and Rate of Growth of GDP per Capita: World and Major Regions, A.D. 1–1998

Region	1	1000	1820	1998	1–1000	1000–1820	1820–1998
	\ Level of Growth (1990 International Dollars)				Annual Average Compound Growth Rate		
Western Europe	450	400	1,232	17,921	−0.01	0.14	1.51
Western Offshoots (e.g., United States, Australia)	400	400	1,201	26,146	0.00	0.13	1.75
Japan	400	425	669	20,413	0.01	0.06	1.93
Latin America	400	400	665	5,795	0.00	0.06	1.22
Eastern Europe and Former USSR	400	400	667	4,354	0.00	0.06	1.06
Asia (excluding Japan)	450	450	575	2,936	0.00	0.03	0.92
Africa	425	416	418	1,368	−0.00	0.00	0.67
World	444	435	667	5,709	−0.00	0.03	0.95

Source: Adapted from Maddison (2003:28)

of the nineteenth century, the great worldwide depression of the 1930s, the recession of the early 1980s, the Asian financial collapse of 1997, and the economic crisis of 2007–2008, the economy has grown reasonably well worldwide, although some parts of the world have historically done a better job than others.

Economic growth is traditionally measured by the growth of gross domestic product (GDP)—a measure of the money value of all goods and services produced and sold in a given time period. Table I.1 and Figure I.2 portray the yearly growth of global GDP during the past two millennia.

Over the long term, but particularly over the past two centuries, the growth of GDP in the global economy, especially among European offshoots (e.g., the United States and Australia)

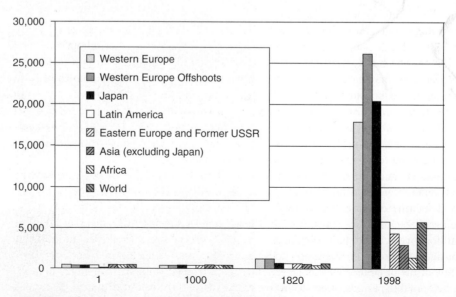

FIGURE I.2   Rate of per Capita GDP Growth by Region from A.D. 1 to 1998

TABLE I.2   **Required Growth in Income and Spending over a Twenty-Five-Year Period**

Year	Required Income Growth 3 Percent (with 0% inflation)		Required Income Growth at 6 Percent (with 0% inflation) or Income Growth at 3 Percent and Inflation at 3 Percent	
	Individual	**Corporate**	**Individual**	**Corporate**
2010	$30,000	$300,000,000	$ 30,000	$ 300,000,000
2015	34,855	348,550,000	40,494	404,940,000
2020	40,495	404,950,000	54,661	546,661,000
2025	47,048	470,048,000	73,783	737,830,000
2035	63,507	635,070,000	134,434	1,344,340,000

and Japan, has been spectacular: a 300-fold increase in the amount of goods consumed, the number of goods produced, and the fortunes that have been made. A global citizen of today is almost nine times as wealthy as his or her counterpart some 200 years ago; in some parts of the world, the average citizen has increased his or her wealth almost 25 times over the same period.

To put perpetual growth into perspective, imagine that in the year 2010 you earned and spent $30,000 a year (or that some corporation earned $300,000,000). A growth rate of about 3 percent a year is necessary to maintain a healthy economy. Consequently, by 2015, you (or the corporation in this case) must earn and spend $34,855 (or $348,550,000) and by 2035, earn and spend $63,507 (or $635,070,000). If we factor in an inflation rate of 3 percent on top of our necessary growth rate, the figures are even higher (see Table I.2).

These increases, of course, could occur only with a steady increase in the money supply. Without the increase, people would not have the means to buy more, employers would not have the means to pay more, and capitalists would not be able to profit more. *But how does the money supply increase? Where does money come from and what or who provides its magical power?*

The Development of Commodity Money

The use of objects as a medium of exchange is likely as old as trade. Thus the use of shells, furs, and other items of value as money are known in small-scale societies throughout the world (see Graeber 2011). The use of precious metals as a medium of exchange can be traced back 5,000 years to Mesopotamia and coins to the seventh century B.C. These are examples of *commodity money*. Commodity money is money that has some value in itself beyond its exchange value. Thus, precious metals used for making coins can be used for making jewelry or other objects of art. Generally, the value of the coins is equal to the value of the metals used. As such, the use of coins for trade involves the exchange of one thing of value (e.g., a shirt) for another thing of equivalent value (e.g., an equal amount of gold).

But coins had a big disadvantage: They were difficult to store and to transport. Furthermore, it was not uncommon for people to melt the coins and use them for some other purpose, thus preventing them from circulation. This is where the first bit of magic comes in; people began to substitute paper for coins. "Exchange" or "demand" notes—paper certificates that could be exchanged for a valuable commodity, generally gold or silver—were first used in China in the twelfth century and became common in Europe in the fourteenth and fifteenth centuries (Williams 1997). Thus, a trader in Milan might buy textiles from someone in Bruges and pay with a paper note backed by gold that the seller could retrieve from a third party. Generally, banks or governments issued exchange notes or paper money, but virtually anyone could do it.

Theoretically, these notes represented a specific amount of some valuable metal—usually gold or silver—that could be retrieved on demand by the holder of the note.

The issuing of paper money was a huge step in helping to accelerate economic growth because there was potentially no limit to the amount of money that could be created. This was the first step in money magic: Paper, which was essentially worthless, now had the same value as gold, silver, or other precious metals. In a wonderful book, *Money and Magic: A Critique of the Modern Economy in the Light of Goethe's Faust,* economist Hans Binswanger (1994) describes how Johann Wolfgang von Goethe, who served as finance minister at the Weimar court, used his classic work *Faust* (published in two parts in 1808 and 1832) for a commentary on the industrial economy, and, more specifically, on the nature of money. The original Faust, on whom the story is based, was a magician, an alchemist. In Goethe's book, Faust makes a bargain with Mephistopheles—a devil—and together they create a new society based on paper money. Binswanger suggests the alchemist's attempts to convert lead into gold were abandoned

> not because they were futile, but because alchemy in another form has proved so successful that the arduous production of gold in the laboratory is no longer necessary. It is not vital to alchemy's aim, in the sense of increasing wealth, that lead actually be transmuted into gold. It will suffice if a substance of no value is transformed into one of value: paper, for example, into money. (Binswanger 1994:9)

There was, however, a big loophole with commodity money. Banks or other entities that issued money were under no legal obligation to have on hand an amount of gold or silver equivalent to the deposits they held or the amount of paper money they issued. Banks practiced what is called *fractional reserve banking*; this means simply that they had to keep on hand only a fraction of the money or gold deposited assuming that not everyone would demand their gold deposits at the same time. They settled on about a 1:10 ratio; that is, for every dollar deposited, they could lend out ten paper dollars, even though they did not have on hand the gold on which the money was based. This gave to banks, and other private financial institutions, the power to literally create money out of thin air. On the one hand, banks profited from the interest on the

The issuing of paper money was a huge step in helping to accelerate economic growth.
(Rafael Ben-Ari/Fotolia.)

loans, and people had more money to spend. On the other hand, problems occurred when, after an economic boom, the economy slowed down and depositors demanded their gold. Unable to pay all their depositors because they had issued notes in excess of the amount of gold they had on hand, banks failed and people lost their savings.

In 1913, the U.S. government tried to address some of these problems by creating the Federal Reserve Bank to control and stabilize the money supply. The Federal Reserve Bank, a private corporation, creates money by lending it to the federal government. The debt assumed by the government becomes an asset (i.e., money owed to the Federal Reserve) that the Federal Reserve then distributes to member banks who, following the fractional reserve requirement, can lend it out or invest it at a 10:1 ratio to earn interest and/or dividends. Money simply represents debt. It is lent into existence (see Brown 2010; Hallsmith and Lietaer 2012). Paper money was still tied to gold, and a person could retrieve paper for gold, but the Federal Reserve could ensure that banks had enough money on hand, or could quickly acquire it, to honor withdrawals. In that way, banks could honor requests for gold but be able to create new money by making loans. But the Federal Reserve could still not address the limitations imposed on economic growth by tying money to a fixed commodity. Solving that problem required another bit of magic in the form of another government decree.

The Shift from Commodity to Fiat or Debt Money

The next stage in the evolution of money occurred in 1931 when the United States stopped allowing people in the country to convert paper money into gold. The value of money was still tied to the value of gold, and exchanges with foreign governments still occurred in gold. Then in 1971, the U.S. government declared that its currency would no longer be backed by gold, or anything else for that matter. This marked the final shift from commodity to fiat or debt money— paper that was used as evidence of a claim to economic value but that, legally, was not redeemable for anything.

As might be expected, with dollars backed by nothing, the money supply could rapidly grow, and theoretically could then match or exceed the growth or potential growth of the economy. More importantly, the Federal Reserve in the United States (which serves as the U.S. central bank) and central banks in other countries could develop ways to control the money supply, ensuring that it grew fast enough to keep up with economic growth but not so fast that inflation resulted. Inflation would occur when the amount of money exceeded the value of goods and services that people demanded, thus driving up the prices as buyers competed for scarce resources. If, however, the supply of goods and services exceeded the money supply, prices would decline as sellers competed for limited dollars, which would lead to deflation. Thus, balancing the amount of money in circulation with the goods and services that could be purchased was a major challenge for central banks, such as the U.S. Federal Reserve.

When we think of money, we think of bills and coins. But that is only a small part (5 percent to 10 percent) of the money supply. The rest exists only as figures on paper (or in computers) in banks and in the records of other financial institutions. Debt money, for example, simply represents a promise by the borrower of money to repay it at some future date.

Table I.3 and Figure I.3 show the kinds of money, or money stocks, in circulation in the United States along with their growth since 1959.

In sum, the money supply in 2007 was more than forty-six times larger than it was in 1959. You can perhaps begin to see why money represents a magical process. Because fiat or debt money is backed by nothing other than the legal power of the nation-state, but can be converted into all kinds of goods and services, we have further succeeded in the alchemist's goal of taking something that is essentially worthless (paper) and turning it into objects of value (whatever we can obtain with this paper).

But, as Faust learned in his bargain with the devil, there is often a price to pay for access to the philosopher's stone.

TABLE I.3   Increase in U.S. Money Supply from 1959 to 2009 (in billions)

Years	Currency	M1	M2	M3	Non-M2 M3	Percentage of Change in M3
1959–1970	416.1	1,959.1	5,074.2	5,256.1	202.0	—
1971–1980	731.6	2,910.3	10,252.8	11,905.2	1,652.6	127
1981–1990	1,661.3	6,102.2	24,088.3	31,002.9	6,916.4	160
1991–2000	3,681.8	10,550.1	37,696.1	49,151.9	11,428.7	59
2001–2009	6,175.0	11,896	58,268.5	140,701.3[1]	31,993.3[2]	186

M1 = Currency, traveler's checks, demand deposits, and other checkable deposits

M2 = M1, retail MMMFs, savings, and small-time deposits

M3 = M1, M2, large time deposits, RPS, Eurodollars and institutional money funds, available at http://www.federalreserve.gov/releases/h6/hist/h6histb.txt

[1] The Federal Reserve stopped publishing M3 data in 2006. The data from 2006 to 2009 is estimated with information available at http://www.shadowstats.com/alternate_data

[2] This includes estimated data from 2006 to 2009.

The Consequences of a System of Debt Money

The key thing to remember about debt money is that every dollar that is created is someone's debt. Money is lent into existence. Consequently every dollar, euro, or pound must earn interest. The interest it earns goes to the bank and the people who buy the debt. This is not the only way to create money; money can be distributed, or given as a reward for some action. Think about airline miles; when people travel they get bonus miles that they can use to purchase airline tickets, or a host of other things such as gas gift certificates. Lending money into existence has advantages—theoretically only people who are capable of paying it back will get it; and, lending money with a requirement that it be repaid with interest disciplines people to work. However, debt money also concentrates wealth in the hands of a few, and, perhaps most importantly, it also exerts constant pressure for economic growth at any cost in order to maintain the interest payments on the money lent. Put another way, the money supply can grow, and continue to do so only if there is a corresponding amount of economic activity. That is, when money is lent into existence it must earn itself and the interest. But, how does the money continue to grow?

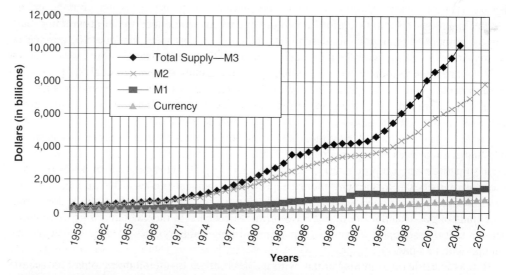

FIGURE I.3   U.S. Money Supply by Type, 1959 to 2008

To answer this question economist Barbara Garson deposited $50,000 (a publisher's advance on the book she was writing) in a small rural bank, the Bank of Millbrook, New York, and asked them to help her trace what happened to her money. The bank couldn't just hold it, because they had to pay interest on the deposit. The money had to keep moving and growing. So while giving Garson 2½ percent interest, they immediately sold it to Chase Bank at 4½ percent; but Chase, of course, had to move it out at a still higher rate. As Garson said,

> I thought of my money as the raw material that banks need and want in order to make more money. But I was beginning to sense, however fuzzily, that it could also be a hot potato that Millbrook passed to Chase and Chase had to pass quickly to the next guy. *Whoever held it, even for a second, had to pay interest. Which means he had to be able to collect interest. If he couldn't, he got burned.* (Garson 2001:39–40 emphasis added)

Thus Chase lent money to a Brooklyn fish company, among others, which, Garson discovered, got much of its fish from East Asia, and to an oil company in Malaysia that was building a new refinery. Marveling at the power of money to mobilize people and resources, Garson traveled to Malaysia to see how her money was at work and discovered that thousands of people were getting jobs directly and indirectly through the money invested in the refinery. She also spoke to the fishermen in the area, some of whose catch may have been going to the Brooklyn fish market and discovered that the oil refinery polluted coastal waters and forced the fishermen to go farther out to sea for their catch. They talked to Garson about the good old days and the catches they used to bring home and the amount of work they have to do today to succeed.

"Some fisherman are lazy," one of the fishermen commented, "If they caught a lot today, they don't go out tomorrow. But I think differently. If we catch a lot today we go out tomorrow, catch more."

But another man, says Garson, politely disagreed. "You're free to do what you want. You can go out three day a week or twenty days a month. *You stop when you have enough.*"

While she says that she didn't realize it at the time, she later thought it was the most subversive thing she heard in all her travels: "The one thing my money could not do," she says, "was stop"(Garson 2001:105–106).

Thus for economic system to work, the money that is lent into existence must keep working, in perpetuity, to earn more. But, as Garson found out, it continues to grow only at a cost, in this case to coastal environments. And this highlights another problem with debt money—the limit on things into which money can be converted. Although the money supply might be unlimited, the goods and services that people can buy with their money are not. But if economic growth (and the supply of money) must increase every year (and must increase at a rate of at least 3 percent to maintain a healthy economy), then so must the things that money can buy. When money was tied to and limited by a commodity such as gold, the money supply was constantly trying to keep up with the goods and services available. However, once money was uncoupled from anything of value and could infinitely grow, the situation was reversed and goods and services began to chase the money supply. Thus, where we used to have a situation where we needed more and more gold to grow, now we simply need more and more stuff. In other words, *the money supply must grow if the economy is to remain healthy, and for the money supply to grow, there must be a steady increase in the goods or services that money can buy.* It is from this simple fact that many of the problems we discuss in this book derive.

Consequently, for the economy to grow, there must be a constant conversion of things that have no monetary value into things that do—that is, there must be constant commodification, because money can only grow through a process whereby nonmonetary wealth, goods, or values are converted into things of monetary worth (see, e.g., Bourdieu 1986:243). In this conversion process lies the genius of capitalism. In it also lies the secret of our Faustian bargain. Through the operation of a myriad of rules, regulations, values, and laws, the culture of capitalism encourages

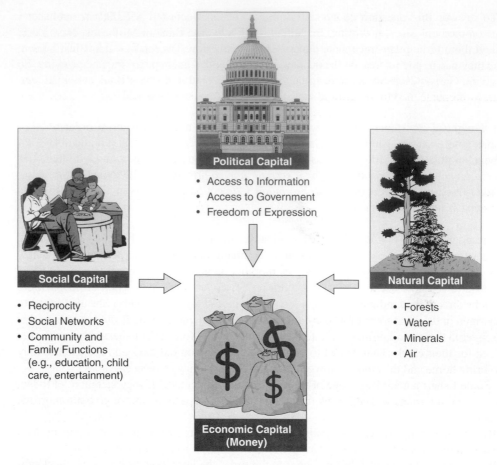

FIGURE I.4   The Conversion of Natural, Political, and Social Capital into Money

the conversion of items and activities that have no intrinsic monetary worth—but that are nevertheless valuable and even necessary in other ways—into items and activities that can be bought and sold in the marketplace. Thus, trees, lakes, and mountains must be converted into things that can be sold in the marketplace; activities once associated with family life and given freely, such as child care, food preparation, and education, must be converted into monetary activities; and freedom itself can be exchanged for money as powerful corporations use their money to gain political access and power (see Figure I.4).

We discuss this process of capital conversion in more detail in Chapter 13, but for now it is sufficient to appreciate why this conversion is necessary to fulfill the prime directive of perpetual economic growth.

In sum, then, our culture works largely on a magical principle in which money, an item of no intrinsic value, perpetually increases in quantity by being lent into existence while we work to convert more and more nonmonetary capital into goods and services that this money can buy. Of course, this is a simplification of everything that must be done to keep the system working. In the next four chapters, we describe how the consumer, the laborer, the capitalist, and the nation-state operate to maintain this magic act. In Part II we'll examine what economists term *the externalities of the working of the market*, such as the environmental damage witnessed by Barbara Garson, and in Part III we'll explore the ways that groups of people have found to resist the sometimes-negative consequences on their lives from these externalities. The final chapter will propose some of the actions that are necessary to remedy the problems we will explore.

This book does suggest that what we term *capitalism* has been distorted by a financial system that requires perpetual growth, and that this growth is unsustainable. Not everyone agrees; some, including most mainstream economists, argue that sustained economic growth can solve many of the problems that we'll be examining. Consequently much of this book is designed to explain how we got where we are and weigh the evidence of whether the harms done by a commitment to perpetual economic growth are greater or lesser than the good. For example, there seems to be a split globally of how to respond to the economic collapse of 2007–2008 and the debt problems faced by many countries. On the one side are those who want to cut government spending, and on the other those who look to government to compensate for the decline in consumption. There is also a split between those who think that government debt is the major problem, and others who feel that growing economic inequality is the major issue. One thing this book will attempt to do is put those sentiments in perspective and show how each side has a point; nevertheless, the problems stem from the distortions that have arisen in our economy.

Constructing the Consumer

The consumer revolution is a strange chapter in the ethnographic history of the species. For what may have been the first time in its history, a human community willingly harbored a nonreligious agent of social change, and permitted it to transform on a continual and systematic basis virtually every feature of social life.

—GRANT MCCRACKEN, *Culture and Consumption*

The … metamessage of our time is that the commodity form is natural and inescapable. Our lives can only be well lived (or lived at all) through the purchase of particular commodities. Thus our major existential interest consists of maneuvering for eligibility to buy such commodities in the market. Further, we have been taught that it is right and just—ordained by history, human nature, and God—that the means of life in all its forms be available only as commodities.… Americans live in an overcommodified world, with needs that are generated in the interests of the market and that can be met only through the market.

—STEPHEN FJELLMAN, *Vinyl Leaves*

The culture of capitalism is devoted to encouraging the production and sale of commodities. For capitalists, the culture encourages the accumulation of profit; for laborers, it encourages the accumulation of wages; and for consumers, it encourages the accumulation of goods. In other words, capitalism defines sets of people who, behaving according to a set of learned rules, act as they must act.

There is nothing natural about this behavior. People are not naturally driven to accumulate wealth. There are societies in which such accumulation is discouraged. Human beings do not have an innate drive to accumulate commodities; again, there are plenty of societies in which such accumulation is discouraged. People are not driven to work; in fact, contrary to popular notions, members of capitalist culture work far more than, say, people who live by gathering and hunting (see, e.g., Schor 1999). *How does* culture, *as anthropologists use the term, encourage people to behave in some ways and not in others? Specifically, how does the culture of capitalism encourage the accumulation of profit, wages, and commodities? How does it, in effect, encourage perpetual growth and what amounts to perpetual change?*

It is not easy to describe the effects of culture on people's lives; anthropologists have noted that culture consists of all learned beliefs and behaviors, the rules by which we order our lives, and the meanings that human beings construct to interpret their universes and their places in them. Yet, using these abstract descriptions, it is difficult to understand how pervasive our culture can be in determining our view of the world. It may help, therefore, to provide a metaphor for culture in the form of a practice of another culture: the sandpaintings of the Navajo of the American Southwest.

Among the Navajo people there is a healing practice in which a curer, using colored sand, cornmeal, or other bits of material, draws on the ground a miniature representation of the universe. Although there are perhaps a thousand versions of these drawings, each contains vital elements of what, for the Navajo, define the general conditions of existence. Navajo conceptions of space are indicated by symbols of the world's directions and that of social life by the distribution of Navajo houses (*hogans*) and mythic beings; values are represented in the stories and chants associated with each sandpainting. Material items critical to Navajo existence (e.g., horses or ritual items) are also portrayed. Once the work is completed, the patient sits on or in the sandpainting, and a curing ceremony, accompanied by chanting and prayer, proceeds. Illness, the Navajo claim, is the result of persons' losing their proper place in the world; the aim of the ceremony is to restore the patient to that place. When the ceremony is completed and harmony restored, the sandpainter destroys the painting.

Navajo sandpaintings serve as therapeutic stages on which a person's place in the universe is defined and ritually enacted.
(Chuck Place/Alamy.)

Navajo sandpainting contains all the elements of what anthropologists often mean by the term *culture*. Like the sandpainting, a culture serves to define the universe as it is supposed to exist for a people. The sandpainting contains the key elements and symbols that people use to locate themselves in physical and social space. It affirms the place of the person in the created world and the values that govern people's lives. Like the sandpainting, particular cultural representations serve as therapeutic frames that communicate to us who and what we are and how we figure in the larger order of things. These representations are therapeutic because they help people resolve the contradictions and ambiguities that are inherent in any cultural definition of reality and self.

Furthermore, every society has its sandpainters, those individuals who are given or who take responsibility for representing the universe to others and who have the power to define those elements that are essential for others in locating and defining their identities. In some societies, as among the Navajo, it is the curer, shaman, mythmaker, or storyteller; in others, it is the priest, poet, writer, artist, singer, or dancer. In capitalism, the sandpainter works in churches, synagogues, or mosques; in theaters; through television sets; at sporting events; or in the shopping malls that reaffirm the vision of abundance central to the consumers' view of the world. Contemporary sandpainters, who include marketing specialists, advertisers, government agents, corporate public relations specialists, entertainers, and journalists, create a vision of the world designed to maximize the production and consumption of goods. They have helped to create a culture in which the prime elements are commodities and in which the consumer's first duty is to buy (or "Shop till you drop," as a popular bumper sticker advises). It is a culture in which virtually all our everyday activities—work, leisure, the fulfillment of social responsibilities, and so on—take place in the context of commodities, and in which shopping, like the sandpainting cure, serves as a therapeutic activity. These contemporary sandpainters construct for us a culture in which at one time or another every individual assumes the identity of consumer. The question we need to explore first is, *How was the universe of the consumer and the consumer her- or himself created?*

REMAKING CONSUMPTION

The consumer did not, of course, appear full blown in the early twentieth-century United States. Mass consumption of certain goods—notably addictive substances such as tobacco, opium, rum, gin, coffee, and tea—arguably fueled the Industrial Revolution and even Europe's colonial domination of Asia, Latin America, and Africa. This consumption also defined the methods by which later commodities were produced, distributed, and consumed (see, e.g., Trocki 1999). But, since these items were physically addictive and required little marketing, merchants generally paid little attention to how these and other goods were marketed or displayed, assuming that when people needed their products, they would buy them. It was this attitude in the United States of a century ago that was to undergo a profound change.

The change did not occur naturally. In fact, the culture of nineteenth-century America emphasized moderation and self-denial, not unlimited consumption. People, workers in particular, were expected to be frugal and save their money; spending, particularly on luxuries, was seen as "wasteful." People purchased only necessities—basic foodstuffs, clothing, household utensils, and appliances—or shared basic items when they could. If we look at a typical inventory of the possessions of an American family of 1870–1880, we find a pattern very different from that of today. In 1870, 53 percent of the population lived and worked on farms and produced much of what they consumed. One Vermont farmwife recorded making 421 pies, 152 cakes, 2,140 doughnuts, and 1,038 loaves of bread in one year (Sutherland 1989:71). Household items were relatively simple—a dinner table, wooden chairs, beds, and perhaps a carpet or rug. There were a few appliances to aid housework—cookstoves, eggbeaters, apple parers, pea shellers, and coffee mills—but most other housework required muscle; even hand-cranked washing machines were not available until the late 1870s. Although most people, except the poorest or most isolated families, did buy some ready-made clothing, most of the items people wore were made at home and were largely functional. Furthermore, because the vast majority of American families lived on farms, most of the family capital was invested in farming tools and implements. There were, of course, exceptions. The wealthy members of society competed with each other in the ostentatious display of wealth and luxury, as they had for centuries. But they represented a small percentage of the population.

Of course, Americans did not yet have electricity, the automobile had yet to be invented, and the money supply was far more limited than it is today. Nevertheless, to transform buying habits, luxuries had to be transformed into necessities. In America, this was accomplished largely in four ways: a revolution in marketing and advertising, a restructuring of major societal institutions, a revolution in spiritual and intellectual values, and a reconfiguration of space and class.

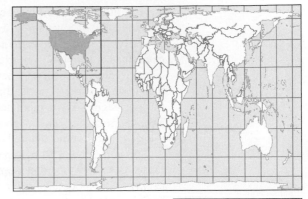

The United States

Marketing and Advertising

First, there was a major transformation of the meaning of goods and how they were presented and displayed. For most of the eighteenth and nineteenth centuries, retailers paid little attention to how goods were displayed. The first department store—Bon Marché—opened in Paris in 1852, allowing people to wander through the store with no expectations that they make a purchase. Enterprises such as Bon Marché were devoted to "the arousal of free-floating desire," as Rosalind Williams put it (McCracken 1988:25). The display of commodities helped define bourgeois culture, converting the culture, values, attitudes, tastes, and aspirations of the bourgeoisie into goods, thus shaping and transforming them (Miller 1994).

But Bon Marché was an exception. In stores in the United States, most products were displayed in bulk, and little care was taken to arrange them in any special way. Prepackaged items with company labels did not even exist until the 1870s, when Ivory Soap and Quaker Oats appeared (Carrier 1995:102). Shop windows, if they existed, were simply filled with items that had been languishing in back rooms or warehouses for years. Even the few large department stores of the mid-nineteenth century, such as that of Alexander Turney Stewart, the Marble Palace in New York, paid little attention to display. It was not until the 1890s and the emergence of the department store in the United States as a major retail establishment that retailers began to pay attention to how products were presented to the public.

The department store evolved into a place to display goods as objects in themselves. When Marshall Field's opened in Chicago in 1902, six string orchestras filled the various floors with music, and American Beauty roses, along with other cut flowers and potted palms, bedecked all the counters. Nothing was permitted to be sold on the first day, and merchants in the district closed so that their employees could visit Field's. Later, elaborate theatrical productions were put on in the stores, artworks were exhibited, and some of the most creative minds in America designed displays that were intended to present goods in ways that inspired people to buy them. The department store became a cultural primer telling people how they should dress, furnish their homes, and spend their leisure time (Leach 1993).

Advertising was another revolutionary development that influenced the creation of the consumer. The goal of advertisers was to aggressively shape consumer desires and create value in commodities by imbuing them with the power to transform the consumer into a more desirable person. Before the late 1880s, advertising was looked down on and associated with P. T. Barnum–style hokum. In 1880, only $30 million was invested in advertising in the United States; however, by 1910, new businesses, such as oil, food, electricity, and rubber, were spending $600 million, or 4 percent of the national income, on advertising. By 1929, advertising was an $11 billion enterprise, and by 1998, the amount spent globally on advertising reached

$437 billion. By 2012, global advertising expenditures reached $498 billion (Lee 2012), or more than the GDP of Sweden.

By the early twentieth century, national advertising campaigns were being initiated and celebrities were being hired to offer testimonials to their favorite commodities. Advertising cards, catalogs, and newspaper ads became a regular feature of American life. Outdoor advertising—billboards, signs, and posters—appeared everywhere. Electrical advertising—neon and flashing signs—were marketed, and Broadway became famous as the "Great White Way." Today, advertising plays such a ubiquitous part in our lives that we scarcely notice it, even when it is engraved or embroidered on our clothing.

Another boon to merchandising was the idea of fashion: the stirring up of anxiety and restlessness over the possession of things that were not "new" or "up-to-date." Fashion pressured people to buy not out of need but for style—from a desire to conform to what others defined as "fashionable."

It is hardly surprising, then, that the garment industry in America led the way in the creation of fashion; its growth in the early 1900s was two or three times as great as any other industry. By 1915, it ranked only behind steel and oil in the United States. Fashion output in 1915 was in excess of $1 billion; in New York alone, 15,000 establishments made women's clothes. New fashion magazines—*Vogue, Cosmopolitan,* and the *Delineator*—set fashion standards and defined what the socially conscious woman should wear, often using royalty, the wealthy, and celebrities as models. In 1903, the fashion show was introduced in the United States by Ehrich Brothers in New York City; by 1915, it was an event in virtually every U.S. city and town. Relying on this popularity, the first modeling agency was founded in New York by John Powers in 1923 (Leach 1993:309). The entertainment industry contributed by making its own major fashion statements as American women of the 1920s sought to imitate stars such as Clara Bow.

The importance of fashion hasn't changed, and fashion magazines remain, as film critic Manohla Dargis (2009) put it, "temples of consumption." Reviewing the documentary, The September Issue, about the creation of a single issue of Vogue, she notes that the glossy images, expensive clothes, and accessories displayed in its pages are about creating desires and transforming wants into needs. The magazine, of course, wants to sell the stuff that adorns its pages; but, more than that, it wants to instill in the reader sets of aspirations. It seeks to define tastes using attractive models and celebrities to define what the well-dressed woman is supposed to wear.

Another addition to the marketing strategy was service, which included not only consumer credit (charge accounts and installment buying) but also a workforce to fawn over customers. Customers became guests.

William Leach suggested that service may have been one of the most important features of the new consumer society. It helped, he said, mask the inequality, poverty, and labor conflicts that were very much a part of the United States at this point in its history. If one wanted to understand how consumer society developed, Leach said, one could look at the rise of service. As economic inequality rose in America, and as labor conflict increased, Americans associated service with the "promise of America." Service conveyed to people the idea that everything was all right, that they had nothing to worry about, and that security and service awaited them. Service expressed what economists then and now would refer to as

> the "benevolent side" of capitalism, that is, the side of capitalism that gave to people in exchange for a dependable flow of profits—a better, more comfortable way of life. In this view, capitalism did not merely "strive for profits" but also sought "the satisfaction of the needs of others, by performing service efficiently." "Capital," said one turn-of-the-century economist, "reigns because it serves." (Leach 1993:146–147)

The Transformation of Institutions

The second way in which American buying habits were changed was through a transformation of the major institutions of American society, each redefining its function to include the promotion of consumption. Educational and cultural institutions, governmental agencies, financial institutions, and even the family itself changed their meaning and function to promote the consumption of commodities.

Before 1900, the contributions of universities to the capitalist economy largely dealt with how to "make" things—that is, with the production of commodities. Virtually no attention was paid to selling or keeping track of what was sold. For example, there was no systematic examination of mass retailing, credit systems, or banking offered by America's schools or universities. In the twentieth century, however, that began to change. For example, in New York City there was the good-design or arts-in-industry movement; schools, such as the Pratt Institute and the New York School of Fine and Applied Arts (now Parsons School of Design), developed and began to prepare students to work in the emerging sales and design industries and in the large department stores. The University of Pennsylvania's Wharton School for Business and the Harvard School for Business introduced programs in accounting (virtually nonexistent before then), marketing, and sales. In 1919, New York University's School of Retailing opened; in the mid-1920s, Harvard and Stanford established graduate business schools as did such schools as Northwestern and other universities in Michigan, California, and Wisconsin soon after. Today, there are virtually no two-year or four-year colleges that do not offer some sort of business curriculum.

Museums also redefined their missions to accommodate the growth of the consumer culture. The American Museum of Natural History and the Metropolitan Museum of Art in Manhattan, the Brooklyn Museum, and the Newark Museum—all heavily endowed by wealthy patrons such as J. P. Morgan—began to make alliances with business. Curators lectured to designers on Peruvian textiles or primitive decorative art. The head of the American Museum of Natural History, Morris D'Camp Crawford, assisted by the head of the anthropology department, Clark Wissler, urged businesspeople and designers to visit the museum. Special exhibits on the history of fashion and clothing were arranged, and Wissler even borrowed the window-display techniques of New York department stores for his exhibits (just as window-display designers had borrowed the idea of the mannequin from anthropologist Franz Boas's exhibit of foreign cultures at the 1893 World's Columbian Exposition in Chicago). The editor of *Women's Wear* magazine praised the museum for being "the most progressive force in the development of the designer" (Leach 1993:166).

The second set of institutions to aid in the development of consumer culture comprised agencies of the local and federal governments. The state, as an entity, had long taken a lively interest in commerce within its borders (as we'll see when we examine the history of global capitalist expansion in Chapter 3). But prior to the twentieth century, the state's concerns focused largely on the manufacture of commodities, the organization of business, the control of labor, and the movement of goods. It wasn't until the twentieth century that state agencies began to concern themselves with the consumption end of the business cycle. In fact, it may not be an exaggeration to say that the government did more to create the consumer than did any other institution.

Nothing better represents the increasing role of the federal government in the promotion of consumption than the growth of the Commerce Department under Herbert Hoover, who served as its head from 1921 until his election as president in 1928. When the Commerce Building opened in Washington in 1932, it was the biggest office structure in the world (and was not surpassed in size until the Pentagon was built a decade later). At the time, it brought together in one building virtually all the government departments that had anything to do with business, from the Patent Office to the Bureau of Foreign and Domestic Commerce (BFDC), then the most important agency of the department. From 1921 to 1930, the congressional appropriation for the BFDC rose from $100,000 to more than $8 million, an increase of 8,000 percent. The number of BFDC staff increased from 100 to 2,500.

Hoover clearly intended the Department of Commerce to serve as the handmaiden of American business, and its main goal was to help encourage the consumption of commodities. For example, between 1926 and 1928, the BFDC, under Hoover's direction, initiated the Census of Distribution (or "Census of Consumption," as it was sometimes called) to be carried out every ten years. (It was unique at that time; Britain and other countries did not initiate government-sponsored consumer research until the 1950s.) It detailed where the consumers were and what quantities of goods they would consume; it pointed out areas where goods were "overdeveloped" and which goods were best carried by which stores. The Commerce Department endorsed retail and cooperative advertising and advised merchants on service devices, fashion, style, and display methods of all kinds. The agency advised retail establishments on the best ways to deliver goods to consumers, redevelop streets, build parking lots and underground transportation systems to attract consumers, use colored lights, and display merchandise in "tempting ways." The goal was to break down "all barriers between the consumers and commodities" (Leach 1993:366).

Hoover also emphasized individual home ownership. In his memoirs, he wrote that "a primary right of every American family is the right to build a new house of its heart's desire at least once. Moreover, there is the instinct to own one's own house with one's own arrangement of gadgets, rooms, and surroundings" (Nash 1988:7). The Commerce Department flooded the country with public relations materials on "homebuying" ideas, producing a leaflet entitled *Own Your Own Home,* along with the film *Home Sweet Home.* They advocated single-dwelling homes over multiunit dwellings and suburban over urban housing. The leaflet recommended a separate bedroom for each child, saying it was "undesirable for two children to occupy the same bed—whatever their age." Regardless of the reasons for these recommendations, the materials produced by the Commerce Department all promoted maximum consumption. Thus, the government responded, as much as did educational institutions, to the need to promote the consumption of commodities.

Another step in creating a consumer economy was to give the worker more buying power. The advantage of this from an economic perspective is not easy to see. From the point of view of an industrialist or an employer, the ideal situation would be to pay as low a wage as possible to keep production costs down and increase profits. However, each producer of goods would prefer other producers to pay high wages, which would allow the other producers' workers to buy more products. The idea that higher wages would serve as an incentive for laborers to work harder or that higher wages might allow the worker to become a consumer occurred relatively late to factory owners and investors. The working class, they assumed, would work only as hard as they needed to get their basic subsistence, and to pay them more would only result in their working less. And when an occasional economic boom gave workers the spending power to consume at a higher level, the middle and upper classes would condemn them for their lack of thrift.

The economic power derived from turning workers into consumers was realized almost by accident. As industry attempted to increase efficiency, it developed new methods. Henry Ford introduced the assembly line, one of the apparently great innovations, to the manufacturing of automobiles. Workers occupied positions on the line from which they did not move ("Walking," Ford said, "is not a remunerative activity") and from which they would perform a single task. It was a process that required almost no training and that "the most stupid man could learn within two days," as Ford said. In essence, each worker had to repeat the same motion every ten seconds in a nine-hour workday.

Workers resisted this mind-numbing process. When Ford introduced his assembly line, absenteeism increased and worker turnover surged. In 1913, Ford required 13,000 to 14,000 workers to operate his plant, and in that year 50,000 quit. But Ford solved the problem: He raised wages from the industry standard of two to three dollars per day to five dollars, and he reduced the working day to eight hours. Soon labor turnover fell to 5 percent, and waiting lines appeared at Ford hiring offices. Furthermore, production costs for Ford's Model T fell from $1,950 to $290, reducing the price to consumers. Most importantly, the rise in wages made Ford workers consumers of Ford automobiles, and, as other manufacturers followed suit, the automobile industry grew. By 1929, there were 23 million automobiles in the United States; by 1950, there were more than 40 million. Today, including light trucks, there are 1.3 cars for every individual.

In addition to the money coming from higher wages, buying power was increased by the expansion of credit. Credit, of course, is essential for economic growth and consumerism, because it means that people, corporations, and governments can purchase goods and services with only a promise to pay for them at some future date. Buying things on credit—that is, going into debt—has not always been acceptable in the United States. It was highly frowned upon in the nineteenth century. It was not fully socially acceptable until the 1920s (Calder 1999), at which time it promoted the boom in both automobile and home buying.

The increased ease of obtaining home mortgages was a key to the home-building boom of the 1940s, 1950s, and 1960s, a boom that in turn fueled subsidiary industries—appliances, home furnishings, and road construction. By 1960, 62 percent of all Americans could claim to own their own home—up from 44 percent in 1940. By 2008, U.S. homeowners owed more than $10 trillion in mortgages. Home mortgages had the further function of disciplining the workforce by forcing it to work to make credit payments. At the same time, homeowners gained a capital asset that served as a hedge against inflation. Automobile loans also added to consumer debt and, similarly, fueled subsidiary economic growth—malls, highways, vacation travel, and so on. Credit cards gave holders a revolving line of credit with which to finance purchases. U.S. household debt reached over $13 trillion in 2008, before falling to $11½ trillion in 2012 as a result of the 2007–2008 recession, while 20 percent of American households have more debt than assets, or 40 percent when real estate is factored out. This debt represents enormous confidence in the future of the economy because this money does not exist. Lenders in our economy simply assume that the money will exist when it comes time for people to repay their debts.

None of this would have been possible without a government financial policy that put limits on interest rates ("usury ceilings"), passed "truth-in-lending" laws, made it easier for certain groups (women and minorities) to borrow, and offered subsidized student loans. Thus, credit increased consumer debt while creating a "mass market" for consumer goods, which served further to stimulate economic growth (see Guttmann 1994).

In addition to changes in the way workers were viewed and the expansion of credit, there had to be a change in the way retail establishments were organized. The emergence of the consumer was accompanied by an enormous growth in retail chain stores. Until this point, people shopped in small stores or large family-owned department stores. The 1920s saw the rise of the large retail conglomerates. In 1886, only two chains operated more than five stores; in 1912, 177 companies operated 2,235 stores; by 1929, nearly 1,500 companies were doing business in 70,000 outlets. In 2012, Wal-Mart alone had over 8500 stores worldwide, and, with over 2 million employees, is the largest employer in the world (Copeland and Labuski 2013).

The Transformation of Spiritual and Intellectual Values

In addition to changing marketing techniques and modifying societal institutions to stimulate consumption, there had to be a change in spiritual and intellectual values from an emphasis on such values as thrift, modesty, and moderation toward a value system that encouraged spending and ostentatious display. T. J. Jackson Lears argued that, from 1880 to 1930, the United States underwent a transformation of values from those that emphasized frugality and self-denial to those that sanctioned periodic leisure, compulsive spending, and individual fulfillment (Lears 1983). This shift in values, said Lears, was facilitated in American life by a new therapeutic ethos, an emphasis on physical and psychological health. This shift was promoted in part by the growth of the health professions and the popularity of psychology, along with the increasing autonomy and alienation felt by individuals as America ceased being a land of small towns and became increasingly urban. Advertisers capitalized on these changes by altering the way products were advertised; rather than emphasizing the nature of the product itself, they began to emphasize the alleged effects of the product and its promise of a richer, fuller life. Instead of simply being good soap, shoes, or deodorant, a product would contribute to the buyer's psychological, physical, or social well-being (Lears 1983:19).

Clothing, perfumes, deodorant, and so on, would provide the means of achieving love; alcoholic beverages would provide the route to friendship; and the proper automobile tires or insurance policy would provide the means of meeting family responsibilities. Commodities would be the source of satisfaction and a vital means of self-expression. Ponder, for example, the following description by a forty-year-old man of the relationship between himself and his expensive Porsche:

> Sometimes I test myself. We have an ancient, battered Peugeot, and I drive it for a week. It rarely breaks, and it gets great mileage. But when I pull up next to a beautiful woman, I am still the geek with glasses. Then I get back into my Porsche. It roars and tugs to get moving. It accelerates even going uphill at 80. It leadeth trashy women ... to make pouting looks at me at stoplights. It makes me feel like a tomcat on the prowl.... Nothing in my life compares—except driving along Sunset at night in the 928, with the sodium vapor lamps reflecting off the wine-red finish, with the air inside reeking of tan glove-leather upholstery and the ... Blaupunkt playing the Shirelles so loud that it makes my hairs vibrate. And with the girls I will never see again pulling up next to me, giving the car a once-over and looking at me as if I was a cool guy, not worried, instead of a 40-year-old schnook writer. (Belk 1988:148)

In the late nineteenth century, a series of religious movements emerged that became known as *mind-cure religions.* William James, in his classic 1902 book *Varieties of Religious Experience,* drew attention to the mind-cure movements, although he was not the first to use the term. These movements—New Thought, Unity, Christian Science, and Theosophy, among others—maintained that people could simply, by an act of will and conviction, cure their own illnesses and create heaven on earth. These movements were, as William Leach (1993:225) phrased it, "wish-oriented, optimistic, sunny, the epitome of cheer and self-confidence, and completely lacking in anything resembling a tragic view of life." There was no sin, no evil, no darkness, only, as one mind curer said, "the sunlight of health."

These movements held that salvation would occur in this life and not in the afterlife. Mind cure dismissed the ideas of sin and guilt. God became a divine force, a healing power. Proponents argued that Americans should banish ideas of duty and self-denial. As one early twentieth-century advocate said,

> If you want to get the most out of life, just make up your mind that you were made to be happy, that you are a happiness machine, as well as a work machine. Cut off the past, and do not touch the morrow until it comes, but extract every possibility from the present. Think positive, creative, happy thoughts, and your harvest of good things will be abundant. (Leach 1993:229)

These new religions made fashionable the idea that, in the world of goods, men and women could find a paradise free from pain and suffering; they could find, as one historian of religion put it, the "good" through "goods."

Popular culture also promoted the mind-cure ideology. As examples, there were L. Frank Baum's *The Wonderful Wizard of Oz,* which Leach characterized as "perhaps the best mind cure text ever written," and the Billikens doll, a squat Buddha-like figure, sometimes male and sometimes female, that represented the "god of things as they ought to be." Its success was without parallel in the toy trade and helped incite the doll craze in America. Billikens, it was said, would drive away petty annoyances and cares. One contemporary put it this way: "An atmosphere of gorged content pervades Billikens. No one can look at him [or her] and worry."

The popularity of the Billikens doll signaled change in spiritual values: It was now permissible to seek self-fulfillment in this life and find elements of satisfaction in manufactured commodities. The world was a good place: There was no misery; poverty, injustice, and inequities were only in the mind. There was enough for everyone.

These changes were not unique to America. Many of the same changes occurred in other nations, most notably Great Britain, Germany, and France (Carrier 1995), and are occurring now all over the world. The consumer revolution of the early twentieth century was not the first of its kind either—it evolved with great intensity and rapidity in America.

Thus, by the 1930s, the "consumer" as a category of person had, as Lizabeth Cohen (2003) points out, replaced the "citizen," adopting a spiritual and intellectual framework that glorified the continued consumption of commodities as personally fulfilling and economically desirable—a moral imperative that would end poverty and injustice.

Pillow Pets, the latest craze in stuffed toys, are a direct descendent of the Billikens doll, a figure designed to drive away worries and cares and convince people that the world is a good place with plenty for everyone. (Yumeto Yamazaki/AFLO/Newscom.)

The Reconfiguration of Time, Space, and Class

The creation of the consumer did not stop in 1930. Since that time, the institutions of our society, particularly those of corporate America, have become increasingly more adept at creating sandpaintings in which people inhabit worlds whose very nature requires the continuous consumption of goods. The need to consume has reordered our organization of time, reconstructed our living space, created new spaces for the encouragement of consumption, and altered the ways that we view one another.

Into the early nineteenth century in the United States, holiday celebrations—most religious, but some secular—marked each year. Washington's Birthday, for example, was one of the most important (see, e.g., Schmidt 1995:47). But holidays were not generally times for gift giving and consumption. In fact, most people, particularly merchants and trades people, viewed holidays and festivities as impediments to work discipline, and they made an effort to reduce their number.

By the late nineteenth century, however, retailers began to recognize the commercial potential of holidays. In 1897, the trade journal *Dry Goods Economist* mocked those who viewed holidays as "an interruption of business" instead of an opportunity for "special sales and attractive displays." The modern retailer, they said, knew that there was "never a holiday" that did not make for increased business. Thus, as Leigh Eric Schmidt observes, "holidays, rather than being impediments to disciplined economic advancement, were seen as critical for consumption and profit" (Schmidt 1995:37).

Valentine's Day is a good example. Until the fourteenth century, St. Valentine was known largely for his "steadfastness in the face of torturous martyrdom." English poet Geoffrey Chaucer is generally credited with laying the foundation for the pairing of St. Valentine with lovers when, in his *Parliament of Fowls,* he wrote that birds were said to choose their mates on St. Valentine's Day (Schmidt 1995:40ff.). Thus, St. Valentine became the patron saint of lovers. On St. Valentine's Day in Scotland, young women would try to divine their future mates, while among the elites it became a day for romantic poetry and gift giving, gloves being a popular item. By the 1840s and 1850s in the United States, the practice of exchanging cards became widespread. By the late nineteenth century, the meaning of the term *valentine* had changed. Instead of referring to a person's sweetheart or betrothed, it came to refer to a commodity, a commercial product that could be consumed like any other. By the end of the nineteenth century, department stores were filling their windows with love missives, jewelry, and other suggestions for gifts. In 1910, a traveling salesman by the name of Joyce C. Hall began a postcard business specializing in Valentine missives that would evolve into Hallmark Cards. By the 1990s, Hallmark had 40 percent of the American greeting card business (Schmidt 1995:100). Of course, other holidays, such as Christmas, soon followed Valentine's Day as occasions for mass consumption, and by the early 1920s, flowers for Mother's Day became firmly fixed in the holiday firmament. Thus, our organization of time, our calendar of festivities, became redefined to promote consumption.

The need to create consumers also redefined our conception of space. Home ownership, for example, particularly of the product-greedy single-family home, cast people out from city centers into the sprawling suburbs, which necessitated new roads and more cars, and, in the end, virtually destroyed public transportation. Retailers and developers quickly realized the possibilities inherent in these new communities; people, they reasoned, had an endless desire to consume. "Our economy," said Macy's board chairman Jack Isodor Straus, "keeps on growing because our ability to consume is endless. The consumer goes on spending regardless of how many possessions he or she has. The luxuries of today are the necessities of tomorrow" (Cohen 2003:261). But it was also believed that suburbanites were growing reluctant to travel to urban centers to shop. The solution was to bring the market to the people, and retailers and developers relocated shopping areas from city centers to spacious shopping centers and malls. Consumers gave various reasons for shifting their shopping from downtown to shopping centers, but the most important issues seemed to involve convenience—easy accessibility (malls and shopping centers were always constructed adjacent to new highways), easy parking, improved store layouts, increased self-service, simplified credit with charge plates, and greater availability of products. Market researchers concluded that shoppers were attracted to the ease and "progressiveness" of mall shopping. Consumers seemed to share the developers' sense that shopping centers were the modern way to consume (Cohen 2003:268).

The new ease of shopping, however, came with some costs. Shopping centers and malls were, unlike city centers, private spaces in which owners could control political activities. They were also easily accessible only to people with automobiles, thus removing from the suburban landscape those shoppers at the low end of the social ladder. In addition, they redefined the nature of social interaction; shopping malls. Bauman (1998:25)

> are so constructed as to keep people moving, looking around, keep them diverted and entertained no end—but in no case looking too long—by any of the endless attractions; not to encourage them to stop, look at each other, think of, ponder, and debate something other than the objects on display—not to pass their time in a fashion devoid of commercial value.... Hence a territory stripped of public space provides little chance for norms being debated, for values to be confronted, to clash and to be negotiated.

In addition to defining the times and spaces in which we live and shop, marketers also redefined categories of people. In the early days of advertising, and up until the 1960s, manufacturers and retailers pitched their products and services to the mass market, continually stimulating demand by offering new products, changing styles, and so forth. But in the 1950s, a new theory of marketing gained acceptance; rather than marketing products and services to a vast, undifferentiated middle class, sellers would differentiate or segment the market, appealing to the desires and needs of each special group. A new field, psychographics, emerged that became so sophisticated that the chief executive of Spiegel Company would boast that armed to the teeth with information, the marketer was "the friend who knows them [consumers] as well as—perhaps better than—they know themselves" (Cohen 2003:299). Target marketing singled out children and minorities for pointed appeals; marketers used "lifestyle branding"— selling products by attracting consumers to a particular way of life rather than the good itself. Advertisers segmented by class and income, and then by gender and then age. They categorized consumers with statistical precision and gave them labels such as "blue blood estates," "shoguns and pickups," and "[H]ispanic mix residents," singling these groups out for direct marketing, telemarketing, and Internet shopping solicitation. "Rather than sell commodities in as much volume as possible to the masses," says Lizabeth Cohen (2003:299), "modern-day marketers, equipped with advanced psychographic tactics, identify clusters of customers with distinctive ways of life and then set out to sell them idealized lifestyles constructed around commodities." Today, of course, there are companies that scour the internet for personal information that enable advertisers to customize the ads that appear on people's Facebook pages (Tynan 2010).

Magazines probably represent the clearest example of segmentation—note the shift from the dominant magazines of the 1930s, 1940s, and 1950s (*Life, Look, Saturday Evening Post*) and examine a typical magazine rack today. We might ask ourselves to what extent has the market segmentation created or exaggerated social and cultural divisions that might otherwise not exist, leaving people with less and less to share.

As Lizabeth Cohen (2003:318) points out, if any kind of segmentation epitomized the goals of marketers and advertisers, it was segmenting by age. First targeting teenagers and then children, they succeeded, with the help of governments, schools, and other institutions, in redefining childhood itself.

KINDERCULTURE IN AMERICA: THE CHILD AS CONSUMER

The Role of Children in Capitalism

Anthropology teaches us that, much like the rest of our culture, childhood is socially created— that is, childhood and the ways it is defined vary from society to society and from era to era. Childhood in nineteenth-century America was very different from what it is today. Prior to the nineteenth century, the major role of children in a capitalist economy was as workers (Lasch 1977:14ff.). There were few industries that did not employ children at some level, and there were few families whose children did not contribute economically through either farm or factory labor. In twentieth-century America, this began to change. Social movements that for decades worked to restrict child labor finally convinced state and federal legislatures to pass laws making child labor illegal. These developments signaled a transformation of children from workers to consumers. Although this may not have been the intent of the reformers, children were to contribute far more to the national economy as consumers than they ever did as laborers.

It wasn't until the beginning of the twentieth century that retailers began to target children as a discrete group of consumers. As late as 1890, there was not a children's market worth considering; children ate, wore, and played with what their parents made for them. Germany was by far the largest producer of children's toys, and there were few, if any, factories in the United States producing children's clothing. Nor was there any market for infants' or children's foods. Yet by 1915, the baby clothing industry was one of the largest in the United States, with seventy-five factories operating in New York State alone. Toy production increased by 1,300 percent between 1905 and 1920. One reason was the destruction of the German toy industry during World War I. Another was the development of new toys in the United States that became international sensations, such as the racist Alabama Coon Jigger, a laughing, prancing, mechanical black male. But, most importantly, retailers were beginning to appreciate the profits that could be made from children's commodities.

Retailers also began to take note of psychologists' discovery of the "natural desire" of "little people" for goods and toys, heeding the psychologists' advice that "every attention shown the child binds the mother to the store," or the observation that if they cultivated consumers "as kids [they would] have them as customers for a lifetime." Santa Claus became one of the major vehicles for selling toys; his commercialization hit its peak in the 1920s.

Child psychologists and home economists also advised parents that children needed toys for exercise and toys to relax; children, they said, should have their own playrooms. These same experts lectured at department stores, advising parents of the educational values of toys. With this new emphasis on the child as consumer, by 1926, America had become the greatest producer of toys and playthings in the world. There were toys for the backyard, camping, the beach, and the "little private room which every child desperately needs to fulfill his or her individuality." Play, said the experts, "is the child's business; toys the material with which he works" (Leach 1993:328).

The federal government played a major role in redefining childhood. In 1929, Herbert Hoover sponsored a White House Conference on Child Health and Protection. The conference report, *The Home and the Child,* concluded that children were independent beings with particular concerns of their own. The child, the report said,

> is often an alien in his home when it comes to any consideration of his special needs in the furnishings and equipment of the home. He belongs nowhere. He must accommodate himself to an adult environment—chairs and tables are too big and too high for him; there is no suitable place for his books and his toys. He moves in a misfit world with nothing apportioned to his needs. Often this results in retarding his physical, mental, and social development. (White House 1931)

The report advised parents to give their children their own "furniture and eating equipment" suitable to each child's age and size; it further advised parents to provide playrooms inside the house and to fill the backyard with "toys, velocipedes, sawhorses, wagons, wheelbarrows, slides, and places to keep pets." The report noted that "Generally a sleeping room for each person is desirable." As a child grows "older and becomes more social he wants games and toys that he can share with his friends." When the family decides on "the purchase of a piece of furniture or a musical instrument" of common interest, it is important to consult the children. Take them shopping for their own "things and let them pick them out by themselves."

> Through such experiences personality develops.... [These] experiences have the advantage also of creating in the child a sense of personal as well as family pride in ownership, and eventually *teaching him that his personality can be expressed through things.* (White House 1931 [emphasis added]; see also Leach 1993:371–372)

Thus, in the span of some thirty years, the role of children in American life changed dramatically; they became, and remain, pillars of the consumer economy, with economic power rivaling that of adults. Children have become a main target of advertisers; as one marketing specialist told the *Wall Street Journal,* "even two-year-olds are concerned about their brand of clothes, and by the age of six are full-out consumers" (Durning 1992:120). Marketing researchers estimate that children ages two to fourteen directly influence $188 billion of parental spending, indirectly influence another $300 billion, and spend themselves some $25 billion. Teen spending alone jumped from $63 billion in 1994 to $94 billion in 1998, to some $175 billion by 2003, and to over $200 billion in 2007 (see Market Research Portal 2006; McNeal 1999; Zollo 1999). Children see about 40,000 ads a year on TV alone, not to mention those delivered to them on their cell phones, music devices, instant messaging, and video games, and spend almost as much time on media as they do sleeping. (see Rideout, Roberts, and Foehr 2010:1).

Advertisers and marketing specialists, including anthropologists and psychologists, devise all sorts of campaigns to appeal to children and are often criticized for the messages they communicate. But some advertising executives are quite candid in their objectives. As one said, "No one's really worrying about what it's teaching impressionable youth. Hey, I'm in the business of convincing people to buy things they don't need" (*Business Week,* August 11, 1997:35). Advertisers work on such things as the "nag factor," explaining to clients that children's nagging inspires about a third of a family's trips to a fast-food restaurant, video store, or children's clothing store (Ruskin 1999). Advertisers explicitly work on a child's desire to be accepted and on their fear of being "losers." As one ad agency president put it,

> Kids are very sensitive to that. If you tell them to buy something, they are resistant. But if you tell them that they'll be a dork if they don't, you've got their attention. You open up emotional vulnerabilities, and it's very easy to do with kids because they're the most emotionally vulnerable. (Harris 1989)

As colleges and universities adapted to the need to persuade people to consume with new academic courses and programs, primary and secondary schools were adapting by providing marketers with access to children. Channel One is a marketing company that delivers ten minutes a day of TV news to some 8 million students in 12,000 schools, provided students also watch two minutes of advertising. "The biggest selling point to advertisers," says Joel Babbit, former president of Channel One, lies in "forcing kids to watch two minutes of commercials." As Babbit (Ruskin 1999) put it,

> [T]he advertiser gets a group of kids who cannot go to the bathroom, who cannot change the station, who cannot listen to their mother yell in the background, who cannot be playing Nintendo, who cannot have their headsets on.

The Social Construction of Childhood

In the early part of the twentieth century, retail establishments, particularly the new department stores, took the lead in redefining the world of children. They produced their own radio programs for children and put on elaborate shows. Macy's, which by the late 1920s had the largest toy department in the world, put on playlets for children in makeshift theaters or in store auditoriums. The most popular department store show was *The Wizard of Oz;* when the show was put on at Field's in Chicago, the children wore green-tinted glasses to better appreciate the "Emerald City."

In this era, the event that most symbolized the reconstruction of childhood was Christmas. Christmas became a time of toy giving in America in the 1840s. By the 1870s, this holiday was appropriated by retail establishments as a way to sell goods; people at that time had already begun to complain that Christmas was becoming overcommercialized (Carrier 1995:189). But it wasn't until the early twentieth century that retail establishments turned Christmas into a spectacle that appealed to children especially. By the mid-1920s, nearly every city in America had its own "radio" Santa Claus. Gimbel's in New York received thousands of letters addressed to Santa Claus; each was carefully answered by staff and signed "Santa," with the name of each child carefully indexed for future use (Leach 1993:330). In 1924, Macy's inaugurated its Thanksgiving Day parade, which ran from 145th Street to West 34th Street and culminated with the appearance of Santa Claus standing on Macy's 34th Street marquee waving to the throngs below.

Thanksgiving also came to mark the beginning of the Christmas buying season, a time when Americans spend some 4 percent of their income on Christmas gifts and when department stores sell 40 percent of their yearly total of toys and 25 percent of their candy, cosmetics, toiletries, stationery, greeting cards, and books. (By the early 1990s, Americans were spending about $37 billion on Christmas gifts, a sum greater than the gross national product [GNP] of all but forty-five countries in the world [see Restad 1995:160]. By 2006, Americans were spending over $700 a person, a total of $457.4 billion, during the "winter holidays," including Christmas [Roysdon 2006].) The government did its part in defining the Christmas buying season when

Fred Lazarus Jr., who was to become president of Ohio's Federated Department Stores, persuaded President Franklin Roosevelt in 1939 to move Thanksgiving Day from November 30, its traditional date, to November 23 to add one more week to the Christmas buying season. Congress made that official in 1941 when it moved the Thanksgiving celebration from the last Thursday in November to the fourth Thursday. The government thus assured that it could fall no later than November 28, guaranteeing a minimum four-week shopping spree (Restad 1995:162).

Santa Claus represents one of the more elaborate ways in which the culture of capitalism shields its members, particularly children, from some of its less savory features. The story of Santa Claus represented a world in which consumer, capitalist, and laborer were idealized: Commodities (toys) were manufactured by happy elves working in Santa's workshop (no factories at the North Pole, and certainly no Chinese assembly plants) and were distributed, free of charge, to good boys and girls by a corpulent, grandfatherly male in fur-trimmed clothes. It is perhaps ironic that when political cartoonist Thomas Nast created what has become the contemporary image of Santa Claus in 1862, he modeled Santa's costume after the fur-trimmed clothes worn by the wealthy Astor family (Carrier 1995:189).

Nast also created Santa's workshop, perhaps in nostalgic remembrance of prefactory production. Writers as early as the 1870s recognized the irony of this idealized version of Christmas and toy production. One magazine editorial in 1873, commenting on a picture of Santa's elves working gaily in some magical workplace, turning out dolls, boats, tops, and toy soldiers, compared it with the reality of the poor, working six days a week in factories (Restad 1995:149). William Waits, in his book *The Modern Christmas in America* (1992), suggested that Santa's major role was to "decontaminate" Christmas gifts, removing the stigma of factory industry (Waits 1992:25).

Others, of course, played a major role in transforming childhood, but we can do no better than to trace the trajectory of this transformation from its beginning in the stories of L. Frank Baum and his Emerald City to its logical culmination in Walt Disney World.

Walt Disney World
(Ian Dagnall/Alamy.)

THE APPROPRIATION OF CHILDHOOD, PART I: BAUM'S EMERALD CITY Pre-1900 children's stories were very different from those common today. The most famous were the stories of Jacob and Wilhelm Grimm. The Grimm brothers took traditional European folktales, most of which contained fairly gruesome and bizarre plots (cannibalism, incest, murder, etc.), and rewrote them so that they could be used as tools for the socialization of children. Each rewritten tale contained a moral lesson. But, as with nineteenth-century religion, government, and economic institutions, these stories lacked the power to produce the necessary mind-cure impulse to consume. Consequently, there emerged new kinds of stories in which the world was cleansed of the darkness of the Grimm's stories and presented as a happy place full of desirable things. The leader in this reconstruction of the child's universe was Baum.

Baum came from a well-to-do New York state family and had moved with his wife, Maud Gage (whose mother, Matilda Joslyn Gage, was a prominent nineteenth-century feminist leader), in the late 1880s to Aberdeen, South Dakota, where he opened a large retail store (Baum's Bazaar). In 1891, economic depression hit Aberdeen, and Baum went broke. He moved his family to Chicago, where he began to write the stories that would make him famous. In addition, he took a lively interest in the art of window display, becoming an advisor to some of the largest department stores in the city.

Baum had always loved the theater, and he combined that with his interest in business to make window displays into theatrical productions, showing off retail goods to their best advantage. The quality of the goods mattered little to Baum; how they looked, their "selling power," was what mattered. He soon founded the National Association of Window Trimmers and developed a manual and later a journal, *The Show Window,* devoted to window displays. (The journal changed its title to *Display World* in the 1920s; it exists today as *Visual Merchandising.*) Baum's general message was to "use the best art to arouse in the observer the cupidity and longing to possess the goods" (Leach 1993:60).

Baum's personal philosophy was compatible with the various mind-cure movements of the late nineteenth and early twentieth centuries. "People do not sin and should not feel guilt," he wrote in 1890 in the *Aberdeen Saturday Pioneer.* "[T]he good things in life are given to be used." The "rainy day" theory of saving was all right, according to Baum, as long as it wasn't used as an excuse to deny oneself comforts. Who, he asked,

> will be the gainer when Death calls him to the last account—the man who can say "I have lived!" or the man who can say "I have saved?... To gain all the meat from the nut of life is the essence of wisdom. Therefore, "eat, drink, and be merry— tomorrow you die." (Leach 1993:247)

Baum's books were filled with goods and mechanical inventions and landscapes of edible fruits, cakes, cookies, all intended to assure readers that the world was a good place. They were, said William Leach, affirmative, Americanized fairy tales. In fact, Baum's explicit goal was to revolutionize children's literature. In his introduction to the first edition of *The Wonderful Wizard of Oz,* Baum wrote,

> The time has come for a series of newer "wonder tales" in which the stereotyped genie, dwarf and fairy are eliminated, together with all the horrible and blood-curdling incidents devised by their authors to point to a fearsome moral to each tale.... *The Wonderful Wizard of Oz* was written solely to please children of today. It aspires to being a modernized fairy tale, in which the wonderment and joy are retained and the heartaches and nightmares are left out. (Leach 1993:251)

The story of *The Wizard of Oz* can be interpreted as a tribute to our ability to create illusions and magic, to make people believe in spite of themselves. In Baum's stories, the Wizard is exposed as a charlatan, a "common man" with no special powers; but he is powerful because he can make others do what he wants, make them believe in the unbelievable. He is a confidence man. People adored him even as he escaped from Oz in a balloon and was remembered as the man who "built for us this beautiful Emerald City." Baum, said William Leach, created a benign trickster, consumer society's version of the capitalist. *The Wizard of Oz* represented a new spiritual–ethical climate that modeled itself on a version of the child's world in which dreams of self-fulfillment through consumption were legitimized and any negative consequences of consumption were banished. In brief, Baum's work represented but one of the sandpaintings of capitalism, one that appropriates childhood to represent a world in which the purpose of life is to consume.

Yet, as sophisticated as Baum was in creating an ethos that encouraged people to buy, the master of the art was to be Walt Disney.

THE APPROPRIATION OF CHILDHOOD, PART II: WALT DISNEY AND THE CREATION OF DISNEY WORLD It is difficult to say when the child's universe, created to turn children into consumers, began to be used to entice adults. Perhaps the glorification of "youth" in advertising and the upward extension of childhood to include the teens were manifestations of this phenomenon. Regardless, the appropriation of childhood as a vehicle to encourage consumption at all ages and rationalize capitalism culminated in the creation of Walt Disney World. Disney and other major American corporations have created what Shirley Steinberg and Joseph Kincheloe (see Kincheloe 1997) call *kinderculture,* the promotion of an ethos of pleasure for the purpose of enticing adults as well as children to consume.

Walt Disney World is the ultimate sandpainting of the culture of capitalism. Instead of a single sandpainter using bits of colored sand and grain to create a picture barely large enough to contain a single person, a corporation has used millions of tons of concrete, wood, plastic, and glass to create the "home of childhood," a miniature universe that promotes innocence and trust, that allows people to leave the "real world" behind, and that encourages (in fact, insists) that participants put themselves in the hands of Disney. However, as Stephen Fjellman (1992:13) warned,

> these hands bear watching, for in their shaping of things lies danger. It is not just that our movements are constrained with the promise, usually fulfilled, of rewards. What is important is that our thoughts are constrained. They are channeled not only in the interests of Disney itself, but also in the interests of the large corporations with which Disney has allied itself, the system of power they maintain, and the world of commodities that is their life's blood.

If we look beyond the pleasantries, said Fjellman, we find that the environment is totally controlled and that there is a degree of discipline at work in this model world that rivals the discipline of a fascist state. And the control is real. In creating Walt Disney World, the Disney Corporation secretly bought forty square miles of Central Florida real estate (twice the size of Manhattan) and was granted almost feudal powers over the land by the state. Disney World has its own government, it sets the rules, and it controls the message. But what is the message of the Disney World sandpainting? To answer this question, let's examine two aspects of Disney World: its depiction of American history and its representation of progress and the future.

History, or *distory,* as Mike Wallace (1985) called it, is everywhere at Walt Disney World, appropriated, like childhood, in the service of the Disney message. The history, of course, is highly idealized. At Disney World, historical figures such as Thomas Edison, Davy Crockett, Benjamin Franklin, and Mark Twain are used as spokespersons for Disney, lending their authority to the Disney message. Fragments of Abraham Lincoln's speeches, most often taken out of context, are read to us by robots; and Leonardo Da Vinci, the Disney model of the prophetic visionary, is everywhere. At Disney World, there is a conscious attempt to present the history of capitalism without the warts. Disney World designers are quite forthright and unapologetic about their intent. As one Disney spokesperson explained, "We are not telling history like it really was but as it should have been" (Fjellman 1992:31). Another Disney "imagineer," as the designers are called, explains "Disney realism" as a "sort of utopian nature, where we program out all the negative, unwanted elements and program in the positive elements" (Wallace 1985:35).

The center of Disney World (and the original Disneyland in California) is Main Street, a highly idealized, turn-of-the-century remodeling of life as it should have been, a consumer's paradise, scaled down to five-eighths of actual size. The street or square is filled with shops and taverns; people are defined by what they sell. Main Street cultivates a nostalgia for an imagined past without classes, crime, or conflict—a time of continuous consumption, "a supermarket of fun."

On one level, Disney World is an extension of the shop windows designed by L. Frank Baum in the 1890s; on another it serves as an explicit model for the modern shopping mall. Urban planner James Rouse based a number of his town designs and historical shopping malls (Faneuil Hall in Boston, Harborplace in Baltimore, and South Street Seaport in New York) on Disney's Main Street (Wallace 1985:42; see also Kowinski 1985).

At the Hall of Presidents, Disney takes viewers through U.S. history in twenty-nine minutes flat. Disney does recognize, in a fashion, that U.S. history was not all that perfect. After all, the average adult visitor to Disney World is a well-educated professional who could not have been ignorant of the historical injustices in the United States' past. Consequently, Disney World provides Frederick Douglass to speak to the oppression of blacks, Chief Joseph represents indigenous peoples, Susan B. Anthony speaks about the concerns of women, and John Muir serves to remind visitors that progress often came at the expense of the environment. However, each is a highly sanitized symbol of opposition to racism, sexism, and environmental devastation. In "distory," these figures do not remind us of persistent problems in the social fabric; rather they are presented as opportunities to overcome barriers. This is also bad, if not outright false, history.

For example, Disney appropriates for its version of indigenous people in American history the story of Chief Joseph and the Nez Percé. In 1877, the U.S. government, largely at the insistence of settlers who wanted the land, unilaterally revised previous treaty commitments and attempted to resettle all Nez Percé in the Walla Walla Valley of Washington on smaller reservations. One group, led by Chief Joseph and the war chief Looking Glass, refused and, after some young warriors killed a trader accused of selling bad whiskey to the Indians, fled the area, heading east into Idaho, Wyoming, and Montana in an attempt to reach Canada. They were pursued by the command of General Oliver O. Howard, whom Joseph's band defeated in battle after battle or consistently outmaneuvered. The campaign, one of the most bloody and heroic of the Indian wars, ended when Joseph and the remnants of his band were finally surrounded by one of the three army commands that had set out to intercept them. In blizzard conditions on October 5, 1877, only forty miles from the Canadian border, Joseph met with the army's commanders to surrender. His surrender speech, among the most famous speeches in American history, was written down by an army lieutenant. At Walt Disney World, Chief Joseph, in robot form, once again delivers his speech; the Disney version is as follows (Fjellman 1992:104):

> *Enough, enough of your words.*
> *Let your new dawn lead to the final sunset on my people's suffering.*
> *When I think of our condition, my heart is sick.*
> *I see men of my own race treated as outlaws, or shot down like animals.*
> *I pray that all of us may be brothers, with one country around us, and one government for all.*
> *From where the sun now stands, I will fight no more forever.*

However, except for the famous final line, that was not what Joseph said. Here is the original speech as recorded that day in 1877 (Beal 1963:229):

Tell General Howard I know his heart. What he told me before I have in my heart.
I am tired of fighting. Our chiefs are killed. Looking Glass is dead. The old men are

all killed. It is the young men who say yes or no. He who led the young men is dead. It is cold and we have no blankets. The little children are freezing to death. My people some of them have run away to the hills and have no blankets, no food; no one knows where they are, perhaps freezing to death. I want time to look for my children and see how many of them I can find. Maybe I will find them among the dead. Hear me my chiefs, I am tired; my heart is sick and sad. From where the sun now stands, I will fight no more forever.

There is a significant difference between the Disney version and the one recorded on the battlefield. Instead of freezing children, the death of the elderly, and a military campaign that ended only after the deaths of hundreds of American soldiers and Nez Percé warriors, Joseph's surrender speech has been turned by Disney into a testimonial to brotherhood and the nation-state.

In telling history "as it should have been," Disney paints a picture of an American past of which people can be proud, while subtly justifying whatever excesses may have been committed. As in the land of Oz, everything has happened for the better.

Epcot (Experimental Prototype Community of Tomorrow) is a more adult attraction than Fantasyland or some of the other venues of Disney World. Epcot was Walt Disney's pet project at the time of his death in December 1966. It was to be a utopian city of 20,000-plus residents that would attract urban planners and experimenters from all over the world. But Walt Disney died, and corporate Disney turned the project into a gigantic, corporate advertisement, using the 1939 World's Fair in New York as its guide and having pavilions depict the corporate version of the history of progress. Thus, at Epcot, Exxon presents the history of energy, while AT&T does communications. Transportation is presented by General Motors, the land by Kraft, the home by General Electric, and imagination by Kodak. Perhaps even more interesting, at the heart of each corporate pavilion is a ride, a setting much like a sandpainting, in which seated passengers travel through tunnels that open to huge dioramas filled with robots, videos, holograms, and other technological marvels.

Throughout the Epcot pavilions there is this message: Technology equals progress, and progress is natural—and perhaps even American. There have been some problems along the way, the corporate exhibits tell us. "We" have made mistakes—but "we" (corporations) are working to solve those problems. "We" polluted the air, "we" abused the environment. Thus, the imagineers admit that there were problems in the past but reject corporate responsibility for them, putting the corporations at the forefront of the ecology movement. History is defined for us as "a record of the invention of commodities which allow man to master his environment" (Wallace 1985:44). Progress is defined as the availability of emancipatory consumer goods. The World of Tomorrow promotes capitalist development as inevitable, spreading the message that history was made by inventors and businesspeople and that the corporations are the legatees of this past. It tells us, as Mike Wallace (1985:47) observed, that "citizens can sit back and consume."

But who is Disney World for? It is supposed to be for children, but it really represents the appropriation of childhood to encourage the consumption of commodities and, more importantly, once again to shield the consumer from the negative side of corporate capitalism. Walt Disney World is now the single biggest tourist attraction in the entire world. Approximately one-tenth of the population of the United States travels there each year. But it is not a universal attraction. By and large, it attracts people of relatively high incomes, 75 percent of whom are professionals or managers. Only 3 percent are black and 2 percent Hispanic. Seventy-one percent are from outside Florida. As Wallace (1985:53) said,

A process of class self-affirmation seems to be at work. Certainly, Disney World seems intent on providing reassurance to this class, on presenting it with its own pedigree. EPCOT's seventies-style liberal corporatism seems tailor-made for professionals and technocrats. It's calibrated to their concerns—nothing on labor, heavy on ecology, clean, well-managed, emphasis on individual solutions, good restaurants—and it provides just the right kind of past for their hippier sensibilities. *Perhaps, therefore, professionals and managers (many of whom, after all, function as subalterns of capital) flock there because it ratifies their world.* Perhaps they don't want to know about reality—past or present—and prefer comforting and plausible stereotypes. [emphasis added]

Or as O'Toole Fintan (1998:21) put it,

Places like Disney World grapple with the problem of an audience that already knows about the exploitation and violence that its way of life requires for maintenance, but that needs, for its own well-being, to maintain a civilized distance from that knowledge.

Walt Disney World is only one manifestation of the tendency or necessity in capitalism to mask the unpleasant side effects of capitalist production and consumption. People may choose to do something that is harmful to others, but they do so according to a cultural logic that makes it the "right" choice. Our culture makes choosing even easier by masking the sometimes-devastating consequences of our choices. Thus, the process of insulating the consumer from truths that might reduce consumption is built into the culture of capitalism; this denial determines in many ways how we view the world. Put another way, the world as seen from the consumer's point of view is very different from the world as seen from the perspective of worker, capitalist, or people of other cultures around the world. One of the tasks of this book is to try to help the reader appreciate these other points of view.

EXPORTING THE CONSUMER

The construction of the consumer in the Western industrial countries took a century to accomplish. In the rest of the world it is taking less than a decade. According to recent studies, some 1.7 billion people, 27 percent of the world's population, can be counted as members of the consumer society—270 million in the United States and Canada, some 350 million in Western Europe, and 120 million in Japan. The rest live in developing countries—240 million in China, and 120 million in India alone. In 2006, China became the world's number two automobile market and in 2011 a total of 14.5 million sedans, sport utility vehicles, and multipurpose vehicles were shipped to dealers.

The Chinese government fully supports this development (as it bulldozes ancient city centers to construct broad avenues to accommodate the automobile) and is planning a countrywide highway network. If growth continues at that pace, by 2015 China will have more automobiles on the road than the United States (Gallagher 2006; Halweil and Mastny 2004:xvii, 3).

Capitalism, writes William Leach (1993:388), "had achieved a new level of strength and world influence, especially in the wake of the collapse of communism." It also, he concluded,

appears to have a nearly unchallenged hold over every aspect of American life, from politics to culture, so much so that the United States looks like a fashion bazaar to much of the rest of the world. For some Americans the continued power of consumerism has led to further degradation of what it means to be an American or of what America is all about. For others, this evolution has only enhanced the country's appeal, making it appear more than ever an Emerald City, a feast, a department store to which everyone is invited and entitled. Just as cities in the United States once operated as generators of consumer desire for internal markets, today America functions similarly on a global scale.

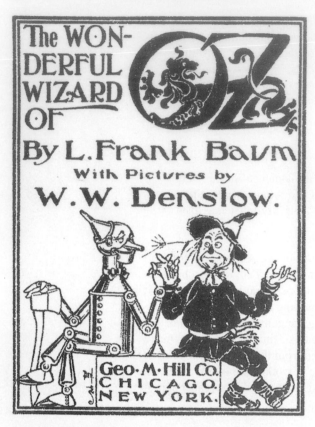

The Wonderful Wizard of Oz, similar to the store display windows that Baum designed, was filled with all the good things in life, assuring the reader that the world is full of things to consume and enjoy.   (Bettmann/Corbis.)

The phenomenon by which people around the world want to emulate consumer capitalism represents what Joseph Nye (2003) calls "soft power." We see this power in Hollywood, which dominates the cultural industries. Countries such as India and Hong Kong try to emulate Hollywood's style while modeling for their audiences' lifestyles and values that they seek to acquire. Information industries around the world are dominated by Anglo-American news. People know what happens in the world because they get the news from AP or Reuters, CNN or NBC (Sisci 2002). We also see this power in the increasing popularity of American sports figures around the world: Michael Jordan, LeBron James, and Tiger Woods are often more familiar names to residents of China or Indonesia than are the countries' leaders (see, e.g., LaFeber 1999).

The rapidity of this global consumer transformation is most evident in India and China, the two most populous countries in the world, with more than one-third of the total global population. Take the case of Rajesh Julka, a thirty-four-year-old resident of the Indian city of Kolkata. In 1996, Julka couldn't afford to replace his ten-year-old television. His father had just retired, and his mother was trying to run a beauty parlor from one of the rooms in their congested ground-floor apartment. Julka was unemployed and trying to establish a sari-making operation. But by 2003, within the span of seven years, he had turned into what Indrajit Basu (2003) calls an "Indian yuppie." He married, had a child, and has since acquired a $100,000 condominium while replacing his cell phone every three months. He bought three new cars during the past four years and recently bought a $2,500 notebook PC during his July holiday to Singapore. "I can't resist buying newer models of electronic goodies," he says. He now also owns three televisions.

Rajesh Julka represents a burgeoning consumer-conscious Indian middle class that has grown to some 445 million people, larger than the entire population of the United States. This middle class is developing new spending patterns; from 1999 to 2002, they spent 4 percent less of their income on groceries and almost 5 percent more on eating out and taking vacations. Spending on personal care went up 2.5 percent during the same period, whereas saving and investing went down almost 7 percent. And because more than 45 percent of India's population is under nineteen years of age, consumption levels are likely to increase at a far faster rate than in industrial countries. In 2011 consumer spending in India reached almost $1 trillion and is expected to increase to $3.6 trillion by 2020, and India's share of global consumption will more than double to 5.8 percent (Bidwai 2003; FirstPost 2011).

And the most prominent symbols of consumer culture are the glitzy, air-conditioned, chrome-and-glass malls, replete with boutiques, restaurants, discos, bars, and theaters that are appearing in India. In addition to the twenty already existing, some 240 megamalls are under construction, forty-three of them in one of the wealthy suburbs of Delhi (Bidwai 2003).

The strategies that created the consumer in the United States were used to equal effect in India. Harold Wilhite (2008:148) notes that in Trivandrum, the capital of the Indian state of Kerala, almost every home is equipped with three things: a mixmaster (mixie), a designated place for prayer, and a television. Since 1995, when cable television became available in Trivandrum, everyone has taken to watching the evening soap operas. TV has replaced cinema as the most popular entertainment, and women, he notes, watch on average about four hours a day. In India in 2009, the court granted a woman a divorce on the grounds that her husband refused to let her watch her favorite soap opera (BBC 2009). And television, as it did in the United States, vastly increased the amount of advertising peopled watched.

Television may be one of the most important contributors to the export of consumption to countries in the periphery. In the United States, Juliet Schor's (1999) research found that for every hour of television people watched, they spent an additional $200.

While it is difficult to measure the effect that television watching has in India, Wilhite notes that the principal sponsor of one soap opera saw its sales rise 300 percent in the two years the series was shown. And, says Wilhite, people watch and enjoy advertisements, citing them as reasons for buying products. As in the United States, television in India has targeted children, who claim to want 75 percent of what they see advertised on television.

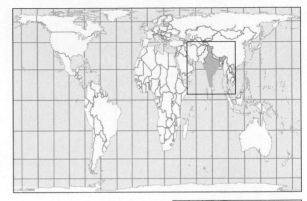

India

What is happening in India is also happening to the most populous country in the world, China. China has averaged GDP growth from 8 percent to 10 percent for more than a decade. GDP for 2011 was US$7.2 trillion, slightly less than half of the United States' $15 trillion economy. And growth and consumer spending continue to soar. Retails sales in 2008 totaled $1.59 trillion, almost 22 percent higher than the previous year, but have been declining slightly because of the global recession.

The same tools that functioned to construct the consumer in the United States are at work in China. In 2010, $120 billion was spent on advertising in China, up from $57 billion in 2006, and $11 billion in 2002 (Ng 2010). Chinese are becoming homeowners, as Americans did in the 1950s. Housing reforms turned over vast amounts of state-owned housing to the people who lived in them at discounts of up to 80 percent. Other laws ensured private property ownership. Home ownership is transforming asset-poor renters into homeowners and driving the purchases of refrigerators, stoves, air conditioners, and cars.

As in the United States, the Chinese consumer is being leveraged through mortgages, auto loans, credit cards, and consumer finance. Credit cards are in their absolute infancy. In 2003, about a million credit cards had been issued—one for every 1,300 people; in 2008, there were 140 million to 150 million credit cards and the rate was increasing at over 97 percent a year. Mortgages were made available only in 2000, auto loans in 2001. Auto ownership, fueled by credit, exploded upward: China had only two cars per 1,000 people in 1997; by 2010 it has reached forty cars per 1,000 persons (compared to 765 per 1,000 in the United States). And perhaps there is no better evidence of the spread of consumerism in China than the mushrooming of fast-food restaurants. There are almost 500 McDonald's in China, and the company plans on doubling that number over the next few years. New restaurants will even have drive-throughs to accommodate the rapid growth of cars in China. The restaurants have become so ubiquitous in Asia that when Chinese, Korean, Japanese, or Taiwanese kids visit America and spot a McDonald's they exclaim that "They have our kind of food here!" (Watson 2000:131).

In the cases of both China and India, one factor in the rising wave of consumption is the same baby boomers (people born at the end of World War II) who fueled consumption in the United States, except that in the case of Asia there are 1 billion of them. In addition, just as children began to move from their parents' homes after 1950 in the United States, they are leaving their parents in Asia. These new households require refrigerators and stoves, pots and pans, and toasters and stereos (Berthelsen 2003; Wilhite 2008).

The responses to these trends are the same as they were in the United States; emerging economies have encouraged the growth of consumer spending and the spread of supermarkets, chain stores, and malls. Wal-Mart and the French Carrefour chain now have nearly fifty stores

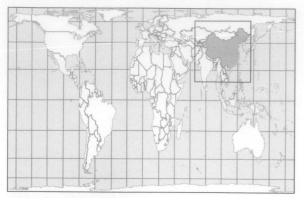

China

in China, a phenomenon that is already beginning to wreak havoc on mom-and-pop operations across Asia. Thailand has begun to experience protests against big-box operators such as Wal-Mart, similar to the protests the United States experienced for a decade (Berthelsen 2003).

CONCLUSION

A couple of days after al Qaeda operatives crashed two planes into the World Trade Center and another into the Pentagon on September 11, 2001, U.S. congressional members met to plan a message to the stunned public. "We've got to give people confidence to go back out and go to work, buy things, go back to the stores—get ready for Thanksgiving, get ready for Christmas," said one member of Congress, echoing the message of the president. "Get out," he said, "and be active, participate in our society" (CNN 2001). The fact that after one of the most shocking events in U.S. history, government officials were urging citizens, above all, to shop and work is ample testimony of the significance of consumption in the effective working of our economy, and, indeed, for our whole society. It is to the consumer that government and business look to supply the impetus for the continued expansion of the economy and the accumulation of capital.

We mentioned earlier that consumption on the scale evident in capitalist culture is unprecedented and is not natural—that is, there is no innate desire in human beings to acquire an ever-greater quantity of stuff. In truth, not everyone agrees with this assumption. Scholars such as James B. Twitchell (2002, 2004) argue that human beings, throughout history, have sought material luxury and that although overconsumption does indeed have its dark side, it has its light side as well—"getting and spending," as he puts it (2004:17), "have been the most passionate, and often the most imaginative, endeavors of modern life." By emulating the consumption-driven lifestyle of capitalist culture, he says, people around the world are being drawn closer together.

Twitchell's defense of luxury is well argued and, insofar as luxury is attainable by all, perhaps something to be considered. But that is a problem: Can the level of wealth enjoyed by members of capitalist culture (remembering that it is twenty-five times greater, on average, than that enjoyed by citizens of two centuries ago) be attained by all but a very few? And if it can be attained, what is the cost of everything else that we must sacrifice? Francesco Sisci (2002) expresses the dilemma well:

> The American victory in the soft war creates the desire of the citizens of the world to become American, with its values, wealth and security umbrella. However, it is impossible for America to grant the American dream to all people who dream it, either in the U.S. or abroad. The danger of creating a desire that cannot be satisfied— whether desire for a certain product or a certain civilization—is the backlash that will follow: waves of protest and dissatisfaction that will translate into a wish to return to one's own history.

CHAPTER 2

The Laborer in the Culture of Capitalism

I have read in E. P. Thompson's The Making of the English Working
Class *that the first man who attempted to establish a labor union
in England at the end of the 18th century was arrested, tried for
sedition, found guilty, drawn and quartered in a public square by
attaching draft horses to each of his arms and legs and pulling him
apart. He was then disemboweled and his guts were burned. Then
they hanged what was left of him. One gathers from this that the
propertied classes were slow to accept the idea of organized labor.*

—ROBERT HASS, *Washington Post,* September 5, 1999

*The capitalist system makes it very much easier for people not to
realize what they are doing, not to know about the danger and
hardship, the despair and humiliation, that their way of life implies
for others.*

—EDMUND WILSON, *The Shores of Light*

The consumer may drive the culture of capitalism, but without the laborer, there would be no commodities to consume. Yet the emergence of the laborer—the person who survives by selling his or her labor—is a recent historical phenomenon. In past centuries most people had access to land on which to grow their own food, selling whatever surplus they produced, or they owned tools (implements for weaving or metalworking, for example) for producing other objects for sale or trade. Thus, to understand capitalism, it is necessary to examine why people choose or are forced to sell their labor. Before we examine this, it is essential to have a fundamental understanding of the workings of the capitalist economy.

Capitalism is not an easy term to define. Pierre Proudhon, who first used the term in 1861, called it "an economic and social regime in which capital, the source of income, does not generally belong to those who make it work through their labor" (Braudel 1982:237). The term *capitalism* does not appear in the writings of Karl Marx and did not gain currency until 1902, when the German economist Werner Sombart used it to denote the opposite of socialism. But

Part of the genius of the culture of capitalism is its ability to produce vast quantities of goods, such as these Nike products that consumers all over the world clamor to buy.
(Hugh Threlfall/Alamy).

definitions alone won't help us to understand fully the dynamics of something as complex as a capitalist economy. We need to understand the major characteristics of capitalism to appreciate how it has permeated our lives as an economic and a cultural system.

Few people will deny that the genius of capitalism lies in its ability to produce goods—commodities for people to buy and consume. Let's start our excursion into capitalism with a product, beginning with something nearly all of us buy at one point or another—sneakers—and examine, briefly, the largest manufacturer of sneakers, Nike, Inc. Today most of the sneakers—and clothes—we wear are assembled overseas because large corporations, such as Nike, have increasingly relocated assembly factories from their home countries to countries on the periphery. Consequently, the clothes we wear; the TVs, stereos, and compact discs (CDs) we listen to; and the computers we use are at least partly produced by a person in another part of the world. This situation creates a clash of cultures that can be illuminating for what it tells us about other cultures and what it may tell us about ourselves. The effects that these factories have on other countries highlight the distinctive features of the capitalist economy and perhaps approximate the impact of early capitalism on our own society. But first let us digress briefly to an understanding of the economic logic of capitalism and, particularly, the role of labor within this economic system.

A PRIMER ON THE ELEMENTS OF CAPITALISM

Let's run through a quick primer on the economics of capitalism and its development. Briefly stated, the economics of capitalism grew out of the interactions of the following five items:

1. Commodities (C). There are basically two types of commodities: capital goods and consumer goods. Capital goods, such as land, raw materials, tools, machines, and factories, are used to produce consumer goods (e.g., television sets, VCRs, computers, and houses) to be sold to others.
2. Money (M). Money is, among other things, a standardized means of exchange. It serves to reduce all goods and commodities to a standard value. By putting a monetary value on something (e.g., a forest), it can be compared with any other commodity (e.g., government bonds). Money, thus, greatly facilitates the exchange of commodities.
3. Labor power (lp). Labor power is the work that is needed to transform one type of commodity into another (e.g., steel into an automobile).
4. Means of production (mp). Another term for capital goods—that is, the machines, land, and tools with which other commodities are produced.
5. Production (P). The combination of lp and mp to produce commodities.

In precapitalist societies or noncapitalist production, as in capitalist production, people either make or obtain commodities—food, clothing, shelter, and the like—to use. These commodities have what economists call *use value*. If someone needs a shirt, they make it; if they need food, they gather, hunt, or grow it. Occasionally, they may trade for what they need or even buy it. Thus, a farmer might barter some corn (C) in exchange for a shirt (C′) or use money to purchase it, but the object is always to obtain something for use. We can diagram this type of exchange as follows:

$$C \rightarrow C' \text{ or } M \rightarrow C'$$

In capitalism, people produce or obtain goods not for their use, but for the purpose of exchange—that is, their object is to produce or obtain commodities (C), not to obtain another commodity (C') but to get capital or money (M). The goods have what is called *exchange value.* Thus, in a business transaction, when a person buys a commodity at one price and sells it at a higher price, the commodity is said to have an exchange value.

$$M \rightarrow C \rightarrow M'$$

Some people might argue that this exchange is capitalism, although most would call it *mercantile exchange,* suggesting that the formula for capitalism is incomplete. You still need one more development: to combine labor and the means of production in a unique way. From this perspective, fully developed capitalism looks like this:

$$M \rightarrow C \rightarrow P \rightarrow C' \rightarrow M'$$

or

$$M \rightarrow C \rightarrow \frac{mp}{lp} \rightarrow C' \rightarrow M'$$

Thus, a manufacturer or producer has money (M) to buy commodities (C; e.g., raw material, machines, and labor) that are then combined (mp/lp) to manufacture commodities that carry a value greater than C (C'). The sale of these commodities permits the producer to receive a sum of money greater than M (M') that constitutes profit. Note that at this point, labor is considered a commodity to be purchased or rented, in the same way that raw materials, machines, factories, or land are purchased or rented. Labor becomes a factor of production in the same way that raw materials, land, or machines are factors of production. In addition, at this point the accumulation of wealth comes to consist increasingly of productive capital (raw materials, machines, and factories).

Let's apply the formula to our sample capitalist enterprise, the Nike corporation. Nike invests money (M) to buy commodities (C) consisting of such things as leather, rubber, machines to make textiles, and factories (mp), which they combine with labor (lp) and the people who design, produce, and assemble the commodity—sneakers—[C'] that they then sell for money [M']. The object of this entire process is to get M' to exceed M as much as possible. That constitutes the profit—the bottom line, so to speak.

Furthermore, Nike doesn't simply keep M'—it reinvests it in commodities and recombines it with mp and lp in order to repeat the process and earn/accumulate still more money and profits. (Figure 2.1 is a diagram of the cyclical nature of capitalist production.)

However, in the real world of finance, there are other factors to consider. For example, producers of commodities do not often have the money (or capital) to start the production cycle on their own; they have to borrow money from banks or sell stock to investors to raise money to obtain the means of production and pay the labor power to produce goods. Consequently, some of the profits take the form of principal and interest to repay investors' loans. The higher the rate of interest that the manufacturer offers investors, the easier it is to obtain loans. Moreover, the producer (Nike, for example) doesn't have to put its profits back into producing more sneakers. It may invest that money elsewhere with the possibility of earning greater profits; in other words, the manufacture and sale of sneakers may produce a profit of 10 percent, but if those profits can be reinvested elsewhere at 12 percent, so much the better.

This reveals one dilemma that Nike and other producers of commodities face: Making a profit is not enough. They must give their investors (the banks, stockholders, and so on) who

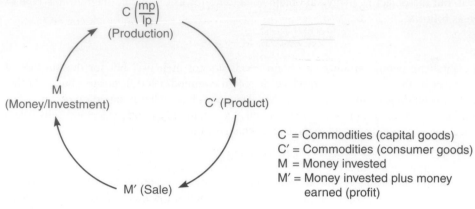

FIGURE 2.1 Cycle of Capitalist Production

supplied the money or capital to start the cycle of production enough of a return on their money so that they do not take it elsewhere. If they go elsewhere (and investors in today's world, as we shall see, have an enormous number of investment options), Nike may find it harder to locate investors and put together the money necessary to restart the cycle. Consequently, they may have to pay higher interest rates and charge more for their products. In that case, however, they might not sell as many units, especially if Adidas or Reebok can sell their sneakers for less.

In order to make a profit, it is imperative to keep the money spent on factories, machines (mp), and labor (lp) as low as possible. In fact, according to some economists, the ability to minimize the production costs of mp and lp will determine the success or failure of the company. (We will return to that in a moment.)

Parenthetically, it is noteworthy that corporations that do not issue stock, and, hence, don't have to worry about satisfying investors, are able to offer workers better incomes, benefits, and working conditions than corporations that are more dependent on investors and banks for working capital. For example, among the present giants of the chocolate industry, only the Mars Company, though a formidable competitor in the market, has the most ethical standards in the business. It remains a family business and, despite having a turnover bigger than McDonald's, has never been quoted on the stock exchange. The founder of the company, Forest Mars, insisted on generosity to the workforce and service to customers; Mars aims to make only a 3 percent return after taxes, and the salaries of employees, or "associates" as they are called, are higher than those in comparable firms, while directors earn less (Fernandez-Armesto 2002:199).

Regardless, it is clear that the capitalist production process is very much a money-making game: Investors and manufacturers put money in at one end of the production process and get more money out of the other end in the form of profits or interest. It is very much like a hypothetical device that engineers call a *black box*. Engineers assume that the black box produces something, but for the purposes of design and planning, they do not concern themselves with how things are produced—that is, with the internal functioning of the box. They simply assume that if they put something into it—fuel, electricity, and so on—they will get something out (e.g., power and movement).

For most capitalist producers or investors, capitalism or capitalist enterprises such as corporations, banks, bonds, or stocks are like black boxes: You put money in one end and get more money out the other (see Figure 2.2).

It is, of course, a highly complex business to know where to put the money, how much to invest, and so forth. But it is the amount of the return rather than the way it is generated that is of utmost importance.

FIGURE 2.2   The Black Box

Nevertheless, it is in the black box that commodities are produced and consumed. It is also in the black box that we find the patterns of social, political, economic, ecological, and ideological life that either promote or inhibit the conversion of money into more money.

Thus, capitalism is more than an economic system; its operation has far-reaching consequences for almost all aspects of our existence. Most of us order our lives in some way to produce and consume commodities that generate the profits and interest that make the capitalist system work. But although most people who invest money do not concern themselves with how it is produced, others who are affected by this almost magical transformation often conceptualize the process in profound ways. For example, peasant farmers in Colombia have a way of conceptualizing capitalist exchange that may help us understand its essential elements and its cost.

The Baptism of Money

After losing their land to large farmers and being forced to supplement their farming activities with wage labor, peasants in the lowlands of Colombia developed the practice of illicitly baptizing money in a Catholic Church—instead of baptizing a newborn child. When presenting a child to the priest to be baptized, a person would hold a peso note that he or she believed received the priest's blessing instead of the child. The note, thus magically transformed and given the name of the child, would, it was believed, continually return to and enrich its owner by bringing with it other notes. In other words, the note would become interest-bearing capital that continued to generate more and more money. Peasants tell stories of such notes disappearing from cash registers, carrying with them all the other notes, and of the store owner who saved his money only because he heard two baptized notes fighting for possession of the drawer's contents.

The idea that money is animate, that it can magically bring back more money, may at first seem strange to us, but Michael Taussig (1977) argued that the Colombian view of money is very close to our own—the major difference having to do with their conception of the black box.

The major feature of capitalism is that money can be used to make more money. To do so, the money must be invested in goods that must be sold, or invested in factories in which people work to make goods to be sold, and so on. Yet, we often talk as if it is the money itself that makes the money, or as if money somehow has a life of its own. We speak of "the *sagging* dollar," "cash *flows*," or "putting our money to *work*." The news will report that "earnings have *surged* ahead" or that we have "*climbing* interest rates." Factories are even referred to as "*plants*" where our "money *grows*."

In other words, our language conveys the notion that capital has an innate property of self-expansion. It is talked about as if it were a living being that reproduces itself (just as the Colombian peasant believes baptized money has a life of its own and can reproduce itself).

The belief that money has a life of its own is beautifully illustrated in Benjamin Franklin's classic letter *Advice to a Young Tradesman* (1748). Here is Franklin's advice:

> Remember, that money is of the prolific, generating nature. Money can beget money, and its offspring can beget more, and so on. Five shillings turned is six, turned again it is seven and three pence and so on, till it becomes a hundred pounds. The more there is of it, the more it produces every turning, so that the profits rise quicker and quicker. He that kills a breeding-sow, destroys all her offspring to the thousandth generation. (Taussig 1977:140)

The attitude expressed by Benjamin Franklin and expressed daily in our own lives is one that Karl Marx called *commodity fetishism*. Fetishism attributes life, autonomy, and power to inanimate objects—dolls, sticks, places, or, in capitalism, money or other commodities. But commodity fetishism also performs another function. By attributing animate life to money, by speaking of it as if the money itself produces money, we mask and hide the actual manner in which money begets money—the exploitation of labor, land, and people. In this magical way of thinking, we begin to perceive money as being able to generate value and yield interest in the same way that pear trees bear fruit or pigs bear piglets. The whole process of capital investment, making a profit, finding the cheapest labor, and so on, comes to appear natural because the real source of profits and the noneconomic consequences of capitalism are largely hidden from view.

Money, however, does not produce money by itself. It requires other things, and this is where the Colombian peasant belief about the baptism of money is quite profound. Colombian peasants' practice of baptizing money so that it brings back more money is a rational interpretation of our own view of money but with one addition: For the Colombian peasant, the process is immoral. It is immoral because it is money rather than the child that is baptized; profit can come only at the cost of the child's soul. In this way, the Colombian peasant is offering a critique of the capitalism that has been imposed on his society in the past century by the expanding world system.

These peasants are also posing key questions: *How does capitalism perform its magic, converting money into more money, and do we pay a price for that conversion?*

THE CONSTRUCTION AND ANATOMY OF THE WORKING CLASS

As noted in the introduction to Part 1, capitalism involves interactions among three sets of people—consumers, laborers, and capitalists—each doing what it is supposed, indeed has, to do. The construction of the consumer took place largely in the twentieth century. The nineteenth century witnessed the development of the working class. Although the flowering of the consumer occurred largely in the United States, the laborer was mainly a creation of the British economy, a creation that gradually migrated from Great Britain to the rest of the world.

Characteristics of the Working Class

The new working class was unlike any that had existed before. Four characteristics of this new category of persons stand out: (1) Members of this class were by necessity mobile, free to move to wherever workers were needed, unhampered by property or family connections; (2) they were segmented or divided by race and ethnicity, age, and gender; (3) they were subject to new kinds of discipline and control; and (4) they were militant, often protesting the conditions in which they were placed. Let's examine each of these characteristics in turn.

LABOR MOBILITY   First, the new laborers were remarkably geographically mobile, moving temporarily or permanently to sources of employment. Most were mobile because they had been forced off their land or because the products they produced were no longer in demand. Take the situation of the Italian worker, for example. Beginning in the 1870s, the sale of public domain and church lands created a situation that allowed large landholders to add to their land, whereas small landholders were squeezed out as prices for agricultural products declined, in part because of the importation of Russian wheat. A blight destroyed many vineyards, and cheap imported goods disrupted local handicrafts. In the 1860s, some 16,000 people emigrated permanently; in the 1870s, the number grew to 360,000; and between 1881 and 1901, the number rose to 2 million, 80 percent of whom had been agricultural laborers.

The countries to which these Italian migrants scattered, including Australia, Canada, and most often the United States, quickly utilized the cheap labor in factories, railroads, mines, stockyards, and oil fields. In the period between 1820 and 1860, the main contingents of immigrants came from Ireland (2 million), southwestern Germany (1.5 million), and the British Isles (750,000). More English, Swedes, and Germans arrived between 1860 and 1890; again they were mainly displaced agriculturists driven off their land by the importation of cheap American and Russian wheat (as Mexican farmers are currently being displaced by the importation of cheap American corn).

In 1890, the source of the new immigration shifted to southern and eastern Europe and consisted largely of displaced peasants from Italy, the Austro-Hungarian Empire, the Balkans, and Poland, along with Jews from Russia.

Coal miners in Pennsylvania had been British, Irish, and German prior to 1890, but after that time they were increasingly Polish, Slovakian, Italian, and Hungarian. After 1890, the textile mills of New England that had been run by French Canadians, English, and Irish were run by Portuguese, Greeks, Poles, and Syrians. In the garment trades, Russians, Jews, and Italians replaced Germans, Czechs, and Irish.

Some 90,000 indentured Chinese laborers were sent to Peru between 1849 and 1874; more than 200,000 were sent to the United States between 1852 and 1875, where they were employed in fruit growing, processing and panning for gold, and railroad construction. Some 10,000 to 14,000 Chinese were used in the construction of the Central Pacific Railroad of California. Thus the nineteenth century saw the greatest migration of human beings that the world had ever seen as millions, no longer able to support themselves, relocated in an effort to sell their labor.

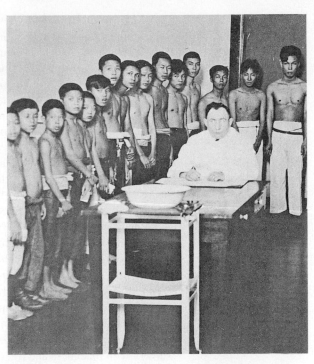

Geographic mobility is one characteristic of the laborer in the culture of capitalism. Here, Chinese boys await medical examinations at Angel Island immigration station in San Francisco around 1910. (The Granger Collection, NYC.)

SEGMENTATION A second characteristic of the working class was that they were divided, or segmented, by race, religion, ethnicity, age, and gender. The new working class split into two broader categories: a labor aristocracy better able to defend its prerequisites through union organization and political influence, and workers who had to accept lower wages and less secure jobs. These divisions were often reinforced by the use of gender, racial, or ethnic distinctions that relegated certain groups such as blacks and, earlier in the century, the Irish to only the lowest-paying jobs. Capitalism did not create these racial and ethnic distinctions, but it did help in defining and reinforcing them and their economic consequences (Wolf 1982:380).

Ironically, the ethnic identities of new immigrants rarely coincided with their self-identification. They first thought of themselves as Hanoverians or Bavarians rather than Germans; as members of a village parish (*okolica*) rather than Poles; as Sicilians, Neapolitans, and Genoans rather than Italians; and as Tonga or Yao rather than "Nyasalanders." In effect, migrants had to be socialized to see themselves as members of particular ethnic groups. They were, as Wolf (1982:381) said, "historical products of labor market segmentation under the capitalistic mode."

The ethnic or racial groupings created or reinforced by capitalist culture often came into conflict with each other as they competed for scarce jobs and resources. The case of the Irish in England and the United States is telling. In the mid-nineteenth century, Karl Marx (1972:293–294) made the following observation about the relationship between English workers and newly arrived Irish laborers:

> Every industrial and commercial center in England now possesses a working class divided into two hostile camps, English proletarians and Irish proletarians. The ordinary English worker hates the Irish as a competitor who lowers his standard of life. In relation to the Irish worker he feels himself a member of the ruling nation and so

turns himself into a tool of the aristocrats and capitalists of his own country against Ireland, thus strengthening their domination over himself. He cherishes religious, social, and national prejudices against the Irish worker. His attitude towards him is much the same as "poor whites" to the "niggers" of the former slave states of the USA. The Irishman pays him back with interest in his own money. He sees the English worker at once the accomplice and the stupid tool of the English domination in Ireland.... This antagonism is the secret of the impotence of the English working class, despite their organization.

In the United States, the same degree of ethnic antagonism developed, particularly between the Irish and blacks. Irish leaders in the early nineteenth century generally were strong critics of slavery and supporters of its abolition. However, once the Irish emigrated to the United States, they, who in their own country were treated almost as badly by British rulers as African Americans were in the United States by whites, became strongly proslavery and antiblack. What accounted for this change in attitude?

Noel Ignatiev (1995), in his book *How the Irish Became White,* maintained that during the first half of the nineteenth century in America, free African Americans competed successfully in the North for relatively good jobs. Before the Irish arrived in large numbers in the United States, the distinction between freedom and slavery was blurred by such intermediate conditions as chattel slavery, indentured servitude, and imprisonment for debt. But the American Revolution had eliminated these intermediate economic categories and reinforced the tendency to equate slavery with blackness and freedom with whiteness. If blacks, then, were allowed to work in the same jobs as the Irish, the Irish would be assigned to the same social category as blacks. In fact, the Irish risked being considered lower in status than blacks, largely because as slaves, blacks had value that the Irish did not. As one official of an Alabama stevedoring company put it, "The niggers are worth too much to be risked here; if the Paddies are knocked overboard, or get their backs broke, nobody loses anything" (Ignatiev 1995:109). Consequently, the Irish did all they could to distance themselves from blacks, including supporting slavery. But the major task of the Irish was to ensure that blacks did not have access to the same jobs that they did.

Gradually, by taking the menial jobs that had been done by blacks, as they were encouraged to do by priests, the Irish began to dominate the ranks of the unskilled laborer—by 1855, the Irish made up 87 percent of New York City's 23,000 unskilled laborers. In 1851, *The African Repository,* a magazine devoted to African American concerns, wrote (Ignatiev 1995:111) that

> in New York and other Eastern cities, the influx of white laborers has expelled the Negro almost en masse from the exercise of the ordinary branches of labor. You no longer see him work upon buildings, and rarely is he allowed to drive a cart or public conveyance. White men will not work with him.

"White men will not work with him," became the rallying cry of labor in elbowing out blacks from jobs that were then taken over by Irish; as Frederick Douglass said, "In assuming our avocation [the Irishman] has assumed our degradation."

The key to the distinction between white and black became work; *white* meant doing "white man's work," whereas *black* meant doing "black man's work." The distinction was arbitrary because many jobs that became white man's work when reserved for the Irish had been performed by blacks earlier. "White," Ignatiev pointed out, was not a physical description, but rather a term of social relations. This distinction resulted, then, in a situation in which to be "white" the Irish had to work in the jobs from which blacks were excluded (Ignatiev 1995:111). Thus, a division of labor was hardened into a distinction of race and ethnicity.

Of course, the workforce was segmented in other ways, most notably by gender and age, with women and children assigned to the lowest-paying and most menial jobs, a development we will explore below.

DISCIPLINE   The new working class was mobile and divided by race, ethnicity, gender, and age. In addition, it had to be disciplined. Central to this process was the factory. The factory is a relatively recent historical phenomenon, having developed largely in the late eighteenth and early nineteenth centuries in Europe (although factory production in textiles may have existed as early as the fifteenth century). Prior to its development, most work (e.g., weaving, spinning, and pottery making) was done in homes or small shops. But with the work scattered from town to town and house to house, manufacturers had difficulty maintaining product standards and supplying the workers with raw materials. Factories solved these problems.

The first factories were modeled on penal workhouses and prisons. Spinning mills were built and installed in brick buildings four or five stories high and employed several hundred workers. The iron and cast-iron mills of the metal industry brought together several blast furnaces and forges and a large workforce (Beaud 1983:66). These settings may have increased the efficiency of production, but the new job discipline required of workers also created tensions between workers and their employers that, at various points in the years to follow, would result in situations approaching civil war.

The factory setting, for example, necessitated workers being disciplined to accept a new conception of time. Time, another of the things we take for granted, is subject to cultural definition. Our time is dictated, by and large, by our means of measuring it—clocks and watches. Time in other societies tends to be task oriented or dictated by natural phenomena: In Madagascar, it might be measured by rice cooking (about one-half hour); in seventeenth-century Chile, the time needed to cook an egg was the time it took to say an Ave Maria aloud; in Burma, monks rose when there was enough light to see the veins in their hands; in oceanside communities, the social patterning of time depended on the ebb and flow of tides. In his classic account of the life of the Nuer of the Sudan, British anthropologist E. E. Evans-Pritchard (1940:103) noted that

> the Nuer have no expression equivalent to "time" in our language, and they cannot, therefore, as we can, speak of time as though it were something actual, which passes, can be wasted, can be saved, and so forth. I don't think they ever experience the same feeling of fighting against time because their points of reference are mainly the activities themselves, which are generally of a leisurely character. Events follow a logical order, but they are not controlled by an abstract system, there being no autonomous points of reference to which activities have to conform with precision. Nuer are fortunate.

Historian E. P. Thompson (1967) noted that until the emergence of modern notions of time, work patterns were characterized by alternating bouts of intense labor and idleness, at least whenever people were in control of their own working lives. He has even suggested that this pattern persists today but only among some self-employed professionals, such as artists, writers, small-farm owners, and college students.

This is not to say that preindustrial work was easy. Thompson (1967:58) described the typical day of a farm laborer in 1636: He rose at 4:00 A.M. and cared for the horses, ate breakfast at 6:00 A.M., plowed until 2:00 or 3:00 P.M., ate lunch, attended to the horses until 6:00 in the evening, ate supper, did other chores till 8:00 P.M., cared for the cattle, and then retired. However, this was during the height of the laboring year on the farm, and it was probably the laborer's wife, says Thompson, who labored the hardest.

It is difficult to say precisely when the Western concept of time and work began to change. Clocks were not widespread in Europe until the seventeenth century, although most towns probably had a church clock. But by the early 1800s, our present sense of time was well established.

Time was an entity that should not be wasted. "Time," as Benjamin Franklin wrote in *Poor Richard's Almanac*, "is money." At about the same period, the idea that idleness was wicked began to gain currency. As *Youth's Monitor* phrased it in 1689, time "is too precious a commodity to be undervalued.... This is the golden chain on which hangs a massy eternity; the loss of time is insufferable, because irrecoverable" (Thompson 1967:58). Leisure time, in general, was attacked; in some religious circles, seeking amusement was considered to be sinful. Anything that did not contribute to production was discouraged.

At about the same time, the school was being used to teach a new time and work discipline. Social reformers in the late eighteenth century suggested that poor children be sent at the age of four to workhouses where they would work and be given two hours schooling each day. As one person said,

> There is considerable use in their being somehow or other, constantly employed at least twelve hours a day, whether they can earn their living or not; for by these means, we hope that the rising generation will be so habituated to constant employment that it would at length prove agreeable and entertaining to them. (Thompson 1967:84)

Thus, by the middle of the nineteenth century, through the supervision of labor, fines, bells and clocks, money incentives, preaching, and schooling, a new time discipline was imposed on society at large and on the laborer in particular.

RESISTANCE   Finally, in addition to its mobility, segmentation, and discipline, the new working class was characterized by a new militancy that would lead to the closest thing the world has seen to a "world revolution." Early in 1848, the French political thinker and chronicler of American democracy Alexis de Tocqueville addressed the French Chamber of Deputies, saying what many Europeans feared. "We are sleeping," he said, "on a volcano.... Do you not see that the earth trembles anew? A wind of revolution blows, the storm is on the horizon" (Hobsbawm 1975:9).

At about the same time, the thirty-year-old Karl Marx and his twenty-eight-year-old friend Friedrich Engels were drafting the *Manifesto of the Communist Party,* which appeared in London in February 1848. Perhaps within days, revolutionaries in France declared the establishment of a new republic; by March, the revolution had moved into Germany, Hungary, and Italy; within weeks, the governments of an area today encompassing France, Germany, Austria, Italy, Czechoslovakia, Hungary, part of Poland, Belgium, Switzerland, Denmark, and the old Yugoslavia were all overthrown. However, within six months of the outbreak, the movement faltered, and within eighteen months, only the new government of France remained, and it was trying to put distance between itself and the insurrectionists. The only long-lasting change was the abolition of serfdom in what had been the Hapsburg Empire.

Although the rebels had the support of moderates and liberals in the various countries, their movements were, nevertheless, "social revolutions of the labouring poor," as Hobsbawm (1975:15) put it. The revolutions were an expression of developing patterns of conflict between the rich and poor, each group developing its spokespersons. On the one side were people such as Jean-Baptiste Say in France and David Ricardo and Thomas Robert Malthus in England who argued that the poor had only themselves to blame for their condition. On the other side were those such as Karl Marx, Friedrich Engels, Robert Owen, Henri Saint-Simon, and Charles Fourier who blamed the exploitation of labor for poverty. The debate is not unlike the ones still being argued over such issues as welfare and the role of the state in alleviating poverty. Malthus argued, for example, that

> it is not in the power of the rich to supply the poor with an occupation and with bread, and consequently, the poor, by the very nature of things have no right to demand these things from the rich.... No possible contributions of sacrifices of the rich, particularly in money, could for any time prevent the recurrence of distress among the lower members of society. (Beaud 1983:78)

It is a matter of morality, said Malthus, that those who are poor must not produce children until they can adequately provide for them. To those who violate this rule, there should be no pity:

> To the punishment, therefore of nature he should be left, to the punishment of want. He has erred in the face of a most clear and precise warning, and can have no just reason to complain of any person but himself when he feels the consequences of his error. All parish assistance should be denied him; and he should be left to the uncertain support of private charity. He should be taught to know that the laws of nature, which are the laws of God, had doomed him and his family to suffer for disobeying their repeated admonitions.... It may appear to be hard that a mother and her children, who have been guilty of no particular crime themselves, should suffer for the ill conduct of the father; but this is one of the invariable laws of nature. (Malthus 1826:343)

One French industrialist wrote matter-of-factly that "the fate of the workers is not that bad: their labor is not excessive since it does not go beyond thirteen hours.... The manufacturer whose profits are poor is the one to be pitied" (Beaud 1983:101).

Of course, those arguing against supplying the poor with necessities were concerned also that if they were given food and shelter, they would have no reason to labor.

For others, such as Karl Marx and Friedrich Engels, society was being divided into two hostile camps and classes—the bourgeoisie and the proletariat:

> Masses of laborers, crowded into the factory, are organized like soldiers. As privates of the industrial army, they are placed under the command of a perfect hierarchy of officers and sergeants. Not only are they the slaves of the bourgeoisie class, and of the bourgeoisie State, they are daily and hourly enslaved by the machine, by the overlooker, and above all, by the individual bourgeoisie manufacturer himself. The more openly this despotism proclaims gain to be its end and aim, the more petty, the more hateful and the more embittering it is. (Marx and Engels 1848/1941:14)

The proletariat must, said Marx and Engels, embody the suffering, rise against it, and produce a society free from the exploitation of one class by another. It must free itself but only by transcending the inhumane conditions of present-day society. Marx had attempted in his writings to create a scientific theory of the fall of capitalism, in the same way that Adam Smith and David Ricardo had tried to create a scientific theory of the rise of capitalism. The results were not only a blueprint to be used by union organizers and revolutionaries but also the creation of two utopian ideologies—that of capitalism and of socialism—which would do battle into the twentieth century.

These, then, are some of the characteristics of the laborer and the relationship between labor and capital as established in the nineteenth century. There were other features as well, such as the increased vulnerability of the laborer to hardship and the greater likelihood of impoverishment. To understand better how the laborer was constructed, let's turn to the contemporary world. In countries all over the world, the nineteenth-century processes through which the laborer was constructed are being repeated. We see this most clearly in the growth of overseas assembly plants.

The Growth of Overseas Assembly Plants

In capitalism, profits and interest depend on the difference between the cost of producing a product and the price at which it is sold. If someone has a monopoly on a product, and if people need it, producers can charge as much as necessary to maintain or increase profits. But if other companies produce the same merchandise, it is likely that the price a company can charge will be determined by what others charge. Thus, Nike can charge 200 dollars for its sneakers, but if its competitors are charging only fifty dollars for the same product, Nike had better lower its price, convince people that its product is worth the difference, or face bankruptcy. Consequently, profit must come, not from increasing the price that people pay, but from controlling the cost of producing the product. Cost increase can be contained by controlling the cost of raw materials and machines—the means of production—or by controlling the price of labor.

The activity of work is common to all societies. In gathering and hunting societies, women and men spend a portion of their time gathering wild foods and hunting game; in pastoral societies, people spend time herding and caring for animals; and in agricultural societies, they work at tending fields, harvesting and storing crops, and so on. But work in the black box of capitalism takes a different form. In fact, some economists believe the key to understanding the way money creates more money is understanding the way labor figures in the production process. For them, profit comes directly from what they call the *surplus value of labor.*

As we noted earlier, to produce commodities for sale, labor must be purchased and combined with the means of production. For example, I might buy cloth and make shirts to sell. I may pay two dollars for the cloth and sell the shirt for ten, thereby making a profit of eight dollars. Where does that profit come from? One obvious place is the labor that went to convert the cloth into a shirt. In this case we might say the labor was worth eight dollars. But what if, instead of making the shirt myself, I paid someone else to do it but paid him or her only two dollars and still sold the shirt for ten. The value of the labor that went into making the shirt is still eight dollars, but the worker I hired received only two; I get to keep the other six dollars. It is this money that constitutes the *surplus value of labor.*

Obviously, then, one way for a company to maximize profits is to maximize the surplus value of labor and pay workers as little as possible. Another way to increase profits is to get the laborer to produce more in the same period of time. Thus, if I paid my shirtmakers an hourly or daily wage, I could double my profits by getting them to produce two shirts in the time that they used to produce one shirt. This I could do by getting them to work faster or by improving the technology or process of shirt-making to make it more efficient.

Companies that produce commodities such as textiles, electronic goods, and toys are labor intensive—that is, they require human labor more than improved technology to manufacture their products and are, consequently, always trying to minimize what they pay workers. Given the economic logic of capitalism, this makes perfectly good sense: The more they save on labor costs and the less they charge for their product, the more they will attract consumers. Furthermore, the more they sell, the greater their profits and greater the return for investors and stock owners. Thus, the role of labor in the black box is critical to our understanding of the amount of profit the box can generate.

There are various ways that producers can keep labor costs down. For example, they can import labor from peripheral areas, particularly for low-paying jobs. In 2011, there were 24.4 million foreign-born persons in the U.S. labor force, comprising 15.9 percent of the total (Bureau of Labor Statistics 2012). Many of these people worked as poultry plant workers, meatpackers, gardeners, hotel maids, seamstresses, restaurant workers, building demolition workers, and fruit and vegetable pickers (Greenhouse 2000). Corporations are also making use of the growing prison population; in the United States there are more than 2 million inmates, more than any other country in the world. Presently, thirty states have enacted laws allowing the use of convict labor by private enterprise who now employ more than 80,000 prisoners. Then there is slave labor. Kevin Bales (1999:8) estimates that there are 27 million slaves in the world today, largely in the form of bonded labor in India, Pakistan, Bangladesh, and Nepal. Bonded laborers give themselves into slavery as security for a loan or when they inherit a debt from a family member. Clearly, the greatest source of cheap labor exists in the periphery where, officially, more than 189.9 million people were unemployed in 2007 and that figure is expected to increase by 5 million or more in response to the economic crisis of 2008 (Blankenburg and Palma 2009:532). It is there that corporations often go to reduce their labor costs.

Corporations in core countries, such as the United States, made much use of foreign labor in the nineteenth century. However, as previously discussed, most of that labor moved to the source of employment, traveling largely from Europe and Asia to work in American mines, railroad yards, and factories. By 1900, 14 percent of the population of the United States was foreign born (see Haugerud, Stone, and Little 2000). Once jobs were filled, however, the immigrants or their descendants who filled them were not anxious to see more immigrants arrive and compete for their jobs. Consequently, they lobbied through unions, churches, and political parties for the government to pass restrictive immigration laws. When Chinese laborers were brought over to help build the transcontinental railroad, groups such as the Knights of Labor protested, even demanding that the Chinese get out of the laundry business. As a result, the U.S. Congress passed the Chinese Exclusion Act of 1882, and anti-Chinese agitation broke out on the West Coast, marking one more stage in the emergence of racism in the United States.

Although importing laborers from overseas worked for a time, corporations soon found that they could more easily tap into pools of cheap labor by relocating their manufacturing processes, when possible, to countries on the periphery of the world system whose governments were committed to economic development through industrialization. For example, to facilitate the establishment of assembly plants, governments in Indonesia, Malaysia, Guatemala, and Mexico, among others, created in their countries *free trade zones,* areas in which large corporations were permitted to deliver goods to be assembled—cut cloth for wearing apparel, electronic components, and so on—and for which they were not required to pay tariffs, provided that the items were not then sold in the country in which they were assembled. In exchange, the multinational corporations, such as Nike, agreed to hire local workers. The home countries, such as the United States, contributed by passing legislation that allowed corporations to transfer the assembled goods back to the United States, paying an import tariff only on the labor cost of each product, rather than on the total value of the product. Thus, the sneakers you wear were probably cut by machines in the United States, shipped to Indonesia or Vietnam to be assembled, and then shipped back to the United States to be distributed and sold there and elsewhere in the world. As an economic arrangement, almost everyone seems to benefit from the growth of assembly plants:

* Nike and other companies are able to compete with other manufacturers by paying workers in Third World countries a fraction of what they would have to pay American workers.
* Workers in the Third World find employment.
* Consumers pay less for their clothes, electronic devices, toys, and so on.
* Investors get a higher return on their money.

It seems that the only ones who don't benefit are the American workers who lose their jobs (over 5 million in the past twenty-five years).

As a result, the growth in assembly plants was dramatic. In 1970 there were an estimated 1,000 women working in manufacturing in Malaysia, for example; by 1980, there were 80,000 concentrated in textiles, electronics, and food processing. In Mexico, the number of *maquiladoras,* as assembly plants are called, grew from virtually none in the 1960s to 1,279 employing 329,413 people in 1988, to more than 3,000 employing more than 1 million workers in 2012 (Hodder 1999; Rosenberg 2012). However, there are some problems. Critics have cited assembly plant workers' poor working conditions, their low pay, the actions of foreign governments in discouraging the formation of workers' unions, and the loose environmental regulations that have in some cases resulted in considerable environmental degradation around free trade zones. Furthermore, as corporations seek out new areas of cheap labor, they abandon old sites, such as Mexico, in favor of new sites, such as China or Vietnam. Consequently, after hitting a peak in 1999, the number of *maquiladora* workers in Mexico is on the decline.

In 1995, in response to abuses, American labor and children's rights groups called for a boycott of all garments assembled in Bangladesh to protest the estimated 25,000 to 30,000 children working in garment factories there. The United States is Bangladesh's biggest apparel customer, with nearly 50 percent of Bangladesh's $1.6 billion in garment exports arriving in the United States. In some assembly factories in El Salvador, where women earn $4.51 for the day, or 56 cents an hour, union organizers are often summarily dismissed, bathrooms are locked and can be used only with permission, and talking on the job is prohibited. In Guatemala, workers are required to work overtime at a moment's notice and are dismissed if they refuse. There have been reports of systematic violence against union organizers in Mexico, El Salvador, and Guatemala. And, as we shall see, assembly plants have far-reaching consequences on the societies and cultures of the cities and countries in which they are located.

The Creation of Free Labor

One defining feature of capitalism is the creation of a class of people who are willing to sell their labor. There must be a working class and, subsequently, a demand for jobs. A key question, then, is, *Why do people, particularly the workers, play the game of capitalism?* For example, if the pay is poor and working conditions harsh, *why do people work in assembly plants?* Aren't these workers, as some argue, lucky to have their jobs?

Although the United States is and has been largely a wage economy in which the vast majority of people, in effect, sell their labor to companies, we sometimes forget, as mentioned earlier, that the existence of a so-called working class is a relatively recent development. In the United States, and particularly in countries such as Malaysia and Mexico until recently, most people earned their livings from the land or from what they themselves produced and sold. Thus, we need to ask, *Why people exchanged a life of relative independence as farmers and craftspeople for a life of dependent wage labor?*

In Malaysia and Mexico, countries trying to industrialize and attract foreign manufacturers such as Nike, political developments in the nineteenth and early twentieth centuries led to the systematic dispossession of peasants from their land and to the increased importation of cheap products (e.g., textiles and iron implements) that put local artisans out of business. For example, up to the nineteenth century, Malaysia consisted of small states ruled over by sultans and so-called big men who extracted tribute from peasants. Peasants held use-rights to land and could pass on to children whatever land they worked but no more than that. The center of life was the *kampung,* or village. However, British colonialists took over the land and converted its use to the production of cash crops, leaving the unlanded population to seek labor on large plantations or migrate to cities in search of jobs. There was still more than enough land in Malaysia for everyone to farm, but it was used instead to produce crops, such as palm oil, for export rather than to produce food for the local population.

In Mexico a similar history has left most of the population without land to produce food. In the early nineteenth century, the vast majority of the Mexican population lived in villages. The land was divided among the residents but owned collectively. People were given the right to use land but not the right to sell it. Then, in the mid-nineteenth century, legislation was passed in Mexico declaring communally held lands to be illegal, giving peasants legal rights to their own land, which they could then also sell or mortgage to repay debts. The result was that wealthy persons—largely Americans—bought up huge tracts of land. By 1910, the year of the beginning of the Mexican Revolution, more than 90 percent of the population was landless and forced to work on large agricultural estates or migrate to the cities in search of jobs. In the course of half a century, the vast majority of the Mexican population was transformed from an autonomous peasantry working their own land to a population of dependent wage laborers.

The process of land dispossession has continued to the present time (as will be discussed later), not only in Mexico and Malaysia but also in many other parts of the world. This has resulted in a large population of landless people with only their labor to sell. Furthermore, as so-called free trade opens countries to goods from the United States and other wealthy countries, local farmers and craftspeople who cannot compete with large multinationals lose their livelihoods and are forced onto the labor market. As a result, the governments of these countries are under great pressure to facilitate the growth of jobs for the population. It is into these situations that American, Japanese, German, and British corporations, among others, have come to build assembly plants.

Assembly factories, however, involve a paradox. In countries such as Malaysia and Mexico, the men traditionally were the wage laborers, but women are sought by corporations, such as Nike, as employees. The women, for some reason, are willing to accept a wage level less than that needed for subsistence. Thus, we need to ask, *Why are there jobs that pay less than a living wage, and why do certain categories of people seem relegated to them?*

The Segmentation of the Workforce

One consequence of the growth of offshore assembly plants was the entrance into the labor market of a new working population of young, single women between the ages of sixteen and twenty-four. *Why do the assembly plants choose to employ young women, and why is it that women choose to work under sometimes unpleasant conditions?* The answer to this question requires us to understand how and why labor is segmented into different levels.

Take, for example, the case of Malaysia. Aihwa Ong (1987) spent two years studying assembly plants in Malaysia owned by Japanese and American corporations. One of the first questions she asked was this: Why did the plants prefer to hire young women? Plant managers that she interviewed gave a number of reasons. One Japanese manager told Ong (1990:396–397) that "females [are] better able to concentrate on routine work" and "young girls [are] preferable than older persons, that is because of eyesight." Another explained, "You cannot expect a man to do very fine work for eight hours [at a stretch]. Our work is designed for females.... [I]f we employ men, within one or two months they would have run away.... Girls [*sic*] below thirty are easier to train and easier to adapt to the job function."

The idea that women are somehow more suited biologically for assembly plant work is widespread in developing countries. For example, a brochure designed to bring foreign investments into Malaysia says this about its female workforce:

> Her hands are small and she works fast with extreme care. Who, therefore, could be better qualified *by nature and inheritance* to contribute to the efficiency of a bench assembly production line than the oriental girl? (Ong 1987:152 [emphasis added])

Young women, such as these uniformed workers at a Nike assembly plant in Vietnam, comprise the vast majority of workers at overseas assembly plants.
(AP Photo/Richard Vogel.)

In Mexican *maquiladoras* the situation is much the same. María Patricia Fernández-Kelly (1983) was also interested in the effects of the assembly plants on women. To study these effects, she found a job in a *maquiladora* to share the experiences of the workers and to meet the women and learn about their lives. She, too, found that companies preferred to hire young females because managers believed that women have higher skill levels; are more docile; and are more willing to comply to the monotonous, repetitive, and exhausting assignments. Men are described by managers as more restless or rebellious, less patient, more likely to unionize, and less tolerant of the working conditions. As one manager related to Fernández-Kelly (1983:181),

> We hire mostly women because they are more reliable than men, they have finer fingers, smaller muscles and unsurpassed manual dexterity. Also, women don't get tired of repeating the same operation nine hundred times a day.

Assembly plants in both Malaysia and Mexico also preferred single women because managers believed that older, married women had too many other obligations; were often unwilling to work night shifts; and may have accumulated enough wage increments to be paid more than a new, young, single woman would earn.

There is also a large population of unemployed women that assembly factories can choose from. In Malaysia and Mexico, there are three applicants for every available position. Thus one *maquiladora* manager could announce to a conference organized by the American Chamber of Commerce that the 30 percent unemployment rate in Ciudad Juárez allows for high employee selectivity. Moreover, village elders in Malaysia and family heads in Mexico are eager to send otherwise non-wage-earning women to work in the assembly plants.

There is another reason, however, for the employment practices of assembly plants, one that tells us even more about the black box of capitalism: You don't have to pay women and children as much as you have to pay men. Nor do you have to pay foreign workers as much as domestic workers. By extension, you do not have to pay people of color as much as you pay whites—that is, the contemporary labor force in peripheral countries, such as Mexico and Malaysia, is already segmented through various forms of social discrimination, as was the labor force in nineteenth-century North America and Europe. Whether or not a capitalist economy creates this type of discrimination, reinforces it, or simply takes advantage of it where it exists is arguable. Regardless, there is no question that, at least to some extent, social discrimination and prejudice—sexism, racism, and discrimination against immigrants—is profitable. It is an important part of the black box. But why?

Let's return to basic economics. Modern industries can be loosely divided into two types. There are *primary industries* whose markets are well defined, whose profits are relatively certain, whose capital investment is high, and who are able to pay good wages and ensure decent working conditions. Primary industries have traditionally included automobile manufacturing, communications, and energy industries, to name a few. They require a well-paid, well-trained, and relatively content workforce.

Then there are *secondary industries* that include the fast-food industry; agriculture; electronics; and, most notably, the clothing, garment, and/or textile industries. Within secondary industries there is intense competition, uncertain or changing demand, a lower profit margin, and a greater dependence on unskilled labor. Secondary industries are the least desirable for workers because to stay competitive, these companies must pay the lowest wages and yet maximize worker output. These are the industries most likely to expand operations to poorer countries. They are also the companies that are likely to hire the most vulnerable and the lowest-ranking members of a population. Traditionally, these people have been women, children, or members of subjugated groups. Thus, when corporations locate assembly factories abroad, they are, in effect, expanding the secondary labor market.

Of course, the hiring of women for low-paying, labor-intensive work has long been a feature of industrial capitalism. Women and children formed the bulk of the factory workforce at the beginning of the Industrial Revolution in the late eighteenth and early nineteenth centuries. In 1851, 31 percent of the labor force in England consisted of women, 45 percent of whom were in manufacturing. In the English textile industry of 1840, more than 75 percent of the workforce consisted of women and children. The locating of assembly plants overseas is simply the latest version of utilizing a socially vulnerable workforce to secure low-paid labor. This expansion of the secondary labor market abroad, however, has had the following economic consequences for workers and corporations at home and abroad:

- It has meant the transfer of jobs abroad and resulting unemployment at home.
- It has widened the gap between primary and secondary labor in the United States.
- From the perspective of workers in peripheral countries of the world system, it has meant the development of poorly paid, unstable jobs with little opportunity for promotion.

The process of targeting the most vulnerable segment of the population for low-wage jobs also affects the meaning that societies give to specific tasks. For example, the division between skilled and unskilled jobs is often not based on the nature of the work, as one would suppose; instead, it is based on who is doing the work. In other words, the work that women do in assembly factories is not necessarily less skilled than other work; it is considered unskilled because it is performed by women. Fernández-Kelly discovered this when she tried to learn the sewing techniques of women in Mexican garment *maquiladoras.* She could barely keep up with them; it required a skill level equal to or greater than many jobs that we call "skilled." In Brazil, women are hired to tend grapevines to produce the large, unblemished grape that consumers in industrial countries desire. The work is skilled (e.g., involving the grafting of vines), but because the work is done by women, it is described as requiring "manual dexterity, delicacy, and nimbleness of fingers" (Collins 2000:102). Thus, work that women do is defined as "unskilled" because it is done by women, just as work that blacks or the Irish did in the nineteenth century was defined as unskilled because it was done by blacks or Irish.

From the corporation's standpoint, however, the transfer of secondary jobs to underdeveloped countries and the ensuing expansion of a cheap labor reserve pool afford corporate employers the greatest degree of political and economic control over workers. They are able to employ the most socially vulnerable sector of the working class, the people least likely to organize, demand better wages, or press for better working conditions. As one Mexican *maquiladora* worker put it, men are unwilling to perform the monotonous labor; women are more shy and submissive and are more used to following orders. They are more easily intimidated and forced to obey. They are the easiest to discipline.

In sum, then, for corporations, women represent a major source of inexpensive, transient labor; thus, women, although making up the vast majority of assembly plant workers throughout the world, occupy few skilled or managerial positions. And because they occupy the lowest positions, women can be hired and fired, depending on the overseas demand for such things as textiles, shoes, plastics, electrical appliances, and, increasingly, electronics.

In spite of the often poor pay and harsh working conditions that women working in assembly plants endure, some economists and public policymakers argue that such employment is necessary if women are ultimately to gain access to better positions and change their often subjugated positions in societies around the world. They argue that the money that women earn gives them control over resources that they would otherwise not have, that as families become dependent on the income that these women bring into their households, their positions in society will improve. Some also argue that the creation of this kind of work is a necessary stage of economic development and will eventually lead to better lives for all. We must remember, however, that if the labor market remains divided between primary and secondary industries, then someone must continue to do the low-paying work. Women may escape low-paying jobs, but only, as the Irish in the nineteenth century learned, if there is another group to take their place.

Control and Discipline

In nineteenth-century America, as young men and women sought work in the growing factory towns and cities, factory owners, as well as local citizens, faced a problem. These young people had been integrated into the social institutions of their hamlets and villages. As members of families and churches, they were expected to conform to certain standards of behavior; deviance from those standards could bring condemnation, punishment, and even social ostracism. But in the towns and cities to which they moved, migrant workers often were freed from such constraints, free to experiment with behaviors previously denied to them. Consequently, men often gained reputations as "rowdies," or "hoodlums," whereas women were labeled "immoral" or "loose." Thus the creation of free labor created a problem: *How do you control the new labor force?*

For example, in turn-of-the-twentieth-century New York City, thousands of young women found employment in factories and used their newfound freedom and the wages they earned for shopping, dating, dancing, or going on excursions to recreation areas such as Coney Island. However, their behavior alarmed some people who saw it as immoral; consequently, groups of social reformers organized and proposed ways to "protect" working women from these "temptations." Some of their solutions to the problem resulted in the formation of social and religious clubs and associations for young women such as the Young Women's Christian Association (YWCA).

These organizations also served another function: They relieved the fears of the parents of these young workers who otherwise might have been reluctant to allow the women to migrate to cities and factory towns.

As in nineteenth-century America and Great Britain, employment in the new assembly plants of such countries as Malaysia and Mexico often requires young men and women to leave their homes and move to cities, freeing them from the traditional constraints imposed by family and church, and, thus, freeing them to spend their leisure time in nontraditional activities. Take, for example, the situation of the largely female workforce in the new assembly plants of Malaysia. Most of the women are young, generally ranging from sixteen to twenty years old. In their villages, they would have lived at home, perhaps attended school, and been involved in various household chores under the direction of their mothers. Dating would have been rare and, when it occurred, would have been carefully supervised by parents. Marriages would have likely been arranged by parents. Factory work, however, allows these same young women to earn wages, a portion of which they control. Although most workers contribute one-half or more of their earnings to their families, they are free to spend the rest on themselves. Some use it for typing or academic classes to prepare for civil service jobs, in effect attempting to control their own job prospects and "careers." Some become consumers, taking shopping trips to town or going to the movies, "making jolly with money," as they say. They exchange traditional *kampung* garb for tight T-shirts, jeans, and Avon makeup, trying to achieve what they call the "electric look."

Because Malaysian working women are now expected to save money to contribute to their own wedding expenses—money that had been traditionally supplied by their families—they feel justified in choosing potential spouses. Sexual freedom may be increasing, as indicated by an increase in abortions, and women are beginning to cross social boundaries, having "illicit" relationships and marrying men of other ethnic groups (e.g., Chinese), something traditional family and church authorities would never have allowed.

One consequence of the growth of the number of working women in Malaysia is a stream of criticism about the loose morals of factory girls, especially from Islamic fundamentalists. The Malay media portrays factory women as pleasure seekers and spendthrifts engulfed in Western consumer culture. A story about prostitution might carry sensational headlines such as "Factory Girls in Sex Racket."

All of this has resulted in a call for greater control of working women, in spite of the fact that similar behavior, such as dating and moviegoing, among upper-class college students has not received the same notice. Even the academic community and religious and state officials have claimed to recognize the problem of declining morals of young women and proposed measures, such as counseling and recreational activities, to arrest the decline. There have also been public calls for control of working women's leisure time, despite the fact that they tend to work about three hours a day more than do women engaged primarily in traditional household chores.

In some ways, the newfound freedom of factory workers is as welcome by businesspeople as it is by the young. Their new income—and their willingness to spend a portion of it on themselves—has turned young village men and women into consumers who buy many of the products they make. But the new freedoms create yet another problem. Capitalist enterprise requires a disciplined and reliable workforce; with old forms of discipline falling away, new forms must be developed to replace them. The question is this: How is that done?

Although family and church are largely absent from the lives of working young men and women, factory managers try to use these traditional institutions to control their workers. Malaysia is an Islamic country, and according to Islamic practice, parents are obligated to care for their children up to age fifteen, and traditional customs decree that children must also care for their parents. Thus, children, particularly women, are obligated to return to their parents the care that they gave them. One of the major appeals made to young women by factory owners and managers is that they use their wages to pay back part of what they owe their parents.

Factory managers also seek to maintain discipline by building relations with people in the women's home villages, thus enlisting their help in controlling workers. For example, managers make donations to community organizations in the villages that supply workers. They also devise regulations to help parents monitor the activities of their daughters. When workers commute from their villages to the factories, the managers deliver workers to their homes by bus, or they allow parents to see overtime forms so they know how much time their daughters were spending at work and at other activities. These efforts enhance the prestige of managers in the eyes of village elders, whose moral support could then be obtained for the social control of working daughters.

Corporations also use traditional family values to encourage workers to comply with company goals (Ong 1987:169). Thus, managers tell workers that they are part of "one big family." One factory had posters proclaiming the company philosophy:

- To create one big family
- To train workers
- To increase loyalty to company, country, and fellow workers

Managers portray themselves as parent figures to the larger community from which women workers come, and although workers complain of too much control, parents rarely tell their daughters to quit.

Religion is also used as a means of discipline (Ong 1987:185). Because Malaysia is an Islamic country, the government includes special departments and agencies that have jurisdiction over the application of religious law. For example, under the current interpretation of religious law, Muslims may be arrested for *khalwat,* "proximity" between a man and a woman who are not immediate relatives or married to each other. Those caught in situations that simply suggest sexual intimacy but not necessarily in the sex act are fined or sentenced to jail for a few months. Muslims arrested for *zinah*—that is, illicit sexual intercourse—may be more severely punished. As a result of the increase in the number of young women working in assembly factories, there have been more raids by the government's religious department on the poor lodgings and cheap hotels used by the workers.

Then there is the factory discipline itself. We mentioned earlier that eighteenth- and nineteenth-century factories were modeled after prisons. Modern assembly plants have much the same character. In Malaysian assembly plants, workers are sometimes watched through glass partitions. In one factory, for example, three supervisors and twelve foremen controlled

530 operators. Discipline was verbally enforced as women workers were scolded by overvigilant foremen for wanting to go to the prayer room, the clinic, or the toilet. Some foremen would even question workers in a humiliating manner about their menstrual problems or nonwork activities. Others were reported to have forced women to run laps around the assembly plant as a form of punishment for reporting late to work or not meeting their production quotas.

As in prisons, clothing can be used to instill discipline. Malaysian workers are required to wear factory overalls that they complain are too tight and which they are not allowed to unbutton. They are also required to wear heavy rubber boots. These clothes are very different from the loose-fitting clothes and sandals Malaysians traditionally wear while working.

Assembly plants also bring with them a Western, factory-oriented sense of the relationship between work and time to which contemporary assembly workers must adapt. Traditionally, in Malaysia, for example, young girls carried out their household or farm tasks relatively free from modern time and work discipline; their activities were interspersed with social visits, usually free of female supervision and always free of male supervision. If there was anything to mark the passage of time, it was the cycle of daily Islamic prayer.

Female workers in the factories, however, are clocked in daily for eight consecutive hours with two fifteen-minute breaks and a half-hour lunch break. Every month their work schedules are changed. Women begin to divide their lives into "work time" and "leisure time." They were watched over by overzealous foremen, screened before they could leave their work benches to go to the toilet, and fined if they were late for work (in spite of the fact that pay was based on piecework). This is in vivid contrast to the traditional work routine where there was no distinction between work and life and no conflict between labor and "passing the time of day."

People in Malaysia are aware of the shift from traditional social time to the capitalist clock time, and they have developed their own ways to critique it. Ong (1987:112) told the story of a married couple, Ahmad and Edah, who, say their neighbors, driven by the desire for wealth, carefully spend their time on capital accumulation at the expense of social obligations. Their neighbors said their obsession with time was the result of a *toyal,* a spirit helper that they raised to filch money from neighbors. The *toyal,* they concluded, turned the tables on the couple by driving them even harder to use all their time to accumulate wealth.

Resistance and Rebellion

Capitalism requires a disciplined working class—people willing to work for wages that allow enterprises to make their necessary profit. But herein lies a problem: In general, people do not readily accept discipline and control and will seek a way to resist, either directly or indirectly.

Resistance to capitalist discipline can take direct forms—worker protests, formation of unions, and even revolution (subjects examined in later chapters). Resistance may also take the form of a moral critique, such as that of Colombian peasants who see capital accumulation represented in the baptism of money as the loss of a child's soul. Such indirect forms of resistance are not unique to the peoples of the periphery of the world system. For example, one of the stories that comes down to us from early industrial Europe is that of Rumpelstilskin. Folktales are more than simply stories; they are statements about people's beliefs. Often they are morality tales that dramatize the consequences of proper or improper behavior. Jane Schneider (1989), for example, suggested that the meaning of the Rumpelstilskin tale lies in the development of the linen industry in early modern Europe. In fact, in many ways, it offers a critique of capitalist production not unlike that of the Colombian peasants.

In one version of the Rumpelstilskin story, a father brags that his daughter is able to spin straw into gold. The king, hearing of this boast, offers to take the girl as his wife if she is able to spin the straw in his castle into gold. The girl tries, fails, then enters into a pact with a strange dwarf who promises to spin the straw into gold for her, but only if she promises to give him her firstborn child. The girl accepts, Rumpelstilskin spins the straw into gold, and she marries the king and has a child. The dwarf comes to claim his fee but is distressed by her tears and grief and offers her a way out. If she can guess his name, he will free her from the contract. She does, of course, much to Rumpelstilskin's dismay.

We have forgotten much of what this tale meant to sixteenth- and seventeenth-century European peasants. For example, one of the main industries of the period was linen production. Linen was produced by spinning flax straw into linen thread that was woven into a fabric that was sold for gold coins. So straw, in effect, really was spun into gold. Moreover, the spinning process was performed largely by young women. A woman's spinning skill was not only a source of money, but also a quality men sought in wives—as the king sought in his future wife. Furthermore, the story contains a pact with a demon, and the price is the firstborn. Thus, as in the Colombian baptism of money, we find the symbolic statement that the generation of wealth comes only with social and personal sacrifice, often of children's souls.

Malaysian assembly plant workers have also found a subtle, generally symbolic means of expressing their resistance to capitalist discipline. It takes the form of spirit possession. Although Malaysia is a Muslim country, Islam exists side by side with indigenous beliefs about magic and spirits. Thus, in the 1980s, assembly plant managers in Malaysia—especially American and Japanese managers—were unexpectedly confronted with an epidemic of spirit possessions in their factories (Ong 1987:204). Forty Malaysian operators were possessed in one large American electronics plant; three years later, in another incident, 120 operators were possessed. The factory was shut down for three days while a spirit-healer (*bomoh*) was called in to sacrifice a goat to the possessing spirit on the premises.

Another American microelectronics factory was closed down when fifteen women were possessed. According to factory personnel officers, possessed girls began to sob and scream hysterically. When it looked as though the possession would spread, the other workers were immediately ushered out. The women explained that the factory was "dirty" and consequently haunted by a *datuk*.

The Malay universe is still full of spirits moving between the human and nonhuman domain. Spirit possession seemed to express themes of filth, anger, and fierce struggles. Particularly prominent in the possession episodes were spirits such as *toyal,* who help their masters gain wealth out of thin air, and the *pontianak,* who threaten the lives of newborn infants.

Aihwa Ong suggested that the women were not reacting to anything as abstract as industrial capitalism but against a sense of violation, of a dislocation in human relations, in much the same way the Colombian peasants reacted to wage labor with the notion of the baptism of money and the sacrifice of children's souls.

Beliefs about the baptism of money in Colombia, sacrificing firstborns in sixteenth- and seventeenth-century Europe, and spirit possession of factory workers in Malaysia are examples of the widespread critiques of capitalism that we find among people confronting capitalist production for the first time. Such beliefs are ways that people find to express their sense that capitalist production brings a modicum of economic betterment at high social and personal costs.

CONCLUSION

A major assumption of this book is that it is impossible to understand the modern world and its problems—population growth, hunger, poverty, environmental degradation, health, war, religious upheaval, and so on—without understanding the capitalist economy that, with its goal of accumulating more and more wealth, has in the past four to five centuries redefined and created new social and cultural forms and altered traditional cultural institutions to serve its own purposes. Capitalism has been characterized here as a black box whose purpose is to convert money into more money, to take monetary investments and convert them into profits, dividends, and interest. For most people, this process is as magical as is the behavior of baptized money among Colombian peasants.

We began to examine how the black box performs its conversion by looking at the growth of overseas assembly plants and the creation, segmentation, and disciplining of the labor force necessary for the box to function at its greatest efficiency. Historically, free labor has been created by removing people from the land or destroying the small-scale industry that allowed them to support themselves. In different countries this was done in different ways, but the overall result has been the creation of populations whose sole means of support is in the sale of their labor. This is as true in industrialized countries as it is in developing or undeveloped countries. In fact, all of us who depend on wage employment—from nuclear physicists to garment workers—constitute the pool of "free" labor. This labor pool is further divided along a continuum comprising at one end relatively well-paid, desirable jobs in industries or enterprises that require a well-trained workforce, and at the other end relatively low-paying, undesirable jobs in industries that are highly competitive and dependent on the existence of a cheap labor supply. Industries and enterprises that depend on a cheap labor supply are able to take advantage of social divisions and discrimination that generally follow lines of gender, race, age, and country of origin to minimize labor costs and control the labor force.

In creating or taking advantage of the increasing supply of cheap labor, the capitalist economy must also develop ways to maintain workforce discipline, which it does through the factory system, the redefinition of time, and the use of traditional institutions, such as the family and the church. Yet, in spite of the new forms of discipline, workers offer resistance in the indirect form of masked criticism—as in the baptism of money, spirit possession, or moral tales such as that of Rumpelstilskin—or through direct forms of protest and the organization of unions.

The mobility, segmentation, and disciplining of the workforce is, of course, only one feature of modern capitalism, and an examination of labor is only the beginning of an understanding of how the black box is able to transform money into more money. It is necessary to examine additional components. In order to do so, let us turn to other major questions: How did the entire system develop historically? How did the black box evolve to where it is today? Most specifically, *How and why did the capitalist evolve from the merchant trader?*

3

The Rise and Fall of the Merchant, Industrialist, and Financier

From the fifteenth century on, European soldiers and sailors carried the flags of their rulers to the four corners of the globe, and European merchants established their storehouses from Vera Cruz to Nagasaki. Dominating the sealanes of the world, these merchants invaded existing networks of exchange and linked one to the other. In the service of "God and profit" they located sources of products desired in Europe and developed coercive systems for their delivery. In response, European craft shops, either singly or aggregated into manufactories, began to produce goods to provision the wide-ranging military and naval efforts and to furnish commodities to overseas suppliers in exchange for goods to be sold as commodities at home. The outcome was the creation of a commercial network of global scale.

—ERIC WOLF, *Europe and the People without History*

When I think of Indonesia—a country on the Equator with 180 million people, a median age of 18, and a Moslem ban on alcohol—I feel I know what heaven looks like.

—DONALD R. KEOUGH, *President of Coca-Cola*

Five years hence, commentators will look back to the birth of the credit derivative market as a watershed development.

—BLYTHE MASTERS, *Derivatives Group of J. P. Morgan*

At no other time in human history has the world been a better place for capitalists. We live in a world full of investment opportunities—companies, banks, funds, bonds, securities, and even countries—into which we can put money and from which we can get more back. These moneymaking machines, such as the Nike corporation, have a ready supply of cheap labor, capital, raw materials, and advanced technology to assist in making products that people all over the world clamor to buy. Moreover, governments compete for their presence, passing laws and making treaties to open markets, while maintaining infrastructures (roads, airports, power utilities, monetary systems, communication networks, etc.) that enable them to manufacture products or provide services cheaply and charge prices that remain competitive with other investments. Nation-states maintain armies to protect investments and ensure that markets remain open. Educational institutions devote themselves to producing knowledgeable, skilled, and disciplined workers, while researchers at colleges and universities develop new technologies to make even better and cheaper products. Our governments, educational institutions, and mass media encourage people to consume more and more commodities. Citizens arrange their economic and social lives to accommodate work in the investment machines and to gain access to the commodities they produce. In return, the investment machines churn out profits that are reinvested to manufacture more of their particular products or that can be invested in other enterprises, producing yet more goods and services. Never before have people had so much opportunity to accumulate great wealth. Among the 400 richest Americans in 1999, 298 of them were worth a billion dollars or more, and the top 400 had a net worth of $1.2 trillion, about one-eighth of the total gross domestic product (GDP) of the United States (see Forbes 2000b).

But there are economic, environmental, and social consequences of doing business and making money. We live in a world in which the gap between the rich and poor is growing, a world that contains many wealthy and comfortable people and more than 1 billion people without enough to eat. Then there are the environmental consequences of doing business: Production uses up the earth's energy resources and produces damaged environments in return. There are health consequences as well, not only from damaged environments but also because those too poor to afford health care often do without it. There are the political consequences of governments' using their armed forces to maintain conditions that they believe are favorable for business and investors. And, finally, there are the occasional economic collapses in which the economies of whole countries suddenly decline, throwing millions of people out of work and wiping out vast wealth.

In the long view of human history, these conditions are very recent ones. For most of human history, people have lived in small, relatively isolated settlements that rarely exceeded 300 or 400 individuals. And until some 10,000 years ago, virtually all of these people lived by gathering and hunting. Then in some areas of the world, instead of depending on the natural growth of plant foods and the natural growth and movements of animals, people began to plant and harvest crops and raise animals themselves. This was not necessarily an advance in human societies—in fact, in terms of labor, it required human beings to do the work that had been done largely by nature. The sole advantage of working harder was that the additional labor supported denser populations. Settlements grew in size until thousands rather than hundreds lived together in towns and cities. Occupational specialization developed, necessitating trade and communication between villages, towns, cities, and regions. Political complexity increased, chiefs became kings, and kings became emperors ruling over vast regions.

Then, approximately 400 or 500 years ago, patterns of travel and communication contributed to the globalization of trade dominated by "a small peninsula off the landmass of Asia," as Eric Wolf called Europe. The domination by one region over others was not new in the world. There had existed prior to this time civilizations whose influence had spread to influence those around them—the Mayan civilization in Central America, Greek civilization of the fourth millennium B.C., Rome of the first and second centuries A.D., and Islamic civilization of the eighth and ninth centuries. But there was an important difference. The building of these empires was largely a political process of conquest and military domination, whereas the expansion of Europe, although certainly involving its share of militarism, was largely accomplished by economic means—by the expansion and control of trade.

Now let's shift our focus to the development of the capitalist—the merchant, industrialist, and financier—the person who controls the capital, employs the laborers, and profits from the consumption of commodities. This will be a long-term, historical look at this development, because if we are to understand the global distribution of power and money that exists today and the origins of the culture of capitalism, knowledge of its history is crucial.

Assume for a time the role of a businessperson, a global merchant, or merchant adventurer, as they used to be called,[1] passing through the world of the past 600 years. We'll begin searching the globe for ways to make money in the year 1400 and end our search in the year 2013, taking stock of the changes in the organization and distribution of capital that occurred in that time. Because we are looking at the world through the eyes of a merchant, there is much that we will miss—many political developments, religious wars, revolutions, natural catastrophes, and the like. Because we overlook these events does not mean they did not affect how business was conducted—in many cases, particularly in the case of war and war debts, they had profound effects. But our prime concern is with the events that most directly influenced the way in which business was conducted on a day-to-day basis and how the pursuit of profit by merchant adventurers influenced the lives of people all over the world. Our historical tour will concentrate on five issues:

1. An understanding of how capital came to be concentrated in so few hands and how the world came to be divided into rich and poor. There were certainly rich people and poor people in 1400, but today's vast global disparity between core and periphery did not exist then. *How did the distribution of wealth change, and how did one area of the world come to dominate the others economically?*

2. An understanding of the changes in business organizations and the organization of capital—that is, *who controlled the money?* In 1400, most business enterprises were small, generally family-organized institutions. Capital was controlled by these groups and state organizations. Today we live in an era of multinational corporations and financial institutions, many whose wealth exceeds that of most countries. We need to trace the evolution of the power of capital over our lives and the transformation of the merchant of 1400 into the industrialist of the eighteenth and nineteenth centuries, then into the investor and financier of the late twentieth and early twenty-first centuries. *How and why did these transformations in the organization of capital come about?*

3. The increase in the level of global economic integration. From your perspective as a merchant adventurer, you obviously want the fewest restraints possible on your ability to trade from one area of the world to another; the fewer the restrictions, the greater the opportunity for profit. Such things as a global currency, agreement among nations on import and export regulations, ease of passage of money and goods from area to area, and freedom to employ whom you want and to pay the lowest possible wage are all to your advantage; furthermore, you want few or no government restrictions regarding the consequences of your business activities. *How did the level of global economic integration increase, and what were the consequences for the merchant adventurer, as well as others?*

4. Fourth, *how do we explain the occasional collapse of national and global economies, such as the one that began in 2007 in the United States and spread to the rest of the world?* Not only do such economic downturns force banks and businesses into bankruptcy, wipe out trillions of dollars of wealth, and throw millions of people out of work, they also threaten the stability of governments and the entire foundation of market economies.

5. Most importantly, *where did the necessity for perpetual economic growth come from? That is, how did an economy arise in which people had to spend, earn, and produce more this year than last and more next year than this, in perpetuity?*

With these questions in mind, let's go back to the world of 1400 and start trading.

---

[1] The name is taken from a sixteenth-century English trading company, The Merchant Adventurers, cloth wholesalers trading to Holland and Germany with bases of operation in Antwerp and Bergen-op-Zoom and later Hamburg. The company survived until 1809.

THE ERA OF THE GLOBAL TRADER

A Trader's Tour of the World in 1400

If, as global merchants in 1400, we were searching for ways to make money, the best opportunities would be in long-distance trade, buying goods in one area of the world and selling them in another (see Braudel 1982:68). If we could choose which among the great cities of the world—Cairo, Malacca, Samarkand, Venice, and so on—to begin trading, our choice would probably be Hangchow, China. China in 1400 had a population of 100 million and was the most technologically developed country in the world. Paper was invented in China probably as early as A.D. 700 and block printing as early as 1050. China of 1400 had a thriving iron industry; enormous amounts of coal were burned to fuel the iron furnaces—the coal used in northern China alone was equal to 70 percent of what metalworkers in Great Britain used at the beginning of the eighteenth century. The explosive power of gunpowder was harnessed around A.D. 650 and by 1000 was used by Chinese armies for simple bombs and grenades. Cannons were in use by 1300, some mounted on the ships of the Chinese navy, and by the fourteenth century, the Chinese were using a metal-barreled gun that shot explosive pellets (Abu-Lughod 1989:322ff.).

If you were to tour the Chinese countryside, you would have been struck by the networks of canals and irrigation ditches that crisscrossed the landscape, maintained by wealthy landowners or the state. China was governed by a royal elite and administered largely by mandarins, people selected from the wealthy classes and who were exempt from paying taxes. State bureaucrats were also selected and promoted through civil service examinations open to all but those of the lowest rank of society (e.g., executioners, slaves, beggars, boat people, actors, and laborers [Hanson 1993:186]). China produced some of the most desired trade goods in the world, particularly silk, spices, and porcelain.

The economic conditions in China also favored traders. There were guilds and associations of merchants, such as jewelers; gilders; antique dealers; dealers in honey, ginger, and boots; money changers; and doctors. China had its own currency system. In the Middle East and Europe, governments issued money in the form of coins of precious metals whose value depended on their weight. In China there was not only copper coin but also paper money (cotton paper stamped with a government seal) to provide merchants with a convenient means of exchange. Paper money also allowed the state to control the flow of money in and out of the country. Precious metals, such as gold and silver, could not be used by foreigners in trade, so foreign traders were forced to exchange their gold or silver for paper money, which they then exchanged for gold and silver when they left. Because they had usually purchased Chinese commodities to sell elsewhere, they usually left with less gold and silver than when they arrived (Abu-Lughod 1989:334).

China was also politically stable. The rulers, members of the Ming Dynasty, had successfully rebelled against the Mongols in A.D. 1368. The Mongols, nomadic horsemen who roamed the vast steppes of Central Asia, conquered China in 1276 and set up their own dynasty, the Yuan. The Mongols, eager to establish trade with the rest of the world, had created relatively safe trade routes to the rest of Asia, the Middle East, and Europe. At least at first, the Ming appeared to want to maintain that trade, sending its impressive navy as emissaries to ports along the Indian Ocean.

The city of Hangchow was situated between the banks of the Che River leading to the sea and the shore of an enormous artificial lake. According to Ibn Battuta, an Arab trader who visited the city in the 1340s, the city extended more than six to seven square miles and was surrounded by walls with five gateways through which canals passed. Thirteen monumental gates, at which its great thoroughfares terminated, provided entry to the city. Situated on the hills overlooking the city were the imperial palace and homes of the wealthy state bureaucrats and merchants; at the opposite end of the city were the houses of the poor—crowded, narrow-fronted, three- to five-story houses with workshops on the ground floors. The main thoroughfare, the Imperial Way, was 3 miles long and 180 feet wide, crowded with carriages drawn by men or tiny horses.

The splendor and wealth of fifteenth- and sixteenth-century China is portrayed in this engraving of a mandarin's terrace and garden. (Fine Art/ Historical Picture Archive/ Corbis.)

The city was a trader's paradise. Inside the city were ten markets as well as teahouses and restaurants where traders could meet and arrange their business. Outside the city were a fish market and wholesale markets. Ibn Battuta said it was "the largest city on the face of the earth." Sections of the city contained concentrations of merchants from all over the world. Jewish and Christian traders from Europe were in one; Muslim traders were in another, with bazaars and mosques, and muezzins calling Muslims to noon prayer. The bazaars of Chinese merchants and artisans were in yet another section. In brief, Hangchow would have been an ideal place to sell merchandise from Europe, the Middle East, or other parts of Asia and to purchase goods, such as spices and silks, that were in demand in other parts of the world.

Silk was particularly desired by foreign traders because its light weight and compactness made it easy to transport and because China had a virtual monopoly in the silk trade. Syrian traders had smuggled silkworms out of China in the thirteenth century, and in 1400 one could purchase silk in India and Italy; but, the quality of Chinese silk was superior. Because the production of silk was likely in the hands of Chinese merchants, you would have purchased it directly from them. You might also purchase Chinese porcelain, especially if you planned to travel by ship because porcelain could be used as ballast by ships returning to the Middle East or Europe (see Figure 3.1).

Your next task would be to arrange to transport your goods to where you planned to sell them. Let's assume you had orders from merchants in cities such as Venice, Cairo, and Bruges, where Chinese goods were in demand. Your first task is to get your goods to the Mediterranean. You could go overland through China, through central Asia to northern India, or to ports on the Black Sea, then travel to European ports such as Venice and Naples. The trip overland through Asia to Europe would take you at least 275 days using pack trains—camels over the deserts, mules through the mountains, ox carts where roads existed, human carriers, and boats. The overland route was popular in the thirteenth and fourteenth centuries, when the Mongols had, through their conquests, unified Central Asia and issued safe conduct passes to traders. In 1400, however, with the Empire fragmented, you may have risked raiding by nomadic bands of Mongol horsemen.

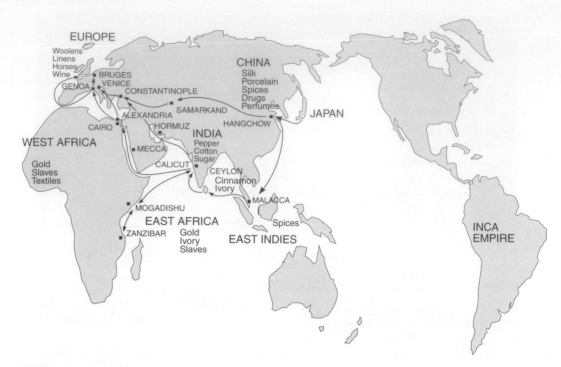

FIGURE 3.1 Major Trade Routes in 1400

A safer route in 1400 would have been the sea route, down the east coast of China, through the Strait of Malacca to Southern India, and then either through the Persian Gulf to Iran and overland, through Baghdad to the Mediterranean, or through the Red Sea to Cairo, and finally by ship to Italy.

Traveling through the Strait of Malacca and into Southeast Asia, you would have found powerful elites ruling states from their royal palaces, surrounded by armed retainers, kin, artisans, and specialists. Beyond this was a peasantry producing rice to support themselves and the elites. These were the civilizations that built Angkor Thom and Angkor Wat in Cambodia. You would likely have been more at home, however, in the seaports that dotted the Strait of Malacca, which owed their existence to trade. Occasionally, these ports would merge with inland kingdoms such as Majapahit in Java. The main city of the area in 1400 was Malacca, founded by pirates led in rebellion twenty years earlier by a prince from Majapahit. The prince converted to Islam, attracting to Malacca wealthy Muslim merchants, and by 1400 Malacca was a city of 40,000 to 50,000 people containing traders from sixty-one nations. The Portuguese Tomé Pires, writing a century later, said, "Whoever is lord of Malacca has his hands on the throat of Venice" (Wolf 1982:58). While in Malacca, you likely would have obtained additional trade goods to take West. Spices, particularly cinnamon (at one time in Egypt considered more valuable than gold), were highly valued because they were easy to transport and brought high profits in the Middle East and Europe.

From Malacca you probably would have traveled along the coast of Southeast Asia and on to India, whose wealth in 1400 rivaled that of China. Southeast India had a thriving textile industry. Farmers grew cotton and passed it on to spinners, who made thread for the weavers. There is some evidence that merchants provided cotton and thread to spinners and weavers and paid the artisans for what they produced. There was a sophisticated technology: a vertical loom, block printing, and the spinning wheel, probably introduced from Turkey. But cotton and textiles were not the only items you might have obtained in India for trade; there were also dyes, tannins, spices, oil seed, narcotics, lumber, honey, and ivory (see Wolf 1982).

From India you might travel to East Africa, where from Bantu-speaking peoples you might have obtained slaves, ivory, leopard skins, gold from Zimbabwe, and rhinoceros horns (still believed in some parts of the world to be an aphrodisiac).

Leaving East Africa, you would have journeyed up the coast through the Red Sea to Cairo or through the Persian Gulf, through Iraq to Baghdad, and on to Constantinople and the Eastern Mediterranean. You would have found the Islamic countries of the Middle East favorable to business, with a sophisticated body of law regulating trade, including rules for the formation of trading partnerships and the extension of credit. One law allowed people to pay for merchandise at a later date at a higher price, a convenient way around the Islamic prohibition of lending money at interest. Bags of gold coin whose value was printed on the outside, and whose contents were apparently never checked, served as money. There were bankers who changed money, took deposits, and issued promissory notes, another way of extending credit and making loans. Merchants kept their accounts by listing credits and debits. Thus, all the rudiments of a sophisticated economy—capital, credit, banking, money, and account keeping—were present in Islamic trade (Abu-Lughod 1989:216ff.).

From Cairo you could join a caravan to go south through the Sahara to West Africa, where textile goods were in demand and where you might obtain slaves or gold. Virtually two-thirds of the gold circulating in Europe and the Middle East came from West Africa. Or you might travel a short way to Alexandria, still a major city. From there you would travel by ship on the Mediterranean to one of the city-states of Italy, such as Venice or Genoa. Italy was the center of European and Mediterranean trade. At European fairs, Italian traders would set up a bench (*banco,* from which *bank* is derived) with their scales and coins, enabling traders to exchange currency from one area of the world for another. Italian bankers monopolized the international exchange of money and credit and pioneered the *bill of exchange.* This was a document in which a buyer agreed to deliver payment to a seller at another time and place in the seller's home currency. In the absence of any widely recognized currency, the bill of exchange greatly facilitated foreign trade (Abu-Lughod 1989:93).

You might then join other merchants from Genoa, Pisa, and Milan who formed caravans to take goods—such as silks and spices from the Orient or the Middle East; alum, wax, leather, and fur from Africa; dates, figs, and honey from Spain; and pepper, feathers, and brazilwood from the Middle East—over the Alps to the fairs and markets of western and northern Europe, a trip taking five weeks. Or you could send your goods by ship, through the Mediterranean and the North Sea to trading centers such as Bruges.

Once you reached northern or western Europe, you had already left the wealthiest part of the world. After the decline of the Roman Empire, western Europe was a backward area, exploited for its iron, lumber, and slaves. Urban areas had declined, and artisan activity retreated to rural areas. Moreover, Europe had been devastated in the fourteenth century by bubonic plague: In the mid-fourteenth century, Europe's population was about 80 million (Abu-Lughod 1989:94). By 1400, plague had reduced it by 45 percent, to between 40 million and 50 million. The plague likely originated in Central Asia or China. It traveled the trade routes, striking Chinese cities as early as 1320 and first striking Europe in Caffa, on the Black Sea, in 1346. It arrived in Alexandria in 1347, probably from Italian ports on the Black Sea. At its height in Alexandria, it killed 10,000 people a day, finally killing 200,000 of the city's half-million people. It struck Italy in 1348, appeared in France and Britain the same year, and reached Germany and Scandinavia a year later.

Feudalism was still the main form of political and economic organization in Europe. Kings bestowed lands, or fiefs, to subjects in return for their loyalty and service. Lords "rented" land to peasants, generally for a share of the produce, which they used to pay tribute to the kings and to finance their own expenses.

Woolen textiles were the most important products of northern and western Europe in 1400. Flanders (western Belgium and northwest France), the textile center of northern Europe, had virtually monopolized the purchase of raw wool from England, and woolen textiles from Flanders were in demand throughout Europe and in other parts of the world.

Let's assume you have sold the commodities you brought from China and realized a handsome profit. The question is, *What to do with your capital and profits?* You might buy Flemish textiles in Bruges or, depending on the political circumstances, travel to England to buy textiles. You might buy land or finance other traders in return for a share of their profits. If, however, you decided to undergo another trade circuit, returning east would be your likely alternative. The Americas were probably unknown and certainly unreachable. You might have traveled down the European coast to West Africa, where European textiles were in great demand and where you could obtain slaves and gold. But while the wind patterns of the Eastern Atlantic would have carried your ship to West Africa, they made it impossible, given the sailing technology, to return by sea, and you would be forced to return overland across northern Africa. Your likely trade route, then, would have been back to Italy and east through the Mediterranean to India, the East Indies, and China.

What if you had been able to cross the sea to the Americas? What would you have found in 1400? No one left a written record of life in the New World just prior to the arrival of Europeans. Archaeologists, however, have created a record from what was left behind. You would have discovered elaborate trade routes extending from South America into North America and the remains of great civilizations in Central Mexico and the Yucatán Peninsula.

The Inca were just beginning their expansion, which would produce the Andean Empire confronted by Pizarro in 1532. Inca society in 1400 was dominated by the Inca dynasty, an aristocracy consisting of relatives of the ruling group, local rulers who submitted to Inca rule. Men of local rank headed endogamous patrilineal clans, or *ayllus,* groups who traced descent to a common male ancestor and who were required to marry within their clan. These groups paid tribute to the Inca aristocracy by working on public projects or in military service. Women spent much of their time weaving cloth used to repay faithful subjects and imbued with extraordinary ritual and ceremonial value. The state expanded by colonizing new agricultural lands to grow maize. It maintained irrigation systems, roads, and a postal service in which runners carried information from one end of the empire to another. Groups that rebelled against Inca rule were usually relocated far from their homeland (Wolf 1982:62–63).

If you had traveled into the Brazilian rain forests, you might have encountered peoples such as the Tupinambá, who lived on small garden plots while gathering and hunting in the forests. Sixteenth-century traveler Calvinist pastor Jean de Léry concluded that the Tupinambá lived more comfortably than ordinary people in France (Maybury-Lewis 1997:13).

In Mexico in 1400, the Aztecs were twenty years from establishing their vast empire with its capital at Tenochtitlán. In the Caribbean there were complex chieftainships with linkages to the civilizations of Mesoamerica and the Andes. A merchant of 1400 would have been able to follow trade routes that spread from Mexico into the southeastern and northeastern United States, encountering descendants of those who archaeologists called the Mississippians. In this society, goods and commodities were used to indicate status and rank. A trader would have encountered towns or ceremonial centers focused on great terraced, earthen platforms. The Mississippians relied on the cultivation of maize, beans, and squash, called "the three sisters" by the Iroquois. You might have met the Iroquois at the headwaters of the Ohio River, the Cherokee in the southern Appalachians, the Natchez on the lower Mississippi River, and the Pawnee and the Mandan on the Missouri River. On the surrounding prairies you would have encountered the peoples of the Northwest, the buffalo hunters of the plains (the horse, often associated with the Plains Indians, wouldn't arrive for another century), and the Inuit hunters of the Arctic and subarctic. These civilizations and cultures might, in later centuries, have provided a lucrative market for the sale and purchase of goods had not other events led to their devastation.

As we complete our global tour, the barriers to commerce are striking. For example, most political rulers were not yet committed to encouraging trade. Although states might value trade for the taxes, tolls, and rents they could extract from traders, merchants were still looked down on. Rulers generally viewed trade only as a way to gain profit from traders and merchants, and some states even attempted to control some trade themselves. In China, for example, trade in salt was monopolized by the government. Religious authorities in Europe, the Middle East, and China discouraged trade by extracting high taxes or forbidding loans at interest.

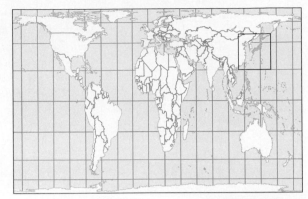

Geography was obviously a major barrier: Trade circuits might take years to complete. Roads were few and ships relatively small and at the mercy of winds and tides. Security was a problem: A merchants' goods were liable to be seized or stolen, or merchants might be forced to pay tribute to rulers along the way.

Economically, there were various restrictions. We were a long way in 1400 from anything resembling a consumer economy. Most of the world's population lived on a subsistence economy—that is, they produced themselves whatever they needed to exist. In Europe, for example, where 90 percent of the population was rural, people might buy an iron plow, some pots, and textile products, but that was all. Consumers tended to be the urban dwellers, largely the clergy, aristocracy, and the small middle class consisting of artisans, merchants, and bureaucrats. Furthermore, if people wanted to buy more, there was virtually no currency with which to do it; even if all the gold and silver of Europe had been in circulation, it would have amounted to only about two dollars per person (Weatherford 1988:14).

Japan

Thus, overall, the world of 1400 seemed little affected by trade. China and India were probably the richest countries in the world, and there is little doubt that royal rulers controlled most of the wealth, largely through the extraction of tribute from peasants, artisans, and traders. Much of this they redistributed in the form of gifts, feasts, and charity. Moreover, the people who worked the soil, as those who remained gathering and hunting at the fringes and outside the world system, had ready access to food. Though there is evidence of periodic famine in which thousands perished, it is unlikely that, as now, close to one-fifth of the world's population in 1400 was hungry. Thus, although a growing system of trade was beginning to link more of the world's people together, there had yet to develop the worldwide inequities that exist today. This, however, would rapidly begin to change over the next one hundred years.

The Economic Rise of Europe and Its Impact on Africa and the Americas

Two events dominate the story of the expansion of trade after 1400: the increased withdrawal of China from world trade networks and the voyage of Vasco da Gama around the southern tip of Africa. These events resulted in a shift in the balance of economic dominance from a country of 100 million occupying most of Asia to a country of 1 million occupying an area just slightly larger than the state of Maine.

The date and reason for China's withdrawal from its position of commercial dominance is something of a mystery and subject to considerable academic debate (see, e.g., Frank 1998; Landes 1998). The ruling dynasty moved the capital of China inland and allowed its powerful navy to gradually disintegrate. Regardless of the reasons for these actions, they resulted in a diminished role for China in global trade, and Portugal, with the most powerful navy in the world, was quick to fill the vacuum left by China in the East Indies. Portugal used its navy to dominate trade and supplemented trading activities with raiding (Abu-Lughod 1989:243).

Japan also took the opportunity after China's withdrawal to expand its trading activity in Southeast Asia. In the fifteenth century, Japan, like England, was a feudal society divided into an upper nobility, the *daimyo,* or great lords; the samurai, vassals of the daimyo; and the *chonin,* or merchants, who were looked down on by the nobility. There was contact between Japan and Europe by the mid-sixteenth century, and Christian missionaries soon established themselves in Japan. But around 1500, Japan was involved in heavy trade with China, trading

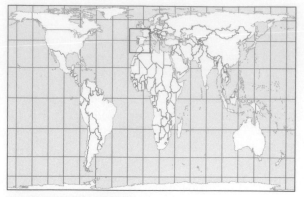

Portugal

refined copper, sulfur, folding fans, painted scrolls, and, most important, swords. One trade expedition carried 10,000 swords to China and returned with strings of cash, raw silk, porcelains, paintings, medicines, and books. Thus, in the fifteenth century, Japan was beginning economic expansion to areas vacated by China (Sanderson 1995:154).

Technological advances in boat building were partially responsible for Portugal's power. Around 1400, European boat builders combined the European square rigger with the lateen rig of the Arabs, the square rig giving ships speed when running and the lateen rig allowing the boat to sail closer to the wind. They also equipped their ships with cannons on the main and upper decks by cutting holes in the hull. The result was a speedy and maneuverable galleon, half warship and half merchantman (Wolf 1982:235).

Equally important for Portugal was location. Prior to the fifteenth century, Portugal was at the edge of the world system. The Mediterranean was controlled by the city-states of Italy and by Islamic powers. The Americas were seemingly out of reach, even if traders were aware of them. The west coast of Africa was inaccessible by boat unless one sailed south down the coast and returned overland. But once the route east to India and China was restricted, action shifted to the Atlantic, and as Africa and the Americas became readily accessible, Portugal was suddenly at the center of world trade.

It was the era of discovery and conquest, of the voyages of Columbus, of efforts to find alternative routes to China and the East Indies. Columbus believed he had discovered China or Cipangu (Japan), and as late as 1638, the fur trader Jean Nicolet, on meeting Winnebago Indians on the shores of Lake Michigan, wore a Chinese robe he brought to wear when meeting the Great Kahn of China (Wolf 1982:232).

Much is made in popular culture and history books of the spirit of adventure of early "explorers" such as Marco Polo, Vasco da Gama, and Christopher Columbus. But they were less explorers than merchant sailors. Their motivation was largely economic; they were seeking alternative ways to the riches of China and the East Indies. One might say that European economic domination, to the extent it was fueled by the wealth of the Americas, was due to the accidental discovery of two continents that happened to be in the way of their attempts to find alternative routes to China, Japan, and India.

If you were a global trader in the sixteenth century whose starting point was Lisbon, Portugal, you had a choice of trade routes. You could go east to the Middle East, India, or Southeast Asia, all kept open to Portuguese traders by Portugal's navy. You could go south along the African coast, or follow Columbus's route to the New World. Or you could simply trade into the rest of Europe. All routes could prove profitable. In our reincarnation as a Portuguese trader, let's first go south to Africa.

Let's assume you have the capital to hire a ship to carry yourself and your goods to Africa. You would probably be carrying Mediterranean wine, iron weapons, perhaps horses (much in demand in Africa), and a consignment of textiles possibly consisting of Egyptian linen and cotton. *What sort of commodities would you acquire in Africa for trade in Europe?*

Africans were already producing the same things as Europeans—iron and steel (possibly the best in the world at the time), elaborate textiles, and other goods. As a trader, you would have been interested in the textiles made in Africa, which were in demand in Europe. You would also have been anxious to trade in gold mined in West Africa, the source until that time of most of the gold in Europe and the Middle East. But your real interest would likely have been slaves.

The institution of slavery goes back well into antiquity. The ancient Greeks kept slaves, and slave labor was used throughout the Middle East and Europe in 1500. Muslims enslaved Christians, Christians enslaved Muslims, and Europeans enslaved Slavs and Greeks. Coal

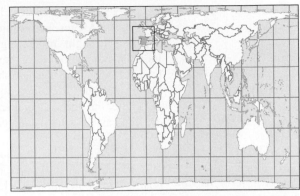

miners in Scotland were enslaved into the seventeenth and eighteenth centuries, and indentured servitude was widespread in Europe. However, there was about to be a huge surge in the demand for slave labor from the new colonies being established in the Americas.

The nature of the slave trade has long been a contentious issue among historians. Many believe the slave trade was forced on Africa, if not by direct military intervention, then by economic extortion, as Europeans offered guns and horses needed by rulers to maintain their authority in exchange for slaves. But there is increasing evidence that the slave trade was largely an African institution in which Europeans and others were only too happy to partake. Slavery in Africa was different from slavery in Europe, however, and different from what it was to become in the Americas.

Spain

Slaves were regarded traditionally in Africa as subordinate family members, as they were in Europe going back to Aristotle's time. Thus, slaves in Africa could be found doing any duties a subordinate family member might do. To understand the African institution of slavery, it is also necessary to understand that among people in African states, there was little notion of private property; for example, land was owned by "corporate kinship groups," networks of related individuals who together owned land in common. People were given the right to use land but not to own it. Slaves comprised the only form of private, revenue-producing property recognized in African law. Slaves could produce revenue because if you had the labor in the form of family members, wives, or slaves, you could claim the use of more land. African conceptions of property are reflected also in the fact that, whereas in Europe taxes were paid on land, in Africa taxes were paid on people, "by the head" (Thornton 1992).

The size of African states may have reflected the lack of concern with land as property. John Thornton (1992:106) estimated that only 30 percent of Atlantic Africa contained states larger than 50,000 square kilometers (roughly the size of New York State), and more than half the total area contained states of 500 to 1,000 square kilometers. Africans generally went to war not to acquire land, as in Europe, but to acquire slaves, with which more land could be worked.

Given these attitudes toward land and labor, there existed in Africa at the time of European arrival a large slave population and a thriving slave market. Slaves were a major form of investment; a wealthy African could not buy land but could acquire slaves and, as long as land was available, claim more land to use. Moreover, slaves, because they were property, could be inherited by individuals, whereas land, because it belonged to the corporate kin group, could not. Investing in slaves would have been the wealthy African's equivalent of a European investing in land, and if you were not using slaves, you could sell them (Thornton 1992:87). Thus, European traders found ready sources of slaves, not because Africans were inveterate slave traders but because in Africa the legal basis for wealth revolved around the idea of transferring ownership of people (Thornton 1992:95).

Once you obtained the slaves, you might have obtained a special ship to transport them back to Europe or to one of the Atlantic Islands, where they were in demand as workers on the expanding sugar plantations. Sugar in the sixteenth century was still a luxury item, used by the wealthy to decorate food or as medicine. The primary areas of supply were around the Mediterranean—Egypt, Italy, Spain, and Greece. But with the opening of the Atlantic, sugar plantations were established first on the Canary Islands and the Azores and later in the Caribbean. Sugar production was a labor-intensive activity, and slaves from Africa supplied much of that labor. From 1451 to 1600, some 275,000 slaves were sent from West Africa to America and Europe. In the seventeenth and eighteenth centuries, sugar would begin to play a major role in the world economy; but in the sixteenth century, its possibilities were only beginning to be recognized.

Let's assume that after buying slaves in Africa and selling them in the new sugar plantations of the Azores, you resume your journey and go west to the Americas. The opening of the Americas brought into Portugal and Spain vast amounts of gold and silver plundered from the Inca and Aztec empires and extracted from mines by slave and indentured labor. When Pizarro invaded Peru and seized Atahualpa in 1532, he demanded and received a ransom of a roomful of gold but killed the emperor anyway. When Cortes conquered the Aztec, he demanded gold; after the Aztec's counterattack, Cortes's fleeing men carried so much loot that one-quarter drowned as they fell from a causeway into a lake, so burdened down were they by their cargo (Weatherford 1988:7).

At the time of the conquest of the Americas, there was approximately $200 million worth of gold and silver in Europe; by 1600, that had increased eight times. Some 180 to 200 tons of gold, with a contemporary value of $2.8 billion, flowed into Europe, much of it still visible in the robes, statuary, and sacred objects of European churches (Weatherford 1988:14).

Most of the silver came from San Luis Potosí. Cerro Rico ("rich hill" in Spanish), the mountain above Potosí in Bolivia, is the richest mountain ever discovered, virtually a mountain of silver. In 1545 slaves and indentured laborers recruited from the indigenous population began digging silver out of the mountain, forming it into bars and coins, and sending it to Spain. By 1603, there were 58,800 Indian workers in Potosí, 43,200 free day laborers, 10,500 contract laborers, and 5,100 labor draftees. By 1650, Potosí rivaled London and Paris in size, with a population of 160,000 (Wolf 1982:136).

The amount of currency in circulation worldwide increased enormously, enriching Europe but eroding the wealth of other areas and helping Europe expand into an international market system. China reopened its trading links to Europe and took in so much silver that by the mid-eighteenth century, its value had declined to one-fifth what it had been prior to the discovery of America. The gold from the Americas also had the effect of destroying the African gold trade (Weatherford 1988).

Gold and silver were not the only wealth extracted from the New World. Spain imported cochineal, a red dye made from insects (it took 70,000 dried insects to produce one pound of cochineal), indigo (blue dye), and cocoa. Portuguese traders established sugar plantations on the northeast coast of Brazil.

The cost of the European expansion of trade to the Americas, at least to the people of the Americas, was enormous. It resulted in the demographic collapse of the New World, what Eric Wolf called "the great dying" (1982:133).

There is broad disagreement about the population of the Americas at the time of the European conquest. Alfred E. Kroeber (1939), one of the founders of American anthropology, estimated that the total population of the Americas was about 8.4 million, of which 900,000 were in North America. Harold Herbert Spinden, relying on archaeological evidence, suggested there were 50 million to 75 million people in the Americas in A.D. 1200. Henry F. Dobyns (1983), working with archaeological evidence, estimates of the carrying capacity of given environments, and historical documents, estimated 90 million to 112 million in the hemisphere and 12.5 million in the area north of Mexico. The disagreement reflected in these numbers is not unimportant, for it involves an important legal question: *Did the "discovery" of the New World permit Europeans to move on to unoccupied wilderness, or did they displace and destroy a settled indigenous population?* If the latter is the case, then European claims of legal ownership of the land based on the doctrine of *terra nullius*—land belonging to no one—would be legally invalid.

There is little doubt, we think, that the higher estimates are closer to the actual population of the Americas. In 1500, Europe, a fraction of the size of the Americas, had a population of 45 million; France alone had a population of 20 million, and tiny Portugal 1 million. And this was after the bubonic plague epidemics. There seems little doubt that the environment and societies of the Americas were capable of supporting large populations. The peoples of the Americas built empires, palisaded settlements, temples, great pyramids, and irrigation complexes. There was certainly an adequate supply of foodstuffs to support a large population; most of our diet today comes from plants domesticated first in the New World, including corn, potatoes, sweet potatoes, tomatoes, squash, pumpkins, most varieties of beans, pepper (except black), amaranth, manioc, mustard, some types of rice, pecans, pineapples, bread fruit, passion fruit, melons, cranberries, blueberries, blackberries, vanilla, chocolate, and cocoa.

In 1496, Bartolomé Colón, Christopher's brother, authorized a headcount of adults of Española, the present-day Haiti and Dominican Republic, then the most populous of the Caribbean Islands. The people of the island, the Tainos, created a culture that extended over most of the Caribbean. Colón arrived at a count of 1.1 million working adults; if we add children and the elderly, and consider that disease and murder had already diminished the population, there must have been at least 2 million and as many as 8 million on that island alone (Sale 1991:160–161). Thus, it is hardly unreasonable to suppose that the population of the Americas as a whole was upward of 50 million to 100 million people.

The scale of death after the arrival of the Europeans is difficult to conceive and rivals any estimate made for the demographic consequences of a nuclear holocaust today. When the Spanish surveyed Española in 1508, 1510, 1514, and 1518, they found a population of under 100,000. The most detailed of the surveys, taken in 1514, listed only 22,000 adults, which anthropologists Sherburne Cook and Woodrow Borah estimated to represent a total population of 27,800 (Cook and Borah 1960). Thus, in slightly more than twenty years, there was a decline from at least 2 million to 27,800 people. Bartolomé de Las Casas, the major chronicler of the effects of the Spanish invasion, said that by 1542 there were only 200 indigenous Tainos left, and within a decade they were extinct. Cook and Borah concluded that in Central America, an estimated population of 25.3 million was reduced by 97 percent in a little more than a century. In all, it is estimated that 95 percent to 98 percent of the indigenous population of the Americas died as a consequence of European contact.

Many died in battles with the invaders; others were murdered by European occupiers desperate to maintain control over a threatening population; and still others died as a result of slavery and forced labor. But the vast majority died of diseases introduced by Europeans to which the indigenous peoples had no immunity.

The most deadly of the diseases was smallpox. It arrived sometime between 1520 and 1524 with a European soldier or sailor and quickly spread across the continent, ahead of the advancing Europeans. When Pizarro reached the Incas in 1532, his defeat of a divided empire was made possible by the death from smallpox of the ruler and the crown prince. When a Spanish expedition set out from Florida for the Pacific in 1535, they found evidence of the epidemic in West Texas. Dobyns (1983) assumed that virtually all the inhabitants of the hemisphere were exposed to smallpox during that one epidemic. *What would the mortality rate have been from this one pathogen alone?*

Dobyns (1983:13–14; see also Stiffarm and Lane 1992) estimated that in the epidemic of 1520–1524, virtually all indigenous peoples—certainly those in large population areas—would have been exposed to smallpox, and because there would have been no immunity, the death rate, judging by known death rates among other Native American populations, must have been at least 60 percent to 70 percent. Dobyns claimed that Spanish reports of the time that half of the native population died most certainly were underestimates.

This was not the only smallpox epidemic. Dobyns calculated that there were forty-one smallpox epidemics in North America from 1520 to 1899, seventeen measles epidemics from 1531 to 1892, ten major influenza epidemics from 1559 to 1918, and four plague epidemics from 1545 to 1707, to name a few. In all, he said, a serious epidemic invaded indigenous populations on average every four years and two and half months during the years 1520 to 1900.

Thus, the occupation of the New World by Europeans was not so much an act of conquest as it was an act of replacing a population ravaged by pathogens that Europeans carried with them. Depopulation was not the only consequence of the economic expansion of Europe into the Americas. The deaths of indigenous peoples proved a boon to the slave trade, as Europeans transported millions of Africans to the plantations and mines to replace the dying indigenous laborers. Much of the remaining native population gathered around mining communities and Spanish agricultural estates, providing a surplus labor supply, producing cheap crafts and agricultural products, and paying tribute and taxes to the colonizers (Wolf 1982:149). Their descendants today still suffer economic and social discrimination at the hands of descendants of European and indigenous unions.

In 1776, Adam Smith wrote in *The Wealth of Nations* that "the discovery of America, and that of a passage to the East Indies by the Cape of Good Hope, are the two greatest and most important events recorded in the history of mankind" (Crosby 1986:vii).

A decade later there was a debate among the savants of France over whether the discovery of the New World was a blessing or a curse. Abbé Guillaume Reynal, author of a four-volume study of trade between Europe and the East and West Indies, wrote a paper to answer this question. In it he listed the gains that Europe had received and discussed the costs to the peoples of Asia and the Americas. He concluded:

> Let us stop here, and consider ourselves as existing at the time when America and India were unknown. Let me suppose that I address myself to the most cruel of the Europeans in the following terms. There exist regions which will furnish you with rich metals, agreeable clothing, and delicious food. But read this history, and behold at what price the discovery is promised to you. Do you wish or not that it should be made? Is it to be imagined that there exists a being infernal enough to answer this question in the affirmative! Let it be remembered that there will not be a single instant in futurity when my question will not have the same force. (Sale 1991:366–367)

The Birth of Finance and the Tulip Bubble of 1636–1637

The next, and perhaps the most important, stage in the evolution of the capitalist was the birth of finance. Finance may be understood, as the third Lord Rothschild put it, as the "movement of money from point 'A', where it is, to point 'B', where it is needed" (see Ferguson 2008:62–63). It may also be properly understood as the art of making money with money, the major mark of a capitalist economy (see Hart 2000:10; Polanyi 1944:68–69). The easiest way to make money with money is to lend money at interest, an act probably as old as money itself. But lending implied certain preconditions that, until relatively recently in global history, were rarely met. First, it had to be permissible. Many religious texts, including the Old Testament, the New Testament, and the Koran, discourage or condemn loans at interest. It was not until the fifteenth and sixteenth centuries that such prohibitions were relaxed in Europe. Second, lending money requires that there be a pretty good chance that the lender gets his or her money back with interest. In other words, the lender had to be able to accurately assess the risk that the borrower would not default and set interest rates accordingly. Third, finance required the development of institutions to facilitate lending, borrowing, credit, investment, and the like. Banks, stock and bond markets, and bodies of financial law and the means to enforce it were prerequisites of a modern financial system.

Without finance and financiers, it would have been difficult, if not impossible, for nation-states to make war; finance large-scale trading voyages; establish trading companies; build canals, dams, and railroads; and so on. But the possibility of making money with money also assumed that at the close of a transaction—the loan, the investment, and so on—there was more money than at the beginning. And it is here that we begin to appreciate the requirement of our economy for perpetual economic growth. The more that is lent or invested (and the higher the interest rates), the more money has to be generated to meet the terms of the investment or loan. When people cannot repay their loans or when investors fail to profit from their investments, financial collapse can ensue. Without the necessary growth, borrowers, including nation-states, may default on their loans; banks may collapse; or currency may widely fluctuate in value. And such crises are fairly frequent. In their study of global financial crises, Carmen M. Reinhart and Kenneth S. Rogoff (2009:34) note that since 1800, there have been at least 250 cases where whole countries have defaulted on their loan obligations. And over the course of the last 200 years, advanced economies have had, on average, 7.2 banking crises lasting an average of 7.2 years each.

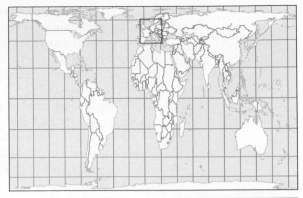

Knowing that the process of making money with money involves some risk, let's resume our time voyage as a merchant adventurer; *how could we have made money with money?* The place to have begun would have been the Netherlands of the sixteenth and seventeenth centuries. After Portugal, it was the Dutch that began to dominate the global economy of that period. The Dutch were initially best able to exploit the new developments in trade, partially because of their large merchant fleet and the development of the *fluitschip,* a light and slender vessel that carried heavy cargoes. But, more importantly, it was in the Netherlands that the first modern economy emerged, one in which making money with money, that is, moving it from where it was to where it was needed (or demanded) for a price, became accepted and normal (see de Vries and van der Woude 1997).

The Netherlands

As in the case of Portugal, it is difficult to understand how a small country with virtually no natural resources other than a tiny fish (herring) could come to dominate the economic world. But it may not be too much to say that the Dutch were the first to realize the full potential of money and to develop the whole field of finance. The Dutch did not invent finance, but they were the first to use it in a large-scale and public way. It would not be inaccurate to say that the Dutch were great investors, and, perhaps for that reason, the Netherlands is sometimes cited as the first modern economy to be characterized by sustained economic growth (see North and Thomas 1976).

The Dutch invested money in all sorts of things. In the period from 1610 to 1640, for example, Dutch citizens invested at least 10 million guilders (when annual average income was 200–400 guilders) in new capital-intensive technologies such as windmill pumping techniques to drain water and in increasing farmland for crops to feed the growing urban populations (see de Vries and van der Woude 1997:29). They also invested money in the building of canals to connect cities and towns and in draining peat bogs, their major energy source.

Dutch citizens also made money financing the public debt. In 1600, the state owed some 5 million guilders, and the public could buy state bonds paying some 8 percent to 16 percent interest (de Vries and van der Woude 1997:114). By 1660, some 65,000 people (out of some 220,000 households) had invested money in state bonds in order to gain the interest on the bonds, and, consequently, make money with money.

One of the most successful investments you might make at the time as a merchant adventurer would be in the United or Dutch East Indian Company (Vereenigde Oost-Indische Compagnie or VOC). The VOC was the first multinational corporation and the first to sell stock. It was also incredibly profitable, paying an average of 18 percent annual return on investments for almost 200 years.

Until that period, most investments in long-distance trading voyages involved one round-trip voyage only. But with increasing competition from Portugal and England, Dutch merchants with the help of the government set up the "United East Indies Company," granting the company exclusive trading rights over Asian trade, along with the authority to build forts, raise armies, and negotiate treaties with Asian rulers. To finance the company, the board, made up of seventeen lords and representing the first board of directors, issued stock in the company. The initial offering raised some 6.45 million guilders, and the shares were bought by everyone from the wealthiest members of society to their servants.

Initially the company was to function for twenty years, and an accounting to investors was to be provided only after that time. Consequently, the only way that investors could withdraw their investment was by selling their shares. Thus the joint-stock company and the stock market were established at about the same time. A considerable number of people wanted to buy and sell shares and therefore a special structure was built in Amsterdam for people to gather and buy and sell shares in the VOC.

Since a stock market cannot function effectively without banks, in 1609 the city of Amsterdam established the Amsterdam Exchange Bank to settle accounts between lenders and debtors and the bank soon began to accept VOC shares as collateral for loans, thus linking the stock market and the supply of credit. When banks began to lend money to buy shares, the outline of a new kind of economy based on investment, credit, and debt began to emerge (see Ferguson 2008:132).

Since much of the investment and debt was tied to the VOC, its success was essential to the maintenance of the economy. That is, if the investments in the VOC didn't pay off, people would have been unable to settle their debts or recoup the money that they had invested. Thus, the VOC had to grow the economy. And this it did.

The VOC's strategy was to establish "factories" in the areas it controlled, producing things (e.g., textiles and iron implements) to use to trade for local goods, such as spices, lumber, or handicrafts, which were shipped back and sold in Europe. In many cases, the successful working of the factories required ruthless exploitation of indigenous communities as well as armed confrontation with competing companies. As Jan Pieterszoon Coen, governor-general of the VOC put it, "We cannot make war without trade, nor trade without war."

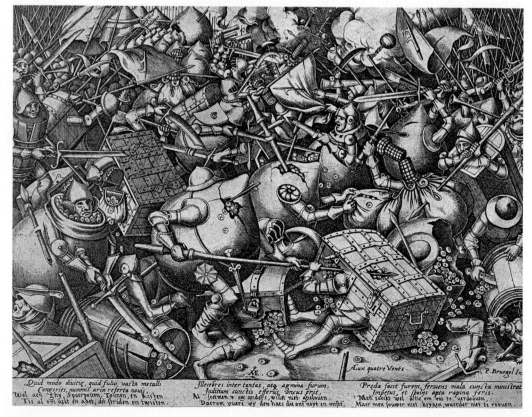

Pieter van der Heyden's sixteenth-century painting *The Battle about Money* conveys the growing concerns about making more money. The Dutch inscription on the bottom warns that "It's all for money and goods, this fighting and quarreling." (Heyden, Pieter van der (c. 1530 - after 1572). After, Pieter Bruegel the Elder (c. 1525–1569). *The Battle of the Money Bags and the Strong Boxes*, 1570–1600. Engraving; second state of four, sheet: 9 5/16 × 11 15/16 in. (23.6 × 30.4 cm). Harris Brisbane Dick Fund, 1926 (26.72.40). The Metropolitan Museum of Art, New York, NY, U.S.A. Image copyright © The Metropolitan Museum of Art. Image source: Art Resource, NY.)

With armies at their disposal, and fleets of fast-sailing ships available, the volume of trade controlled by the VOC increased yearly. In the 1620s, 50 VOC ships returned laden with goods from Asia; by the 1690s the number was 156, and from 1700 to 1750 the tonnage of Dutch ships doubled.

As trade increased, so did the value of VOC stock. From 1602 to 1733 the value of VOC stock rose from par (100) to 786 guilders. In addition, the dividends paid to shareholders by 1650 were eight times the purchase price, yielding an annual return of 27 percent, rivaling that of the most profitable present-day hedge funds.

But not all Dutch investments of the period worked out as planned; the Dutch not only can be said to have invented finance, they were also responsible for the first financial bubble and collapse. As mentioned earlier, the Dutch were avid investors and financial speculators. For example, as early as the 1550s, they invested in futures contracts. There were agreements between buyers and sellers that a specific commodity, such as grain or herring, could be purchased at a specific price at some time in the future. A futures contract was a way to reduce financial risk; the buyer would be guaranteed the right to buy a commodity at a price they could predict, and the seller was guaranteed a price for his or her product that they estimated would be profitable, regardless of whether the market prices of these commodities rose or fell.

By the seventeenth century, futures contracts were being written on such trade items as pepper, coffee, cacao, brandywine, whale bone, and whale oil. However, unlike the earlier futures market, many of the contracts in the seventeenth century represented speculation on prices; that is, purchasers had no intention of taking possession of the goods, just as sellers did not possess the goods. People essentially were betting that the prices of the goods would either rise or fall; if they won their bet, they profited. If not, they lost. And if many people speculated or bet on a specific commodity, and enough lost their bet, the whole economy could be thrown into disarray. Thus, we have the Dutch tulip mania of 1636/1637.

Beginning in 1635, during a decade when shares in the VOC were doubling in value, tulips, to most Dutch, looked like a good thing. Tulips enjoyed great popularity among the Dutch, who appreciated their aesthetic quality and the many-colored patterns of the flowers. Since some patterns were more desirable than others, prices of tulip bulbs varied immensely.

Tulip bulbs can propagate through the formation of outgrowths on the mother bulb, and when the bulbs are invaded by a mosaic virus, it produces an effect called "breaking" that results in multicolored flower patterns that are highly desired. However, the presence of these patterns can be verified only between June, when the bulbs can be removed from the ground, and September, when they must be replanted. Single bulbs were sometimes worth modest fortunes. A single Semper Augustus bulb sold for 5,500 guilders at a time, again, when the average yearly income was 200 to 400 guilders.

In the fall of 1636, the trade in tulips began to accelerate as ordinary Dutch citizens began to purchase tulip futures, specifying the kind of tulip they wished to purchase and entering into contracts with sellers. Most of the buyers had no intention of taking possession of the tulip bulbs, betting that the prices would rise and that they could then sell the rights to buy the tulips to people who wanted the bulbs. Often the sellers did not have any bulbs, but were betting that they could get them at a price less than they were offered from the buyers. Thus, as de Vries and van der Woude (1997:150) put it, "citizens crowded into taverns to buy and sell bulbs they could not deliver and did not want to receive." They were betting on the future price of bulbs.

Since there was no bank credit, payment was often promised in kind. In one case, for a pound of White Crown bulbs (a particularly common variety), one buyer offered FL 525 to be

In the attempt to make money with money, a single Semper Augustus bulb sold for 5,500 guilders at a time when the average yearly income was 200 to 400 guilders.
(Edward Owen/Art Resource, NY.)

paid on delivery of the bulbs (presumably the following June) and put four cows as a down payment. Other down payments consisted of "tracts of land, houses, furniture, silver and gold vessels, paintings, a suit and a coat, a coach and dapple-gray pair." Another buyer of a single Viceroy bulb, valued at FL 2,500, paid "two *lasts* (a measure that varied by commodity and locality) of wheat, four of rye, eight pigs, a dozen sheep, two oxheads of wine, four tons of butter, a thousand pounds of cheese, a bed, some clothing and a silver beaker" (Kindleberger 1978:109).

Then in February of 1637, for reasons that are unclear, prices being offered began to collapse, and investors who had depended on the rise in prices faced economic ruin. Since they had given the sellers only a portion of the agreed-upon price, they had to somehow come up with the rest, which they often did not have. Furthermore, the sellers, who had used the contracts as collateral for loans, had to come up with additional collateral that they didn't have. But since the futures contracts were, at the time, unenforceable in court, there was no incentive to honor the contracts. Thus investors lost large sums of money or the goods that they had used as down payment on their bulb purchases, while sellers were often not able to collect anyway. Many amateur investors went bankrupt. In spite of this, in the seventeenth century, the Dutch remained devoted investors, continuing to put their money in VOC stock or canal building, paintings, and clocks.

The lessons of the VOC and the "tulip bubble" are that for investors to profit and for borrowers to pay their debts, there must be some form of economic growth, either as an increase in trade, as with the VOC, or as an increase in the value of assets, such as tulip bulbs. If growth occurs, profits are made and debt is repaid. If it doesn't, investors experience losses and borrowers may default on their loans.

In addition, the period marked the increase in activities that required the gathering of large amounts of capital, usually through borrowing. Thus, states borrowed to wage war, merchants to engage in long-distance trade, and investors to speculate on commodities. And, as projects became larger and more expensive, greater sums of money had to be borrowed, lent, and repaid, all requiring perpetual economic growth.

Thus, the financial inventions of the Dutch Republic ushered in a new kind of economy, one in which making money with money became a significant feature of economic life, and in which economic growth became a necessity. There have also been repeated instances, as we will see, of speculative bubbles bursting and threatening to bring down whole economies, the most recent example being the collapse of housing values in the United States, as well as other countries, in 2007, which we will examine in more detail shortly.

THE ERA OF THE INDUSTRIALIST

By 1800, England had militarily, politically, and economically subdued her closest rivals of the early eighteenth century—France and Holland. British commerce thrived, fueled largely by the growth of industry, particularly textiles, and the related increase in the availability of cheap labor. And although Britain lost her American colonies, politically if not economically, she gained in many ways a wealthier prize—India.

But the big news was the industrial development of England. From 1730 to 1760, iron production increased 50 percent; the first iron bridge was built in 1779 and the first iron boat in 1787. In 1783 Watt produced the double-effect steam engine. From 1740 to 1770, consumption of cotton rose 117 percent, and by 1800, mechanized factories were producing textiles at an unprecedented rate.

Social scientists often pose two related questions: *What made England take off? And why was there an industrial revolution at all?* These are more than academic questions. As planners in so-called economically undeveloped countries attempt to improve peoples' lives through economic development, they often look to the history of Great Britain to discover the key ingredients to economic success. England became, to a great extent, the model for economic development, the epitome of progress, or so it was believed, particularly in Great Britain.

The reasons for the Industrial Revolution in England and the emergence of the capitalist economy are varied, and although analysts disagree on which were the most important, there is general agreement on those that played some part. They include the following (see, e.g., Wallerstein 1989:22ff.):

1. **An increase in demand for goods.** This demand may have been foreign or domestic, supplemented by increased demands for largely military products from the state. The textile industry was revolutionary also in its organization of labor and its relationship to the foreign market, on which it depended for both raw materials (in the case of cotton) and markets. Historian Eric Hobsbawm argued that there was room for only one world supplier, and that ended up being England (Hobsbawm 1975).

2. **An increase in the supply of capital.** An increase in trade resulted in greater profits and more money, and these profits supplied the capital for investment in new technologies and businesses.

3. **A growth in population.** Population increased dramatically in England and Europe in the eighteenth century. From 1550 to 1680, the population of western Europe grew by 18 percent, and from 1680 to 1820, by 62 percent. From 1750 to 1850, England's population increased from 5.7 million to 16.5 million. Population increase was important because it increased the potential labor force and the number of potential consumers of commodities. But there is disagreement as to why population increased and on the effects it had on industrialization.

    Some account for the increase with lower mortality rates attributable to smallpox inoculation and an improved diet related to the introduction of new foodstuffs, such as the potato. Life expectancy at birth rose from thirty-five to forty years (Guttmann 1988:130). Others attribute the rise in population to an increase in fertility. Indeed, families were larger in the eighteenth century. In England between 1680 and 1820, the gross reproduction rate (number of females born to each woman) went from two to nearly three and the average number of children per family from four to almost six. Later we examine the relationship of population growth to industrialization because it is key to understanding the rapid growth of population today.

4. **An expansion of agriculture.** There was an expansion of agricultural production in England in the eighteenth century that some attribute to enclosure laws. These laws drove squatters and peasants from common lands and forests from which they had drawn a livelihood. The rationale was to turn those lands over to the gentry to make them more productive, but this also had the effect of producing a larger landless and propertyless population, dependent on whatever wage labor they might find. Regardless, some argue that the increased agricultural yields allowed the maintenance of a larger urban workforce.

5. **A unique English culture or spirit.** Some, notably sociologist Max Weber, attribute the rise of England to the development of an entrepreneurial spirit, such as the Protestant ethic, that motivated people to business success in the belief that it would reveal to them whether or not they were among God's elect (Weber 1958).

6. **State support for trade.** Some claim that a more liberal state structure imposed fewer taxes and regulations on businesses, thus allowing them to thrive. The state did take action to support trade and industry. There was continued political and military support for extending Britain's economy overseas, along with domestic legislation to protect merchants from labor protest. A law of 1769 made the destruction of machines and the buildings that housed them a capital crime. Troops were sent to put down labor riots in Lancaster in 1779 and in Yorkshire in 1796, and a law passed in 1799 outlawed worker associations that sought wage increases, reduction in the working day, "or any other improvement in the conditions of employment or work" (Beaud 1983:67).

7. **The ascendance of the merchant class.** Stephen Sanderson (1995) attributed the development of capitalism to an increase in the power of the merchant class. There has always

been, he suggested, competition between merchants and the ruling elites, and although elites needed merchants to supply desired goods and services, they nevertheless looked down on them. But gradually the economic power of the merchant class grew until, in the seventeenth and eighteenth centuries, the merchant emerged as the most powerful member of Western, capitalist society. Capitalism, said Sanderson (1995:175–176), "was born of a class struggle. However, it was not, as the Marxists would have it, a struggle between land-lords and peasants. Rather, it was a struggle between the landlord class and the merchants that was fundamental in the rise of capitalism."

8. A revolution in consumption. Finally, some attribute the rapid economic growth in England to a revolution in the patterns of retailing and consumption. There was a growth in the number of stores and shops and the beginning of a marketing revolution, led by the pottery industry and the entrepreneurial genius of Josiah Wedgewood, who named his pottery styles after members of the Royal Family to appeal to the fashion consciousness of the rising middle class.

Regardless of the reasons for England's rise and the so-called Industrial Revolution, there is little doubt that in addition to the traditional means of accumulating wealth—mercantile trade, extracting the surplus from peasant labor, pillage, forced labor, slavery, and taxes—a new form of capital formation increased in importance. It involved purchasing and combining the means of production and labor power to produce commodities, the form of wealth formation called *capitalism* that we diagramed earlier as follows:

$$M \rightarrow C \rightarrow mp/lp \rightarrow C' \rightarrow M'$$

[Money is converted to commodities (capital goods) that are combined with the means of production and labor power to produce other commodities (consumer goods) that are then sold for a sum greater than the initial investment.] *How did this mode of production differ from what went before?*

Eric Wolf offered one of the more concise views. For capitalism to exist, he said, wealth or money must be able to purchase labor power. But as long as people have access to the means of production—land, raw materials, tools (e.g., weaving looms and mills)—there is no reason for them to sell their labor. They can still sell the product of their labor. For the capitalistic mode of production to exist, the tie between producers and the means of production must be cut; peasants must lose control of their land, artisans control of their tools. These people, once denied access to the means of production, must negotiate with those who control the means of production for permission to use the land and tools and receive a wage in return. Those who control the means of production also control the goods that are produced, and so those who labor to produce them must buy them back from those with the means of production. Thus the severing of persons from the means of production turns them not only into laborers but into consumers of the product of their labor as well. Here is how Wolf (1982:78–79) summarized it:

> Wealth in the hands of holders of wealth is not capital until it controls means of production, buys labor power, and puts it to work continuously expanding surpluses by intensifying production through an ever-rising curve of technological inputs. To this end capitalism must lay hold of production, must invade the productive process and ceaselessly alter the conditions of production themselves.… Only where wealth has laid hold of the conditions of production in ways specified can we speak of the existence or dominance of a capitalistic mode. There is no such thing as mercantile of merchant capitalism, therefore. There is only mercantile wealth. Capitalism, to be capitalism, must be capitalism-in-production.

Wolf (1982:100) added that the state is central in developing the capitalist mode of production because it must use its power to maintain and guarantee the ownership of the means of production by capitalists both at home and abroad and must support the organization and discipline of work. The state also has to provide the infrastructure, such as transportation, communication, judicial system, and education, required by capitalist production. Finally, the state must regulate conflicts between competing capitalists both at home and abroad, by diplomacy if possible, by war if necessary.

The major questions are, *How did this industrially driven, capitalist mode of production evolve, and what consequences did it have in England, Europe, and the rest of the world?*

Textiles and the Rise of the Factory System

Assume once again your role as a merchant; let's examine the opportunities and problems confronting you as you conduct business. Typical textile merchants of the early eighteenth century purchased their wares from specialized weavers or part-time producers of cloth or from drapers, persons who organized the production of cloth but did not trade in it. The merchant then sold the cloth to a consumer or another merchant who sold it in other areas of Europe or elsewhere. The profit came from the difference between what the merchant paid the artisan or draper and what the customer paid. This is not a bad arrangement. It does not require a large capital outlay for the merchant because the artisan has the tools and material he or she needs, and as long as there is a demand for the cloth, there is someone who will buy it.

But as a merchant, you face a couple of problems. First, the people who make the cloth you buy may not produce the quantity or quality that you need, especially as an expanding population begins to require more textiles. Moreover, the artisan may have trouble acquiring raw materials, such as wool or cotton, further disrupting the supply. What can you do?

One thing to do is increase control over what is produced by "putting out"—supplying the drapers or weavers with the raw materials to produce the cloth— or, if you have the capital, buy tools (looms, spinning wheels, and so on) and give them to people to make the cloth, paying them for what they produce. Cottage industry of this sort was widespread throughout Europe as merchants began to take advantage of the cheaper labor in rural areas, rather than purchasing products from artisans in towns and cities. In England of the mid-eighteenth century, there was probably plenty of labor, especially in rural areas, supplied by people who had been put off their land by enclosure legislation or because of failure to pay taxes or repay loans. In the land market of the eighteenth century, there were far more sellers than buyers (Guttmann 1988).

Another problem English textile merchants faced in the mid-eighteenth century was that the textile business, especially in cotton, faced stiff competition from India, whose calico cloth was extremely popular in England. How do you meet this competition? The first thing England did was to ban the import of Indian cloth and develop its own cotton industry to satisfy domestic demand. This not only helped protect the British textile industry, but it also virtually destroyed the Indian cotton industry; before long, India was buying British cotton textiles. The result was summed up in 1830 in testimony before the House of Commons by Charles Marjoribanks (Wallerstein 1989:150):

> We have excluded the manufactures of India from England by high prohibitive duties and given every encouragement to the introduction of our own manufactures to India. By our selfish (I use the word invidiously) policy we have beat down the native manufactures of Dacca and other places and inundated their country with our goods.
>
> And in 1840, the chairman of Britain's East India and China association boasted that this Company has, in various ways, encouraged and assisted by our great manufacturing ingenuity and skill, succeeded in converting India from a manufacturing country into a country exporting raw materials. (Wallerstein 1989:150)

The next, and to some extent inevitable, stage in textile production was to bring together in one place—the factory—as many of the textile production phases as possible: preparing the raw wool or cotton, spinning the cotton yarn and wool, weaving the cloth, and applying the finishing touches. This allowed the merchant or industrialist to control the quantity and quality of the product and control the use of materials and tools. The only drawback to the factory system is that it is capital intensive; the merchant was now responsible for financing the entire process, whereas the workers supplied only their labor. Most of the increase in cost was a consequence of increased mechanization.

Mechanization of the textile industry began with the invention by John Kay in 1733 of the flying shuttle, a device that allowed the weaver to strike the shuttle carrying the thread from one side of the loom to the other, rather than weaving it through by hand. This greatly speeded up the weaving process. However, when demand for textiles, particularly cotton, increased, the spinning of thread, still done on spinning wheels or spindles, could not keep up with weavers, and bottlenecks developed in production. To meet this need, James Hargreaves introduced the spinning jenny in 1770. Later, Arkwright introduced the water frame, and in 1779 Crompton introduced his "mule" that allowed a single operator to work more than 1,000 spindles at once. In 1790 steam power was supplied. These technological developments increased textile production enormously: The mechanical advantage of the earliest spinning jennies to hand spinning was twenty-four to one. The spinning wheel had become an antique in a decade (Landes 1969:85). The increase in the supply of yarn—twelve times as much cotton was consumed in 1800 than in 1770—required improvements in weaving, which then required more yarn, and so on.

The revolution in production, however, produced other problems: *Who was going to buy the increasing quantity of goods that were being produced, and from where was the raw material for production to come?*

The Age of Imperialism

The results of the Industrial Revolution in Europe were impressive. The period from 1800 to 1900 was perhaps one of the most dynamic in human history and, certainly until that time, the most favorable for accumulation of vast fortunes through trade and manufacture. Developments in transportation, such as railroads and steamships, revolutionized the transport of raw materials and finished commodities. The combination of new sources of power in water and steam,

Power loom weaving in a nineteenth-century cotton textile factory. Note that all the workers are women. (Bettmann/Corbis.)

a disarmed and plentiful labor force, and control of the production and markets of much of the rest of the world resulted in dramatic increases in the level of production and wealth. These advances were most dramatic in England and later in the United States, France, and Germany. In England, for example, spun cotton increased from 250 million pounds in 1830 to 1,101 million pounds in 1870. World steam power production went from 4 million horsepower in 1850 to 18.5 million horsepower twenty years later; coal production rose from 15 million tons in 1800 to 132 million tons in 1860, and 701 million tons in 1900. The consumption of inanimate energy from coal, lignite, petroleum, natural gasoline, natural gas, and water power increased sixfold from 1860 to 1900; railway trackage went from 332 kilometers in 1831 to 300,000 kilometers in 1876. The Krupp ironworks in Germany employed seventy-two workers in 1848; there were 12,000 by 1873.

There was also a revolution in shipping as ocean freight costs fell, first with the advent of the narrow-beamed American clipper ship and later with the introduction of the steamship. A clipper ship could carry 1,000 tons of freight and make the journey from the south coast of China to London in 120 to 130 days; in 1865 a steamship from the Blue Funnel Line with a capacity of 3,000 tons made the journey in seventy-seven days. The construction of the Suez Canal, completed in 1869 with the labor of 20,000 conscripted Egyptian *fellaheen,* or peasants, cut the travel time from England to eastern Asia in half—although it bankrupted the Egyptian treasury and put the country under Anglo-French receivership. These events initiated a military revolt that the British stepped in to put down, consequently cementing the British hold on Egypt and much of the Middle East. Politically, the United States emerged as a world power, and Japan was building its economy and would be ready to challenge Russia. The Ottoman Empire was on its way to disintegrating as France, England, and Russia sought to gain control over the remnants.

But it was not all good news for the capitalist economy. There was organized worker resistance to low wages and impoverished conditions, resistance and rebellion in the periphery, and the development of capitalist business cycles that led to worldwide economic depressions. Thus, although business thrived in much of the nineteenth century, it had also entered a world of great uncertainty. First, with the expansion of the scope of production, capital investments had increased enormously. It was no longer possible, as it had been in 1800 when a forty-spindle jenny cost six pounds, to invest in the factory production of textiles at fairly modest levels. Furthermore, there was increased competition, with factory production expanding dramatically in Holland, France, Germany, and the United States. There was the constant problem of overproduction, when supply outstripped demand and resulted in idle factories and unemployed workers. Unlike agricultural production—there seemed always to be a market for food—industrial production depends on the revolution in demand or, as Anne-Robert-Jacque Turgot put it, "a transformation of desires" (Braudel 1982:183). Until the eighteenth century, manufacturers launched their enterprises only when profit was guaranteed by subsidies, interest-free loans, and previously guaranteed monopolies. Now manufacturers simply had to hope people would buy their products.

Moreover, there were speculative bubbles that burst, leading to investors' losing millions of dollars. The big mania in 1840s England was railroad stock. Piqued by Queen Victoria taking her first train trip in 1842, British interest in building railroads surged, particularly among landowners who would benefit by the rise of land values adjacent to railroads.

In England, George Hudson was the first to fan the public interest, building and acquiring thousands of miles of track and publicizing the virtues of rail travel. He charged high tariffs and paid low wages, leading to various accidents, but paying shareholders in his railroad a dividend of 9 percent. And anyone could start a railroad: All you needed were a collection of people, permission from parliament, an engineer, and the sale of subscriptions to raise the money necessary to build. Parliament thought of regulating the growth of railways more strictly, but backed down after objections from speculators, such as George Hudson. By 1844, with interest rates low and railways returning 10 percent dividends, the interest in railways was growing. In 1845, sixteen new railroad schemes were projected. People readily bought shares in proposed rail lines with promises of 10 percent dividends.

By 1845, 20,000 speculators had each subscribed for more than two pounds worth of shares, including 157 members of parliament and 257 clergymen. Many had contracted beyond their means. Two brothers who subscribed for 37,500 pounds' worth of shares were the sons of a charwoman living in a garret on a guinea a week. They hoped to sell at a profit. Many bought shares in railways that would never be approved by parliament.

Newspapers and members of parliament all warned that it was sheer speculation and that everyone knew a crash would come, but believed that they would escape and get out before prices declined. By June, there were plans for 8,000 miles of new railways, four times the size of the existing system and twenty times the length of England. By the summer of 1845, some railway scrip showed a profit of 500 percent and still more railways were being proposed and subscribed.

But by October of 1845, the boom was over and the worth of railway script crashed. Parliament was forced to pass the Dissolution Act, allowing the railways to disband but requiring speculators to purchase the script that they contracted for at the height of the craze. Many were financially ruined.

Then there was the Great Global Depression of 1873 that lasted essentially until 1895. The depression was, of course, not the first economic crisis, but the financial collapse of 1873 revealed the degree of global economic integration, and how economic events in one part of the globe could reverberate in others. The economic depression began when banks failed in Germany and Austria because of the collapse of real estate speculation. At the same time, the price of cast iron in England fell by 27 percent because of a drop in demand. The drop in iron prices increased British unemployment, while European investors, needing to cover their losses from real estate, withdrew their money from American banks. This led to bank collapses in the United States. In England, from 1872 to 1875, exports fell by 25 percent, the number of bankruptcies increased, and rail prices fell by 60 percent. In France, the Lyon stock market crashed in 1882; bank failures and rising unemployment followed. Competition among railroads decreased profits and led to the collapse of railroad securities in the United States (Beaud 1983:119–120; see also Guttmann 1994).

The depression of 1873 revealed another big problem with capitalist expansion and perpetual growth: It can continue only as long as there is a ready supply of raw materials and an increasing demand for goods, along with ways to invest profits and capital. Given this situation, *If you were an American or European investor in 1873, where would you look for economic expansion and continued economic growth?*

The obvious answer was to extend European and American power overseas, particularly into areas that remained relatively untouched by capitalist expansion—Africa, Asia, and the Pacific. Colonialism had become, in fact, a recognized solution to the need to expand markets, increase opportunities for investors, and ensure the supply of raw material. Cecil Rhodes, one of the great figures of England's colonization of Africa, recognized also the importance of overseas expansion for maintaining peace at home. In 1895 Rhodes said,

> I was in the East End of London yesterday and attended a meeting of the unemployed. I listened to the wild speeches, which were just a cry for "bread," "bread," and on my way home I pondered over the scene and I became more than ever convinced of the importance of imperialism.... My cherished idea is a solution for the social problem, i.e., in order to save the 40,000,000 inhabitants of the United Kingdom from a bloody civil war, we colonial statesmen must acquire new lands for settling the surplus population, to provide new markets for the goods produced in the factories and mines. The Empire, as I have always said, is a bread and butter question. If you want to avoid civil war, you must become imperialists. (Beaud 1983:139–140)

P. Leroy-Beaulieu voiced the same sentiments in France when, to justify the conquest of foreign nations, he said,

> It is neither natural nor just that the civilized people of the West should be indefinitely crowded together and stifled in the restricted spaces that were their first homes, that they should accumulate there the wonders of science, art, and civilization, that they should see, for lack of profitable jobs, the interest rate of capital fall further every day for them, and that they should leave perhaps half the world to small groups of ignorant men, who are powerless, who are truly retarded children dispersed over boundless territories, or else to decrepit populations without energy and without direction, truly old men incapable of any effort, of any organized and far-seeing action. (Beaud 1983:140)

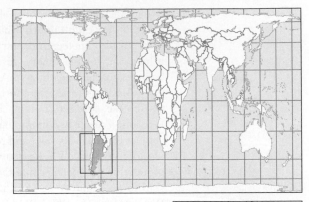

Argentina

As a result of this cry for imperialist expansion, people all over the world were converted into producers of export crops as millions of subsistence farmers were forced to become wage laborers producing for the market and to purchase from European and American merchants and industrialists, rather than supply for themselves, their basic needs. Nineteenth-century British economist William Stanley Jevons (Kennedy 1993:9) summed up the situation when he boasted,

> The plains of North America and Russia are our cornfields; Chicago and Odessa our granaries; Canada and the Baltic are our timber forests; Australasia contains our sheep farms, and in Argentina and on the western prairies of North America are our herds of oxen; Peru sends her silver, and the gold of South Africa and Australia flows to London; the Hindus and the Chinese grow tea for us, and our coffee, sugar, and spice plantations are all in the Indies. Spain and France are our vineyards and the Mediterranean our fruit garden, and our cotton grounds, which for long have occupied the Southern United States are now being extended everywhere in the warm regions of the earth.

Wheat became the great export crop of Russia, Argentina, and the United States, much of it produced in the United States on lands taken from the Native Americans. Rice became the great export of Southeast Asia, spurred by Great Britain's seizure of lower Burma in 1855 and its increase in rice production from 1 million to 9 million acres. Argentina and Australia joined the United States as the major supplier of meat as cattle ranchers in Australia and the United States turned indigenous peoples into hired hands or hunted them to extermination, as did the ranchers in California into the late nineteenth century (see Meggitt 1962).

In 1871 a railroad promoter from the United States built a railroad in Costa Rica and experimented in banana production; out of this emerged in 1889 the United Fruit Company that within thirty-five years was producing 2 billion bunches of bananas. The company reduced its risk by expanding into different countries and different environments and by acquiring far more land than it could use at any one time as a reserve against the future.

The demand for rubber that followed the discovery of vulcanization in 1839 led to foreign investments in areas such as Brazil, where one major supplier increased production from 27 tons in 1827 to an average of 20,000 tons per year at the end of the nineteenth century. The laborers who collected the rubber were workers who had lost their jobs with the decline in the sugar industries and Indians, who were sometimes held captive or tortured or killed if they didn't collect their quota of rubber. The wives and children of those Indians who ran away would be killed if they didn't return (Taussig 1987).

In the nineteenth century, palm oil became a substitute for tallow for making soap and a lubricant for machinery, resulting in European military expansion into West Africa and the conquest of the kingdoms of Asante, Dahomey, Oyo, and Benin.

Vast territories were turned over to the production of stimulants and drugs, such as sugar, tea, coffee, tobacco, opium, and cocoa. In the Mexican state of Chiapas and in Guatemala, legislation abolished communal ownership of land. Land could now be privately owned and subject to purchase, sale, and pawning, allowing non-Indians to buy unregistered land and fore-close mortgages on Indian borrowers (Wolf 1982:337). These lands were then turned to coffee production and, later, cattle ranching. In Ceylon, common land was turned into royal land and sold to tea planters. In 1866 diamonds and gold were discovered in the Orange Free State of West Africa. By 1874, 10,000 Africans were working in the European-owned diamond mines. By 1884, there were almost 100,000 and 255,000 by 1910. In 1940 there were 444,000.

Colonization was not restricted to overseas areas; it occurred also within the borders of core states. In 1887, the U.S. Congress passed the General Allotment Act (the "Dawes Act") to break up the collective ownership of land on Native American reservations by assigning each family its own parcel, then opening unallotted land to non-Native American homesteaders, corporations, and the federal government. As a consequence, from 1887 to 1934, some 100 million acres of land assigned by treaty to Native American groups was appropriated by private interests or the government (Jaimes 1992:126).

At first glance it may seem that the growth in development of export goods such as coffee, cotton, sugar, and lumber would be beneficial to the exporting country because it brings in revenue. In fact, it represents a type of exploitation called *unequal exchange*. A country that exports raw or unprocessed materials may gain currency for their sale, but they then lose it if they import processed goods. The reason is that processed goods—goods that require additional labor—are more costly. Thus, a country that exports lumber but does not have the capacity to process it must then reimport it in the form of finished lumber products, at a cost that is greater than the price it received for the raw product. The country that processes the materials gets the added revenue contributed by its laborers.

Then there is the story of tea and opium and trade in China. China, of course, was a huge prize, but the British and western European nations had a problem with trade into China: Chinese products, notably tea, were in high demand, but there was little produced in England or the rest of Europe that the Chinese wanted or needed. However, there was a market in China for opium, virtually all of which was produced and controlled by the British East India Company. Opium was illegal in China, but the government seemed incapable of stopping the smuggling that was hugely profitable for British, American, and French merchants. When, in 1839, the Chinese government tried to enforce laws against opium sales by seizing opium held by British merchants in warehouses in Canton, the British government sent in troops and effectively forced the Chinese government to stop enforcing opium laws. An analogy today might be the Colombian government sending troops to the United States to force acceptance of Colombian cocaine shipments. Moreover, using its military superiority, the British demanded and received additional trading rights into China, opening a market not only for opium but for British textiles as well.

The British-led opium trade from India to China had three consequences. First, it reversed the flow of money between China and the rest of the world. During the first decade of the nineteenth century, China still took in a surplus of $26 million; by the third decade, $34 million left China to pay for opium. Historian Carl Trocki (1999) suggests, in fact, that the opium trade financed British colonial expansion in the nineteenth century. Second, it is estimated that by the end of the nineteenth century, one out of every ten Chinese had become an opium addict. Third, cotton exports to India and China had increased from 6 percent of total British exports in 1815 to 22 percent in 1840, 31 percent in 1850, and more than 50 percent after 1873 (Wolf 1982:255ff.).

Thus, as a merchant adventurer, your economic fortune has been assured by your government's control over foreign economies. Not only could you make more money investing in foreign enterprises, but also the wealth you accumulated through trade and manufacturing gained you entry into a new elite, one with increasing power in the core countries. Power was no longer evidenced solely in the ownership of land but in the control of capital. In England, for example, the great families of high finance and international trade, businesspeople, manufacturers, shipowners, bankers, parliamentarians, jurists, and families of the aristocracy and gentry, all crisscrossed by ties of marriage and kinship, became the new ruling class. This new elite depended on business and industry to a great extent for their economic power: In the eighteenth century, landed inheritance accounted for 63.7 percent of national wealth in Great Britain; toward the end of the nineteenth century, that figure had decreased to 23.3 percent. Meanwhile, during the same period, wealth linked to capitalist development increased from 20.8 percent to almost 50 percent.

In the United States, a new capitalist elite emerged during and after the Civil War, as people such as J. P. Morgan, Jay Gould, Jim Fisk, Cornelius Vanderbilt, and John D. Rockefeller—most of whom made their fortunes in dealings with the U.S. government—emerged as a new bourgeoisie. More importantly, they were the driving force behind the emergence of a relatively new form of capital organization—the multinational corporation.

THE ERA OF THE CORPORATION, THE MULTILATERAL INSTITUTION, AND THE CAPITAL SPECULATOR

Although the imperialist activities of the core powers allowed their economies to grow, they also created international conflict on a scale never before imagined. In 1900, each of the great powers sought to carve out a sphere of domination in Asia, Africa, and South and Central America that, with the help of nationalism, racism, and xenophobia, turned economic competition into political and military conflict. These conflicts fed on myths of national or racial superiority—British, French, American, white, and so on—and the supposed civilizing mission of the West (Beaud 1983:144). At the Berlin Conference of 1885, great European powers met to carve up zones of influence and domination in Africa, laying the groundwork for levels of colonization from which Africa still has not recovered.

Attempts to extend or defend these zones of economic influence triggered what was until then the bloodiest war ever fought—World War I. Eight million people were killed. Britain lost 32 percent of its national wealth, France 30 percent, Germany 20 percent, and the United States 9 percent. Germany was forced to pay $33 billion in reparations. Industrial production fell in all countries except the United States. Then the Russian Revolution cut off huge markets for European and American products, while colonized countries demanded independence.

The United States emerged from World War I as the world's leading economic power: Its national income doubled, and coal, oil, and steel production soared. However, workers' real wages and the power of labor unions declined; new forms of factory organization led to greater fatigue—there were 20,000 fatal industrial accidents per year in the 1920s, and the courts blocked the formation of new unions and the application of social laws, such as those prohibiting child labor. It was an era of the rise of a new, great economic power—the corporation.

The Rise of the Corporation

From your perspective as a merchant adventurer, the most important development of the early twentieth century was the merger frenzy in the United States that would be unrivaled until the 1990s. Companies such as Ford, General Motors, and Chrysler in automobiles; General

Electric and Westinghouse in the electric industry; Dupont in chemicals; and Standard Oil in petroleum dominated the market. In 1929, the 200 largest companies owned half of the country's nonbanking wealth. Since then, of course, corporations have become one of the dominant governance units in the world. By 1998, there were more than 53,000 transnational corporations (French 2000:5). From their foreign operations alone they generated almost $6 trillion in sales. The largest corporations exceed in size, power, and wealth most of the world's nation-states and, directly or indirectly, define policy agendas of states and international bodies (Korten 1995:54). As a merchant adventurer, you have now entered the corporate age. *What kind of institution is the corporation, and how did it come to accumulate so much wealth and power?*

Technically, a corporation is a social invention of the state; the corporate charter, granted by the state, ideally permits private financial resources to be used for a public purpose. At another level, it allows one or more individuals to apply massive economic and political power to accumulate private wealth while protected from legal liability for the public consequences. As a merchant adventurer, clearly you want to create an institution in which you can increase and protect your own profits from market uncertainties (Korten 1995:53–54).

The corporate charter goes back to the sixteenth century, when any debts accumulated by an individual were inherited by his or her descendants. Consequently, someone could be jailed for the debts of a father, mother, brother, or sister. If you, in your role as merchant adventurer, invested in a trading voyage and the goods were lost at sea, you and your descendants were responsible for the losses incurred. The law, as written, inhibited risky investments. The corporate charter solved this problem because it represented a grant from the crown that limited an investor's liability for losses to the amount of the investment, a right not accorded to individual citizens.

The early trading companies, such as the Dutch East India Company and the Hudson's Bay Company, were such corporations, and some of the American colonies themselves were founded as corporations—groups of investors granted monopoly powers over territory and industries. Consequently, corporations gained enormous power and were able to influence trade policy. For example, in the eighteenth century, the English parliament, composed of wealthy landowners, merchants, and manufacturers, passed laws requiring all goods sold in or from the colonies to go through England and be shipped on English ships with British crews. Furthermore, colonists were forbidden to produce their own caps, hats, and woolen or iron goods.

Suspicion of the power of corporations developed soon after their establishment. Even eighteenth-century philosopher and economist Adam Smith condemned corporations in *The Wealth of Nations*. He claimed corporations operated to evade the laws of the market by artificially inflating prices and controlling trade. American colonists shared Smith's suspicion of corporations and limited corporate charters to a specific number of years. If the charter was not renewed, the corporation was dissolved. But gradually American courts began to remove restrictions on corporations' operation. The U.S. Civil War was a turning point: Corporations used their huge profits from the war, along with the subsequent political confusion and corruption, to buy legislation that gave them huge grants of land and money, much of which they used to build railroads. Abraham Lincoln saw what was happening and just before his death is said to have wrote that

> corporations have been enthroned.... An era of corruption in high places will follow and the money power will endeavor to prolong its reign by working on the prejudices of the people ... until wealth is aggregated in a few hands ... and the Republic is destroyed. (Korten 1995:5)

Gradually, corporations gained control of state legislatures, such as those in Delaware and New Jersey, lobbying for (and buying) legislation that granted charters in perpetuity, limited the liabilities of corporate owners and managers, and gained the right of corporations to operate in any way not specifically prohibited by the law. For example, courts limited corporate liability for accidents to workers, an important development in the nineteenth century when fatal industrial accidents from 1888 to 1908 killed 700,000 workers, or roughly one hundred per day. Other favorable court rulings and legislation prohibited the state from setting minimum wage laws, limiting the number of hours a person could work, or setting minimum age requirements for workers.

A Supreme Court ruling in 1886 by a single judge, however, arguably set the stage for the full-scale development of the next stage of the culture of capitalism. The court ruled that corporations could use their economic power in a way they never before had. Relying on the Fourteenth Amendment, added to the Constitution in 1868 to protect the rights of freed slaves, the Court ruled that a private corporation is a natural person under the U.S. Constitution and consequently has the same rights and protection extended to persons by the Bill of Rights, including the right of free speech (Hartmann 2002). Thus, corporations were given the same "rights" to influence the government in their own interest as were extended to individual citizens, paving the way for corporations to use their wealth to dominate public thought and discourse. The debates in the United States today over campaign finance reform, in which corporate bodies can "donate" millions of dollars to political candidates, stem from this ruling, although rarely, if ever, is that mentioned. Thus, corporations, as "persons," were free to lobby legislatures, use the mass media, establish educational institutions such as the many business schools founded by corporate leaders in the early twentieth century, found charitable organizations to convince the public of their lofty intent, and in general construct an image that they believed would be in their best interests—all of this in the interest of "free speech." This power

JACK AND THE WALL STREET GIANTS.

This early twentieth-century cartoon depicts Jack, of "Jack and the Beanstalk," confronted by the then "giants" of Wall Street, including John D. Rockefeller, J. J. Hill, J.P. Morgan, and Jay Gould, all watched over by a seemingly helpless President "Teddy" Roosevelt. (Fotosearch/Getty Images.)

was reinforced in 2010 when the U.S. Supreme Court, in a five to four decision, ruled in the case of Citizens United that Congress could not limit the amount of campaign contributions of corporations or unions.

Corporations use this power, of course, to create conditions in which they could make more money. But in a larger sense they used this power to define the ideology or ethos of the emerging culture of capitalism. This cultural and economic ideology is known as *neoclassical, neoliberal, and libertarian economics, market capitalism, or market liberalism* and is advocated in society primarily by three groups of spokespersons: economic rationalists, market liberals, and members of the corporate class. Their advocacy of these principles created what David Korten called *corporate libertarianism,* which places the rights and freedoms of corporations above the rights and freedoms of individuals—the corporation comes to exist as a separate entity with its own internal logic and rules. Some of the principles and assumptions of this ideology include the following:

1. Sustained *economic growth,* as measured by gross national product (GNP), is the path to human progress.
2. *Free markets,* unrestrained by government, generally result in the most efficient and socially optimal allocation of resources.
3. *Economic globalization,* achieved by removing barriers to the free flow of goods and money anywhere in the world, spurs competition, increases economic efficiency, creates jobs, lowers consumer prices, increases consumer choice, increases economic growth, and is generally beneficial to almost everyone.
4. *Privatization,* which moves functions and assets from governments to the private sector, improves efficiency.
5. The primary responsibility of government is to provide the infrastructure necessary to advance commerce and enforce the rule of law with respect to *property rights and contracts.*

However, hidden in these principles, said Korten, are a number of questionable assumptions. First, there is the assumption that humans are motivated by self-interest, which is expressed primarily through the quest for financial gain (or, people are by nature motivated primarily by greed). Second, there is the assumption that the action that yields the greatest financial return to the individual or firm is the one that is most beneficial to society (or, the drive to acquire is the highest expression of what it means to be human). Third is the assumption that competitive behavior is more rational for the individual and the firm than cooperative behavior; consequently, societies should be built around the competitive motive (or, relentless greed and acquisition lead to socially optimal outcomes). Finally, there is the assumption that human progress is best measured by increases in the value of what the members of society consume, and ever-higher levels of consumer spending advance the well-being of society by stimulating greater economic output (or, it is in the best interest of human societies to encourage, honor, and reward the preceding values).

Although corporate libertarianism has its detractors, from the standpoint of overall economic growth, few can argue with its success on a global scale. World economic output has increased from $6.7 trillion in 1950 to almost $70 trillion in 2011. Economic growth in *each decade* of the last half of the twentieth century was greater than the economic output in all of human history up to 1950. World trade increased from total exports of $308 billion in 1950 to $5.4 trillion in 1998. In 1950, world exports of goods was only 5 percent of the world GNP; by 1998, this figure was 13 percent (French 2000:5).

There were still, however, some problems for the merchant adventurer in the early twentieth century. As corporations rose to power in the 1920s and 1930s, political and business leaders were aware that corporations, by themselves, could not ensure the smooth running of the global economy. The worldwide economic depression of the 1930s and the economic disruptions caused by World War II illustrated that. That every country had its own currency and that it could rapidly rise or fall in value relative to others created barriers to trade. Tariffs and import or export laws inhibited the free flow of goods and capital. More importantly, there was the problem of bringing the ideology of corporate libertarianism, and the culture of capitalism in general, to the periphery, especially given the challenge of socialism and the increasing demands of colonized countries for independence. The solution to these problems was to emerge from a meeting in 1944 at a New Hampshire resort hotel.

Bretton Woods and the World Debt

In 1944 President Franklin D. Roosevelt gathered the government financial leaders of forty-four nations to a meeting at the Mt. Washington Hotel in Bretton Woods, New Hampshire. From your perspective as a merchant adventurer, it was to be one of the most far-reaching events of

TABLE 3.1 The Bretton Woods Institutions

Institution or Agency	Function
International Monetary Fund (IMF)	To make funds available for countries to meet short-term financial needs and to stabilize currency exchanges between countries
International Bank for Reconstruction and Development (World Bank)	To make loans for various development projects
Global Agreement on Tariffs and Trade (GATT)	To ensure the free trade of commodities among countries

the twentieth century. The meeting was called ostensibly to rebuild war-ravaged economies and to outline a global economic agenda for the last half of the twentieth century. Out of that meeting came the plan for the International Bank for Reconstruction and Development (the World Bank), the International Monetary Fund (IMF) to control currency exchange, and the framework for a worldwide trade organization that would lead to the establishment in 1948 of the General Agreement on Tariffs and Trade (GATT) to regulate trade between member countries. Although GATT was not as comprehensive an agreement as many traders would have liked, its scope was widely enlarged on January 1, 1995, with the establishment of the World Trade Organization (WTO). The functions of these agencies are summarized in Table 3.1.

The IMF constituted an agreement by the major nations to allow their currency to be exchanged for other currencies with a minimum of restriction, to inform representatives of the IMF of changes in monetary and financial policies, and to adjust these policies to accommodate other member nations when possible. The IMF also has funds that it can lend to member nations if they face a debt crisis. For example, if a member country finds it is importing goods at a much higher rate than it is exporting them, and if it doesn't have the money to make up the difference, the IMF will arrange a short-term loan (Driscoll 1992:5).

The World Bank was created to finance the reconstruction of Europe after the devastation of World War II, but the only European country to receive a loan was Holland, then engaged in trying to put down a rebellion of its Southeast Asian colonies. The World Bank then began to focus its attention on the periphery, lending funds to countries to foster economic development, with, as we shall see, mixed results.

The GATT has served as a forum for participating countries to negotiate trade policy. The goal was to establish a multilateral agency with the power to regulate and promote free trade among nations. However, because legislators and government officials in many countries, particularly the United States, objected to the idea of an international trade agency with the power to dictate government trade policy, the creation of such an agency did not occur until the WTO was finally established on January 1, 1995. In essence, the agency can react to claims by member nations that other nations are using unfair trade policies in order to give businesses in their country an unfair advantage (see Low 1993:42). For example, in 1989 the European Union instituted a ban on the importation of beef injected with bovine growth hormones. These hormones are manufactured in the United States by Monsanto Corporation and are used to boost milk production in cows. The hormone was approved in 1993 by the U.S. Food and Drug Administration, but public interest groups maintain that, because it increases udder infections in cows, it requires greater use of antibiotics in cows, and these antibiotics end up in the milk. Some scientists even link the use of the hormone to cancer development (see BGH Bulletin 2000). The United States, on behalf of Monsanto, claimed to the WTO that the ban amounted to an unfair barrier to U.S. beef exports. The WTO ruled in favor of the United States and allowed the U.S. government to impose a 100 percent tariff on $116.8 million worth of European imports, such as fruit juices, mustard, pork, truffles, and Roquefort cheese. Thus, the WTO can rule that a country's food, environmental, or work laws constitute an "unfair barrier to trade" and penalize a country that does not remove them (see French 2000).

One of the most profound influences of the Bretton Woods meeting is the accumulation of the debt of peripheral countries; some consider this "debt crisis" the gravest one facing the world. The reasons for the debt crisis, and the possible impact it can have on everyone's lives, are complex but essential to understand. Overwhelming debt of peripheral countries is one of the major factors in many global problems that we will explore, including poverty, hunger, environmental devastation, the spread of disease, and political unrest.

Three things were particularly important in creating the debt crisis: the change during the last third of the twentieth century in the meaning of money, the amount of money lent by the World Bank and other lending institutions to peripheral countries, and the oil boom of the early 1970s and the pressure for financial institutions to invest that money.

Money, as noted earlier, constitutes the focal point of capitalism. It is through money that we assign value to objects, behaviors, and even people. The fact that one item can, in various quantities, represent virtually any item or service, from a soft drink to an entire forest, is one of the most remarkable features of our lives. But it is not without its problems. The facts that different countries have different currencies and that currencies can rise or fall in value relative to the goods they can purchase have always been barriers to unrestricted foreign trade and global economic integration. Furthermore, there have always been disputes concerning how to measure the value of money itself. Historically, money has been tied to a specific valuable metal, generally gold. Thus, money in any country could always be redeemed for a certain amount of gold, although the amount could vary according to the value of a specific country's currency.

Although the meeting at Bretton Woods would not lead to the establishment of a global currency, the countries did agree to exchange their currency for U.S. dollars at a fixed rate, and the United States guaranteed that it would exchange money for gold stored at Fort Knox at thirty-five dollars per ounce. But in the 1960s, during the Vietnam War and the increase in U.S. government spending on health, education, and welfare programs, the United States was creating dollars far in excess of its gold supply, while at the same time guaranteeing all the rest of the money in the world. As a result, in 1971 the United States declared it would no longer redeem dollars on demand for gold. This totally divorced the American dollar and, effectively, all the other currencies in the world, from anything of value other than the expectation that people would accept dollars for things of value. Money became simply unsecured credit.

Because countries no longer needed to have a certain amount of gold in order to print money, money became more plentiful. How this happened, and the impact it has had on all our lives, requires some elaboration.

We generally assume that governments create money by printing it. And, in fact, when money was linked to gold, there was a limit on how much could be printed. However, with the lifting of these restrictions, most money is now created by banks and other lending institutions through debt. We generally assume, also, that the money that banks lend is money that others have deposited. However, that is not the case; only a fraction of the money that banks lend needs to be in deposits. In effect, whenever a bank lends money, or whenever a product or service is purchased on credit, money has been created. In effect, then, there is virtually no limit on the amount of money that lending institutions can create; furthermore, the interest on the loan payments creates yet more money. Economists call this debt money (Rowbotham 1998:5), or credit money (Guttmann 1994).

Debt provides an important service to the culture of capitalism; it allows people to buy things with money they don't have—thereby fueling economic growth—and it requires people to work in order to pay off their debts. Furthermore, it stimulates greater need for economic growth to maintain interest rates—that is, return on investments. It also means, however, that there is more money that has to be invested and lent, and a considerable amount of that went to peripheral countries. This proved to be a boon not only for individual borrowers but also for peripheral countries seeking to develop their economies. The problems were that the interest on most loans was adjustable (could go up or down depending on economic circumstances) and that debts began to accumulate beyond what countries could repay.

The second factor that led to the debt crisis was the operation of the World Bank. The Bank itself had a problem. European countries, whose economies it was to help rebuild, didn't need the help. With a lack of demand for their services, what could they do? How could the institution survive? The Bank's solution was to lend money to peripheral countries to develop their economies. The plan was to help them industrialize by funding things such as large-scale hydroelectric projects, roads, and industrial parks. Furthermore, the bigger the project, the more the Bank could lend; thus, in the 1950s and 1960s, money suddenly poured into India, Mexico, Brazil, and Indonesia, the Bank's four largest borrowers. From 1950 to 1970, the Bank lent some $953 million. We should not overlook the fact that these loans also benefited wealthy core countries, who largely supplied the construction companies, engineers, equipment, and advisors needed to develop these projects.

But the success of the Bank in lending money created another problem—what economists call net negative transfers; borrowing nations collectively were soon paying more money into the Bank in loan repayments than the Bank was lending out. Put another way, the poor or peripheral nations were paying more money to the rich core nations than they were receiving from them. Aside from the consequences for poor countries, this would ultimately lead to the bank going out of business—its only purpose would be to collect the money it had already lent out. This is not a problem for regular banks because they can always recruit new customers, but the World Bank has a limited number of clients to whom it can lend money. Now what do you do? The Bank's solution was to lend still more.

More than any one person, Robert McNamara, past chief of the Ford Motor Company and secretary of defense during the John F. Kennedy and Lyndon B. Johnson administrations, made the World Bank into what it is today. During McNamara's tenure from 1968 to 1981, the Bank increased lending from $953 million to $12.4 billion and increased staff from 1,574 to 5,201. The result was to leave many peripheral countries with staggering debt burdens. There were other problems as well.

The third source of the debt crisis was the oil boom of the early 1970s. Oil producers were making huge profits ("petrodollars"). The problem was that this money needed to be invested, particularly by the banks into which it went and from which depositors expected interest payments. But banks and other investment agents had problems finding investments. One of their solutions was to lend even more money to peripheral countries.

Thus, by the late 1970s, peripheral countries had borrowed huge sums of money and, with this infusion, were doing generally well. But then financial policies in the wealthy countries precipitated an economic collapse. With their own economies in recession because of the increase in oil prices in the 1970s, core governments reacted by raising interest rates. Countries such as Brazil, Mexico, and Indonesia that had borrowed large sums of money at adjustable, rather than fixed, interest rates suddenly found that they could no longer pay back what they owed. Many couldn't even pay back the interest on the loans. Furthermore, an economic recession in the core nations decreased the demand for whatever commodities peripheral countries had for sale, further undermining their economies.

This all sounds largely like an economic problem that would have little effect on you or me, or on a peasant farmer in Mexico, a craftsperson in Africa, or a small merchant in Indonesia. But, in fact, it has had an enormous impact, and it illustrates how global problems are tied closely to today's merchant adventurers.

There is an old joke that says that when an individual can't pay his or her bank debts, he or she is in trouble, but when a big borrower, such as a corporation or country, can't repay its debts, the bank is in trouble. This, in brief, was the dilemma posed by the global debt crisis for private lending institutions and the World Bank.

The World Bank and the IMF responded to the debt crisis by trying to reschedule the repayment of debts or extending short-term loans to debtor countries to help them meet the financial crises. However, to qualify for a rescheduling of a debt or loan payment, a government had to agree to alter its fiscal policies to improve its balance-of-payments problems—that is, it had to try to take in more money and spend less. But how do you do that? There are various ways, all creating serious problems in one way or another. For example, countries had to promise to manage tax collecting better; sell government property; increase revenues by increasing exports; reduce government spending on social programs, such as welfare, health, and education; promise to refrain from printing more money; and take steps to devalue their currency, thus making their goods cheaper for consumers in other countries but making them more expensive for their own citizens.

Although these measures are rarely popular with their citizens, governments seldom refuse IMF requests to implement them because not only might they not receive a short-term loan, but agencies, such as the World Bank, and private capital controllers, such as banks and foundations, would also then refuse to make funds available. There is pressure on the World Bank and IMF to forgive or reduce debt, and forty-one of the poorest countries in the world have been targeted for debt relief of some sort (see Jubilee 2000). But for most countries, the interest alone on their debts dictates economic, environmental, and social policies that are devastating.

First, debt means that countries must do whatever they can to reduce government expenses and increase revenue or attract foreign investment. Reducing government expenses means cutting essential health, education, and social programs. The results are apparent when you compare high-, middle-, and low-income countries on such measures as income, life expectancy, and schooling (see Table 3.2).

Second, the effects on environmental resources are equally devastating. To increase revenues, countries must export goods and resources. Because most indebted countries, particularly those in sub-Saharan Africa, have little industrial capacity, they must export raw materials, such as minerals and lumber. This requires dismantling whatever environmental regulations may have existed. But because so many countries (including the wealthy countries of the world) are in debt, each must adopt the same export strategy, thus driving down the prices they receive for their exports (see Rowbotham 1998:89).

Third, there is the question, *Where did all the money that was lent to peripheral countries go?* Because "capital flight"—money leaving the periphery—increased dramatically during the period of rising debt, the prevailing view is that loans were siphoned off by the elites in the periphery and invested back in the core. For example, while the IMF and other financial

---

TABLE 3.2   **Comparison Between High-, Middle-, and Low-Income Countries for GDP, GDP per Capita, Debt, and Other Variables, 2007–2008**

	High-Income Countries	Middle-Income Countries	Low-Income Countries
GDP (current US$) (billions)	43,189.9	16,826.9	568.5
GNI per capita, Atlas method (current US$)	39,345	3,260	524
External debt stocks (% of GNI)	—	24.5	35.2
Life expectancy at birth, total (years)	79	69	59
Population, total (millions)	1,068.5	4,650.7	972.8
Population growth (annual %)	0.7	1.1	2.1
School enrollment, primary (percent net)	95.0	88.5	77.6
Surface area (sq. km) (thousands)	35,300.1	79,484.9	19,310.5

Source: Data from *World Bank Data and Statistics*, http://web.worldbank.org/WBSITE/EXTERNAL/DATASTATISTICS/0,,contentMDK:20535285~menuPK:1192694~pagePK:64133150~piPK:64133175~theSitePK:239419,00.html

institutions were lending billions to restore the Russian economy after the fall of communism, $140 billion (U.S.)—almost $2 billion per month—fled Russia during the first six years of market reforms. The World Bank estimates that between 1976 and 1984, capital flight from Latin America was equal to the area's whole external debt (Caufield 1996:132). Capital flight from Mexico alone from 1974 to 1982, invested in everything from condominiums to car dealerships, amounted to at least $35 billion. "The problem," joked one member of the U.S. Federal Reserve Board, "is not that Latin Americans don't have assets. They do. The problem is they are all in Miami" (Caufield 1996:133).

Finally, debt is not only a problem of poor countries. Most countries in the world are heavily in debt, and they must continue to grow to repay it. In 2009, Dubai, part of the United Arab Emirates, which had a per capita income of over $44,000, found itself overextended, threatening to default on its debt (Thomas 2009), and other countries such as Ireland, Greece, and East European countries face a similar situation. Table 3.3 provides an illustration of the external

TABLE 3.3 External Debt, Debt as a Percentage of GDP, and Investor Credit Rating[1] (1–100 with 100 the highest) of Selected Countries, 2007, 2011

Country	Gross External Debt ($)[2]	External Debt as a Percentage of GDP	Investor Credit Rating	External Debt per Capita
	2011	2011	2011	2011
United States	14,959,000,000	99,46	89.4	47,664
Hungry	216,000,000	110.3	53.1	21,706
Italy	2,494,000,000	136.6	66.5	40,724
Australia	1,283,000,000	139.9	89.7	58,322
Spain	2,392,000,000	169,5	64.7	50,868
Greece	564,920,000	178.9	19.6	50,792
Germany	5,674,000,000	183.9	89.8	69,788
Portugal	511,940,000	207.3	46.5	47,483
Austria	847,950,000	241.3	88.2	103,160
Finland	478,840,000	244.8	92.5	90,984
Norway	653,290,000	246,9	94.8	138,783
France	5,632,000,000	254.4	85.2	85,824
Sweden	995,000,000	262.3	92.9	109,318
Hong Kong	939,830,000	265.7	85.6	131,380
Denmark	591,400,000	283.2	89.1	106,680
Belgium	1,457,000,000	353.7	79.4	139,613
Netherlands	2,590,000,000	367	90.8	154,820
Switzerland	1,332,000,000	391.3	94.1	174,022
United Kingdom	10,157,000,000	451.4	85.8	161,110
Ireland	2,226,000,000	1,239	51.9	478,087

Source: See Paul Toscano, "Countries Overloaded with Debt," *CNBC*, http://www.cnbc.com/id/33506526; Institutional Investor, *Global Rankings*, http://www.institutionalinvestor.com/Research/3633/Global-Rankings.html

[1] Investor Credit Rating may be interpreted as the extent of investor confidence in the growth of the economy. More information is available at http://rru.worldbank.org/businessplanet/.

[2] Gross external debt is the combined total of liabilities, plus interest, that corporations, private citizens, and the government owe to entities outside their borders.

debt of selected countries; this is money owed to entities outside the country. Table 3.3 also provides information on investor confidence in each country (in terms of investor ratings, which work much like the credit ratings of individuals, the higher the number, the more likely you will realize profit on your investment). As a merchant adventurer, this gives you an idea of whether or not you'd like to do business in a country.

The debt problems of both poor and wealthy countries once again remind us that, as a merchant adventurer, you must expect periodic financial crisis, often related to debt. It is debt, for example, that played a major role in the financial crisis of 2007–2008, as we'll see next.

THE "SECOND GREAT CONTRACTION"

In the summer of 2007, the world began to enter what some have called the "second great contraction" (Reinhart and Rogoff 2009), the first being the global economic depression of the 1930s. As we have seen, being a merchant adventurer has its risks and opportunities. But there are also risks of a financial collapse that can not only wipe out great financial gains but also throw millions out of work and place national and local governments on the brink of collapse. The common explanation for this latest global financial collapse is that it resulted from the bursting of a housing bubble in the United States. The story is that low interest rates in the United States along with high cash inflows from overseas, particularly China, sent Americans on a house-buying spree that sent home prices soaring at an unprecedented rate. The bubble was further fueled by the "subprime mortgages," loans to people with few financial resources who soon defaulted on their loans. When people began to default, and banks stopped lending, the housing market collapsed, resulting in the crash of home values and the wiping out of trillions of dollars of wealth. Most explanations for the crash focused on human greed, homebuyers purchasing more than they could afford, and banks, seeking greater and greater incomes, lending far more than they should have. However, as we will see, it was a little more complex than that.

Regardless, the housing crash brought major banks to near collapse and resulted in a near-meltdown of the entire economic system. The consequences were severe. Since 2007, according to the IMF, if we include losses to the financial sector, to corporations, to homeowners, and to unincorporated businesses, the total global equity loss will total some US$40 trillion, or about two-thirds of the world's GDP. In human terms, the International Labour Organization estimates that worldwide unemployment could rise by at least 30 million people, and possibly as much as 50 million people, while more than 200 million people, mostly in developing economies, will fall into poverty (see Blankenburg and Palma 2009).

To understand the story of the second great contraction we need to begin with a gigantic oil spill—the Exxon-Valdez disaster of March 24, 1989, when the oil tanker owned by Exxon Oil Company ran aground in Prince William Sound, Alaska, and spilled 10.8 million U.S. gallons into the sea. The merchant adventurers of our story were finance people who worked at J. P. Morgan, one of the largest investment banks in the United States. As anthropologist and financial journalist Gillian Tett (2009) tells it, Exxon approached its bank, J. P. Morgan, for a 5 billion dollar loan in order to cover possible penalties to the company because of the oil spill. The bank had no problem with the loan itself: Exxon was one of its best customers and one of the most profitable companies in the world. But it was concerned about the reserve requirement, a rule imposed by international regulatory agencies, that banks keep in reserve a portion of what is owed to protect them against default. The same reserve requirement applies to bank deposits; for example, if you deposit $1,000 in the bank, the bank may lend out about $900 of that to others, but it must keep $100 out of every $1,000 in order to meet depositors' demands for withdrawals. It must keep only 10 percent, because no one expects everyone to want to withdraw their money (or fail to pay their loans) all at once. But banks have problems with reserve requirements, because money that has to be held in reserve is money that is not working, that is not bringing in interest or fees. For banks to pay interest, they must invest deposits (or sell them). Thus a problem that banks have is, *How can they put the money they hold in reserve to work?*

At J. P. Morgan, a group in the derivatives department headed by Peter Hancock thought they had a perfect solution. They approached the European Bank for Reconstruction and Finance (EBRF), which had lots of money at their disposal, and asked whether, for a fee, they would insure the Exxon loan. That is, in the unlikely event that Exxon defaulted on its obligation, whether EBRF would make good on the loan. Once EBRF agreed to do this, the derivatives team at J. P. Morgan went to bank regulators and asked the regulators to reduce the reserve requirement on the Exxon loan, since, they argued, it was now insured, and even if Exxon failed to pay, they would then collect from EBRF. The regulators agreed, and J. P. Morgan was able to off-load the credit risk from the Exxon loan. They called this new financial instrument a "credit default swap." This may seem like a fairly esoteric banking deal, but it set the stage for the economic disaster to follow.

The team at J. P. Morgan reasoned that they could use the same financial strategy on other loans that it held as it had on the Exxon loan. J. P. Morgan had outstanding about 10 billion dollars of loans to some 307 major corporations. What if they took those loans and shifted them to a dummy corporation (thus removing them from the J. P. Morgan books), divided those assets in the form of the interest on the loans of the new corporation into smaller packages, and then sold them to investors (see Figure 3.2). They called these securities Broad Index Securities Trust Offerings, or BISTROs. These securities were a form of financial derivative, a financial instrument whose worth was linked to some other asset. These are the same sorts of financial instruments or contracts that Dutch investors were buying when they invested in tulips or that commodity traders bet on when they invest in the future value of corn, hog backs, or soy. Furthermore, what if they could find a large insurance company to guarantee those loans in the same way as the EBRF had guaranteed the Exxon loan? If they could do that, they reasoned, the bank regulators would let them greatly reduce the reserve requirements on the 10 billion dollars of loans from the 307 corporations, which will reduce the risk exposure of the bank, thus freeing up millions of additional dollars for investment. They approached Joseph Caffano, the head of a

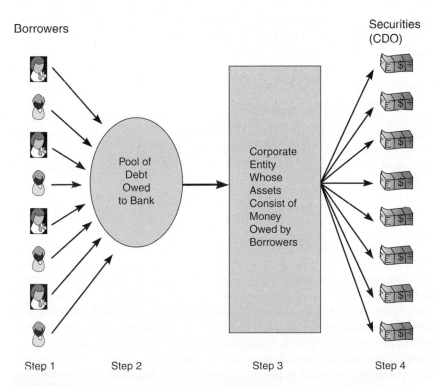

FIGURE 3.2 The Process of Creating Collateral Debt Obligation (CDOs)

small department at the giant insurance company AIG, and, for a modest fee, Caffano committed AIG to insure the securities issued on the corporate loans. And, finally, regulators agreed to lower the bank's reserve requirement.

The team at J. P. Morgan celebrated, not because they thought they had put one over on the regulators, but because they had come up with a financial innovation that could free up billions, if not trillions, of dollars for investment and, consequently, help to speed economic growth. Furthermore they had effectively dealt with the risk of loan default by insuring against it and, at the same time, distributing risk among a larger group, thus diluting the possible loss of any one person or financial entity. They had, they thought, contributed to a better financial world. As one of the members of the J. P. Morgan derivatives team put it, "Five years hence, commentators will look back to the birth of the credit derivative market as a watershed development" (Tett 2009:56).

When other banks heard about the financial innovations of the derivatives team at J. P. Morgan, they enthusiastically followed suit, packaging loans or debt that they held into securities to sell to investors. These securities were also insured by AIG and others and seemed to have so little risk that investment rating services gave them double and triple A ratings, the same given to government-issued securities.

Then, Bayerische Landesbank, a large German bank, approached the derivatives people at J. P. Morgan and asked them to package some $14 billion U.S. home mortgages into securities to sell; however, that posed a problem. Unlike corporate loans, which had a long history that enabled banks to estimate the probability of default, there was no corresponding information for housing mortgages. Thus, it was difficult to assess how risky these securities would be. J. P. Morgan went ahead with the German bank, but only after building in additional safeguards against default, and, after doing one more BISTRO deal, discontinued that line of development.

Other banks, however, partially to keep up with their competition, bundled trillions of dollars of home mortgages and other forms of debt (credit card loans, auto loans, commercial loans, etc.) into collateral debt obligations (CDOs) and sold them to eager investors from pension funds, banks, insurance companies, and anyone else who hoped to make an almost certain profit buying triple A or double A securities. One turning point may have come when large banks entered into agreements with home mortgage companies to buy any mortgage they sold to homebuyers in order to meet the demand from investors for more of these securities. Mortgage companies could then make millions of dollars in fees for selling a mortgage to a homebuyer, with little concern about the homebuyer's ability to pay, since they were then selling the loan, sometimes the same day, to larger banks. These companies were so anxious to give mortgages that they offered them with no down payment, even, in some cases, offering mortgage buyers a free car or a household of furniture. In some circles, these were called "liar loans," because there was no background check on borrowers' income or resources, "neutron loans," because they killed the people but left the houses standing, or, finally, "ninja loans," no income and no assets. If the homebuyer expressed concern about repaying the mortgage, they were offered mortgages with low initial payments and told that if they had a problem once payments increased, they could, with home prices rapidly rising, sell the home at a profit or refinance the loan.

Of course, it didn't work out. The simplest way of looking at the collapse is that trillions of dollars were bet on the premise that the value of an asset—houses in this case—would continue to increase, when, in fact, the values collapsed. As buyers defaulted on their loans, the value of the securities based on those loans either greatly declined or were impossible to sell because no one knew how much they were worth. Furthermore, derivatives based on commercial loans, credit card debt, and automobile loans were threatened by defaults. With banks losing money, holding assets of unknown worth and not knowing the financial state of other institutions and borrowers, and insurance companies unable to compensate investors for their losses, banks stopped lending, and the whole financial system threatened to freeze. Remember that finance is based on moving money, for a price, from where it is to where it is needed, and now, in the fall of 2007, it stopped moving. The insurance companies and banks that had guaranteed the securities were forced to pay out billions of dollars they didn't have and were on the verge of collapse until the U.S. government came to the rescue with a trillion-dollar bailout. But the resulting banking crisis stopped the flow of money and credit and forced the massive selling of assets (stocks, real estate, etc.) by people who needed to meet debt obligations. This further decreased asset value, affecting millions of businesses and throwing millions of people worldwide out of work.

The second great contraction followed the path of many banking crises (see Reinhart and Rogoff 2009). An inflow of money resulting from foreign investment and low interest rates set off a flurry of spending and investment, driving up prices until the process became unsustainable and

One of the major consequences of an economic crisis is the loss of jobs. In the United States alone, the second great contraction resulted in at least 15 million job losses. (Sherwin McGehee/Getty Images.)

resulted in financial collapse. We had seen the same thing happen with Dutch tulips and British railway stock, where people bet, wrongly, that an asset would continually increase in value. But it would be a mistake to attribute these financial crises to greed. Instead, to understand it, we must examine the internal logic of our financial system, and, again, the imperative for perpetual economic growth.

As we mentioned earlier, once a segment of the economy depends on making money with money, perpetual growth must ensue. That is, once money is lent or invested, the money must, so to speak, work to produce more money to account for both the original amount lent or invested (the principal), plus the interest, dividend, or profit. The amount of growth required depends, obviously, on the interest, dividend, or profit required. If there is insufficient growth to generate the additional money, loans go unpaid, and/or dividends or profits unrealized. Thus, going back to the present crisis, as long as house prices continued to grow, the system worked well; but once they ceased growing and in fact declined, the entire economic system was threatened.

A simple example should suffice. Take a household that is earning $150,000 a year. They purchase a house for $600,000 at 7 percent interest over ten years; the monthly payment is $6,965, but the total interest paid over the course of the loan is $235,981. The $600,000 (that is the value of the house) has been created by the bank by extending the loan, and that remains in the form of a fixed asset (the house). The remaining $235,981, that is the interest payment, represents new money that does not yet exist. The household has to produce that, and to do so, it must produce, on average, $23,598 a year, or 15.7 percent a year of their total initial income in order to pay off the debt.

There are, of course, many other variables that need to be considered to calculate the actual necessary growth rate (rates of inflation, the cost of rolling over portions of the debt, the extent to which the money invested produces, or doesn't produce, new money, and so on). But it does illustrate why, in an economy devoted to making money with money, perpetual growth in the form of increased economic activity is necessary.

We have already seen how debt in the case of developing or emerging countries threatens their economic survival. The money that was borrowed, in most cases, did not, for various reasons (declining commodity prices, unfair trade practices, rising energy costs, corruption, etc.), generate the rate of economic growth necessary to produce the money needed to repay the

TABLE 3.4 U.S. Total Debt by Sector (January 1, 2012)[1]

Debt Type	Debt Amount (Trillion)	Debt Per Person
Federal Government Sector	$15.22	$ 49,097
State and Local Government Sector	$ 3.01	$ 9,677
Household Sector	$13.22	$ 42,445
Business Sector	$11.63	$ 37,516
Financial Sector	$ 13.6	$ 43,871
Other	$ 2.24	$ 7,226
Sum of all government and private sector debt	**$ 58.9**	**$190,000**

[1] Data from Grandfather Economic Report, http://grandfather-economic-report.com/debt-summary-table.htm.

principal and interest on the loan. Thus, countries defaulted in their loans, were forced to accept structural adjustment programs that cut services, or were forced to sell assets, often at bargain-basement prices.

The question of how much growth is necessary given a specific level of debt is important because of the significant increase in debt obligations over the past few decades, particularly in the United States. Table 3.4 shows the current debt obligations of different segments of the U.S. economy as of January 2009 (Hodges 2009).

Much of this debt is newly created; for example, 80 percent of it was created since 1990; in 1981 household debt was 48 percent of GDP, while in 2007, it was 100 percent. Private sector debt was 123 percent of GDP in 1981 and 290 percent by late 2008. The financial sector has been in a leveraging frenzy: Its debt rose from 22 percent of GDP in 1981 to 117 percent in late 2008 (see Crotty 2009:575).

The question that never gets addressed is, *What is the rate of economic growth required to honor all of these debt obligations? That is, how much growth is necessary before the rates of default impact financial institutions to the extent that credit dries up, businesses fail, unemployment rises, more defaults ensue, and so on?* The numbers chosen for the household debt example mentioned earlier were not arbitrary. The $600,000 represents the approximately $60 trillion debt held by all sectors of the U.S. economy in 2010, and the $150,000 income represents the approximately $15 trillion U.S. GDP, that is, the total value of goods and services produced each year. Thus, if the average interest on all of these debts, which range from 1 percent on U.S. Treasury notes to 20 percent or more on credit card debts, is, say, 7 percent and the average term of the debt or investment is ten years, the economy must produce well over $20 trillion in new money. That is, the economy must grow at a rate of 15 percent a year, a rate virtually impossible to achieve.

There is another factor, which receives little attention, that contributes to our understanding of economic growth and financial crises—that is, the wealthier a country becomes, the more difficult it is to maintain economic growth. That is why emerging economies, such as China, India, and Brazil, can grow from 6 percent to 10 percent a year, while wealthy economies struggle to attain the necessary 3 percent to 5 percent (see Figure 3.3).

The implication is that our modern merchant adventurers must continue to come up with new and innovative ways to make more and more money. That is why the derivatives team at J. P. Morgan was told, "You will have to make at least half your revenues each year from a product which did not exist before" (Tett 2009:7–8).

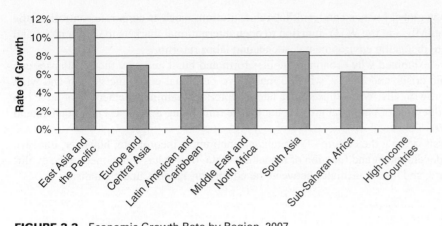

FIGURE 3.3 Economic Growth Rate by Region, 2007

Thus, the current economic crisis has more to do with the internal logic of our economic system—particularly the need for perpetual growth—than it does with any intrinsic human characteristic, such as greed. In general, the economy works, and sometimes doesn't work, because of people operating according to specific cultural prescriptions and not because of any innate characteristic.

CONCLUSION

We began this chapter with the goal of trying to understand five historical developments that have had a profound influence on today's world and in the development of the culture of capitalism—the increase in the division of world wealth, changes in the organization of capital, the increase in the level of economic globalization, the reasons for periodic financial crises, and why our economies have to perpetually grow. We found that the division of wealth has grown enormously, between both countries and areas of the world. In 2000 more than 1.2 billion people lived in absolute poverty, earning the equivalent of less than one dollar per day. The three top ultrarich people, including Microsoft's Bill Gates, own more than the gross national product of the forty-eight poorest nations combined. Furthermore, the gap is increasing. According to the UN World Development Report of 1997, of the 173 countries in the study, seventy to eighty have lower per capita incomes than they did have ten or thirty years ago. People in Africa consume 20 percent less than they did twenty-five years ago. The UN report pointed out that the 20 percent of the world's population living in the wealthiest countries consume 86 percent of the world's goods and services. The poorest 20 percent consume only 1.3 percent.

The organization of capital has changed dramatically. We began our journey with capital largely in the hands of individual merchants, family groups, or limited partnerships and ended with the era of capital controllers, such as transnational corporations, multilateral institutions, and investment firms. In 1400, it might take a global merchant a year's journey from one area of the world to another to complete an investment cycle of buying and selling goods; today a capital controller can transfer billions from one area of the world to another without ever leaving his or her computer.

We have seen global economic integration increase to the extent that global trade is easier today than trade between adjacent towns was in 1400, as trade treaties dissolve regional and country boundaries, freeing capital to migrate where it is most likely to accumulate. Furthermore, we have seen how global financial and multilateral institutions, such as corporate controllers, the World Bank, the IMF, and the WTO, function to open international markets to corporations and force countries to dismantle environmental, social, and labor reforms.

Fourth, we examined why economic bubbles form and burst and why these collapses can lead to economic crisis, and finally, why we must have perpetual economic growth and what happens when growth fails. We will need, in a later chapter, to examine whether or not there is a way out of this dilemma of perpetual growth, but for the time being it is important to understand its consequences.

Our analysis of how the culture of capitalism functions is incomplete, however, until we understand the development and function of the nation-state, how it has functioned in the evolution of the culture, and how it mediates between the consumer, laborer, and capitalist.

The Nation-State in the Culture of Capitalism

We have about 50% of the world's wealth but only 6.3% of its population. This disparity is particularly great as between ourselves and the peoples of Asia. In this situation, we cannot fail to be the object of envy and resentment. Our real task in the coming period is to devise a pattern of relationships which will permit us to maintain this position of disparity without positive detriment to our national security. To do so, we will have to dispense with all sentimentality and day-dreaming; and our attention will have to be concentrated everywhere on our immediate national objectives. We need not deceive ourselves that we can afford today the luxury of altruism and world-benefaction.

—GEORGE F. KENNAN, *Director of Policy Planning,*

U.S. State Department, 1948

Due to the unqualified and unstoppable spread of free trade rules, and above all the free movement of capital and finances, the "economy" is progressively exempt from political control; ... Whatever has been left of politics is expected to be dealt with, as in the good old days, by the state—but whatever is concerned with the economic life the state is not allowed to touch; any attempt in this direction would be met with prompt and furious punitive action from the world markets.

—ZYGMUNT BAUMAN, *Globalization: The Human Consequences*

Imagine an alien from another planet who lands on Earth after a nuclear holocaust has destroyed all life but has left undamaged terrestrial libraries and archives. After consulting the archives, suggested Eric Hobsbawm (1990), our observer would undoubtedly conclude that the last two centuries of human history are incomprehensible without an understanding of the term *nation* and the phenomenon of *nationalism*.

The nation-state, along with the consumer, laborer, and capitalist, is, we suggest, an essential element of the culture of capitalism. It is the nation-state, as Eric Wolf (1982:100) suggested, that guarantees the ownership of private property and the means of production and provides support for disciplining the workforce. The state also has to provide and maintain the economic infrastructure—transportation, communication, judicial systems, education, and so on—required by capitalist production. The nation-state must regulate conflicts between competing capitalists at home and abroad, by diplomacy if possible, by war if necessary. The state plays an essential role in creating conditions that inhibit or promote consumption; controls legislation that may force people off the land to seek wage labor; legislates to regulate or deregulate corporations; creates the base money supply by borrowing from the central bank; initiates economic, political, and social policies to attract capital; and controls the legitimate use of force. Without the nation-state to regulate commerce and trade within its own borders, there could be no effective global economic integration. *But how did the nation-state come to exist, and how does it succeed in binding together often disparate and conflicting groups?*

Virtually all people in the world consider themselves members of a nation-state. The notion of a person without a nation, said Ernest Gellner (1983:6), strains the imagination; a person must have a nationality as he or she must have a nose and two ears. We are Americans, Mexicans, Bolivians, Italians, Indonesians, Kenyans, or members of any of more than 200 states that currently exist. We generally consider our country, whichever it is, as imbued with tradition, a history that glorifies its founding and makes heroes of those thought to have been instrumental in its creation. Symbols of the nation—flags, buildings, monuments—take on the aura of sacred relics.

By the middle of the twentieth century, the attainment of nationhood had become a sign of progress and modernity. To be less than a nation—a tribe, an ethnic group, or a regional bloc—was a sign of backwardness. Yet fewer than one-third of the more than 200 states in the world are more than thirty years old; only a few go back to the nineteenth century, and virtually none go back in their present form beyond that. Before that time, people identified themselves as members of kinship groups, villages, cities, or, perhaps, regions, but almost never as members of nations. For the most part, the agents of the state were resented, feared, or hated because of their demands for tribute, taxes, or army conscripts.

States existed, of course, and have existed for 5,000 to 7,000 years. But the idea of the nation-state, of a people sharing some bounded territory, united by a common culture or tradition, common language, or common race, is a product of nineteenth-century Europe. Most historians see the French Revolution of 1789 as marking the beginning of the era of the nation-state. Yet, in spite of the historical newness of the idea, for many people nationality forms a critical part of their personal identity. Some of the questions we need to explore are as follows: *How did the nation-state come to have such importance in the world? Why did it develop as it did, and how do people come to identify themselves as members of such vague abstractions? Finally, why does the nation-state kill as often as it does?*

The question of killing is important, because today most killing and violence is either sanctioned by or carried out by the state. This should not surprise us: Most definitions of the state, following Max Weber's (1947:124–135), revolve around its claim to a monopoly on the instruments of death and violence. "Stateness," as Elman Service (1975) put it, can be identified simply by locating "the power of force in addition to the power of authority." Killing by other than the state, as Morton Fried (1967) noted, will draw the punitive action of organized state force.

The use of force, however, is not the only characteristic anthropologists emphasize in identifying the state; social stratification, the division of societies into groups with differing access to wealth and other resources, is also paramount. Yet even here the state is seen as serving as an instrument of control to maintain the privileges of the ruling group, and this, too, generally requires a monopoly on the use of force (see Cohen and Service 1978; Lewellen 1992).

Thus, to complete our description of the key features of the culture of capitalism, we need to examine the origin and history of the state and its successor, the nation-state; we also need to understand the role of violence in the maintenance of the state and the role of the state in the maintenance and growth of the economy.

THE ORIGIN AND HISTORY OF THE STATE

The Evolution of the State

States represent a form of social contract in which the public ostensibly has consented to assign to the state a monopoly on force and agreed that only it can constrain and coerce people (Nagengast 1994:116). Philosophers and political thinkers have long been fascinated by the question of why the state developed. Seventeenth-century philosopher Thomas Hobbes assumed the state existed to maintain order, and that without the state, life would be "nasty, brutish, and short." However, anthropologists have long recognized that some societies do very well without anything approaching state organization; in fact, "tribes without rulers," as they were called, represented until 7,000 to 8,000 years ago the only form of political organization in the world. Government in these societies was relatively simple. There might be a chief or village leader, but their powers were limited. In gathering and hunting societies, most decisions were probably made by consensus. Village or clan chiefs may have had more authority than others, but even they led more by example than by force. Power, the ability to control people, was generally diffused among many individuals or groups.

The state as a stratified society presided over by a ruling elite with the power to draw from and demand agricultural surpluses likely developed in the flood plains between the Tigris and Euphrates in what is now Iraq 4,000 to 5,000 years ago. The fortified cities of Uruk and Ur, forming the state of Sumeria, had populations of 40,000. States developed independently in Egypt, the Indus River Valley of India, the Yellow River Valley of China, and, later, Mesoamerica and Peru.

Anthropologists have long been concerned with the idea of the origin of the state (see Lewellen 1992). *Why didn't human aggregates remain organized into small units or into villages or towns of 500 to 2,000 persons? What made the development of densely settled cities necessary? Why, after hundreds of thousands of years, did ruling elites with control of armed force emerge to dominate the human landscape?*

One theory is that as the population increased and food production became more complex, a class of specialists emerged and created a stratified society. Who comprised this class or why they emerged is an open question. Karl Wittfogel (1957), in his "hydraulic theory" of state development, proposed that Neolithic farmers in the area where states developed were dependent on flooding rivers, such as the Tigris, the Nile, and the Yellow rivers, to water their fields and deposit new soil. But this happened only once each year; so to support an expanding population, farmers began to build dikes, canals, and reservoirs to control water flow. As these irrigation systems became more complex, groups of specialists emerged to plan and direct these activities, and this group developed into an administrative elite that ruled over despotic, centralized states.

Others propose that an increase in population, especially where populations cannot easily disperse, requires more formal means of government and control and will lead to greater social stratification and inequality. These theories of state development emphasize the integrative function of the state and suggest that it evolved to maintain order and direct societal growth and development.

However, another framework emerges from the work of Marx and Engels. In this framework, early societies were thought to be communistic, with resources shared equally among members and little or no notion of private property. However, technological development permitted production of a surplus of goods, which could be expropriated and used by some persons to elevate their control or power in society. Asserting control permitted this elite to form an entrepreneurial class. To maintain their wealth and authority, they created structures of force.

Anthropologists' major criticism of this framework is that there is little evidence of this kind of entrepreneurial activity in prehistoric societies; moreover, it is difficult to apply notions such as "communism" and "capitalism" to early societies. However, Morton Fried (1967) proposed that differential access to wealth and resources creates stratification, and once stratification emerges, it creates internal conflict that will lead to either disintegration of the group or to the elite imposing their authority by force.

Yet another view proposes that external conflict is the motivation for state development: Once a group united under a strong central authority develops, it could easily conquer smaller, less centralized groups and take captives, land, or property. Following this line of reasoning, if smaller groups were to protect themselves from predator states, they, too, had to organize, the result being the emergence of competing states with the more powerful ones conquering the weaker ones and enlarging their boundaries. Robert Carneiro (1978) reasoned that war has served to promote consolidation of isolated, politically autonomous villages into chiefdoms of united villages and into states. At first, war pits village against village, resulting in chiefdoms; then it pits chiefdom against chiefdom, resulting in states; and then it pits state against state, creating yet larger political units.

It should be clear that these theories are not mutually exclusive; the emergence of states may be a result of any one or a combination of factors. Thus, other theorists, such as Marvin Harris (1971) and Kent Flannery (1972; 1973), propose that the evolution of the state required the interaction of various factors such as control of birth rates, nature of food resources, and the environment.

Regardless of why the state emerged as a human institution, it is clear that by 1400 the world was very much divided into states and empires ruled by groups of elites who maintained their positions through the use of force. But the states of prehistoric times—the city-states of ancient Greece, the Roman Empire, the Chinese dynasties—were very different from the modern nation-state. It is doubtful that subjects of the Ming Dynasty or Roman Empire identified themselves as members of a state, let alone a nation. It is unlikely that a British or French soldier of the sixteenth or seventeenth century felt he owed allegiance to his "nation"—to his king or queen, perhaps, but not to anything so abstract as a "country." The nation-state is a very recent historical development, one we need to understand to appreciate its role in the culture of capitalism.

The History and Function of the Nation-State

The state as it exists today is obviously very different from the state that evolved 7,000 years ago or the state as it existed in the years 1500 or 1800. We have gone from being states to being nations or nation-states. The differences are important. A state is a political entity with identifiable components. If someone asked citizens of the United States to identify a constituent of the "state," they could point to federal buildings (e.g., the Congressional Office Building, the White House, and federal courthouse) or name federal bureaucracies (e.g., Congress, the Internal Revenue Service, and the Department of Agriculture); they could list the things that the state requires of them—to pay taxes, register for Social Security, obtain citizenship, or vote. However, if someone asked them what constituted the "nation," to what, other than the flag, could they point? Other than being "patriotic," what could they say is required of them by the "nation"? The American nation is a far more abstract concept than the American state; a nation, as Benedict Anderson (1991:5–6) put it, is "an imagined political community." Yet in the past 200 years, states have evolved to nations or nation-states. *But why did a new form of political entity develop, and what function did it perform?*

The modern state, suggested historian Fernand Braudel (1982:515–516), has three tasks: to secure obedience and gain a monopoly on force with legitimate violence; to exert control over economic life to ensure the orderly circulation of goods and to take for itself a share of the national income to pay for its own expenditure, luxury, administration, or wars; and to participate in spiritual or religious life and derive additional strength by using religious values or establishing a state religion. We examine later the use of violence by the state and the use of religious values. Let's first examine the state control of economic life.

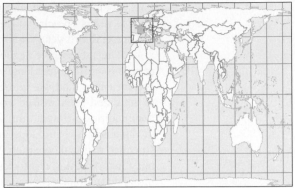

The state has probably always been involved in its subjects' economic life in one way or another. The ancient state existed partly to protect the privileges of the elites by ensuring production of resources, offering protection from other elites, and extracting surplus wealth from a largely peasant population. Traders supplied wealth to the elite in the form of taxes, tributes, and fees required to do business. The state also performed some functions for the trader—it might mint

France

coins and produce paper money, establish standards for weights and measures, protect the movement of merchants and goods, purchase goods, and create and maintain marketplaces where merchants could sell their products. But the ancient states probably did little actively to encourage trade, and in many ways they may have inhibited it. For example, they may have taxed the merchant to an extent that making a profit became difficult. The elite may have limited the goods that merchants could trade or limited the market for goods—for example, by claiming exclusive rights to wear certain kinds of clothes or furs, hunt certain animals, eat certain foods, and inhabit certain sites.

In sixteenth- and seventeenth-century Europe and Japan, states began to take a truly active role in promoting and protecting trade, recognizing that the state's wealth depended on the success of its manufacturers and traders. They began to protect their manufacturers and traders by imposing protective tariffs on goods from other states, using military force to open markets in peripheral areas, and granting trading monopolies to firms within their borders. States created and maintained ports, built roads and canals, and, later, subsidized railroad construction.

The state was also involved in the consumption of goods, either by purchasing goods or, again, using its military or bargaining power to open up foreign markets to its merchants. One of the most lucrative sources of manufacturers' profits was (and still is) the sale to governments of weapons and other goods and services (food, clothing, and transportation) necessary to maintain the military and other government services. Although ostensibly the military existed in core countries to protect the state against foreign invaders, it was far more often used to create and maintain colonies necessary for the success of domestic manufacture and trade and to maintain domestic order. Finally, the state organized, entitled, and directed financial institutions, such as banks, which ensured the ready availability of capital.

The nation-state, said Immanuel Wallerstein (1989:170), became the major building block of the global economy. To be part of the interstate system required that political entities transform themselves into states that followed the rules of the interstate system. This system required for its operation an integrated division of labor, along with guarantees regarding the flow of money, goods, and persons. States were free to impose constraints on these flows but only within a set of rules enforced collectively by member states or, as it usually worked out, a few dominant states.

At the beginning of the nineteenth century, the new capitalist state faced two problems. The first was political. With the downfall of the doctrine of the divine right of kings and the absolute state, political leaders faced a crisis of political legitimacy. *On what basis could they claim control of the state apparatus that had become so critical for the emergence and success of the "national economy"?* A second and related problem was economic: *How could the state promote the economic integration of all those within its borders?* Although the English state could claim control over England, Scotland, and Wales, and the French state over the regions of France (Bretagne, Picardie, Provence, Languedoc, etc.), the situation in the countryside did not reflect that control. At the beginning of the nineteenth century, few residents of the British

Isles would identify themselves as Britons; few residents of the state of France would identity themselves as French—at least 25 percent of them didn't even speak French. Germany and Italy, of course, didn't yet exist.

Thus, the degree of economic integration of regions was weak or nonexistent. Not only did people speak different languages, but they also used different currencies, had different standards and measures, and were downright hostile to state officials. Wages and prices varied from area to area, and standardized vocational training was virtually nonexistent. Furthermore, tastes in commodities differed; things manufactured or produced in one area might not appeal to people in other areas. Thus, local economies existed either side by side with or independent of the so-called national economy. While countries such as England, France, and the Netherlands were busy incorporating territories in South and North America, Asia, Africa, and the Middle East into their national economies, they hadn't yet fully incorporated members of their own states.

There was, however, a single solution to both the political and the economic problem: to turn states into nations—groups of people who shared a common culture, language, and heritage and somehow belonged together (or thought they did), worked together, and shopped together. This was not easy to accomplish because virtually all of the major European states in the eighteenth and nineteenth centuries were hodgepodges of languages, cultures, and religions. When Garibaldi united a group of provinces into what was to become Italy, less than 3 percent of the population spoke Italian as their native language. German became the language of Germany only because Joseph II arbitrarily decided it should be. Thus nations had to be created: Frenchmen, Italians, Germans, and Americans had to be manufactured by convincing them they had something in common, preferably loyalty and devotion to their respective states.

If members of a state would see themselves as sharing a common culture—a common heritage, language, and destiny—state leaders could claim to represent the "people," whoever they might be, and the people could be more easily integrated into the national economy. They would, ideally, accept the same wages, speak the same language, use the same currency, have similar skills and similar economic expectations, and, even better, demand the same goods. The question is, *How do you go about constructing a nation?*

CONSTRUCTING THE NATION-STATE

It has been argued by some, especially ardent nationalists of various persuasions, that nation-states are expressions of preexisting cultural, linguistic, religious, ethnic, or historical features shared by people who make up or would make up a state. For many of the nineteenth-century German writers who were instrumental in creating the idea of the nation-state—Johann Gottfried von Herder, Johann Gottlieb Fichte, and Wilhelm Freiherr von Humboldt—nations were expressions of shared language, tradition, race, and state. Thus, today we see some of the citizens of Quebec claiming that their cultural heritage and language differentiate them from the rest of Canada and entitle them to nationhood, Kurds aspiring to their own state on the basis of cultural unity, Bosnian Serbs demanding their own state on the basis of their ethnic purity, and Sikhs demanding their own state based on their mode of worship.

However, the more generally held view, certainly among scholars, is that nation-states are constructed through invention and social engineering. Traditions, suggested Eric Hobsbawm, must be invented. People must be convinced that they share or must be forced to share certain features, such as language, religion, ethnic group membership, or a common historical heritage, regardless of whether they really do. As Hobsbawm and Ranger (1983:1) put it,

> "Invented tradition" is taken to mean a set of practices, normally governed by overtly or tacitly accepted rules and of a ritual or symbolic nature, which seek to inculcate certain values and norms of behavior by repetition, which automatically implies continuity with the past. In fact, were it possible, they normally attempt to establish continuity with a suitable historic past.

Sir David Wilkie's painting *Chelsea Pensioners Reading the Gazette of the Battle of Waterloo* represents the power of the nation-state to transcend boundaries of age, gender, class, ethnicity, and occupation.
(North Wind/North Wind Picture Archives.)

Creating the Other

An understanding of how the nation-state and, by extension, people's national identities are constructed is critical to understanding nationalism and ethnicity. Let's begin by examining some of the ways Great Britain and France, pioneers in nation building, went about the task. Linda Colley (1992) illustrated how this was done in Great Britain. Colley's book includes a painting by Sir David Wilkie, *Chelsea Pensioners Reading the Gazette of the Battle of Waterloo,* that caused a sensation when it was exhibited at the Royal Academy in 1822.

The painting depicts a crowd celebrating the news of the British victory over Napoleon at Waterloo. The distinguishing feature of the painting is its clear identification of people from all over Britain. There are Welsh, Scottish, and Irish soldiers; women and children; rich and poor; and even a black military bandman. It is, Colley said, a celebration of patriotism that transcends boundaries of age, gender, class, ethnicity, and occupation. It is war, the painting suggests, that forged a nation by uniting this diverse group against a common enemy. Even the signs on the taverns celebrate past wars and victories. According to Colley, Wilkie recognized the importance of war in nation building and that uniting diverse people and groups against outsiders is one of the most effective ways to create bonds among them (1992:366–367).

Outsiders, however, can be used in more symbolic ways to build national unity. For example, Colley suggested that the making of the British nation from its culturally and linguistically diverse populations would have been impossible without a shared religion, and that British Protestantism allowed the English, Scots, and Welsh to overcome their cultural divergence to identify themselves as a nation. However, that would not have been so effective had their religion not also distinguished them from their arch rival, Catholic France.

Furthermore, the founding of a colonial empire created additional Others from whom members of the British nation could distinguish themselves. Britons thought the establishment of an empire proved Britain's providential destiny, that God had chosen them to rule over other peoples and to spread the Gospel. Contact with manifestly alien peoples fed Britons' belief about their superiority. They could favorably compare their treatment of women, wealth, and power. The building of a global empire corroborated not only Britain's blessings, but what Scottish socialist Keir Hardie called the indomitable pluck and energy of the British people (Colley 1992:369).

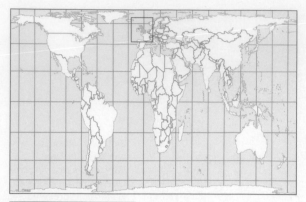

Great Britain

Thus, one of the most effective ways to construct a nation is to create some Other against whom members of the nation-state can distinguish themselves. That Other needn't be a country; it may be a category of persons constructed out of largely arbitrary criteria, such as racial characteristics or religion. Thus, a group may insist that only people of a particular skin color or religion or who speak a particular language can be citizens of their nation. War, religion, and the creation of colonies full of subjugated peoples provided for Britons a sense of their collective identity as a people, allowing them to overcome their own significant differences in language, culture, and economic status. Of course, people must find it in their own self-interest as well to proclaim their identity as members of a nation-state. As Colley pointed out, men and women became British patriots to obtain jobs in the state or to advertise their standing in the community. Some believed that British imperialism would benefit them economically or that a French victory would harm them. For some, being an active patriot served to provide them full citizenship and a voice in the running of the state.

Yet the creation of hated or feared Others through such means as war, religion, and empire building is probably not in itself sufficient to build loyalty and devotion to a nation. If it were, the nation-state would likely have emerged well before it did. Constructing a nation-state also requires a national, bureaucratic infrastructure that serves in various ways to unite people.

Language, Bureaucracy, and Education

Eugen Weber, in his book *Peasants into Frenchmen* (1976), provides a classic account of nation building. He documents how peoples in France were administratively molded into a nation by bringing the French language to the countryside, by increasing the ease of travel, by increasing access to national media, by providing military training, and, most importantly, by creating a national educational system. Weber (1976:486) compares the transformation of peasants into citizens of a French nation-state to the process of colonization and acculturation: Unassimilated masses had to be integrated into a dominant culture. The process, he suggests, was akin to colonization, except it took place within the borders of the country rather than overseas. *What kind of transformation of national identity did take place in France in the nineteenth century?*

At the beginning of the nineteenth century, even after the French Revolution, a significant portion of rural France still lived in worlds of their own. Few if any would have called themselves "French." The peasants of France were for the most part subsistence farmers, producing not for market or cash but for themselves and their families. People spent their lives in their villages. Scholars estimate that one-fourth of the residents of France did not speak French, including half the children who would reach adulthood in the last quarter of the nineteenth century. Arnold van Gennep would write as late as 1911 that "for peasants and workers, the mother tongue is patois, the foreign speech is French" (Weber 1976:73).

State officials saw linguistic diversity as a threat not to administrative unity but to ideological unity, a shared notion of the interests of the republic, a oneness. Linguistic and cultural diversity came to be seen as imperfection, something to be remedied (Weber 1976:9). As a result, in the 1880s, at the insistence of the government, the French language began to infiltrate the countryside, a process more or less completed by 1914, although even in 1906 English travelers in France had problems communicating in French.

With the homogenization of language came the homogenization of culture. Local customs began to be replaced; dress and food preferences became standardized. Although many aspects of local culture began to disappear, some were adopted as national symbols. The beret, worn only by Basques in 1920, became by 1930 a symbol of France; by 1932, some 23 million were manufactured, one for every French citizen.

Another sign of state integration and the decline of local traditions and values is the decay of popular feasts and rituals that celebrated the unity of local groups and their replacement by private ceremonies and rituals along with a few national holidays. Communal celebrations, such as Christmas, New Year, and Twelfth Night, turned into family affairs. Where once they were public rituals, baptisms, first communions, and marriages became private ceremonies. Renewal ceremonies that glorified time (the season), work (harvest), or the community (through its patron saint) disappeared as the redistribution of goods, once done through ritual at these ceremonies, was now managed more efficiently (and more stringently) by the state (Weber 1976:398). The replacement of local holidays and festivals with national holidays also allowed these occasions to be turned into periods of massive consumption and gift giving, similar to Valentine's Day, Easter, Mother's Day, and Christmas in the United States (Schmidt 1995).

National unity in France was also evidenced by the growth of patriotism. In the early nineteenth century, draft evasion in the provinces was high; for most, the military was a foreign institution. There was great tax resistance. Even toward the end of the nineteenth century, some French citizens had never heard of Napoleon; national authority was embodied in the tax collector and the recruiting sergeant. This is not to say, as Weber (1976:114) pointed out, that the French were unpatriotic, only that they had no uniform conception of patriotism. As he said, "patriotic feelings on the national level, far from instinctive, had to be learned."

Thus, in the nineteenth century, people living within the boundaries of the French state gradually learned to be French. *But how did this happen? How were peasants turned into French citizens?* As with Great Britain, war and the struggle against outsiders certainly played a role in the conversion. The war against Prussia in 1870–1871 was a significant unifying event for most residents of France. The expansion of a colonial empire helped create Others to whom the French could feel superior. But more significant was the fact that, as Weber points out, there were far-reaching changes in the infrastructure and bureaucracy of France.

New roads were built, connecting people to others to whom they had never been connected; the growth of the railroads further increased mobility and contact between people of different regions. The railroads helped to homogenize tastes. Although we now associate the French with wine drinking, wine was not common in the countryside in the first half of the nineteenth century; it became more available only with the railroads. The roads and railroads brought peasants into a national market; it allowed them to grow and sell crops they couldn't sell before and to stop growing those they could purchase more cheaply, bringing ruin to some local enterprises no longer protected by isolation. Fashions from the cities began to penetrate the countryside. And the roads and railroads set people on the move. In the early part of the nineteenth century, if people migrated to find work, they almost always returned. This was no longer true by the end of the century.

As more people spoke French and became literate, they gained access to newspapers and journals, which in turn increased knowledge of national affairs and interests, demonstrating that events at the national level affected their lives. Military service increased identification with the state. Prior to the 1890s there was little sense of national identity in being a soldier; soldiers were either feared or thought to bring bad habits to their communities. Local men who joined the army were forced to conform when they returned to their villages lest their newly learned habits affect others. Many returned not even having learned to speak French. But the war with Prussia seemed to mark the beginning of a national identity in the rank and file of the military and among the peasants. The army began to become a school for the fatherland. Furthermore, for most recruits, life in the army was better than life at home; the army ate better, dressed better, and was healthier than the average French citizen. Toward the end of the century, more and more soldiers did not return to their villages after finishing their military obligations.

As important as all these agents of nation building were in France and other countries, perhaps none was as important as the school. Weber credited the school with being the ultimate source of acculturation that made the French people French.

At the beginning of the century, educational conditions were abysmal in France, as in most countries; some teachers couldn't read, and some classes were conducted by nuns who could read only prayers. In 1864, a French school inspector commented that none of the children understood what they read, and when they could read, they could not give an account of it. Furthermore, schooling in the countryside had little practical benefit; it could not improve the lives of students economically or socially. Although improving education in the countryside had been a goal of the state since the 1830s, great changes occurred only in the 1880s, when the state began to subsidize education and every hamlet with twenty children or more was required to have a school.

It was clear to state officials that education was necessary as a "guarantee of order and social stability" (Weber 1976:331). "To instruct the people," one said, "is to condition them to understand and appreciate the beneficence of the government" (Weber 1976:331). Clearly there was an explicit link in the minds of state officials between education, nation building, national identity, and economic expansion. Following is a passage from a first-year civics textbook that helped students in "appreciating their condition":

> Society (summary): (1) French society is ruled by just laws, because it is a democratic society. (2) All the French are equal in their rights: but there are inequalities between us that stem from nature or from wealth. (3) These inequalities cannot disappear. (4) Man works to become rich; if he lacked this hope, work would cease and France would decline. It is therefore necessary that each of us should be able to keep the money he has earned. (Weber 1976:331)

Schooling was to be the great agent of nationalism. As one teacher said in 1861, it would teach national and patriotic sentiments, explain the benefits of the state and why taxes and military service were necessary, and illustrate for students their true interest in the fatherland. In 1881, another wrote that future instructors must be taught that "their first duty is to make [their charges] love and understand the fatherland." By the 1890s, officials considered the school "an

Third graders in Palo Alto, California, pledge their allegiance to their nation-state (Russell Curtis/Science Source.)

instrument of unity," an "answer to dangerous centrifugal tendencies," and the "keystone of national defense" (Weber 1976:332–333).

The best instrument of indoctrination, said school officials, was history, which, when properly taught, "is the only means of maintaining patriotism in the generation we are bringing up." In 1897 candidates for the *baccalauréat moderne* were asked to define the purpose of history in education; 80 percent replied essentially that it was to exalt patriotism (Weber 1976:333).

Before 1870, few schools had maps of France; by 1881, few classrooms, no matter how small, were without one. By the end of the century, the educational system seemed to be accomplishing its task, as evidenced by boys in rural France who began to enact the exploits of historical heroes.

Ernest Gellner (1983:34) drew the connection between nation building, education, and economic integration even more tightly. According to Gellner, work in industrial society no longer means working with things; rather it involves working with meanings, exchanging communications with other people, or manipulating the controls of machines, controls that need to be understood. It is easy to understand the workings of a shovel or a plow; it is another thing to understand the complex process through which a button or control activates a machine. As a consequence, a modern capitalistic economy requires a mobile division of labor and precise communication between strangers. It requires universal literacy; a high level of numerical, technical, and general sophistication; mobility where members must be prepared to shift from area to area and from task to task; and an ability to communicate with people they don't know in a context-dependent form of communication, in a common, standardized language. To attain the standard of literacy and technical competence needed to be employable, people must be trained, not by members of their own local group but by specialists. This training could be provided only by something like a "national" education system. Gellner (1983:34) went so far as to suggest that education became the ultimate instrument of state power, that the professor and the classroom came to replace the executioner and the guillotine as the enforcer of national sovereignty, and that a monopoly on legitimate education became more important than the monopoly on legitimate violence to build a common national identity and to provide the training necessary for the full integration of national economies.

Violence and Genocide

While creating a feared or hated Other, a national bureaucracy, and an educational system are essential in constructing the nation-state, violence remains one of the main tools of nation building. In fact, there is a view, shared in anthropology by Pierre van den Berghe (1992), Leo Kuper (1990), Carole Nagengast (1994), and others, that the modern nation-state is essentially an agent of genocide and ethnocide (the suppression and destruction of minority cultures). Given the glorification of the nation-state as a vehicle of modernization, unity, and economic development, this seems a harsh accusation. Yet there exists ample evidence that one of the ways states have sought to create nations is to eliminate or terrorize into submission those within its borders who refuse to assimilate or who demand recognition of their status as a distinct ethnic or national group. In the United States, the attempt first to kill all indigenous peoples, then forcibly to assimilate those who remained, followed by a policy of "benign neglect," is but one example of state hostility to cultural variation, as we shall see. The claim that states are agents of death and oppression against minority or even majority groups (e.g., South Africa, Sudan, and Pakistan) is often provided in daily news reports.

Between 1975 and 1979, in one of the worst cases of state killing in the twentieth century, the government of Cambodia, the Khmer Rouge, systematically killed as many as 2 million of its 7 million citizens. These killings were carried out in the name of a program to create a society without cities, money, families, markets, or commodity-money relations. Millions were disemboweled, had nails driven into the backs of their heads, or were beaten to death with hoes.

This program involved destroying what the leaders saw as the enemy classes—imperialists (e.g., ethnic Vietnamese, ethnic Chinese, and Muslim Chams), feudalists (the leaders of the old regime, Buddhist monks, and intellectuals), and comprador capitalists (ethnic Chinese). The goal was as much nationalistic as it was socialistic—to return Cambodia and the Khmer race to its previous glory. They took over a country devastated by U.S. bombing during the Vietnam War and ended up killing millions who they deemed didn't belong (Kuper 1990). But the Khmer Rouge's killing of its citizens, while reaching an intensity matched by few states, was hardly an exception. As Carole Nagengast (1994:119–120) wrote,

> The numbers of people worldwide subjected to the violence of their own states are staggering. More than a quarter of a million Kurds and Turks in Turkey have been beaten or tortured by the military, police, and prison guards since 1980; tens of thousands of indigenous people in Peru and Guatemala, street children in Brazil and Guatemala, Palestinians in Kuwait, Kurds in Iraq, and Muslim women and girls in Bosnia have been similarly treated. Mutilated bodies turn up somewhere every day. Some 6,000 people in dozens of countries were legally shot, hung, electrocuted, gassed, or stoned to death by their respective states between 1985 and 1992 for political misdeeds: criticism of the state, membership in banned political parties or groups, or for adherence to the "wrong" religion; for moral deeds: adultery, prostitution, homosexuality, sodomy, or alcohol or drug use; for economic offenses: burglary, embezzling, and corruption; and for violent crimes: rape, assault, and murder.

In a series of books on state killing, R. J. Rummel (1994) documented the carnage committed by states against their own citizens: 61 million Russians from 1917 to 1987; 20 million Germans from 1933 to 1945; 35 million Chinese killed by the Chinese communist government from 1923 to 1949 and 10 million killed by the Chinese nationalists; almost 2 million Turks from 1909 to 1918; and almost 1.5 million Mexicans from 1900 to 1920. In total, Rummel (1994:9) said, almost 170 million men, women, and children from 1900 to 1987

> have been shot, beaten, tortured, knifed, burned, starved, frozen, crushed, or worked to death; buried alive, drowned, hung, bombed, or killed in any other of the myriad ways governments have inflicted death on unarmed, helpless citizens and foreigners. The dead could conceivably be nearly 360 million people. It is as though our species has been devastated by a modern Black Plague. And indeed it has, but a plague of power not germs.

Rummel attributed state killing to power and its abuses, claiming it is largely totalitarian regimes that resort to democide, genocide, or ethnocide. Democracies also kill, as evidenced in the twentieth century by indiscriminate bombings of enemy civilians in war, the large-scale massacre of Filipinos during U.S. colonization of the Philippines at the turn of the century, deaths in British concentration camps during the Boer War in South Africa, civilian deaths in Germany as a result of the Allied blockade, the rape and murder of helpless Chinese in and around Peking in 1900, atrocities committed by Americans in Vietnam, the murder of helpless Algerians by the French during the Algerian War, and the deaths of German prisoners of war in French and U.S. prisoner-of-war camps after World War II. But Rummel said even these prove his point about power, for virtually all of these cases were committed in secret behind a trail of lies and deceit by agencies and power holders who were given the authority to operate autonomously and shielded from the press. Even attacks on German and Vietnamese cities were presented as attacks on military targets. He concluded that as we move from democratic through authoritarian and to totalitarian governments, the degree of state killing increases dramatically (Rummel 1994:17).

Pierre van den Berghe (1992:191) attributed state killing not to the misuse of authority but to nation building itself. Taking what he called a frankly anarchist position, he said,

> the process euphemistically described as nation-building is, in fact, mostly nation-killing;... the vast majority of so-called "nation-states" are nothing of the sort; and... modern nationalism is a blueprint for ethnocide at best, genocide at worst.

Van den Berghe said that the nation-state myth has been allowed to persist because international bodies, such as the United Nations, insist that internal killing is a state matter, a "gentlemen's agreement" between member states not to protest the butchering of their own citizens. Also, scholars perpetrate the myth with the use of nation-state designation. The result is to legitimize genocide in the interests of building nation-states that function to further economic and political integration.

Carole Nagengast (1994:122) proposed that state-sponsored violence serves to aid in the construction and maintenance of the nation-state. She examined not only state killing but also the institutionalization of torture, rape, and homosexual assault. The purpose of this state-sponsored violence is not to inflict pain but to create what Nagengast called "punishable categories of people," to create and maintain boundaries and legitimate or delegitimate specific groups. State violence against its own citizens, she suggested, is a way to create an Other, an ambiguous underclass that consists on the one hand of subhuman brutes and on the other hand of superhuman individuals capable of undermining the accepted order of society. Arrest and torture serve to stigmatize people and to mark them as people who no one wants to be. Arrest and torture become, in effect, a way of symbolically marking, disciplining, and stigmatizing those categories of people whose existence or demands threaten the idea, power, and legitimacy of the nation-state. Furthermore, because the torture and violence are committed only against "terrorists," "communists," or "separatists," it becomes legitimate. "We only beat bad people," said a Turkish prison official in 1984. "They are no good, they are worthless bums, they are subversives who think that communism will relieve them of the necessity of working." He revealed with apparent pride that he had "given orders that all prisoners should be struck with a truncheon below the waist on the rude parts, and warned not to come to prison again." "My aim," he said, "is to ensure discipline. That's not torture, for it is only the lazy, the idle, the vagabonds, the communists, the murderers who come to prison" (cited Nagengast 1994:121).

Terrorist acts are often depicted as being extralegal—that is, committed by persons outside state control. Yet there is considerable evidence that most terror is applied by states to integrate or control a reluctant citizenry. As Jeffery Sluka (2000:1) puts it,

> If terrorism means political intimidation by violence or its threat, and if we allow the definition to include violence by states and agents of states, then we find that the major form of terrorism in the world today is practiced by states and their agents and allies, and that quantitatively, anti-state terrorism pales into relative insignificance in comparison to it.

Death squads operate outside the law but with the tacit approval of the state. Thus their actions carry out state goals of eliminating dissidents without due process of law but are enough removed from official state agencies to allow the state "plausible denial." Rarely are members of death squads punished, and many are also members of official state agencies, such as the police, militia, or army.

Targets of death squads are often portrayed by the state as "terrorists" or subversives but tend to be anyone that challenges the status quo. These include people who organize unions, offer Bible classes, propose land reforms, or advocate tax increases on the rich. They include clergy, labor organizers, human rights activists, social workers, journalists, and so on. Victims include women, children, the elderly, and relatives of activists. More recently, particularly in Latin America, victims include street children.

Few countries are immune to the operation of state-sanctioned death squads. In the United States, for example, there were 4,743 recorded lynchings from 1882 to 1968. Of these people who

There were 4,743 lynchings in the United States from 1882 to 1968. These "death squads" acted with impunity and were never prosecuted by the state. (Bettmann/ Corbis.)

were lynched, 3,446 were black. People were never prosecuted for participating in a lynching, and they frequently requested to have their pictures taken next to the victim, often turning the photograph into a postcard (Allen 2000).[1]

Core countries play a major role in supporting violent regimes in the periphery by either training officers or offering direct military aid. Virtually all this military support is used, not to defend against foreign invasion, but to suppress political dissent or unionization or to discipline a resistant citizenry. And the financial cost of maintaining militaries and supplying client states is high (see Table 4.1). Alexander George in his book *Western State Terrorism* concludes that

> the plain and painful truth is that on any reasonable definition of terrorism, taken literally, the United States and its friends are the major supporters, sponsors, and perpetrators of terrorist incidents in the world today…. [M]any, probably most, significant instances of terrorism are supported, if not organized, by the U.S., its partners, and their client states. (George 1991:1–2)

TABLE 4.1 **Military Spending, World Share, Spending per Capita, Share of GDP, and Change from 1999 to 2008 of Fifteen Countries with the Highest Military Spending**

Rank	Country	Spending ($ Bn.)	Percent of GDP	World Share (%)
—	**World Total**	**1,630**	**2.6**	**100**
1	United States	711.0	4.7	41
2	China	143.0	2.0	8.2
3	Russia	71.9	3.9	4.1
4	United Kingdom	62.7	2.6	3.6
5	France	62.5	2.3	3.6
6	Japan	59.3	1.0	3.4
7	Saudi Arabia	48.2	8.7	2.8
8	India	46.8	2.5	2.7
9	Germany	46.7	1.3	2.7
10	Brazil	35.4	1.5	2.0
11	Italy	34.5	1.6	2.0
12	South Korea	30.8	2.7	1.8
13	Australia	26.7	1.8	1.5
14	Canada	24.7	1.4	1.4
15	Turkey	17.9	2.3	1.0

Source: *Military Expenditures: SIPRI Yearbook, 2011*

---

[1] Many of these are available at www.withoutsanctuary.org/ along with a movie narrated by James Allen.

SPIN, FREE TRADE, AND THE ROLE OF ENERGY IN THE GLOBAL ECONOMY

In March of 2003, the United States, Great Britain, and a small number of military personnel from forty other countries invaded Iraq. The invasion and subsequent occupation of Iraq are clearly one of the first defining moments of the twenty-first century. Its consequences dominated U.S. electoral politics, preoccupied the media, and resulted in the deaths of hundreds of thousands of Iraqis, Americans, and others, along with the displacement of millions more at an ultimate cost of over one trillion dollars. The question is, *What can we learn about the role of the nation-state from this event and from the wider involvement of the United States in the Middle East?* More specifically, *What does it tell us about the role of the nation-state in marshaling support for its actions and for its function of maintaining the health and growth of the economy?*

Iraq

To answer these questions, we first need to provide a brief history of recent U.S. involvement in the Middle East, and particularly its history of relations with three countries—Saudi Arabia, Iran, and Iraq—who together hold almost 45 percent of the known world petroleum reserves.

U.S. involvement in the Middle East, particularly in Middle East politics, began largely in May of 1933, when Standard Oil of California (today's Chevron) gained the right to drill for oil in Saudi Arabia, formalizing the agreement with the Saudis by forming a partnership known as the Arabian-American Oil Company (Aramco). Aramco worked hard at making the partnership work at the cultural level, insisting that employees follow strict Saudi laws and building power plants, roads, schools, and other needed facilities. By 1980, Saudi Arabia had bought 100 percent of Aramco's shares and in 1988, with little objection from the United States, took over total management of the company, changing the name to Saudi Aramco.

The United States has maintained remarkably cooperative relations with the Saudis, gaining much prestige in Saudi Arabia and the rest of the Arab world in 1956 when it sided with Egypt against Great Britain, France, and Israel, who had attacked Egypt in 1956 when it asserted control over the Suez Canal. The United States has always been adamant that no country interfere with its access to Saudi oil, the largest known deposit in the world.

In 1953, Iran, with the fifth-largest oil deposits in the world, became a U.S. interest when a democratically elected government led by Mohammad Mossadeq nationalized the British Anglo-Iranian Oil Company. Seeing British interests threatened, the United States joined Great Britain, and, working largely through the U.S. Central Intelligence Agency (CIA) and with Iranian army officers, overthrew Mossadeq on the pretext that he had communist leanings. They lent their support to the shah Mohammed Reza Pahlavi, who had briefly reigned when his father, Reza Pahlavi, abdicated in 1941 and who ruled more as a dictator than a constitutional monarch. As a result of U.S. participation in the overthrow of Mossadeq, U.S. firms gained a 40 percent share in Iranian oil and the right to maintain military bases in Iran. Largely because of the repressive nature of the shah's government, he was deposed in 1979 when a popular revolution drove him from power and installed a fundamentalist Islamic government headed by Islamic cleric Ayatollah Khomeini. The Iranian Revolution had two serious consequences for the United States: the loss of access to Iranian oil and the loss of military bases in Iran.

The year 1979 was also eventful because Iraq, with the second-largest oil reserves in the world, officially acquired a new leader, Saddam Hussein al-Tikriti. In 1963, Saddam had been among a group of army officers who, with CIA help, overthrew and killed General Abdel-Karim Kassem, who had angered the United States by legalizing the Communist Party in Iraq and enacting land reforms while granting autonomy to the Kurdish population in the north of the country. In 1980 Saddam invaded Iran. When it looked like Iraq might lose the war, the

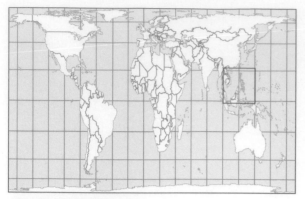

The Philippines

United States supplied arms and intelligence to Iraq, which finally signed a treaty with Iran in 1989 after the deaths of some 1.5 million people. The United States remained on good terms with Saddam until 1990, when, in a territorial dispute, Saddam invaded Kuwait. The United States and its allies responded by launching Operation Desert Storm to "liberate" Kuwait. The United States easily succeeded in driving the Iraqi army out of Kuwait, and then led the United Nations in applying economic sanctions against Iraq and limiting the country's ability to acquire any goods (including medicines) that conceivably could be used for military purposes. UNICEF estimated that at least 500,000 children died for lack of medicines as a consequence of the sanctions. Then, in March of 2003, the U.S.-led coalition invaded Iraq.

To illustrate the role of the nation-state, mainly the relationship to capitalists (particularly multinational corporations), we need to examine the following questions, each of which is raised by the Iraq invasion. First, *how does a nation-state, especially one with a representative government, gain support for policy decisions and collective action such as the invasion of another country?* Second, *how does the invasion of Iraq relate to the nation-state's stewardship of the economy, especially its relationship to multinational corporations?* Finally, given the importance of Middle Eastern petroleum supplies, *what is the role of nation-states in the availability of energy supplies, and what is the role of oil, and energy in general, to the workings of national economies?*

Manufacturing Consent: Spin

Manufacturing consent, a term suggested by Edward S. Herman and Noam Chomsky (2002), refers to the efforts of governments and corporations to manipulate the manner in which policies and events are represented by the mass media and, consequently, interpreted by citizens. The effort of President George W. Bush's administration to justify the invasion of Iraq is a good example. There is significant evidence that even before the attacks of September 11, 2001, on the World Trade Center and the Pentagon, the administration wanted to invade Iraq and that even after 9/11 was advised that public opinion first had to be prepared for an invasion (Johnson 2004:227). The administration consequently launched a public relations campaign to convince people that removing Saddam Hussein would be essential for America's "war on terror."

There were claims ("slam dunks," according to the head of the CIA, George Tenet) that Saddam had weapons of mass destruction, none of which were ever found. Then the president floated scenarios in which Iraq could use drones to target the United States with chemical or biological weapons. The secretary of defense, Donald Rumsfeld, told newsmen that the government had "bulletproof" evidence of links between Iraq and al Qaeda and that Iraq had offered safe haven to bin Laden and Taliban leaders. Of course, the president later admitted that there were no such links, although in February of 2006, three years after the invasion, 90 percent of the American troops fighting in Iraq still believed that Saddam was directly responsible for 9/11 (Zogby 2006).

Political pundits and politicians later attacked the questionable reasons given for the invasion of Iraq. But all governments, including those of the United States, have generally used spin to justify military action, to manufacture consent that going to war is in some national interest. To justify the war against Spain in 1898, which resulted in the United States driving Spain from Cuba and annexing the Philippines, the U.S. government claimed (with significant help from the news media and without evidence) that the Spanish were responsible for the explosion that destroyed the battleship *Maine* in Havana Harbor. In April of 1917, Woodrow Wilson established the Committee on Public Information (CPI) to marshal support from a reluctant citizenry for the United States' declaration of war against Germany. The CPI gained media support for the war, distributed posters depicting alleged German atrocities, and recruited influential members of American towns and cities to give supposedly spontaneous four-minute talks to community groups in support of the war.

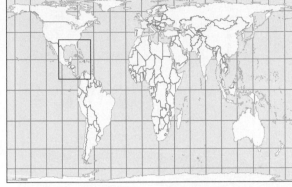

Cuba

In 1962, after Fidel Castro installed a communist government in Cuba, and after a failed U.S.-supported invasion to depose Castro failed, the chair of the joint chief of staff, General Lyman Lemmitzer, sent a memo to Secretary of Defense Robert McNamara proposing that the military kill innocent Americans in the street, sink boats carrying refugees from Cuba, and conduct terrorist attacks in American cities—and blame Cuban agents to justify a U.S. invasion of Cuba. Named Operation Northwoods, it was signed by all members of the staff. McNamara ignored the memo and two months afterward forced Lemmitzer's retirement (Bamford 2002:778–791; see also Johnson 2004:301).

President Lyndon Johnson justified U.S. military action in Vietnam in 1964 by claiming that the North Vietnamese had attacked an American warship on "routine patrol" in the Gulf of Tonkin and gained a congressional resolution that justified U.S. military intervention in Vietnam. In fact, the warship was on an intelligence-gathering mission to assist South Vietnam forces attacking North Vietnam. The president claimed that there was a second attack, which never occurred. As Congress voted to authorize military action, the *New York Times* said that the president had gone "to the American people with the somber facts," while the *Los Angeles Times* urged Americans to "face the fact that the Communists, by their attack on American vessels in international waters, have themselves escalated the hostilities."

At the start of the first Gulf War in 1991, President George H. W. Bush said that Iraqi soldiers had invaded a Kuwaiti hospital, pulled 312 babies from their incubators, and "scattered them across the floor like firewood." But according to the doctors in Kuwait, there were only a few incubators and few if any babies in them at the time of the invasion. After the war, it was revealed that Kuwait had hired the Washington public relations firm Hill & Knowlton to peddle this story, and on October 10, 1990, arranged for an "eyewitness" to testify before Congress that it had indeed happened. That witness, who turned out to be the daughter of the Kuwaiti ambassador to Washington, had not been anywhere near a hospital in Kuwait City in August 1990. Other "witnesses" who claimed to have seen Iraqi atrocities later acknowledged that they had all been coached by Hill & Knowlton (Cohen 2002; Johnson 2004:230; Regan 2002).

Spin is not, of course, unique to government. Corporations, public interest groups, and even religious leaders try to depict the world in ways that are, for one reason or another, in their own interests. But another reason for spin is a general distrust among the elite of nation-states of democratic decision making. Fareed Zakaria (2003), former editor of the journal *Foreign Affairs,* warned that too much democracy threatens liberties and that public-spirited elites should act as "social stabilizers" and not be accountable to "public whim." Central banks, the European Union, and the World Trade Organization (WTO) are examples of some of the elite organizations that he suggests we need in order to temper what he calls "illiberal democracy." Zakaria's argument reflects the political writings of people from Aristotle to Edmund Burke, all warning about the dangers inherent in giving people the right to have too much of a say in their lives and in their government. *Where did this distrust come from, and how did it give rise to the need to manufacture consent?*

To begin answering these questions, let's go back to the late nineteenth and early twentieth centuries, a period when civic participation and social activism were thriving in the United

During World War I, the U.S. government established the Committee on Public Information to gain support for the war against Germany. (World History Archive/ Alamy.)

States. It was a time, also, when corporate prerogatives were being called into question and when social movements were driven by popular appeals to equality and social justice. At the same time, elites were warning again about the dangers of democracy. One of the most influential of these warnings came from French sociologist Gustave Le Bon in his book *The Crowd: A Study of the Popular Mind* (first published in 1895). In *The Crowd,* Le Bon warned of the power of the masses, which had been set loose and was overtaking the historical stage. The question given "scientific" legitimacy by Le Bon was how to assert control over "the mob"? Le Bon's question is credited by some, including media scholar Stuart Ewen (1996), with leading to the creation of the whole field of public relations and the emergence of "spin," attempts to "engineer consent," and mold public opinion to the interests of nations, elites, corporations, and fee-paying clients.

Edward Bernays was central to this development. Bernays, whose name is recognizable to few, is listed by some as one of the hundred most important people of the twentieth century. Bernays, often called "the father of spin," was born in 1891 to a powerful and wealthy Austrian family (he was a nephew of Sigmund Freud). Bernays was a public relations genius: He got his start working for the U.S. CPI during World War I. He originated the orchestration of public events to advertise products, as when he convinced women's rights marchers in New York City to hold up Lucky Strike cigarettes as "Torches of Freedom." Bernays was the advisor and confidant of presidents, world leaders, and corporate heads for over eighty years. Interviewed when he was almost 100 years old by Stewart Ewen, Bernays expressed a clearly hierarchical view of society in which an "intelligent few" have been charged with influencing the tide of history. Public relations, he said, is a response "to a transhistoric concern: the requirement, for those people in power, to shape the attitudes of the general population" (Ewen 1996:11). He even suggested that an eleventh article be added to the Bill of Rights—in addition to the freedom of speech, freedom of assembly, and freedom of the press, he said, we should add "the freedom to persuade."

Bernays, of course, was not alone in his sentiments. Guided by public relations pioneers such as Ivy Lee and Walter Lippmann, popular opinion and culture began to be seen as something that must be controlled for the good of society. Particularly concerned in the early twentieth century were corporations whose practices were coming under increased scrutiny and attack by journalists, government agencies, and the public at large.

Corporations hired public relations consultants to sell policy decisions, and soon a social science emerged that specialized in mass psychology and manipulation. These public relations people saw themselves as "news engineers." They proposed to get out "facts" to enable the public to understand the soundness of corporate policy. Government and corporate campaigns to influence public opinion led to the doctrine of what historian Robert B. Westbrook called *democratic realism,* the idea that it was best to strictly limit government by the people and to redefine democracy as, by and large, government for the people by enlightened and responsible elites (Ewen 1996:147).

The masters of spin had a low opinion of public intelligence. Journalist Walter Lippmann, for example, thought the public incapable of seeing the world clearly, much less understanding it. But, he said, the scientifically trained person could engineer "pseudo-environments" to persuade people to see the larger political environment, and to this end, the mass media, was critical.

Particularly frightening to elites during the 1930s were the economic and social policies of Franklin D. Roosevelt's New Deal, which threatened corporate autonomy. Furthermore, Roosevelt was particularly effective in presenting the reasons for his policies by trying to educate the public, rather than simply control it. For example, in his first of thirty-one "Fireside Chats," he outlined the intricacies of the banking system, why so many had failed in the preceding months, and what must be done to make them secure again. Roosevelt, Ewen writes,

> struck a bargain with popular activism. Exhibiting trust and affection for the public, not fear, he encouraged ordinary people to examine even his own New Deal programs and provide suggestions—if required—for more suitable actions to be taken. (1996:257–258)

Alarmed conservatives and businesspeople countered the New Deal with the National Association of Manufacturers (NAM) and launched a campaign to convince the public that what was good for business was good for them. They produced pamphlets such as *What Is Your American System All About,* which told people they had a choice of what kind of country they lived in, one in which "the citizen is supreme and the government obeys his will," or one in which "the state is supreme and controls the citizen."

Some of the strategies included distributing newspaper articles with a pro-business spin addressing Depression concerns such as the uneven distribution of wealth and class antagonisms. They had six professedly independent scholars from Princeton, New York University, Stanford, and University of Southern California take turns writing newspaper columns attacking economic aspects of the New Deal and published a series of booklets called *You and Industry* for schools, colleges, and public libraries. *Young America,* distributed weekly to schools, contained articles offering a user-friendly portrayal of capitalism. They also produced documentaries for theaters such as the ten-minute series *America Marches On* narrated by Lowell Thomas describing America as the greatest industrial system the world has ever seen. They also moved to drama, producing a fifteen-minute weekly radio show called *The American Family Robinson,* which chronicled the lives of ordinary Americans and portrayed businesspeople as heroes and labor organizers as villains. They also spent millions on billboards upholding "the American Way" and describing the glories of life in America and the evils of communist "collectivism." For example, the American Medical Association (AMA) launched a campaign in 1949 to scuttle what looked like a promising plan for federally insured health coverage by linking the plan to communism. The spotlight was shifted from health care needs to the evils of government intervention. In all, they spent $1.4 million to defeat the proposal (the equivalent of over $10 million today).

Today, while spending hundreds of millions of dollars on public relations, corporations try to mask their involvement in spin by forming citizen groups, such as the National Wetlands Coalition (with its logo of a duck flying over a swamp), sponsored by oil and gas drilling companies and real estate developers fighting for reducing restrictions on the conversion of wetlands to drilling sites and shopping malls. Keep America Green, sponsored by the bottling industry, argues for antilitter campaigns rather than mandatory recycling legislation.

Protected by the free speech provision of the First Amendment, corporations marshal huge public relations efforts on behalf of their agendas. In the United States, the 170,000 public relations employees whose job it is to manipulate news, public opinion, and public policy in the interests of their clients outnumber news reporters by 40,000. A study in 1990 discovered that almost 40 percent of the news content of a typical U.S. newspaper originates as public relations press releases, story memos, and suggestions. The *Columbia Journalism Review* reported that more than half the news stories in the *Wall Street Journal* are based solely on corporate press releases (Korten 1995:148).

Thus an important function of the state and its corporate supporters is to use the political and economic power at their disposal to manufacture consent for actions and policies that it believes are essential, and convince the public that these actions and policies are in their interest. Thus, even basic foreign policy decisions, many advise, must be done covertly. Contemporary political analysts such as Charles Krauthammer and Robert D. Kaplan advise that American global domination is best done covertly and secretly, since if left to its own devices, the U.S. public would disarm and place constraints on executive power (Johnson 2004:68).

The elites' low regard for public participation also requires removing from democratic decision making anything having to do with economic policy. In fact, one of the curious facts about attempts by nation-states to engineer consent is how infrequently economic factors are incorporated into spin to justify war. We go to war, say the media managers, to protect citizens from attack (Saddam's drones or biological weapons) or for humanitarian purposes (to "bring democracy" or "to free people from tyranny"), never for economic purposes. Yet, as we'll see next, economic factors were very prominent in the invasion of Iraq.

Markets and Free Trade

One of the major criticisms voiced by policymakers and the media of the U.S.-sponsored invasion of Iraq was that, while the initial phase of the invasion went well, there was no plan for what to do next. Consequently, the story goes, an insurgency was allowed to develop that undermined the plans to install a democratic state. What went basically unnoticed, particularly by the popular media, was that, in fact, the administration had drawn up an elaborate set of well-planned economic reforms that were imposed on Iraq by the Coalition Provisional Authority (CPA) immediately after the invasion. These reforms reveal another role of the modern nation-state—to provide to corporate sponsors unregulated access to markets and resources and to establish rules, laws, and regulations that maximize the ability of corporations to profit—rules, laws, and regulations that likely would not be supported by the general population of a democratic state.

The United States put together the CPA after the invasion to govern Iraq prior to the holding of democratic elections. However, before elections could be held, the director of the CPA, L. Paul Bremer, imposed a set of orders that were intended to turn Iraq into a model demonstration of "free trade" and neoliberal economic theory.

These orders included (Coalition Provisional Authority ND) the following:

- Suspending all tariffs, customs duties, import taxes, or licensing fees on goods and services entering or leaving Iraq.
- Granting full immunity from Iraqi law to all security firms brought in to work in Iraq.
- Privatizing some 200 state-owned enterprises, permitting 100 percent foreign-ownership of Iraqi businesses.
- Allowing investors to take 100 percent of the profits they made in Iraq out of the country with no requirement that the profits be reinvested.
- Prohibiting any requirement that foreign companies hire local workers, recognize unions, or reinvest any profits back into the country.
- Allowing foreign banks to open in Iraq and take a 50 percent interest in Iraqi banks.
- Lowering the corporate tax rate from 40 percent to a flat 15 percent.

These orders constituted a corporate wish list of rules and regulations that virtually no democratic legislature could openly support, let alone implement. Furthermore, the CPA planned to build these rules into the Iraqi constitution so that they would have to be acknowledged by any subsequent Iraqi government. This was particularly important because without guarantees that these economic policies would be retained by future Iraqi governments, no corporation or bank or investor would risk investing money in the Iraq economy (see Klein 2004).

Thus, some of Bremer's first acts as head of the CPA was to fire 500,000 state workers, most of them soldiers, but also doctors, nurses, teachers, publishers, and printers (partly because they were members of Saddam Hussein's political party, Baath Arab Socialist); open the border to unrestricted imports (much to the dismay of local Iraqi businesspeople); and privatize some 200 state-owned companies producing everything from cement to washing machines. In fact, U.S. corporations were brought in to supply the occupation with cement that could have been supplied by Iraqis at a fraction of the cost. "Getting inefficient state enterprises into private hands," Bremer said, "is essential for Iraq's economic recovery" (Klein 2004). It is noteworthy that in the beginning of 2007, with the rising possibility of a U.S. defeat in Iraq, the Pentagon began a program to reopen state-run factories in order to provide jobs for the mass of Iraqi unemployed put out of work by the CPA (Glanz 2007).

The actions of the CPA in Iraq represent the kinds of "free trade" regulations that corporations lobby for, but which are rarely enacted in their pure form because of objections from small businesspeople, unions, or citizens in general. In fact, in any democratic system where representatives have a say, such reforms are very difficult to enact, as thirty years of efforts in Latin America, Asia, the United States, and Europe attest. Iraq represented a situation in which free trade reforms could be imposed by force with no interference from democratic institutions. But force is not the only way to prevent democratic procedures from interfering with free trade reform.

Corporations have enormous power, as we noted in Chapter 3. The economic resources available to corporations rival those available to most countries and one of the major priorities of corporations is advancing the doctrine of "free trade." This involves working with nation-states to remove the so-called barriers to trade. These barriers include the following:

- taxes and tariffs on goods entering or leaving a country
- subsidies, tax breaks, or other forms of preferential treatment that countries might give to domestic businesses, such as payments to farmers or tax breaks to specific businesses
- social or environmental laws, such as those regulating the age of workers, working conditions, or laws restricting environmental damage by corporations
- customs and cultural traditions (e.g., the midday siesta in Spain)

The question is, *Other than conquering a country militarily, in what other ways can these barriers be removed, particularly if a large portion, or even a majority of the population, objects?*

First, nations or groups of nations can agree among themselves to remove barriers to trade. For example, the United States and Australia implemented a free trade agreement in January 2005. The North Atlantic Free Trade Agreement (NAFTA) between Canada, the United States, and Mexico is another example, as is the Asian-Pacific Economic Cooperation Forum (APEC) that includes some twenty-one countries. Generally these agreements stipulate that countries cannot give preferential treatment to domestic business and must lower or remove tariffs on goods traded between member countries. It may also mean that countries cannot impose labor or environmental laws on businesses or corporations from other member countries if they are deemed an unfair restriction on trade. Typically these agreements must be ratified by democratically elected bodies, but once they are ratified, control over many economic rules and laws passes to unelected individuals empowered to hear disputes between countries, or between countries and corporations.

A second way that barriers to trade can be removed is through actions of multilateral organizations such as the International Monetary Fund (IMF) or the World Bank. Generally, if a country is in debt to the IMF and must renegotiate the repayment of the loan, the IMF will insist that the country do everything it can to promote foreign investment in the country; this typically involves removing the sorts of barriers to trade mentioned earlier. Thus, the IMF insisted that Jamaica, which is heavily in debt to the IMF, open the country to foreign corporations wishing to do business there. One result was the virtual destruction of Jamaican agriculture, because Jamaican farmers could not produce and sell produce in their own country as cheaply as could American agribusiness. In these cases, democratically elected representatives have virtually no choice but to follow IMF directives; otherwise the country will be cut off from loans from other financial entities and will likely lose any possibility of attracting foreign capital and investment.

A third way to reduce barriers to trade is through membership in the WTO. As we noted in the last chapter, the goal of the WTO is to foster free trade. For example, Japan, because of public concerns about pesticide residues in foods, required testing whenever a poisonous chemical was used to fumigate imported fruits and nuts against infestation by coddling moths. But since Japan's safety standards were higher than those set by the WTO, the United States complained to the WTO that this regulation constituted a barrier to trade, and the WTO ruling body agreed.

It is fair to ask, who benefits from free trade? It clearly benefits corporations that are guaranteed access to global resources, labor supplies, and consumers. It also benefits consumers by lowering the prices for goods and services. And it disproportionately benefits wealthy nations who are able to impose sometimes unfair trading practices on poor countries. For example, the WTO requires third world countries to remove all subsidies for agriculture but allows EU and U.S. subsidies to continue because they were in place before the WTO agreement. Finally, overall, free trade may contribute to economic growth by accelerating both production and consumption.

Who, then, is hurt by free trade? First, small farmers and businesspeople who cannot compete with large corporations. Mexican peasants did relatively well selling their corn when the government assisted them with money for fertilizers and placed import tariffs on U.S. corn farmers. However, once NAFTA removed those protections, Mexican farmers could not sell their corn in Mexico as cheaply as large U.S. farmers could. This does not necessarily mean that small-scale farms in countries such as Jamaica and Mexico are less efficient; instead, farmers in countries such as the United States receive hidden subsidies of one sort or another. One reason Jamaican farmers could not compete with U.S. farmers is because the interest rates (dictated by the IMF) that they had to pay on loans were much higher than interest rates paid by U.S. farmers. Because of the support that the U.S. government gives to oil companies, U.S. farmers also pay less for energy than Jamaican farmers or farmers in poorer countries. Thus, in spite of the ideology of free trade, farmers in Europe and the United States are given distinct economic advantages over farmers in poorer countries.

Hurt also by free trade are laborers who, because of the terms of many free trade agreements, are denied effective labor representation, or, as we noted in Chapter 2, are forced to compete with laborers in other countries who, for various reasons, must accept lower wages. And, as we'll see in Chapter 5, laborers are also restricted by immigration laws. Thus while goods, services, and capital may freely flow across borders, workers may not. Finally, another category of persons harmed by free trade are citizens who are exposed to unregulated products and environmental hazards.

Energy and Technology

There is little question that the invasion and occupation of Iraq involved oil. U.S. presidents and policymakers have long made it clear that protecting access to Middle Eastern oil for the United States and its allies is critical to both national security and the economy in general. In 1980 President Jimmy Carter described access to oil in the Persian Gulf as a "vital interest" and said that the United States would use "any means necessary, including military force" to overcome an attempt by a hostile power to block that flow (Klare 2004:4). U.S. military leaders made an explicit reference to Iraq in the joint chiefs of staff report *Strategic Assessment 1999* when they noted that an "oil war" in the Persian Gulf was a serious possibility and that U.S. forces might be used to ensure adequate supplies. They suggested also that a war could eliminate the influence of Saddam Hussein and gain U.S. control of Iraqi oil, while at the same time gaining access to the energy-rich area of Central Asia (Johnson 2004:226).

One question is, *How has oil, or energy in general, come to play the role it has in global politics, and in what way does it affect the role and function of the nation-state?*

Fossil fuels are, by far, the major source of global energy, with oil the dominant source (see Figure 4.1).

Generally speaking, up until recently, energy sources have been relatively plentiful; in 2000 oil was selling for under twenty dollars a barrel, coal was still plentiful (although highly polluting), and natural gas deposits seemed more than adequate. However, in the first years of the twenty-first century, energy outlooks became alarming. The price of oil at one point reached seventy dollars a barrel, and some oil geologists predicted that we would soon reach "peak oil," meaning that the total amount of petroleum produced would begin to decline. Largely because of the economic growth of China and India, global oil usage jumped 450 percent from 15 million barrels a day in 1955 to 83.7 million barrels a day by 2005. The United States alone consumes over 20 million barrels (840 million gallons) of oil a day, and global demand is projected to be 118 million barrels per day by 2030 (Bodman 2006).

The United States is largely dependent on foreign oil. Table 4.2 provides information for the years 2006 to 2011 on the top fifteen countries from which the United States imports its oil. U.S. oil imports have declined, partly because of the economic contraction of 2007–2008 and

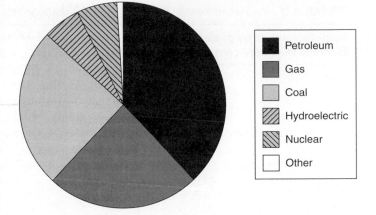

FIGURE 4.1
Global Energy Sources, 2006

TABLE 4.2 U.S. Petroleum Imports by Country of Origin: Thousand Barrels per Day, 2006–2011

Country	2006	2007	2008	2009	2010	2011
Canada	2,353	2,455	2,493	2,479	2,535	2,706
Mexico	1,705	1,532	1,302	1,210	1,284	1,205
Saudi Arabia	1,463	1,485	1,529	1,004	1,096	1,195
Venezuela	1,419	1,361	1,189	1,063	988	944
Nigeria	1,114	1,134	988	809	1,023	817
Iraq	553	484	627	450	415	460
Algeria	657	670	548	493	510	358
Angola	534	508	513	460	393	346
Russia	369	414	465	563	612	621
United Kingdom	272	277	236	245	256	158
Ecuador	278	203	221	185	212	192
Kuwait	185	181	210	182	197	191
Norway	196	142	102	108	89	113
Colombia	155	155	200	276	365	422
Brazil	193	200	258	309	272	249
All Countries	13,707	13,468	12,915	11,691	11,793	11,360

Source: U.S. Energy Information Administration. US Imports by Country of Origin, http://www.eia.gov/dnav/pet/ pet_move_impcus_a2_nus_epU0_Im0_mbblpd_a htm

TABLE 4.3   Projected Energy Consumption (quadrillion Btu) by Selected Region, 2010–2030

Regions (ranked by projected increase in energy consumption)	2010	2015	2020	2025	2030	Projected Annual Percent Increase
China	79.9	99.0	119.8	142.5	169.8	5.0
India	20.0	24.0	28.4	33.1	38.7	3.8
Africa	18.3	22.1	25.0	28.3	32.6	3.4
Central and South America	29.2	34.8	40.7	47.2	53.9	3.4
Middle East	25.9	30.4	34.5	39.4	44.6	3.1
Brazil	11.1	13.0	14.7	16.8	18.9	2.9
Mexico	8.1	9.5	11.0	12.7	14.5	2.8
South Korea	11.1	12.8	14.1	15.4	16.9	2.5
Russia	34.6	39.4	44.4	49.4	54.6	2.4
Canada	15.8	17.1	18.2	19.4	20.6	1.6
United States	110.2	118.7	127.2	136.6	146.4	1.5
Australia/New Zealand	6.7	7.2	7.7	8.3	8.8	1.4
European Union	85.5	89.4	92.2	96.1	101.2	0.9
Japan	23.1	24.1	24.7	25.5	26.2	0.6
Total World	524.2	594.2	666.0	745.6	835.4	2.6

Source: Energy Information Administration, http://www.eia.doe.gov/oiaf/ieo/excel/ieohtab_1.xls

partly because of increased natural gas production from the environmentally risky process of hydrofracking.

Adding to concerns about sufficient energy resources, especially oil, is the fact that some oil-producing countries, many of which were subject to colonial rule, are distrustful of foreign involvement or have groups protesting or rebelling against the central government. The oil-producing areas of Nigeria, for example, have been subject to attacks by groups that have suffered from environmental devastation due to oil exploration and drilling (Klare 2004:127). And global energy consumption in general is projected to increase at a rate of 2.6 percent a year (see Table 4.3).

Given the projected energy crisis that many see approaching, *is it fair to ask, why it is that we can't reduce our energy dependence?* One answer is that economic growth is directly tied to energy consumption. It is probably no accident that the increase in petroleum usage since 1950 (450 percent) is close to the percentage increase in the money supply (see Table I.3). Generally, each percent of GDP growth requires 0.27 percentage increase in energy usage (Martenson 2011:150). The production of money begins with energy. Energy is required to fuel our technologies, which in turn produce goods and services that are transformed into money. Thus, one of the keys to maintaining economic growth is the constant acceleration of production through the use of energy-dependent technology (see Robbins 2005).

We can see how the process works with the recent history of agriculture. Agriculture and animal husbandry were, perhaps, the first areas to which technology was applied to accelerate production. Virtually all of the food crops and domesticated animals that comprise the Western diet existed 2,000 years ago. Today Western farmers and ranchers just grow and raise them faster and with less human labor. In the nineteenth century, the advent of mechanized agriculture—the steel plow; the mechanical reaper; and the "combine," which combined the machines for reaping and threshing wheat—cut the labor time for each bushel of wheat harvested from sixty-one to three hours. In cereal production in general, output per worker more than tripled between 1840 and 1911 with 60 percent of the increase attributable to mechanization (Rosenberg 1982).

In the latter half of the twentieth century, the so-called green revolution (which we will discuss in more detail in Chapter 6) further reduced labor time by substituting nonhuman energy (largely subsidized by nation-states) in the form of chemical herbicides, pesticides, and fertilizers for human energy. Technology has also contributed to the accelerated growth of domesticated animals. A grass-fed steer in 1750 would not attain maximum weight until it was five or six years old. By 1950, grain feeding would bring the steer to market in two or three years. But with today's use of oil-based herbicides to increase pasturage, protein supplements, growth hormones, forced feeding of grain, and antibiotics to ward off infections, a typical steer can reach its slaughter weight of some 1,200 pounds in fourteen to sixteen months (Pollan 2002). Now, with the advent of genetic engineering, researchers are further accelerating the growth and size of animal species such as salmon, trout, catfish, and oysters, as well as plants.

The cost of accelerating food production is a vastly increased need for energy, particularly petroleum. As Richard Manning (2004) puts it, we "eat oil." Manning is referring to the development of energy-dependent agriculture that has emerged in the past half century (see Chapter 6). A modern American farm, says Manning, requires the energy equivalence of four tons of TNT per acre per year; Iowa farms, in total, require the energy equivalence of 4,000 Nagasaki bombs. Every calorie that we eat is backed by at least a calorie of oil; the production of one calorie of breakfast cereal requires four calories of energy. If the rest of the world ate the same way as people in the United States did, global fossil-fuel reserves could be gone in seven years (see Manning 2004).

In addition, the use of technology to accelerate capital accumulation does not apply only to food. We can find technology making everything go faster (see Gleick 2000) in virtually every area of the economy, from transportation to communication to commodity production to the pace of work. It is no accident that the wealthier a country, the more fast paced the life of its citizens (see Levine 1997). Time is, as many a capitalist has remarked, money. And technology, and the energy that runs it, overcomes time.

For these reasons, it is essential for nation-states to ensure that their citizens have adequate and increasing access to energy sources. Furthermore, the cost of the energy must be low enough to allow a significant difference in value between it and the goods and services into which the energy is ultimately converted. In other words, it makes little economic sense if the profit from the sale of a bushel of corn is equal to the cost of the energy needed to produce it. Thus, it is crucial for nation-states to ensure access to energy and to cheap energy. At this point in history, fossil-based fuels (oil, coal, and natural gas) are the cheapest sources of energy.

The problem, of course, is that as nation-states compete for cheap energy sources and access to foreign markets and resources, the risk of violent conflict increases. Consequently, military power becomes more important. At this point in time, the United States is clearly the strongest military power in the world and used that power, as in Iraq and Afghanistan, to maintain access for producers to energy and markets, and spinning military action to both maintain public support for its actions while minimizing global condemnation. But this has consequences.

Chalmers Johnson (2004:285ff.) suggests that the battery of military bases required to ensure U.S. access to energy and markets carries with it what he calls the "sorrows of empire," which will ultimately change the nature of the nation-state. These "sorrows" include a state of perpetual war that will lead to more violent attacks against U.S. citizens and to an increase in reliance by smaller states on weapons of mass destruction; a loss of democracy and constitutional rights to an increasingly imperial presidency; a "shredded principle of truthfulness," as propaganda and spin are used to glorify war; power and the military itself; and, finally, economic decline and neglect of education, health, and individual well-being as more and more economic resources are spent to maintain the military empire. In addition, the maintenance of empire requires the militarization of society in general. For example, the requirement for the United States to maintain a standing military and staff the more than 750 bases around the world requires the "professionalization" of the armed forces, producing people who will fight because they are told to, because it is their job, regardless of the political goals of military operations. In World War II, we needed propaganda to convince the armed forces that they were fighting against evil: Today it is enough to be simply ordered into war. As Johnson put it,

> With public support slackening, the military high command turned to inculcating martial values into the troops, making that the most vital goal of all military instruction, superseding even training in the use of weapons. These values were to include loyalty, esprit de corps, tradition, male binding, discipline and action—generally speaking, a John Wayne view of the world. (2004:58)

CONCLUSION

The state emerged some 7,000 to 8,000 years ago to politically integrate largely heterogeneous peoples and cultures. Military conquest was the main vehicle for its creation and maintenance. Two hundred to three hundred years ago, the nation-state developed to fulfill a new need—that of economic integration. Military conquest as a device was not entirely abandoned, but new strategies of integration, such as improved means of communication and transportation, national education systems, and the ideology of nationalism, became preferred means of attaining desired economic ends.

The nation-state helped create the type of people—laborers and consumers—required to maintain and protect the interests of the capitalist. It created and maintained an unprecedented division of labor and imposed a shared culture that enabled workers to communicate with precision while thirsting for the commodities that labor produced and which served as the basis of the elite's wealth.

More importantly, terror and violence remained state instruments of integration, serving to eliminate those who refused to assimilate into the new ideal of the nation-state or to mark as undesirable Others against whom the majority could unite. As a consequence, millions have died as victims of their own governments.

The need to maintain economic growth, to convince an often reluctant citizenry to support government policy, even if it goes against their interests, has also led to a dependence upon spin by both governments and corporations. It has also led to global militarization as nation-states compete to open access for their corporations to resources and markets of other nation-states and to protect vital energy resources that serve as the foundation of national economies and, indeed, societies.

With this discussion of the nation-state, we conclude our outline of the culture of capitalism and the origins of and relations among consumer, laborer, capitalist, and nation-state. These relationships may seem complex, but they are written on virtually every commodity we possess. For example, sneakers were once for kids or tennis or basketball players. Consumers of this commodity have been cleverly created through massive advertising campaigns involving, among other things, endorsements from popular sports figures, which not only make the shoes fashionable but also allow Nike and other corporations to sell them for up to hundreds of dollars. To make their shoes, Nike has, as they should do to please their investors, sought out cheap sources of labor. The labor for a pair of Nike sneakers costs less than one dollar per pair, and the total amount Nike spends on labor is about the same as that paid to major sports figures for endorsements. As a consequence, Nike earns billions of dollars, returning much of it to banks and investors and using some to influence government legislation that would be favorable to its interests. To help generate this profit, nation-states support the entire operation by supporting and maintaining communication networks, financial institutions, and favorable labor legislation, and maintain markets and access to necessary resources. Without the nation-state, businesses could not prosper, and consumers could not buy, at least not as cheaply as they do.

Thus, countries such as Vietnam and Indonesia offer tax breaks to Nike and control and discipline their labor forces to ensure an inexpensive and docile workforce, many of whom use their wages to purchase Nike products.

Thus, although the historical, social, cultural, economic, political, and ideological factors that have helped create and maintain the culture of capitalism are in their totality complex, they can be identified in virtually every element of our culture, at least for those who care to look. Furthermore, as we shall see, these same factors contribute in one way or another to virtually every global issue that we discuss in the remainder of this book.

PART TWO

The Global Impact of the Culture of Capitalism: Introduction

Our thesis is that the idea of a self-adjusting market implied a stark utopia. Such an institution could not exist for any length of time without annihilating the human and natural substance of society; it would have physically destroyed man and transformed his surroundings into a wilderness. Inevitably, society took measures to protect itself, but whatever measures it took impaired the self-regulation of the market, disorganized industrial life, and thus endangered society in yet another way. It was this dilemma which forced the development of the market system into a definite groove and finally disrupted the social organization based upon it.

—Karl Polyani, *The Great Transformation* (1944)

A problem faced by every society is how to distribute wealth—that is, *what are the principles established in a society that determine people's access to desired resources?* In the rare case where wealth is plentiful and people are few, there is, theoretically, no problem; everyone gets what they want. But if resources are scarce, or if, for whatever reason, human wants are great, some way must be devised to determine who gets what. In traditional societies, the most common ways of distributing goods were through sharing or gift giving, principles that we still recognize and use. If people had more than they needed, or others had less, resources were freely given. In the case of gift exchange or in systems of reciprocity, people gave things to others or helped with some task in the expectation that at some time in the future the recipient of the gift would offer some return. It is quite possible, theoretically, to organize even large-scale societies using the principles of sharing and gift exchange as the major means to distribute resources (see Graeber 2001).

Tribute or taxes are other ways to distribute wealth. In this case, goods or services—in the form of crops, animals, crafts, textiles, or money—are delivered or paid to a central authority (i.e., chief, lord, king, or state) that, after keeping a portion for its own expenses, redistributes the rest. Taxes that we pay to the government, for example, are used to finance government functions, while the remainder, ideally, is redistributed to fund such things as education, welfare, health programs, infrastructure (roads, water systems, waste removal, etc.), and the military.

Finally, there is the market. Marketplaces are thousands of years old. For centuries, traders, artisans, and farmers brought their goods to marketplaces and traded them for other goods or sold them for money. Virtually every town and city in the world going back thousands of years had its marketplaces or systems of markets where people could go and purchase or trade for whatever they needed. Today, of course, virtually the entire world is a marketplace. When we speak of "the market," we are referring to a principle of wealth distribution rather than a specific place, although the principle is the same; people produce things or supply services for other people in exchange for money.

Ideally people will supply only those goods and services for which there are demands, and, generally, a balance will be established regarding what is demanded and what is supplied. In his classic work *The Wealth of Nations* (1776), Adam Smith saw the workings of the market as an "invisible hand" by which a benevolent God administered a universe in which human happiness was maximized, an ideal system whereby each person, seeking his or her own ends, would contribute to the betterment of society as a whole. Thus, by seeking money and wealth, each person would work toward supplying what others needed or demanded. For Smith, the market represented a utopian vision in which wealth was perpetually created for the benefit of all.

For the market to work as Smith predicted, however, certain conditions had to be met, and three were particularly critical. First, to benefit from the market, individuals had to be able to exert demand, and to do that, they had to have money. If a person had no money, no one was going to produce anything for her or provide him or her with any services. Second, you had to have competition between people supplying goods and services to the market; with competition, producers were forced to auction their goods and services to buyers who were able to choose the best and most efficient among them, thus continually forcing producers to provide the best and the least expensive goods and services. Third, there had to be a means of enforcing contracts, a means of upholding the rule of law, and a means to supply information to people about the products and services available; each of these was to be the function of the state.

There is no doubt that the market as a means of distributing goods and services is highly efficient. However, because the conditions that Smith outlined for the working of the market are rarely met, most societies divide goods and services between those that should be supplied only by the market (e.g., luxury goods and other nonessentials) and those goods or services that should be available to everyone regardless of their ability to pay. In the United States, for example, education is considered a service that is so essential to the workings of a democratic society that it is available (indeed required) for everyone, at least to a point. Food, water, shelter, and health care are, to some degree in most societies, available to people outside the market. Thus, an additional function of the state is to decide what is and what is not too important to be left to the operation of the market.

But in addition to the problem of deciding what should be left to the market and what should be provided outside the market, there is the problem of what economists call *market externalities*. These are specific consequences of the workings of the market; some are positive, but most are negative. For example, operating with no regulation, the market can have dire consequences on the environment as more and more people exploit natural resources to produce goods and services that people demand. The sickness and death that result from the inability of people to pay for food is a market externality, as is the unequal distribution of wealth and its consequences.

In addition, in the same way that societies can vary regarding what should be distributed by the market and what should be available to all regardless of their ability to pay, societies can also vary to the extent to which they allow producers, manufacturers, and corporations to externalize their costs. For example, for years tobacco companies did not have to pay for the damage to smokers' health; the cost was externalized and paid by customers or by the general population in the form of health and insurance costs. The following chapters are, in one way or another, about market externalities, but it might help to better illustrate what we mean by *externalities* by examining a couple of items of our culture and the effects that their production and operation have on the larger society.

A PRIMER ON MARKET EXTERNALITIES: POLANYI'S PARADOX

In his classic book on the Industrial Revolution *The Great Transformation* Karl Polanyi posed what might be called "Polanyi's paradox": *How is it possible to get the market to perform efficiently without, at the same time, "annihilating the human and natural substance of society"?*

The paradox is beautifully illustrated in an ingenious piece of work called *Stuff: The Secret Lives of Everyday Things* by John C. Ryan and Alan Thein Durning (1997). They describe what happens in the rest of the world to supply an average North American with the stuff of everyday life such as a cup of coffee, a newspaper, a T-shirt, shoes, a car, a hamburger, French fries, and a glass of cola.

The coffee, for example, required around a hundred beans from a coffee tree grown, perhaps, on a small farm in Colombia; ranchers cleared the hillside to pasture cattle, while poor farmers used the less productive area to plant coffee and fruit trees. Prior to the 1980s, dense trees covered the coffee plants and harbored numerous birds and other wildlife. However, in the 1980s, these trees were cut down while farmers planted high-yielding varieties of coffee, in the process increasing soil erosion and decimating the bird population. With the absence of birds and other insect eaters, pests increased, thus requiring the use of more pesticides, applied by workers clothed in T-shirts and shorts who unavoidably inhaled residues of pesticides into their lungs. Because coffee is the second most traded commodity in the world, prices are low, as are the less-than-a-dollar-a-day wages that relegate workers to crowded shantytowns. After picking the beans for our cup of coffee, workers hand-fed the beans into a diesel-powered crusher, with the pulp dumped into the river. Dried by the sun, the remains of the beans (one pound of beans to two pounds of pulp) were shipped to New Orleans on a freighter made in Japan of Korean steel mined on the lands of indigenous peoples in western Australia and powered by Venezuelan oil.

Once in New Orleans, the beans were roasted for thirteen minutes at 400 degrees in ovens fueled by natural gas from Texas. Packed in bags constructed of polyethylene, nylon, aluminum foil, and polyester, the coffee was shipped in an eighteen-wheeler getting six miles to a gallon to a local warehouse and then taken by a smaller truck to our local grocery. From there, we brought it home in a large brown paper sack made in paper mills in Oregon, traveling by car and using about a one-fifth of a gallon of gasoline. Once home, we measured out the beans in a plastic scoop molded in New Jersey and spooned them into our Chinese-made grinder consisting of aluminum, copper, and plastic parts. We poured the coffee into an unbleached paper filter and into our plastic-and-steel drip coffeemaker. The water came by pipe from our local reservoir via a water-processing plant and was then heated to some 200 degrees, the electricity coming from our local gas-, coal-, oil-, or nuclear-powered utility. We drank from a cup made in Taiwan and added sugar from the cane fields that had once been sawgrass marshes south of Lake Okeechoobee, denuded of some 75 percent to 95 percent of its animal life largely by the growth of sugarcane fields.

That, of course, is only a partial story of our cup of coffee (see, e.g., Tucker 2011), but it should serve as an idea of the secret life or biography of a cup of coffee (see Kopytoff 1988). For the coffee consumer, the main economic consideration is its market price, about ten dollars a pound, or three dollars a cup. The problem is that the market price doesn't include the cost of the market externalities such as the damage to the environment caused by the coffee's production and distribution, the health and impoverished lives of the coffee workers, or the waste and decimation of water resources in the production process. These represent the externalized costs of coffee and are simply passed on to others or to future generations. The external costs of things are rarely calculated and, consequently, never directly paid. In fact, the economy could not function as it does if we had to pay the money costs of externalities (see Wallerstein 1997). Table II.1 provides some idea of how market factors—the things that go into the production, sale, distribution, and disposal of goods and services—translate into market externalities.

We can also understand Polanyi's paradox by examining an example of the market working as perfectly as it can—the case of Wal-Mart stores. The explicit goal of Wal-Mart is to sell

TABLE II.1 Market Factors and Negative Externalities

Market Factors	Possible Market Externality
Labor costs	Low wages, slavery, poverty, disease, hunger, alienation
Extraction of raw materials	Habitat devastation, pollution, military expansion
Transportation and distribution	Infrastructure creation and environmental consequences, pollution, etc.
Disposal costs	Pollution, disease, habitat destruction
Manufacturing and production costs	Environmental pollution, resource depletion
Advertisement and market expansion	Exploitation of children, conversion of relations of reciprocity into market relations, etc.
Maintaining market-friendly laws and regulations	Corruption, military expansion, distortion of the political process, etc.

things at the lowest cost. It even has a policy that a commodity that is unchanged from one year to the next be sold at a *lower* cost. This formula has worked extremely well, particularly for price-conscious shoppers. As of January 31, 2009, Wal-Mart operated 891 discount stores, 2,612 super centers, 153 Neighborhood Markets, and 602 Sam's Clubs in the United States. By 2012, Wal-Mart alone had over 8,500 stores worldwide, and, with over 2 million employees, is the largest employer in the world (Copeland and Labuski 2013). The company ranks second in sales in the world ($447 billion in 2012). In the United States, it is the largest grocer, toy seller, and furniture retailer. Wal-Mart is now the largest private employer in Mexico. Economists credit Wal-Mart for the nonexistent inflation in the United States and for about 12 percent of the economy's productivity gains in the second half of the 1990s. And admirers credit Wal-Mart with making goods more readily available to the poor. Analysts say that grocery prices, for example, drop an average of 10 percent to 15 percent in markets Wal-Mart has entered (see Fishman 2003).

Wal-Mart succeeds in lowering prices by pressuring its over 21,000 worldwide suppliers to be efficient and produce things at lower costs, savings that it then passes on to consumers. In effect, Wal-Mart is acting as Adam Smith's "invisible hand." Former labor secretary Robert B. Reich said, "Wal-Mart is the logical end point and the future of the economy in a society whose preeminent value is getting the best deal" (Lohr 2003).

But the sticker price of a Wal-Mart item is only part of the story, and this is where Polanyi's paradox comes in: In addition to the direct cost of an item (the sticker price), there is the externalized cost, as in the case of coffee. In order to provide the lowest prices, Wal-Mart forces those companies that supply their goods to reduce production and labor costs. In the United States, this has resulted in the shutting down of hundreds of factories and the loss of thousands of jobs as companies shift operations to countries with cheaper labor costs. Carolina Mills, which supplies thread yarn and finishing materials to apparel makers, half of whom sell to Wal-Mart, has closed ten of seventeen factories and reduced its labor force from 2,600 employees to 1,200 because its customers couldn't compete with clothing imported into the United States by Wal-Mart. In some cases, even companies that don't sell to Wal-Mart have had to reduce costs in order to compete. Hoover, for example, has been the leading name in vacuum cleaners in the United States for over a hundred years. Recently, Hoover's sales dropped 20 percent because of cheaper models being made in China for Wal-Mart. Hoover's parent company, Maytag, demanded that its workers in Ohio take a cut in insurance and other benefits; otherwise the company would move its production facilities to *maquiladoras* in Ciudad Juarez, Mexico (Fishman 2003).

Wal-Mart is one example of how commodities can be produced more cheaply by externalizing the costs of production and distribution.
(Marc F. Henning/Alamy.)

Wal-Mart imports 12 percent of all Chinese exports, and even in China, where wages are low, they insist on even more "efficiency." The Ching Hai Electric Works Co. in Shajing, China, makes several million electric fans per year, selling them under many of the world's leading brands and under two of their own. The workers were paid thirty-two dollars per month, about 40 percent below China's minimum monthly wage of fifty-six dollars per month. In the late 1990s, Wal-Mart demanded that the price of the fans be lowered, and they have since fallen from approximately seven dollars to four dollars per fan. But to do this, the manager of the plant fired half the workforce while continuing to produce the same number of fans. Consequently, the remaining workers must work fourteen hours a day (Fishman 2003).

The loss of jobs, the low pay, the environmental damage done in areas where environmental laws don't exist or aren't enforced, and the health costs to underpaid and overworked laborers represent the cost of commodities that don't appear in the sticker price. And it is probably not inaccurate to say that *as the sticker price of items goes down, the externalized costs go up.* The situation was summed up well by Steve Dobbins, president of thread maker Carolina Mills: "We want clean air, clear water, good living conditions, the best health care in the world," he said, "yet we aren't willing to pay for anything manufactured under those restrictions" (Fishman 2003).

Thus, to produce goods at the cheapest cost, certainly an admirable economic goal, we must use up more environmental and social capital. But it doesn't stop there. As corporations such as Wal-Mart succeed, they are able to exert political influence that dwarfs that of ordinary citizens in a democracy. For example, in 2012, Wal-Mart donated over two million dollars to favored political candidates, 54 percent going to Republicans and 46 percent to Democrats (Open Secrets ND). In 2011, Wal-Mart allocated almost 8 million dollars to lobbying activities that bought mention on 49 different Congressional legislative actions. Political contributions clearly translate into political influence, replacing corporate legislative agendas, which include rules and laws that increase market externalities, for those of citizen voters. While these agendas may on occasion overlap, they are clearly not the same.

Many of the problems we will be looking at in the following chapters—such as poverty, hunger, disease, environmental destruction, and ethnic conflict—represent, at least in part, market externalities, part of the cost of the goods and services that we crave. This fact is, or should be, relatively transparent. It certainly is no secret that Wal-Mart forces its suppliers to cut wages, reduce or eliminate health benefits, and move operations to places with no unions, few environmental regulations, and little if any worker protection. It is also no secret that the transport of goods from halfway around the world uses vast energy resources, or that local stores, if they are not put out of business by Wal-Mart, are forced to cut wages or lay off employees. *Why, then, are people not more concerned about market externalities?*

As we've mentioned, one of the tasks of the culture of capitalism is to mask from its members (or to allow its members to mask from themselves) the negative consequences of the market's operation. Corporations spend billions, for example, to distance themselves from the processes used to manufacture and distribute their products. They hide the "dirt" in the biographies of commodities through advertising and public relations efforts. They hide the effects of their production and distribution practices by controlling the information that is allowed to reach the public or through legislative or legal measures to discourage public criticism. The language we use often helps us hide negative market externalities. We speak of "malnutrition" rather than "starvation," somehow implying that it is the fault of the victim. Deadly riots, massacres, and genocides are blamed on "ancient hatreds," while the underlying economic factors are obscured or ignored. "Environmentalists" are labeled a "special interest group," rather than as properly concerned citizens. We develop ideologies that seek to explain global problems in ways that distance the problems from the operation of the market. One of the tasks of the following chapters is to examine some of the ways that we hide from ourselves, or ways that others hide from us, the consequences of our demand for perpetual economic growth. We'll begin, therefore, with one of the most common explanations for global problems—population growth.

5

Population Growth, Migration, and Urbanization

There is not now, nor has there ever been, too much global migration. The world would clearly be better off with more migration. The problem is, therefore, not that there is too much global migration, but, rather, that we do not yet have effective ways whereby the gainers from global migration can compensate the losers. The problem is not global migration. The problem is a lack of political will.

—TIMOTHY J. HATTON AND JEFFREY G. WILLIAMSON,
Global Migration and the World Economy

... the cities of the future, rather than being made out of glass and steel as envisioned by earlier generations of urbanists, are instead largely constructed out of crude brick, straw, recycled plastic, cement blocks, and scrap wood. Instead of cities of light soaring toward heaven, much of the twenty-first century urban world squats in squalor, surrounded by pollution, excrement, and decay. Indeed, the one billion city dwellers who inhabit postmodern slums might well look back with envy at the ruins of the sturdy mud homes of ÇatalHüyük in Anatolia, erected at the very dawn of city life nine thousand years ago.

— MIKE DAVIS, *Planet of the Slums*

Some modern research on the genetic structure of human populations suggests that we are all descended from a relatively small number of individuals, and no more than a few families, who lived in Central Africa as recently as 100,000 to 200,000 years ago. By 15,000 years ago, their progeny numbered 15 million (the present population of Mexico City). The world population at the time of Christ had increased to about 250 million (a little more than the present population of Indonesia) and on the eve of the Industrial Revolution had tripled to about 700 million (a little more than twice the size of the current population of the United States). In the following two centuries, the population increased at an annual growth rate of 6 per 1,000,

TABLE 5.1   Population, Annual Growth, Doubling Time, Projected Growth, 10,000 B.C. to A.D. 2050

Year	10,000 B.C.	0	1750	1950	2000	2025 (projected)	2050 (projected)
Population (millions)	16	252	771	2,330	6,100	7,810	9,039
Annual growth (%)	0.008	0.037	0.064	1.845	1.400	1.000	—
Doubling time (years)	8,369	1,854	1,083	116	51	70	—

Source: United Nations, 1998. *Revision of the World Population Estimates and Projections,* www.popin.org/pop1998/; Population Reference Bureau, 2011. *2011 World Population Data Sheet,* http://www.prb.org/Publications/Datasheets/2011/world-population-data-sheet/data-sheet.aspx/

reaching 2.5 billion by 1950. In the following five decades, it has more than doubled, at a growth rate of 18 per 1,000, to reach more than 6 billion in 2000. We passed 7 billion in 2012, and the UN estimates that we will almost reach 9 billion by 2050 (United Nations 2004). Growth in world population is summarized in Table 5.1.

The rate of population growth over the last sixty years has prompted concern that the world is poised on the brink of disaster; that we are running out of enough food to sustain the growing population; and that population growth is responsible for poverty, environmental destruction, and social unrest. Moreover, so the argument goes, economic development in poor countries is impossible as long as populations continue to rise, because any increase in economic output must be used to sustain the increased population instead of being invested to create new jobs and wealth. These concerns have led to concerted efforts by international agencies and governments to control the rate of population growth, especially in peripheral countries where it is highest (see Table 5.2).

A number of people, however, seriously question whether population growth is a problem. Some economists argue that population growth is a positive factor in economic development; some environmentalists claim that environmental destruction is a result of rapid industrialization and capitalist consumption and investment patterns, not population growth; and some religious authorities are opposed to any form of birth control.

In addition to growing, the earth's human population is moving. Over the past two centuries there have been major waves of global migration, the first from about 1870 to 1920 when some 600,000 to a million people a year moved, largely from Europe to the New World, and the second, beginning around 1980 and continuing today. Migration, along with population growth, has also generated alarm, so much so that political parties in the United States, Europe, and Australia have made controlling immigration a significant (if not only) policy concern.

TABLE 5.2   Population and Projected Population Growth for World Regions, 2009

	Population (millions)	Births per 1,000 Population	Deaths per 1,000 Population	Rate of Natural Increase (%)	Projected Population 2025	Projected Population 2050
World	6,810	20	8	1.2	8,087	9,421
More Developed	1,232	12	10	0.2	1,282	1,318
Less Developed	5,578	22	8	1.4	6,805	8,103
Less Developed (excluding China)	4,246	26	8	1.7	5,329	6,666
Least Developed	828	35	11	2.4	1,151	1,657

Source: Population Reference Bureau, 2009, http://www.prb.org/pdf09/09wpds_eng.pdf

As we shall see, however, the situations, both in terms of population growth and migration, are more complex than presented in public debates. To understand better the demographic and ideological issues involved in the population debates, we need first to examine the major frameworks used to explain population growth, the Malthusian or neo-Malthusian position, and the framework provided by demographic transition theory. We will try to show how they are seriously flawed, ethnocentric, and self-serving for core nations. Then we examine some of the factors known to determine how many children are born and specifically examine what anthropology can contribute to the debate over population growth. Then we will examine the issue of migration, particularly the economic impacts of both legal and illegal immigration, and finally examine urbanization and the growth of global slums.

THE MALTHUSIANS VERSUS THE REVISIONISTS

Interest in the effects of increasing population dates back at least as far as Reverend Thomas Malthus's famous *Essay on the Principle of Population,* written in 1798. This essay outlines his well-known argument that whereas population "increases in a geometrical ratio," the resources for survival, especially food, "increase only in an arithmetical ratio" (see Livi-Bacci 1992:76). Without preventive checks to control fertility, such as "moral restraint" or "marriage postponement," argued Malthus, population will constantly increase, deplete resources, and bring into play "positive checks"—famine, disease, and war—that will return population to a balance with resources.

Malthus had some historical confirmation for his ideas. For example, he predicted that as population rose and the demand on resources increased, food prices (e.g., that of grain) would increase and result in increased mortality rates. Indeed, this seemed to have been the case in Europe in the seventeenth and eighteenth centuries. Likewise, he predicted that a decreased demand because of population decrease would result in lower prices, decreased mortality, and a subsequent rise in population, exactly as occurred in Europe after the plague epidemics of the fourteenth century.

Malthus predicted that disaster was imminent. What he failed to foresee was that in the face of increasing population, innovations in agricultural techniques would result in constantly increasing food production. Even though the world population today is at least six times what it was in 1800, there is still more than enough food produced worldwide to support the population.

In spite of Malthus's failed predictions, others have recently revived his message, arguing that, although Malthus may have been wrong in his early projections, no one could foresee the explosive growth of population in the past fifty years. Food production, they say, is now beginning to fall behind population growth, and even innovations that improve production are only stopgap measures. Neo-Malthusians may disagree on how close we are to disaster, but they unanimously agree that unless we take measures to reduce population growth, especially in the periphery, the whole planet faces ruin. The consequences of this population growth, they say, are now all around us in overcrowded cities, polluted environments, increased crime, and massive immigration. But their arguments have the most far-reaching implications in policies regarding economic development. It is impossible, according to neo-Malthusians, for poor countries to escape poverty when their populations grow at a rate greater than 2 percent per year because resources that could be used to increase living standards must instead go to maintaining the people added to the population. Thus, any economic innovations will provide only temporary relief because the gains are quickly offset by the increase in population. They conclude that the only way economic development can provide benefits is for these countries to lower their birth rates. The governments of most countries must agree, because 127 countries, representing 94 percent of the world's population, express support for family planning.

Economist J. F. Meade (1967; see also Livi-Bacci 1992) provided a parable to illustrate what he saw as the folly of population growth. He tells of two imaginary countries, Sterilia and Fertilia. Sterilia is a coastal country with a democratic government and an ethnically mixed population. Fertilia, an inland country with a homogeneous population, is ruled by upper-class landowners who have little contact with the outside world. Both countries were colonized, and both received their independence at the same time and had similar demographic characteristics—high fertility (birth rate) and high mortality (death rate). Mortality, however, was sharply reduced in both countries by DDT spraying, which eliminated malaria-bearing mosquitoes, and penicillin administration, which controlled several diseases.

Sterilia's government promoted economic development and to that end instituted a well-organized family planning program. The imperial elite of Fertilia, however, did little to control their growing population. Consequently, the surplus rural population flooded into the cites, and economic capital had to be used to support the growing number of poor, leaving little to invest in education, roads, communications, and health. People in Sterilia, however, began having smaller families and were able to save money, which became capital for economic investment. Their well-fed, healthy, efficient workers produced and sold products and goods that earned more money to be invested in education, creating a still more efficient and profitable workforce. Consequently, Sterilia surged ahead, with growing commerce, increasing literacy, and expanding health programs, whereas Fertilia became trapped in a spiral of increasing poverty. The moral of Meade's parable is clear: Those countries that institute successful programs of birth control will prosper; those that do not will suffer economic and social decline. *But is that really true?*

The Case of India and China

We do have a real-life Sterilia and Fertilia—China and India, countries that together represent 38 percent of the population of the periphery. Since the early 1950s, India, the Fertilia of our parable, has promoted family planning programs but with little success. When early attempts to convince couples to have fewer children failed, the government tried more coercive means, attempting to pass laws requiring sterilization after the third child (one province passed such a law but never enforced it). When that failed, the government attempted to convince women to use an intrauterine device, but this failed because of exaggerated rumors about the dangers of the devices. Oral contraceptives were never authorized for use in India. Consequently, the policy of population reduction has not been successful. Although the birth rate fell from 5.97 children per woman in 1950 to 3.3 in 2000, increases in life expectancy decreased the population growth rate over the same period from 2 percent to only 1.8 percent per year.

China, our real-life Sterilia, embarked on a concerted effort to control population growth in 1970, twenty years after India. In 1980 they developed a program to ensure that their population of 996 million would not exceed 1.2 billion by the year 2000. The government instituted policies to raise the age at which people could marry, increase birth intervals, and limit the number of children couples could have to two. Provincial leaders were assigned birth quotas, and groups were formed to encourage the use of contraceptives, sterilization, and abortion, which was widespread, free, and did not require the husband's consent. Later, a one-child policy was encouraged by providing incentives for those complying (higher wages, larger houses, priority for children's education, and free medical care) and penalties for those not complying (wage cuts, smaller houses, and lower priorities for education and medical care).

In spite of public resistance and a population with a large number of women of reproductive age, China has succeeded where India failed. Population growth fell from 2.2 percent in 1970 to 1.4 percent in 1990 and to 0.877 percent in 2000. Whereas India's population in 2025 will be four times what it was in 1950, China's population will have increased by a factor of less than three. One would predict, therefore, that the rate of economic growth will be higher in China than in India.

But that hasn't happened. As we noted in Chapter 1, both countries have among the most thriving economies in the world. India's growth rate was more than twice the world average—more than 9 percent in 2006 and 2007, falling to about 5 percent in the wake of 2008 global downturn. China's economy grew at almost 8 percent in early 2009, in spite of the global

This billboard in China promotes family planning and idealizes the single-child nuclear family. The fact that the child is female is a significant attempt to make acceptable a single female child in a society in which only males can continue the ancestral line.
(Alain Le Garsmeur/ Documentary/Corbis.)

downturn, after averaging some 8 percent to 11 percent over the previous decade. Moreover, if we compare economic growth and standard of living as measured by the gross domestic product (GDP) of poor countries in general to population growth in those countries, there is no relationship. If we measure progress, as some have suggested, by an index of social freedom, India ranks well above China (see Livi-Bacci 1992:186–187). There are still significant differences between India and China: China has done notably better in improving the quality of life of the bulk of its population, ranking ahead of India in areas such as literacy, health care, life expectancy, and nutrition. But these improvements are largely attributed to China's social policies and seem to have little to do with the rate of population growth.

Economists and demographers who have examined the connection between economic development and population growth in other countries have discovered little evidence that population growth inhibits economic development. In fact, historically, population growth correlates with economic prosperity, whereas population decline or stability is generally associated with economic stagnation or decline. For example, from 1820 to 1987, the population of the four leading Western nations (Great Britain, France, Germany, and the United States) grew by a factor of 5.5, whereas their combined GDP (in constant prices) increased by ninety-three. In other words, while population increased five times, production increased seventeenfold. After reviewing studies that examine the relationship between demographic and economic growth, demographer Massimi Livi-Bacci (1992:145) concluded that during the past two centuries, population growth has not hindered economic development and that quite possibly the reverse is true, with the countries that experienced the greatest population increase assuming the leading role in the global economy.

Does the real-life failure of the parable of Fertilia and Sterilia mean there is no connection between population growth and economic development? That's difficult to say, but it does suggest that the connection is obscured by factors that probably cancel each other out. It also means population growth has not been an insurmountable obstacle to economic development.

The Issue of Carrying Capacity

Even if we accept the idea that population has not yet inhibited economic growth, *can we say, as many neo-Malthusians do, that although we haven't felt the impact yet, the reduced doubling time of the population will soon result in the human population exceeding the carrying capacity of the earth?* Biologists use the term *carrying capacity* to denote the maximum number of organisms a given environment will support. For example, we can examine the types of food that sustain wolves in a specific environment and, by calculating how much of that food is available, estimate the number of wolves the environment will support. This is the kind of assumption Malthusians make about the human population: Given food and other resources on the planet, how many people can survive before those resources are depleted? For example, David Pimentel and his associates (1999) estimate that, because of declining fertile land, declining water resources for irrigation, and declining fertilizer usage, by the year 2100, the world will be able to support only a population of 2 billion people living at a standard half that of the United States in the 1990s.

However, the problem with applying the theory of carrying capacity to human beings is that our capacity for culture and symbolic thought enables us constantly to alter our diets and the way we exploit the environment for food. It is true, for example, that a given environment will support only so many people who live by gathering wild plants and hunting wild animals. But when a gathering and hunting society exceeded the population a given area could support and were restricted from migrating to another area, they could and did begin to plant and harvest their own plants and herd and breed their own animals. Later, when agricultural populations began to grow, they started farming and developing techniques that allowed them to grow more food on the same land. Human beings are capable of constantly changing the rules of subsistence by altering their resource base. In fact, estimates of the Earth's carrying capacity vary widely, from 7.5 billion to 147 billion, depending on the technology employed to produce food (Cohen 1995; Livi-Bacci 1992:207). Consequently, it is difficult if not impossible to predict when our ability to provide for additional people will end, if ever. And that is one of the major arguments between Malthusians and Revisionists.

If we conclude that the alarms raised by neo-Malthusian arguments are unsubstantiated, it is fair to ask, *Why do Malthusian alarms dominate the dialogue about the so-called problems of population growth?* More specifically, *Why are their arguments so attractive to politicians and policy planners, and why do people so readily accept their assumptions?*

The Ideology of Malthusian Concerns

One of the important questions addressed by anthropologists concerns why people believe what they do about themselves and the world—that is, *What social purpose or function does a particular belief serve?* For example, if people believe that witches exist and that they will punish people who harm others, the belief will serve to enforce proper social behavior. If people believe that gazing at someone with envy can harm that person, members of that society will be reluctant to flaunt their wealth, fearing it might attract an "evil eye." It is legitimate to examine the social function or purpose of any viewpoint, even those that are scientifically founded. Regardless of whether Malthusian assumptions are correct, it is legitimate to ask what social interests or purposes might be advanced by their acceptance (see Barnes 1974). Put another way, *Do Malthusian arguments about population growth mask other concerns or social interests?*

For example, population growth was not, for Thomas Malthus, the major issue. What concerned him was the rising number of poor in England, why they should exist, and what should be done about them. Poverty, according to Malthus, was not a consequence of expanding industrialism, enclosure laws that evicted people from common lands, or the need of manufacturers for a source of inexpensive labor; it arose from the laws of nature, the discrepancy between the powers of reproduction and the ability to expand food production. People were poor because there were too many of them and because they kept having children in spite of their poverty. Providing relief to the poor, argued Malthus, would simply encourage them to have more children. Instead, they should be forced to delay marriage (Malthus was opposed to all forms of birth control). In 1834, encouraged to a large extent by Malthus's writings, the British government revised the so-called Poor Law, repealing various forms of relief that had been in place for centuries and leaving the destitute to decide whether their condition required their access to public shelters, which were deliberately made into places of horror (Polgar 1975:86).

The Malthusian position assumes that if poverty exists, it must be because of overpopulation, which is the fault of those people who, because of a lack of moral standards, refuse to change their reproductive behavior. There also may have been in the Malthusian position a fear that the army of the poor gathering in cities such as London would stimulate revolution, much as it did in France in 1787.

Malthus's ideas did not go unchallenged during the nineteenth century. Karl Marx, as we examined earlier, saw poverty not as a consequence of excess population but as a condition produced by the capitalist mode of production, which required a surplus of labor, an "industrial reserve army" condemned to compete for wages, with the losers doomed to unemployment and underemployment. It is their exclusion or partial exclusion from the economy and their dependence on wage labor, not their numbers, said Marx, that determined their impoverished condition.

Malthusian explanations for poverty and demographic theory were resurrected by neo-Malthusians after World War II. In his 1968 book *The Population Bomb,* biologist Paul Ehrlich, whose work is among the most influential in reviving Malthusian theory, described how he came to discover the significance of the population problem. It dawned on him, he said, "one stinking hot night in Delhi."

> As we crawled through the city [in a taxi], we entered a crowded slum area. The temperature was well over 100 degrees and the air was a haze of dust and smoke. The streets seemed alive with people. People eating, people washing, people sleeping. People visiting, people arguing and screaming. People thrust their hands through the taxi window, begging. People defecating and urinating. People clinging to buses. People herding animals. People, people, people, people. As we moved slowly through the mob, hand horn squawking, the dust, noise, heat, and cooking fires gave the scene a hellish aspect. Would we ever get to our hotel? All three of us were, frankly, frightened … since that night I've known the feel of overpopulation. (Ehrlich 1968:15)

As political scientist Mahmood Mamdani (1972) pointed out, had Ehrlich been in Times Square in New York or Picadilly Circus in London, he would have been in the midst of an even larger population, but those situations would not likely have led Ehrlich to fear overpopulation. Ehrlich was disturbed not by the number of people but by their poverty and the physical threat posed by a poor and potentially unruly populace.

In addition to those who blamed the poor for their poverty and targeted them for population reduction, Malthusian demographic and social theory also appealed to eugenicists, those who saw poverty as a consequence of faulty genes rather than national social or economic policy. Eugenic theory is rooted incorrectly in Charles Darwin's ideas about natural selection and "fitness." Eugenicists reason that Darwin's ideas can be applied to human populations and that if people with defective genetic endowments had more offspring than those with superior genetic endowments, the quality of the human race (or German "race" or British "race") would decline. Consequently, for eugenicists, it makes sense to promote policies that discourage or prevent people with defective genes from reproducing, while encouraging people with superior genes to have as many offspring as possible. Clearly, they reason, people are poor because they have a faulty heredity.

Whether a place is perceived as "overpopulated" or not, often depends on its degree of opulence. Although these crowded streets of Seoul, South Korea, are packed, few would see a "population problem." The poverty represented by this line of beggars in Varanasi, India, would more likely create concerns about "overpopulation."   (Left: AP Photo/Yun Jai-hyoung. Right: DIPTENDU DUTTA/AFP/Getty Images.)

Eugenics has long been discredited by most scientists, although it sometimes appears in modified forms, as it has recently in the debate over the inheritance of intelligence and IQ (see Cohen 1998; Robbins 2008:210ff.). But in the heyday of eugenics in the 1920s, groups such as the Committee to Study and Report on the Best Means of Cutting Off the Defective Germ-Plasm of the United States concluded, "Society must look upon the germ-plasm as belonging to society and not merely to the individual who carries it" (Polgar 1975:189).

Another advocate of Malthusian demography, Garrett Hardin, wrote,

> How can we reduce reproduction? ... But in the long run a purely voluntary system selects for its own failure: non-cooperators outbreed cooperators. So what restraints shall we employ? A policeman under every bed? ... We need not titillate our minds with such horrors, for we already have at hand an acceptable technology—sterilization.... If parenthood is only a privilege, and if parents see themselves as trustees of the germ plasm and guardians of the rights of future generations, then there is hope for mankind. (Polgar 1975:190)

We will probably never know how many women in the world or in the United States were sterilized by those who felt they were ridding the population of "defective" genes. In *The Legacy of Malthus* (1977), Allan Chase estimated that up until 1975, half of the 1 million sterilizations performed yearly in the United States were involuntary.

It should be apparent that it is difficult historically to separate advocates of birth control from racist and eugenic agendas. In the past, and perhaps today, programs to control or reduce population have often masked racist and sexist policies aimed at controlling the poor. Early concerns about population growth were directed at the poor in the core—the urban poor of England, blacks and Native Americans in the United States, immigrants, and the rural poor. It was not until the 1950s that Western nations began to concern themselves with the fertility of people in the periphery. One question is, *Why, in the 1950s and 1960s, did population growth in the periphery begin to concern Western governments?*

One reason may be the same as that for concern over poor populations in the core: It cost money to try to help them. Malthusians like Paul Ehrlich embraced ideas such as those advocated by William and Paul Paddock, who in their 1967 book *Famine—1975* advocated using the military triage policy for food aid. The Paddocks recommended that the United States use its excess food production to halt starvation only in those countries that would submit to its power:

> During the coming Age of Food that nation which has the most food will be, if it uses that food as a source of power, the strongest nation. This will be, then, clearly an era which the United States can dominate—if the United States picks up the challenge. (Paddock and Paddock 1967:232)

Furthermore, advocates of population control share a concern for mass migration of the poor to their countries as well as for social unrest that could upset economic and political stability in the countries of the periphery. For example, a National Security Study memorandum produced in 1974 by the National Security Council at the request of U.S. secretary of state Henry Kissinger (Mumford 1996) concluded that population growth in the periphery is a threat to U.S. national security for four reasons: (1) Larger nations will gain greater political power, (2) populous nations may deny the United States access to needed strategic materials, (3) a growing population will include a large number of young people who may be more likely to challenge global power structures, and (4) the growing population may threaten U.S. investors in those countries. The memorandum targets India, Brazil, Egypt, Nigeria, Indonesia, the Philippines, Bangladesh, Pakistan, Mexico, Thailand, Turkey, Ethiopia, and Colombia as the countries of greatest concern.[1]

Thus, as Steven Polgar (1972;1975) suggested, U.S. foreign policy was driven less by a concern for overpopulation than by a concern that increasing population in the periphery hindered the possibility of raising the income level (and purchasing power) of people in the periphery and by a concern that increased populations might represent a political and economic threat to the United States. Polgar said that population concerns in core countries stem not from a fear of overpopulation but from a change in the role of exploited countries. People in the periphery were needed at first for labor and later for markets. In fact, until the 1940s, core countries were unconcerned with population growth in the periphery, and they complained it was too slow. Once the need for certain raw materials declined as synthetics were developed, and as the poverty of these people precluded their being turned into consumers, they ceased being useful, especially because they became potential revolutionaries, migrants, and criminals. The subjects became burdens.

Not everyone who believes there is a population problem or that poverty is a consequence of overpopulation is a racist or an imperialist. But people have been far too ready to accept the basic Malthusian assumptions without question. The consequence is that Malthusian explanations for poverty, environmental destruction, disease, and social unrest may mask other, more pertinent, reasons for these problems and divert our attention from them. But it is not only Malthusian assumptions that have dominated the public discussions about population.

DEMOGRAPHIC TRANSITION THEORY

The other framework that dominates discussions of the population problem is the *theory of demographic transition* (see Table 5.3).

According to this theory, world population growth increased only very slowly from human beginnings to around 1750. This relatively steady state of population growth was maintained largely because high birth rates were offset by high death rates. Toward the end of the eighteenth century and the beginning of the nineteenth, mortality began to decline in developed countries

---

[1] The original memorandum is available online at Africa 2000 at www.africa2000.com/INDX/nssm200.htm. A link can also be found at the Web site for this book at www.plattsburgh.edu/legacy/Population_Resources.htm.

TABLE 5.3 Stages of Demographic Transition			
	Birth Rate	**Mortality Rate**	**Rate of Population Growth**
Stage 1	High	High	Stable
Stage 2	High	Low	Accelerated
Stage 3	Low	Low	Stable

because of advances in medicine and sanitation, whereas birth rates remained the same; consequently, population rose rapidly. Then, because of population pressures and the availability of contraception, birth rates declined to close to "replacement levels" and the rate of population growth stabilized, at least in the developed countries (see Coale 1974).

The population rise in the periphery came later, beginning in the mid-twentieth century, but was particularly explosive because mortality rates were reduced much more quickly than in core countries, especially among children. Fertility rates in the periphery, according to demographic transition theory, are only now beginning to decline in response to population growth. This occurs when the increasing costs of education and child care in modernizing societies, along with the availability of modern forms of contraception, provide the incentives and means for people to reduce their family size.

The demographic transition model shares assumptions with neo-Malthusian theory: It, too, links lowered fertility with economic development. However, instead of arguing that economic development requires lower fertility, demographic transition theorists suggest that lowered fertility will result from economic development. The problem with this model is that it makes some decidedly ethnocentric assumptions.

First, it assumes that throughout history, fertility rates have always been uniformly high. Demographic transition theorists reason that high fertility rates were necessary to balance the number of deaths that occurred because of the harsh living conditions of preindustrial peoples. Yet there was clearly an ethnocentric bias in this assumption; although demographic theorists recognized that fertility rates among preindustrial Europeans did vary depending on the age at which marriage occurred, as we'll see, they assumed that preindustrial non-Europeans would not or could not control their fertility rates.

Second, the demographic transition model assumes that the only way of stabilizing population growth is to make available Western methods of birth control and contraception. As we shall see, the model significantly ignores variations in fertility that are based on various economic and social factors as well as the fact that preindustrial populations were significantly healthier than previously thought.

Third, it assumes that the resistance of people in poor countries to adopt Western standards of fertility is the result of irrational thinking, outmoded religious values, or traditional or fatalistic worldviews. Fertility control, in contrast, is consistently viewed as rational and modern (Caldwell 1982:119).

Finally, some claim that demographic transition theory has its own ideological bias—that its goal is to provide an alternative to Marx's idea of a surplus reserve of workers. As we noted earlier, Marx saw capitalism as creating a surplus population because competition for scarce jobs would allow merchants, manufacturers, and governments to keep wages as low as possible. If labor were scarce, however, employers would have to compete for laborers and wages would increase. If Marx were correct, one would have expected colonial governments to encourage population growth in the periphery, rather than restrict it. In fact, that is exactly what happened. In the early twentieth century, colonial governments in Africa worried about the low population and subsequent lack of laborers and did everything they could to increase the birth rate.

Demographic transition theorists blame high population growth in the periphery on the people themselves, arguing that capitalist expansion, rather than causing the problem of population growth, can cure it. In other words, demographic transition models see economic development as an answer to the problem; Marx viewed economic development as a cause (O'Brien 1994).

Demographic transition theorists generally ignore the fact that human populations have consistently adjusted fertility rates to local economic and social conditions. Moreover, if that is so, we can assume that high fertility in peripheral countries is not solely the result of a lack of ability to control births and that it is not, given the context of people's lives, irrational. In other words, high fertility rates are not the result of ignorance, outmoded religious values, or lack of education, but the result of social or economic factors that people, largely women, react to in order to adjust the size of their families. However, to understand how populations regulate their size without having access to modern means of birth control, we need to answer the question, *How have human societies historically controlled the size of their population?*

A Primer on the Determinants of Population Growth and Decline

At its simplest, worldwide population growth is a factor of only two things—births and deaths. If the rate of death is lower than the rate of birth, population increases. If deaths exceed births, population declines. In regional populations, migration also contributes to population increases or declines, but for now let's focus on natural increases or decreases. The question is, *What economic, social, and cultural factors dictate birth and death rates?*

FERTILITY Birth rates are a factor of the number of children born in a given population; this is determined by biological and social factors, including the frequency of births during a woman's fecund period and the portion of the fecund period—between puberty and menopause—used for reproduction.

Frequency of births—the interval between births—is determined by a number of factors, including the following:

- Period of infertility after birth: There is a period after birth when ovulation does not occur.
- Time between ovulation and conception: Although some women may conceive during the first ovulation after giving birth, others do not. The average is five to ten months.
- Average length of pregnancy (nine months).
- Fetal mortality: About one in five recognized pregnancies ends in miscarriage. (The actual percentage of interrupted pregnancies, including those that are unrecognized, may approach 80 percent.)
- Presence or absence of birth control techniques.

Of these factors, the length of time between births and the presence or absence of birth control techniques provide for most of the variation in birth rates. Length of time between births can be influenced by various cultural factors. For example, breast-feeding suppresses ovulation. In societies in which children are not weaned until the age of three, four, or five years, breast-feeding leads to greater intervals between births. Attitudes toward breast-feeding vary significantly: In some societies it is encouraged and expected; in others it is discouraged, perhaps because of concerns about body image or because it has sexual connotations.

Economic and consumption patterns may also influence breast-feeding. For example, breast-feeding in the periphery has markedly decreased in the past thirty to forty years because of increased advertising and sales of powdered infant formula. Thus, cultural or social factors that inhibit breast-feeding, especially in the absence of modern birth control methods, may result in shorter spacing between births and an increase in fertility and population growth.

Many societies practice a postpartum sexual taboo, a rule that women should not have sexual intercourse for a set period of time after the birth of a child. The period can vary from a few months to a few years, but regardless of the length, the taboo is likely to increase birth spacing.

Thus, even leaving aside the influence of modern birth control techniques, the spacing of births through so-called natural means may vary from eighteen to forty-five months (1.5 to 3.5 years).

A second major factor in fertility is the fecund period used for reproduction, or the number of years in which a woman can conceive. This, too, can vary considerably because of cultural, social, or economic factors. Biological fecundity is the period shortly after the onset of menses until the onset of menopause; this can range from eleven years of age to over fifty years of age, although the average is fifteen years of age to forty. More importantly, however, is cultural fecundity, the age at which a woman becomes sexually active. This is determined in most societies by age at marriage, which varies, on the average, from fifteen to twenty-five years of age.

Combining the minimum and maximum period between births attributable to natural factors with the minimum and maximum age at marriage produces two very different population growth scenarios (see Livi-Bacci 1992:13). Assuming a fifteen-year reproductive period (fecundity lasting from age twenty-five to age forty) with a maximum interval between births produces a fertility rate of 4.3 children per woman:

$$\frac{\text{15-year reproductive period}}{\text{3.5-year birth interval}} = 4.3 \text{ children}$$

However, assuming a reproductive period of twenty-five years (fecundity lasting from age fifteen to age forty) and minimum birth spacing of 1.5 years produces a fertility rate of 16.7 children per woman:

$$\frac{\text{25-year reproductive period}}{\text{1.5-year birth interval}} = 16.7 \text{ children}$$

The latter condition is not likely to be realized because it does not account for the increased risk of death or pathological conditions resulting from childbearing that may lower fecundity; in fact, the highest fertility rates recorded range from eleven to twelve children per woman. However, the aforementioned projections provide some idea of the possible range of differences in fertility rates based solely on cultural factors, such as age at marriage and age of weaning, independent of the availability and use of modern contraceptive techniques.

Anthropologists have also examined the extent to which other cultural practices, such as polygamy and monogamy, affect birth rates. For example, some predict that polygamy—the practice of a man having more than one wife—might lower birth rates because the frequency of intercourse with each wife would be lower than in a monogamous marriage. Studies, however, have been inconclusive. Frequency of sexual intercourse itself is another culturally determined variable that may affect fertility rates but which also has not been shown to influence fertility rates significantly (see Nag 1975).

DEATH   A second major determinant of population growth is death, particularly the average life expectancy in a population. Most important is the percentage of the reproductive period realized in the life expectancy ranges. For example, in a population with a life expectancy of twenty years, the number of women who live through their full reproductive period is far less than in a population with a life expectancy of sixty years. In fact, demographers have calculated that with a life expectancy at birth of twenty years, only 29.2 percent of the potential reproductive period is lived, whereas with a life expectancy of eighty years, 98.2 percent of the potential fecund period is lived (Livi-Bacci 1992:19).

Most demographers have assumed that mortality rates in preindustrial societies were consistently high, but, as we shall see, that is probably mistaken. It seems we have consistently underestimated the general health levels of preindustrial societies.

The other major mortality factor in population growth is infant mortality, especially because this is where the greatest variation in life expectancy rates occur. It is also an area in which control on population growth can be exercised with the practice of infanticide and abortion. For example, one factor in death rates may be preference for male or female children, a preference that may be determined by economic needs. In societies that practice traditional agriculture, there is evidence that boys and girls are equally valued as farm workers. In early industrial society, however, when wage labor began to be more prevalent, there was a preference for boys, a preference that gradually began to subside as women entered the factory workforce (Harris and Ross 1987a:156).

MIGRATION   Migration is another factor in population growth rates. Although migration may not appear to influence world population, it can influence regional patterns of population growth and decline (and, consequently, influence global population; see Manning 1990). For example, migration can affect reproductive rates: A population in which many people migrate may feel reduced population pressure, which may result in earlier marriages and rising birth rates. If more men migrate, fewer women may marry, causing the birth rate to decline. Migration rates may in turn be affected by cultural factors: In agricultural areas that practice impartible inheritance, in which land is passed on undivided to an older or younger child, those who do not inherit are more likely to migrate out; in agricultural societies that practice partible inheritance, in which land is divided among some or all children, people are less likely to leave.

Other factors can influence the rate of population growth, such as the percentage of a population of childbearing age and factors relating to environmental constraints. But what is important, and sometimes ignored by demographic transition theorists, is that populations have in the past been able to maintain population stability without modern methods of birth control; dramatic increases in population growth have sometimes occurred because of economic or social factors, not because modern health or sanitation practices reduced death rates. Because this is critical for understanding some of the biases in alarmist projections of population growth, let's examine a few historic cases of demographic transitions.

Some Examples of Demographic Change

To illustrate how the cultural and social factors previously outlined can influence rates of population growth independent of modern birth control methods, let's look briefly at three cases of demographic change: the case of prehistoric gathering and hunting societies, the story of French Canadian fertility, and demographic changes in Ireland in the late eighteenth and early nineteenth centuries. We will see, as Marvin Harris and Eric Ross (1987a) noted, that historic populations did adjust their fertility rates to fit local economic and environmental conditions.

THE FIRST DEMOGRAPHIC TRANSITION   One of the assumptions of demographic transition theorists is that preagricultural peoples suffered from high mortality that was balanced by correspondingly high fertility to keep the population from dying out. Let's examine the first great demographic transition of 10,000 to 12,000 years ago, when human populations began to switch from gathering and hunting to agriculture.

We know from archaeological evidence and research that, among gatherers and hunters, population growth rates before 10,000 B.C. were slow. However, chemical and anthropometric analysis of skeletal remains and ethnographic studies reveal that gatherers and hunters had fewer health problems than later agricultural and industrial peoples; in addition, the rate of infant mortality was comparable to or well below that of European rates up to the nineteenth century and below those of peripheral countries through the mid-twentieth century (Cohen 1994:281–282). Moreover, life expectancy was relatively high, around thirty years—higher than some nineteenth-century Western countries and higher than that in many peripheral countries until recently. If

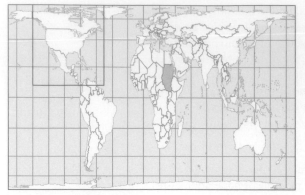

Canada

infant mortality was lower than many have assumed and life expectancy was higher yet the rate of population growth was low, then there must have been other means of controlling population size.

Assuming life expectancy varied from twenty-five to thirty-five years and that a woman's reproductive period extended from ages fourteen to twenty-nine, with birth spacing of twenty-three months, we would expect six births per woman; if three of these children survived, there would be a 50 percent increase in population for each generation. Because we know this did not occur, there must have been some limit placed on population growth. War and conflict between groups, given what we know about conflict among gatherers and hunters, cannot account for that much population loss, and episodic disasters would not have occurred with the frequency required to check population at that level.

The only other way population growth could have been limited is through a check on fertility. Research among contemporary gatherers and hunters, such as the Ju/wasi of Namibia studied by Nancy Howell (1979), shows that they have on average 4.7 children, well below the average in the periphery of six to eight. Howell suggested that the leanness characteristic of these populations is associated with late menarche, irregular ovulation, long postpartum amenorrhea (suppression of menses), and early menopause. She also suggested that an active physical life stimulated the contraceptive hormone prolactin in gathering and hunting populations, as does exercise in contemporary female athletes. Probably of greater influence is prolonged breast feeding, which would have suppressed ovulation and resulted in greater birth spacing. Moreover, it is likely that abortion and infanticide played a major role in keeping population growth levels at near zero (Cohen 1994; Polgar 1972).

Regardless of the reason, gatherers and hunters do have lower fertility rates than sedentary neighbors, and research shows that their fertility levels increase when they settle. In other words, gathering and hunting peoples were able to control fertility and adjust it to changing conditions.

THE FRENCH CANADIANS People have not only been able to maintain low fertility levels when conditions required it, but they have also been able to increase their rate of growth. French Canadians represent a classic case of demographic success. In the seventeenth century, 15,000 people migrated from France to what is now Quebec; some of these moved on, and in 1680 the population was about 10,000 people. In 100 years, from 1684 to 1784, the population grew from 12,000 to 132,000—an elevenfold increase representing an annual growth rate of 2.4 percent. Because only approximately one-third of the original settlers established families, it is estimated that the vast majority of the current 8 million French Canadians are descended from some 1,425 women.

The demographic success of French Canadians was due not to declining death rates but to high birth rates resulting from early marriages. Probably because of a higher proportion of males in the population, women married at ages fifteen to sixteen; moreover, unlike women in France, widows in Quebec had little trouble remarrying and consequently giving birth to more children. Thus, women in Quebec averaged only twenty-five months between pregnancies, compared to twenty-nine months in France. Finally, there was a lower mortality rate and a life expectancy five years greater in Quebec than in France, perhaps because low population density kept down the spread of disease. Of the Quebec pioneers who began families, each couple had 6.3 children, of whom 4.2 married; consequently, the population doubled in thirty years. The 4.2 children of each family in turn produced an average of thirty-four offspring—that is, each original couple had more than fifty children and grandchildren. Moreover, daughters of pioneers had even higher fertility rates than their mothers and grandmothers; those marrying between fifteen and nineteen years of age had an average of 11.4 offspring, compared to 10.1 for the original pioneers marrying between the ages of fifteen and nineteen (which contrasted with 9.5 in northwest France, where most of the pioneers came from).

Table 5.4 compares the number of offspring of women in the area from which the pioneers migrated with that for pioneer women and their offspring.

The fertility rate of French Canadians in the eighteenth century is among the highest ever recorded. Finally, some people assume religion was a factor in the fertility of Quebec women; however, today, with Catholicism still the dominant religion in Quebec, as it was in the seventeenth and eighteenth centuries, the province has one of the lowest birth rates in the world.

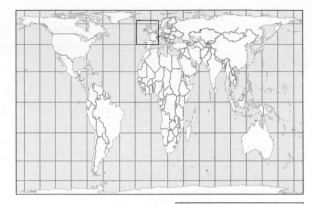

Ireland

THE CASE OF IRELAND The case of Ireland reveals some of the mechanisms through which people can raise their fertility levels in response to local economic conditions and demands of colonial powers. At the beginning of the eighteenth century, population growth in Ireland was relatively low. People married late, reducing the fecund period, and mortality was high, life expectancy generally being under thirty years. Then from 1780 to 1840, the population doubled from 4 million to more than 8 million. There seems little doubt that the reason was that women began to marry earlier, between ages fifteen and twenty, and in some areas even younger (Connell 1965:425). The question is, *Why were Irish women marrying earlier?*

Marriages in Ireland were arranged but only when the prospective bride and groom had access to land to farm. Before the late eighteenth century, marriage occurred at a relatively late age—between twenty and twenty-five years for women—because there was not enough land to support early marriage. Two things happened that increased the availability of land and encouraged earlier marriages. Virtually all the farms in Ireland were owned by British landlords who extracted rents from the tenants. Their profits rose when a new landholding was created, so they had a vested interest in increasing the number of farms. In addition, population was rising in England in the late eighteenth century, increasing the demand for food, particularly corn. Therefore, landlords who increased their number of farms and the amount of land devoted to corn production could realize greater profits. As a result, landlords subdivided farms into smaller and smaller plots, reclaimed swamps, and extended farming into mountainous areas.

Families were able to subsist on smaller plots of land than before because of the potato. Introduced to Ireland in the sixteenth century, the potato had become the staple subsistence crop of the Irish farmer. Potato cultivation is very productive: An acre of potatoes can feed a family of six, including their livestock. A barrel of 280 pounds of potatoes can feed a family of five for a

TABLE 5.4 **Fertility Rates of Women in Northwest France Compared to Pioneer Women in Quebec and Their Offspring**

Age at Marriage	No. of Offspring, NW France	No. of Offspring, Pioneer Women, Quebec	No. of Offspring, Daughters of Pioneers
15–19	9.5	10.1	11.4
20–24	7.6	8.1	9.5
25–29	5.6	5.7	6.3

Source: See also MassimiLivi-Bacci, 1992. *A Concise History of World Population*. Cambridge: Blackwell.

week at a daily consumption rate of eight pounds per person. Estimates are that people ate about ten pounds a day, which, along with a liter of milk, would provide some 3,800 calories along with all necessary nutrients. This allowed landlords to divide land into smaller parcels, providing a greater number of farms.

Thus, from 1791 to 1831, the amount of agricultural land increased, whereas the size of individual farming plots became smaller. The result was an increase in the number of farming plots, which permitted people to marry earlier, resulting in a rate of population increase of greater than 1 percent per year.

In 1845, a potato fungus struck, destroying the harvest of 1846 entirely and leading to the great famine of 1846–1847. This and epidemics resulted in 1.1 million to 1.5 million deaths and an exodus from Ireland of 200,000 people per year. The average age at marriage increased from twenty-three to twenty-four in 1831–1841 to twenty-seven to twenty-eight by 1900, and one-fifth of the population never married. As a result, the population of Ireland decreased from 8.2 million in 1841 to 4.5 million in 1901.

In sum, the cases of the gatherers and hunters, Quebec pioneers, and Irish peasants reveal that, contrary to the assumptions of demographic transition theory, populations historically adjusted their fertility rates when they needed to adapt to local social and economic conditions, and they did so without the benefits of modern contraception. This raises the question, *Why are populations in the periphery not, for the most part, lowering their fertility rates in the face of increasing population and supposedly declining economic resources?*

POPULATION GROWTH IN THE PERIPHERY

Traditional demographic transition theory, and most public policy and government analysts, suggests that the rapid rise in population in the poor nations is because of lowered mortality, itself a result of the importation of Western medical technology and public health measures. There is no question that life expectancy has increased remarkably in the periphery since 1950 and that a reduction in child mortality is the biggest factor in mortality decline.

Population growth in the periphery, however, began "exploding" well before the introduction of Western medicine and public health measures. Egyptian population grew in the nineteenth century from 2.5 million to 9 million, whereas the Mexican population grew from 5.8 million to 16.5 million. Cuba's population rose from 550,000 in 1800 to 5.8 million in 1953 (Wolf 1969:281). Furthermore, we saw how in Ireland the population increased not because of improvements in health but as a consequence of the economic demands of English landlords. The question is, *How and why did the economic expansion of the world capitalist economy change reproductive behaviors?*

Some anthropologists, such as Carol R. Ember (1983), suggest that, in general, fertility increased with the intensification of agricultural activities promoted by colonizers in the Third World. Ember pointed to evidence that women reduce birth spacing as agricultural activities intensify, partly to compensate for the increased domestic work for women when men increase their agricultural labors.

Thus, it should be no surprise that populations grew under colonialism. As long as the production of commodities for export was essential to economic growth in the core, and as long as profits exceeded the costs of maintaining the colonies, policies that led to increases in the labor force served colonial aims (Polgar 1972:207). If there was any concern about population on the part of colonial rulers, it was too low. One Frenchman complained in 1911 that Equatorial Africa lacked labor for its development (Cordell 1994:137). Women in Africa, like women elsewhere, responded to colonial economic pressures by increasing their fertility rates. For example, in villages in the Sudan, after the British established cotton growing in the 1920s to produce raw materials for its textile mills and increased the need for workers either to grow cotton or to replace those removed from subsistence agriculture, women began to wean their children earlier so they could become pregnant again (O'Brien 1994).

Wealth Flows Theory

It is clear, then, that people, particularly women, can and do adjust fertility in response to local economic and social conditions, and they do so without the assistance of Western methods of contraception. Yet fertility rates, while dropping in some countries, remain high in most. The question is, *Why does the demand for children in developing countries remain high?* Among the reasons generally given are the following:

- The cost of raising children in rural areas is low, and in terms of cost, children may represent a net gain economically.
- For security in old age. Surveys in Indonesia, the Koreas, Thailand, Turkey, and the Philippines reveal that 80 percent to 90 percent of parents expect economic assistance from children in their old age.
- Cultural factors encourage people to see children as an affirmation of family values, a guarantee of family continuity, and the expression of religious principles.

Beginning with the idea that people in some societies resist attempts to limit fertility because of the economic benefits of children, demographer John Caldwell (1982) formulated the *wealth flows theory* to explain the reproductive decisions made by families. There are, according to Caldwell, only two types of reproductive strategies that families can adopt: One occurs where there is no economic gain to restricting fertility; the other occurs when there is an economic gain. Furthermore, where it is beneficial to have children, people will maximize family size; where it is not economically beneficial, people will minimize family size. In other words, when children contribute wealth to the family, when wealth flows from children to parents, parents will maximize the number of children they produce; when wealth flows from parents to children, parents will minimize family size. Caldwell defined *wealth* in broad terms to include money or wages as well as economic security, labor assistance, prestige, the expansion of social and political networks, and so on.

The Yoruba of Nigeria, for example, desire large families because they increase the size of the security system in times of need, increase the number of cooperating individuals in less

Family form has much to do with family reproductive strategies. The many children in the extended Nigerian family pictured on the left are expected to contribute to its wealth, whereas the small number of dependents of the typical Western nuclear family, such as this one above in Boston, are expected to be a drain on family resources. (Left: Bruce Paton. Right: Juan Carlos Tinjaca/ Shutterstock.)

serious situations, and expand the range of economic and political contacts of family members. They also increase the number of political allies and the number of relatives who attend family ceremonies, both of which enhance prestige and status. For both urban and traditional Yoruba, family numbers are taken as signs of political strength and affluence. Moreover, a large family provides a springboard for success in the modern economy by supplying funds for education or personal connections to aid in finding jobs (Caldwell 1982:136). Children perform services not only by producing goods but also by providing services that adults regard as children's work—carrying water; collecting fuel, messages, and goods; sweeping; looking after siblings; and caring for animals. Adult children help with labor and gift-giving and assist in making family contributions to community ceremonies, funerals, and birth ceremonies. Adult children also care for aging parents and contribute to farms and businesses in such a way that aged parents can still participate. Finally, parents can invest in training or education of children to maximize later returns. When surveyed, 80 percent of Yoruba said that children are better than wealth, and even that children are wealth. Only 6 percent said that children consume wealth.

In core countries, however, children clearly consume wealth. For example, the U.S. Department of Agriculture estimates that in the United States, a child born in 2008 in the highest income group will "cost" $483,750 until the age of eighteen, while a child born in the lowest income group will "cost" $200,340 (see Table 5.5).

TABLE 5.5 Estimated Annual Expenditures[1] on a Child Born in 2008, by Income Group, Overall United States (USDA 2009)

		Income Group		
Year	*Age*	**Lowest ($)**	**Middle ($)**	**Highest ($)**
2008	<1	8,500	11,610	19,250
2009	1	8,760	11,960	19,840
2010	2	9,030	12,330	20,440
2011	3	9,380	12,750	21,090
2012	4	9,660	13,140	21,730
2013	5	9,960	13,540	22,390
2014	6	9,980	13,920	23,090
2015	7	10,280	14,340	23,790
2016	8	10,590	14,780	24,520
2017	9	11,810	16,180	26,330
2018	10	12,170	16,680	27,130
2019	11	12,540	17,190	27,960
2020	12	13,520	18,670	30,650
2021	13	13,940	19,240	31,580
2022	14	14,360	19,830	32,540
2023	15	14,830	21,150	36,030
2024	16	15,280	21,800	37,130
2025	17	5,750	22,460	38,260
Total	**—**	**200,340**	**291,570**	**483,750**

[1] Estimates are for the younger child in husband-wife families with two children and assume an average annual inflation rate of 3.05 percent.

As a result of his research, Caldwell (1982:140) concluded that

> the key issue here, and, I will argue, the fundamental issue in demographic transition, is the direction and magnitude of intergenerational wealth flows or the net balance of the two flows—one from parents to children and the other from children to parents—over the period from when people become parents until they die.

Furthermore, said Caldwell, for intergenerational wealth flow to change, there must be a fundamental change in family structure; programs that simply emphasize family planning or increase the availability of contraception will not provide incentives to reduce fertility. Given these conclusions, the questions are, *What kinds of changes are required in family structure to reduce fertility, and if in some circumstances fertility decline is desirable, under what economic and social circumstances will families be motivated to have fewer children?*

The Social Implications of Wealth Flows Theory

Wealth flows theory highlights an area of research that demographers have tended to neglect—the relationship between family structure and fertility. Anthropologists have been traditionally concerned with kinship and family relations because in small-scale and preindustrial societies, kinship, more than any other factor, tends to define a person's relationship to everyone else. In small villages and towns, for example, it is not unusual for everyone to be related in some way to everyone else and for everyone to know exactly what those relations are. In fact, in many societies, in the absence of kin, a person is viewed with suspicion and hostility. Many anthropologists who have lived and done fieldwork in such communities have had the experience of being assigned some fictional kinship designation—the sister, brother, daughter, or son of someone in the community.

One of the major distinctions that anthropologists make about different types of families is between the *nuclear family* and the *extended family*. The nuclear family consists of a father, mother, and children. This is the standard family unit in most Western countries and (although not the most common) in the United States. In other societies, extended families consisting of mothers and/or fathers and brothers, sisters, parents, grandparents, and others are the norm. Extended family structure can also vary considerably depending, for example, on whether a person is considered to be more strongly tied to his or her father and his kin (*patrilineal descent*), to his or her mother and her kin (*matrilineal descent*), or equally to both (*bilateral descent*).

Whether a society emphasizes nuclear family ties or extended family ties can obviously have great significance on patterns of family relations. In nuclear families, for example, parents or siblings are clearly responsible for the care of children; in extended families, children may be cared for by parents, siblings, members of the mother's or father's family, grandparents, and so on. In nuclear families, resources (income, possessions, etc.) are shared among mother, father, and children; in extended families, resources may be shared and distributed among a far greater number of individuals.

Furthermore, emotional ties may vary considerably. In a patrilineal extended family, a man may have closer ties to his brother than to his wife, or a woman may have closer ties to a brother or sister than to her husband. In nuclear families, the main tie is between husband and wife, and their main obligation is to their children. The question is, *What implications do population control programs have for family structure and relations?*

If wealth flow is the main determinant of fertility in a society, then fertility behavior will change only if there is a shift from extended family structures, in which wealth almost always flows from children to parents, to nuclear family structures, in which wealth almost always flows from parents to children. In Nigeria, for example, government efforts at reducing fertility have met with almost no success, even among modernized urban families. This is because the extended family, even in the cities, remains the norm. In the few instances of *demographic*

Barbados

innovators—those who have changed their fertility behavior—there has been a marked change in attitudes toward family and children to the emotional and economic patterns that resemble those found in nuclear families. These people have withdrawn emotionally from ancestors and extended family relatives and become more involved with their children and their children's future. They give more emotion and wealth to their children than they expect to get back. Caldwell (1982:149) speculated that those couples who have adopted the Western form of family, and consequently Western notions of family size, have probably done so not because of population control and family programs but because of the long-standing attempt by missionaries, colonial administrators, and educational authorities to persuade people to abandon their traditional family structure and adopt a Western family ideal.

To the extent that such efforts are successful and that population control and family planning programs contribute to these efforts, we will see a loss of extended families along with the patterns of emotional, economic, and social ties that characterize them, and the adoption of emotional, economic, and social characteristics of the Western family. In other words, fertility change requires a nucleation of obligations, expenditures, and emotions in which conjugal family ties take precedence over all external relationships and that foster the belief that what parents owe their children is more important than what children owe their parents. The Western nuclear family is also marked by a greater emphasis on the rights of individuals to act independently of the family by, for example, choosing a spouse on the basis of mutual attraction, choosing a residence independent from one's parents, choosing a career, and making decisions together with a spouse about family size.

The Question of Gender and Power

The United Nations Population Fund report *The State of the World's Population, 2000* (UNPF 2000:2), concludes that the status of women is one of the prime determinants of fertility and population growth. They conclude that if

> women had the power to make decisions about sexual activity and its consequences, they could avoid many of the 80 million unwanted pregnancies each year, 20 million unsafe abortions, some 500,000 maternal deaths (including 78,000 as a result of unsafe abortion), and many times that number of infections and injuries. They could also avoid many of the 333 million new sexually transmitted infections contracted each year.

Anthropologists suggest also that relations between husbands and wives may be as important as the influences of extended and nuclear family structure in influencing fertility. In situations where there is high unemployment, where women have limited access to economic resources and must depend on men and children for economic contributions or economic security, fertility will be high. This is clearly revealed in the research of W. Penn Handwerker (1989) in Barbados.

In the 1950s, according to Handwerker, the West Indian family was characterized by weak conjugal bonds, a relative absence of stable nuclear units, weak bonds between fathers and children, and strong bonds between mothers and children. Family interactions among men, women, and children tended to take place in visiting relationships, consensual cohabitation, and legal marriage, which tended to occur late if at all. Consequently, 80 percent of births occurred outside of marriage.

Historically, marriage patterns were a function of sugar production and the demand for sugar on the world market. The British freed their Barbados slaves in 1833, but the freed slaves were still dependent on wage labor in the sugarcane fields. Furthermore, to replace slaves who left, the British encouraged the migration of thousands of indentured laborers from India and the East Indies. As a result, the population of Barbados increased in the nineteenth century from 60,000 to 200,000. Because the sugar growers controlled the economy, and because there was a more than adequate workforce competing for available jobs, wages were low. To get a job, a laborer often needed the patronage of someone connected to the sugar growers. As a result, living conditions for the bulk of the black laborers were among the worst in the British West Indies. Infant mortality, for example, was 25 percent in the early 1900s and remained as high as 15 percent into the 1950s.

Handwerker claimed that the scarcity of jobs created severe competition among the poor for available work, such that men and women could optimize their resources only by exploiting each others' weaknesses. Because only men were employed on the sugar plantations, they earned most of the money, money they used to gain sexual conquests, rum, and unquestioned authority. Meanwhile, women exploited men's desire for sex, their absence from the home, and their distance from children to attach the children emotionally to themselves and distance them from their fathers.

This does not mean women didn't have jobs—60 percent worked from age fifteen to age fifty-five. Their work was low-paying manufacturing work, or they worked as seamstresses, domestics, and petty traders. Wages were so low that one woman commented, "You are lucky if a daughter can earn enough to help herself, let alone help you" (Handwerker 1989:77). To survive, a woman needed to supplement her income with that of a man.

These patterns of male–female relations resulted in a family pattern in which women attracted men as cohabitants, boyfriends, and, later, husbands in a unit in which men sought to dominate and control women. Men continued to meet their social obligations by working long hours, often at several jobs, providing an adequate material base for their wives and children; they exercised absolute authority in the home and spent free time with either men or other women. Women, needing men for economic support, submitted reluctantly, often complaining that their husbands or coresidents simply wanted a slave and expressing a desire to be treated as equals. Yet because of the pattern of out-migration of men, and the resulting greater number of women, men were able and expected to have extramarital affairs.

The result was a family in which men had minimal emotional attachments to their wives and children, whereas women worked to maintain close ties to their children. Women used sex to cement the tie to men, and, according to Handwerker's informants, children were by-products of the exchange. Moreover, older children were expected to help support their mothers and even to protect them from their fathers or stepfathers. As Handwerker (1989:88) said,

> Women could optimize or improve their resource control only by unrestricted childbearing. Getting pregnant and bearing children tended to be viewed as both a woman's duty and as her goal, and mothers generally took the view that their children owed them support for bringing the children into the world.

Even the belief system worked to enhance high fertility. Women believed that abstention from sex was unhealthy and that a woman who failed to bear all the children she was capable of bearing would suffer from high blood pressure and other diseases. "You have children until you can have no more," one woman in her fifties put it. Thus, patterns of economic exploitation created a family form in which women, acting according to the logic of their social and economic conditions, maximized the number of children they would have.

Beginning in the 1960s, however, family structure slowly began to change in response to changing economic conditions. The colonial sugar economy declined to the point that sugar represented only about 6 percent of domestic output and 10 percent of employment. Manufacturing and tourism grew, and with it the importance of education for access to jobs. Connections to people of influence mattered less. More importantly, women gained access to jobs unavailable to them before.

As a consequence, the Barbadian family of the 1980s was very different from the family of the 1960s and earlier. Women expect their husbands to be companions, and there have been equivalent expectations on the part of husbands. Although women still suffer from job discrimination, education provides them with access to better-paying jobs as technical specialists, secretaries, receptionists, business executives, university employees, and lawyers. From 1950 to 1980, the percentage of women working in manufacturing increased from less than 15 percent to more than 50 percent. The competition for resources between men and women lessened, and the exploitative pattern of relations decreased. Marriages came to resemble more the so-called companionate marriages that emerged in England in the nineteenth century (Stone 1976); men began to enjoy their families, and their lives began to center more on their wives and children.

This did not occur without conflict, however. Because the stronger emotional ties within the nuclear family required weakening to some extent ties outside the family, especially between sons and mothers, relations between wives and mothers-in-law became strained as they competed for the affections of husbands. Regardless, the family of the 1980s came to resemble the idealized Western nuclear family. Women viewed children as a cost rather than as a future resource, and young Barbadian women explicitly denied owing anything to their parents.

With the change in family patterns, there has been a dramatic decrease in fertility, from a birth rate of about five per woman in the 1950s to a low of about two in the 1980s. Handwerker (1989:210) concluded that changes in patterns of family relations, not large-scale population control programs of the sort advocated by the Cairo Population Conference, will determine fertility. It is not knowledge of contraceptive techniques or a population problem per se that inhibits women from having smaller families but an issue of power relations. Family planning programs, said Handwerker,

> should not be expected to bring about fertility transition because they can neither create the jobs nor provide the education necessary for many jobs that would permit women to achieve meaningful control over their own lives. The "right" to have a small family is not a real option for women who are dependent for basic material well-being on their children.

Issues of Immigration

Migration, particularly of illegal or undocumented immigrants, is another issue that has raised political alarms in wealthy countries. Presently over 200 million or one out of every 35 persons in the world resides in a country other than that in which they were born. The prevailing pattern, as one would expect, is for people in poor countries to migrate to richer ones in search of jobs. As Jeffery Kaye (2010:3) puts it, "migrants go where the grass in greener." Mexicans seek to enter the United States, while Guatemalans try to go to Mexico. Bangladeshis try to go to Kosovo or Great Britain, while sub-Saharan Africans want to go to Spain or Italy, and Bolivians to Argentina. See Table 5.6 for a list of selected countries by foreign-born population.

Immigration policy is a major issue in both developed and developing countries. While countries from which people migrate support immigration, for reasons we'll explore, the vast majority of people in the developed world desire strong immigration controls.

To examine why immigration is such an emotional topic, we need to answer the following questions: *How has migration varied historically? Why do people emigrate? What are the economics of migration? How does it affect wages and the economies of both the host and sending countries? What is the impact of illegal immigration and how have countries tried to regulate immigration? What is a sensible immigration policy?*

TABLE 5.6 Countries by Number of Immigrants (2005)

Country	Number of Immigrants	Estimated Number of Illegal Immigrants[1]	Percentage Total of All Immigrants in the World	Immigrants as a Total of National Population
United States	38,355,000	12–20 million	20.56	12.81
Russia	12,080,000	10–12 million	6.474	8.483
Germany	10,144,000		5.437	12.31
Ukraine	6,833,000		3.662	14.7
France	6,471,000	200,000–400,000	3.468	10.18
Saudi Arabia	6,361,000		3.409	25.25
Canada	6,200,000	35,000–120,000	3.272	18.76
India	5,700,000	A few hundred thousand to 20 million.	3.055	0.517
United Kingdom	5,408,000	550,000–950,000	2.898	8.982
Spain	4,790,000		2.567	10.79
Australia	4,097,000	100,000	2.196	19.93
People's Republic of China	3,852,000	100,000	2.064	0.2944
Pakistan	3,254,000		1.744	1.984
United Arab Emirates	3,212,000		1.722	71.4
Hong Kong	2,999,000		1.607	42.59
Israel	2,661,000		1.426	37.87
Italy	2,519,000		1.35	4.288
Kazakhstan	2,502,000		1.341	16.88
Cote d'Ivoire	2,371,000		1.271	13.06
Jordan	2,225,000		1.193	39.01
Japan	2,048,000		1.098	1.599
Iran	1,959,000		1.05	2.861
Singapore	1,843,000		0.9878	42.6
Palestinian Territories	1,680,000		0.9004	45.38
Ghana	1,669,000		0.8945	7.548
Kuwait	1,669,000		0.8945	62.11
Switzerland	1,660,000		0.8897	22.89
Malaysia	1,639,000	800,000	0.8784	6.15
Netherlands	1,638,000		0.8779	10.05
Argentina	1,500,000		0.8039	3.871
Turkey	1,328,000		0.7118	1.814
Uzbekistan	1,268,000		0.6796	4.768

Source: World Population Policies 2005, *United Nations, Department of Economic and Social Affairs,* March 2006. ISBN 978-92-1-151420-9. See also List of countries by foreign-born population in 2005. Wikipedia. http://en.wikipedia.org/wiki/List_of_countries_by_foreign-born_population_in_2005

[1]See Illegal Immigration, Wikipedia. http://en.wikipedia.org/wiki/Illegal_immigration#cite_note-134

Figures for the number of illegal immigrants are rough estimates at best, which is why estimates for the United States range from 10 to 20 million. Different interest groups will also skew the numbers to support their political or economic agenda. The number also depends to some extent on enforcement procedures of a given country, both in border controls and detection procedures. For that reasons estimates will probably run from one-fifth to one-half of the number of legal immigrants.

Between 1870 and 1920, almost 28 million people arrived in the United States from Europe, while another 10 to 11 million migrated to South America.
(The Bridgeman Art Library Ltd/Alamy.)

Argued that America was for those who were born here

History of Migration

The first great wave of immigration involved the first human ancestors moving out of Africa and into Europe, the Middle East, and Asia. Some of those Asian immigrants crossed the land bridge of the Bering Straits and into North and South America sometimes between 10,000 and 20,000 years ago. The movement of Europeans into the New World after 1500 marked another migration milestone, as did the involuntary movement of some 10 million Africans into North and South America.

The next great wave occurred with the Industrial Revolution when demands for both skilled and unskilled labor surged, and industrializing regions and countries sought to attract immigrants, even subsidizing their travel. The first legislation regarding immigration in the United States in 1864 sought to increase the number of immigrants. At first during the early part of the nineteenth century rates of migration tended to be small, first because travel was difficult, and, second, because most people were too poor to afford to move. But, steamship and railroad travel in the latter half of the nineteenth century made travel easier, while increases in wealth afforded people increased opportunities to emigrate. Between 1870 and 1920, almost 28 million people arrived in the United States from Europe, while another 10 to 11 million migrated to South America.

The first instance of opposition to European immigration in the United States occurred in the 1850s. The Order of the Star Spangled Banner, or "Know-Nothing" Party, was formed to protest the entry of Irish immigrants fleeing the potato famine. They argued that America should be for those born here, and argued that the Irish were loyal to a foreign power—the Pope. In the United States the first action to restrict immigration, which we mentioned in Chapter 2, was the Chinese Exclusion Act of 1882, enacted in response to protests, largely in California, that Chinese immigrants were taking jobs from native workers. (See Table 5.7 for a history of U.S. legislation regarding immigration.) There was also evidence that by increasing the availability of labor, wages declined and unemployment increased. Thus studies suggest wages of the average American, absent immigration after 1870, would have been 11 percent to 14 percent higher than they were (Hatton and Williamson 2005:125).

In addition, as voting rights were extended to more people in liberal democracies such as the United States, Great Britain, and Australia, politicians were forced to pay more attention to native workers' concerns that their economic welfare was being threatened by the influx of immigrants. Concerns increased as the source of European immigrants gradually switched from northern Europe, where increased industrialization lessened people's motivation to emigrate, to southern and eastern Europe. The influx of desperately poor Italians, Slavs, Ukrainians, and Jews, with no English-language skills raised fears that they could never assimilate to life in the United States. In 1907, the U.S. Congress created a committee, the Dillingham Commission, to study the life of immigrants, and in 1911 they issued a forty-one-volume report that led to the next restrictive legislation, the Literacy Act of 1917 (see Table 5.7).

However, there were counter pressures. While native laborers feared that immigrants threatened their wages, if not their jobs, and others felt threatened by the cultural diversity represented by the immigrants, employers in agriculture, industry, and business welcomed the rise in laborers willing to work for less. This conflict between labor and business continues to define the policy debates about immigration in the United States and elsewhere.

TABLE 5.7   The History of U.S. Legislation to Regulate and Control Immigration

Date	Legislation	Description
1864	An Act to Encourage Immigration	This was the first action taken by the United States federal government regarding immigration. Prior to that it was seen as a state prerogative.
1882	The Asian Exclusion Act	Essentially prohibited the immigration of Chinese citizens. The legislation was a reaction to protests, largely in California, claiming that Chinese workers were taking jobs of U.S. workers.
1891	The Immigration Act of 1891	Established an Office of the Superintendent of Immigration within the Treasury Department.
1917	The Literacy Act	The act established a literacy test for prospective immigrants, imposed a "head" tax, and excluded categories of people including "idiots," alcoholics, and anarchists.
1921	Emergency Quota Act	Limits were established for the number of immigrants from different countries. The limit for any country was 3 percent of the total from that country in the United States according to the Census of 1910. The quotas allowed for 356,000 total but limited the number from countries whose citizens were seen as having a problem assimilating and likely to end in poverty. Asian restrictions remained in place and there were no quotas from Western Hemisphere countries.
1924	Johnson-Reed Act	Lowered the total quota for immigrants from 356,000 to 165,000 and established the Border Patrol.
1942–1960	Mexican Farm Labor Program—1942–1964	The "Bracero Program," as it was called, was initially prompted by a demand for manual labor during World War II and began with the U.S. government bringing in a few hundred experienced Mexican agricultural workers to California. Texas initially opted out of the program in preference for an "open border" policy, but was denied braceros by the Mexican government until 1947 due to perceived mistreatment of Mexican laborers. The number admitted under the program ranged from just over 4,000 in 1942 to almost 450,000 in 1959.
1965	Immigration and Nationality Act	Also called the "family reunification act," because its main provision was to allow relatives of people in the United States to join them. It allotted 20,000 immigrants for each Eastern Hemisphere country with a maximum total of 170,000 a year. 64 percent of the spots were reserved for relatives of U.S. citizens, with 30 percent allotted to various employment categories. Most notably the act removed the exclusion of Asians and Africans.
1985	The Immigration Reform and Control Act	The major provision was to grant amnesty to some 3 million illegal immigrants. It also made it illegal to hire an illegal immigrant, but, after protests form business leaders, softened the law so that it read "to knowingly hire an illegal immigrant."
1990	Immigration Act of 1990	With some modifications, largely governs present U.S. immigration policy. The 1990 revisions introduced an annual quota of 675,000 divided into three classes: 480,000 were allotted to family members of U.S. citizens, employment-based visas were increased from 54,000 to 140,000, and 55,000 were allocated to diversify immigration from countries with relatively low immigrant presence in the United States. Homosexuality was removed as grounds for exclusion.
1996	Illegal Immigration Reform and Immigrant Responsibility Act	This act states that immigrants unlawfully present in the United States for 180 days but less than 365 days must remain outside the United States for three years unless they obtain a pardon. If they are in the United States for 365 days or more, they must stay outside the United States for ten years unless they obtain a waiver. If they return to the United States without the pardon, they may not apply for a waiver for a period of ten years. Also enhanced funding for border surveillance.

The Immigration Act of 1921 established quotas for countries according to the number from that country already in the United States (see Table 5.7). These restrictive acts, along with the economic depression of the 1930s, brought the first wave of massive immigration to a halt, as an average of fewer than 50,000 people a year entered the United States in the 1930s (Hatton and Williamson 2008:183).

The immigration restrictions of the 1920s did benefit U.S. workers, particularly blacks, who had been crowded out of the northern labor market by European immigrants. The migration of blacks from the south into the industrialized north between 1910 and 1950 helps account for the leveling of incomes through the middle third of the twentieth century (Hatton and Williamson 2008: 197). And, since North Americans were not excluded in the immigration acts of the 1920s, the percentage entering from Canada and Mexico rose from 12.9 percent of all immigrants in 1910, to 45.4 percent from 1920 to 1929. Mexican immigration rose by 320,000 in that decade (Hatton and Williamson 2008:186).

The next great global movement of people began after WW II and continues today. It has differed from the previous pattern in five ways. First, Europe declined as a source of immigrants and became a major destination, surpassing the United States in that regard. Second, Latin America changed form being a prime destination for migrants, to becoming a major source. In fact, from 1960 to 1980, Latin America went from hosting 1.8 million foreign-born to providing 1.8 million migrants, a change of 3.6. million in only twenty years (Hatton and Williamson 2008:208). While only about a fifth of all U.S. immigration originated south of the border in the 1950s, almost half (47.2 percent) did so in the 1990s, half of that coming from Mexico.

The third post–WW II shift came in Asia where immigration, largely from India, China, Korea, the Philippines, and Vietnam into the United States increased largely as a result of the United States' 1965 Immigration Act that removed Asian restrictions (see Table 5.7). The demand for migrant labor in the oil-rich Persian Gulf countries marked a fourth change, with the annual flow of migrants going from less than 100,000 in 1973 to nearly 1 million in 1991. Persian Gulf countries preferred Asian workers over Arab migrants because Asians were less likely to permanently settle in the countries and were less of a political threat.

Finally, with the collapse of the Soviet Union and the subsequent removal of restrictions on emigration, the flow of immigrants from eastern Europe to western Europe surged from about 240,000 a year to 1.2 million a year between 1985 and 1989.

The Economics of Immigration

Much of the political debate about immigration has to do with who wins and who loses economically. Clearly, historically, the benefits to the migrant are considerable. Even back in the nineteenth century, a Norwegian could increase his income 3.7 times by immigrating to the United States, and an Indian from Madras working on a sugar plantation in British Guinea could increase his income by five times. Overall in the late nineteenth century, during the peak of European migration to the New World, wages in the New World were double that of Europe. Today, wages in the wealthy countries of the world are five times that of the Third World (Hatton and Williamson 2008:215). In the Philippines, for example, a nurse earns about $260 a month. It is not surprising then that when in 2004 more than 50,000 Filipino-trained nurses were working in the United States, at the same time the Philippines was experiencing a shortage of nurses. Between 2000 and 2007, almost 78,000 nurses left the Philippines. In fact, with doctors in the Philippines making on average $4,000 a year, more than 6,000 between 2000 and 2008 retrained as nurses to migrate to the United States or elsewhere (Kaye 2010:34–35).

Employers also gain from immigration. One estimate is that the 11 percent increase in labor supply from immigration between 1980 and 2000 reduced the wages of the nonmigrant worker by 3.2 percent (Hatton and Williamson 2008:293). This is one of the reasons that business and agricultural groups favor liberal immigration laws. When Texas and Arizona

TABLE 5.8   Total Remittances (in US$ millions) in 2010 by Top Receiving Country and Percent of GDP of Selected Countries in 2009

	World	$440,077			0.7%
1	India	53,131	1	Tajikistan	35.1%
2	China	51,300	2	Tonga	30.3%
3	Mexico	21,997	3	Samoa	26.5%
4	Philippines	21,373	4	Lesotho	26.2%
5	Bangladesh	10,804	5	Nepal	23.8%
6	Nigeria	10,045	6	Moldova	22.4%
7	Pakistan	9,683	7	Lebanon	21.9%
8	Lebanon	8,409	8	Kyrgyz	21.7%
9	Vietnam	8,000	9	Haiti	21.2%
10	Egypt	7,725	10	Honduras	17.6%
11	Indonesia	7,250	11	El Salvador	16.5%
12	Morocco	6,452	12	Jamaica	15.8%
13	Ukraine	5,595	13	Jordan	14.3%
14	Russian	5,477	14	Guyana	13.7%
15	Serbia	4,896	15	Serbia	12.6%

Source: Remittances data, Development Prospects Group, World Bank, 2011, http://www.migrationinformation.org/dataHub/remittances/All_profiles.pdf

lawmakers, under strong pressure from largely Republican and conservative antiimmigrant groups, passed legislation designed to stop the influx of undocumented Mexican laborers, business groups, which were also largely Republican, had to publically oppose the legislation. Given the power of agricultural and business groups in the United States, it is surprising that immigration laws are as strict as they are, but, perhaps, unsurprising, that enforcement of these laws is generally lax.

Another winner is the country from which people emigrate. One source of gain to source countries comes in the form of remittances, money that migrants bring home or send home to friends and relatives (see Table 5.8). In some cases, some 10 percent or more of a country's GDP, or national income, comes from money brought or sent back by emigrants. And the amounts in Table 5.8, which are based on money sent through formal banking channels, may be underestimated by anywhere from 10 percent to 90 percent. Remittances are such an important part of national incomes that some countries, such as the Philippines, India, Vietnam, Sri Lanka, Indonesia, and Bangladesh, have special government offices to encourage and assist emigrants, and airports have special signs wishing them good luck as they leave.

In addition, there is evidence that money sent home by immigrants significantly reduces child mortality rates and increases educational levels of households that receive remittances (Hatton and Williamson 2008:333). And a further benefit is that as migrants leave, they reduce the number of people competing for jobs and which raises average wages. The only drawback is that migrants tend to be the most educated in the source country, although what is lost in economic productivity is more than made up for by remittances.

In sum then, some of the winners in the migration sweepstakes are:

- the migrants and their families, either those that accompany them or those that stay behind
- employers, renters, businesses, and likely consumers in the host country
- the economy of the source country, along with workers who remain in the source country

Other winners include:

- the global employment services who earn billions for their services
- the wire services that send remittances
- the smugglers who charge $1,400 to $5,000 or more to help migrants enter countries illegally, and the people and industries that earn billions trying to stop them.

Those who lose are laborers, generally the unskilled, in the host country, who may see a reduction in their wages of anywhere from 3 percent to 9 percent (Hatton and Williamson 2008:304–305). Other losers are the illegal immigrants who die (200 or more each year on the U.S.-Mexican border, and thousands more in Europe and Asia) trying to reach their destination. Some claim that taxpayers who support public services, such as schools, health facilities, and social services utilized by immigrants, lose, and we'll examine that claim below.

Understanding Illegal Immigration

There are an estimated 25 to 32 million undocumented immigrants in the world, and that is probably an underestimate. In the United States there are an estimated 12 to 20 million illegal immigrants (see Table 5.6), some 59 percent from Mexico and approximately half being individuals who overstayed a visa permitting them to enter the country legally.

It is fair to say that illegal immigration represents a failure of neoliberal free-trade doctrine. Free trade promotes the movement of goods, services, and capital, but traps in place those made redundant by those same policies. Free trade, as we examined in Chapters 3 and 4, is based on the idea that the free flow of commodities, services, and capital increases economic activity in general, and produces overall economic benefits for all. Over the past fifty years, in fact, with multi- and bilateral trade agreements and the establishment of the World Trade Organization (WTO) most barriers to the flow of commodities, services, and capital have diminished or been removed. Thus consumers can enjoy the lower prices of goods made in China, U.S. corporations can employ people in the Philippines or in India to answer customers' phone inquiries, and banks and other financial institutions are free to buy shares in the banks or invest in enterprises of other countries. At the same time, however, the growth in economic inequality between countries, in part because of these agreements, creates more of a desire for those in poor countries to seek economic opportunities in richer countries. This is the opposite of the situation in the nineteenth and early twentieth century when the movement of commodities, services, and capital was restricted by tariffs and laws, while labor was free to move where it was most in demand.

For example, the North American Free Trade Agreement (NAFTA) between Canada,

The debate over immigration policy is as intense as ever in both the United States and Europe. A major conflict is between businesses, which welcome immigrants willing to work for less, and native workers, who feel threatened with lower wages. (Dennis Brack/DanitaDelimont.com/ Danita Delimont Photography/Newscom.)

Mexico, and the United States allowed American farmers to flood the Mexican market with corn, displacing thousands of Mexican farmers. Theoretically, the most productive and profitable agricultural techniques of U.S. producers won out over the less productive and less profitable Mexican producers. With free trade, those displaced should be free to seek employment where they could be more productive, but are prevented from doing so by restrictive immigration laws. In 1994, the Mexican government was close to bankruptcy and was saved by a loan that allowed Mexico to repay its debts to Wall Street Banks. But, in exchange, the Mexican government had to raise interest rates on loans and loosen the rules regarding foreign ownership of banks. But the rise in interest rates that, in part, allowed the Mexican government to repay its loan ahead of schedule, resulted, according to a 2008 report by the Mexican Senate, in the bankruptcy of hundreds of thousands of Mexican businesses and the loss of millions of jobs. The report concluded that the economic collapse would result in 6 million Mexicans seeking employment in the United States (see Kaye 2010:50–51). It is probably no coincidence that after the signing of NAFTA, the United States doubled the number of border agents.

In Senegal, as Jeffrey Kaye notes, the traditional dish is *thieboudienne*. To prepare this dish, fry some onions and fish; stir in tomato paste, rice, and water; and bring to a boil. Then add vegetables such as carrots, sweet potatoes, turnips, eggplant, and cabbage and simmer until done. Yet, for Senegalese, buying these items from Senegalese producers is now almost impossible. Fishing declined by half from 1997 to 2005 because industrial-size trawlers from Europe, Japan, and the United States depleted the fish stocks. Senegalese farmers can't compete with the factory-style agriculture of the United States and Europe whose produce sells more cheaply in Senegalese markets than local produce. Senegal imports 80 percent of its rice, although it has the capacity to produce all it needs. With jobs destroyed, and the collapse of the Senegalese economy in the 1990s, the only option left for many Senegalese was to migrate, either legally or illegally. Thus the 2009 United Nations Development Report estimates that the emigration rate is 4.4 percent (United Nations 2009:145).

Economists are almost unanimous in agreeing that, overall, unrestricted immigration increases global well-being. Estimates of the economic benefits range from a doubling of the world's GDP, to an increase of 10 percent. Another study estimates that a transfer of 16 million migrants to wealthy countries, 8 million skilled and 8 million unskilled workers, would raise world GDP by $156 billion or 0.6 percent, and would result in a 1 percent drop in skilled wages and a 0.6 percent drop in unskilled wages in the host country. It would raise skilled wages by 5 percent and unskilled wages by 0.1 percent in the less developed source country (Hatton and Williamson 2008:371).

Another reasons for favoring unrestricted migration is the aging problem. Worldwide in 1950, there were twelve persons of working age for every person age sixty-five or older. By 2010, that number shrunk to nine. By 2050, this elderly support ratio—the number of people one to sixty-five years of age, divided by the number over sixty-five—which indicates levels of potential social support available for the elderly, is projected to drop to four. This is particularly serious in Europe, although not quite as much in the United States. Since pension programs require working adults to support retirees, there will be fewer of the former and more of the latter.

In order to keep the elderly support ratio constant at 2000 levels—4.3 for Europeans and 5.2 in the United States—a significant number of immigrants are required. New U.S. immigration would need to be 14.3 million per year in 2000–2025 and 11.9 million per year in 2025–2050, roughly *fifteen times* that based on current rates. Net EU immigration would have to be even higher, 8.6 million and 18.4 million per year, or *forty to seventy times higher* than what is currently projected (Hatton and Williamson 2008:377).

Yet, in spite of the advantages offered by immigrants—legal and illegal—polls taken over the last two decades find that people in the wealthy countries overwhelmingly support more restrictive immigration laws, especially when it comes to stopping illegal immigrants. Cries of

"We have lost control of our borders," are common both in the United States and Europe. The question is, is immigration fair to taxpayers?

The most common concern is that illegal immigrants constitute a financial burden on taxpayers. Immigrants, in general, are more likely to receive benefits from one or more welfare programs, 19.7 to 13.3 percent for native families. Since Latin American families tend to have more children, they also receive a higher share of education benefits. And immigrants who are poor, also pay less tax.

One study commissioned by the U.S. Congress calculated that the net fiscal burden per immigrant-headed household in 1996 was between $1,613 and $2,206 representing a fiscal cost of between $166 and $226 per nonimmigrant household (Hatton and Williamson 2008:308). Thus the cost to a California household was about $2,000. Another study by the Federation for American Immigration Reform (FAIR) concluded that illegal immigration costs U.S. taxpayers about $113 billion a year, or $1000 per U.S. household (Martin and Ruark 2010:1).

However, others questioned these studies because they simply estimate the taxes paid by illegal immigrants and subtract it from an estimate of the public services (health, education, and social services) received. For example, a study commissioned by Americans for Immigration Reform (AIR) concludes that ending illegal immigration would result $1,757 trillion in lost spending, $651.511 billion in annual lost output, and 8.1 million lost jobs (Perryman Group 2008:5). A third study by the Immigration Policy Center (Hanson 2009) examines the data and includes that gains and losses from illegal immigrants basically balance out.

The debate is likely to continue; one reason is that it is difficult to separate economic arguments about immigration—legal and illegal—from social attitudes, prejudices, and racism, particularly given the fact that most migrants come from poor countries. Generally speaking, countries do welcome migrants who are most like them. Australia, as well as Canada and the United Kingdom, has a point system to determine a person's eligibility to immigrate (see Table 5.9). You might want to determine your score.

In sum, we can conclude that countries still largely control their borders, particularly if they were willing to enforce penalties on employers who hire illegal immigrants. However, given the political power of business and corporations, and the economic losses they would incur if they were unable to utilize immigrant labor, governments tend to be unwilling to enforce such laws. The result is a system where the government attempts to play up its efforts to restrict immigration to satisfy antiimmigrant sentiment, while at the same time providing little financial support for enforcement, thus satisfying business and corporation needs for cheaper labor.

For the migrant, particularly an undocumented one, the result is a shadow existence whose fate lies largely with border agents and employers. Michael Kearney (1991) points out that even such things as border patrols function not so much to apprehend illegal migrants as to force them to accept low-paying jobs while not claiming benefits accorded to other laborers. He cited the example of migrant Mixtecs, who walk through the mountains in winter to find work and who, because of their work ethic, are desired by American employers. They don't understand why the *Migra* (border patrol) seek to apprehend them, forcing them to work harder and faster before they are apprehended and forcing them to take whatever work at whatever wages they can. But, as Kearney (1991:61) indicates, that is exactly the point of the *Migra;* it is not intended to stop migrants from coming into the United States to work; rather it functions to discipline them to work harder and accept low wages.

Urbanization and the Growth of Slums

In 1950 there were 86 cities in the world with a population of more than 1 million; today there are 400 and by 2015 there will be at least 550. Cities absorbed nearly two-thirds of the global population growth since 1950, and are currently growing by a million babies and migrants each week (see Table 5.10). And in the developing world, the vast majority of urban dwellers

TABLE 5.9   Australian Immigration Point System
http://www.migrationmatters.com/australiapoints.php
Estimate Your Points with the Migration Matters Skilled Migration Points Calculator. Pass is 65 Points

Age

18–24	◯	25 points
25–32	◯	30 points
33–39	◯	25 points
40–44	◯	15 points
45–49	◯	0 points

English Language

Competent English–IELTS 6 or below	◯	0 points
Proficient English–IELTS 7	◯	10 points
Superior English–IELTS 8	◯	20 points

Australian work experience in nominated occupation or a closely related occupation *

No Australian work experience	◯	0 points
One year Australian	◯	5 points
Three years Australian	◯	10 points
Five years Australian	◯	15 points
Eight years Australian	◯	20 points

Overseas work experience in nominated occupation or a closely related occupation *

No overseas work experience	◯	0 points
Three years overseas	◯	5 points
Five years overseas	◯	10 points
Eight years overseas	◯	15 points

Qualifications (Australian or recognised overseas)

No recognized qualification	◯	0 points
• Offshore recognised apprenticeship • AQFIII/IV completed in Australia • Diploma completed in Australia	◯	10 points
Bachelor degree (including a Bachelor degree with Honours or Masters)	◯	15 points
PhD	◯	20 points

Additional:

Designated language	▣	5 points
Partner skills	▣	5 points
Professional Year	▣	5 points
Sponsorship by state or territorygovernment	▣	5 points
Sponsorship by family or state or territory government to regional Australia	▣	10 points
Study in a regional area	▣	5 points

Points Total:

0 points

TABLE 5.10 Global Percentage of Urban Population by Region: 1950–2040 (Projected)

Year	World % urban	Latin America and the Caribbean % urban	Asia % urban	Africa % urban	United States % urban	Europe % urban	More Developed Regions % urban	Less Developed Regions % urban	Least Developed Regions % urban
1950	29.4	41.4	17.5	14.4	64.2	51.3	54.5	17.6	7.4
1955	31.4	45.3	19.2	16.2	67.2	54.1	57.7	19.6	8.4
1960	33.6	49.3	21.1	18.6	70	57	60.9	21.8	9.5
1965	35.5	53.3	22.9	21.2	71.9	60	63.9	24	11.1
1970	36.6	57.1	23.7	23.5	73.6	62.8	66.6	25.3	13
1975	37.7	60.7	25	25.6	73.7	65.2	68.7	27	14.7
1980	39.4	64.3	27.1	27.8	73.7	67.3	70.1	29.5	17.2
1985	41.2	67.4	29.8	29.8	74.5	68.7	71.3	32.3	19
1990	43	70.3	32.3	32	75.3	69.8	72.3	34.9	21
1995	44.8	73.1	34.8	33.9	77.3	70.3	73.2	37.5	22.7
2000	46.7	75.5	37.4	35.6	79.1	70.8	74.1	40.1	24.3
2005	49.1	77.3	40.9	37.3	80.7	71.6	75.9	43	26.1
2010	51.6	78.8	44.4	39.2	82.1	72.7	77.5	46	28.1
2011	52.1	79.1	45	39.6	82.4	72.9	77.7	46.5	28.5
2015	53.9	80.2	47.6	41.1	83.3	73.8	78.8	48.7	30.3
2020	56	81.5	50.5	43.2	84.4	74.9	80	51.3	32.7
2025	58	82.5	53.1	45.3	85.2	76.1	81.1	53.6	35.2
2030	59.9	83.4	55.5	47.7	86	77.4	82.1	55.8	38
2035	61.7	84.3	57.8	50.1	86.8	78.6	83.1	57.9	40.8
2040	63.5	85.1	60	52.6	87.5	79.9	84.1	60	43.8
2045	65.3	85.9	62.2	55.1	88.2	81	85	62	46.8
2050	67.2	86.6	64.4	57.7	88.9	82.2	85	64	49.8

Source: Population Division of the Department of Economic and Social Affairs of the United Nations Secretariat, *World Population Prospects: The 2010 Revision* and *World Urbanization Prospects: The 2011 Revision*

TABLE 5.11 Level of Urbanization, 2000 and 2020 (Projected) and Slum Population, 2001 by Region

	Level of Urbanization (%)		Estimated Urban Slum Population 2001	
	2000	2020	in thousands	%
Developed Regions	75.3	79.9	54,068	6
Europe	73.4	77.6	155,344	6.2
Other	78.4	83	21,006	5.7
Developing Regions	40.4	51.3	869,918	43
Northern Africa	51.7	59.7	21,355	28.2
Sub-Saharan Africa	34	45.7	166,208	71.9
Latin American and the Caribbean	75.4	81.8	127,567	31.9
Eastern Asia	38.2	55.1	193,824	36.4
South-Central Asia	29.8	37.8	262,354	58
South-Eastern Asia	37.5	51.1	56,781	28
Western Asia	64.7	69.8	41,311	33.1
Oceania	26.4	33.8	499	24.1

Source: Compiled from data in *UN-HABITAT. 2003*.

live in slums. In 2001, there were an estimated 924 million slum dwellers in the world, representing about 32 percent of the world's total urban population (see Table 5.11). In the least developed countries, some 78.2 percent of urban residents live in slums (UN-HABITAT 2003:vi).

The movement to the cities by unemployed rural laborers is another side to the failure of neoliberal free trade. Most of the migrants to the cities have been displaced by the influx of foreign produce and commodities, or displaced by the working of foreign capital. But unable, because of restrictive immigration laws, to seek employment in rich countries, they flock instead to the cities of their home country in search of employment that rarely exists. Instead they enter the informal economy making do however they can, as we'll examine in Chapter 6. Being poor, they settle on any piece of vacant land available, generally areas unsuitable for middle-class residents, such as hillsides, swamps, toxic dumps, alleyways, rooftops, or whatever spaces are available. In Cairo, squatters unearthed tombs of sultans in which to make a home (Davis 2006:33). In Hong Kong, which is one of the richest places in the world, one-quarter of a million people live in slums. Single men erect wire around their sleeping spaces to prevent theft. These bed-space apartments average 38.3 people in an area of 194 square feet, or less than 7 by 3 feet per person. Los Angeles is the first-world capital of the homeless, with 100,000 homeless people (Davis 2006:35).

Slums represent in another way the failure of neoliberal economics. Capital, as we noted earlier, will not work to provide goods and services for those who can't pay for it. Essentially, if you have no money, you don't exist. Furthermore, part of the neoliberal agenda is to reduce, privatize, or eliminate government services. Consequently, while the need for federal, state, or municipal governments to build urban infrastructures—sewage treatment plants, roads, police and fire services, clean water, etc.—increases, their ability to do so is undercut by global capital. As Mike Davis (2006:137) describes, urban slums are deep in the shit that urban residents have struggled for centuries to dispose of.

In the least developed countries of the world, some 78.2 percent of urban residents live in slums, as rural residents flow to cities in search of wage labor, erecting shelters on unoccupied land.
(Peter Treanor/Alamy.)

Authorities try to deal with these slums by ignoring them, or, if the need arises, try to destroy them. As Brazil prepares to host the Olympics in 2016, it planned to build a waterside park and an Olympic village for the athletes, only to find 4,000 people living in a squatter settlement taking the city to court to prevent the razing of their homes. Unlike China's preparation for the Beijing Olympics, where thousands of families were forcibly relocated to make room for Olympic venues, *favela* dwellers in Brazil are supported by a network of activists. In spite of that, some 170,00 people may face eviction ahead of the World Cup and Olympics (Romero 2012).

The battles faced by squatter settlements mirror the struggles of illegal immigrants trying to carve out a space for themselves on the margins of civilization.

As Mike Davis points out, there was nothing inevitable about the growth of slums. Castro in Cuba, and the rulers of Brazil, Algeria, and elsewhere where progressive governments came to power, tried to address the influx of people from the countryside with state-built housing, but only China and Cuba had any level of success.

Perhaps the most comprehensive study of slums was pioneered by the World Bank economist Branko Milanovic in his work *The Challenge of Slums: Global Report on Human Settlements 2003* (UN-HABITAT 2003). Slums, it concludes, are characterized by insecurity of tenure, a lack of basic services, especially water and sanitation, inadequate and sometimes unsafe building structures, overcrowding, and location on hazardous land. Residents are poor, have limited or no access to credit, and suffer inordinately from waterborne diseases such as cholera and typhoid. Women, and the children they support, tend to suffer the most.

On a more positive note, the report observes that slums are often the first stopping off point for immigrants, providing low-cost housing that allows immigrants to save money for entering urban society. Slum dwellers try to make an honest living in the informal economy, and form networks of social, economic, and political support. They provide much of the labor force for the cities and are melting pots for different groups and cultures. And slum dwellers are not devoid of the material appurtenances of modern life. One study in Bangkok, Thailand, found that virtually all slum households had a color television, almost all had a refrigerator, and two-thirds had a washing machine and a CD player, although only 15 percent had a bathroom with hot water (UN-HABITAT 2003:xxx).

But in spite of the efforts of those living in urban poverty to make the best of horrid living conditions, the situation is severe enough that the World Bank warned that urban poverty could become "the most significant and politically explosive problem of [this] century" (Davis 2006:20).

CONCLUSION

Western scientific and popular discussions of population growth have been dominated by two frameworks. The Malthusian perspective predicts that population growth threatens the world with starvation, poverty, environmental destruction, and social unrest. The demographic transition theory, while sharing the Malthusian concern over population growth, predicts that, as in the wealthy countries, population in poorer countries will eventually stabilize if they adopt Western programs of economic development designed to bring them into the modern world. From an anthropological perspective, both views are faulty, because both assume the connections between population growth and economic development, and both ethnocentrically assume the reasons for population rise and decline in premodern societies. Furthermore, the Malthusian position has a clear class and, perhaps, ethnic bias in its tendency to blame the victims of poverty and environmental decline for their economic, social, and ecological state, ignoring the effects of the historical expansion of capitalism. The ethnocentrism of demographic transition theory is evident in its assumptions that modernization will result in lowered fertility because, somehow, modernity encourages rationality in choices about family size. However, as we have seen, there is nothing irrational about large families in societies where the family is a major source of economic support and security, and where the wealth received from children throughout one's life far exceeds the wealth that flows to children.

We examined the relationship between fertility and family structure, describing John Caldwell's intergenerational wealth flows theory, and demonstrated that lowering fertility requires a change in family structure from an extended family pattern to a nuclear family pattern. We also noted that unless women gain access to economic resources, it remains in their interest to maximize fertility. Yet, if fertility decline is a major priority for international agencies and countries, and if, as anthropological research indicates, such a decline requires the adoption of the Western nuclear family along with its values, attitudes, and consumption patterns, we need to examine the consequences of such a change. In particular we need to consider whether the social and economic effects of such a change are worth whatever might be gained by slowing population growth.

And finally we examined the global movement of peoples, either from country to country, or from rural areas to cities, displaced by the dynamic of globalization and in search of employment, occasionally finding it, or, if not, entering the world of the informal economy, a subject we'll examine in the next chapter.

6

Hunger, Poverty, and Economic Development

> *The persistence of widespread hunger is one of the most appalling features of the modern world. The fact that so many people continue to die each year from famines, and that many millions more go on perishing from persistent deprivation on a regular basis, is a calamity to which the world has, somewhat incredibly, got coolly accustomed.... Indeed, the subject often generates either cynicism ("not a lot can be done about it") or complacent irresponsibility ("don't blame me—it is not a problem for which I am answerable").*

—JEAN DRÈZE AND AMARTYA SEN, *Hunger and Public Action*

> *Poverty is the main reason why babies are not vaccinated, why clean water and sanitation are not provided, why curative drugs and other treatments are unavailable and why mothers die in childbirth. It is the underlying cause of reduced life expectancy, handicaps, disability and starvation. Poverty is a major contributor to mental illness, stress, suicide, family disintegration and substance abuse. Every year in the developing world 12.2 million children under 5 years die, most of them from causes which could be prevented for just a few US cents per child. They die largely because of world indifference, but most of all they die because they are poor.*

—WORLD HEALTH ORGANIZATION, *World Health Report*

At the end of World War II, public officials and scientists from all over the world predicted that with advances in modern technology it would be possible by the end of the twentieth century to end poverty, famine, and endemic hunger in the world. Freed from colonial domination and assisted by new global institutions, such as the United Nations and the World Bank, the impoverished countries of Africa, Asia, and Latin America, people assumed, would follow paths to economic development blazed by the core countries.

Today these optimistic projections have been replaced by hopelessness and resignation as 1.2 billion people are estimated to still live on less than one dollar per day, and almost 3 billion on less than two dollars per day. Estimates of the number of people with insufficient food range from 800 million to well over a billion, virtually one-sixth of the world's population. Children are particularly vulnerable; food aid organizations estimate that 250,000 children per week, almost 1,500 per hour, die from inadequate diets and the diseases that thrive on malnourished bodies.

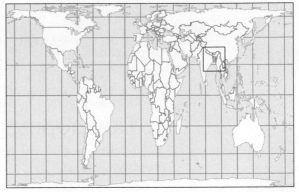

In 2008, the Food and Agriculture Organization of the United Nations estimated that more than 900 million, or about 13 percent of the global population, are afflicted with hunger. Of those suffering from hunger, 94 percent live in developing nations. Most are subsistence farmers, landless families, or people working in fishery or forestry. The remainder live in shantytowns on the fringes of urban areas. A quarter of the hungry are children.

Bangladesh

Common misunderstandings about world hunger should be quickly dispelled:

- First, world hunger is not the result of insufficient food production. There is enough food in the world to feed 120 percent of the world's population on a vegetarian diet, although probably not enough to feed the world on the diet of the core countries. Even in countries where people are starving, there is either more than enough food for everyone or the capacity to produce it.
- Second, famine is not the most common reason for hunger. Although famines, such as those in recent years in Ethiopia, Sudan, Somalia, and Chad, receive the most press coverage, endemic hunger—daily insufficiencies in food—is far more common.
- Third, famine itself is rarely caused by food insufficiency. When hundreds of thousands starved to death in Bangladesh in 1974, it was not because of lack of food. In fact, there was more food than there had been in the years leading up to the disaster and more food than was produced in the years following. The starvation resulted from massive unemployment brought on by flooded farmland and high food prices brought on by a fear of food shortages. People starved to death because they couldn't afford to buy food and had no land to grow their own.
- Finally, hunger is not caused by overpopulation. Although growing populations may require more food, there is no evidence that the food could not be produced and delivered if people had the means to pay for it. This does not mean population and food availability play no role in world hunger; rather, it indicates that the relationship is far more complex than it appears.

The questions are, *Why do people continue to starve to death in the midst of plenty?* More importantly, *is it still possible to believe that poverty and hunger can be eliminated? If so, how? And if not, how can the poor adapt to their conditions?*

To answer these questions, we need to know about the nature and history of food production and to understand the reasons why people are hungry. There is a prevailing view that hunger is inevitable, but that need not be the case. We examine some possible solutions to world hunger, how specific countries, some rich and some poor, have tried to ensure that people have adequate food, and how people actively seek to cope with poverty.

THE EVOLUTION OF FOOD PRODUCTION: FROM THE NEOLITHIC TO THE NEOCALORIC

Until recently in world history, virtually everyone lived on farms, grew their own food, and used whatever surplus they produced to pay tribute or taxes, to sell at local markets, and to keep for seed for the following year. Since the beginning of the Industrial Revolution, people have left the land in increasing numbers, converging on cities and living on wages. As late as 1880, half of the U.S. population was engaged in agriculture; this figure decreased to 38 percent by 1900, and to 18 percent by 1940. Today, less than 2 percent of Americans feed the other 98 percent, as well as millions of others around the world who purchase the products of American agriculture (Schusky 1989:101). This shift of the population from farming to other sources of livelihood is intensifying all over the world. *Why do people leave the land on which they produce their own food to seek wage employment, which requires that they buy food from others?*

To answer this question, we need to understand the history of agriculture, why food production has changed, and how economic and agricultural policies have resulted in increased poverty and hunger.

From Gathering and Hunting to the Neolithic

For most of their existence, human beings produced food by gathering wild plants—nuts, roots, berries, and grains—and hunting large and small game. Generally, these people enjoyed a high quality of life. They devoted only about twenty hours per week to work, and archaeological studies and research among contemporary gathering and hunting societies indicate that food was relatively plentiful and nutritious. Life span and health standards seem to have been better than those of later agriculturists. Consequently, a major question for anthropologists has been why human populations that lived by gathering and hunting began to plant and cultivate crops. Before 1960, anthropologists assumed that domesticating plants and animals provided more nourishment and food security than gathering and hunting. But when, in the 1960s, the research of Richard Lee and James Woodburn (see Devore and Lee 1968) revealed that the food supply of gatherers and hunters was relatively secure and that the investment of energy in food production was small, speculation turned to the effects of population increase on food production. Mark Cohen (1977) suggested that increases in population densities may have required people to forage over larger areas in search of food, eventually making it more efficient to domesticate and cultivate their own rather than travel large distances in search of game and wild plants. Even then the shift from gathering and hunting to domestication of plants and animals must have been very gradual, emerging first on a large scale in Mesopotamia about 10,000 years ago during the Neolithic era. From that point until 5,000 years ago, settlements domesticated such plants as wheat, barley, rye, millet, rice, and maize and began to domesticate animals such as sheep, goats, pigs, camels, and cattle. Traditionally, animals have served as a farmer's food reservoir, fed with surplus grains in good times and killed and eaten when grain became scarce. Some, such as sheep, goats, cattle, and camels, eat grasses that human beings cannot eat, thus converting cellulose to protein for human consumption in the form of meat and dairy products.

Slash and burn, or *swidden, agriculture* is the simplest way of cultivating crops; although it is highly efficient when practiced correctly and requires considerable knowledge of local habitats. In swidden agriculture, a plot of land is cleared by cutting down the vegetation, spreading it over the area to be used for planting, and then burned. Seeds are planted, and the plants cultivated and then harvested. After one to three years of use, the plot is more or less abandoned, and a new area cut, burned, and planted. If there is sufficient land, the original plot lies fallow for ten years or more until bushes and trees reestablish themselves; then it is used again. Of the four major factors in agricultural production—land, water, labor, and energy—swidden agriculture is land intensive only. It uses only natural rainfall and solar energy and requires about twenty-five hours per week of labor. For tools, swidden agriculture requires only an ax or machete and a hoe or digging stick.

Swidden agriculture is still practiced in much of the periphery, but only recently have researchers begun to appreciate its efficiency and sophistication. Burning vegetation, for example, once thought only to add nutrients in the form of ash to the soil, also kills pests, insects, and weeds. When practiced correctly, it is environmentally sound because it re-creates the natural habitat. Swidden agriculturists must choose a site with the proper vegetation and desirable drainage and soil qualities. They must cut and spread the brush properly and evenly to maximize the burn and the heat. Cuttings that dry slowly must be cut earlier than those that dry quickly. Unlike in monoculture—the growing of a single crop—swidden plots are planted with a variety of foodstuffs as well as medicinal plants and other vegetable products. Swidden agriculturists must know when to abandon a plot so that grasses do not invade and prevent regeneration of brush and forest. Furthermore, abandoned plots are rarely truly abandoned, being used to grow tree crops or attract animals that are hunted for food.

Just as there is debate as to why gatherers and hunters began to practice agriculture, there is some question as to why swidden agriculturists began to practice the more labor-intensive irrigation or plow agriculture. These techniques do not necessarily produce a greater yield relative to the labor energy used; however, they do allow use of more land more often by reducing or eliminating the fallow period. Land that in swidden agriculture would lie fallow is put into production. Irrigation agriculture also allows continual production on available land, sometimes allowing harvest of two or three crops in a year. Moreover, it permits the use of land that could not be used for agriculture without irrigation. Ester Boserup (1965) suggested that increasing population density required more frequent use of land, eliminating the possibility of allowing land to lie fallow to regain its fertility. Thus, plow and irrigation agriculture, while requiring greater amounts of work, does produce more food.

The productivity comes at a cost, however. Of the four agricultural essentials—land, water, labor, and energy—irrigation requires more water, labor, and energy than swidden agriculture. In addition, irrigation generally requires a more complex social and political structure, with a highly centralized bureaucracy to direct the construction, maintenance, and oversight of the required canals, dikes, and, in some cases, dams. Furthermore, irrigation can be environmentally destructive, leading to salinization (excess salt buildup) of the soil and silting. For example, it is estimated that 50 percent of the irrigated land in Iraq and 30 percent in Egypt is waterlogged or salinized (Schusky 1989:72). Irrigated sites may also be used to dump sewage and often harbor disease-carrying parasites and insects, resulting in an increase in such diseases as cholera, typhoid, schistosomiasis, and malaria. Irrigated areas also serve as a haven for weeds. Finally, the shift to plow or irrigation agriculture changed the division of labor between men and women (Boserup 1970). Generally, in swidden agriculture, men clear the land and women burn the cuttings and care for the crops. In some areas today, such as sub-Saharan Africa, women do the majority of the agricultural labor. However, in plow or irrigation agriculture, women tend to do less of the labor—their labor shifts to domestic chores, and often the total amount of women's labor increases as their agricultural labor decreases (Ember 1983).

If we surveyed the world of 2000 years ago, when virtually all of the food crops now in use were domesticated and in use somewhere, we would find centers of irrigation agriculture in China, Mesopotamia, Egypt, and India, with later developments coming in the Andes and Mesoamerica. Plow agriculture was practiced extensively in areas of the Middle East and Europe. But where agriculture was necessary, swidden agriculture, if population levels and state demands for tribute permitted it, must have been by far the most common. Moreover, until the twentieth century, there was little change or improvement in agricultural techniques.

Capitalism and Agriculture

The next great revolution in food production was a consequence of the growing importance of world trade in the sixteenth through eighteenth centuries and the gradual increase in the number of people living in cities and not engaged in food production. The expansion of trade and growth of the nonfarming population had at least four profound consequences for agricultural production.

First, food became a commodity that, like any other commodity, such as silk, swords, or household furniture, could be produced, bought, and sold for profit. Second, the growth of trade and the number of people engaged in nonagricultural production created competition for labor between agricultural and industrial sectors of the economy. Third, the growth of the nonagricultural workforce created greater vulnerability on the part of those who depended on others for food. The availability of food no longer depended solely on a farmer's ability to produce it but also on people's wages, food prices, and an infrastructure required for the delivery, storage, and marketing of food products. Finally, the increasing role of food as a capitalist commodity resulted in the increased intervention of the state in food production. For example, food prices needed to be regulated; if they were too high, people might starve and industrial wages would need to increase; if they were too low, agricultural producers might not bring their food to market. Import quotas or tariffs needed to be set to maximize food availability on the one hand and protect domestic food producers on the other. New lands needed to be colonized, not only to produce enough food but also to keep food production profitable. The state might also regulate agricultural wages or, as in the United States, not regulate them. (Although the United States has had a minimum wage for industrial workers since 1937, there is still no minimum wage for farm workers.)

As it turned out, the most important change in food production inspired by the transformation of food into a capitalist commodity was the continual reduction of the amount of human energy and labor involved directly in food production and the increase of the amount in nonhuman energy in the form of new technologies, such as tractors, reapers, and water delivery systems. The results of this trend continue to define the nature of agricultural production in most of the world.

Reducing labor demands in agriculture and increasing technology accomplishes a whole range of things that contribute to trade and profit in both the agricultural and industrial sectors. First, substituting technology for human labor and reducing the number of people involved in agriculture makes agriculture more profitable. Labor costs are reduced and agricultural wealth is concentrated in fewer hands. Increasing technology also creates a need for greater capital investments. As a result, those people with access to capital—that is, the more affluent—are able to profit, forcing the less affluent to give up their farms. This further concentrates agricultural wealth. The increase in the need for capital also creates opportunities for investors (banks, multilateral organizations, and commodity traders) to enter the agricultural sector, influence its operation by supplying and/or withholding capital, and profiting from it.

Second, reducing the number of people in agriculture and concentrating agricultural wealth to ensure profits of those who remain helps keep food prices and, consequently, industrial wages relatively low. This creates a danger of food monopolies and the potential for a rise in prices. For example, cereal production in the United States is controlled by only a few companies, and the prices of processed cereals such as cornflakes and oats are exorbitant as 0.04 cents of corn generates $4.00 of cornflakes Yet, as long as consumers are able to pay, the government is content not to intervene. As it is, food cost as a percentage of the cost of living in the United States is among the lowest in the world.

Third, reducing agricultural labor frees labor to work in industry and creates competition for industrial jobs, which helps keep wages low—that is, the more the number of people who are dependent for their livelihood on jobs, the lower the wages industry needs to pay.

Finally, to keep labor costs down and increase the amount of technology required for the maintenance of food production, the state must subsidize the agricultural sector. In the United States, for example, the government has financed irrigation and land reclamation projects, conducted agricultural research, and subsidized farm prices and/or energy costs. The U.S. government also subsidized agriculture by investing billions of dollars in food aid, buying surplus U.S. farm products, and using them for foreign aid (although this aid often created a dependence on U.S. farm products while forcing local producers out of business).

In sum, the results for the capitalist economy of the reduction of agricultural labor and the subsequent increase in technology are:

- a capital-intensive agricultural system dependent on the use of subsidized energy
- the exploitation of domestic farm labor and of foreign land and labor to keep food prices low and agricultural and industrial profits high
- a large labor pool from which industry can draw workers, whose wages are kept down by competition for scarce jobs and the availability of cheap food

It is important to note that until the 1950s, the technological intensification of agriculture did not substantially increase yield—that is, though an American corn farmer needed only 100 hours of labor to produce one hectare (2.41 acres) of corn, the amount of corn produced was no greater than that produced by a Mexican swidden farmer, working ten times as many hours using only a machete and hoe. In other words, although mechanization made the American farm more economical by reducing labor energy and costs, it did not produce more food per hectare (Schusky 1989:115). One question we need to ask is, *What happens when we export the American agricultural system to developing countries?*

The Neocaloric and the Green Revolution

The culmination of the development of capitalist agriculture, a system that is technologically intensive and substitutes nonhuman energy for human energy, was dubbed the *neocaloric revolution* by Ernest Schusky. For Schusky, the major characteristic of the neocaloric revolution has been the vast increase in nonhuman energy devoted to food production in the form of fertilizers, pesticides, herbicides, and machinery.

David Pimentel and Marcia Pimentel (1979) provided a unique perspective on the neocaloric. Their idea was to measure the number of kilocalories[1] produced per crop per hectare of land and compare it to the amount of both human and nonhuman energy expended in kilocalories to produce the crop. Their work dramatized both the efficiency of traditional forms of agriculture and the energy use required of modern capitalist agriculture.

For example, to produce a crop of corn, a traditional Mexican swidden farmer clears land with an ax and machete to prepare it for burning and uses a hoe to plant and weed. Pimentel and Pimentel (1979:63) figured that crop care takes 143 days and the worker exerts about 4,120 kilocalories per day. Thus, labor for one hectare amounts to 589,160 kilocalories. Energy expended for ax, hoe, and seed is estimated at 53,178 kilocalories, for a total of 642,338 kilocalories. The corn crop produced yields about 6 million kilocalories, for an input–output ratio of one to eleven—that is, for every kilocalorie expended, eleven are produced, a ratio that is about average for peasant farmers. Nonhuman energy used is minimal, consisting only in the fossil fuel (wood, coal, or oil) used in producing the hoe, ax, and machete.

Now let's examine plow agriculture with the use of an ox. One hour of ox time is equal to four hours of human time, so labor input for one hectare drops to 197,245 kilocalories from 589,160 kilocalories. But the ox requires 495,000 kilocalories to maintain. Moreover, the steel plow requires more energy in its manufacture, so fossil fuel energy used rises to 41,400, with energy for seeds remaining at 36,608, for a total of 573,008. However, the corn yield drops significantly to half, so the input–output ratio drops to 1:4.3. The reason for the drop is likely

---

[1] A calorie or gram calorie is the amount of heat needed to raise the temperature of one gram of water from one degree Celsius to fifteen degrees Celsius. The kilocalorie (kcal) or kilogram calorie is 1,000 gram calories or the amount of heat needed to raise the temperature of one kilogram of water from one degree Celsius to fifteen degrees Celsius. It can also be conceptualized as follows: One horsepower of energy is the same as 641 kilocalories; one gallon contains 31,000 kilocalories; if used in a mechanical engine that works at 20 percent efficiency, one gallon of gasoline is equal to 62,000 kilocalories of work, or one horse working at capacity for a ten-hour day, or a person working eight hours per day, five days per week, for 2.5 weeks.

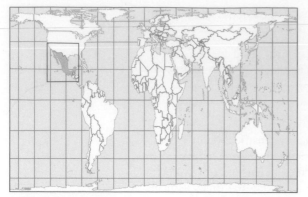

Mexico

the lowering of soil fertility. If leaves, compost, or manure is added to the soil, yields might increase, but so would the energy required to gather and spread the fertilizer.

Finally, if we consider a corn farmer in the United States in 1980, we find that, using modern farming machinery, herbicides, insecticides, fertilizers, transport, and irrigation, the farmer produces about 7,000 kilograms of corn per hectare, almost seven times that produced by the Mexican swidden farmer but at a cost of almost 25 million kilocalories. Consequently, the input–output ratio is 1:3.5, far below the ratios of most "primitive" swidden farmers. In fact, in the United States, the ratio of kilocalories used in crop production to kilocalories produced declined from 3.7:1 in 1945 to 2.8:1 in 1970. The question is, *Why has modern agriculture become so energy intensive?*

The intensification of the use of technology in agriculture is largely the result of what has been called the *green revolution*. The green revolution began with research conducted in Mexico by American scientists in the 1940s and 1950s sponsored by the Rockefeller Foundation. Their goal was to develop higher-yielding hybrid strains of corn and wheat suitable for Mexican agriculture. Soon the research produced dramatic results all over the world as farmers began using specially produced strains of crops such as wheat, corn, and rice, called *high-yielding varieties* (HYVs). The productivity of the new seeds lay largely in their increased capacity for using fertilizer and water. Whereas increased use of fertilizer and water did not increase the yields of old varieties (in fact, it might harm them), it vastly increased the yields of the new varieties. Consequently, more and more farmers around the world adopted them. Use of these new varieties was encouraged by the petrochemical industry and fertilizer production plants, which sought to expand their markets. Thus, research efforts to develop HYV plants were expanded in India, the Philippines, and Taiwan, encouraged by the U.S. Agency for International Development (USAID) and the Rockefeller Foundation.

But the green revolution soon ran into some problems. First, the new plants required greater inputs of fertilizer and water. Because of the added energy costs, farmers often skimped on fertilizer and water use, resulting in yields similar to those prior to the adoption of the new crops. Consequently, farmers returned to their previous crops and methods. Second, the Organization of Petroleum Exporting Countries (OPEC) oil embargo in 1973 raised oil prices, and because fertilizers, irrigation, and other tools of the green revolution were dependent on oil, costs rose even higher. Some people began to refer to HYV as *energy-intensive varieties* (EIVs).

The expense was increased further by the amount of water needed for fertilizers. Early adaptations of the new technology tended to be in areas rich in water sources; in fact, most of the early research on HYV was done in areas where irrigation was available. When the techniques were applied to areas without water resources, the results were not nearly as dramatic. It also became apparent that the energy required for irrigation was as great in some cases as the energy required for fertilizer.

In addition, the green revolution requires much greater use of chemical pesticides. If farmers plant only a single crop or single variety of a crop, it is more susceptible to the rapid spread of disease, which, because of the added expense, could create catastrophic financial losses. Consequently, pesticide use to control disease becomes crucial. Furthermore, because the crop is subject to threats from insect and animal pests at all stages of production—in the fields, storage, transportation, and processing—pesticide costs rise even further.

Finally, the new fertilizers and irrigation favor the growth of weeds; therefore, herbicides must be applied, further increasing energy expenditure.

One result of the change from subsistence farming, in which the major investment was land, to a form of agriculture that is highly land, water, and energy intensive is, as Ernest Schusky (1989:133) noted, to put the small farmer at a major disadvantage because of the difficulty in

TABLE 6.1 Changes in Number of U.S. Farms by Size, 1950–1992

Size of Farm (in acres)	1992	1969	1950	Percent Change
1–59	1,310,000	1,944,224	4,606,497	−172
260–499	255,000	419,421	478,170	−47
500–999	186,000	215,659	182,297	+0.08
1,0001	173,000	150,946	121,473	+58
Total	1,925,000	2,730,250	5,388,437	−166

Source: Adapted from Eric Ross, *Beyond the Myths of Culture: Essays in Cultural Materialism.* New York, Academic Press, 1980; and 1992 USDA Census of Agriculture. http://www.agcensus.usda.gov/Publications/1992/index.php

raising the capital to finance the modern technological complex. The result in the United States and elsewhere is the concentration of agricultural wealth in fewer hands and a constant reduction in the number of small family farms (see Table 6.1).

It is in livestock production, however, that the neocaloric revolution really comes into focus. One innovation of the past hundred years in beef production was feeding grain to cattle. By 1975, the United States produced about 1,300 kilograms of grain for every person in the country. But 1,200 kilograms of that was fed to livestock. Dairy cows are relatively productive compared to beef cattle; it takes about 190 kilograms of protein to produce sixty kilograms of milk or about thirty-six kilocalories of fossil energy to produce one kilocalorie of milk protein. Beef get about 40 percent of their protein from grazing and 60 percent from grain. If we calculate the energy that goes into grain production and the operation of feedlots, the productive ratio is as low as one kilocalorie produced for every seventy-eight kilocalories expended.

If we factor in processing, packaging, and delivery of food, the energy expenditure is even higher. David Pimentel estimated that the American grain farmer, using modern machinery, fertilizer, and pesticides, uses eight calories of energy for every one calorie produced. Transportation, storage, and processing consume another eight fossil calories to produce one calorie (see Schusky 1989:102).

As Schusky said, in a world short on energy, such production makes no sense, but in a world of cheap energy, particularly oil, especially if it is subsidized by the nation-state, it is highly profitable. The real problem comes when agricultural production that substitutes fossil fuel energy for human energy is exported to developing countries. To begin with, there is simply not enough fossil energy to maintain this type of production for any length of time. One research project estimated that if the rest of the world used energy at the rate it is used in the United States, the world's petroleum resources would be exhausted on the food supply alone in the next ten to twelve years (Schusky 1989:119).

Furthermore, in countries with large rural populations, the substitution of energy-intensive agriculture for labor-intensive agriculture will throw thousands off the land or out of work, resulting in more people fleeing to the cities in search of employment. And because modern agriculture is capital intensive, the only farmers who can afford to remain will be those who are relatively wealthy, consequently leading to increasing income gaps in rural as well as urban areas. Where the green revolution has been successful, small-farm owners have been driven off the land to become day laborers or have fled to cities in search of jobs, as commercial investors bought up agricultural land. Or more wealthy farmers have bought their neighbors' farms because only they had the capital to invest in fertilizers and irrigation.

Then there is the potential for *green revolution II,* the application of genetic engineering to agricultural production. Genetically engineered crops are controversial, largely because of claims that they have not been rigorously tested and because we do not know yet what effects the crops may have on the environment or on the people who eat them. Clearly, claims by agribusiness

such as Monsanto Corporation, that such crops will help us feed the hungry are, as we
disingenuous at best. Furthermore, in some cases, genetically engineered crops simply
ect the damage done by capitalist agriculture. For example, there is the much touted
ce," a genetically engineered variety with vitamin A that is a cure for blindness that
ne 300,000 people a year. Yet, as Vandana Shiva (2000) notes, nature ordinarily pro-
dant and diverse sources of vitamin A; rice that is not polished provides vitamin A, as
ch as bathua, amaranth, and mustard leaves, which would grow in wheat fields if they
rayed with herbicides.

all it is clear that we have developed a system of food production that is capital intensive,
e, state-subsidized agribusiness, minimizes the use of labor, and subsequently makes
more people dependent on wage labor with which to obtain food. In the culture of capitalism,
access to food is determined almost entirely by the ability to pay, not by the need to eat.

THE POLITICS OF HUNGER

The obvious consequence of the reduction of labor needed for food production and the concentration of food production in fewer hands is that the world's population is more dependent on
wage labor for access to food. Consequently, people are more vulnerable to hunger if opportunities for employment decrease, if wages fall, or if food prices rise; they can starve even in the
midst of food availability. This is not to say that lack of food is never a factor in hunger, but it is
rare for people to have economic resources and not be able to acquire food.

The role of food in a capitalist economy has other important consequences. For example,
food production is not determined necessarily by the global need for food; it is determined by
the market for food—that is, how many people have the means to pay for it. That is why world
food production is rarely at its maximum and why it is difficult to estimate how much food could
be produced if the market demand existed. The problem is that there are not enough people with
sufficient income to pay for all the food that could be produced, and so-called overproduction
would result in lower prices and decreased profitability. For that reason, in many countries, food
production is discouraged. Furthermore, land that could be used to grow food crops is generally dedicated to nonfood crops (e.g., tobacco, cotton, and sisal) or marginally nutritious crops
(e.g., sugar, coffee, and tea) for which there is a market. Finally, the kind of food that is produced
is determined by the demands of those who have the money to pay for it. For example, meat is
notoriously inefficient as a food source, but as long as people in wealthy countries demand it, it
will be produced in spite of the fact that the grain, land, and water required to produce it would
feed far more people if devoted to vegetable crops. Thus, people in Mexico go hungry because
land is devoted to the production of beef, which few Mexicans can afford, but which brings high
prices in the United States.

In sum, we need to understand the economic, political, and social relations that connect people to food. Economist Amartya Sen (1990:374) suggested that people command food
through entitlements—that is, their socially defined rights to food resources. Entitlement might
consist of the inheritance or purchase of land on which to grow food, employment to obtain
wages with which to buy food, sociopolitical rights such as the religious or moral obligation of
some to see that others have food, or state-run welfare or Social Security programs that guarantee adequate food to all. Not all of these kinds of entitlements exist in all societies, but some exist
in all. From this perspective, hunger is a failure of entitlement. The failure of entitlement may
come from land dispossession, unemployment, high food prices, or lack, suspension or collapse
of state-run food security programs, but the results are that people may starve to death in the
midst of a food surplus.

Viewing hunger as a failure of entitlements also corrects ideological biases in the culture of capitalism, the tendency to overemphasize fast growth and production, the neglect of
the problem of distribution, and hostility to government intervention in food distribution. Thus,
rather than seeing hunger or famine as a failure of production (which it seems not to be), we can

focus on a failure of distribution (see Vaughn 1987:158). Furthermore, we are able to appreciate the range of possible solutions to hunger. The goal is simply to establish, reestablish, or protect entitlements, the legitimate claim to food. Seeing hunger as a failure of entitlement also focuses on the kinds of public actions that are possible. For example, access to education and health care are seen in most core countries as basic entitlements that should be supplied by the state, not by a person's ability to pay. And most core countries see basic nutrition as a state-guaranteed entitlement, in spite of recent attempts in countries such as the United States to cut back on these entitlements. Thus, by speaking of entitlements, we can focus on the importance of public action in dealing with world hunger.

To understand the range of solutions to hunger, we also need to distinguish between the more publicized instances of famine, generally caused by war, government miscalculations, civil conflict, or climatic disruptions; food poverty, in which a particular household cannot obtain sufficient food to meet the dietary requirements of its members; and food deprivation, in which individuals within the household do not get adequate dietary intake (Sen 1990:374).

To illustrate, let's take a look at two situations of hunger: first, the more publicized instance of famine and then the less widely publicized endemic hunger.

The Anatomy of Famine

Famines have long been a part of history. As early as the fourth century B.C., administrators in India wrote of measures to avert famines, and the people of India have been subject to massive famines throughout its history. China has also suffered major famines. The latest occurred in 1958–1961, when 15 million to 30 million people starved to death.

Many historic famines were caused by crop failures, climatic disruptions, and war. Archaeologists have speculated that widespread climatic changes reduced the yields of Mayan agriculturists and resulted in the destruction of Mayan civilization. Yet it is clear that, even historically, famines resulted from entitlement failures rather than insufficient food (Newman 1990). Even during the Irish potato famine of 1846–1847, when one-eighth of the population

An image that emerged from the famine in Somalia in 1992.
(Bernard Bisson/Sygma/ Corbis.)

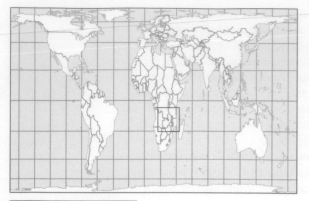

Malawi

starved to death, shiploads of food, often protected from starving Irish by armed guards, sailed down the Shannon River, bound for English ports and consumers who could pay for it.

We can better appreciate the dynamics of famine and the importance of entitlements by examining a famine crisis in the African country of Malawi in 1949. It was by no means the most serious famine in Africa in the past sixty years, but Megan Vaughn (1987), in her analysis of it, provides answers to the key questions, *Who starves and why?*

The famine began with a drought. The lack of rain was first noticed after Christmas 1948 and drew serious attention when in January, normally the wettest month of the year, there was no rain at all; it remained dry until some rain fell in March.

In some areas the first and second plantings of maize, the main food crop, failed completely, and wild pigs, baboons, and hippos devastated the remaining crops. Old people who remembered the last famine in 1922 said there were signs of a major crisis, and within a few months it was apparent that people were starving. The British colonial government began to organize relief efforts, sending agricultural representatives into the countryside to organize the planting of root crops, replanting of crops that failed, and opening food distribution camps. By the time the rains came in October, there were reports of real malnutrition and of hundreds of children and adults starving to death. Many died, ironically, at the beginning of 1950 as the maize crop was being harvested, many from eating the crop before it ripened (Vaughn 1987:48).

According to Vaughn, women suffered most from the famine. The question is, *What happened to women's food entitlements that resulted in their being the most severely affected?* To answer this question, we need to know a little about food production, the role of kinship in Malawi life, and the changing role of women in African economies.

Malawi at the time was under British control; agriculture was divided between cash crop agriculture—tobacco was the most important crop—and subsistence agriculture, the growing of such crops as maize, sorghum, and a few root vegetables. In addition, many people worked at wage labor, either in the formal employment sector, for European or Indian farmers or merchants, or the government, or in the informal employment sector, working on farms owned or worked by Africans. Cash could also be earned through migrant labor, almost exclusively a male domain, although women could earn money making and selling beer or liquor.

The predominant form of kinship structure was matrilineal—that is, people traced relations in the female line. The most important kin tie was between brother and sister, and the basic social unit was a group of sisters headed by a brother. Under this system, rights to land were passed through women, men gaining rights to land only through marriage. Traditionally, women would work their land with their husbands, who lived with them and their children. In this system, a woman's entitlement to food could come from various sources: her control of land and the food grown on it, sharing of food with matrilineal kin, wages she might earn selling beer or liquor or working occasionally for African farmers, or wages her husband or children might earn. In addition, during the famine, the government established an emergency food distribution system from which women could theoretically obtain food. *What happened to those entitlements when the crops failed?*

Changes in the agricultural economy and the introduction of wage labor under European colonial rule had already undermined women's entitlements (Boserup 1970). The British colonial government was under pressure, as it was in other parts of Africa, to produce revenue to pay the cost of maintaining the colonies. Consequently, they introduced cash crops such as coffee, tea, cotton, and tobacco. The latter proved to be the most profitable in Malawi and was the major cash crop when the famine struck. But cash cropping was generally a male prerogative and provided wages for African men only when they worked for Europeans or Indians. Cash cropping by Europeans and Indians also took land that might have been used for food crops, contributing to a growing land shortage for Africans. Thus, in addition to providing new ways for men to gain economic power, European practices led to the decrease of women's power in the agricultural sector. This combination of changes in access to land, decreasing amounts of land available for Africans, and the growing importance of wage labor for men made women more dependent on men for their food entitlements when the famine struck.

When the famine became evident to the British authorities, they took measures that further reduced women's entitlements. First, partly to conserve grain and partly because of a fear of social disorder, they forbade the making and sale of beer, removing a major source of income for women. Next, they assumed the family unit consisted of a husband, wife, and children, presided over by the husband, and, consequently, refused to distribute food relief to married women, assuming they would obtain food from their husbands. However, many husbands were traveling to seek work elsewhere to buy food, and they might or might not send food or money home. Next, the government food distributions gave preference to those, mostly urban people, who were employed in the formal economy by Europeans, Indians, or the government, neglecting those in the rural economy such as part-time women laborers. Furthermore, Europeans and Indians, who had ample food supplies during the famine, often shared with their workers who, again, were mostly men. Many of these men, of course, were conscientious husbands, fathers, brothers, and uncles and shared the food they received. But some did not, either keeping it for themselves or selling it at high prices on the black market.

To make matters worse, as the famine wore on, social units began to fragment. This is a common feature of famines. Raymond Firth (1959) reported that during the early phases of a famine on the island of Tikopia, families recognized extended kin ties in the sharing of food, but as the famine wore on, food was shared only within individual households. In Malawi, the situation was even worse; at the beginning of the famine, there seems to have been sharing within the main matrilineal kin group, but as it wore on, the sharing unit became smaller and smaller until people ate secretly. Because one of a woman's entitlements consisted of food received from relatives, this would have further reduced the amount of food she received. Finally, divorce rates apparently increased significantly, particularly in families where the husband was a migrant laborer, further isolating women and reducing their food entitlements.

In sum, then, the most vulnerable portion of the population was women without male support but for whom the colonial authorities took no responsibility, married women whose husbands had abandoned them, and wives of long-term migrants who did not remit money (Vaughn 1987:147). In addition, of course, the children of these women suffered and died disproportionately.

The lesson of the Malawi famine is that starvation can be very selectively experienced within a population because of the distribution of food entitlements. Given the amount of food already available in the areas most affected by the famine and the food available through relief efforts, it is unlikely that anyone had to starve. But many did.

The Anatomy of Endemic Hunger

Although famine as a cause of hunger has decreased, endemic hunger caused by poverty has increased. One problem with endemic hunger is that it goes largely unnoticed or ignored, particularly by the press who prefer to cover the more spectacular instances of famine and by governments whose economic and social policies might be held responsible for the hunger. Yet endemic hunger is a far more serious problem. India, for example, which has done an excellent job of famine prevention, has done poorly in solving the problem of endemic hunger. Consequently, every eight years, more Indians die as a result of hunger than Chinese died in the famine of 1958–1961. Yet the deaths in India do not receive nearly the public attention that is given to famine. One of the questions we need to ask is, *How and why is endemic hunger ignored, unrecognized, and sometimes denied by state agencies, as well as by the hungry themselves?*

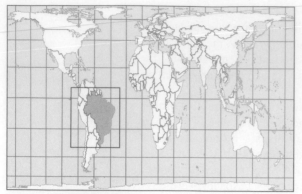

Brazil

Governments often refuse to recognize hunger because it marks an admission of failure to provide adequately for its citizens. And hunger sometimes goes unrecognized because it is assumed to be a medical problem, rather than a problem of food entitlements. Doing anthropological fieldwork in Mali, Katherine A. Dettwyler (1994:71–73) encountered a little girl with swelling of the face, hands, feet, and abdomen, classic symptoms of *kwashiorkor,* a disease that results from a diet that is sufficient in calories but deficient in protein. The girl's mother said she had *funubana,* "swelling sickness," and asked Dettwyler for medicine for her daughter, failing to recognize that what her daughter needed was extra meat or milk. When Dettwyler suggested just that, the mother responded by saying the little girl wasn't hungry and that she needed medicine. For the mother it continued to be a medical problem, not a food problem.

The denial of hunger prevents the development of programs to alleviate it. More insidiously, when hunger goes unrecognized or unacknowledged, problems that are a consequence of hunger, such as poor work performance, poor academic achievement, and stunted growth, are attributed to other factors, such as lack of motivation or cultural background.

To illustrate how social, economic, and cultural factors converge to produce hunger in the midst of plenty, as well as the complexity of identifying hunger and even admitting it exists, let's examine the case of starvation in Brazil in the 1980s. Brazil was not and is not a poor country; in fact, it is presently among the top ten to fifteen economies in the world ranking with India and China as a growing economic power. During the period of great optimism following World War II, Brazil was one of the first of the so-called underdeveloped countries to embark on a concerted policy of economic and industrial development. A large number of Brazilians have become very wealthy, yet 40 percent of its population lives in poverty, and, until recently, it had one of the highest rates of infant mortality in Latin America. Exploring why this happened will help us understand the dynamics of world hunger.

Brazil set out to develop economically by imitating the pattern followed by core countries such as England, France, and the United States. The strategy was to build industry, export cash crops, and create jobs, with the idea that the wealth created would "trickle down" to others in society. However, that didn't happen. Instead, peasants once able to secure a reasonable subsistence through simple agriculture are deprived of land, through either expropriation of land or privatization of communal land, and forced to work as wage laborers on the surviving farms or to flee to cities to seek work, often ending up in the shantytowns that surround the cities. Their wages are insufficient to buy food, and structural adjustment policies imposed by international lending institutions forced the reduction of social support programs. One thing stands out: The vast majority of the population becomes dependent on others for food, food they must buy and which must be affordable. Unfortunately, in many cases, they do not have the means to buy food, or prices keep it out of reach. The problem of hunger and poverty was, in the 1980s, particularly severe in northeastern Brazil.

Sugar dominated the economy of northeastern Brazil for more than 400 years. Fueled by a growing European demand for sugar, Portuguese colonists established plantations in the sixteenth century and imported slaves to grow and process sugarcane. The colonization of Brazil and the nature of the economic relations created by sugar production created a pattern of class relations that remained largely intact through the mid-twentieth century. A plantation-owning elite ruled over a large peasant population that cut sugarcane for wages, using unused land to grow their own food crops. A few others worked for wages in the sugar mills and refineries. However, as the sugar industry expanded and as technological improvements were made in the 1950s and 1960s because of government policies to expand production for export, many peasants were evicted from the land, fleeing to the cities in search of jobs. Poverty was widespread, and even people with jobs did not earn enough to meet family expenses. For example, in northeastern Brazil in 1989, the legal minimum monthly income was forty dollars, whereas food expenses alone for a family of four were four times that amount.

To make matters worse, in the mid-1980s, Brazil and other countries could not keep up their payments to the World Bank and other Western financial institutions from which they had borrowed to industrialize and, consequently, threatened to default on their loans. To help these countries avoid default, the World Bank allowed them to renegotiate their loans. These countries had to agree to change their economies by, among other things, reducing government spending on such things as public education, welfare, housing, and health, entitlement cutbacks that resulted in still greater hardships for the poorest portion of the population.

In 1982, Nancy Scheper-Hughes returned to the shantytown Alto do Cruzeiro, located in the city of Bom Jesus da Mata, where she had worked as a Peace Corps volunteer in 1965. The shantytown consisted of 5,000 rural workers, one-third of whom lived in straw huts. The vast majority of residents had no electricity, and water was collected by the women twice a day from a single spigot located in the center of the community. Most men and boys worked as sugarcane cutters during the harvest season. A few men and some women worked in the local slaughterhouse. Other than this part-time work, there was little employment. Many women found jobs as domestics among the middle- and upper-class families or sold what they could in the market. Many women and children worked in the cane fields as unregistered workers at less than minimum pay.

The economics of hunger in the shantytowns is simple—there is not enough money to buy food. Because of the economic situation in Brazil, Scheper-Hughes reported that in 1987–1988, groceries cost twice what they did in

A homeless mother and child trying to survive on the streets of a Brazilian city.
(Sean Sprague.)

1982. Furthermore, a basic subsistence costs one and a half times minimum wage. Many of the residents do not make minimum wage and are unemployed from February to September when there is no cane to cut. Furthermore, fresh vegetables that some used to grow or that were available from relatives in the countryside are no longer available because so many have been forced off the land by the sugarcane growers. In the 1960s, brown beans cooked with slices of native squash, pumpkin, and onions were a staple; now the beans are cooked with only a little salt and flavoring. Dried beef was once available but is now prohibitively expensive and has been replaced by salted fish caught in the polluted river that passes through town. Even dried beans have become prohibitively expensive, and dried cornmeal has taken its place.

With jobs scarce, available wages inadequate, land unavailable to grow food, and government assistance inadequate or nonexistent, residents of the shantytown scramble as best they can to acquire food. In fact, according to Scheper-Hughes, slow starvation is a primary motivating force in the social life of the shantytowns. People eat every day, but the diet is so meager that they are left hungry. Women beg while their children wait for food, and children's growth is stunted by hunger and malnutrition. Children of one and two years of age cannot sit unaided and cannot or do not speak. Breastbones and ribs protrude from taut skin, flesh hangs in folds from arms, legs, and buttocks, and sunken eyes stare vacantly. The plight of the worker and his or her family is, according to Scheper-Hughes (1992:146), "the slow starvation of a population trapped … in a veritable concentration camp for more than thirty million people."

Perhaps the most tragic result of hunger is the death of infants. Approximately 1 million children younger than five years of age died each year in Brazil. Northeastern Brazil, which accounted for 25 percent of child deaths, had an infant mortality rate of 116 of every 1,000 live births, one of the highest in the world at the time. And not all deaths were reported. Scheper-Hughes estimates that in northeastern Brazil, two-thirds of infants who died do so without a medical diagnosis.

Scheper-Hughes found that reliable statistics on infant mortality in the shantytowns were difficult to acquire. She finally obtained statistics for selected years in the 1970s, all of which indicated an infant mortality rate of 36 percent to 41 percent. From information she collected by combing public records, Scheper-Hughes found the following infant mortality rates for Bom Jesus da Mata: 49.3 percent in 1965; 40.9 percent in 1977; 17.4 percent in 1985; and 21.1 percent in 1987.

Although the infant mortality rate in northeastern Brazil has generally declined, the decline, said Scheper-Hughes (1992:280), is misleading. Instead of a decline in infant mortality, there is a "modernization of child mortality," characterized by containing child death to the poorest families and by a change in the major reported causes of child death from the "old killers" (diseases now controlled by immunization) to "new killers," especially infant malnutrition and dehydration caused by diarrhea.

News reports and government studies about poverty in Brazil do mention the problem of infant mortality, but they generally attribute it to malnutrition and disease. But Scheper-Hughes's study revealed a more basic problem: People, especially infants and children, are not only malnourished, a term that implies simply a poor diet, but are also in fact starving to death. Yet even medical authorities rarely mention starvation. When Scheper-Hughes examined medical records of children and infants who died, she found that in 34.8 percent of cases, the cause of death was cessation of heartbeat and respiration; in 22.2 percent it was listed as dehydration. Only 3.4 percent were attributed to malnutrition and only 1.7 percent to diarrhea. One wonders, wrote Scheper-Hughes (1992:303),

> amid the sea of froth and brine that carried away the infants and babies of the Alto do Cruzeiro, what kind of professional prudery it was that "failed to see" what every mother of the Alto do Cruzeiro knew without ever being told. "They die," said one woman going to the heart of the matter, "because their bodies turn to water."

One way to mask the evidence of starvation is to turn it into a medical problem; the medicalization of hunger is exactly what Scheper-Hughes discovered in Brazil. People interpret the symptoms of starvation, even in children, as conditions that require medical treatment rather than food.

One of the things anthropology teaches about the human capacity for culture is that people place experiences in systems of meaning that allow them to make sense of their experiences. Illness and disease are no exception; different people define differently what constitutes illness as opposed to something that is not illness. Moreover, people will define what constitutes a medical problem (e.g., infant diarrhea) as opposed to, say, a social problem (e.g., hunger). In northeastern Brazil, hunger, a social problem, has been redefined as a medical problem. How and why this has been done reveals much about how human beings construct their own world of experience and how people construct systems of meaning that best enhance their social or political interests.

One of the major traditional illness syndromes in Brazil, and indeed in much of Latin America, is *nervos,* assumed to be a wasting sickness that leaves the victim weak, shaky, dizzy, tired, depressed, and disoriented. When people are suffering from these symptoms, they say they are sick with *nervos.* People believe *nervos* is the result of an innately weak and nervous body. In years past when people thought they suffered an attack of *nervos,* they drew on their traditional store of herbal medicines and the practical knowledge of elderly women in the household. Today they seek medical help from one of the local clinics; now *nervos,* a traditional disease category, is thought to be treatable by modern medicine.

But there was another more insidious change in how people defined their physical condition: Symptoms associated with hunger began to be talked about as *nervos*—that is, hunger and *nervos* became synonymous. This was not always the case. Starvation and famine have long been a feature of life in northeastern Brazil; people frequently complained of *fome* (hunger) and its terrifying end, *delirio de fome,* the madness that signaled the end of life from starvation. But hunger is rarely mentioned today. If a person is weak, tired, or dizzy, he or she will not complain of hunger and seek food but instead complain of *nervos* and seek medicine to cure it. In other words, people who may be suffering from hunger and who twenty years ago would have defined themselves as suffering from *fome* now define themselves as suffering from *nervos,* an illness separate from hunger that simply happens or is the result of innate weakness. Moreover, if weakness, fatigue, dizziness, and other symptoms that may be related to slow starvation simply happen, then no one is at fault and social causes of the problem can be ignored.

Nancy Scheper-Hughes (1992:174) said a hungry body represents a potent critique of the nation-state in which it exists, but a sick body implicates no one and conveys no blame, guilt, or responsibility. Sickness simply happens. The sick person and the sick social system are let off the hook. A population suffering from starvation, however, represents a threat to the state that requires economic and social solutions—social programs, jobs, or land redistribution. *Nervos,* a sickness, is a personal and "psychological" problem that requires only medical intervention and faults no one, except perhaps the person suffering from it. Sickness requires little state action, other than supplying the occasional prescription of tranquilizers, vitamins, or sleeping pills. Instead of the responsible use of state power to relieve starvation and hunger, there is a misuse of medical knowledge to deny that there is a social problem at all.

Scheper-Hughes (1992:207) related the story of a young single mother who brought her nine-month-old child to the clinic, explaining that the baby suffered from *nervoso infantil.* She complained that the small, listless, and anemic child was irritable and fussy and disturbed the sleep of family members, especially the grandmother, who was the family's economic mainstay. Herbal teas did not work, and the grandmother threatened to throw them out if the child did not sleep. The doctor refused to give her sleeping pills for the child and instead wrote a prescription for vitamins. The doctor failed to acknowledge the mother's real distress, as well as the child's state of malnutrition, and the vitamins served virtually no purpose other than to redefine the infant's condition from starvation to sickness or malnutrition.

On other occasions, children will be brought to doctors with severe diarrhea, a classic symptom of starvation. Simple rehydration therapy, feeding the child special fluids, will usually cure the diarrhea for a time. But the child is still returned to an environment where, with lack of food, the problem is likely to recur until after being "saved" perhaps a dozen times the child finally dies of hunger.

The question, said Scheper-Hughes, is *how do people come to see themselves as primarily nervous and only secondarily hungry? How do they come to see themselves as weak, rather than exploited? How does overwork and exploitation come to be redefined as a sickness for which the appropriate cure is a tonic, vitamin A, a sugar injection? Why do chronically hungry people "eat" medicines and go without food?*

One reason is that since hungry people truly suffer from headaches, tremors, weakness, irritability, and other symptoms of nervous hunger, they look to doctors, healers, political leaders, and pharmacologists to "cure" them. They look for strong-acting medicines, so they line up at clinics and drugstores until they get them. One cannot, said Scheper-Hughes, underestimate the attractiveness of drugs to people who cannot read warning labels and who have a long tradition of "magical medicines."

Furthermore, she said, health is a political symbol subject to manipulation. Slogans such as "health for all by the year 2000," or "community health," filter down to poor, exploited communities where they serve as a cover for neglect and violence. There is power and domination to be obtained by defining a population as sick or nervous and in need of the power of politicians and doctors:

> The medicalization of hunger and childhood malnutrition in the clinics, pharmacies, and political chambers of Bom Jesus da Mata represents a macabre performance of distorted institutional and political relations. Gradually the people of Bom Jesus da Mata have come to believe that they desperately need what is readily given to them, and they have forgotten that what they need most is what is cleverly denied. (Scheper-Hughes 1992:169–170)

Conspiracy by medical workers is not necessary to effect this transformation. Doctors and clinic workers themselves accept the magical efficacy of cures; either that or they are demoralized to the extent that they prescribe drugs as the only solution they have to ills they are ill-prepared to solve but called on to treat. As one doctor (cited Scheper-Hughes 1992:204) said:

> They come in with headaches, no appetite, tiredness, and they hurt all over. They present a whole body in pain or in crisis, with an ailment that attacks them everywhere! That's impossible! How am I to treat that? I'm a surgeon, not a magician! They say they are weak, that they are nervous. They say their head pounds, their heart is racing in their chest, their legs are shaking. It's a litany of complaints from head to toe. Yes, they all have worms, they all have amoebas, they all have parasites. But parasites can't explain everything. How am I supposed to make a diagnosis?

SOLUTIONS AND ADAPTATIONS TO POVERTY AND HUNGER

What solutions are there to the problem of world hunger and the poverty that ultimately causes it? Is it best to focus on economic development or, as some call it, growth-mediated security systems, assuming so-called market mechanisms will improve people's lives? Or are famine and endemic hunger best addressed by public support systems in the form of state-financed food and nutrition programs, state-financed employment, or cash distribution programs? And, more importantly, in the absence of any effective solution, *how do the poor adapt to their plight?* The answers to these questions are not easy. Some argue, for example, that state-run programs take money needed for economic development and divert it to programs that may in the short run alleviate poverty and hunger but in the long run will simply aggravate the problem by undercutting the growth of private enterprise. This is the position generally taken by multilateral organizations, such as the World Bank and the International Monetary Fund (IMF), which insist on limitations or cutbacks in state spending as conditions for loans or structural adjustment programs to assist countries in debt. Others respond that state-run antipoverty programs represent an investment in the human capital necessary for economic development—that a population that is hungry, undernourished, and subject to disease is less productive. To answer these questions, we first examine the role of economic development in reducing poverty and hunger, then examine what has been termed the *informal economy* and how people adapt and sometimes take advantage of economic activities outside the purview of the nation-state.

Economic Development

The concept of "economic development" can be traced to U.S. president Harry S. Truman's inaugural address before Congress in 1949 in which he referred to the conditions in "poorer" nations and described them as "underdeveloped areas." At that point, multilateral institutions, such as the World Bank and the IMF, were mobilized to further development goals, often recommending massive economic and social changes and a total reorganization of societies deemed to be "undeveloped." For example, the 1949 World Bank report sent back from Colombia (and similar to that of hundreds to be issued in subsequent years) advised that

> piecemeal and sporadic efforts are apt to make little impression on the general picture. Only through a generalized attack throughout the whole economy on education, health, housing, food, and productivity can the vicious circle of poverty, ignorance, ill health, and low productivity be decisively broken. (International Bank for Reconstruction and Development [IBRD]1950:xv)

Proponents of economic development point to successes in raising life expectancy rates worldwide, lowering infant mortality rates, and raising literacy rates. They can point to the development of successful national economies in South Korea, Malaysia, and Brazil, among others.

Critics, however, paint a different picture. They argue that the goal of economic development to raise the living standards of people in the periphery, sixty years after its inception, has largely failed. A higher percentage of the world's population, they say, is hungrier today than in 1950. Studies by the very institutions at the forefront of development, such as the World Bank and IMF, conclude that the goals of development have not been met. Although poverty rates had declined somewhat in East Asia (from 26.6 percent in 1987 to 15.32 percent in 1999) and the Middle East (from 4.3 percent to 1.95 percent), elsewhere they have remained the same or increased. The poverty rate in Latin America and the Caribbean remains at 15.57 percent, at 39.99 percent in South Asia, and at 46.30 percent in sub-Saharan Africa (Chen and Ravallion 2000). In eastern Europe, the number living in poverty has climbed from 0.24 percent (1.07 million) in 1987 to 5.14 percent (24 million) in 1999. Furthermore, the absolute number living in poverty in the periphery increased over the same period from 1.1 billion to almost 1.2 billion. If the number of people living on less than two dollars a day is added, those living in poverty number 2.8 billion people.[2] Furthermore, the projects that were to promote "development" have notably decreased people's quality of life. Hundreds of millions of people have been displaced from their communities and homes or thrown off their land by World Bank hydroelectric and agricultural megaprojects. Instead of lifting the standard of living of peripheral countries, there has been a doubling of the degree of economic inequality between rich and poor countries in the past forty years. As one study concludes,

> there is no region in the world that the [World] Bank or [International Monetary] Fund can point to as having succeeded through adopting the policies that they promote—or, in many cases, impose—in borrowing countries. (Weisbrot, Naiman, and Kim 2000:3)

In addition, the economic crash of 2007 threatens to negate any economic gains of the past ten to twenty years. As we noted earlier, worldwide unemployment could rise by at least 30 million people, and possibly as much as 50 million people, while more than 200 million people, mostly in developing economies, will fall into poverty (see Blankenburg and Palma 2009).

The question, then, is, *Why, up to this point, has the economic development initiative largely failed?*

---

[2] The figures of $1.25 and $2.00 a day used by the World Bank, the United Nations, and other international agencies to measure poverty may also be misleading. In the United States, for example, poverty is measured, not by an arbitrary dollar amount, but by the costs of necessities such as food, clothing, shelter, and education. In 1996 in the United States, that amounted to $11 a day per person. The poverty standard used by the United Nations Development Program (UNDP) reports a lower poverty rate in Mexico than the United States, and a lower rate for Jamaica than Canada (see, e.g., Chossudovsky 1997, n.d.). Furthermore, most declines in global poverty rates are due largely to China where the number in poverty has been reported reduced by almost 400,000 people since 1981. The problem is that by shifting from a largely socialist to a market economy, people with little or no income, but who nevertheless received food, housing, and other benefits, now had to earn money to acquire necessities. Therefore they may or may not be better off.

There are three features of the economic development program that we need to examine. The first is the tendency to define the goals of development and an acceptable standard of living in the very limited terms of *income* and *gross national product* (GNP). Income and the level of production has become the measure of the worth of a society.

Second, economic development embodies an ideology that assumes that the culture and way of life of the core is universally desirable and should be exported (or imposed, if necessary) on the rest of the people of the world. As Wolfgang Sachs (1999:5) notes, "development meant nothing less than projecting the American model of society on the rest of the world."

Third, the concept of development greatly increased the power of core governments over the emerging nation-states of the periphery. If development was to be the goal, then "undeveloped" or "underdeveloped" countries must look to the expertise of the core for financial aid, technological aid, and political help. Furthermore, by embracing development as a goal, leaders of peripheral states gain military assistance and support that permit many of them to assume dictatorial powers over the rest of the population.

In his book *Seeing Like a State: How Human Schemes to Improve the Human Condition Have Failed* (1998), James C. Scott examines a series of failed development projects. Among these, says Scott, are the design and building of cities such as Brasilia, the Soviet collectivization of agriculture, the Russian revolution itself, and compulsory villagization in Tanzania. All were characterized, he says, by the same basic features, as previously mentioned, of economic development programs.

First, all these projects engaged in a form of economic reductionism; social reality was reduced to almost solely economic elements, ignoring institutions and behaviors essential to the maintenance of societies and environments. Reductionism of this sort is attractive to nation-states because it makes populations and environments more "legible" and, consequently, amenable to state manipulation and control. The guiding parable for understanding this reductive tendency is, for Scott, that of the "scientifically" managed forest.

Scientific forestry emerged in Prussia and Saxony in the last half of the eighteenth century. It viewed the forest almost solely as a source of revenue for the timber that might be annually extracted. Missing in this view was the foliage that might be fed to animals, game that might be hunted by farmers, or social interactions for which the forest served as a backdrop. Consequently, the first scientifically planted forests were set only with "productive" trees; anything that was thought to interfere with timber production was eliminated. Underbrush was cut, flora and fauna eliminated, and so on. The result in the first generation of trees was impressive; however, forestry officials soon found that the new forest was living off the capital of rich soil created by the disordered forest, and by the second and third generations, timber production had declined dramatically and the soil itself lost the capacity to produce. Thus, without all of the "worthless" elements of the forest, the forest itself collapsed.

The language of capitalism, says Scott, constantly betrays its tendency to reduce the world to only those items that are economically productive. Nature, for example, becomes "natural resources," identifying only those things that are commodifiable. Plants that are valued become "crops"; those that compete with them are stigmatized as "weeds." Insects that ingest crops are called "pests." Valuable trees are "timber," whereas species that compete with them are "trash" trees or "underbrush." Valued animals are "game," or "livestock," whereas competitors are "predators" or "varmints" (Scott 1998:13). In the language of economic development, the focus is on GNP, income, employment rates, kilowatts of electricity produced, miles of roads, labor units, productive acreage, and so on. Absent in this language are items that are not easily measured or that are noneconomic (e.g., quality of social relations and environmental aesthetics).

The second ingredient in failed projects, says Scott, is what he refers to as "high modern ideology." This ideology is characterized by a supreme (or, as Scott refers to it, a "muscle-bound") version of self-confidence in scientific and technical progress in satisfying human needs, mastering the environment, and designing the social order to realize these objectives. This ideology emerged as a by-product of unprecedented progress in the core and was attributed to science and technology. High modern ideology does not correspond to political ideologies and can be found equally on the left and the right. Generally, however, it entails using state power to bring about huge, utopian changes to people's lives.

The idea of economic development is a product of high modern ideology. It represents an uncritical acceptance of the idea of scientific and technological progress, and an unrestrained faith in the wisdom of core economic, scientific, and technological principles. The green revolution and the attempt to widely apply the technology of genetic engineering discussed earlier are but two other products of high modern ideology.

Scott is careful not to reject outright the application of high modern ideology. In some cases it can and has led to significant improvements in peoples' lives. Thus, economic reductionism and high modern ideology are not, in themselves, sufficient to contribute to a failed project. For failure to occur, there is a third ingredient—an authoritarian state. When high modern ideology and the nation-state's tendency to reduce the world to legible, manipulative units is combined with an authoritarian state willing, and able to use the full weight of its coercive power, to bring these high modernist designs into being, along with a civil society that is unable to resist its manipulations, the stage is set for a development disaster. As Scott says,

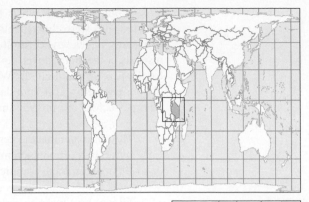

Tanzania

> the legibility of a society provides the capacity for large-scale engineering, high-modernist ideology provides the desire, the authoritarian state provides the determination to act on that desire, and an incapacitated civil society provides the leveled social terrain on which to build. (1998:5)

To illustrate how the goals of economic development and modernization can lead to disruption, Scott describes the *ujamaa* village campaign in Tanzania from 1973 to 1976. It represented a massive attempt to permanently settle most of the country's population in villages planned, partly or wholly, by officials of the central government (Scott 1998:221).

Clearly, the village scheme emerged from a desire of the Tanzanian state to make its population more legible and manipulable. At the beginning of the development scheme, there were some 11 million to 12 million rural Tanzanians living in scattered settlements, growing crops and herding animals, using techniques developed over generations. As the natural forest contained elements to sustain it, so these settlements sustained themselves with local knowledge and practice built up over the years. From the viewpoint of the state, however, these populations were economically unproductive, disordered, and, somehow, primitive. The project, which succeeded in moving more than 13 million people into 7,684 villages (Scott 1998:245), was to transform the citizenry into producers of exportable crops, strung out along paved roads where state services could be easily delivered and where the population could be easily monitored. Furthermore, the success of the villagization program could be easily tracked by counting the number of people moved, the number of villages built, and so on.

Clearly, the project was driven by a high modern ideology imported from the West that assumed that "modern" settlement patterns, agricultural techniques, and modes of communication were clearly superior to those practiced by the indigenous population. In fact, notes Scott (1998:241), these premises were holdovers from the colonial era. Project designers and supporters assumed that African cultivators and pastoralists were backward, unscientific, and inefficient. They assumed that only through the supervision or, if necessary, coercion by specialists in scientific agriculture could they contribute to a modern Tanzania.

Finally, as with most development schemes, there had to be an authoritarian state to impose the program and to suppress resistance to it. From the beginning, Tanzanians were skeptical about villagization. Whereas they had knowledge of the areas in which they lived, the new, selected sites were chosen without consideration of water or fuel resources, and they feared that being in villages would result in overcrowding for people and domestic animals. To meet this resistance, the state moved its machinery into place to force compliance. It was, said officials, for the people's own good. "We cannot tolerate," said Tanzanian president Julius Nyerere, "seeing our people live a 'life of death' " (Scott 1998:230). All of this was keeping with World Bank reports, such as one in 1964 that said,

> How to overcome the destructive conservatism of the people and generate the drastic agrarian reform which must be effected if the country is to survive is one of the most difficult problems political leaders of Tanzania have to face. (Scott 1998:241)

Given the situation, violence was inevitable. The police and militia were given authority to move people, first threatening that they would not be eligible for famine relief if they did not move, later forcing them to tear down and load houses and belongings onto trucks. In some cases, houses were burned or run over with trucks. When people realized that resistance was futile, they saved what they could move and fled the new villages at the first opportunity (Scott 1998:235–236).

As might be expected, the results of villagization were disastrous. Huge imports of food were necessary from 1973 to 1975 because of the immediate decline of agricultural production, the cost of which would have bought a cow for every Tanzanian family. Some 60 percent of the new villages were built on semiarid land that required long walks to reach farm plots. Peasants were moved from fertile farmlands to poor lands or land on which the soil was unsuitable for the crops the government demanded farmers grow. Villages were located at a distance from crops, which left the crops open to theft and pests. The concentration of people and livestock resulted in cholera and livestock epidemics, while herding cattle in concentrated areas devastated both rangeland and livelihoods (Scott 1998:247). Instead of achieving legitimacy, the villagization campaign created an alienated and uncooperative peasantry for which Tanzania would pay a huge financial and political price.

Of course, the scheme was not totally Tanzanian. It resembled hundreds of colonial schemes, built on the supposed promise of modern science and technology, as well as projects still supported by the World Bank, the USAID, and other development agencies. That it was a disaster should come, in retrospect, as no surprise, in spite of the conviction of virtually everyone involved that it would vastly improve the life of the subjects. More disturbing yet is that the Tanzanian government, at the urging of the World Bank and the U.S. government, continues to relocate indigenous peoples with similar negative results (see, e.g., Fratkin 1997a;1997b).

Based on his examination of failed projects, Scott (1998:348) concludes that the major fault is that the project planners thought they were smarter than they really were and that they regarded the subjects of their plans as far more stupid and incompetent than they really were. By trying to impose a vision of modernization and progress built largely on economic criteria and a vision of life that emerged in the West, high modern ideologues fostered the social and cultural equivalent of unsustainable, impoverished, monocropped, and "scientifically managed" forests, environments devoid of the social stuff that enable people in communities to form cooperative units and work together to achieve common goals.

The Nature and Growth of the Informal Economy

Having a job in a market economy is essential. Employment is, for the vast proportion of the world's population, the major means of entitlement to necessary goods and services. But what happens when there are not enough jobs? Presently there are at least 195.2 million people unemployed in the world, along with some 1.37 billion working poor—those working but living on less than the equivalent of U.S.$2.00 per day. Unemployment most affects people aged 15 to

24 (some 86.3 million of them), representing 44 percent of total unemployed (International Labor Organization 2007). There are various reasons for unemployment other than the obvious fact that there are not enough jobs. Many of the unemployed are recent migrants fleeing economically depressed rural areas and moving to cities in search of jobs. In 2007, for the first time, more than half of the world's population lived in cities, a percentage that is expected to climb to two-thirds by 2030. *But what happens in areas where people go in search of employment, but there are no jobs? More to the point, what steps do people take independent of the nation-state to escape poverty?*

Economic policymakers, as well as the media, often convey the impression that the poor passively accept their economic circumstances or are in poverty because they somehow lack initiative. Missing from these conceptions is the consideration of how the poor and unemployed adapt by tapping into the informal or underground economy and surviving on income that never appears in any government accounts. The informal economy consists of economic activities that are illegible to the state, which is one reason why it is difficult to track the income earned from these sources. These activities range from babysitting, to auto repair, to begging, to the sale of children and women, to the incredibly complex and global enterprise of illegal drug sales. In the United States, activities forming part of the underground economy might include a plumber taking cash for a repair, a gang member selling cocaine, a pawnbroker fencing stolen goods, farmers employing illegal immigrants, textile manufacturers running a sweatshop, border dwellers smuggling cigarettes, or people selling fake Rolexes or pirating CDs (Schlosser 2003:4). The informal economy is often the residue of nation-state attempts to regulate a commodity or activity by banning or taxing it or by controlling its distribution. Such attempts provide spaces for the informal economy by providing people the opportunity to either sell a banned commodity (e.g., illegal drugs) or provide the commodity or activity at lower costs (e.g., smuggled cigarettes).

Anthropologist Keith Hart (2000) was one of the first to name and draw attention to the informal economy. During his research in the city of Accra in Ghana, he noted that the masses of surplus laborers were not "unemployed" but rather worked for erratic and low returns. The streets of Accra, Hart said, were

> teeming with life, a constantly shifting crowd of hawkers, porters, taxi-drivers, beggars, pimps, pickpockets, hustlers—all of them doing their best to get by without the benefit of a real job of the sort found in national economic statistics. (2000:149–150)

Participants in this informal economy were not limited to the poor, although they, particularly women (see Carr and Chen 2001), depended on it for their survival more than anyone else; virtually everyone, even those who were part of the formal economy, took part. Informal opportunities included everything from market gardening and brewing to gambling, theft, and political corruption. Hart (2000:151–154) describes the case of Atinga who, getting out of the army, invested his last salary payment to divide his living quarters in two by setting up a partition and opening a bar in which he sold gin. He would buy a barrel of gin for about four or five pounds and sell it by the drink or bottle. Profits were minimal because many of his clients could only pay on credit, if at all, but he managed to make a little while looking for a more permanent job. He finally got a job as a night watchman, turning the bar over to his wife to run. However, business declined and his wife drank most of the gin. Occasionally his income would rise when he was able to purchase a stray dog for meat and soup sold at the bar, but ultimately he left with his family while his landlord's wife took over the enterprise.

While activities such as these might seem a minor feature of an economy, in totality, they represent a significant part of the global GDP and have a major impact on other aspects of the economy. While there is no agreement on the size of the informal economy, most acknowledge that it is vast and growing. The International Monetary Fund estimates that illicit funds amount to between U.S.\$590 billion and U.S.\$1.5 trillion, or 1 percent to 5 percent of the world GDP.

And that is probably a significant underestimate. In the United States alone, it is estimated to be some 9.4 percent of the total economy, or some $650 billion. In other countries it is even larger, ranging from 12.5 percent of the GDP in Great Britain; 27 percent in Italy; 40 percent in Brazil; 45 percent in Russia; and 51 percent in the Ukraine (Schlosser 2003:5–6). The informal economy in Asia is estimated to range from 45 percent to 85 percent of the nonagricultural GDP and 80 percent of the nonagricultural GDP of Africa (Carr and Chen 2001). The UN estimates that the money generated by organized and unorganized crime alone—illicit gambling, illegal arms trade, human smuggling, traffic in body organs, car theft, prostitution and racketeering, and, most of all, drug sales—is about U.S.$1 trillion. Furthermore, the money-laundering activities that accompany illegal enterprises have a significant impact in the global economy, even being implicated in the financial crises that hit Mexico in 1994–1995 and Thailand in 1997 (Fabre 2002).

Anthropologist Christian Geffray's (2002) courageous work examining illegal drug networks in the Amazon provides us with an excellent case study of how informal economies develop, how they intersect with the formal economy, and how they impact local and regional economies. In the 1970s, the World Bank financed construction of the BR 364 highway in Brazil, through the rain forests of the state of Rondônia. Prior to the road construction, the forests were occupied only by indigenous groups and *caboclos,* local populations that lived along the rivers and worked for entrepreneurs (e.g., rubber merchants) who lived in the towns. But the roads brought in hundreds of thousands of mostly poor people who wanted to try out their luck on the frontier. The first phase of the emergence of an informal economy comprised the activities of Bolivian cocaine traffickers who set up laboratories on the Bolivian side of the Mamoré River and began smuggling supplies (e.g., ether, kerosene, and acetone) for coca processing from Rondônia in exchange for processed cocaine. Among those involved in the smuggling were gold prospectors (*garimpeiro*) working on the river. The *garimpeiro* worked on balsa rafts pumping alluvial deposits from the riverbed and processing it on the surface. As Geffray (2002:34) put it, the cocaine producers and dealers and "thousands of often penniless Brazilian gold prospectors, isolated in the forest and abandoned by society, faced each other on either side of the river."

The divers were under severe mental and physical stress and often relieved their tension of working underwater for hours at a time by crossing the river and getting coca paste to smoke. These workers would occasionally trade gold for cocaine and spread it among the poor and working-class populations of the area. Gradually the cocaine made its way to Brazilian cities where the unemployed and working-class population could engage in small-scale dealing. Meanwhile, in Rondônia, the drug traffic led to a lively trade in stolen goods (vehicles, aircraft, farm machinery, electronic equipment, cattle, etc.) exchanged for cocaine. Larger traffickers in drugs or stolen goods then began to invest their money in legal enterprises as a means of laundering the money earned in the informal economy. (Money laundering is a process in which funds that are obtained illegally are made to appear as though they originated from a legitimate source [e.g., see Steel 2006]. For example, drug traffickers laundered money by investing in balsa rafts used by gold prospectors so they could claim that the money they earned in the drug trade came from gold prospecting.)

Thus, the money brought in through the informal economy began to feed the formal economy. The process by which formal and informal economies intersect is illustrated in Rondônia by the career of Jabes Rabelo. His family owned coffee warehouses, and Jabes Rabelo began to use money he earned as a drug trafficker to purchase coffee from local producers. Since his goal was not to make money in the coffee trade but to exchange his illegal drug money into legal coffee money, he paid coffee producers well above the market value of their coffee and sold the coffee to processors at prices below what others were selling it at. This had a number of side effects: First, it drove legitimate coffee dealers (those not using drug money) out of business because they couldn't pay the high prices that drug traffickers were willing to pay, and it artificially raised the profits of the coffee producers. In effect, coffee production was being subsidized by cocaine money. It also ingratiated the drug traffickers with local coffee producers and others in the population who benefited directly or indirectly from the illegal trafficking in drugs and other goods. Finally, it provided those who succeeded in the informal economy with money with which to either bribe government officials (another feature of the informal economy) or to run for elected office themselves. Thus, Jabes Rabelo invested his dirty money into rural trade that allowed him to take control of the whole coffee market and, in the process, establish a network of alliances within the elites. His role in subsidizing the coffee business led the elites to elevate him to a "Citizen of Honour," bragging that one of its citizens was the state's biggest buyer and exporter of coffee. Rabelo's control and subsidization of the producers enabled him to build broad support and become the *de facto* benefactor of thousands of people in rural areas; consequently, he had little difficulty being elected a federal deputy. Each year at Christmas and Easter he would send out trucks full of toys, chocolate eggs, and other gifts to children of the poor and provide drinks at charity events. The arrest in 1991 of his brother, who possessed 540 kilos of cocaine, did nothing to affect Rabelo's popularity (Geffray 2002:39).

Geffray's description of the evolution of the informal economy of Rondônia—one he characterizes as a "society ruled by drug trafficking" (2002:45)—illustrates how an informal economy emerges, the extent to which thousands of people come to depend on it, and how it can dominate a local economy. It also illustrates how the informal economy can allow the emergence of new elites who, financed by their profits from the informal economy, gain power through patronage and election to public office.

The Nature and Scope of the Informal Economy of Drugs

Illegal drugs are clearly one of the most important commodities produced, distributed, and sold in the global informal economy. Drugs, in general, have been a mainstay of the global economy for well over 300 years. Tobacco is a good example. It originated in the Americas and was first observed by Europeans during Columbus's first voyage when sailors saw Taino Indians smoking leaves rolled into large cigars. It was brought back to Europe, but for most of the sixteenth century, it was largely a novelty item until its cultivation became global and the increased supply annually drove down the price. By 1670, the Dutch were using on average 1.5 pounds per person, and the English over a pound. Its use spread rapidly, particularly as prices decreased, and was fashionable in Europe in the nineteenth century; by 1925, the French were using about three pounds per person. By 1950, American men and women were purchasing 15,000 cigarettes a second, and by the mid-1990s, there were 1.1 billion smokers in the world, about one-third of the population over fifteen, smoking 5.5 trillion cigarettes a year, or a pack a week for every person on the planet (Courtwright 2001). But tobacco, as with other widely traded addictive substances such as coffee and tea, has never been deemed illegal. It has, however, been widely taxed and regulated, its addictive quality guaranteeing nation-states a steady income. The state's attempt at extracting income from tobacco's sales also cemented its status in the informal economy as people sought to evade the taxes and fees associated with its use.

Three other widely traded addictive substances—opium, cannabis, and coca, which were widely used in products such as cough syrups, soft drinks, and various tonics—were ultimately declared illegal, first in the United States in 1914. However, by making opium, cannabis, and coca illegal, the state created a group of commodities that became the pillars of the informal economy.

It is difficult to calculate the place of illegal drugs in the global economy. The United Nations Office on Drugs and Crime (UNODC 2006:17) estimates that the global drug trade generates $320 billion a year in revenue, or some 0.9 percent of the world's GDP, equal to the GDP of all but 12 percent of the countries in the world. Put another way, the sale of drugs is equal to 12 percent of the global export of chemicals (U.S.$794 billion), 14 percent of global agricultural exports (U.S.$674 billion), and exceeded the global exports of ore and minerals (U.S.$79 billion). Cannabis is the most widely grown and used drug (some 162 million people), followed by amphetamine-type stimulants (some 35 million people), and ecstasy (almost 10 million people). Opiate users number some 16 million, of which 11 million use heroin and 1.3 million cocaine

(United Nations 2005:9). In all, some 200 million people, or some 5 percent of the global population, used an illegal drug at least once. Practically speaking, if the legal suppression of the drug trade actually succeeded, much of the world economy from Bolivia to Afghanistan to Northern California could collapse (Henson 2005).

In many ways, the informal economy in drugs is simply another economic sector that works like any other. There are the producers, generally small farmers in Afghanistan, Colombia, or the United States, doing what they have to do to make a living; there are the buyers and processors, often organized into large gangs or cartels; and there are the large-scale distributors and the small retailers, whose profits are small and risks great.

To understand the importance of drugs in the informal economy, especially for the poor, let's examine the role they played in two different places and eras: London in the early eighteenth century and New York in the late twentieth century.

London may have provided the first "drug craze." The drug involved was gin. Distilled beverages had been available to the English working classes since the late sixteenth century but were too expensive to be used for other than medical purposes among the poor. But when grain production in England increased, cheap gin produced from the grain became available and the amount of it consumed increased annually from about a third of a gallon per person in the early 1700s to about 2.2 gallons per person in 1743. Seeking to raise revenue, the government placed an excise tax on drinks and required licenses for those who sold gin, thus providing an opportunity for small sellers to hawk drinks at cheaper prices.

Taking advantage of the opening created by the government's attempt to tax gin were the thousands of new immigrants arriving in the city without employment or housing, driven off the land by enclosure movements. Gin was appealing first as a source of solace and second as a source of employment. These immigrants were mostly young and poor with few ties to family, employers, or the larger community, and, as such, were a worry to the elite. But the increased use of and thriving informal economy in gin led to the passage of a series of legislative acts attempting to further control both the sale of gin and the people who could use it. Most of the early gin acts were rarely enforced (London had no formal police force in the eighteenth century), but the Gin Act of 1736, which required sellers to purchase a license for fifty pounds, also offered a fee of five pounds for information leading to a conviction of someone selling gin without a license. This created an army of informers made up of essentially the same strata of society from which the gin sellers came.

But the informal economy in gin continued to thrive. For many, the selling of gin made the difference between poverty and destitution. They sold gin in hovels; "gin shops"; or out of wheelbarrows, baskets, and even boats. And women were among the major peddlers. As Jessica Warner describes it in her book *Craze: Gin and Debauchery in an Age of Reason,* selling gin appealed to women because it required little or no capital, it did not require membership in professional organizations, and it was one of the few occupations that women were not excluded. It was, as Warner (2002:51) put it, a means of economic survival. But women were also at greater risk; while they accounted for only about 20 percent of the known gin retailers in London, they accounted for 70 percent of the people charged under the Gin Act of 1736.

With so many dependent on the informal economy for gin and the addictive quality of the commodity feeding its sales, the London elite and the government became more concerned about its consumption. However, they had to contend with not only the informal sellers and consumers, but also with those among the elite who profited from gin sales. These included the grain growers and sellers whose product was converted into gin. It also included the state, which used the money from gin taxes to finance England's war with France. But those arguing for increased regulation of gin generally prevailed. They reasoned that drunkenness was a direct cause of such things as robberies, assaults, and even murders, their claims given credence by the occasional deaths, injuries, and fights attributed to gin consumption reported widely in newspapers and pamphlets. They also felt that the poor's consumption of distilled beverages was above their station in life. They argued that by reducing drunkenness, they could reduce lawlessness and

The different attitudes of the British toward gin and beer, and people who used each, are depicted in these eighteenth-century prints by William Hogarth, *Gin Lane* (left) and *Beer Street* (right).   (Left: *Gin Lane* is a print issued in 1751 by William Hogarth (1697–1764) an English painter, printmaker, in support of what would become the Gin Act. It depicts the evils of the consumption of gin/Universal History Archive/UIG/The Bridgeman Art Library. Right: William Hogarth (1697–1764), *Beer Street in London*, engraving, 1751/De Agostini Picture Library/A. Daglı Ortı/The Bridgeman Art Library)

increase the respect of the working poor for their employers. Hard work and low wages, they thought, would keep down the cost of British exports and keep the poor in their place (Warner 2002:112). Ironically, there was never any attempt to regulate beer consumption in spite of the fact that the average Londoner consumed some thirty gallons a year. The conflicting attitudes toward gin and beer are evident in two prints by William Hogarth—*Gin Lane* and *Beer Street*. The former depicts lives of misery and destitution, while the latter a street filled with productive enterprise (see illustration).

But the attempts to control gin by unleashing an army of informers turned neighbor against neighbor, creating attitudes of mistrust and provoking riots and protest. In other words, the attempts at regulation created, in many ways, a worse situation than the offense it was supposed to stop (Warner 2002:159–160).

The protests and riots that ensued after the passage of the Gin Act of 1736 led to the gradual nonenforcement of the regulation and a gradual increase in gin consumption to about two and a half gallons a year per person. Then public concern led to the passage of the Gin Act of 1751, which raised excise tax on gin to 4.5 pence a gallon, barred distillers form selling gin, and banned it in prisons, workhouses, and poorhouses. It enacted stricter standards for eligibility to obtain a license. Consumption dropped, as it had in 1736, but began to rise again in 1756 until the government banned altogether the manufacture of spirits from domestic grains because of crop failures.

There are a number of lessons to be learned from the gin craze in eighteenth-century London, such as the role of drugs in the informal economy and attitudes toward and attempts to regulate addictive drugs. But before we examine those, let's go to New York City of the 1980s and Philippe Bourgois's study of the drug economy of East Harlem, or *el Barrio*. Like London of the early eighteenth century, East Harlem was the destination for hundreds of thousands of immigrants, largely from Puerto Rico. Like most of the migrants to London, many had been semisubsistence peasants on private plots or haciendas or were workers on sugar plantations or assembly plants. And like the arrivals in London, many found it difficult to get jobs in the formal economy (the area had a 40 percent unemployment rate), turning instead to the informal sector to survive.

For women, activities in the informal economy included babysitting, working "off the books" as seamstresses, tending bar at social clubs, taking in boarders, or engaging in prostitution. Men's jobs tended to be more visible: street-corner car repairs, working for unlicensed contractors, selling "numbers," or selling drugs. Drugs were the multibillion-dollar foundation of the underground economy in *el Barrio*. Cocaine, crack, and heroin were the most prevalent drugs and were easily accessible, says Bourgois:

> The street in front of my tenement was not atypical, and within a two block radius I could…obtain heroin, crack, powder cocaine, hypodermic needles, methadone, Valium, angel dust, marijuana, bootleg alcohol, and tobacco. Within one hundred yards of my stoop there were three competing crack houses selling vials at two, three, and five dollars. Just a few blocks farther north down, in one of the local "pill mills," a doctor wrote $3.9 million worth of Medicaid prescriptions in only one year, receiving nearly $1 million for his services. Ninety-four percent of his "medicines" were on the Department of Social Services' list of frequently abused prescription drugs. (1995:3–4)

The 1980s drug scene in the United States was dominated by the use of crack cocaine, a combination of cocaine and baking soda that could be smoked and that delivered an almost instantaneous high. As London had the "gin shop," East Harlem had the "crack house." These were run by dealers who would hire managers and lookouts for a share of the income, often bringing in hundreds of dollars a night, although, as Bourgois (1995:91) points out, most street-level dealers remained penniless because of their need to spend lavishly. In addition, working in the informal drug economy was dangerous. Bourgois indicates that when you calculate the risks (getting beat up or killed), the off-time (jail or crack house closings by police), the poor working conditions, the conditions of the clientele, and legal costs, employment in the crack economy is generally much worse than legal employment. Thus, many of the drug dealers that Bourgois worked with sought jobs or business opportunities in the formal economy, generally with little success.

As in London, women were a significant part of the drug underground economy of *el Barrio*. Women, says Bourgois, were forced into a balancing act between the two state agencies that dominated their lives—the penal system and the welfare system. Given the attack on welfare of the 1980s launched by the Reagan administration, it was virtually impossible to maintain a family on welfare alone. Consequently, women had to supplement their income with off-the-books jobs, maintain two or more Social Security cards, or sell drugs. Those who became drug users themselves often turned to prostitution to maintain their habit. Welfare was complicated by the city practice of requiring recipients to requalify every six months and cutting off benefits if they couldn't supply accurate documentation. As a result, some 10 percent to 15 percent of New York City recipients were being terminated each year.

Thus, the poor of East Harlem were hit by a double economic plague: Because of global trade liberalization, manufacturing jobs for which the new migrants were most qualified were being sent overseas, some 800,000 of them from the 1960s through the early 1990 in New York City alone. At the same time, the government was reducing its support for the poor. These conditions created a situation where desired commodities (crack and other drugs), easy (although restricted) availability, and a surplus supply of laborers created a thriving informal economy.

But participation in the informal economy carried a stigma and, at the same time, provided the state with an opportunity to blame the victims and diminish its responsibility for poverty and hunger. In the cases of both gin and crack, a drug and those associated with it were blamed for societal problems for which the drugs were symptoms rather than causes. For example, children were prominent in both the gin and crack debates; in Hogarth's *Gin Lane,* a baby is plunging to its death as its mother drinks, while another sits uncared for by the coffin of its mother. In the late 1980s, critics started claiming that our children were being taken from us by crack. Politicians joined with journalists to condemn the mothers of babies addicted to crack cocaine. The *San Jose Mercury News* noted that "the image of bad women destroying their babies in the womb fits perfectly with the politics of demonizing drugs and regulating pregnancy" (Warner 2002:210). Rather than demonizing an ethnic group or social class, the crack epidemic of the late 1980s and 1990s, says Warner (2002:278–279), assaulted women, the family, and motherhood. Inner-city women who smoked crack were accused of having lost the "mother-nurture instinct." One reason for this was the fact that for the first time in U.S. history, women comprised half the addicts on the streets, and because they were often the only family providers, they brought toddlers and newborns with them to the crack houses.

In commenting on Hogarth's print *Gin Lane,* Warner says,

> It is a remarkable print—easily Hogarth's best—and it succeeds as propaganda because it identifies cause and effect in terms that are as stark as they are seemingly irrefutable. Gin is cause and poverty its effect. It is a very appealing equation: take away gin and away goes poverty and in comes the jolly prosperity of *Beer Street.* The converse is a little trickier, for it forces us to do something about it. This approach was, of course, even less popular in eighteenth century England than it is today. Poverty and gin were inextricably linked, but which came first? Most of London's working poor led lives of unspeakable misery before the advent of gin; moreover, their lives, as measured by real wages, were even more wretched after its demise. It was not gin that made people poor; it was poverty that made them drink. (2002:213)

The problem, says Warner (2002:212), is assuming that any drug such as gin or crack cocaine is the cause of the poor health and behavior of users. Such an assumption removes the nation-state from any responsibility for the environments that make drugs attractive as commodities. It is, to some extent, the equivalent of "medicalizing" hunger. If it is the weakness and criminality of the poor that is responsible for their condition, then the nation-state and those who control it are absolved of responsibility.

But the criminalization of certain commodities and activities has another insidious consequence. The history of drugs is characterized by the association of certain commodities or activities with marginalized groups of people. In eighteenth-century London, gin was associated with the poor, while beer and other distilled beverages were associated with the elite or the working class. Likewise, in the United States, specific drugs have been selectively associated with marginalized groups: Opium at the turn of the century was associated with Chinese immigrants, marijuana with Mexican immigrants, and cocaine with African Americans, while other drugs, alcohol, coffee, and tobacco were associated with mainstream populations and considered acceptable.

But by criminalizing only those drugs associated with marginalized populations, the nation-state may bring judicial authorities to bear on those groups; they become objects of legitimate suspicion, surveillance, and control. Thus, to the extent that marginalized populations engage in activities that are criminalized, it permits the state to selectively deprive them of many rights held by other members of society. The case of marijuana is illustrative. It was perfectly legal until the 1920s when it became associated with Mexican immigrants. In the 1930s, when Mexican immigrants were competing for scarce jobs, marijuana was demonized as the "evil weed" and criminalized in the Marijuana Tax Act. The 1936 film *Reefer Madness* tells the story of high school students who are lured into trying marijuana, which results in a hit-and-run accident, a suicide, a rape, and a descent into madness. Then in the 1960s and 1970s, marijuana began to be associated with the white middle-class student counterculture. Consequently, marijuana laws were relaxed, and government commissions removed marijuana from the list of dangerous drugs. In the 1980s, conservative parent groups convinced the government to criminalize marijuana once again, although the black arrest rate for marijuana offences are 2.5 times the rate for whites, probably reflecting the degree of discretion that allowed the police in making arrests (NORML 2000).

As a consequence of the criminalization of drugs, the United States has the largest prison population in the world—over 2.2 million people, or 1 of every 136 people. In 2005 in the United States, 1,846,351 people were arrested for drug violations; of those, 786,545 were marijuana related, and 696,074 (37 percent of all drug arrests) were for possession alone (Office of National Drug Control Policy 2007).

CONCLUSION

It is apparent that hunger is not caused by a lack of food, but rather by some people's lack of ability to purchase food. It is also apparent that the poverty that causes hunger is a consequence of global economic forces, such as the financial debt that peripheral countries accumulated in the 1970s. Other instances of hunger and famine are generally a consequence of political unrest. Even in relatively wealthy countries, such as Brazil, the growing gap between rich and poor that has seemingly resulted from growing integration into the world economy results in thousands dying of starvation.

We have seen, furthermore, that economic policies of the wealthy countries are not designed to help the poor countries but to further the interests of corporate and political agendas. As we have seen, economic development programs have, by and large, done very little to help their intended beneficiaries, and in many cases have created enormous suffering, economic hardships, and environmental devastation.

However, we examined the types of adaptations the poor sometimes make to their condition, engaging the informal economy and the financial opportunities it offers, as well as the price they sometimes pay in government surveillance and prosecution.

7 Environment and Consumption

If the life-supporting ecosystems of the planet are to survive for future generations, the consumer society will have to dramatically curtail its use of resources—partly by shifting to high-quality, low-input durable goods and partly by seeking fulfillment through leisure, human relationships, and other nonmaterial avenues.

—ALAN DURNING, *How Much Is Enough?*

A man is rich in proportion to the things he can afford to let alone.

—HENRY DAVID THOREAU, *Walden*

"Sustainable," we think, has now to be understood ideologically, as the effects that the majority of people can be persuaded to find tolerable, as the necessary environmental consequence of an ever more necessary growth process.

—ELAINE HARTWICK AND RICHARD PEET

All animals alter their environments as a condition of their existence. Human beings, in addition, alter their environments as a condition of their cultures—that is, by the way they choose to obtain food, produce tools and products, and construct and arrange shelters. But culture, an essential part of human adaptation, can also threaten human existence when short-term goals lead to long-term consequences that are harmful to human life. Swidden agriculture alters the environment but not as much as irrigation agriculture and certainly not as much as modern agriculture with its use of chemical fertilizers, pesticides, and herbicides. Domesticated animals alter environments, but keeping a few cattle for farm work or cows for dairy products does far less damage than maintaining herds of thousands to supply a meat-centered diet.

The degree to which environments are altered and damaged is determined in part by population and in part by the technology in use. Obviously, the more people in a given area, the more potential there is for environmental disruption. Tractors and bulldozers alter the environment more than hoes or plows. But the greatest factor in environmental alteration—in the use of raw materials, the use of nonhuman energy, and the production of waste—is consumption. Because of our level of consumption, the average American child will do twice the environmental damage of a Swedish child, three times that of an Italian child, thirteen times that of a Brazilian child, thirty-five times that of an Indian child, and 280 times that of a Chadian or Haitian child (Kennedy 1993:32).

The United States alone uses over 20 percent of the world's energy and accounts for over 20 percent of the world's carbon emissions that are responsible for global warming (see Table 7.1). The United States and Canada have by far the highest per capita rates of energy usage and carbon emissions of any countries on earth. They are also the countries most resisting the implementation of the Kyoto Accord, an international agreement negotiated in 1992 to reduce global carbon emissions to 1990 levels. One of the questions that we must ask is, *why are some of the most powerful nations on earth resisting measures to preserve it?*

One of the best ways to appreciate the impact of lifestyle on the environment is through the method of the ecological footprint developed by Mathis Wackernagel and William E. Rees (1996). The ecological footprint calculates the amount of land available to supply necessary resources and absorb waste given the consumption patterns of individual countries. They estimate, for example, that some 15 acres (6.4 hectares) of land are required to maintain the consumption level of the average person from a high-consumption country. The problem is that in 2006, worldwide there were only 4.5 acres (2.1 hectares) of ecologically productive land for each person (see Table 7.2). For example, each person in the United States requires some 22.3 acres to maintain his or her consumption levels; but the country as a whole can support only 10.9 acres for each person, leaving a deficit of 11.3 acres. If we calculate how many acres a U.S. consumer uses by considering the number of acres available to each person on earth, the deficit increases to 17.8 acres. Wackernagel and Rees conclude that the deficit is made up in core countries by drawing down the natural resources of their own countries and expropriating the resources, through trade, of peripheral countries. In other words, someone has to pay for our consumption levels, and it will either be our children or inhabitants of the periphery of the world system.[1]

Figure 7.1 illustrates that, globally, we are already drawing on more than the total biocapacity available to us, and, in effect, requiring almost one and half earths to meet our total consumption needs.

Our consumption of goods obviously is a function of our culture. Only by producing and selling things and services does capitalism in its present form work, and the more that is produced and the more that is purchased the more we have progress and prosperity. The single most important measure of economic growth is, after all, the gross national product (GNP), the sum total of goods and services produced by a given society in a given year. It is a measure of the success of a consumer society, obviously, to consume.

The production, processing, and consumption of commodities, however, require the extraction and use of natural resources (wood, ore, fossil fuels, and water) and require the creation of factories and factory complexes, which create toxic by-products, whereas the use of commodities themselves (e.g., automobiles) creates pollutants and waste. Yet, of the three factors to which environmentalists often point as responsible for environmental pollution—population, technology, and consumption—consumption seems to get the least attention. One reason, no doubt, is that it may be the most difficult to change; our consumption patterns are so much a part of our lives that to change them would require a massive cultural overhaul, not to mention severe economic dislocation. A drop in demand for products brings on economic recession or even depression, along with massive unemployment.

Thus, given the need to maintain economic growth, convincing people to significantly reduce their consumption patterns, or convincing governments to implement policies to reduce consumption is no easy task. Consumption is as much a part of our culture as horse raiding

---

[1]You can calculate your individual footprint at http://www.myfootprint.org/.

TABLE 7.1 Population, Energy Use, and Carbon Emissions of Selected Countries, 2004, 2009

Country	Population in 1000s		Total Energy Consumption (in quadrillion BTU*)		Percentage of World Consumption		Per Capita Consumption (million BTU)		Total Carbon Emissions (million metric tons)		Percentage of World Emissions		Motor Vehicles per 1,000 People
	2004	2009	2004	2009	2004	2009	2004	2009	2004	2009	2004	2009	2009
United States	298,213	307.006	100.414	94.546	22.5	21.0	342,7	0.308	5,912.21	5,427.06	21.9	17.0	802
China	1,315,844	1,323.591	59.573	90.257	13.3	15.1	45,9	0.068	4,707.28	7,204.885	17.4	22.7	47
Russia	143,202	140.041	30.062	26.816	6.7	6.3	208,8	0.191	1,684.84	1,448.460	6.2	4.6	271
Japan	128,085	127.078	22.624	20.597	5.1	4.7	177,7	0.162	1,262.10	1,104.603	4.7	3.5	589
Germany	82,689	82.329	14.693	13.460	3.3	2.9	178,3	0.163	862.23	762.952	3.2	2.4	564
India	1,103,371	1,156.897	15.417	21.688	3.5	3.9	14,5	0.018	1,112.84	1,622.698	4.1	5.1	18
Canada	32,268	33.487	13.600	13.042	3.0	2.9	418,4	0.389	587.98	551.246	2.2	1.7	607
France	60,496	62.982	11.250	10.657	2.5	2.3	186,1	0.169	405.66	395.504	1.5	1.3	598
United Kingdom	59,668	62.258	10.038	8.905	2.2	1.9	166,5	0.143	579.68	518.969	2.2	1.6	384
Italy	58,093	58.157	8.265	7.319	1.9	1.7	142,3	0.125	484.98	408.462	1.8	1.3	672
Brazil	186,405	198.739	9.078	10.287	2.0	2.1	49,3	0.051	336.71	414.662	1.2	1.3	209
Mexico	107,029	111.211	6.609	6.995	1.5	1.6	63	0.062	385.46	432.37	1.4	1.4	276
Saudi Arabia	24,573	25.328	6.100	7.834	1.4	1.5	236,5	0.309	233.44	438.246	0.9	1.4	—
Indonesia	222,781	240.271	4.686	6.052	1.0	1.0	19,7	0.025	307.68	417.586	1.1	1.3	79
Nigeria	131,530	149.229	1.012	0.772	0.2	0.2	8,1	0.005	93.95	74.142	0.3	0.23	—
Bangladesh	141,822	153.700	0.658	0.947	0.1	0.2	4,7	0.006	37.90	54.388	0.1	0.2	3
Guatemala	12,599	13.276	0.180	0.215	0.04	0.1	15,4	0.016	10.68	12.681	0.04	0.04	98
World Total	6,464,750	6,776.917	446.442	482.972	—	—	70,1	66.1	27,043.57	29,777.65	—	—	95

*BTU = British thermal unit. It is the amount of heat that increases the temperature of a pound of liquid water one degree.

Sources: U.S. Energy Information Administration, http://www.eia.gov/cfapps/ipdbproject/IEDIndex3.cfm?tid=90&pid=44&aid=8; Vehicle Information from the World Bank, http://data.worldbank.org/indicator/IS.VEH.NVEH.P3/countries?display=default.

TABLE 7.2 Ecological Bio-Capacity and Footprint for World and Selected Countries, 2006

	Population (in millions)	Bio-Capacity (in acres)	Ecological Footprint of Consumption (in acres)	Ecological Deficit or Reserve (by national capacity)	Ecological Deficit or Reserve (by global capacity)
World	6,592.9	4.5	6.4	−1.9	—
High-Income Countries	1,022.1	8.3	15.0	−6.7	−10.6
Middle-Income Countries	4,281.1	4.2	4.4	−0.2	0.1
Low-Income Countries	1,277.0	2.5	2.5	−0.1	2.0
Selected Countries					
United States	302.8	10.9	22.3	−11.3	−17.8
Canada	32.6	42.2	14.2	28.0	−9.7
China	1,328.5	2.1	4.6	−2.5	−0.1
India	1,151.8	0.9	1.9	−1	2.6
Japan	128.0	1.5	10.2	−8.6	−5.7
United Kingdom	60.7	3.9	15.1	−11.2	−10.6
Greece	11.1	3.4	14.2	−10.9	−9.7
Italy	58.8	2.6	12.2	−9.6	−7.7
Ireland	4.2	10.5	20.2	−9.7	−15.7
Netherlands	16.4	2.6	11.4	−8.8	−6.9
Russian Federation	143.2	15.6	11.0	4.7	−6.5
Germany	82.6	4.6	10.0	−5.4	−5.5
France	61.3	7.0	11.4	−4.4	−6.9
Qatar	0.8	9.7	23.9	−14.2	−19.4
Saudi Arabia	24.2	3.2	8.6	−5.4	−4.1
Korea, Republic of	48.1	0.7	9.2	−8.5	−4.7
Egypt	74.2	0.8	3.5	−2.7	1.0
Algeria	33.4	2.0	4.7	−2.7	−0.02
Angola	16.6	8.3	2.3	6.0	2.2
Nigeria	144.7	2.2	4.0	−1.8	0.05
Turkey	73.9	3.6	7.0	−3.4	−2.5
Argentina	39.1	17.4	7.4	10.0	−2.9
Chile	16.5	10.1	7.6	2.5	−3.1
Peru	27.6	10.1	4.4	5.6	0.1
New Zealand	4.1	29.8	18.7	11.0	−14.2
Mexico	105.3	4.2	8.0	−3.8	−3.5

Source: Global Footprint Network, 2008, http://www.footprintnetwork.org/en/index.php/GFN/page/ecological_footprint_atlas_2008/.

and buffalo hunting were part of Plains Indian culture; it is a central element. Consequently, there is no way to appreciate the problem of environmental destruction without understanding how people are turned into consumers and how luxuries are turned into necessities—that is, *Why do people choose to consume what they do, how they do, and when they do? How are our tastes formed*? Take sugar, for example. In 1997, each American consumed in his or her soft drinks, tea, coffee, cocoa, pastries, breads, and other foods sixty-six pounds of sugar (USDA 2000). In addition, Americans consume almost 200 grams, or fifty-three teaspoonfuls, of caloric sweeteners each day (Gardner and Halweil 2000:31). Why? Liking the taste might be one answer. In fact, a predilection for sweets may be part of our biological makeup. But that doesn't explain why we consume it in the form of sugarcane, beet sugar, and high-fructose corn syrup and in the quantities we do. Then there is meat. Modern livestock production is one of the most environmentally damaging and wasteful forms of food production the world has known. In 1961 the world produced 71 million tons of meat. In 2007, it was estimated to be 284 million tons, and it is expected to double by 2050 (Bittman 2008). And Americans eat more meat per capita than all but a few other peoples.

Some environmentalists argue that we can change our destructive consumption patterns if we desire. But *is our pattern of consumption only a matter of taste and of choice, or is it so deeply embedded in our culture as to be virtually impervious to change?*

To begin to answer this question, we shall examine the history of sugar and beef, commodities that figure largely in our lives but involve environmental degradation. The combination of sugar and beef is appropriate for a number of reasons:

1. The production and processing of both degrade the environment; furthermore, the history of sugar production parallels that of several other things we consume, including coffee, tea, cocoa, and tobacco, that collectively have significant environmental effects.
2. Neither is terribly good for us, at least not in the quantities and form in which we consume them.
3. Both have histories that closely tie them to the growth and emergence of the capitalist world economy. They are powerful symbols of the rise and economic expansion of capitalism; indeed, they are a result and a reason for it.
4. With the rise of the fast-food industry, beef and sugar, fat and sucrose have become the foundations of the American diet, accounting for more than one-half of the caloric intake of North Americans and Europeans (Gardner and Halweil 2000:15). Indeed, they are foundation foods of the culture of capitalism symbolized in the hamburger and Coke, a hot dog and soda, and the fat-and-sucrose dessert—ice cream.

How many planets we'd need if everyone lived like a resident of the following:

Balanced Budget	Global Deficit
United States 5 planets	
United Kingdom 3.4 planets	
Argentina 1.7 planets	
South Africa 1.5 planets	
China 1.0 planet	
India 0.4 planet	
World Average 1.4 planets	

FIGURE 7.1
Number of Planets Required to Support Different Lifestyles
Source: Info Grafik (with permission).

THE CASE OF SUGAR

The history of sugar reveals how private economic interests, along with economic policies of the nation-state and changes in the structure of society combined to convert a commodity from a luxury good believed to have health benefits into a necessity with overall harmful health consequences. In the process, it vastly increased the exploitation of labor (first in the form of slavery, then in migrant labor), converted millions of acres of forest into sugar production (in the process expelling millions from their land), and changed the dietary habits of most of the world. It illustrates how our consumption patterns are determined in capitalism and why we engage in behavior that may be environmentally unsound and personally harmful. The story of sugar is an excellent case study of how the nation-state–mediated interaction of the capitalist, the laborer, and the consumer produces some of our global problems.

Sugar Origins and Production

Sugarcane, until recently the major source of sugar, was first domesticated in New Guinea, then grown in India and the Middle East. The processing of sugarcane into sugar is complex and environmentally damaging. There are various kinds of sugar plants, most of which grow quickly after regenerating from cuttings left in the fields after harvests or from the controlled planting of cuttings. The stalk matures in nine to eighteen months and must be cut when the juice in the stalk contains the most sucrose. The juice must be extracted quickly before it rots or ferments; it is squeezed from the cane by chopping, pressing, or pounding, then heated to evaporate the liquid, leaving crystals from which centrifugal machines extract most of the molasses. The molasses may be used as a sweetener or, more importantly, processed into rum. The raw sugar that remains after the molasses is extracted can be consumed as is, turned into a liquid syrup, or processed further to obtain the granular white sugar that most Americans and Europeans favor.

Sugar production alters the environment in a number of ways. Forests must be cleared to plant sugar, wood or fossil fuel must be burned in the evaporation process, waste water is produced in extracting sucrose from the sugarcane, and more fuel is burned in the refining process. When Spain sought to expand sugar production into the Atlantic islands in the sixteenth century, it colonized the Canary Islands, then inhabited by the Guanche. The Spaniards transformed the Canarian ecosystem, clearing the forests and hillsides to make way for cane fields and to obtain fuel for the fires of the *ingenio,* or sugar house. Within a few decades, wood was so scarce that the government tried, in vain, to protect the forests from the lumberjacks (Crosby 1986:96). The Guanche were also gone within a century. When sugar production expanded in the seventeenth century, the sugar refineries of Antwerp caused so much pollution that the city banned the use of coal. Contemporary sugar production in Hawaii has destroyed forests, and waste products from processing have severely damaged marine environments. "Big sugar," as the sugar industry is called in Florida, is largely responsible for the pollution, degradation, and virtual destruction of the Everglades.

Sugar, therefore, like virtually all commodities, comes to us at a heavy environmental cost. Yet people did not always crave sugar. For that to happen, a luxury had to be converted into a necessity; a taste had to be created.

Uses of Sugar

By A.D. 1000, when sugar was grown in Europe and the Middle East, it was a highly valued trade item and a luxury. Sugar was used largely as a spice and a medicine and was available only to the wealthy. In Arabian medical works from the tenth and fourteenth centuries, for example, sugar was an ingredient in virtually every medicine. So useful was sugar as a medicine that one way of expressing desperation or helplessness was the saying, "Like an apothecary without sugar" (Mintz 1985:101). According to one source, "nice, white sugar" from the Atlantic islands cleaned the blood and strengthened the chest, lungs, and throat; when used as a powder, it was good for the eyes; and when smoked, it was good for the common cold. Mixed with cinnamon, pomegranate, and quince juice, it was good for a cough and fever (Mintz 1985:103).

Sugar was also used for decoration, mixed with almonds (marzipan) and molded into all kinds of shapes, the decorations becoming central to celebrations and feasts. And it was used as a spice in cooking and, of course, as a sweetener. It was also used as a preservative. We still use sugar to preserve ham, and it is often added to bread to increase its shelf life. But through the seventeenth century, even with its diverse uses, it was an expensive luxury item reserved for the upper classes.

The Development of the Sugar Complex

As a luxury item, sugar brought considerable profits for those who traded in it. In fact, it was the value of sugar as a trade item in the fifteenth and sixteenth centuries that led Spain and Portugal to extend sugarcane production, first to the Atlantic Islands, then to the Caribbean islands, and finally to Brazil, from which, beginning in 1526, raw sugar was shipped to Lisbon for refining.

Modern economists like to talk about the spin-off effects of certain commodities—that is, the extent to which their production results in the development of subsidiary industries. For example, production of automobiles requires road construction, oil and petroleum production, service stations, auto parts stores, and the like. Sugar production also produced subsidiary economic activities; these included slavery, the provisioning of the sugar producers, shipping, refining, storage, and wholesale and retail trade.

The increased demand for sugar in the eighteenth and nineteenth centuries represented a boom for West Indies sugar plantations and created a demand for more laborers, including slaves and children. (Lordprice Collection/Alamy.)

The slave trade was a major factor in the expansion of the sugar industries. Slaves from Europe and the Middle East were first used on the Spanish and Portuguese plantations of the Canary Islands and Madeira, but by the end of the fifteenth century, slaves from West Africa were working the fields. The growing demand for and production of sugar created the plantation economy in the New World and was largely responsible for the expansion of the Atlantic slave trade in the sixteenth, seventeenth, and eighteenth centuries. From 1701 to 1810, almost 1 million slaves were brought to Barbados and Jamaica to work the sugar plantations.

Money was to be made also from the shipment of raw sugar to European refineries, more yet from the wholesale and retail sale of sugar, and probably more yet from the sale by European merchants of necessary provisions to the plantation owners. Investors in Europe, especially England, put money into the sugar industry in the development of plantations, the sale of provisions to the colonial plantations, in shipping, or in the slave trade. Attorneys, grocers, drapers, and tailors invested small amounts to form partnerships to finance slave-buying expeditions to Africa and the subsequent resale of slaves to buyers from the sugar plantations of the New World. Thus, it was during the sixteenth and seventeenth centuries that sugar became the focus of an industry, a sugar complex that combined the sugar plantations, the slave trade, long-distance shipping, wholesale and retail trade, and investment finance.

The Expansion of Sugar Production

It was not until the late seventeenth century that sugar production and sales really began to influence sugar consumption in Europe. Sugar consumption increased fourfold in England and Wales from 1700 to 1740 and doubled in the next thirty-five years. From 1663 to 1775, consumption increased twentyfold. Sugar consumption rose more rapidly than that of bread, meat, and dairy products in the eighteenth century. Although the per capita annual consumption in 1809 of eighteen pounds of sugar per person does not compare to our present consumption of almost seventy pounds, it was more than sufficient to generate large profits.

Why did people in England begin to consume sugar in greater and greater quantities? First, increased sugar production led to reduced prices, making it accessible to more people, although its use was still largely confined to the upper and emerging middle classes of English society. One reason prices remained as high as they did was the imposition of high import tariffs on sugar produced in other countries. Second, the benefits of sugar were widely touted by various authorities, notably popular physicians. Dr. Frederick Slare found sugar a venerable cure-all. He recommended that women include at their breakfast—bread, butter, milk, and sugar. Coffee, tea, and chocolate were similarly "endowed with uncommon virtues," he said, adding that his message would please the West Indian merchant and the grocer who became wealthy on the production of sugar. Slare also prescribed sugar as a dentifrice, a lotion, a substitute for tobacco in the form of snuff, and for babies. Sidney Mintz (1985:107–108) said of Slare that although his enthusiasm for sugar is suspect, it is more than a curiosity because it relates to so many aspects of what was then still a relatively new commodity; furthermore, by stressing sugar's value as a medicine, food, and preservative, he was drawing additional attention to it.

A third reason that sugar consumption increased in the eighteenth century was its use as a sweetener for three other substances, all bitter and all technically drugs (stimulants)—tea, coffee, and cocoa. All of these were used in their places of origin without sugar, in spite of their bitterness. All three initially were drinks for the wealthy; by the time they were used by others, they were generally served hot and sweetened.

Fourth, sugar's reputation as a luxury good inspired the middle classes to use it to emulate the wealthy—sugar was a sign of status. The powerful used sugar for conspicuous consumption, as a symbol of hospitality and the like. When sugar was a luxury, the poor could hardly emulate these uses, but as the price declined and as its use expanded, sugar became available to the poor to use in much the same way as their social betters.

Finally, sugar consumption increased because the government increased its purchase of sugar and sugar products. After the capture of Jamaica and its sugar plantations from the French in 1655, the British navy began to give its sailors rum rations, set in 1731 at half a pint per day and later increased to a pint per day for adult sailors. The government also purchased sugar to distribute to poorhouse residents.

Thus, sugar production and consumption increased, as did the amount of land devoted to its production and the number of sugar mills and refineries, distilleries producing rum, and slaves employed in the whole process. Most importantly, the profits generated by the sugar trade increased dramatically.

The Mass Consumption of Sugar

By 1800, British sugar consumption had increased 2,500 percent since 1650, and 245,000 tons of sugar reached European consumers annually from the world market. By 1830, production had risen to 572,000 tons per year, an increase of more than 233 percent. By 1860, when beet sugar production was also rising, world production of sucrose increased another 233 percent to 1.373 million tons. Six million tons were produced by 1890, another 500 percent increase (Mintz 1985:73).

Two acts by the British government helped spur this massive increase in sugar production and consumption. First, the government removed tariffs on the imports of foreign sugar. This made foreign sugar more accessible to British consumers and forced domestic producers to lower their prices, making it affordable to virtually all levels of British society. Second, England abolished slavery during the years 1834–1838 (it had abolished the slave trade in 1807). This had the effect of forcing technological improvements, but it also spurred the creation of a labor pattern that exists to the present. The freed slaves were without land and tools and were dependent on whatever labor they could get. As Mintz (1985:176) noted, although freed from the discipline of slavery, they were reduced to laborers by the discipline of hunger. The surplus supply of labor was increased when the British Foreign Office went to the aid of the planters in the West Indies by helping them import contracted laborers from India, China, and elsewhere. The freed slaves, unable to secure a livelihood independent of the sugar industry or to use collective bargaining, settled into obscurity until they reentered British consciousness as migrants to England more than a century later.

The lower price of sugar increased its use in tea and stimulated a dramatic rise in the production of preserves and chocolate. More importantly, it must have been apparent to sugar producers and sellers that there was a fortune to be made by increasing the availability of sugar to the working mass of England. Certainly, there were those who worked hard to expand its availability.

Sidney Mintz's history of sugar reveals how much social, political, and economic power had to do with increased sugar consumption. Planters, slavers, shippers, bankers, refiners, grocers, and government officials, all profiting in one way or another from increased sugar consumption, exercised power to support the rights and prerogatives of planters, the maintenance of slavery, the availability of sugar and its products (molasses, rum, and preserves) and products associated with it (tea, coffee, and cocoa), and to supply it to the people at large at prices they could afford. Thus, the consumption of sugar was hardly only a matter of taste—it had to do with investments, taxes, the dispensation of sugar through government agencies, and a desire to emulate the rich, among other things. It also had to do with convenience and the changes in household structure, labor, and diet that accompanied the Industrial Revolution.

Rural workers in England in the eighteenth and nineteenth centuries typically had diets that consisted of oatmeal, porridge, milk, homemade bread, and vegetable broth. Although it was simple, the diet was relatively nutritious. In the industrial cities, however, it could be costly. Fresh food in general would have been more costly in the city, and food preparation, especially if it needed cooking, required fuel, which cost yet more money. Furthermore, urban women were, as noted earlier, also working in the factories twelve to fourteen hours per day, reducing the time they could spend on food preparation.

As a result, the diet of the urban working class and poor was transformed to one dominated by tea, sugar, store-bought white bread, and jam. Hot tea replaced vegetable broth. Jams (50 percent to 65 percent sugar) were cheaper than butter to put on bread, were easily stored, and could be left open on shelves for children to spread on bread in the absence of adults. In other words, the cultural and social constraints of time and cost created in the urban, industrial setting combined with the convenience of sugar and the prodding of those who profited from its sale to shape the diet of the British working class. It was an ideal arrangement, for, as E. P. Thompson (1967) noted, after providing profits to plantation and refinery investors, sugar provided the bodily fuel for the working people of Britain. Sugar is also what Sidney Mintz referred to as a "drug food," a category that includes coffee, tea, cocoa, alcohol, and tobacco—foods that deaden hunger pangs and stimulate effort without providing nutrition and do so cheaply. That is one reason why they have been transformed from upper-class luxuries to working-class necessities.

Modern Sugar

Sidney Mintz (1985:180–181) suggested that the consumption of goods such as sugar is the result of profound changes in the lives of working people, changes that made new forms of foods and of eating seem "natural," as new work schedules, new sorts of labor, and new conditions of life became "natural." This does not mean that we lack a choice in what we consume but that our choice is made within various constraints. We may have a choice between a McDonald's hamburger and a Colonel Sanders chicken leg during a half-hour lunch break. The time available acts to limit our choice, removing, for example, the option of a home-cooked vegetarian lunch.

Sugar has become, as it did for the nineteenth-century British laborer, a mainstay of the fast-food diet in the United States, the perfect complement to fat. Both fat and sugar are made more attractive by the clever use of language. The fat side of our diet is advertised with words like "juicy," "succulent," "hot," "luscious," "savory," and "finger-licking good." The sugar side is advertised as "crisp," "fresh," "invigorating," "wholesome," "refreshing," and "vibrant." And the sugar in soft drinks serves as the perfect complement to hamburgers and hot dogs because it possesses what nutritionists call "go-away" qualities—removing the fat coating and the beef aftertaste from the mouth.

Thus, sugar fits our budgets, our work schedules, and our psychological needs while at the same time generating monetary profits and growth.

THE STORY OF BEEF

The story of beef is very much like that of sugar, except that livestock breeding has been indicted for even greater environmental damage than sugar production, largely because of the vast amount of land needed to raise cattle. As an agricultural crop, sugar is quite efficient; although it has little nutritional value, it is possible to get about 8 million calories from one acre of sugarcane; to get 8 million calories of beef requires 135 acres. In addition, much of the beef we eat is grain fed to produce the marbling of fat that makes it choice grade and brings the highest prices; as mentioned earlier, 80 percent of the grain produced in the United States is fed to livestock. In addition, two-thirds of U.S. grain exports go to feed livestock in other countries. Thus, to the amount of land needed for rangeland, we must add the farmland devoted to animal feed; moreover, as we saw in Chapter 6, this grain production requires tons of chemical fertilizer, pesticides, and herbicides, all of which negatively alter the environment.

Cattle raising consumes a lot of water. Half the water consumed in the United States is used to grow grain to feed cattle; the amount of water used to produce ten pounds of steak equals the household consumption of a family for an entire year. Fifteen times more water is needed to produce a pound of beef protein than an equivalent amount of plant protein. There are also environmental problems associated with beef waste products; a feedlot steer produces forty-seven pounds of manure per day (Ensminger 1991:187), not to mention the methane gases that contribute to the destruction of the ozone layer. Even more pollution is produced by the slaughter, refrigeration, transport, and cooking of beef.

Cattle raising has also been criticized for its role in the destruction of tropical forests. Hundreds of thousands of acres of tropical forests in Brazil, Guatemala, Costa Rica, and Honduras, to name only a few countries, have been leveled to create pasture for cattle. Because most of the forest is cleared by burning, the extension of cattle pasture also creates carbon dioxide and contributes significantly to global warming. In addition, with increasing amounts of fossil fuel needed to produce grain, it now takes a gallon of gasoline to produce a pound of grain-fed beef.

Much of the rangeland of the United States has been devastated by livestock herding to the point that it has become desert. Currently, 2 million to 3 million cattle graze on 306 million acres of public land. According to the General Accounting Office (GAO), more plant species are being threatened by cattle grazing than by any other single factor, and populations of pronghorn, antelope, and elk have virtually disappeared from Western rangelands.

The same problems are occurring in areas of Africa that have a long tradition of cattle raising. When cattle populations were managed by traditional means and for traditional consumption, there was little environmental damage. When attempts were made to introduce Western livestock-raising practices and technologies to increase the number of cattle and develop a larger beef export industry, pasture was turned to desert and wild animals disappeared, largely because of overgrazing by cattle (Rifkin 1992:216).

In addition, beef is terribly inefficient as a source of food. By the time a feedlot steer in the United States is ready for slaughter, it has consumed 2,700 pounds of grain and weighs approximately 1,050 pounds; 157 million metric tons of cereal and vegetable protein are used to produce 28 metric tons of animal protein. Finally, beef in the quantities that Americans consume it is unhealthy, being linked to cardiovascular disease, colon cancer, breast cancer, and osteoporosis.

Americans are among the highest meat consumers in the world and the highest consumers of beef. More than 6.7 billion hamburgers are sold each year at fast-food restaurants alone. Furthermore, we are exporting our taste for beef to other parts of the world. The Japanese, who in the past consumed only one-tenth the amount of meat consumed by Americans, are increasing their consumption of beef. McDonald's sells more hamburgers in Tokyo than it does in New York City.

Historically, few societies have made meat the center of their diet. If we look around the world, we find that most diets center on some complex carbohydrate—rice, wheat, manioc, yams, and taro—or something made from these—bread, pasta, tortillas, and so on. To these are added some spice, vegetables, meat, or fish, the combination giving each culture's food its distinctive flavor. But meat and fish are generally at the edge, not the center, of the meal (Mintz 1985). Moreover, regardless of whether we simply like meat, *Why do American preferences run to beef?* Anthropologists Marvin Harris and Eric B. Ross (1987b) have some interesting answers that may help us understand why, in spite of the environmental damage our beef consumption causes, we continue to eat it in such quantities. The answers involve understanding the relationships among Spanish cattle, British colonialism, the American government, the American bison, indigenous peoples, the automobile, the hamburger, and the fast-food restaurant.

Creating a Taste for Beef

The story of the American preference for beef begins with the Spanish colonization of the New World. The Spanish, as noted earlier, introduced the so-called cattle complex to the New World, where it became established in Argentina; areas of Central America, particularly northern Mexico; and Texas. By the 1540s, cattle were so numerous around Mexico City that the Spaniards had to train Native Americans to handle them. Fortunes were made in cattle in the sixteenth century on meat and leather.

In Argentina, the number of feral cattle increased so rapidly on the pampas that by the seventeenth century, meat was eaten three times a day, and animals were killed for their hides and the meat left to rot. One seventeenth-century traveler wrote of Argentina,

> All the wealth of these inhabitants consists in their animals, which multiply so prodigiously that the plains are covered with them ... in such numbers that were it not for the dogs that devoured the calves ... they would devastate the country. (Rifkin 1992:49)

In colonial America, however, pigs, not beef, were the meat of choice. Eric Ross (1980) pointed out that the preference for beef or pork is related in part to environmental factors. Pigs tend to be raised in forested areas and can be maintained in areas of relatively dense populations because they eat the same food as human beings. In densely populated West Germany in 1960, the ratio of cattle to hogs was 0.06 to 1, whereas in sparsely populated Argentina, with its large tracts of rangeland, it was 11.2 to 1. Another reason pork was preferred in America was that the preservation process—smoking, salting, and pickling—improved the flavor of the meat, whereas for beef it did not. In fact, pork was the meat of choice in the United States until the 1960s, when beef overtook it. Although meat consumption in the United States has declined since the 1970s, beef is still preferred (see Table 7.3).

TABLE 7.3 U.S. per Capita Meat Consumption, 1900 to 2015 (in pounds)

Year	Beef	Pork
2015 (projected)	62.9	48.4
2009	60.4	48.0
2008	65.8	49.1
2007	66.5	50.9
2006	65.5	49.5
2005	65.3	50.0
2004	65.0	51.0
2000	67.0	51.0
1998	64.9	49.1
1996	65.0	49.9
1993	61.5	48.9
1990	64.0	46.4
1977	125.9	61.6
1975	120.1	54.8
1970	113.7	66.4
1960	85.1	64.9
1950	63.4	69.2
1940	54.9	73.5
1920	59.1	63.5
1900	67.1	71.9

Source: Ross (1980:191); U.S. Bureau of the Census (1990, 1993, 1994); USDA/NASS Agricultural Statistics (2000), http://www.nass.usda.gov/Publications/Ag_Statistics/2000/index.asp; http://www.nass.usda.gov/Publications/Ag_Statistics/2000/index.asp; http://www.ers.usda.gov/publications/oce071/oce20071d.pdf.

The Emergence of the American Beef Industry

On the eve of the Industrial Revolution, England was the beef-eating capital of the world, with 100,000 head of cattle slaughtered annually in London. But in the nineteenth century, with its population increasing and more people migrating to the factory towns and cities, England began to look toward its colonies and ex-colonies for food, especially meat. Eric Ross (1980) suggested that the motivation was not simply to get food but to keep meat prices low in order to keep wages low and allow industry in Great Britain to remain competitive with industries in other countries. As we saw earlier, the British increased cattle production in Ireland by increasing the amount of land devoted to pasture, pushing people onto smaller plots of land and increasing dependence on the potato. When the potato blight hit Ireland in 1846–1847 and millions starved, the export of Irish grain and livestock intensified. In fact, because of the massive out-migrations caused by the famine, English landlords were able to intensify cattle production even more; from 1846 to 1874, the number of Irish cattle exported to England climbed from 202,000 to 558,000, and more than 50 percent of the total landmass of Ireland was devoted to cattle raising.

England next turned to Argentina, where the development of the refrigerated steamer permitted the shipment of fresh beef to England. In the 1870s, English, Scottish, and Irish colonists already owned 45 percent of the sheep and 20 percent of the cattle herds in Argentina, and English demand and English capital helped develop the Argentine beef business. One of the greatest nineteenth-century fortunes made in England, that of the Vesteys, was made by dominating the Argentine meat market.

Who was eating all this meat? It was not the working class, whose breakfast consisted of little more than bread, butter or jam, and tea with sugar and whose dinner might include a meat by-product, such as Liebig's extract (made from hides and other residue), or inferior cuts. The gentry, however, apparently consumed vast quantities. Beef, in fact, had been for some time the choice of the British well-to-do. For example, in 1735 a group of men formed the Sublime Society of Beef Steaks, most renowned for the invention of the sandwich by one of its members. The society consisted largely of members of the British elite but also included painters, merchants, and theatrical managers. It existed until 1866. Twice a year the group would meet for dinner, at which, according to the society's charter, "beef steaks shall be the only meat for dinner" (Lincoln 1989:85).

A typical breakfast in1887 for British nobility might contain a variety of fish, poultry, game (probably killed on the estate), sausage, mutton cutlets, along with filets of beef, with a side table of cold cuts such as tongue and ham, and perhaps a round of spiced beef (Harris and Ross 1987b:35–36).

The army and navy consumed enormous amounts of meat, each sailor and soldier getting by regulation three-fourths of a pound of meat daily; in fact, the diet of the military was vastly superior to that of the bulk of the population. Between 1813 and 1835, the British War Office contracted for 69.6 million pounds of Irish salted beef and 77.9 million pounds of Irish salt pork; as Harris and Ross (1987a:37–38) noted, Irishmen were able to eat the meat of their own country only by joining the army of the country that had colonized theirs. Furthermore, the British military, by distributing rum and meat to their men, helped to subsidize both the sugar and meat industries.

Lying largely untapped in the latter half of the nineteenth century, by either the British or the Americans, were the American Great Plains and the vast herds of Texas longhorns. The longhorn was the remnant of the Spanish herds that ran wild. It was uniquely adapted to the extremes of heat and cold of the prairies; it could eat almost anything, including leaves and prickly pear, and by the 1830s and 1840s, cowboys began to round up the strays and herd them to New Orleans. In the 1830s, there were 100,000 head of cattle roaming Texas; by 1860, there were more than 3.5 million.

But cattle traders faced three problems in trying to make a profit from longhorn cattle. The first problem was shipping cattle to areas in the Midwest from where they could be distributed. They could be driven overland, but that was too costly. The second problem was the availability of rangeland; in the 1860s, the plains were occupied by indigenous peoples and their major food source, the buffalo. The third problem was the quality of the beef; longhorn beef was too lean and tough for British tastes. The solutions to these problems would define the American taste for beef and a good part of the history of the American West.

The problem of transporting cattle to the Midwest and East was solved by a young entrepreneur, Joseph McCoy, who convinced the Union Pacific Railway to construct a siding and cattle pen at its remote depot in Abilene, Kansas, and agree to pay McCoy a commission on every animal he delivered for shipment. The animals would be driven from Texas to Abilene on the Chisholm Trail. McCoy first needed and got the governor of Kansas to lift a quarantine on Texas cattle that had been imposed because of the spread of Texas fever; then he persuaded the Illinois legislature to allow his shipment of cattle into their state. On September 5, 1867, McCoy shipped twenty railway cars of cattle east from Abilene. By 1871, he was shipping 700,000 cattle annually. Through the 1870s, the Chisholm Trail was traveled by herd after herd headed for the slaughterhouses, tables, and leatherworks of the East.

But as the demand for meat, leather, and tallow grew, more land was needed for cattle; the plains, once considered the Great American Desert, were being promoted as a land of a "fairy-tale" grass that required no rain and could support millions of head of cattle (Rifkin 1992:73). Only two things stood in the way of its use—buffalo and Native Americans.

Cattlemen, Eastern bankers, the railroads, and the U.S. Army believed the solution to both problems could be effected by the extermination of the buffalo, and they joined in a systematic campaign to that end. In a period of about a decade, from 1870 to 1880, in one of the world's greatest ecological disasters, buffalo hunters ended 15,000 years of continuous existence on the plains of the American bison, reducing herds of millions to virtual extinction. Stationed in Kansas, Colonel Richard Henry Dodge wrote that in 1871, buffalo around the post were virtually limitless; by the fall of 1873, "there was now myriads of carcasses. The air was foul with a sickening stench, and the vast plain, which only a short twelve months before teemed with animal life, was a dead, solitary, putrid desert" (Rifkin 1992:74).

Buffalo hunters were getting one to three dollars a hide, and heroes such as William F. Cody (Buffalo Bill) were entertaining European royalty on buffalo hunts, while railroad passengers, armed with rifles provided by the conductors, shot the animals from the moving trains. Not everyone approved of the slaughter, and some newspaper editorials condemned it but to no avail. Even the bones were ground up for fertilizer and sold for eight dollars a ton. The "white harvest," as it was called, even engaged indigenous groups, who would bring the bones in wagons for sale at the railroad depots; meat met sugar as "fresher bones" were made into char and used in the refining process to remove the brownish coloration of sugar. In a speech to the Texas legislature in 1877, General Phillip Sheridan said of the buffalo hunters,

> These men have done…more to settle the vexed Indian question than the entire regular army has done in the last thirty years. They are destroying the Indians' commissary; and it is a well-known fact that an army losing its base of supplies is placed at a great disadvantage. Send them powder and lead if you will; but for the sake of lasting peace let them kill, skin, and sell until the buffalo is exterminated. Then your prairies can be covered with speckled cattle and the festive cowboy who follows the hunter as a second forerunner of an advanced civilization. (Wallace and Hoebel 1952:66)

With the buffalo went the Indians of the plains. With their major food and source of ritual and spiritual power removed, they were soon vanquished and confined to reservations on land granted to them by the U.S. government—land that had been taken away from them in earlier treaties.

In one of the great ironies of history, cattlemen made fortunes selling beef to the U.S. government for distribution to Native Americans forced onto reservations and hungry because of the buffalo slaughter. Furthermore, cattlemen grazed their animals on what remained of Native American land, paying them in beef or cash only a fraction of what the grazing rights were worth.

The final problem in the story of England and the Texas longhorn involved the toughness or leanness of plains cattle. The British liked their beef generously marbled with fat. This problem was solved by a historic bargain; Western cattle would be transported to the Midwestern farmbelt and fed corn until their meat was speckled with fat, then shipped by rail and steamer to English ports (Rifkin 1992:58–59). The integration of the plains and the prairie, rangeland and farmland, was so complete that to this day the price of corn is closely linked to the demand for and price of cattle.

As a consequence of the merger of cattle and corn in the 1870s, British banks were pouring millions into the American West. They formed the Anglo-American Cattle Company Ltd. with £70,000 of capital; then the Colorado Mortgage and Investment Company of London bought 10,000 acres of rangeland north of Denver; the Scottish-American Company invested £220,000 in land in Wyoming and the Dakotas. Cattlemen associations were formed that controlled millions of acres and often became spokespersons for foreign cattle barons. In all, the British invested some $45 million in Western real estate, and by the 1880s, America was responsible for 90 percent of beef imported to England (Harris and Ross 1987b:38). By the mid-1880s, 43,136 tons of fresh beef were being shipped yearly to Great Britain (Rifkin 1992:95).

The takeover of the West by the British so alarmed some Americans that in the 1884 presidential election, both parties included planks that would limit "alien holdings" in the United States. The Republican campaign slogan of 1884, "America for Americans," was directed not at poor Latin Americans or Asian migrants or European minorities, as it would be later, but at the British elite. But the British invasion of the American cattle industry had one other long-lasting effect: It defined for the next 100 years the American taste in beef.

In response to both British tastes and Midwestern farm interests, the U.S. Department of Agriculture (USDA) developed a system of grading beef that awarded the highest grade—prime—to the beef with the most fat content, choice grade to the next fattiest, select grade to the next, and so on. Thus, the state participated in creating a system that inspired cattle raisers to feed cattle grain and add fat because it brought the best price, while at the same time communicating to the consumer that, because it was most expensive, the most marbled cuts of beef must be the best.

The federal inspection and grading standards also aided another important sector of the beef industry: the meatpackers. Beef packers wanted to centralize their operations, to bring live animals to one area to be butchered, but most states had laws that required inspection of live animals twenty-four hours before slaughter. Butchers were opposed to the centralized slaughter of beef because, since most animals were slaughtered and butchered locally, centralizing the operation would put many of them out of business. The beef-packing industry lobbied successfully to convince Congress to pass a federal meat inspection system that, unlike state inspection systems, would not affect out-of-state centralized operations (Harris and Ross 1987b:202).

Aided by the government, the meatpacking business proceeded to dominate the production and distribution of beef. Refrigeration technology and the new federal inspection standards allowed individuals, such as George H. Hammond in 1871, Gustavus Swift in 1877, and Philip and Simeon Armour in 1882, to slaughter beef in one area of the country—Chicago—and ship it fresh to any other area of the country. Their growth and domination of the meatpacking industry resulted in the concentration of production in five companies that by World War I handled two-thirds of all meatpacking in the United States. By 1935, Armour and Swift controlled 61 percent of meat sales in the United States.

One of the great technological innovations in meatpacking was the assembly (or, as Jeremy Rifkin [1992] called it, "disassembly") line. Henry Ford is generally credited with developing assembly line technology in the construction of his Model T Ford in 1913. However, even Ford said that he got his idea from watching cattle hung on conveyor belts passing from worker to worker, each assigned a specific series of cuts until the entire animal was dismembered. The working conditions in the meatpacking industry were then, and remain, among the worst of any industry in the country. At the turn of the century, they prompted Upton Sinclair to produce his quasifictional account *The Jungle* (1906), whose descriptions of the slaughterhouses promoted such public outrage that the government acted to regulate the meatpacking industry.

The state has also heavily subsidized our taste in beef by allowing cattlemen to graze cattle on public lands at a fraction of market costs for grazing on private land, thus making beef more affordable and encouraging its consumption. As early as the 1880s, cattlemen were fencing millions of acres of public land—to which they had no title—with the newly invented barbed wire. In fact, at that time, most of the cattle companies grazing their cattle on public land were British. After objections to the practice were raised, the government passed the Desert Land Act of 1887, which awarded land to anyone who improved it. The Union Cattle Company of Cheyenne dug a thirty-five-mile-long ditch, called it an *irrigation canal,* and claimed 33,000 acres of public land (Skaggs 1976:62).

In 1934, Congress passed the Taylor Grazing Act, which transferred millions of acres of public land to ranchers if they took responsibility for improving it. In 1990, some 30,000 cattle ranchers in eleven Western states grazed their cattle on 300 million acres of public land, an area equal to the fourteen East Coast states stretching from Maine to Florida (Rifkin 1992:105–106). These permit holders pay a third to a quarter less than they would pay on private lands.

The victory of beef, however, was not yet complete. To appreciate the story of American beef consumption, we need to understand the role of the American government in creating the legal definition of a hamburger and the infrastructure that encouraged the spread of the automobile.

Modern Beef

Legend has it that the hamburger was invented by accident when an Ohio restaurant owner ran out of pork sausages at the Ohio Fair in 1892 and substituted ground beef on his buns. The hamburger was the rage of the St. Louis World's Fair of 1904, and by 1921, White Castle had opened its hamburger chain in Kansas City. But the hamburger still needed an assist, and it got it from the automobile and the government.

Henry Ford's Model T began the American romance with the automobile, and the number of Americans with cars grew enormously in the twentieth century. There are now as many automobiles as there are licensed drivers in the United States. But it was the surge in highway construction after World War II (a $350 billion project to construct a network of 41,000 miles of superhighways) that made the automobile boom possible. This led to the growth of the suburbs and the fast-food restaurants that were to make beef, and particularly the hamburger, king.

Pork, as mentioned earlier, had always competed with beef for priority in American meat tastes. Whereas beef was more popular in the Northeast and the West, pork was the meat of choice in the South; however, in the Mid-Atlantic states and the Midwest, they were relatively evenly matched. But by the 1960s, beef clearly became the meat of choice for most Americans.

One advantage of beef was its suitability for the outdoor grill, which became more popular as people moved to the suburbs. Suburban cooks soon discovered that pork patties crumbled and fell through the grill, whereas beef patties held together better. In addition, because the USDA does not inspect pork for trichinosis because the procedure would be too expensive, it recommended cooking pork until it was gray, but that makes pork very tough. Barbecued spare ribs are one pork alternative, but they are messy, have less meat, and can't be put on a bun. In 1946, the USDA issued a statute that defined the hamburger:

> *Hamburger.* "Hamburger" shall consist of chopped fresh and/or frozen beef with or without the addition of beef fat as such and/or seasonings, shall not contain more than 30 percent fat, and shall not contain added water, phosphates, binders, or extenders. Beef cheek (trimmed Beef cheeks) may be used in the preparation of hamburgers only in accordance with the conditions prescribed in paragraph (a) of this section. (Harris 1987:125)

Marvin Harris (1987:125–126) noted that we can eat ground pork and ground beef, but we can't combine them, at least if we are to call it a hamburger. Even when lean, grass-fed beef is used for hamburger and fat must be added to bind it, the fat must come from beef scraps, not from vegetables or a different animal. This definition of the hamburger protects not only the beef industry but also the corn farmer, whose income is linked to cattle production. Moreover, it helps the fast-food industry because the definition of hamburger allows it to use inexpensive scraps of fat from slaughtered beef to make, in fact, 30 percent of its hamburger. Thus, an international beef patty was created that overcame what Harris called the "pig's natural superiority as a converter of grain to flesh."

The fast-food restaurant, made possible by the popularity of the automobile, put the final touch on the ascendancy of beef. Ray Kroc, the founder of McDonald's, tapped into the new temporal and work routines of American labor. With more women working outside the home, time and efficiency were wed to each other as prepared foods, snacks, and the frozen hamburger patty became more popular. In many ways, the fast-food restaurant and the beef patty on a bun were to the American working woman of the 1970s and 1980s what sugar, hot tea, and preserves were to the English female factory worker of the latter half of the nineteenth century. They both offered ease of preparation and convenience at a time when increasing numbers of women worked outside the home.

As with sugar, therefore, our "taste" for beef goes well beyond our supposed individual food preferences. It is a consequence of a culture in which food as a commodity takes a form defined by economic, political, and social relationships. We can, as many have done, refuse beef. But to do so requires a real effort, as those who try to follow a strictly vegetarian diet can attest.

In addition, as with much of what Americans do, the matter of beef does not stop in the United States. The United States produces about 9 percent of the world's beef but consumes 28 percent of it. In 2009, Americans consumed 61 pounds of beef per person, and although consumption per capita is declining, the total amount of beef consumed is increasing. The consumption of beef in core countries is having more of an impact on countries in the periphery, and this is likely to worsen as other countries, such as Japan and China, begin to emulate American and European dietary patterns.

THE IMPACT OF PRODUCTION ON THE ENVIRONMENT: THE EFFECTS OF CLIMATE CHANGE

There are various environmental threats posed by our production of stuff: unhealthy air and water, deforestation, the accumulation of both toxic and nontoxic waste, to name just a few. But the one measure that, to a certain extent, encompasses all of those is climate change.

The major source for information on climate change is the Intergovernmental Panel on Climate Change (IPCC), a governmental and United Nations clearinghouse that evaluates scientific data and reports its findings. Given the political implications of its findings, they tend to be conservative. But they conclude, nevertheless, that the temperature of the earth is rising, that the rise is caused by human activities, and that the cause is the emission of carbon from the burning of fossil fuels—oil, gas, and coal. Carbon gases act much like a greenhouse, allowing the sun's heat into the atmosphere, but preventing much of it to radiating back into space. These gases are essential to life on earth: without them the earth would be ice cold and incapable of supporting life. But too much of these gases causes the earth's surface to heat and threatens life in other ways.

The IPCC concludes that the burning of fossil fuels has increased the concentration of carbon dioxide (CO_2) in the atmosphere from about 280 parts per million (ppm) at the start of the Industrial Revolution to about 390 ppm today. Examining the concentration of CO_2 in ice cores, they conclude also that 390 ppm is the highest it has been in 10,000 years. As a result, the earth's average temperature has increased by 1.4 percent since the early twentieth century. Climate scientists believe that anything beyond a 2 degree centigrade increase will lead to dangerous climate change which can lead to food shortages, desertification, increased incidences of disease, coastal flooding, and erratic climate disturbances (see IPCC 2007:30, 37; Parenti 2011:58–580). (See Table 7.4).

The IPCC concludes that as a result of changes over the past fifty years, extreme weather events have increased in frequency and intensity; cold days and nights have increased in frequency, while hot days and nights have become more frequent; heat waves have become more frequent and intense; and the frequency of heavy rainfall, and subsequent flooding have increased along with a rise in the sea level both from increased precipitation and the melting of polar icecaps (IPCC 2007:30).

The row of fast-food restaurants that line streets in virtually every American town and city represents not only the union of sugar and fat but also the fast-paced lives required in a consumer-oriented society. (Bill Bachmann/ Alamy.)

TABLE 7.4 Some Likely Regional Impacts of Climate Change

Africa	By 2020, between 75 million and 250 million of people are projected to be exposed to increased water stress due to climate change. By 2020, in some countries, yields from rain-fed agriculture could be reduced by up to 50 percent. Agricultural production, including access to food, in many African countries is projected to be severely compromised. By 2080, an increase of 5 percent to 8 percent of arid and semiarid land in Africa is projected under a range of climate scenarios.
Asia	By the 2050s, freshwater availability in Central, South, East, and South-East Asia, particularly in large river basins, is projected to decrease. Coastal areas, especially heavily populated megadelta regions in South, East, and South-East Asia, will be at greatest risk due to increased flooding from the sea and, in some megadeltas, flooding from the rivers. Endemic morbidity and mortality due to diarrheal disease expected to rise in East, South, and South-East Asia due to projected changes in the hydrological cycle.
Australia and New Zealand	By 2020, significant loss of biodiversity is projected to occur in some ecologically rich sites, including the Great Barrier Reef and Queensland Wet Tropics. By 2030, water security problems are projected to intensify in southern and eastern Australia and, in New Zealand, in Northland and some eastern regions. However, in New Zealand, initial benefits are projected in some other regions.
Europe	Climate change is expected to magnify regional differences in Europe's natural resources and assets. Negative impacts will include increased risk of inland flash floods and more frequent coastal flooding and increased erosion. In southern Europe, climate change is projected to worsen conditions (high temperatures and drought) in a region already vulnerable to climate variability, and to reduce water availability, hydropower potential, summer tourism, and, in general, crop productivity. Climate change is also projected to increase the health risks due to heat waves and the frequency of wildfires.
Latin America	By mid-century, increases in temperature and associated decreases in soil water are projected to lead to gradual replacement of tropical forest by savanna in eastern Amazonia. Semiarid vegetation will tend to be replaced by arid-land vegetation. There is a risk of significant biodiversity loss through species extinction in many areas of tropical Latin America. Productivity of some important crops is projected to decrease and livestock productivity to decline. Overall, the number of people at risk of hunger is projected to increase.
North America	Warming in western mountains is projected to cause decreased snowpack, more winter flooding, and reduced summer flows, exacerbating competition for over-allocated water resources. In the early decades of the century, moderate climate change is projected to increase aggregate yields of rain-fed agriculture by 5 percent to 20 percent, but with important variability among regions. Cities that currently experience heat waves are expected to be further challenged by an increased number, intensity, and duration of heat waves during the course of the century, with potential for adverse health impacts.
Island Communities	Coastal communities and habitats will be increasingly stressed by climate change impacts interacting with development and pollution. Sea level rise is expected to exacerbate inundation, storm surge, erosion, and other coastal hazards, thus threatening vital infrastructure, settlements, and facilities that support the livelihood of island communities.

Source: Intergovernmental Panel on Climate Change (IPCC) 2007 (IPCC). An Assessment on the Intergovernmental Panel on Climate Change. http://www.ipcc.ch/pdf/assessment-report/ar4/syr/ar4_syr.pdf

Having concluded that climate change is occurring, and that it is caused by the increased use of carbon-based fuels, the question is, what effects is it having and is likely to have, and who stands to lose the most from the changes, and who, if anyone, stands to gain? For example, one study by the Global Humanitarian Forum (GHF)—*The Anatomy of a Silent Crisis*—estimates that climate change adversely affects 300 million people a year, killing 300,000 of them because of floods, droughts, forest fires, and new diseases, and that the economic costs of these changes could reach $600 billion annually (GHF 2009).

More specifically, the IPCC predicts that because of changes in rainfall and other weather events, crop productivity at lower latitudes in dry and tropical regions will decrease and increase the risk of hunger, although it will rise in mid- and high latitudes for some crops. By the 2080s, more people will experience annual flooding, especially in the low-lying river deltas of Asia and Africa. The health status of people will be affected by malnutrition, there will be increased deaths due to diarrheal diseases, and the range of tropical diseases such as malaria will expand.

Overall, the area of the world most likely to be impacted by climate change is the earth's mid-level latitudes which are, therefore, labeled the *Tropic of Chaos* by sociologist Christian Parenti (2011). While the physical impacts of climate change in these areas—rising sea levels, desertification, freak storms, and flooding—are frightening, more so may be the social and political chaos that accompanies these events.

While humanitarian groups have voiced concerns about the impact of climate change in these areas, the potential instability has also drawn attention from government intelligence agencies. They report that weak or failed states will not be able to cope with the effects of climate change and will produce authoritarian governments and terrorist groups, and that the wealthier countries will face a flood of immigrants from the south. They predict that Africa and parts of Asia will face political and social instability from climate change. In Kenya, for example, droughts are becoming more common; whereas seventy or eighty years ago they occurred every ten years, they have been happening every five years now. Since 2000, there have been three major droughts and people are killing each other over water.

Droughts have plagued Uganda since the 1960s and their intensity is increasing putting Uganda, according to the UN, on the edge of a humanitarian catastrophe with food output

Increased flooding, such as occurred in New York and New Jersey as a result of Superstorm Sandy in 2012, is one expected outcome of climate change. (US Air Force Photo/Alamy.)

declining by 30 percent in some areas (see Smith and Vivekananda 2007:79, 82). Over 80 percent of Uganda's 31 million people rely on rain-fed subsistence farming, and with rainfall declining more than 38 percent of children younger than 5 are stunted and 23 percent are underweight (Smith and Vivekananda 2007:38).

Drought in eastern Afghanistan is linked to climate change which has led to a rise in temperature in the mountains and slightly decreased precipitation. The drought was broken by the 2010 monsoon that flooded 20 percent of Pakistan, killing 2000 people and destroying 2.4 million hectares of crops. The economic loss was estimated at $43 billion. It was drought that led to insurrection in the 1970s, which ultimately led to the rise of Taliban. It was also climate change–fueled drought that has led to the failure of food crops resulting in farmers in Afghanistan growing more opium poppies, which are largely drought resistant. A half an acre of poppies, which require one-sixth the amount of water as wheat, can bring about $5,000. The same area of wheat will bring $100 (Parenti 2011:98–99).

Egypt depends on the Nile River, but the Nile is fed by tributaries that pass through nine other countries, each, to one degree or another, anxious to capture some of that water source. Egypt has used recurring military force to control the upper reaches of the Nile, and, until now, agreements with other countries, such as Sudan, apportioning a certain amount of water to each, have prevented full-scale war. But a combination of an increasing demand for water by these countries, along with recurring droughts in the area fueled by climate change, threaten one-third of Africa with economic, social, and political instability (Klare 2001:148ff.).

In 1960, under pressure from the World Bank, India and Pakistan signed the Indus Water Treaty guaranteeing Pakistan 80 percent of the water flowing from the Indus and its main tributaries. According to the treaty Pakistan was to receive 55,000 cusecs (a flow of 1 cubic foot of water per second). But recently Pakistan has complained that India has cut the flow to 13,000 cusecs in the winter and 29,000 in the summer damaging agriculture and needed electric energy. Compounding the problem, Pakistan reports a declining rainfall and overuse of groundwater. It also reports that per capita use of water has fallen over the past fifty years by 80 percent from 5,600 to 1,038 cubic meters a person and is expected to decline to 89 meters per person by 2025 (Parenti 2011:129).

U.S. intelligence services reported to Congress that India can deal with climate change until 2030 but, beyond that, its ability to cope will be reduced by declining agricultural productivity because of decreasing water supplies and increasing cross-border migrations into the country (Parenti 2011:139).

No area of the world will likely escape some negative consequences of climate change. Increases in global temperatures have increased the incidences of heat waves, leading to dehydration and heat stroke. In 2003, a heat wave in Europe killed 35,000 people, the majority over seventy-five years of age, in five countries. It has been estimated that anthropogenic warming has increased fourfold the probability of a weather-related disaster such as the 2003 European heat wave. The likelihood is projected to increase hundredfold over the next four decades (Smith and Vivekananda 2007:33).

Many of these disasters still can be avoided if we can reduce our use of carbon-based fuels. But to do so would require reducing our economic activities and rates of economic growth, and that could lead to massive economic dislocation and ruin. The other option is to make more use of alternative technologies to fuel our economy's productive engines. But there is little likelihood of replacing carbon-based fuels with alternative forms of energy production anytime in the near future.

In 2009 the world produced and consumed 84.4 million barrels of oil a day (mbd) or 30.8 billion barrels for the year. To get the same amount of energy from nuclear power, a popular energy alternative, would require 6,800 reactors, or roughly more that 6,400 more than were operating worldwide in 2009. Or it would require 6 million new wind towers, operating at maximum efficiency, every day of the year, or 17 million running at the efficiency of presently operating towers. Or to get the equivalent amount of energy from solar PV panels, also operating at maximum efficiency, would require covering 2,000 square miles. And, finally, if we converted to biofuel, it would mean converting 16 billion acres of farmland to soybean production, or 135 percent of the total amount of world agricultural land (Martenson 2011:160).

So there is a dilemma; if no effective action is taken to reduce the use of carbon-based fuels, their by-products—largely carbon dioxide—will, to some degree, alter the climate and create widespread suffering and dislocation on a scale no one is prepared to address. The question then, is, why are governments, particularly in the nations most responsible for creating the problem, so resistant to doing anything about it?

The Environment, Sustainability, and the Nation-State

Our eating habits and tastes are, of course, only a single dimension of how our lifestyles, and the need for perpetual growth affect our earth, water, and air. And while most people recognize the dangers posed to the environment and the lives dependent on it, there is disagreement regarding what to do about it. Neoliberals claim that the solution to our environmental problems lies in maintaining and even accelerating economic growth and global economic expansion. More money, they claim, will lead to new solutions and new technologies that will solve environmental as well as social problems. They point to research that suggests that while countries in the initial stages of economic growth may experience increased environmental degradation, once per capita income reaches a certain point, the environment improves (see, e.g., Chua 1999). Critics of globalization, on the other hand, suggest that unrestrained growth will result in, among other things, even greater deforestation, the acceleration of harmful climate change, and further degradation of farmland and water supplies. They point out that even if the research that shows reductions in pollution with a rise in per capita income is useful, and there is much evidence that it is not (see, e.g., Harbaugh, Levinson, and Wilson, 2002), estimates of per capita income at which the environment improves range from about $4,000 to $13,000. Since more than half the world's population earns $5,000 per capita or less, billions must then try to survive in increasingly devastated environments. This issue is likely one of the most important of the twenty-first century. *Do we need to accelerate growth and assume that more money and newer technologies will alleviate environmental damage, or do we seek to transform our economic and social lives to reduce those activities that lead to environmental destruction?*

The problem is that when nation-states have had a choice between growth and environmental destruction, they almost always choose growth. The major goal of government, as presently defined, is to advance trade and do whatever it takes to maintain economic growth. This does not mean that citizen action is ineffective. In the United States, after the publication in 1962 of Rachel Carson's *Silent Spring,* which documented the devastating impact of DDT on the environment, voters demanded governmental action to ensure clean air and water, along with the preservation of other environmental resources. These demands for a cleaner environment led to the passage of the Clean Air Act of 1970 and Federal Water Pollution Control Act of 1972. However, both pieces of legislation, along with virtually every other attempt to pass environmental regulations, have been vigorously opposed by corporate interests. Moreover, any environmental legislation must deal with the negative impact that it may have on economic growth. Democratic governments all over the world, then, face a dilemma: *How do they respond to citizen demands to protect the environment while, at the same time, respond to pressure from corporate interests not to pass legislation that might affect corporate profits and economic growth?* (see Kroll and Robbins 2009).

Generally speaking, governments have adopted three strategies to address this dilemma. The first is to pay lip service to environmental concerns by emphasizing sustainable growth. The idea of sustainable growth gained popularity as a result of the report issued in 1987 by a commission headed by Norwegian prime minister Gro Harlem Brundtland (The World Commission on Environment and Development 1987). The Brundtland Report, *Our Common Future,* defined sustainable development as development that "meets the needs of the present without compromising the ability of future generations to meet their own needs." The problem is, as we noted, whenever economic growth clashes with environmental concerns, economic growth almost always wins. Furthermore, as Hartwick and Peet (2003:209) note, the notion of sustainability itself may simply be an ideological device to convince a majority of citizens that the greatest negative environmental impact is necessary to maintain growth. Sustainability in this sense, they say, may have a number of meanings, including keeping growth going using state intervention, swapping pollution rights in the market, or just minimizing pollution enough to inhibit organized political action. Unorganized action can be dismissed as "deranged anarchism" (Hartwick and Peet 2003:209).

A second strategy that can be adopted by governments to avoid responding to public demands for environmental protection is to displace regulatory power to unelected and largely remote global governance institutions such as the WTO. For example, when researchers discovered that dolphin populations were endangered by tuna fishing, the U.S. government reacted by issuing rules to protect dolphins and banning the importation of tuna from countries whose fishing fleets did not follow those rules. Mexico claimed that this law violated articles of the WTO and appealed to the WTO to have the United States rescind the rules or permit retaliatory tariffs to be applied to U.S. exports. The WTO ruled that the laws protecting dolphins were unnecessary barriers to trade, and the United States had to abandon its dolphin-friendly legislation. The WTO does have a provision (Article XX) ensuring that nothing in the agreement "shall be construed to prevent the adoption or enforcement by any contracting party of measures … [n]ecessary to protect human, animal, or plant life or health," or "[r]elating to the conservation of exhaustible natural resources …" However, in every instance in which an environmental rule was challenged as a barrier to trade, the WTO Dispute Settlement Panel ruled in favor of trade and against the environment (Hartwick and Peet 2003:201–202).

Thus, by assigning the legal right to decide cases in which environmental protection conflicts with economic growth to dispute panels of the WTO, governments can absolve themselves of failing to respond to citizen environmental demands. Allowing multilateral institutions such as the WTO to dictate environmental policy may explain the reluctance of some governments, such as the United States, to enter into multilateral agreements addressing the environment, such as the Kyoto Accord to control global warming or the Basel Convention regulating the disposal of toxic waste. What would occur if two multilateral bodies, one designed to protect the global economy and the other to protect the global environment, disagreed with each other? It may also explain why efforts to form a Global Environmental Mechanism (GEM), as proposed by Daniel C. Esty and Maria H. Ivanova (2003), have been so difficult to implement. Yet, the failure of governments to support the development of a GEM as vigorously as they have supported the WTO is indicative of global governmental priorities.

Finally, the third governmental strategy to avoid taking significant environmental action that conceivably could endanger continued economic growth is to free corporations and the mass media to spin environmental events and news to allay public fears and interests regarding the environment. Beginning in the 1970s, corporations, as Sharon Beder (2002) documents in her book *Global Spin: The Corporate Assault on Environmentalism,* began spending huge amounts on public relations campaigns to convince the public that they were environmentally conscious, while also spending additional millions trying to minimize governmental regulations and countering scientific findings regarding the deterioration of the environment and its consequences on human health. Nowhere was this clearer than in the debate over global warming. Scientists are virtually unanimous in their judgment that global warming is occurring and that it is due largely to human activities (see, e.g., Emanuel 2007) and that it may have serious environmental and economic consequences.[2] Yet the media and some governmental spokespersons in the United States convey the impression that the conclusions about global warming are uncertain and that

---

[2]Some of the more up-to-date information is contained in the Intergovernmental Panel on Climate Change (IPCC) and can be accessed at: http://www.ipcc.ch/.

global warming is still being debated in the scientific community. Yet, one study by Naomi Oreskes (2004) of 928 papers on climate change in refereed scientific journals found that not one disagreed with the general consensus that global warming was occurring and was the result of human activity. Another study (Boykoff and Boykoff 2004) of global warming reporting in over 3,500 stories from the major media outlets (e.g., the *New York Times, Washington Post, Wall Street Journal,* and *Los Angeles Times*) found that in the interest of "balanced reporting," 53 percent of the stories gave roughly equal treatment to the view that global warming is caused by human activity and the view that it is the result of natural fluctuations. Thirty-five percent emphasized the role of human activity, but presented both sides of the debate, and 6 percent emphasized the doubts about the claim that human activity causes global warming. Thus, skeptics, financed largely by oil, coal, and gas corporations, who cannot gain an outlet through the normal scientific channels, are given equal weight in the mass media, creating the impression that there is *no* consensus in the scientific community. Of course, the media also thrive on controversy; consequently it is also in their interest to make it appear that there is no consensus.

John Bellamy Foster concluded that capitalism will never sacrifice economic growth and capital accumulation for environmental reform. Opposition will develop, as we shall see in later chapters, and some changes will be made, as have been made in the United States during the past thirty years, but environmental concerns will never be allowed to threaten the system itself. As Foster concluded (1993:19),

> Where radical change is called for little is accomplished within the system and the underlying crisis intensifies over time. Today this is particularly evident in the ecological realm. For the nature of the global environmental crisis is such that the fate of the entire planet and social and ecological issues of enormous complexity are involved, all traceable to the forms of production now prevalent. It is impossible to prevent the world's environmental crisis from getting progressively worse unless root problems of production, distribution, technology, and growth are dealt with on a global scale. And the more that such questions are raised, the more it becomes evident that capitalism is unsustainable—ecologically, economically, politically, and morally—and must be superseded.

CONCLUSION

We began this chapter by asking why people choose to consume what they do, how they do, and when they do. We concluded that our tastes are largely culturally constructed and that they tend to serve the process of capital accumulation. There is no "natural" reason why we engage in consumption patterns that do harm to the environment. Furthermore, we suggested that of all the contributing factors to environmental pollution, the most difficult to "fix" is our consumption behavior because it serves as the foundation of our culture.

To illustrate, we examined how the American taste for sugar and fat was historically constructed largely to serve the interests of sugar and beef producers. We examined how anthropological research is trying to help peripheral countries in their effort to meet Western demands for products such as beef without destroying their environmental resources.

We examined the issue of climate change, specifically in relation to the social, economic, and political effects. Some areas, particularly the global south, may threaten to become the "tropic of chaos," as changing rainfall patterns may create intense conflict of such things as water resources.

We also examined the dilemma of choosing between economic growth and the environment, concluding, generally, that when there is a choice between maintaining growth and protecting the environment, historically the choice has been growth. We also examined ways that nation-states can resist citizen pressure for environmental protections and the role that sustainability may play to placate citizen demands without sacrificing the imperative for growth.

8

Health and Disease

We live in a globalized world, filled with shared microbial threats
that arise in one place, are amplified somewhere else through
human activities that aid and abet the germs, and then traverse
vast geographic terrains in days, even hours—again, thanks to
human activities and movements. If there is blame to be meted out,
it should be directed at the species Homo sapiens *and the manifest*
ways in which we are reshaping the world ecology, offering germs
like the influenza virus extraordinary new opportunities to evolve,
mutate and spread.

—LAURIE GARRETT, *The Path of a Pandemic*

A thorough understanding of the AIDS pandemic demands a
commitment to the concerns of history and political economy:
HIV…has run along the fault lines of economic structures long
in the making.

—PAUL FARMER, *AIDS and Accusation*

In the halcyon days after World War II, when the advance of science and economic prosperity inspired government leaders and leading academics to predict a coming era of worldwide peace and prosperity, medical professionals were predicting the end of infectious disease. Universal health was set as a realistic and achievable goal. In 1967, the U.S. Surgeon General said it was time to close the door on infectious disease. There was some reason for this optimism. As a result of a worldwide vaccination campaign, smallpox had been completely eliminated, the last case in the world being diagnosed in 1979. Malaria, one of the world's major killers, had been reduced worldwide and even eliminated in some areas by controlling the vector—the mosquito—that spread the disease and through the development and massive distribution of curative drugs. Tuberculosis, the major killer of the nineteenth century, was disappearing. The U.S. Surgeon General declared that measles would be eliminated by 1982 with an aggressive immunization campaign. Jonas Salk developed a vaccine for poliomyelitis, the scourge of childhood, and the development of antibiotics promised to rid us of every infirmary from pneumonia to bad breath. Then, in the space of a decade, everything changed.

AIDS was one of the shocks that changed universal optimism to what Marc Lappé (1994) called "therapeutic nihilism," an attitude common today among hospital personnel that nothing will work to cure patients. But there were other reasons for the change: the emergence of antibiotic-resistant strains of disease; the reemergence of malaria, cholera, and tuberculosis in even deadlier forms; the emergence of other new diseases, particularly Lyme disease, dengue-2, severe acute respiratory syndrome (SARS), avian influenza (H5N1) virus, swine flu (H1N1), and hemorrhagic fevers such as Ebola that result in massive internal bleeding and have mortality rates of up to 90 percent. Measles, supposed to have been eradicated from the United States in 1982, was ten times more prevalent in 1993 than 1983. These developments and others have required medical researchers in biology, epidemiology, and anthropology, among others, to reexamine the relationship between human beings and the microbial world, particularly those pathogens that cause disease. It is clear that we underestimated the ingenuity of microbes to adjust to our adaptations to them and failed to appreciate how our patterns of social, political, and economic relations affect the emergence and transmission of disease.

Each age, it seems, has its signature disease. Bubonic plague in the fourteenth and fifteenth centuries emerged as a result of the opening of trade routes to Asia and was carried by merchants and warriors from the middle of what was then the world system west to Europe and east to China. Syphilis spread in the sixteenth and seventeenth centuries through increased sexual contact of people in towns and cities. Tuberculosis was the disease of the nineteenth century, spread through the air in the densely packed cities and slums of Europe, the United States, and the periphery.

As we shall see, AIDS is very much the signature disease of the latter quarter of the twentieth and the beginning of the twenty-first century, serving as a marker for the increasing disparities in wealth between core and periphery and the accompanying disparity in susceptibility to disease. More than 98 percent of deaths from communicable disease (16.3 million a year) occur in the periphery. Worldwide, 32 percent of all deaths are caused by infectious disease, but in the periphery, infectious disease is responsible for 42 percent of all deaths, compared with 1.2 percent in industrial countries (Platt 1996:11).

Table 8.1 provides some indicators of health by country for the year 2006. It is obvious that income plays a major role in such things as life expectancy, infant mortality, years lost to

AIDS has become the signature disease of the culture of capitalism, striking particularly hard in the poor countries of the periphery, such as Uganda, where this sign advises people to practice safe sex.
(Malcolm Linton/Liaison/Getty Images.)

TABLE 8.1 Health Indicators of Selected Countries by per Capita Income, 2006

Country	Per Capita Income ($)	Per Capita Health Expenses	Health Expenses as Percent of GDP	Adult Mortality Fifteen to Sixty Years (per 1,000 population)	Infant Mortality per 1,000 Live Births	Life Expectancy	Prevalence of HIV per 100,000	Under-5 Mortality Rate per 1,000	Years Lost to Communicable Diseases (percent)	Percentage of Access to Improved Drinking Water	Percentage of Access to Improved Sanitation
United States	44,070	6,714	15.3	109	7	78	508	8	9	99	100
Canada	36,280	3,672	10	72	5	81	222	6	6	100	100
Sweden	34,310	3,119	8.9	64	3	81	107	4	4	100	100
United Kingdom	33,650	2,784	8.4	80	5	79	137	6	10	100	100
Japan	32,840	2,514	7.9	67	3	83	<100.0	4	8	100	100
France	32,240	3,554	11.1	91	4	81	263	5	6	100	100
Spain	28,200	2,388	8.1	75	4	81	380	4	6	100	100
Saudi Arabia	22,300	607	3.4	178	21	70	—	26	22	89	100
Czech Republic	20,920	1,490	6.8	108	3	77	<100.0	4	3	100	99
Russia	12,740	638	5.3	300	10	66	775	13	8	97	87
Mexico	11,990	756	6.2	122	29	74	244	35	27	95	81
Argentina	11,670	1,665	10.1	124	14	75	456	17	18	96	91
Chile	11,300	697	5.3	91	8	78	229	9	17	95	94
Venezuela	10,970	396	5.1	142	18	74	598	21	24	89	83
Iran	9,800	731	7.8	138	30	71	133	35	22	94	83
Cuba	9,500	363	7.1	104	5	78	52	7	10	91	98
Costa Rica	9,220	743	7	95	11	78	235	12	22	98	96
South Africa	8,900	869	8.6	564	56	51	16,579	69	77	93	59
Brazil	8,700	765	7.5	176	19	72	454	20	30	91	77
Jamaica	7,050	240	5.1	177	26	72	1,371	32	30	93	83
Colombia	6,130	626	7.3	131	17	74	509	21	25	93	78
Algeria	5,940	188	3.6	135	33	71	82	38	50	85	94
China	4,660	342	4.5	116	20	73	62	24	23	88	65
Bolivia	3,810	204	6.6	208	50	66	120	61	55	86	43
Indonesia	3,310	87	2.2	212	26	68	106	34	41	80	52
India	2,460	109	4.9	241	57	63	747	76	58	89	28
Pakistan	2,410	51	2	206	78	63	86	97	70	90	58
Vietnam	2,310	264	6.6	155	15	72	421	17	40	92	65
Kenya	1,470	105	4.6	416	79	53	6,125	121	81	57	42
Nigeria	1,410	50	4.1	423	99	48	3,547	191	83	47	30
Malawi	690	70	12.3	533	76	50	12,528	120	89	76	60
Ethiopia	630	22	4.9	326	77	56	—	123	82	42	11
Afghanistan	400	29	5.4	473	165	42	<100.0	257	76	22	30

Source: World Health Organization Data Tables, http://www.who.int/whosis/en/index.html

infectious disease, and so forth. However, income is not the only factor; in the United States, with the most amount of spending per capita on health, many indicators (adult mortality from 15 to 60, infant mortality, life expectancy, etc.) are below that of other countries, which spend far less on health. Nevertheless, one of the major features of global health is the great inequality in the health risks that people face from country to country (see Table 8.2).

TABLE 8.2 Health Risk Factors by Country[1]

Location	Per Capita Alcohol Consumption (liters)	Percentage of Adult Female Obesity	Percentage of Adult Male Obesity	Adolescent Tobacco Use (percent)	Adult Tobacco Use (percent)
Afghanistan	0.01	—	—	9.8	—
Algeria	0.15	—	—	13.8	15.2
Argentina	8.4	—	—	24.9	30
Bolivia	3.23	15.1	—	20.8	31.7
Brazil	5.76	13.1	8.9	17.2	—
Canada	7.8	13.9	15.9	—	21.6
Chile	6.6	25	19	35.5	37.9
China	5.2	3.4	2.4	5.5	31.8
Colombia	5.68	16.6	8.8	32.8	—
Costa Rica	5.65	—	—	18.7	16.8
Cuba	2.26	—	—	10.3	35.9
Czech Republic	12.99	16.3	13.7	35	31
Ethiopia	0.86	0.7	—	7.9	4.3
France	11.43	—	—	—	31.7
India	0.29	2.8	1.3	13.7	18.6
Indonesia	0.09	3.6	1.1	13.5	35.4
Iran	0	19.2	9.1	26.6	17.6
Jamaica	1.74	—	—	19.5	15
Japan	7.59	3.3	2.9	—	29.4
Kenya	1.51	6.3	—	15.1	14.7
Malawi	1.41	2.4	—	18.4	15
Mexico	4.57	28.1	18.6	28.6	24.7
Nigeria	10.57	5.8	—	18.1	7.1
Pakistan	0.01	—	—	10.1	21.1
Russia	10.32	—	—	27.3	48.5
Saudi Arabia	0	—	—	15.9	14.7
South Africa	6.72	—	—	23.6	18.4
Spain	11.68	13.5	13	—	33.7
Sweden	5.96	9.5	10.4	—	22
United Kingdom	11.75	23	22.3	—	35.7
United States	8.61	33.2	31.1	—	23.9
Vietnam	0.85	—	—	2.2	24.3

[1]Data years vary from 2003 to 2006

Source: World Health Organization Data Tables, http://www.who.int/whosis/en/index.html

The fact that each historical epoch has its characteristic illness reveals clearly that how we live—the social and cultural patterns at any point in time and space—largely define the kinds and frequencies of diseases to which human beings are susceptible. The questions we need to ask are, *What do we do that exposes us to disease? What do we do that exposes others to disease? How do we create the conditions for unique interactions between pathogens, their environments, and their hosts? Furthermore, what features of human societies make pathogens more or less lethal?*

Many of the things we discussed in previous chapters are relevant. For example, increases in population density clearly relate to the emergence and frequency of disease, as does the division of the world into rich and poor. Rural workers and peasants crowding into cities, as agricultural land becomes concentrated in the hands of a few, influence disease susceptibility. Public policy that makes economic growth a priority and neglects health programs encourages the spread of disease, as do International Monetary Fund structural adjustment programs in peripheral countries that demand the cutting of health, sanitation, and education programs. The alteration of the environment has enormous consequences for the spread and emergence of disease.

As food is available to those who can pay for it, so, too, are medical cures available largely to those with the money to buy them. In a capitalist medical system, as in a capitalist food system, market demand, not need, determines what and how much is produced. Of the 1,233 new medicines patented between 1975 and 1997, only thirteen—1 percent—were for tropical diseases. One American drug company stumbled on a drug for sleeping sickness, currently infecting some 300,000 people a year, largely in sub-Saharan Africa. The drug company that now owns the patent for the drug, however, has decided not to market it because of the poor profit potential. It did donate the patent to the World Health Organization (WHO), but WHO lacks the financial resources to develop it (see Tardieu 1999). Malaria infects an estimated 500,000 and kills from 1 million to 3 million people a year, mostly in poor countries, yet drug companies invest little to find cures because there is little profit in addressing the needs of the poor. "The poor have no consumer power, so the market has failed them," said Dr. James Orbinski, international president of Doctors without Borders/Médecins Sans Frontières: "I'm tired of the logic that says, 'He who can't pay, dies' " (McNeil 2000). Thus, although drug companies invest some $27 billion a year in research, most of that is for drugs to grow hair, relieve impotence, fight cholesterol, control depression and anxiety, and relieve arthritis and high blood pressure, all problems of the wealthiest 10 percent or 20 percent of the world's population. Those priorities make good economic sense in the short term but, given the rapidity of the spread of disease, endanger everyone.

Infectious disease, of course, is not the only health problem we face. Environmental pollutants, often a direct outgrowth of industrialization, cause sickness. For example, asthma, often aggravated by industrial pollutants, is on the rise. Millions of people face malnutrition and starvation, conditions that further expose them to disease. Commercially promoted products, such as alcoholic beverages and tobacco, endanger health. Cigarette manufacturers produce some five and a half trillion cigarettes a year—almost 1,000 cigarettes for every man, woman, and child on the planet. Asia, Australia, and the Far East are the largest consumers (2,715 billion cigarettes), followed by the Americas (745 billion), Eastern Europe and Former Soviet Economies (631 billion), and Western Europe (606 billion) (World Health Organization 2002). As cigarette sales continue to fall in the core in response to antismoking campaigns and state legislation, cigarette companies, with the support of core governments, have intensified their efforts to sell their products to people in other countries, particularly to women and the young. For example, the United States has used free trade arguments and the threat of economic sanctions to pressure other nations—Thailand, Taiwan, and South Korea—to open their markets to American cigarettes. In such cases it is easy to see a direct connection between the capitalist world system and the onset of disease. However, the relation that exists between the culture of capitalism and infectious pathogens is often more subtle and hidden.

A PRIMER ON HOW TO DIE FROM AN INFECTIOUS DISEASE

Human beings swim in a sea of microbes; we eat them, breathe them, and absorb them through skin openings and membranes. Most do us no harm, and many are useful. Millions of bacteria live in our intestinal system to aid digestion, and in nature they serve as catalysts for decomposition of material that can then be reused by plants and animals. Many we never meet because they exist in distant parts of the world. Some microbes, however, do harm us. Harmful or pathogenic microbes include bacteria, viruses, and parasites that invade our bodies and cause illness and, in some cases, death. The question we need to ask is, *What determines the relationships that we have with the infectious pathogens whose world we share?*

To answer this question, let's ask what is required for a pathogen to kill us—that is, *What does it take for us to die of an infectious disease?* At least four things have to happen. First, we must come into contact with the pathogen or a vector—such as a mosquito, tick, flea, or snail—that carries it. Second, the pathogen must be virulent—that is, have the capacity to kill us. Third, if we come into contact with a deadly pathogen, it must evade our body's immune system. Finally, the pathogen must be able to circumvent whatever measures our society has developed to prevent it from doing harm. As we shall see, human actions are critical in each step.

What actions of human beings increase their likelihood of coming into contact with an infectious pathogen? Various behaviors may serve to expose an organism to an infectious agent. For example, carnivorous animals create an opportunity for pathogens to spread when the animals eat the flesh of other animals; animals that congregate create opportunities for the spread of pathogens by physical contact. Because human behavior is dictated largely by our culture, cultural patterns that characterize human populations play a major role in creating or inhibiting opportunities for pathogens to spread. Actions that change the environment or change the size, density, and distribution of human settlement patterns increase or decrease the likelihood of our meeting an infectious parasite or influence the size of the parasite population. The emergence of Lyme disease is a good example of many of these factors.

Lyme disease was first reported in 1975, when two women, in Old Lyme and Haddam, Connecticut, reported to a Yale physician that their children had strange symptoms, including aching bones, malaise, and neurological symptoms such as poor memory and concentration. Studies revealed that the disease, now spread throughout much of the United States, is carried by four varieties of ticks. The question is, *Why did it suddenly become a major health problem?* The reason apparently has to do with human alterations of the environment along with human settlement and recreational patterns.

In the seventeenth and eighteenth centuries, much of the New England forest was cleared for farming. As farming declined, the forests grew back but with a very different ecology than the one that existed originally: Gone were certain species of animals, such as wolves, bears, and mountain lions, and populations of deer and mice, once controlled by these predators, increased dramatically. Also increasing were the populations of ticks associated with deer and mice and, with the ticks, the *Borrelia* organism, a pathogen they carried in their salivary gland. As human beings built settlements (suburbs) along the forests and ventured into them for recreational activities, they were exposed to the tick. The result was Lyme disease.

As previously noted, coming into contact with a pathogen is not sufficient in itself to kill us. The pathogen must be virulent enough to disrupt critical bodily functions or reproduce so extensively in the body that the damages it causes will result in death. There is obviously a big difference between "catching" a cold and "catching" HIV. We seem to take for granted that some diseases are more severe than others, but the reality is far more complex. A pathogen that is harmless to one host may be lethal in another. There is a herpes virus, for example, that has evolved to survive, spread, and do no harm in one type of monkey but is 100 percent lethal when it infects another type (Garrett 1994:573).

Generally, it is not in the best interest of a parasite, bacteria, or virus to seriously harm its host; it is far better to allow the host to survive, to provide an environment for the pathogen to survive, reproduce, and spread. Furthermore, it is a distinct advantage to the pathogen if the host remains mobile to help the pathogen spread to new hosts. The rhinoviruses that cause the common cold, for example, reproduce in the cells that line the nasal passages; they are shed by sneezing or by a runny nose. If a person with a cold wipes his or her nose with a finger and then touches the finger of another person, the exposed person may inhale the contaminated air or touch the finger to his or her mouth. However the pathogen is spread, it requires the host to move, so killing or disabling the host is counterproductive.

Thus, most microbes that we come into contact with and even those that infect us do us little or no harm. However, there are certain exceptions to the rule that microbes should not harm their host. First, the newer the disease, the more deadly it is likely to be because microbe and host will not have had sufficient time to adapt to each other. Anything that human beings do that exposes them to diseases to which they haven't been previously exposed increases the likelihood that the disease can kill them. As we saw in Chapter 3, the destruction of the peoples of North, South, and Central America in the sixteenth and seventeenth centuries is a case in point. Having never been exposed to such diseases as smallpox, measles, influenza, and in some cases even a common cold, millions died. Something as simple as increased travel can bring people into contact with a disease that is far more lethal for them than for the people who share their environment with the pathogen. Intestinal illnesses that are the bane of travelers are but one example; the traveler can be devastated by a pathogen that people native to the area harbor in their bodies with little or no effect. HIV-2 is carried in the bodies of African green monkeys with apparently little effect, but when it "crossed over" to human beings, the result was fatal.

A second exception to the rule that pathogens should do no harm is when the disease is carried and spread by a vector. When a disease is spread from human to human by another species such as the mosquito, flea, or tick and does not depend on human beings for its existence, reproduction, or transmission, the pathogen is under no selective pressure to spare human beings and can be as virulent as it likes. In fact, extensive multiplication in the human host might be beneficial to the microbe because it increases the likelihood of the vector picking it up and continuing the microbe's reproductive cycle. It might be even better for the host to be disabled if, for example, the host would be less able to protect itself from the vector. As we might expect, pathogens are generally very kind to vectors, generally causing them no harm whatsoever (Lappé 1994:25). What this means is that anything that human beings do to increase their exposure to vector-borne pathogens will increase their likelihood of contracting a deadly disease.

A third exception to the "do-no-harm" rule is when a pathogen is spread by contaminated water or another external medium. For example, diarrheal diseases tend to be more virulent if they are spread by water systems and do not require person-to-person contact. The reason, suggested biologist Paul Ewald (1993:88), is that diseases that are spread by contaminated water lose nothing by incapacitating their host, but they gain a great deal by reproducing extensively in the host. Their large numbers make it more likely that they can contaminate water supplies through the washing of sheets or clothing or through bodily wastes. Thus, human activities that create contaminated water supplies are likely to create more virulent forms of diarrheal diseases.

Finally, the fact that diseases are spread by vectors or external mediums suggests that the virulence of a disease is affected also by the ease of transmission: The easier a disease is to transmit, the more virulent it is likely to be; or, conversely, the more difficult a pathogen is to transmit, the less virulent it will be. If a disease is difficult to transmit, the microbe that can lurk in the body without harming it (thus allowing the host to survive until an opportunity arises to jump to another host) has a decided advantage over a microbe that quickly kills or disables its host. Thus, chronic diseases, such as tuberculosis, can lie dormant for years without doing damage to the host, waiting for an opportunity first to infect the host and then spread to another. However, reasoned Ewald, if the disease is easy to transmit, then it is under no selective pressure to spare the host. Diseases such as Ebola, for example, reproduce so rapidly in the body, and infect virtually every organ, that anyone who comes into contact with any of the victim's bodily fluids is likely to contract the disease.

The notion that diseases that are difficult to transmit are likely to be less lethal has important implications. For example, sexually transmitted diseases in generally monogamous populations should be less virulent, according to Ewald, because the pathogens have to wait longer to be transmitted from host to host. If sexual activity increases, however, it is to the pathogen's advantage to increase rapidly in the body to take advantage of the increased likelihood of transmission. This seems to fit with some developments with HIV, the virus that causes AIDS. In populations in which transmission was more difficult because people had fewer sex partners or were more likely to use condoms, the disease evolved into a less virulent form (Garrett 1994:587).

Even if Ewald's hypothesis that diseases that are easier to transmit are more lethal does not apply universally, its implications are striking. It means, as Ewald (1993:93) suggested, that we should be able to make a pathogen less lethal by increasing the price it pays for transmission; in other words, by making the pathogen more difficult to transmit, we should be able to force it to evolve toward a less lethal form. Thus, by cleaning up water supplies, protecting ourselves from mosquitoes, and reducing the likelihood of the spread of sexually transmitted diseases, we are working to prevent the disease and to make it less deadly when it does occur.

Having examined how human actions bring us into contact with a pathogen and help determine how lethal it is, let's move on to the next step toward our death. Let's assume we have come into contact with a pathogen that is highly virulent to human beings. *Is there anything that can save us?* Fortunately, the human body has evolved a highly sophisticated immune system that generally prevents microbes from harming us. When a microbe infects the body, specific cells of the immune system, T cells, attach themselves to the invader, signaling other cells, macrophages, to envelop and destroy it. Once destroyed, other cells of the immune system call off the attack, lest the system overreacts and destroys its own cells.

It is an ingenious system and, under stable conditions, one that will hold in check most microscopic invaders. However, if an immune system is weakened, for example, by hunger, it is less able to fight off disease. Furthermore, in unstable conditions, when the opportunity exists for rapid changes in the number and type of microbes, the microbes have a decided advantage. Microbes are extremely adept at evolving ways to escape the body's immune system. The reason is that viruses and bacteria mutate and reproduce at a much faster rate than larger organisms, such as human beings. Consequently, if a microbe evolves that can somehow get around the immune system, that particular variety of microbe will have a distinct adaptive advantage, and more of its offspring will survive. Ultimately, this will lead to the emergence of a microbe for which our bodies have no defense.

Simple arithmetic demonstrates how quickly microbes can adapt to changed or threatening environments. Let's assume that a variety of an organism—let's call it X—emerges with a characteristic that gives it only a 1 percent reproductive advantage over another variety—Y—of the same organism. That means that 101 of the X variety will survive in each generation to only 100 of Y. Arithmetically, this means that X will become the dominant form of the organism in only thirty generations. In human terms, thirty generations is a long time—700 to 800 years. But for microorganisms, thirty generations is a very short time—for bacteria that reproduce every twenty to thirty minutes, thirty generations can elapse in a day, at the end of which two bacteria have produced 1 billion.

Because of this ability to adapt so quickly, some microbes have developed the capacity to evade the immune system. The bacterium that causes dengue hemorrhagic fever has evolved to use the immune system to spread from the blood systems to the vital organs. The virus that causes influenza changes so rapidly that infection by one strain does not confer any immunity to subsequent strains. The AIDS viruses evolved to attack and destroy the body's immune system, not only allowing the virus to survive and spread but also creating the opportunity for other diseases, such as tuberculosis, to take root and thrive. In fact, one of the major threats of HIV is that the rapid change in its genetic structure, about 1 percent per year in some varieties, will allow it to evolve resistance to whatever defenses the body or medical researchers may develop.

Assuming, then, that we have met a lethal pathogen and that the body's immune system is unable to destroy it, what next? As far as we know, human beings have always sought to cure whatever illness afflicted them. Ritual and ceremonial cures are known in societies throughout the world, as are the use of plants and other natural resources. However, there is little question that one of the major success stories of the culture of capitalism is the development of measures to protect people from and cure them of infectious disease. The discoveries of the causes of infectious disease and then the development, manufacture, and distribution of vaccines and antibiotics have, in general, extended the human life span in societies throughout the world. Worldwide, life expectancy at birth was forty-eight years in 1955, fifty-nine years in 1975, sixty-five years in 1995, and 68.9 in 2007 (World Bank, World Development Indicators 2009).

Unfortunately, just as microbes can quickly adapt and evade the natural defenses of our immune system, they can also quickly evolve to render modern drugs useless. When antibiotics are overused or used incorrectly or prescribed for viral infections against which they are useless, new varieties that are resistant to existing antibiotics may evolve. Some researchers claim that half of the 150 million antibiotic prescriptions written by American doctors each year are misprescribed or misused in this way. Patients often take a portion of the prescribed dosage and, once they feel better, neglect to take the rest. This results in killing the bacteria most susceptible to the antibiotic but may leave unaffected those that are more resistant. Those resistant bacteria then gradually become the dominant strain of the microbe; even if 99.9 percent of the original strain is destroyed, the survivor is likely to be a superstrain on which existing antibiotics have no effect (Platt 1996:54).

Furthermore, half of the antibiotics used in the United States are used for livestock, aquaculture, and other biological industries. Monocultural farming is a major source of the problem. When only one kind of animal or one kind of crop is grown, a disease outbreak can decimate a business. A commercial chicken farm, for example, may have 100,000 chickens; an aquaculture facility may have thousands of salmon. To protect themselves, growers use antibiotics to fend off disease, creating an opportunity for evolution of drug-resistant strains of pathogens, some of which may be capable of infecting people. Anne E. Platt (1996:52) summed up the problem when she wrote,

> Today, almost all disease-causing bacteria are on the pathway to complete drug resistance. More than a half century after the discovery of antibiotics, humanity is at risk of losing these valuable weapons and reverting to the pre-antibiotic era.

One of the greatest risks we face may come from drug-resistant tuberculosis that is finding its way from poor countries to the rich. The most dangerous source for this disease was the former countries of the Soviet Union. Because of the economic collapse in the 1990s, prison doctors treating tuberculosis were unable to give a full course of drug treatments to patients. The partial treatment triggered the rise of a new dominant strain of the disease that was causing 10,000 new drug-resistant cases a year, each 250 times more expensive to treat than the old strain of the disease. And tuberculosis spreads quickly. More than a dozen passengers on a flight from Paris to New York were infected by a lone Ukrainian infected with the drug-resistant strain (York 1999). Some estimate that, if tuberculosis is not properly treated, 1 billion people will be newly infected—and 35 million will die—in the next two decades.

Thus, we get some idea of how human actions can influence the relationship between infectious pathogens and human bodies, and what it takes in a general sense for us to die of an infectious disease. Next let's examine how this translates to the relationship between disease and culture, and more specifically, how people's behavior in the culture of capitalism contributes to the creation and transmission of infectious disease.

THE RELATIONSHIP BETWEEN CULTURE AND DISEASE

As we have seen, our world is filled with organisms that can cause us harm. Whether we come into contact with them, how deadly they are for us, and whether we can help the body fight them off or reach a mutually beneficial arrangement are greatly influenced by the kinds of lives we lead or, more specifically, the cultures and patterns of social relations that we construct, maintain, and reproduce. Let's examine this a little further and identify some of the specific cultural adaptations of human beings that either encourage or inhibit disease. One of the questions we want to consider is, *How has the emergence of consumer capitalism influenced the spread of disease?* Put another way, *how does the behavior appropriate to our culture expose people to the risk of disease or create opportunities for the creation and spread of infectious pathogens?* To illustrate the relationship between culture and disease, between our behavioral choices and how they affect our relationships with the world of microbes, let's examine what happened to disease during another great cultural transformation in human history—the shift from gathering and hunting to agriculture.

Gathering and Hunting to Early Agriculture

Early gathering and hunting societies were likely afflicted by a range of diseases far different from our own. Small, geographically scattered human populations did not afford infectious diseases the same opportunity for infection and transmission as do large, densely populated modern societies. Most pathogens in early human societies must have depended for their survival on nonhuman hosts. When they infected human beings, it was when people got in the way of the reproductive cycle of the nonhuman host, not because the microbe depended on human beings for its survival.

Contact with wild animals likely exposed early human societies to such diseases as rabies, anthrax, salmonellosis, botulism, and tetanus (Cohen 1989:33). Worm parasites that infested animals' bodies would have been encountered by hunters. Malaria and yellow fever were transmitted by mosquitoes and other diseases by ticks. As Mark Cohen noted in *Health and the Rise of Civilization* (1989), these diseases strike rarely, cannot spread directly from person to person, and do not claim many victims. But because human beings would not have built up an immunity to these diseases and because the offending microbes would not have depended on human transmission, the diseases were often fatal.

There were also categories of disease that could be transmitted from person to person; these would have had to live in hosts for a long time to have the opportunity to spread and must have been transmitted fairly easily by touch; breathing, sneezing, or coughing; and in food or other shared items. Yaws was probably one such disease, as may have been the herpes virus and a variety of intestinal illness (Cohen 1989:37). Because diseases tend to evolve toward less virulent forms the longer they coexist with a population, diseases that we recognize today as mild may have been more serious in earlier human populations.

However, it was during the transition of human societies from gatherers and hunters to sedentary agriculturists that began some 10,000 years ago that whole new relationships developed between culture and disease. By remaining sedentary, people probably came into contact with fewer pathogens, and by remaining in one place, people likely developed greater immunities to localized bacteria, viruses, and parasitic infection. Being sedentary also makes it easier to care for the sick. But, as Cohen pointed out, being sedentary also has some major disadvantages. First, sedentary societies are more likely to engage in long-distance trade, which may increase contact between groups and, as a consequence, spread disease from one group to another. Second, sedentary populations create more favorable conditions for pathogens to spread; permanent shelters attract vermin—insects and rodents—that may carry disease, while the buildup of garbage and human waste may serve in sedentary societies to harbor and spread microbes, especially if water sources are infected with human waste.

Third, alteration of the landscape through horticulture, animal husbandry, and agriculture exposed people to new disease. Malaria-bearing mosquitoes would have thrived in the ponds and bodies of stagnant water created by human environmental intervention. Ponds and irrigation ditches would have provided opportunities for expansion of the snail that carries schistosomiasis.

Fourth, improvements in cooking technology, particularly pottery, may have helped cook food more thoroughly and destroyed disease-carrying microbes, but porous pots may have encouraged the growth of some bacteria. Storage of food for extended periods increased the possibility of bacteria buildup and fungal contamination and attracted disease-carrying vermin.

Finally, regular contact with domesticated animals exposed human populations to additional infections. Living in close contact with animals gives parasites, such as tapeworms, opportunities to involve human hosts in their life cycles as they pass between humans and domestic animals. There is evidence that most human respiratory disease arose after animals were domesticated, and a whole range of diseases now or once common in human beings—measles, smallpox, influenza, and diphtheria—are thought to have had their origins in domestic animals (Cohen 1989).

Today it is estimated that spread of diseases from wild and domesticated animals are responsible for around 2.5 billion cases of human illness and 2.7 million human deaths per year (MacMillan 2012; Robbins 2012).

Cities: "Graveyards of Mankind"

As much as agriculture changed the relationship between microbes and humans, the voluntary or involuntary decisions of people to move to cities shifted the balance in favor of infectious disease. Simply put, the more people per square mile, the more easily an infectious agent could pass from one person to another. For example, as early as 2,000 to 4,000 years ago, writers told of infestations of lice, bedbugs, and ticks that they associated with dense housing conditions and the onset of disease. The chances of a citizen of ancient Rome living to the age of thirty years was one in three, whereas 70 percent of rural residents survived until thirty (Garrett 1994:236). In 430 B.C., an epidemic of an unknown disease in Athens killed half the population.

Although cities have existed for at least 6,000 to 7,000 years, they began increasing dramatically in size during the expansion of the capitalist world system. Cities became the hubs of financial activities and were themselves one of the main reasons for the growth of trade—city residents relying on food from rural agricultural areas and trade items from distant places. Cities also grew as a consequence of the commercialization or capitalization of agriculture because more people were pushed off the land and forced to seek sustenance in the cities of the core and then the periphery.

Five diseases in particular seem to have benefited from the expansion of urban environments—bubonic plague, leprosy (Hansen's disease), cholera, tuberculosis, and syphilis. Bubonic plague, as we saw in Chapter 3, was spread in the fourteenth century by traders and invaders from Central Asia west into Europe and east into China and periodically reemerged with disastrous demographic, economic, and social consequences. Cities tried to protect themselves by banning travelers from entering and by finding scapegoats on which to blame the disease. Tens of thousands of Jews and alleged devil worshippers were slaughtered for this reason, with the city of Strasbourg alone killing 16,000 of its Jewish residents. The Brotherhood of Flagellants, a society of Christian men, beat themselves with leather straps embedded with iron spikes to drive out the sins they believed responsible for the disease (Garrett 1994:238). In 1665, the plague hit London, killing as many as 3,000 people per day.

Leprosy is a particularly good example of an apparent adaptation of a parasite. The disease swept over Europe in 1200, aided by the growing density of cities, disdain for bathing, wool clothing, and sharing of bedding with others to stay warm. The disease is caused by a bacterium passed by human contact that attacks the nerves of the extremities, causing them to go numb. Because there is no feeling in the fingers, toes, and other extremities, injuries go unnoticed by the victim, leading to the characteristic disfigurement and stigmatization of victims. By 1980, most of the world's 5 billion people had antibodies to the bacterium, indicating they had been harmlessly exposed to the disease (Garrett 1994:239).

Cholera struck the world's cities in four devastating pandemics between 1830 and 1896, spreading through contaminated water and sewage systems. In St. Louis in 1849, 10 percent of the population perished; in the city of Mecca in 1847, some 15,000 residents and Muslim pilgrims died, and another 30,000 died in 1865; in London in 1847, 53,000 died. Because the disease seemed to affect the most impoverished segments of the population, those in power assumed it was a result of lower-class "immorality." It was not until 1849 that London physician John Snow demonstrated that the disease was transmitted via water supplies. Snow removed the handle of a pump that was the sole water supply for a cholera-ridden neighborhood, and the local epidemic ended. Yet it was years before authorities were convinced that the disease was transmitted through the water supply and took measures to protect it.

Tuberculosis was the most deadly disease of the nineteenth century. Like others, the bacterium responsible for the disease, *Mycobacterium tuberculosis*, was ancient, dating back to at least 5000 B.C. Tuberculosis is a slow-growing disease, causing illness only after months or years of infection and then ultimately killing the host; however, only about 10 percent of those infected actually develop the disease. It is transmitted through microscopic droplets exhaled by victims, making people who inhabit densely populated, closed spaces—the kind typical of urban slums—particularly susceptible.

The effect of population density on the incidence of tuberculosis is evident in its history in the United States. In 1830, Boston had a crude death rate from tuberculosis of 21 per 1,000, half that of London, which had a far larger population. By 1850, when Boston's population had grown, the death rate was 38 per 1,000. In Massachusetts, tuberculosis rates increased by 40 percent from 1834 to 1853. Then, toward the end of the nineteenth century, for unknown reasons, tuberculosis rates began to decline. In 1900, tuberculosis killed about 200 of every 100,000 Americans; by 1940, before the advent of antibiotic therapy, the rate was 60 per 100,000.

A number of hypotheses have been offered in the ensuing debate over why tuberculosis death rates declined. Some claim that better nutrition enabled people to withstand infection better. Rene Dubos, whose 1952 book *The White Plague* pioneered the study of the connection between human behavior and disease, claimed that the elimination of the deplorable working conditions of men, women, and children during the Industrial Revolution along with improved housing resulted in the decline.

Laurie Garrett (1994:244) suggested that a clue to the decline in tuberculosis can be found in the experience of South Africa. Even with the increased availability of antibiotics and an understanding of the transmission of the disease, death rates for tuberculosis rose 88 percent from 1938 to 1945. Cape Town saw a rise of 100 percent, Durban 172 percent, and Johannesburg 140 percent. Urban rates of infection were as high as 7 percent of the total population, whereas in rural areas, despite poverty and hunger, the rates were less than 1.4 percent. Virtually all cases struck the black and Asian, or "colored," population.

Housing, according to Garrett (1994:245), seemed the most likely culprit responsible for the outbreak. During that period, South Africa had its own industrial revolution and, as in Europe in the eighteenth and nineteenth centuries, required inexpensive labor. Blacks and coloreds, by far the major source of cheap labor, were required by law to live in areas designated by the government and to carry identity cards that stipulated where they could and could not go. The government subsidized housing for the white population, but government-sponsored housing projects for blacks actually declined by 471 percent during this period of expansion, resulting in abysmal living conditions. The South African medical authorities blamed the outbreak on an imagined genetic susceptibility of blacks, thus blaming the victim for an affliction caused by the expansion of the capitalist economy.

Cities also seemed to provide ideal conditions for the emergence of sexually transmitted diseases such as syphilis. The density of population, anonymity of urban life, and influx of single people, especially men, in search of work, promoted greater sexual activity, experimentation, and prostitution.

There is some debate over the origins of syphilis (see Baker and Armelagos 1988). It is carried by a bacterium transmitted in sexual intercourse or at birth from an infected woman to her child. It was first reported in Europe in 1495 among French soldiers (explaining its early designation as the "French disease") fighting against Naples and within two years had spread throughout the world, apparently existing in a deadlier form than it does today. Because the outbreak of the disease coincided with the return of Columbus's sailors from the New World, many scholars believe its origin lay in the Americas, from which it was spread by European conquerors to the rest of the world. Others argue that the rate at which the disease killed indigenous people of the New World suggested a lack of any immunity that would likely have been conferred if the disease were native to that area of the world. Still others (see Hudson 1965) suggest that syphilis is caused by the same bacterium that causes yaws, a common but easily cured childhood skin disease with a worldwide distribution, and that local sanitary conditions determined whether the disease manifested itself as yaws or syphilis. Regardless of its origins, it spread throughout European cities from the sixteenth through the twentieth centuries.

The pace of urbanization from the fifteenth to the nineteenth centuries that created conditions for diseases such as plague, leprosy, cholera, tuberculosis, and syphilis to spread has dramatically increased in the twentieth century, especially in the periphery. In 1950 there were only two megacities—urban areas with 10 million or more people—New York and London. By 1980, there were ten: Buenos Aires, Rio de Janeiro, São Paulo, Mexico City, Los Angeles, New York, Beijing, Shanghai, Tokyo, and London. Currently, over 50 percent of the world's people live in cities of 2,000 or more (Population Reference Bureau 2009). Many of these urban dwellers will be new migrants from rural areas flocking to cities, as they have for centuries, in search of jobs, often after being forced off their land by the continuing concentration of agricultural production and wealth in a few hands and by government policies that function to create cheap labor to fuel economic growth. These densely packed populations will continue, as they have for centuries, to be prime breeding grounds for the creation and dissemination of disease.

When New York and London were reaching megacity status, they were doing so in countries that were the richest in the world. That wealth allowed them to adjust to their growth by building sanitation services, public health networks, and medical services to accommodate growing numbers of people and the special problems created by increasing population density. For the most part, the new megacities, with the exception of some in East Asia, lack that luxury. Not only have they grown at unprecedented rates, but they are also in countries on the brink of economic ruin. The international debt of countries such as Brazil, Egypt, Mexico, and India prevents them from building facilities to accommodate the growing urban populations. Residents live in hastily constructed shantytowns and slums that rival any of those in eighteenth- and nineteenth-century Europe and America for the extent of poverty and disease. Even the richer cities cannot keep up with the growth; in Tokyo in 1985, less than 40 percent of dwellings were connected to proper sewage, and tons of untreated human waste was dumped into the ocean. Hong Kong, another of the more wealthy cities, was dumping 1 million tons of untreated waste each day into the China Sea. In the poor cities, of course, the situation is far worse. In 1980, 88 percent of Manila's population lived in squatter settlements with houses built of scrap wood, cardboard, tin, or bamboo. Nairobi's slums, where 40 percent of the population lived, were deliberately left off official maps of the city (Garrett 1994:251).

A United Nations report reveals that the average child growing up in one of the urban slums of the periphery is forty times more likely to die before his or her fifth birthday of a preventable infectious disease than a rural child in the same country. No country is immune; the extent of neglect of inner-city children in the United States was underscored in 1993 when the WHO announced that the United States had fallen behind Albania, Mexico, and China in childhood vaccination rates, largely because of the collapse of health services to inner-city poor (Garrett 1994:512).

Therefore, human demographic patterns, largely a consequence of labor movement and commerce, continue to generate environments that harbor pathogens and provide ample opportunity for their spread, and help opportunistic pathogens expand their base of operations. A case in point is cysticercosis, a disease produced by tapeworms found in undercooked pork and other animal flesh, which in some forms can infect the brain. Epidemiologists observed that in Mexico City, people were being infected not from eating undercooked pork—those infected could not afford to eat meat—but from the water of the Tula River, highly polluted and the city's primary water source. Tens of thousands of people living in shantytowns downriver from the city's sewage system were being infected. Once a parasite adapts to a new environment, it may easily spread. By 1980, this pathogen had found its way to Los Angeles, carried back by travelers to Mexico, immigrants, or visitors to the United States.

Diseases of Environmental Change

Urban centers emerged as a natural outgrowth of the expansion of commerce, increased industrialization, and the need for financial hubs to serve as links between commercial and industrial centers. However, the environmental and social changes of the past fifty years that have influenced the spread of disease have been more methodical and controlled. Disease, it seems, is becoming an environmental problem. Emerging diseases such as HIV/AIDS, Ebola, West Nile Virus, and, as we discussed, Lyme disease are all the result of human alteration of nature.

We carefully plan and build massive hydroelectric projects that result in the flooding of millions of acres, in the process creating new environments for waterborne infectious parasites. We methodically destroy millions of acres of rain forests, in the process creating new habitats to be exploited by disease vectors. We plan and build roads that bring people into areas where they have never been, thus exposing them to new pathogens. We expand habitats, consequently changing the delicate ecological balances and promoting evolution of microbes that once infected only nonhuman species to infect human beings. We knowingly dump raw sewage into our oceans and waterways, not only spreading disease worldwide but also creating a massive evolutionary medium for new pathogens to develop. In modern warfare, we devastate environments in ways that past armies were incapable of doing, in the process creating opportunity for pathogens to thrive.

For example, in 1985, the Daima Dam was built on the Senegal River by the Mauritanian, Senegalese, and Malian governments. The dam made possible the irrigation of 10,000 hectares of desert soil, converting it into fields of sugarcane, potatoes, mint, and rice. As a result of agricultural expansion, a few members of a local tribe became millionaires (Platt 1996:45). But with the dam came infectious disease. Sanitation in the area is poor, and the irrigation canals, from which people drink, bathe, and wash their clothes, have become infected with strains of diarrheal bacteria. The dam also halted the flow of salt water that once penetrated up to 200 kilometers inland. The salt water had kept the snail population in check, but the dam created ideal conditions for an epidemic of snail-borne schistosomiasis. The first cases were detected in 1988, and by 1990, 60 percent of the population exhibited symptoms. In one village that had profited from growing mint, 91 percent of the people were infected.

Schistosomiasis is an ancient disease. Egyptian mummies have evidence of infection, and the disease was common in China around 200 B.C. during a time of expanding rice cultivation. Today, it ranks second only to malaria among diseases in tropical regions. It infects farmers and fishers who wade in shallow water infected with the snails that carry the disease. It is transmitted when people defecate the larvae of the parasite, which then travels through water supplies and infects other snails and people (Platt 1996:47).

In some areas the disease is so prevalent that it goes unrecognized. Katherine A. Dettwyler (1994:46) was doing anthropological work on disease in Mali and taking urine samples when she received one from a young boy that appeared to be full of blood. The urine contained over 500 *Schistosoma* eggs per milliliter, the highest count measurable with the technique she used. When she gave him a look of consternation, he asked, "What's the matter?" "Does your urine always look like this?" she asked. "Yes," he replied. "Isn't it supposed to? Doesn't everyone's?" She later learned that in some communities, the first appearance of red urine in boys was believed to be equivalent to the onset of menstruation in girls and was thought to indicate sexual maturity. In some communities, celebratory rites of passage were held when boys reached this milestone.

When Brazil completed its highway through the Amazon, a new disease, *oropouche*, began to strike residents of Belém; it affected 11,000 people. When settlers cleared the forest for cacao planting, they disturbed the habitat of a midge that harbored the virus that caused the disease. Discarded cacao shells provided a new breeding ground for the insect, and the explosion of their population in association with human settlements created the opportunity for disease spread.

One reason forest, especially rain forest, destruction unleashes disease is because of the variety of species that exist in forests. A single hectare of rain forest contains more insect species than the entire New England area or all of Great Britain. When human beings destroy that habitat, it brings them into contact with insects and pathogens that are then searching for new habitats and new hosts. Epidemiological studies show that increasing deforestation by 4 percent increases the incidence of malaria by 50 percent (Lozano, Pinedo-Cancino, Patz, 2006).

Thus how human beings alter their surroundings and create new ones has a profound effect on the exposure to disease (see Table 8.3).

TABLE 8.3   Causes of Infectious Disease Emergence and Representative Disease Examples

Cause of Emergence	Infectious Disease
Changing Environmental Conditions	
Deforestation	Malaria, hemorrhagic fever, rabies, Lyme disease
Agriculture and Irrigation	Argentine hemorrhagic fever, Japanese encephalitis, Bolivian hemorrhagic fever, schistosomiasis, influenza (pandemic)
Dam building, road building	Schistosomiasis, malaria, Rift Valley fever
Poor sanitation and hygiene	Diarrheal diseases, malaria, schistosomiasis, lymphatic filariasis, river blindness, dengue, yellow fever, cholera, Guinea worm disease, Japanese encephalitis, salmonella, hemolytic uremic syndrome, cryptosporidiosis, giardiasis
Climate change	Hanta virus, plague, malaria, schistosomiasis, other vector-borne disease
Demographic Changes	
Urbanization	Yellow fever, malaria, dengue, acute respiratory illness, plague, cholera
Increased trade, travel, migration	Cholera, yellow fever, influenza, dengue, dengue hemorrhagic fever, pneumonia, HIV/AIDS, influenza
Deteriorating Social Conditions	
Breakdown in Public Health	Measles, diphtheria, pertussis, tuberculosis, cholera, influenza, HIV/AIDS, other sexually transmitted diseases
War and civil disorder	Malaria, cholera, diphtheria, waterborne diseases
Increased sexual activity	Hepatitis B and C, HIV/AIDS, other sexually transmitted diseases
Intravenous drug use	HIV/AIDS
Overuse of antibiotics	Antibiotic-resistant malaria, tuberculosis, staphylococci, pneumococci, enterococci, gonorrhea, others
Other	
Air-conditioning systems	Legionnaires disease
Ultra-absorbent tampons	Toxic shock syndrome
Unknown	Streptococcus Group A, Ebola

We can see another example of how human beings construct their exposure to disease in the yearly influenza epidemics that fly around the world.

Diseases of Human Ecology: Chickens, Pigs, and Wild Birds

Influenza is a regular phenomenon; each year, the Centers for Disease Control (CDC) tries to establish the strain of influenza that would circulate most widely that year, and develop a vaccine to protect people. The influenza virus is highly contagious, with every droplet emitted by an infected person containing 50,000 to 500,000 virus particles. Influenza attacks the upper respiratory tract, targeting the hairlike cells that line the upper respiratory tract, destroying them, and allowing infection to enter.

The first definitive description of influenza appeared in A.D. 1173 in Europe. The first pandemic, that is, a worldwide spread of the disease, took place in 1580 (Crosby 1976), spreading from Asia to Africa and ultimately North America. There were likely some six to nine pandemics from 1600 to the deadly pandemic of 1918. That epidemic killed from 50 million to 100 million people worldwide, almost 700,000 in the United States alone. Some countries were devastated; Ghana lost 5 percent of its population and Western Samoa 20 percent. There were also serious epidemics in 1957–1958 in which 70,000 died in the United States alone. The CDC estimates that even in a normal flu season 200,000 Americans are hospitalized and 38,000 die, most of whom are over sixty-five.

But what are the chances of another epidemic on the scale of the 1918 influenza, and how deadly would it be? A flu as deadly as the 1918 variety would probably kill some 2 million in the United States alone, while the CDC estimates that a "medium-level epidemic" would hospitalize 740,000 people and kill 207,000. Some more recent influenza strains, such as the so-called "avian" or "bird flu" (H5N1), if it maintained the 30 percent mortality rate evidenced among those who contacted it, would kill 16 million people. And if it could spread as easily as the more recent H1N1 or "swine flu," it could be even more lethal. *But what is influenza, where does it come from, and how does human behavior, particularly the expansion of trade, contribute to its occurrence and spread?*

The Origin of Influenza: Avian Flu and H1N1

Influenza, generally, is a perfect example of a disease of human ecology, involving the transmission of genetic material between wild aquatic birds such as migratory ducks; herons and geese; domestic fowl such as chickens, ducks, and turkeys; domesticated mammals, largely pigs and sometimes horses; and human beings. The influenza virus usually originates in wild birds and does them no harm. As the birds migrate, they can pass on the viruses to domesticated birds via feces, or during competitions over territory, food, or water (see Garrett 2005). The domestic fowl can then spread the virus to other domestic animals, such as pigs, from where it can then spread to human beings. However, it can also spread directly to human beings from wild or domestic birds, as was the case with H5N1, avian flu.

Asia, particularly southern China, has always been a major incubator of influenza for a number of reasons. First, farms commonly combine large numbers of domestic fowl with pigs in pens surrounding people's homes, providing opportunities for the passage of a virus from birds to pigs and to humans. Second, China's dense population has altered the migration routes of wild birds, forcing them to seek food and water in farms, industrial sites, or public parks. But, as we will see, the increased global demand for meat is creating incubators of disease all over the world.

The key to understanding the spread of a flu virus from one species to another and its ability to alter its form regularly lies in its genetic structure. The viruses are made of eight genes composed of RNA wrapped loosely in proteins. Each gene of the influenza virus contains a code that produces two surface proteins, one called hemagglutinin (H), which acts as a grappling hook to anchor the virus to receptor cells of the host. From there it enters the host cell and begins to

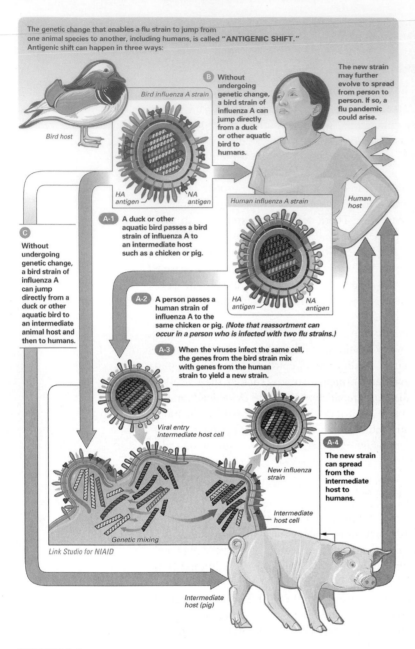

The genetic change that enables a flu strain to jump from one animal species to another, including humans, is called **"ANTIGENIC SHIFT."** Antigenic shift can happen in three ways:

Bird influenza A strain

Bird host

HA antigen   NA antigen

B Without undergoing genetic change, a bird strain of influenza A can jump directly from a duck or other aquatic bird to humans.

The new strain may further evolve to spread from person to person. If so, a flu pandemic could arise.

C Without undergoing genetic change, a bird strain of influenza A can jump directly from a duck or other aquatic bird to an intermediate animal host and then to humans.

A-1 A duck or other aquatic bird passes a bird strain of influenza A to an intermediate host such as a chicken or pig.

Human influenza A strain

Human host

HA antigen   NA antigen

A-2 A person passes a human strain of influenza A to the same chicken or pig. *(Note that reassortment can occur in a person who is infected with two flu strains.)*

A-3 When the viruses infect the same cell, the genes from the bird strain mix with genes from the human strain to yield a new strain.

Viral entry intermediate host cell

New influenza strain

A-4 The new strain can spread from the intermediate host to humans.

Intermediate host cell

Genetic mixing

Link Studio for NIAID

Intermediate host (pig)

FIGURE 8.1
Antigenic Shift
Source: Used with permission. Michael Linkinhoker, Link Studio, LLC, and the National Institutes of Allergy and Infectious Diseases.

reproduce. The other protein is neuramindase (N), which enables the virus to move from cell to cell in the host. There are fifteen different Hs and nine different Ns, which are used to classify each subtype of influenza virus. Thus it was an N1H1 subtype that caused the 1918 pandemic, and an H5N1 subtype that was responsible for the 1997 epidemic (Sherman 2006:398; Barnes 2005:341).

The influenza virus reproduces sloppily and can fall apart and easily absorb genetic material from whatever cells it is infecting. Thus, if another virus is present, the material from one can recombine with the other, and it may switch from being an avian virus to a pig virus, or from a pig virus to a human virus. Pigs generally act as the primary "mixers" for creating hybrid subtypes. They easily get infected by both human and bird subtypes of the same viruses, and when infected by both at the same time, the different subtypes can swap genetic segments to produce a hybrid virus (Barnes 2005:343). The genetic change that enables a flu strain to jump from one animal species to another is called antigenic shift, illustrated in Figure 8.1.

The viruses also readily change to adapt to the immune properties of the host they infect. Thus each subtype can develop its own variants; different variants of the H1N1 have persisted in pig populations for decades, so that the subtype H1N1 that caused the 1918 pandemic reemerged in a less deadly variety of H1N1 in 2009, causing the epidemic of "swine flu." The ability to recombine, change, and reproduce rapidly is one of the influenza virus' adaptive features, for if they remained the same, hosts would develop immunity and no longer be able to spread the virus along the wild bird/poultry/pig/human cycle and it would die out. Constant change, in other words, provides a way around the hosts' immune systems. Generally it seems that every twenty-five years an influenza virus occurs for which there is no immunity (Sherman 2006:398).

The avian flu first was identified in Hong Kong in 1997, killing six people and sickening another eighteen. It rampaged through the Asian chicken populations killing 11 million chickens in Vietnam and Thailand, and, by 2004, 120 million chickens had died or been exterminated, costing the Asian poultry industry some $15 billion. By 2005, it was appearing in pigs. Humans were generally infected by coming into contact with an infected bird. It was extremely virulent, killing some 30 percent of the people it infected. Another strain that appeared in 2003 killed 68 percent of its victims. Fortunately there were only a few suspected cases of human-to-human transmission, the others requiring direct contact with an infected bird. However, the fear is that

TABLE 8.4 CDC Estimates of 2009 H1N1 Cases and Related Hospitalizations and Deaths in the United States from April 2009 to February 13, 2010, by Age Group

2009 H1N1	Mid-Level Range[1]	Estimated Range[1]
Cases		
0 to 17 years	~19 million	~14 million to ~28 million
18 to 64 years	~34 million	~24 million to ~50 million
65 years and older	~6 million	~4 million to ~8 million
Cases Total	~59 million	~42 million to ~86 million
Hospitalizations		
0 to 17 years	~85,000	~60,000 to ~125,000
18 to 64 years	~154,000	~109,000 to ~226,000
65 years and older	~26,000	~19,000 to ~38,000
Hospitalizations Total	~265,000	~188,000 to ~389,000
Deaths		
0 to 17 years	~1,250	~890 to ~1,840
18 to 64 years	~9,200	~6,530 to ~13,500
65 years and older	~1,550	~1,100 to ~2,280
Deaths Total	~12,000	~8,520 to ~17,620

[1] Deaths have been rounded to the nearest ten. Hospitalizations have been rounded to the nearest thousand, and cases have been rounded to the nearest million.

Source: Center for Disease Control, http://www.cdc.gov/h1n1flu/estimates_2009_h1n1.htm

given the propensity of the influenza virus to change and recombine, a more easily transmitted strain could emerge that could pass easily between human hosts, as in the case of "swine" or H1N1 flu.

Swine flu, which through February of 2010 infected some 59 million Americans and killed an estimated 12,000 (see Table 8.4), was first identified in March of 2009. The first cases were identified in La Gloria, Mexico, in a town adjacent to a hog farm or concentrated animal feed operation (CAFO). The first reports speculated that H1N1 originated at the CAFO, but those reports were dismissed as other cases appeared; however, Mexico suffered an immediate decline in tourist revenue as well as losses from closed shops and the cessation of other social activities.

The actual story of the emergence of the recent strain of H1N1 is a perfect illustration of the way the influenza virus is constantly reconstructing itself and exploiting opportunities created by global lifestyles to recombine in available hosts. Tracing the path of H1N1, Laurie Garrett (2009) begins in 2005 in a Wisconsin slaughterhouse where a teenaged boy helped his brother-in-law butcher thirty-one pigs and a week later pin down another pig while it was gutted. Preparing for Thanksgiving, the family bought a chicken and kept it in their home. On December 7 the boy came down with flu; on visiting a local clinic, he fully recovered. As Garrett describes the incident, it would have gone unnoticed except that the influenza virus that infected the boy was unlike any other seen, being a combination of a wild-bird flu, a human type, and a variant found in pigs. When a five-year-old in La Gloria, Mexico, was infected in 2009, it was found to be similar to the swine/bird/human flu first identified in Wisconsin. To illustrate the global reach of the influenza virus, CDC scientists discovered that the H1N1 had pieces of genetic material that matched a human flu first indentified in New Caldonia in 1999, along with two swine types identified in Asia and Wisconsin, and an unknown avian-flu virus. Furthermore, scientists believe that there are genetic elements of the virus that can be traced back to an Indiana pig farm in 1987. In other words, the teenager in Wisconsin was infected by a new virus with bits of genes from three species—birds, pigs, and humans—and the virus had been emerging for possibly twenty years.

The virus also spread from humans to pigs; in 2006 herds in the Midwest were infected with a type of H1N1 that was a close match of the Wisconsin H1N1 variety.

The most significant feature of the emergence of the 2009 variety of H1N1 is the extent to which human beings have created industrial environments for the raising of pigs, cattle, chickens, and other animals that serve as disease sinks for the mixing and emergence of new diseases with the potential for creating pandemics in the human populations.

Furthermore, large-scale animal-raising operations are continuing to grow in response to the growing demand for meat in the emerging economies of the world such as China, India, and Brazil. *In 1980, per capita meat consumption in China was about forty-four pounds a year: It now tops 110 pounds. In 1983 the world consumed 152 million tons of meat a year. By 1997, consumption had risen to 233 million tons. And the United Nations Food and Agriculture Organization estimates that by 2020 world consumption could top 386 million tons of pork, chicken, beef, and farmed fish.* And that means more large-scale animal-raising operations and greater opportunities for various strains of bird, pig, and human viruses to recombine and produce new varieties that could be deadlier than any other we have seen, perhaps rivaling the 1918 pandemic.

AIDS AND THE CULTURE OF CAPITALISM

We mentioned earlier that AIDS is very much the signature disease of our age. By this we mean the conditions for its development and spread were essentially created by our patterns of beliefs, attitudes, and behaviors. AIDS burst on the world in 1981, when physicians in San Francisco and New York began to encounter symptoms in young men that either had been seen previously in older men or were so rare most physicians had never seen them. They turned out to be opportunistic infections, such as rare forms of pneumonia, cancer, and other diseases that attacked bodies whose immune systems had been destroyed. The new disease was first called *gay-related immunodeficiency disease* (GRID) because of its early diagnosis among gay men, but when it was acknowledged to occur in heterosexual populations, the name was changed in 1982 to *acquired immunodeficiency syndrome* (AIDS). In 1983 the disease appeared in Zaire, and some European researchers thought they had unearthed cases in European hospitals as early as 1967 and possibly 1959.

The early 1980s was a turbulent time for AIDS. Researchers were competing to be the first to isolate and identify the virus. Researchers in Europe and Africa could not publish their articles in the leading medical journals because the peer review panels did not believe the disease was transmitted heterosexually and claimed the researchers had missed some other mode of transmission. The Reagan administration, which had made millions of dollars available for research in Legionnaires' disease, was reluctant to release funds for AIDS research, education, and services. Leaders of the religious right in the United States opposed using federal funds for a disease they claimed was God's judgment against immorality and corruption. Pat Robertson, a Baptist minister, founder of the Christian Broadcasting Network, and presidential candidate in 1988, claimed scientists were "frankly lying" when they said AIDS could be spread heterosexually and that condoms would prevent infection. In the meantime, AIDS continued to spread among heterosexuals, gay men, intravenous drug users, and hemophiliacs given HIV-infected transfusions (Garrett 1994:469).

As of 2008, an estimated 28 million people have died from AIDS since the epidemic began, and the Joint United Nation Program on HIV/AIDS (UNAIDS) and the WHO estimate that there are presently almost 34 million to 40 million people worldwide infected with HIV/AIDS (see Table 8.5).

TABLE 8.5 Region HIV and AIDS Statistics, 2001 and 2008

	Adults and Children Living with HIV	Adults and Children Newly Infected with HIV	Adult Prevalence (percent)	Adult and Child Deaths Due to AIDS
Sub-Saharan Africa				
2008	22.4 million	1.9 million	5.2	1.4 million
2001	19.7 million	2.3 million	5.8	1.4 million
Middle East and North Africa				
2008	310,000	35,000	0.2	20,000
2001	200,000	30,000	0.2	11,000
South and Southeast Asia				
2008	3.8 million	280,000	0.3	270,000
2001	4.0 million	310,000	0.3	260,000
East Africa				
2008	850,000	75,000	<0.1	59,000
2001	560,000	99,000	<0.1	22,000
Oceania				
2008	59,000	3,900	0.3	2,000
2001	36,000	5,900	0.2	<1,000
Latin America				
2008	2.0 million	170,000	0.6	77,000
2001	1.6 million	150,000	0.5	66,000
Caribbean				
2008	240,000	20,000	1.0	12,000
2001	220,000	21,000	1.1	20,000
Eastern Europe and Central Asia				
2008	1.5 million	110,000	0.7	87,000
2001	900,000	280,000	0.5	26,000
Western and Central Europe				
2008	850,000	30,000	0.3	13,000
2001	660,000	40,000	0.2	7,900
North America				
2008	1.4 million	55,000	0.6	25,000
2001	1.2 million	52,000	0.6	19,000
Total				
2008	**33.4 million**	**2.7 million**	**0.8**	**2.0 million**
2001	**29.0 million**	**3.2 million**	**0.8**	**1.9 million**

Source: UNAIDS 2009, http://data.unaids.org/pub/Report/2009/2009_epidemic_update_en.pdf

Sub-Saharan Africa has the highest rate with over 22 million infected, or over 5 percent of the population, whereas Eastern Europe and South and Southeast Asia have the fastest rate of growth. In North America, there are over 1.4 million cases of HIV. This total is heavily skewed toward the poorest segments of the population with the incidence of AIDS being 6.5 times greater for blacks and four times greater for Hispanics than for whites.

We now think we know the origin of AIDS—that it likely crossed over from nonhuman primates in Central and West Africa sometime after World War II, infecting only a few people until the late 1970s, when it made its breakthrough worldwide. But there are many questions we need to explore to understand the effects of human culture on the disease. For example, *What features of global culture influenced the spread of the disease? What features of our culture determined the people most at risk for AIDS? How did our culture influence the way people choose to react to the epidemic and to those affected by it?*

How Did the Disease Spread?

AIDS reveals the extent to which we are interconnected in global space. As geographer Peter Gould (1993:66–69) noted, we live in a world in which New York is closer to San Francisco than it is to towns 200 miles away; in which Los Angeles is closer to Miami and Houston than it is to towns in Nevada; and in which Kinshasa, Zaire, is closer to Paris than to villages in the center of the country. Gould meant that people located at the hubs of the capitalist world system, those cities connected by rapid air travel, are more likely to come into contact with each other than they are with people located physically much closer to them. Viewed another way, patterns of contact are characterized by what Gould called "hierarchical diffusion" rather than "spatially contiguous diffusion." In the hierarchical diffusion that characterizes AIDS, or "AIDS space," as Gould called it, the disease jumps from travel hub to travel hub.

This is not the first time global space has been redefined by revolutions in trade and travel. In the earlier eras of sea travel, seaports became economic hubs as well as the major points of distribution for disease. Today, with rapid air travel, economic centers such as Tokyo, New York, Paris, Jakarta, San Francisco, London, São Paulo, Bombay, Johannesburg, and Moscow form the geographic center of the world system and, as a consequence, the epicenters of the spread of AIDS.

With the exception of infected blood supplies, AIDS has to be carried from place to place by people and transmitted directly. There is no vector involved in AIDS as in plague, malaria, or dengue. But human travel provides an effective means of transmission. Therefore, to understand the spread of AIDS, we need to ask why in the culture of capitalism do people travel? Generally, they travel for one of four reasons: tourism, business, labor migration, and war, all of which have had a major role in the spread and distribution of AIDS.

Tourism is essentially a product of industrial capitalism of the nineteenth century. Although the wealthy of Europe had their country estates and cottages for centuries, travel and tourism were relatively new phenomena for the emerging middle class (Hobsbawm 1975:203). Made possible by the development of steamboats and railways, the tourist industry grew throughout the nineteenth and early twentieth centuries. For the British middle class, holiday travel became a serious enterprise in the 1860s and 1870s; this transformed the British coastlines with promenades and piers. In Europe, mountain resorts such as Biarritz were becoming fashionable. Tours through Europe became popular, creating an industry and a form of travel that was probably unique. For the poor, day trips dominated; American resorts such as Coney Island in New York became popular for new immigrants to the United States. In the twentieth century, tourism evolved into a major industry, and most people, certainly in the core, have at one time or another been tourists. Tourism is one of the world's largest industries with tremendous annual growth rates. The industry's gains grew to $439 billion in 1998 (Pera and McLaren 1999).

Tourism has always been associated with disease, as any traveler can tell you who has sampled food and water laden with bacteria to which his or her system had no resistance. It is likely that such perils have confronted travelers for centuries. But in the age of AIDS, it is not only the traveler who is at risk, but also the people in the host country who are equally susceptible.

We have no figures on the number of people who have contracted AIDS as a consequence of tourist travel, but researchers suggest that it has had a major impact on at least two countries hit the hardest by the epidemic, Haiti and Thailand. One reason for their susceptibility is that both were targeted for "sex tours."

Anthropologist and physician Paul Farmer (1992) suggested that the history of HIV/AIDS in Haiti is linked to its history as a tourist destination. In the 1970s, Haiti, the poorest country in the Western Hemisphere,

Advertisements for sex tours, such as this one in Thailand, attract tourists from Europe, North America, and other parts of Asia and create fertile breeding grounds for the AIDS virus and other sexually transmitted disease.
(Andrew Aitchison/In Pictures/Corbis.)

became a major tourist attraction with the closing of Cuba in 1959 to American tourists. Tourist visits to Haiti increased to 100,000 per year by 1970 and to 143,538 by 1979. (Later, the tourist industry was a casualty of the Haitian AIDS epidemic: Tourist visits dropped to 75,000 in the winter of 1981–1982 and to below 10,000 the following winter.)

Tourism in Haiti brought with it an increase in institutionalized prostitution. Poverty and 60 percent to 80 percent unemployment rates made prostitution for males and females one of the only economic alternatives available. The country, particularly the Carrefour area of the capital city Port-au-Prince, gained a reputation for cheap sex. Travel guides published for homosexual men recommended Haiti to tourists.

Whether AIDS was brought to Haiti by American tourists, as some researchers suggest, or in some other fashion is a matter of debate, but it is clear that tourism accelerated the spread of the disease among Haitians and, probably, among tourists. By the late 1980s, the rate of HIV in hotel workers catering to tourists was 12 percent, and Haiti had one of the highest rates of infection in the world. But even when Haitian workers became aware of AIDS, they seemed to treat it as just an "occupational hazard" (Farmer 1992:145).

In Thailand, also, tourism played a major role in the spread of AIDS. HIV/AIDS was relatively late in arriving in Asia, with the first recorded death in 1984, a gay man who had spent time in the United States. By 1987, the rate climbed within months from 15 percent to 43 percent among intravenous drug users. The group hit hardest by AIDS was the commercial sex workers. Among Chiang Mai prostitutes, the rate of infection went from 0.04 percent in 1989 to 70 percent 20 months later (Garrett 1994:489).

Thailand had for years an active trade in both drugs and prostitution, trades that accelerated when Thailand became a major rest and recreation zone for American military personnel during the Vietnam War. Both drugs and prostitution were, and continue to be, major sources of foreign exchange for Thailand's economy. By 1990, Thailand was attracting 5.3 million tourists a year, with a high proportion of single men from Malaysia, Japan, and Taiwan and with special "sex tours" arriving in Bangkok from Japan, the Middle East, and Europe, particularly Germany. As a consequence of the growth in the sex industry, there are 500,000 to 800,000 prostitutes representing some 10 percent of the female population between the ages of fifteen and twenty-four. In the early 1990s in some areas of Bangkok, there was an AIDS infection rate of 90 percent.

Probably because of the economic importance of the sex industry, particularly for attracting tourists, government authorities in Thailand were slow to respond to the threatened epidemic. As cases began to increase in 1987, the government decided not to launch an anti-AIDS campaign

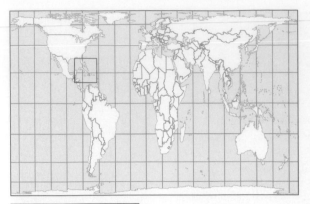

Haiti

for fear of "inciting panic." By 1989, 0.5 percent of all pregnant women were HIV-seropositive, with some northern provinces reporting rates of 3 percent. In 1991 the government reevaluated its policy and noted again that they did not want to create panic. A Bangkok newspaper reported that HIV/AIDS was spread only by anal sex and intravenous drug use, when in fact there were forty times more heterosexual cases than homosexual cases reported. The WHO estimated that, by 1992, 450,000 people in Thailand were infected.

Another form of travel that characterizes the capitalist culture is labor migration. At least since the increase in slave trade in the seventeenth and eighteenth centuries, the world economy has required massive shifts of laborers from one area to another. Although it is difficult to determine exactly the extent of the worldwide transmission of AIDS by migrating workers, there is considerable evidence that this type of travel was a major cause of AIDS transmission in Africa. Male workers travel from rural areas to urban areas in search of work, sometimes visiting prostitutes whose infection rate in some areas approaches 90 percent and sometimes bringing the disease back to their rural villages.

Commercial and business travel were also instrumental in the spread of AIDS. The routes of infection in Africa pass along well-traveled truck and commercial transportation routes. The north–south alignment of AIDS starts at Djibouti at the mouth of the Red Sea, the port city and railway terminal for the city of Addis Ababa, the capital of Ethiopia, to which goods, and AIDS, flow. In 1991 some 50 percent to 60 percent of prostitutes and 1 percent of the general population were reportedly infected with HIV. In the Sudan, 80 percent of the "bar girls" were seropositive for HIV-1. From Uganda to Mozambique, samples of truck drivers indicate that 30 percent to 80 percent are infected. Estimates are that Tanzania has 1.4 million infected people of a total population of 18 million, Zimbabwe has 1.5 million, and Kenya 1.6 million. The highway between Malawi and Durban, South Africa, is known as the "Highway of Death," truckers having an infection rate of 90 percent (Gould 1993:75).

Patterns of AIDS distribution seem to follow commercial routes in North America as well. Paul Farmer (1992:149) noted that the incidence of AIDS in the Caribbean correlates with the degree to which a country is economically integrated into the "West Atlantic system." Excluding Puerto Rico because it is not an independent country, the countries with the highest rates of AIDS—the Dominican Republic, the Bahamas, Trinidad/Tobago, Mexico, and Haiti—are also the countries most dependent on trade with the United States and most linked to the American economy. The country with the highest rates of AIDS—Haiti—was most dependent on U.S. exports.

Finally, the movement of soldiers and refugees precipitated by conflict played a role in the spread of AIDS. Researchers speculating about the origins of AIDS and the factors that may have contributed to its breakout in Central and East Africa have concluded that something dramatic must have happened around 1975 to cause the emergence of the epidemic. The period of 1970 to 1975 was characterized by guerrilla warfare, civil war, tribal conflicts, mass refugee migrations, and striking dictatorial atrocities. Laurie Garrett suggested that such social upheaval may have affected the course of AIDS both directly and indirectly. For example, most African conflict was characterized by rival forces trying to cripple each other economically, politically, socially, spiritually, and militarily. In such conflicts, civilian casualties are high. In any number of military campaigns of the past two to three decades in Central Africa, rape was used (as it was in Bosnia) systematically to terrorize and dominate the enemy. Some armies have tested up to 50 percent HIV-positive. Other human activities resulting from social disruption—including increased multiple-partner sexual activity, famine and malnutrition that further stressed immune systems, large-scale migrations and concentrations of people in refugee camps, increased prostitution, and destruction of health care services—could have further spread the disease (Garrett 1994:367–368).

Who Gets Infected with AIDS?

Rene Dubos (1968) wrote in the 1950s and 1960s of the special vulnerability of the poor to infections; malnutrition, substandard housing, dense population, and lack of access to health care all promote the spread of infectious disease. Paul Farmer in *Infections and Inequality* (1999) documents the link between economic inequality and susceptibility to infectious disease. Certainly poverty played a role in the spread of tuberculosis, cholera, and syphilis. But AIDS has affected the economically marginalized as well as those who are socially and politically marginalized—homosexuals, women, and children.

Public and governmental responses to the AIDS epidemic, especially in the United States, were greatly influenced by the mistaken assumption that it was a disease of homosexual men, in spite of the fact that there was clear evidence of heterosexual transmission in the United States; Europe; and particularly Africa, where it was almost exclusively transmitted by heterosexual relations. We may never know to what extent the association of the disease with a socially marginalized portion of American society delayed research and education efforts, but it is clear that it didn't help.

It is also clear that the poor, globally and in the United States, have been the most frequent victims of the disease. Africa, the poorest area of the world, has by far the highest incidence of AIDS, whereas Eastern Europe, economically

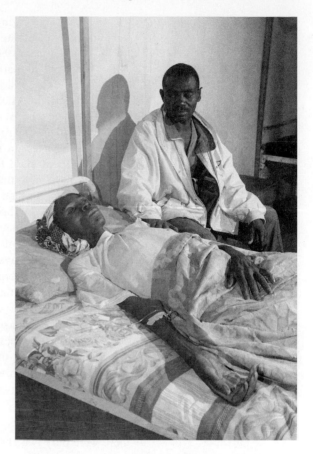

Women, particularly in Africa, comprise the majority of AIDS victims. (imagebroker/ Alamy.)

devastated with the collapse of socialist economies and cutbacks in health services, has the highest rate of growth in HIV/AIDS. Poor countries in other areas of the world are the others most affected. For a particularly apt illustration of a poor and socially marginalized country that suffers disproportionately with AIDS, let's return to Haiti.

Haiti is very much a creation of the capitalist world system. In the sixteenth and seventeenth centuries, the indigenous population (the Taino) were exterminated and the country resettled with African slaves ruled by a European elite. Haiti passed from Spain to France in 1697 and was renamed Saint-Dominique. In 1804, a slave revolt led by Toussaint L'Ouverture succeeded in defeating the French, establishing the country of Haiti, the first, as Paul Farmer referred to it, of the Third World countries.

The new country found itself in a world hostile to the idea of self-governing blacks, a nightmare to every country in which slavery endured, particularly the United States. Every effort was made to undermine black rule in Haiti. The French demanded that Haiti compensate planters for the loss of land, and in the nineteenth century, European gunboats would periodically appear in Haitian ports demanding compensation. By 1900, 80 percent of national revenue was used to pay off international debts, and by the late 1920s, Haiti was being advertised in *Financial America* as a place where "easily directed" Haitian labor could be had for twenty cents per day, as opposed to three dollars per day in Panama.

American domination has continued throughout the twentieth century, as Haiti has lived with a series of despotic rulers supported by the United States. This history left Haiti in 1983 with an annual per capita income of $315 overall and $100 in the countryside. The agricultural situation was so bad that Haiti was a net importer of food, even sugar. Even when Haiti had promise as a recreational playground for other North Americans, the tourist industry collapsed because of

Haiti's reputation as the originator of AIDS. There were few avenues out of poverty in Haiti. The 60 percent unemployment rate combined with the country's dependence on the United States set the stage for what Farmer (1992:189–190) called the "West Atlantic pandemic."

AIDS is not only a marker of poverty, but it is becoming a marker of gender and age as well. We saw in our discussion of famine and hunger that women and children are particularly at risk. In the instance of AIDS, women worldwide represent the majority of all reported cases. The fact that women, who were at the fringe of the epidemic in the mid-1980s, have frequently become victims reflects the role of women in global capitalist culture. Women seem to become infected at younger ages. In many countries, 60 percent of new AIDS infections are among women between the ages of fifteen and twenty-four; in surveys of several African and Asian countries, women younger than twenty-five account for 30 percent of new AIDS cases, compared with 15 percent for men younger than twenty-five.

Women contract the disease largely through heterosexual intercourse; many of these are among women who are monogamous but have male partners who are not. This is in part because of the sexual subordination of women in many countries where men initiate sexual relations and women, especially wives, have little say. The attitudes toward women and sex in many countries inhibit conversation about sexual matters and virtually prohibit AIDS educational campaigns directed toward women. Furthermore, education is hampered by the higher illiteracy rates among women in many countries. Even in countries with well-developed campaigns to educate women about the risk of AIDS, men still often resist condom use because of decreased sensitivity, ignorance about how to use them, or fear that their use will cause sterility.

Women also contract the disease through prostitution, itself a reflection of the limited options available to women, especially in poor countries. As Laurie Garrett (1994:368) said about AIDS and prostitution in Uganda,

> [a]s a business, prostitution was second only to the black market. For most women there were only two choices in life: have babies and grow food without assistance from men, livestock, or machinery, or exchange sex for money at black-market rates.

Finally, the more women are infected with AIDS, the more likely children will be infected. Children are at risk of acquiring the disease at birth. AIDS can be transmitted by infected hypodermic needles; yet, many countries that depend on intravenous drugs are too poor to afford new needles. In some African countries, needles are reused. Intravenous transmission of AIDS to children is not solely a problem of the periphery. In Russia, the collapse of communism and the social and economic chaos that followed virtually destroyed the country's health care system. Syringes were unavailable, and medical personnel, especially in rural areas, were forced to use the same syringes again and again, up to 400 times in some cases. In 1988, AIDS emerged in Elistya, capital of the Kalmyk Republic on the Caspian Sea. A baby had been infected by its mother. The baby was treated by staff who used the same syringes to draw blood samples and administer drugs to all the babies in the hospital's nursery for three months; HIV was unknowingly injected into all the babies on the ward and some of their mothers (Garrett 1994:501).

Socially marginalized members of the capitalist world system face another danger: Once infected with HIV, they are the ones least likely to receive treatment or to receive information to enable them to take measures to avoid the onset of AIDS. As AIDS researcher Renée Sabatier (Garrett 1994:475) noted in reference to AIDS education campaigns,

> I think there is a very real danger that we're going to end up as a [world] society divided between those who were able to inform themselves first and those who were informed late. Those who have access to information and health care, and those who don't. Those who are able to change, and those who aren't. I think there is a real danger of half of us turning into AIDS voyeurs, standing around watching others die.

The announcement in the summer of 1996 of a new drug treatment that restores the body's immune system and holds the AIDS virus at bay is a further development in the ghettoization of AIDS. Although the announcement was greeted with great enthusiasm, and the use of the drug has cut mortality rates in the United States by 75 percent, the treatment costs at least $10,000 to $20,000 per year and is, therefore, beyond the reach of the world's poor. When South Africa moved to make generic versions of HIV/AIDS drugs, or proposed importing the drugs from countries with the lowest prices, actions that could have helped cut the costs 50 percent to 90 percent, the United States raised objections and drug companies sued, although, under heavy public pressure, withdrew the threats. Drugs, however, remain largely unavailable to the poor. Of the 1 million people in Malawi who are HIV-positive, only thirty are on the new drug therapy (Finkel 2000).

Who Gets Blamed?

We saw the phenomenon of blaming the victim when we examined population growth, poverty, hunger, and environmental degradation. Problems generated by core exploitation of the periphery are blamed on the periphery itself. However, nowhere is the phenomenon of blaming the victim more clearly illustrated than in the case of HIV/AIDS, and nowhere was that more clear than in the case of Haiti. When the AIDS epidemic was identified in the early 1980s, Haitians with AIDS were a "wild card": they didn't fit the categories of homosexuals, hemophiliacs, and heroin users. So they were added as a whole category, thus completing the early four-H club (homosexuals, hemophiliacs, heroin users, and Haitians). But this was clearly racist: There was no reason, based on some thirty-four cases, to place all Haitians in a risk group. This would be analogous to claiming that all San Franciscans or all New Yorkers were at special risk to contract and spread the disease. Risk designation was akin to being labeled a carrier. Then, in a leap that surprised few Haitians, AIDS was said to have originated in Haiti.

Bruce Chabner of the National Cancer Institute was quoted in 1982 as saying, "Homosexuals in New York take vacations in Haiti, and we suspect that this may be an epidemic Haitian virus that was brought back to the homosexual population in the United States" (Farmer 1992:201). This epidemic of blame led to widespread discrimination against Haitians in job hiring and a rapid decline in the Haitian tourist industry.

The Haitian government was angry with the CDC because, even when it became evident that the rate of infection was higher in other Caribbean Islands and most U.S. cities, the CDC refused to abandon the designation of Haitians as a high-risk group. In 1985 the CDC finally removed the designation but without comment, refusing to admit it made an error. Then in 1990, the FDA ruled that Haitians could not donate blood. It was an absurd ruling; as one Boston newspaper editorial pointed out, if the FDA was consistent, it would have banned donations from all San Franciscans, New Yorkers, Bostonians, and emigrants from other Caribbean Islands, some of whom had rates of AIDS/HIV as much as ten times greater than Haiti's (see Farmer 1992:220).

Why was Haiti singled out? According to Paul Farmer, largely because the U.S. folk model of Haitians included images of superstitious natives, blacks, immigrants, and the like that symbolized the stigma associated with AIDS. The model was driven to some extent by the media. The *New York Times* wrote that "Haitian voodooists may be unsuspectingly infected with AIDS by ingestion, inhalation, or dermal contact with contaminated ritual substances, as well as by sexual activity" (Farmer 1992:3). This view was furthered by the medical community. Jeffrey Viera, senior author of the paper that put Haitians at risk, blamed the media for stigmatizing Haitians, but he himself made reference to voodoo rituals, the drinking of menstrual blood, and the like. An article in the *Journal of the American Medical Association* entitled "Night of the Living Dead" considered these voodoo origin theories, asking whether necromantic zombies transmit HIV/AIDS (Farmer 1992:3). Blaming Haiti for AIDS was a classic case of blaming the victim.

The view from the periphery concerning the origins of AIDS was quite different than the view from the core. As researchers focused on Africa as the origin of the disease, African officials became sensitive to what they saw as a Western campaign to blame their countries for the epidemic. One result was official government denials that there was any AIDS in African countries, even after the epidemic had clearly become established. One African health minister was fired after admitting to international health agencies that AIDS was present in his country. Not surprisingly, conspiracy theories abounded. One theory was that the American CIA had introduced the disease; another, popular also in core countries, was that AIDS was the result of American germ warfare experiments gone awry.

Haitians saw AIDS as a disease visited on them by resentful Americans. As one Haitian schoolteacher (Farmer 1992:232) put it, "The Americans have always resented Haiti, ever since 1804. Being strong, they can punish us, humiliate us. The AIDS thing was a perfect tool."

When asked if they thought the United States did what they did on purpose, Haitian teenagers in the United States almost universally said yes. Others said that AIDS was created in U.S. laboratories.

Paul Farmer (1992:58), in *AIDS and Accusation,* concluded that questions asked by Haitians and Americans such as

> Is AIDS a product of North American imperialism? Can one person send an AIDS death to another through sorcery? Are Haitians a special AIDS risk group? Are "boat people" disease-ridden and a risk to the health of U.S. citizens?...underscore several of the West Atlantic pandemic's central dynamics—blame, search for accountability, accusation, and racism—that have shaped both responses to AIDS and the epidemiology of a new virus.

CONCLUSION

The disease factors that we examined in this chapter have practical consequences. For example, knowledge of the effects of culturally defined human behavior can help us predict as well as treat disease. Might more careful application of this principle have made a difference? Could we have anticipated the emergence of AIDS, as many medical anthropologists once posited? Would we have let multidrug-resistant tuberculosis get out of hand? Would we have allowed so many antibiotic-resistant strains of disease to develop or relied so much on antibiotics? Would drug-resistant malaria be out of control? Would new diseases such as Lyme disease spread so quickly?

Even if we were to predict, as some scientists did, the dangers of overuse of antibiotics and other things, could we really have done something about it? Even knowing the dangers of AIDS, the U.S. government moved slowly in releasing research funds. Even when it was known that anal sex could transmit AIDS, many in the homosexual community refused to heed advice for safe sex, believing AIDS was simply a tactic to discredit their lifestyles.

We continue to create "disease sinks," populations of poor and marginalized people among whom infectious pathogens thrive and who may serve as breeding grounds for new diseases. If there was some omnipotent microbe responsible for the survival and spread of all infectious pathogens, it could hardly improve on the actions of human beings in the culture of capitalism whose cumulative behavioral choices relegate some of their numbers to these sinks.

The lesson is that although we must be aware of how our behavior puts us in danger of contracting disease, we must also be aware of the factors that promote adoption or rejection of therapeutic regimes necessary to lower our risk of becoming ill, cure us, or inhibit the creation of new and more deadly strains of disease. If biologist Paul Ewald is correct and diseases become more lethal the more easily they are spread, then given the increase in travel, the increase in the number of poor, the cutback of medical and public health services for structural adjustment programs, the ecological destruction of habitats such as rain forests, and the emergence of drug-resistant strains of new and old killers, we are truly on the verge of a pandemic on a scale of that which struck the peoples of North and South America in the sixteenth and seventeenth centuries.

What can be done? That is difficult to say, but it seems that political, religious, and social associations that can marshal forces against largely imaginary social, political, and religious enemies certainly could rally populations to cope with the pathogens that threaten to overwhelm us.

Indigenous Groups and Ethnic Conflict

At the present time indigenous societies that believe it is immoral not to share with one's kin or with those less fortunate than oneself are ... considered backward, for this surely hampers capital accumulation and therefore "progress" as the modern world defines it.

—DAVID MAYBURY-LEWIS, *Indigenous Peoples, Ethnic Groups, and the State*

Official statements frequently justify the extension of government control over tribal populations as an effort to bring them peace, health, happiness, and other benefits of civilization.... But, undoubtedly, the extension of government control was directly related to protecting the economic interests of nonindigenous peoples moving into formerly exclusive tribal areas.

—JOHN BODLEY, *Victims of Progress*

There is a museum exhibit in Jakarta, Indonesia, of a Javanese wedding; the guests are arranged around the bride and groom, each dressed to represent a different Indonesian ethnic group, of which there are hundreds. The exhibit is reminiscent of an early nineteenth-century painting we mentioned earlier by the British painter Sir David Wilkie, *Chelsea Pensioners Reading the Gazette of the Battle of Waterloo,* in which all the various groups that made up the British nation-state and empire—Welsh, Scottish, Irish, black, and so on—are depicted together reading about Wellington's victory over Napoleon. Indonesia is one of the most culturally diverse countries in the world. It is also one of the most officially tolerant toward ethnic diversity. Ethnic tolerance is incorporated into education programs, and "hate speech" is a crime. But it is a tolerance with definite limits. Java is the dominant island in Indonesia, and the museum exhibit suggests, said Anna Lowenhaupt Tsing (1993:24), that minority groups are "invited" into the nation, but only as long as they bow to Javanese standards.

One of the casualties of the expansion of the culture of capitalism is cultural diversity. As noted in Chapter 4, one of the functions of the nation-state is to integrate, peacefully if possible, violently if necessary, the diverse peoples within its borders into a common culture. At best,

Although Indonesia officially recognizes and celebrates cultural diversity, the dominant culture is still Javanese, represented here in the wedding of the son of Indonesian ex-president Suharto (on the far left), Hutomo "Tommy" Mandala Putra (third from left), with Ardhia "Tata" Pramesti Rigita Cahyani (fourth from left).
(AP Photo/Pool.)

minority cultures are integrated into the larger culture in superficial ways—dress, art, dance, music, and food are maintained and represented as the culture itself. At worst, however, policies of the nation-state may lead to ethnocide, the destruction of culture, or, in more extreme instances, genocide, the destruction of a people.

The dilemma of minority groups in the modern nation-state is particularly evident in Indonesia because it officially recognizes and celebrates diversity, but this does not stop the nation-state from systematically destroying the culture of indigenous peoples. In her book *In the Realm of the Diamond Queen* (1993), Anna Lowenhaupt Tsing described the fate of the Meratus Dyak, who subsist on swidden agriculture and gathering and hunting, and, although relatively isolated in the Meratus mountains, they frequently trade with other groups. Their culture requires that they frequently move to establish new garden plots. Individuals also travel to maintain political contact with other Meratus groups, travel being a source of prestige.

According to Tsing (1993:41), however, the Indonesian government sees the Meratus as uncivilized, stuck in a timeless, archaic condition outside modern history. Furthermore, the government attributes their condition to their mobility and travel across the forest landscape. From the state's perspective, Meratus mobility constitutes "semi-nomadism" and labels them as runaways from state discipline and a threat to national security. For the Meratus, however, mobility is a sign of personal autonomy.

In Indonesia, there are more than 1.5 million members of what the government calls "isolated populations." Most, like the Meratus, live in small, scattered mountain settlements. To transform these societies into forms acceptable to the Indonesian government, they established the Management of Isolated Populations, a program that operates, to quote one official document, to guide "the direction of their social, economic, cultural and religious arrangements in accord with the norms that operate for the Indonesian people" (Tsing 1993:92). To meet the goals of the project, the government devised various strategies that amount largely to attempts to discipline these populations and bring them under government control. One strategy is resettlement.

The government builds clustered housing and moves isolated populations to them. The state justifies this housing by saying it is more modern, but in fact it makes everyone visible,

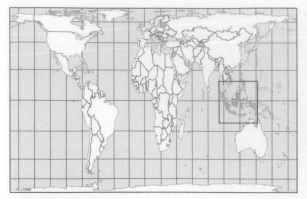

Indonesia

keeps them in one place, enables government control, and in some cases creates settlements designed specifically for military security. The Meratus quickly caught on to the government's game and built their villages with clustered housing so they would "look good if the government comes to visit" (Tsing 1993:93). The government also initiated nutrition programs to reorganize the eating habits of isolated populations. The Meratus were given a demonstration in which locally unavailable meats and vegetables were prepared "the right way." The Meratus were considered unordered in their eating habits; as one village head explained, "[Indonesians] drink in the morning," referring to the typical morning diet of coffee or tea and a pastry, "and then have two meals during the day. We [Meratus] sometimes eat five times a day and sometimes once a day. It's not ordered" (Tsing 1993:93). But eating habits are dictated by work schedules, and in farming or hunting communities, one can eat at very different times. For government planners, even the way food is prepared is supposed to follow national standards; one government official complained that the Meratus butchered a chicken but cooked it without sour spices or chili peppers. To please government authorities, the Meratus leaders now see to it that the chickens are cooked "properly when authorities visit."

The government also exercised control over isolated populations by introducing family planning programs. Once again, there was a distinct difference in how the government saw the program and how the Meratus viewed it. The program was essentially an attempt by the nation-state to discipline the population into following state-mandated views of family form and reproductive practices. In the early 1980s, the state began a program to encourage women to use IUDs or take birth control pills. To advance the program, the government encouraged a local male leader, Pa'an Tinito, to enroll women in the program. He signed up women, but it became apparent that they had little idea of what the program was about and expressed shock when Tinito explained to the men the purpose of contraception. The men were shocked; how could the government possibly want them to limit the size of their population? Weren't communities already too small and weak? The program was ridiculous, and there must be some mistake. Pa'an Tinito responded that the government wanted only a list of women; nothing was said about limiting reproduction. When the supply of oral contraceptives arrived some months later, Pa'an Tinito brought them back to his house and hung them in the rafters, where they stayed (Tsing 1993:109).

In developing relocation, nutrition, and family planning programs, the nation-state was, in effect, imposing standards of social structure and family authority. There should be a fixed and stable "village" consisting of individual families, each with a family "head," generally a man. For the government, to get to women one must go through men. But this is not the way the Meratus were organized, nor was it the way the Meratus saw the situation. Their view of the world differed significantly from that of the nation-state in which they are subjects. The dilemma faced by the Meratus, as well as other indigenous and ethnic groups, is whether one can be simultaneously outside and inside the nation-state. As Tsing (1993:26) put it,

> Marginals stand outside the state by tying themselves to it; they constitute the state locally by fleeing from it. As culturally "different" subjects they can never be citizens; as culturally different "subjects," they can never escape citizenship.

However, whereas nation-states have systematically destroyed the culture of indigenous people, there has been, at the same time, growing divisions among ethnic groups. This problem is most severe in instances where, for one reason or another, one ethnic group enjoys an economic advantage over another. In some instances, as we'll see, the result is genocidal violence.

In this chapter we examine the dilemma of cultural and ethnic divisions in the nation-state. We need to ask, *Why were indigenous cultures destroyed, and what is likely to be the fate of the indigenous cultures that remain in the world? And what is the cause of ethnic conflict and attempted genocides?*

THE FATE OF INDIGENOUS PEOPLES

Who are indigenous or tribal peoples? They certainly include the aboriginal peoples of Australia; the Native Americans of North, South, and Central America; and the peoples of most of the African continent. At the second general assembly of the World Council of Indigenous Peoples, indigenous peoples were defined as follows (Bodley 1990:153):

> Indigenous people shall be people living in countries which have populations composed of different ethnic or racial groups who are descendants of the earliest populations which survive in the area, and who do not, as a group, control the national government of the countries within which they live.

David Maybury-Lewis (1997:7) says the difficulty with this definition is it assumes that should indigenous people gain control of the government, they would no longer be indigenous; however, it is clear they are native to the countries they inhabit and that they claim they were there first and have rights of prior occupancy to their lands. They also have been conquered by peoples racially, ethnically, or culturally different from themselves; they generally maintain their own language and, most importantly, "are marginal to or dominated by the states that claim jurisdiction over them"—that is, indigenous peoples are defined largely by their relationship to the state. Maybury-Lewis (1997:55) concluded that

> many people are stigmatized as "tribal" ... because they reject the authority of the state and do not wish to adopt the culture of the mainstream population that the state represents. They are in fact stigmatized as being "tribal" because they insist on being marginal.

Maybury-Lewis estimated that approximately 5 percent of the world's population fit the description of indigenous peoples; these are the descendants of peoples who have been marginalized in the global capitalist economy.

One of the problems faced by indigenous peoples, as we saw with the Meratus, is that their cultures often conflict with the culture of capitalism. Consequently, the first question we need to explore is, *How is the culture of indigenous peoples incompatible with the culture of capitalism?*

Some Characteristics of Indigenous Peoples

The cultures of indigenous peoples are vulnerable to destruction from capitalist expansion partly because their way of life differs so significantly from that in the culture of capitalism. Although there are significant differences among these cultures, they do tend to share certain characteristics. For example, they tend to be mobile; they may be nomads who threaten state integrity by traversing international boundaries or shifting agriculturists who require large tracts of land or whose frequent movements make them difficult to control.

A second characteristic of small-scale indigenous societies, and one that is quickly undermined by capitalist culture, is their communal ownership of valuable resources, particularly land. Communality creates all kinds of problems in the culture of capitalism. For example, communally held land is not readily sold or purchased, instead requiring group consensus. Financial institutions cannot use communally held land as collateral for an individual's debts because it cannot be repossessed. Furthermore, contrary to some writers' views (see Hardin 1968; Hardin and Baden 1977), communally held lands tend to be subject to greater conservation measures and less subject to exploitation for short-term financial gain. Finally, communal resources and discoveries that are not legally incorporated cannot be protected from capitalist exploitation. For example, the Urueu-Wau-Wau peoples of the Amazon developed from plant extracts an anticoagulant that Merck Pharmaceuticals "discovered" and is attempting to develop, yet no benefits accrue to the Urueu-Wau-Wau, who are threatened with extinction. Thus, as Darrell Posey (1996:7) noted, traditional and communal knowledge that would be recognized as property if held by an individual or a legally designated "natural person," such as a corporation, is deemed in the culture of capitalism to be free for the taking.

A third characteristic of small-scale indigenous groups that is incompatible with capitalist culture is kinship-based social structure. In small-scale societies, most relationships are defined by a person's kin links with others, and the primary social unit tends to be the extended family. The large network of relations that each person can call on for help promotes the sharing of resources and reduces the need to consume and to work to make money. The small, socially isolated nature of family units, such as the nuclear family, makes them more susceptible to state control and discipline. As we shall see, one of the first features of indigenous societies to come under attack is the pattern of kinship relations. This does not mean kinship cannot be used as a basis for control and accumulation of capital; early business enterprises were family based, as noted in Chapter 3, and small family businesses still thrive. Yet, perhaps because of the need for a mobile and socially unattached labor force, extended family units do not do well in the culture of capitalism.

Fourth, most small-scale indigenous societies tend to be relatively egalitarian. As John Bodley (1990:4) notes, equality in social relations reduces the incentive and need to consume because people have far less need to use material possessions to mark their status. Furthermore, nation-states require a political hierarchy to govern effectively. Without a recognized local leader with the power to make decisions, who, for example, will collect the taxes? Who will enforce government directives? Who will ensure that the laws of the nation-state are enforced? As we shall see, one of the first things that nation-states do to control indigenous peoples is to impose a new pattern of authority.

Finally, and perhaps most importantly, indigenous peoples tend to control resources or occupy land desired by members of the capitalist nation-state or the nation-state itself. Thus, as John Bodley (1990:4) writes,

> the struggle between tribes and states has been over conflicting systems of resources management and internal social organization. Tribes represent small-scale, classless societies, with decentralized, communal, long-term resource management strategies, whereas states are class-based societies, with centralized management systems that extract resources for the short-term profit of special interest groups. Understandably, then, the political conquest of tribal areas often brings rapid environmental deterioration and may impoverish tribal peoples.

The Process of Ethnocide

In *Victims of Progress,* Bodley describes the various ways nation-states acted to transfer the rights of resources from indigenous peoples to settlers wishing to exploit the resources for themselves. The process occurs in stages, generally beginning with the establishment of a frontier situation and advancing through military intervention, the extension of government control, and the gradual destruction of indigenous culture through land takeovers, cultural modification, and economic development. Bodley's analysis provides insight into why indigenous peoples have disappeared and gives ample evidence that their "integration" into the modern world was neither voluntary nor beneficial to them.

THE FRONTIER SITUATION   Often the destruction of an indigenous culture begins with the establishment of a frontier, an area perceived to be abundant in natural resources that can be easily exploited but seems not to be controlled by a nation-state. Prior ownership rights and interests of indigenous peoples are considered irrelevant by both the nation-state and invading settlers. For example, in 1909 the London magazine *Truth* published the account of a young American engineer, Walter Hardenburg, describing the brutality of the managers of a British- and Peruvian-owned rubber company in the Putumayo River region separating Peru and Colombia (see Taussig 1987). The article, which described the enslavement, torture, and killing of Indian rubber gatherers, caused a sensation and led the British government to send Roger Casement, then a consular representative in Rio de Janeiro, Brazil, to investigate the charges. Casement had already written a report describing the horrors inflicted by rubber traders on native workers in the Congo, horrors depicted in Joseph Conrad's fictional account *Heart of Darkness* (1972[1902]).

In his report to Sir Edward Grey, head of the British Foreign Service, Casement described again and again the horrors inflicted on the indigenous peoples of the Putumayo region, accounts that he collected from black workers recruited by the rubber companies from Barbados, who themselves, under threat of death, had inflicted the horrors. For example, he wrote to Grey of the fate of Indians who did not fill the quota of rubber allotted to them (Taussig 1987:35):

> The Indian is so humble, that as soon as he sees that the needle of the scale does not mark the ten kilos, he himself stretches out his hands and throws himself on the ground to receive the punishment. Then the chief [of the rubber station] or a subordinate advances, bends down, takes the Indian by his hair, strikes him, raises his head, drops it face downwards on the ground, and, after the face is beaten and kicked and covered with blood, the Indian is scourged. This is when they are treated best, for often they cut them to pieces with machetes.

Casement said that 90 percent of the Indians he saw carried scars from floggings. He described other ways the company managers disciplined and controlled their Indian workers, including deliberately starving them, burning alive those who tried to run away, killing children, and inflicting virtually every form of torture imaginable. Casement's report became the centerpiece of a British House of Commons Select Committee called to investigate the charges against British-owned rubber companies operating in the Putumayo region. Yet virtually nothing was done to change the situation, partly because the British could not assert political control over the region; in fact, one of the most brutal of the company managers later became a head of state.

The kinds of frontier situations described by Hardenburg and Casement almost a century ago, common in most areas of the periphery, still exist today. For example, consider what is happening to the Yanomami Indians of Brazil. Yanomami is the name given the Indians who live along the border between Brazil and Venezuela; in 1980 there were 10,000 Yanomami. They were protected somewhat by their isolation until the 1970s, when the Brazilian military government built a road that passed through Yanomami territory. The highway was never finished, but the traffic it brought to Yanomami country carried with it disease, starvation, and death. The highway brought gold miners, who forced some Yanomami out of their villages and massacred others; federal police were unable or unwilling to expel the miners, and the governor of the area refused to take judicial action against the murderers. Even the Brazilian Indian Service (FUNAI) was literally under attack by uniformed gunmen hired by the miners.

In 1986 the military enlarged a small airstrip that had been used by FUNAI and missionaries, ostensibly to protect the borders against drug trafficking and subversion, but resulting in intensification of the gold rush into Yanomami territory. As a result, by 1988 at least one-fourth of the Yanomami had died and the majority of survivors were sick and starving. When the situation caused an international outcry, the president of Brazil declared that it was impossible to expel the miners from the territory and even proposed demarcating three reserves in the area, not for the

Yanomami group but for the miners (Maybury-Lewis 1997:27). Alcida Ramos (1995:312) in a recent book on the situation among one Yanomami group, the Sanumá, concluded,

> I didn't expect to be around, only ten years after my immersion into an autonomous and healthy culture such as I found among the Sanumá, to see one of the worst examples of cultural devastation in the recent history of Brazilian Indigenism.

MILITARY INTERVENTION Military force was another means of destroying indigenous populations. Clearly, the superiority of European weaponry made the difference in their confrontation with indigenous cultures, although not without some notable losses and defeats at the hands of less-well-armed peoples. In 1860, when the Maori of New Zealand resisted the work of a survey team subdividing a large block of their land, the governor declared martial law and sent in the military to subdue them. The Maori managed to fight for twelve years against a force that at one time numbered 22,000 soldiers, costing the colony 500 people and 1.3 million pounds (Bodley 1990:50).

It was military intervention, of course, that finally subdued the Native Americans on the American Plains in the period from about 1850 to 1880. When Plains nations resisted take-over by Euro-Americans of their land and resources, the U.S. government sent in the military to control them, succeeding, as noted in Chapter 7, only after they destroyed the buffalo herds on which the Native American nations depended.

THE EXTENSION OF GOVERNMENT CONTROL Once indigenous nations were militarily subdued, the next step in the process of cultural transformation was the extension of government control. When the nation-state is able to extend its authority, the indigenous society ceases being an autonomous "nation" and becomes incorporated into the state. In most cases, rulers of the nation-state justified control as bringing to indigenous peoples the benefits of civilization. As John Bodley (1990:58) noted, however, it was directly related to protecting the economic interests of nonindigenous peoples moving into indigenous territory.

Various techniques were used to establish political control. One was simply direct rule, in which a person from the dominant group was appointed, after the military had subdued a population, to administer the subjugated group. The French did this in Africa, appointing French commissioners or heads. More common, and probably more effective, was the technique pioneered by the British in Africa, called *indirect rule*. This involved maintaining and strengthening the role of traditional leaders or creating them when they did not exist and governing through them (Bodley 1990:71).

The base camp program used by Australia to extend governmental control in Papua New Guinea proved to be particularly effective. The territory of Papua New Guinea was relatively isolated; even into the 1940s there were indigenous groups that had never been in direct contact with outside areas. To extend their control, the Australian government would send an armed patrol with trade goods to establish a base camp in an area already under government influence. While the patrol was in camp, they offered highly prized trade goods such as salt, steel tools, and cloth to visitors to establish contact with surrounding villagers. Then they would move out to the villages and ask permission to build a rest house to allow longer visits by the patrol. Although these requests were not always welcome, the villagers were generally convinced by native interpreters. Then more distant villagers would come for trade goods, and the officer would agree to give the goods, but only if the villagers would build a road for the office. When new villagers were visited, gifts would be distributed and perhaps a government-sponsored feast would be given. Peace agreements were drawn up, and native police were strategically placed, after which village chiefs were appointed to act as intermediaries between the village and the government. Then annual visits by patrols were made. The Australian government considered the efforts at pacification successful when labor recruiters seeking workers for coastal plantations were allowed to operate freely in a village. In areas where resistance was more determined and where villagers might desert their homes when patrols were in the area, the patrols might kidnap old people left behind in the village until communications were established with resisters.

This process of peaceful penetration began in the 1920s and has continued uninterrupted, except during World War II, to the present. In 1950, for example, 168,350 square kilometers were not yet fully controlled. By 1970, only 1,735 square kilometers remained uncontrolled (Bodley 1990:66).

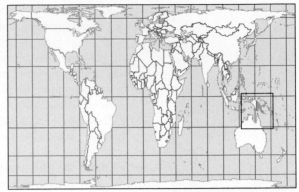

LAND POLICIES The policies of nation-states toward land ownership are some of the more delicate issues in the process of incorporating indigenous peoples or the resources they control into the nation-state. International law, and most governments, generally recognizes that aboriginal inhabitants possess rights to the lands they use. For example, in 1787 the U.S. government declared in the Ordinance for the Government of the Northwest Territory (Fey and McNickle 1970:56)

Papua New Guinea

> [t]he utmost good faith shall always be observed towards the Indians; their lands and property shall never be taken from them without their consent; and in their property rights and liberty, they never shall be invaded or disturbed, unless in just and lawful wars authorized by congress.

However, that policy was honored only as long as the Native Americans had a viable political presence and only as long as there was land that Euro-Americans did not want. Most early treaties recognized Native Americans' rights to land and designated large areas in the West as Native American. However, as European migration increased and as Native American land became desired, the government pressed to renegotiate old treaties, generally finding someone to negotiate with who would sign such treaties. However, even treaties could not protect Native American land from the U.S. Congress, as we saw in Chapter 3; in 1887 Congress passed the Native American Allotment Act (Dawes Act), which led to the appropriation of almost 100 million acres of Native American land (Jaimes 1992:126).

CULTURAL MODIFICATION POLICIES After destroying the autonomy of indigenous peoples and gaining control of their lands and resources, the next step for the nation-state was to modify the culture. Any native custom considered immoral, offensive, or threatening was abolished. Indigenous kinship systems and social organization were particularly threatening to colonists. At various times, such things as the payment of bride price, infant betrothal, polygamy, levirate (a man marrying his brother's widow), secret societies, and traditional kinship duties and obligations in general were attacked or banned. Even into the 1960s, the extended family was particularly criticized by economic development agents as a "drag on economic development and a serious obstacle to economic progress" (Bodley 1990:96).

Unfortunately, in retrospect, anthropologists played an important role, unwittingly or not, in the efforts to modify indigenous cultures and incorporate them into the nation-state. Even Margaret Mead (1961:19–20), one of the great spokespersons for tolerance and understanding of indigenous peoples, was convinced that tribal peoples she worked with wanted to "modernize": "We do not conceive of people being forcibly changed by other human beings. We conceive of them as seeing a light and following it freely," she said.

Development theorists (Goulet 1971:25–26) suggested that "traditional people must be shocked into the realization that they are living in abnormal, inhuman conditions as psychological preparation for modernization."

Ward Goodenough (1963:219), one of the most respected figures in anthropology, noted in his book *Cooperation in Change* that

> the problem that faces development agents…is to find ways of stimulating in others a desire for change in such a way that the desire is theirs independent of further prompting from outside. Restated, the problem is one of creating in another a sufficient dissatisfaction with his present condition of self so that he wants to change it. This calls for some kind of experience that leads him to reappraise his self-image and reevaluate his self-esteem.

EDUCATION FOR PROGRESS   One of the most effective ways indigenous cultures have been modified, as we noted in Chapter 4, is through formal education. As the French, British, German, and American governments used it to integrate those within their borders, so they used it to integrate colonial peoples. As John Bodley (1990:103) said,

> In many countries schooling has been the prime coercive instrument of cultural modification and has proved to be a highly effective means of destroying self-esteem, fostering new needs, creating dissatisfactions, and generally disrupting traditional cultures.

Formal education often conflicted with indigenous teachings and served to undermine them. The schools established by the French in its African colonies taught two subjects, the French language and "morale," meaning ideals of "good habits" such as order, politeness, respect, and obedience. In Italian East Africa, boys were taught to farm and make crafts, whereas girls were taught to cook native foods. Textbooks (see Bodley 1990:104) contained such passages as

> I am happy to be subject to the Italian government and I love Italy with the affection of a son.

or

> Help me, oh God, to become a good Italian.

Indigenous students, carefully dressed in required Western-style clothing, attend class at the Carlisle Indian School. In this class, photographed in 1900, they are debating the resolution "the Negroes of the South should not be denied the right of citizenship." The American government did not grant full citizenship to indigenous people until 1924. (Library of Congress, Prints & Photographs Division, [LC-USZ62-47083].)

Often the first efforts at education were controlled by missionaries. It was a useful partnership for both the church and the nation-state. The missionaries educated indigenous children in the ways of the nation-state while converting them to whatever religious faith they represented. Thus, French Jesuit missionaries opened schools along the St. Lawrence River in 1611 with a government edict to "educate the Indians in the French manner" (Noriega 1992:371).

In the United States, missionaries and church groups played a major role in indigenous education and were paid by the government to develop educational programs. One of the earliest models for missionary schools was the Methodist Episcopal Society, established in 1839 in Leavenworth, Kansas. The school was modeled on a rigid, military-style regimen. Native American students worked a 400-acre farm to raise money to pay for their educations; because there were no labor costs, the school succeeded and became a model for hundreds more missionary-run manual labor schools. Soon separate schools were opened for girls. These schools remained missionary-controlled until the end of the nineteenth century.

By the end of the 1860s, attendance at these schools was mandatory on many Native American reservations. However, it soon became apparent to government observers that day schools on the reservations left students too close to their family and culture. Consequently, the government initiated a program of Indian boarding schools to isolate Native American students from the "contaminating" influences of their own society. In its final form, the boarding school drew heavily from the penal procedures used to break the wills of indigenous resistance leaders and owed much to the efforts of Richard H. Pratt. Pratt was an army captain who believed he could turn Native Americans into whites; he convinced the government to allow him to run an educational program at the prison at St. Augustine, Florida, where captured Cheyenne leaders were held. He founded his first Indian boarding school in Carlisle, Pennsylvania; the school combined the manual labor model perfected by the missionaries with the penal model Pratt perfected in St. Augustine. Carlisle then served as the model for a national network of Indian boarding schools.

Native American children in boarding schools were isolated, given short haircuts, dressed in military-style uniforms, forced to maintain silence during meals, and forbidden to speak in their own language. Family visits were restricted, and children were not allowed to return home, even during vacations. It was not unusual for a child who began at the school at the age of six not to see his or her home or family until the age of seventeen or eighteen. The boarding school program created individuals who, stripped of their own culture and language, did not fit into their culture of origin but were also not accepted by the larger society.

People resisted. The Hopi, for example, hid their children from roving Mormon missionaries who wanted to gather the children and send them to the Intermountain School in Utah. Eventually the local Indian agent called in troops who assisted in the roundup, but not until they were bombarded with rocks from the tops of the mesas and forced to retreat temporarily. Although the boarding schools were gradually phased out, of the 52,000 Native American children over whom the Bureau of Indian Affairs had control, 35,000 were in boarding schools as late as 1973. As Jorge Noriega (1992:381) noted,

> [t]he whole procedure conforms to one of the criteria—the forced transfer of children from a targeted racial, ethnic, national or religious group to be reared and absorbed by a physically dominating group—specified as a Crime Against Humanity under the United Nations 1948 Convention on Punishment and Prevention of the Crime of Genocide.

ECONOMIC DEVELOPMENT The next step in the destruction of indigenous cultures was integrating them into the national economy. This was sometimes achieved through violence, as in slavery and forced labor, and was sometimes far more subtle, coming under the rubric of "economic development." As Bodley (1990:114) pointed out, *development* is a highly ethnocentric term denoting growth, inevitability, and progress; *transformation* is a far more appropriate term in this context.

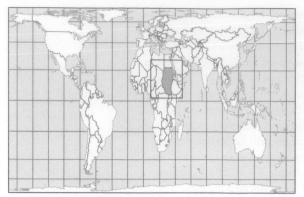

Sudan

Initially, the most common way of incorporating indigenous people into the capitalist economy was through forced labor. Settlers and colonial governments found that many people didn't want or need to work for wages—their consumption needs were modest, and they met their basic needs by growing their own crops or sharing products among kin or other groups. In French West Africa, conscript labor forces were required to spend three years working on highways, railroads, and irrigation projects. In some forced labor situations, the death rate ranged up to 60 percent per year (Bodley 1990:116). Forced labor, common throughout colonized areas, was not internationally outlawed until 1957.

Another technique for forcing indigenous peoples into the capitalist economy was through taxation; forcing people to pay taxes (head taxes, poll taxes, etc.) in cash forced them to labor on white plantations, work in mines, or raise cash crops to pay the taxes. These measures were staunchly defended as necessary to "civilize the savages." U.S. legal authority Alpheus Snow (Bodley 1990:118) wrote in 1921 that "natives simply lack the acquisitive drive characteristic of civilized man, and doing virtually anything that will correct this mental deficiency is permissible and even a moral duty of the state."

Economic change was also fostered through technological development. A good example is the Zande Development Scheme. The Azande were a large population of hunters and shifting cultivators living in scattered homesteads in the southwest corner of Sudan. The British assumed administrative control in 1905 and proceeded to outlaw features of Azande culture that they found threatening, such as shield making, warrior societies, and even iron smelting. In 1911 the entire population was relocated along roads built by conscripted Azande labor and prevented from locating their farm plots in favored places in the forests or along streams. A head tax was introduced in the 1920s to force people to seek wage labor, and importation of British trade goods was encouraged. But the isolation of the area, the self-sufficiency of the population, and the lack of any resource in demand in the rest of the world inhibited the economic integration of the Azande into nation-state. Then in the 1930s, the government decided on an "economic development" program to introduce cotton as a cash crop. The agricultural development expert appointed to study the feasibility of the project called for a conversion of the Azande into

> [h]appy, prosperous, literate communities … participating in the benefits of civilization through the cultivation of cotton and the establishment of factories to produce exportable products on the spot. (Bodley 1990:123)

In 1944 the government justified the project, saying, "We have a moral obligation to redeem its [the southern Sudan's] inhabitants from ignorance, superstition, poverty, malnutrition, etc." (Bodley 1990:123). By 1946, the project was under way with the building of a small complex that included facilities for spinning, weaving, and soap making and employing some 1,500 Azande workers under European supervision. Every man in the district was required to work at least one month per year at $0.85 to $1.30 per month. Furthermore, to facilitate development, 50,000 Azande families, some 170,000 people, were removed from their roadside homes, where they had been forcibly resettled thirty years earlier, and relocated into geometrically arranged settlements and on to arbitrarily selected sites, without consideration of individual desires to be near kin.

The key to the project was the cotton growing, but the Azande had no desire to plant cotton; frustrated officials said the Azande had no "realization of what money could do for them." One solution was to force anyone who refused to grow cotton to do a month's labor on the roads as punishment. Yet, as remarkable as it seems, said Bodley (1990:124–125), the planners really did seem to have been driven by the best of intentions, "to bring progress, prosperity, and the reasonable decencies and amenities of human existence to the Azande." According to one district commissioner, "The object throughout has been to interfere as little as possible with the people's own way of life." In 1965, twenty years after the project began, one Sudanese journalist

> [r]eported enthusiastically that the standard of living in Zandeland was higher: consumption of sugar had doubled in just nine years; there were no naked people left; Azande women were dressed in the fashionable northern Sudanese style; and everyone had bicycles and lived in clean houses equipped with beds and mattresses.... [B]est of all, there were now swarms of children everywhere! (Bodley 1990:125)

By the 1980s, the decline of the cotton market and a civil war in Sudan had left the Azande economy in virtual ruin.

These kinds of projects, of course, are common today. Governments in the periphery turn to areas occupied by the few remaining indigenous cultures in order to raise cash to pay off the debts they accumulated in the 1970s and 1980s. The results, as we shall see, continue to be devastating.

THE GUARANÍ: THE ECONOMICS OF ETHNOCIDE

It is difficult for any member of the culture of capitalism to take an unbiased view of indigenous peoples—that is, not to view such groups as backward, undeveloped, economically depressed, and in need of civilizing. This, of course, is the way indigenous peoples have been portrayed for centuries. Theodore Roosevelt (Maybury-Lewis 1997:4), famous for his campaign to conserve nature, said, "The settler and pioneer have at bottom had justice on their side; this great continent could not have been kept as nothing but a game preserve for squalid savages."

In the nineteenth century, "scientific" theories of evolution and racial superiority allowed people to rationalize the enslavement, confinement, or destruction of indigenous peoples. As late as the 1940s, British anthropologist Lord Fitzroy Raglan (Bodley 1990:11), who was to become president of the Royal Anthropological Institute, said that tribal beliefs in magic were a chief cause of folly and unhappiness. Existing tribes were plague spots: "We should bring to them our justice, our education, and our science. Few will deny that these are better than anything which savages have got." Although many of these attitudes have changed, indigenous peoples still tend to be seen as needy dependents or victims, largely incapable of helping themselves. We tend to see their destruction as a consequence of their weakness, rather than as patterns of behavior and exploitation built into the culture of capitalism.

It may help to change that view if instead of seeing indigenous peoples as needy dependents living largely outmoded ways of life, we consider the resemblance between indigenous societies and a modern, socially responsible corporation that carefully manages its resources, provides well for its workers, and plans for the long term rather than the short term. Looking at indigenous

A Guaraní Indian family ride a horse-drawn cart in Japora County in southern Brazil, on one of the ranches the Guaraní "repossessed," claiming it as ancestral land, January 26, 2004. (Andrew Hay/Reuters/Corbis.)

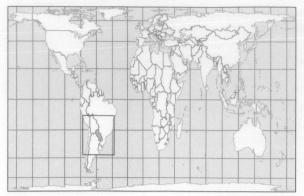

Paraguay

societies in this way may help us better appreciate why they don't survive. The fact is that environmentally and socially responsible corporations do not fare well in the capitalist world; they fail not because of any inherent weakness but because they become targets for takeovers by individuals or groups who, after taking the corporation over, quickly sell off the carefully managed resources solely to make a quick profit, leaving the corporation in ruin and its workers unemployed.

Take the fate of the Pacific Lumber Company. The family-owned company was known as one of the most environmentally and economically sound companies in the United States. It pioneered the practice of sustainable logging on its large holdings of redwoods and was generous to its employees, even overfunding its pension plan to ensure that it could meet its commitments. Furthermore, to ensure the security of its employees, it had a no-layoff policy. Unfortunately, the very features that made the company a model of environmental and social responsibility also made it a prime target for corporate raiders. After Maxxam, Inc., took control of the company in the late 1980s, they doubled the cutting rate on company lands, drained $55 million of the $93 million pension plan, and invested the remaining $38 million in a life insurance company that ultimately failed (Korten 1995:210). It filed for bankruptcy in 2007.

The fate of Pacific Lumber is not unique. Indigenous peoples possess all the characteristics that make them prime targets for takeovers. Like responsible corporations, they have managed their resources so well that those same resources (e.g., lumber, animals, and farmlands) become targets for those who have used up theirs or who wish to make a quick profit. The indigenous peoples become expendable for resources to be exploited. To illustrate, let's look at the case of the Guaraní as described by Richard Reed (1997).

History and Background

Most of the 15,000 Guaraní are settled in the rain forests of eastern Paraguay; they live in 114 communities ranging from three to four houses to more than 100 families. They are a minority population in a country in which most citizens are *mestizo,* or *criollos,* descendants of Europeans who married Guaraní.

When Europeans arrived, more than 1 million Guaraní and related groups lived in the area stretching from the Andes to the Atlantic Ocean. The Guaraní welcomed the first conquistadors, joining them in carving out trade routes to the Andes. The earliest reports of travelers indicate that the Guaraní system of production and standard of living were successful. In 1541 the region's first governor, Cabeza de Vaca (Reed 1997:8), noted that the Guaraní

> [a]re the richest people of all the land and province both for agriculture and stock raising. They rear plenty of fowl and geese and other birds, and have an abundance of game, such as boar, deer, and dantes (anta), partridge, quail and pheasants; and they have great fisheries in the river. They grow plenty of maize, potatoes, cassava, peanuts and many other fruits; and from the trees they collect a great deal of honey.

In addition to their economic success, the Guaraní were a relatively egalitarian society in which a person's place in society was determined by kinship. Leadership was usually determined by age, although political leaders had little or no power of coercion over others.

The Guaraní engaged European markets soon after contact, managing to combine their traditional subsistence activities of swidden agriculture and hunting and gathering with the collection of commercial products from the forests, such as yerba mate, a naturally growing tea;

animal skins; and honey. Anthropologists call this combination of productive activities *agrofor-estry,* the active management of forest resources for long-term production.

To understand *agroforestry* as practiced by the Guaraní, we need to understand a little about the nature of tropical rain forests. They are the most diverse *biosystems* on Earth, containing half the recorded species in the world, although only about 15 percent of these species have even been discovered. They are also among the most fragile ecosystems. A rain forest is a layered system, the top layer, or canopy, provided by large trees protecting the layers underneath it, with each species of plant or animal in lower layers dependent on the others, and all surviving on a very thin layer of soil. Guaraní agroforestry focuses on three activities: horticulture, hunting and gathering, and commercial tree cropping. The agriculture is called *shifting* or *swidden* agriculture, in which small areas of the forests are cut and burned, the ash providing a thin layer of nutrients for the soil. These areas are planted until spreading weeds and decreased yields force the farmer to move to a new plot. The old plot is not abandoned but planted with banana trees and manioc, crops that need little care and that produce for up to four years. In this way, land is gradually recycled back into tropical forest. Furthermore, these plots provide forage for deer, peccary, and other animals, which the Guaraní trap or shoot.

Fishing provides another source of protein—usually the Guaraní fish with poison. They crush the bark of the timbo tree and wash it through the water, leaving a thin seal on top of the water. They wait for the water to be depleted of oxygen, and the stunned fish float to the surface. The Guaraní also fish with hook and lines. Other food sources are honey, fruit, the hearts of palm trees, and roots gathered from the forest floor.

Finally, to earn cash, the Guaraní collect yerba mate leaves, animal skins, oils, and food. In these activities, the Guaraní use the forest extensively but not intensively. For example, they will cut leaves from all yerba trees but take only the mature leaves from each tree every three years, thus promoting the plants' survival. In addition, because the Guaraní harvest from a number of ecological niches and because their consumption needs are modest, they never overexploit a commodity to earn cash.

The Guaraní, therefore, use the forest to supplement their other subsistence activities, integrating this resource into their production system. It is a production system that is modeled after that of the rain forest itself; by incorporating trees, the system preserves or re-creates the forest canopy necessary for the survival of plants and animals below it. Crops grow in the shade of the trees. The surviving diversity of crops and animals ensures the recycling of nutrients necessary for their maintenance. In fact, as Richard Reed (1997:15) noted, "agroforestry often increases ecological diversity."

Agroforestry differs markedly from the typical exploitive forest activities in the culture of capitalism, such as intensive agriculture, lumbering, and cattle raising, activities modeled after factory production. First, indigenous production systems are diverse, allowing forest residents to exploit various niches in the forest without overexploiting any one niche. Second, unlike intensive agriculture, lumbering, or cattle raising, the Guaraní production system depends on the resources of plants and animals themselves rather than on the nutrients of the forest soils. Thus, by moderate use of the soils, water, canopy, and fauna of the forest, the Guaraní ensure that the whole system continues to flourish.

Third, Guaraní production techniques lend themselves to a pattern of social relations in which individual autonomy is respected and in which activities do not lend themselves to a division of labor that leads to status hierarchy. The basic work unit is the family, with both men and women involved in productive labor (farming, gathering food, and collecting commercial products) and reproductive labor (child care, food preparation, and the construction and maintenance of shelters).

Fourth, unlike the activities of the culture of capitalism, the Guaraní mode of production is neither technologically oriented nor labor intensive. The Guaraní spend about 18 percent of their time in productive activities; one-third of that is devoted to horticulture, slightly less to forest subsistence activities, and about 40 percent to commercial activities. Another 27 percent of their time is devoted to household labor. In all, about half their daylight time is spent working; the rest is devoted to leisure and socializing. Reed said that the Guaraní workday is approximately half that of a typical European worker.

Finally, unlike capitalist production, which is tightly integrated into the global system, Guaraní production allows them a great deal of autonomy from the larger society. When prices for their products are too low, the Guaraní stop selling; if prices on store goods are too high, the Guaraní stop buying. Thus, they do not have to rely on commercial markets; their stability is in their gardens, not their labor.

This autonomy can be attributed in part to the Guaraní's modest consumption needs. Food accounts for about 40 percent of the average family's monthly market basket—about two kilograms of rice, pasta, and flour; one kilogram of meat; a half liter of cooking oil; and a little salt. Cloth and clothing is the next most important purchase, perhaps a new shirt or pants (but not both) each year. Another one-fifth of the budget is spent on tools, such as machetes and axes, and an occasional luxury, such as tobacco, alcohol, or a tape recorder. Thus, as Reed (1997:75) noted, the Guaraní engage the global economic system without becoming dependent on it.

Contemporary Development and Guaraní Communities

Guaraní culture and their system of adaptation are, however, being threatened. Since the 1970s, the rate of forest destruction in Paraguay has increased dramatically as forests are cleared to make way for monocultural agriculture and cattle ranching. As a result, Guaraní house lots stand exposed on open landscapes, and families are being forced to settle on the fringes of mestizo towns. Reed made the point that it is not market contact or interethnic relations that are destroying the Guaraní; they have participated in the market and interacted with mestizo townspeople for centuries. Rather, it is a new kind of economic development spawned by the needs of the global economy.

After decades of little economic growth, in the 1970s the Paraguayan economy began to grow at the rate of 10 percent per year. This growth was fueled by enormous expansion of agricultural production, particularly cotton, soy, and wheat. Most of this growth came at the expense of huge tracts of rain forest felled to make way for the new cultivation. As Reed said, since 1970 every effort has been made to convert the land of eastern Paraguay into fields for commodity production. A number of things contributed to rain forest destruction.

First, roads built into the forests for military defense against Brazil contributed to the influx of settlers into the rain forest. Second, large-scale, energy-intensive agriculture displaced small farmers, who flooded to the cities in search of work. This created pressures on these populations to find work or land, but rather than redistribute the vast tracts of cleared land held by wealthy cattle ranchers to peasants, the government chose to entice poor peasants into the forests with land distribution programs. Between 1963 and 1973, 42,000 families had been given land; between 1973 and 1976, 48,000 families were given a total of 4 million hectares of land.

A third factor was international finance. The oil boom of the 1970s, along with changes in currency, allowed core institutions to go on a lending spree as people sought ways to reinvest their profits. Like most other peripheral countries, Paraguay borrowed heavily in the 1970s to build roads, hydroelectric projects, and other things they believed necessary to build an industrial economy. The money that came into the country from the World Bank and other financial institutions needed to be reinvested by Paraguayan financiers, and some invested in farms and cattle ranches in the forests. Finally, to repay the loans, the country needed to raise funds, which it did by expanding agricultural growth in export crops, putting further demands on the rain forest.

The process of environmental destruction soon followed. For example, the Guaraní group Reed worked with (the Itanaramí) suffered their first major incursion in 1972, when the government cut a road into their forest. It was built partly to control the border with Brazil, but it also allowed logging in what had been impenetrable forests. Loggers brought in bulldozers to cut roads directly to the hardwood trees. Lumber mills were positioned along the roads, and the cut lumber was trucked to the capital city, where it was shipped to the United States, Argentina, and Japan. As Reed (1997:85) said, the forests that had provided the Guaraní with shelter and subsistence were cut down so that consumers in the United States, Europe, and Japan could enjoy furniture and parquet floors.

The roads also brought into the Guaraní forest impoverished Paraguayan families in search of land that they illegally cut to create fields in the forests, fields that will bear crops only for a short time before losing their fragile fertility. To complicate matters, Brazilian peasants, many displaced by large-scale agricultural projects in their own country, crossed the border seeking land on which to survive. The area even became home to a Mennonite community seeking to escape the pressures and problems of the larger world.

On the heels of these colonists came agribusiness concerns clearing more forest on which to raise soy and cotton. Within months of their arrival, thousands of hectares of forest were cut down and replaced by fields of cash crops. The road that had brought in the military, loggers, and peasant colonists was now used to haul out produce for foreign markets and for cattle drives to deliver meat to consumers across South and North America.

Thus, in the same way that corporate raiders seize responsible corporations to turn a quick profit, often destroying them in the process, people seeking a profit from the lands of the Guaraní quickly destroyed the forest. The logging companies cut the trees that provided the canopy for the forests as well as the trunks on which vines such as orchids and philodendron climbed. Without the protective cover of the large trees, the enormous diversity of life that thrived beneath the canopy was no longer viable. Faunal populations declined immediately because their habitat was being destroyed and because they were being hunted to extinction by the new settlers. With the flora and fauna decimated, all that remained was a fragile layer of topsoil, which the harsh sunlight and rains quickly reduced to its clay base.

The rate of forest destruction was enormous. From 1970 to 1976, Paraguayan forests were reduced from 6.8 million to 4.2 million hectares. Half of the remaining forest was cut by 1984, and each year thereafter another 150,000 to 200,000 hectares has fallen to axes and bulldozers. At this rate, the Paraguayan forests will be gone by the year 2025.

More to the point for this discussion, with the rain forest went the way of life of the Guaraní. When Reed first began working with the Itanaramí in 1981, they were isolated in the forest, living largely as they had for centuries. By 1995, they were on a small island of forest in an "ocean of agricultural fields."

The Guaraní had no legal title to the land they have inhabited for centuries, such title being claimed by the nation-state; those who bought the land from the government assume they have both a legal and moral right to remove any people occupying the land. Even when Guaraní were allowed to retain their house plots, their traditional system of agroforestry was impossible because their forest was being destroyed and they were forced to seek new and smaller plots. Furthermore, the settlers destroyed their hunting stock, so the Guaraní quickly came to depend for meat on the occasional steer slaughtered by ranchers in the towns, for which the Guaraní had to pay cash. But the ranchers destroyed the stands of yerba mate, a source of cash for the Guaraní, that they had cultivated for centuries.

Gradually, with their traditional production system destroyed, the Guaraní were forced to enter the market economy as cotton or tobacco growers or as wage laborers on the lands they had sustained for centuries. Those who entered the agricultural sector found that the new system of farming was capital intensive and required inputs of fertilizers, herbicides, and insecticides. Families went into debt becoming dependent on mestizo merchants and lenders. Those who chose to work found that wages were often too low to support a family, forcing several or all family members to work. Furthermore, labor required people to travel outside their communities so that even those families who managed to gain access to land on which to garden had little time for it. Because wage labor demands the strongest workers, it is often the youngest and strongest who must leave their communities.

There are other effects. Illness and disease became more prevalent. Suicide, virtually unknown previously in Guaraní communities, increased from a total of six in 1989 to three suicides per month in the first half of 1995. The leadership system collapsed, as religious leaders who earned their authority through their ability to mediate disputes found themselves helpless to mediate the new problems that arose between Guaraní and mestizo or government bureaucrats. Today the government appoints community leaders to make it easier for them to control and negotiate with Guaraní communities. These new leaders derive their power from assistance programs that funnel resources to the Guaraní, but which many leaders use to reward friends and relatives and punish nonkin and enemies.

In sum, the debt assumed by the Paraguayan government to foster economic expansion and the resulting expansion of capital-intensive farming and cattle ranching in the 1980s disrupted Guaraní society more than had four centuries of contact; as a result, its members are dispersing and assimilating into the larger society. It would be easy to condemn the Paraguayan government and other governments whose indigenous peoples are being destroyed. Yet the nation-states are only doing what capital controllers are supposed to do: They are choosing modes of production and ways of life that will bring the greatest immediate monetary return.

DISADVANTAGED MAJORITIES AND THEIR REVENGE

Although indigenous minorities are often endangered by the expansion of the culture of capitalism, it is common also for market expansion to disadvantage indigenous majorities, sometimes with deadly impact.

In the past two to three decades, the software industry has produced the largest group of billionaires and multibillionaires in American history. Just imagine, suggests Yale law professor Amy Chua (2003:19), that all of these billionaires and multibillionaires were ethnic Chinese. Imagine that ethnic Chinese, while being only 2 percent of the U.S. population, controlled most of the largest corporations in America—Time Warner, General Electric, Chase Manhattan, Exxon, Mobil, United Airlines, and Microsoft—along with most banks, plus Rockefeller Center and two-thirds of the best real estate in the country. Then consider that the two-thirds of the country who thought of themselves as "white" were dirt poor, owned no land, and, as a group, had experienced no upward mobility as far back as anyone could remember. If you can imagine this, says Chua,

> you will have approximated the core social dynamic that characterizes much of the non-Western world … [where] free markets have led to the rapid accumulation of massive, often shocking wealth by members of an "outsider" or "non-indigenous" ethnic minority. (2003:19)

In her book *World on Fire* (2003), Amy Chua examines situations where the disadvantaged comprises the majority of the population, whereas a small minority controls most of the wealth. When there is a market-dominant minority, Chua suggests, capitalism and democracy are a volatile combination.

Markets, says Chua, often concentrate spectacular wealth in the hands of market-dominant minorities, whereas, at the same time, democracy increases the power of the impoverished majority. This is the situation of minorities, she says, in countries all over the world: the Chinese in Southeast Asia, whites in South Africa, Lebanese in West Africa, Ibo in Nigeria, Indians in East Africa, Croats in the former Yugoslavia, and Jews in postcommunist Russia. In situations such as this, opportunistic, vote-seeking politicians pit the frustrated "indigenous" majority against the wealthy and resented minority. The resulting violence may take the form of a backlash against the market by targeting the wealth of the minority, it may take the form of a backlash against democracy by forces favorable to the market-dominant minority, or it may take the form of genocidal violence directed against the market-dominant minority itself (Chua 2003:10). Thus, since 1989,

Chua (2003:123) says, the world has seen the proliferation of ethnic conflict, the rise of militant Islam, the intensification of group hatred and nationalism, expulsions, massacres, confiscations, calls for renationalization, and two genocides of magnitudes unprecedented since the Nazi Holocaust.

Chua begins her book by relating the story of her aunt who lived in the Philippines. She was murdered, her throat slit by her chauffeur. Chua was shocked, as were other members of the family, by the brutality of the crime; her aunt was single, fifty-eight years old, and four-feet-eleven-inches tall; her attacker was six foot two. There was little doubt who did it and why; the police report detailed the confessions of the maids who knew and assisted with the murder, and jewelry and other valuables were found missing. At the funeral, Chua asked one of her uncles how the criminal investigation was going, and her uncle replied that the killer had not been found; his wife added that the police had essentially closed the case. Later Chua saw the police report; under the entry "motive for murder," instead of "robbery," there was only one word—"revenge."

Chua's aunt was relatively wealthy, part of the market-dominant ethnic Chinese minority. In the Philippines, millions of Filipinos work for Chinese; virtually no Chinese work for Filipinos. Global markets intensify the Chinese dominance of industry and commerce. If investors want to do business in the Philippines, they deal almost exclusively with Chinese. Although there are a few aristocratic families of Spanish descent, all Philippine billionaires are of Chinese descent. But Filipinos do all the menial jobs, and all peasants are Filipino as are all domestic servants and urban squatters. In Manila there is a twelve-block-wide mountain of fermenting refuse known as the "Promised Land." Surrounding the dump are makeshift shantytowns housing some 100,000 people who eke out livings by scavenging through rotting food and dead animal carcasses. In July of 2000, accumulated methane gas exploded, collapsing the mountain of garbage and killing more than 100 people. When Chua asked her uncle about it, he responded with annoyance, "Why does everyone want to talk about that? It's the worst thing for investment" (Chua 2003:4).

All over Southeast Asia, ethnic Chinese comprise a market-dominant minority. In Burma, some 69 percent of indigenous Burmans cannot compete economically with the 5 percent Chinese minority. In Vietnam in the 1950s, the 1 percent Chinese minority controlled 90 percent of the non-European private economy. In Indonesia—with the help of the IMF and World Bank, and a corrupt indigenous leadership led by the Suharto family that accumulated a personal fortune estimated to be $16 billion—the Chinese, making up 3 percent of the population, owned 70 percent of the private economy. Although most of the Chinese are hard-working members of the middle class with no political connections, the resentments of the indigenous majority erupted in 1998, and rioters looted, burned, and raped their way through the Chinese neighborhood. "It was like Christmas," one woman said after hearing her neighbors trade stories about the various appliances they had carried out from burning Chinese stores. "Less festive were the hundreds of charred corpses lying in the rubble that had been commercial Jakarta" (Chua 2003:153). One result of the riot was that some $40 billion to $100 billion of mostly Chinese-controlled capital fled the country. But most Chinese could not leave what was for most the only home they ever knew. Instead, women purchased stainless steel "anti-rape corsets" developed by a Chinese entrepreneur.

In Russia in the 1990s, a forced privatization plan imposed by the IMF resulted in a situation where only a handful of people managed to monopolize the country's wealth. The wealthiest comprised a group of seven oligarchs, all but one of whom was Jewish. Yet of the some 147 million people in Russia, Jews make up only 1 percent of the population. One result of this concentration of wealth has been growing anti-Semitism, making victims of the thousands of poor or middle-class Jews. Thus, a financial collapse in 1998 in Russia saw a spate of synagogue bombings, the beating of two rabbis, neo-Nazi marches on Moscow, and desecration of Jewish synagogues. In 2002, a new political party was formed calling for a better deal for ethnic Russians and blaming Jews for stealing the country's wealth (Chua 2003:94).

Leveling Crowds

Chua, of course, is not the first to connect poverty with violence or to suggest that capitalism and democracy can be an explosive mixture. Eric Hobsbawm (1964) showed how the best predictor of the occurrence of riots in revolutionary France was the price of food. In the *Federalist Papers,* founders of the U.S. republic, including Alexander Hamilton, James Madison, and John Jay, questioned whether republics are doomed to failure because the "principle of liberty" that allows the free expression of hostility becomes impossible to check. Madison seems to take it as a feature of human nature when he said that

> so strong is this propensity of mankind to fall into mutual animosities … the most common and durable source of factions has been the various and unequal distribution of property. (Beard 1959:13)

Stanley J. Tambiah (1996) examined instances of riots and ethnic violence in South Asia. These riots, in which a dominant ethnic group attacks an ethnic minority—Sinhalese attacking Tamils in Sri Lanka, Hindus rioting against Sikhs in India, and Sindhis attacking Muhajirs in Pakistan—follow the similar pattern outlined by Amy Chua: A majority group, feeling either disenfranchised or oppressed, attacks minority members who have achieved economic success. In 1983 in Colombo, the capital of Sri Lanka, crowds attacked Tamil residences and businesses. Existing tensions, which exploded into a Tamil insurgency and civil war that ended only in 2008, were high after Tamil insurgents killed thirteen soldiers. During the funeral, crowds broke away and began attacking Tamils, burning Tamil businesses, factories, and banks. Tambiah notes that much of the ensuing violence was purposive; rioters came equipped with weapons such as metal rods and knives and carried gasoline. They carried voter lists and the addresses of Tamil property owners supplied by government officials, and the rioters arrived in Tamil areas on government-owned trucks and buses (Tambiah 1996:96). Tambiah notes that the riots may have been encouraged by what he calls "riot captains," such as Sinhalese businesspeople and shop owners who sought to eradicate Tamil competitors, or smugglers, crime figures, or politicians who used the riots to eliminate rivals. The official death toll was 400, but Tambiah says it was closer to 2,000 or 3,000. It was the worst case of communal violence in Sri Lanka's history, and some 150,000 Tamils fled the country as a result.

In 1984, after the assassination of Indian prime minister Indira Gandhi by her Sikh bodyguard, Hindus rioted against Sikhs in Delhi. The riots lasted for days and seemed to increase each day in an orgy of arson, rape, and murder. Trains were stopped before getting into Delhi so that Sikhs could be attacked. Hundreds were burned either semiconscious or dead. From 2,500 to 4,000 people were killed, and crowds destroyed Sikh houses, stores, and religious and educational institutions. Like the Tamils in Sri Lanka, Sikhs were perceived as economically advantaged. And like the riots in Colombo, prominent members of society directed the action. Members of the leading political party and local leaders actually identified Sikh houses, shops, businesses, religious sites, and schools for the mob to attack (Tambiah 1996:113).

Tambiah notes that the rioters in every case he examined represented a crosssection of society—teachers, store owners, government workers, and so on. Although the riots began as a result of some inflammatory incident, they were soon organized and purposive in their action—not simply the action of a disorganized mob. They were sometimes flamed by the media and led by politicians or prominent members of the society. And almost always they involved an ethnic group that perceived itself as economically disadvantaged relative to the group being attacked. He concludes that

> certain kinds of rioting crowds in pursuit of collective entitlements are essentially "levelers," destroying property and life in a public cause that absolves them of individual crime and guilt. The leveling down of an ethnic group as an over-privileged enemy, an acquisitive other, an obstacle to one's own group's prosperity, is

an orgiastic, short-lived action. If the ethnic group that is victimized still has in its possession the specialized knowledge, the material and symbolic capital, the networks that provide access to resources, it can usually pretty quickly recoup and regain its former position thus inviting another act of leveling and conspicuous, methodical destruction of its property. (Tambiah1996:279)

The riots and violence contained, says Tambiah, an element of performance, routinized and ritualized acts that gain public acceptance and that confer on the actors a degree of prestige and legitimacy. There is, he says, a sense of "popular culture" in the violence as it entails public expression of collective values and motivations (Tambiah 1996:223).

Conflict in this sense, he continues, does not represent episodic violence but becomes an everyday and permanent state of affairs; the violence of state security officers on the one hand and armed rebels or opponents on the other becomes what Tambiah (1996:223) calls "a patterned mode of conducting politics by other means."

Genocide as an Externality of the Market

Tambiah emphasizes that economic dislocation of one sort or another always preceded the riots. In Sri Lanka, for example, it was the Sinhalese who suffered most when the ruling party, under pressure from the IMF and World Bank, changed a state-regulated, welfare, and protectionist policy to a capitalist, market-oriented, and free trade policy. This suggests that ethnic violence is not, as Chua suggests, solely an incompatibility between democracy and the market but is also a problem of a group's reaction to sudden economic deprivation brought about by radical market reforms.

There is tyranny in the market, particularly in its neoliberal version. To the extent that all goods and necessities are available only through the market, each person's life must be directed to the acquisition of money. In other words, when large-scale sharing or redistributive mechanisms for obtaining goods are removed, life is possible only through the acquisition of money. Those who refuse to pursue money, or those who, for whatever reason, are excluded from access to it, end up, at best, in abject poverty with no access to life's necessities. Market capitalism in its present form leaves little room for any alternative.

Relations between ethnic groups in countries experiencing interethnic violence in the past two decades were often peaceful prior to some economic upheaval in which peoples' access to money, or the worth of money itself, was removed. One of the most prominent examples is Yugoslavia, the site of one of the worst incidents of genocidal slaughter in the past two decades. It is a case that dramatically reveals how we mask unpleasant externalities of the market.

"ETHNIC CLEANSING" IN YUGOSLAVIA Yugoslavia was formed after World War I by combining six republics—Serbia, Croatia, Bosnia-Herzegovina, Montenegro, Slovenia, and Macedonia. The country evolved a socialist economy modeled, to some degree, after that of the Soviet Union. But in 1991, after the breakup of the Soviet Union, Yugoslavia as a nation-state began to dissolve. Slovenia, the wealthiest of the republics, was the first to secede. Croatia declared its independence at the same time, but because it had a large Serbian minority and a lucrative coastline, the Yugoslav National Army refused to let it go, and a seven-month war followed leaving 10,000 dead. That put Bosnia-Herzegovina, which was 43 percent Muslim, 35 percent orthodox Serb, and 18 percent Roman Catholic, in a bind. If Bosnia-Herzegovina remained in the republic, Serbs, the largest group in a unified Yugoslavia, would get the desirable jobs, and Muslims and Croats would be marginalized. Consequently, with instructions from Western diplomats, Bosnia-Herzegovina held a referendum for independence, and 99.4 percent of the Bosnian-Herzegovinians voted to secede; however, Serbs, who wanted to secede and make Bosnia part of a "Greater Serbia," boycotted the election. In response, the Yugoslav army teamed with local Bosnian Serb forces to create a new Bosnian Serb army of

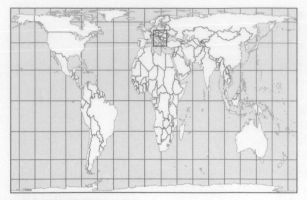

Bosnia-Herzegovina
and Croatia

some 80,000 soldiers. Bosnian Muslims and Croats could not respond militarily because the United Nations imposed an arms embargo on the entire country. Thus, the stage was set for a genocide.

With their military superiority, Bosnian Serbs began to round up Muslim and Croat intellectuals, musicians, and professionals and beat and execute them. The Serbs also used their military superiority to prohibit non-Serbs from holding jobs, meeting in cafeterias, hunting or fishing, gathering in groups of more than three people, selling real estate, or exchanging homes. Sometimes Muslims and Croats were told that they had only twenty-four hours to pack their bags. But that was only the beginning. Serb gunmen knew that their violent deportation and killing campaign of Bosnian Muslims and other non-Serbs would not be enough to ensure the lasting achievement of ethnic purity and so began the campaign of "ethnic cleansing." They forced fathers to castrate their sons or molest their daughters, initiated a campaign to rape and impregnate young women (Power 2002:231), and engaged in mass killings. The result of the "ethnic cleansing" campaign by Bosnian Serbs was that some 200,000 mostly Bosnian Muslims were killed and 2 million people displaced, and a multi-ethnic European republic was divided into three ethnically pure statelets.

Although the violence continued in Yugoslavia until 1997, the conflict in Bosnia-Herzegovina ended in 1995 when the Croatian army overpowered the Serbs and peace accords were signed at a meeting called in Dayton, Ohio, by U.S. president Bill Clinton.

In many ways the genocidal violence in Yugoslavia fits the pattern outlined by Amy Chua when an ethnic majority attacks a market-dominant minority. Yugoslavia was characterized by significant economic differences between Slovenia and Croatia in the north (per capita income of $6,737 in 1997) and Serbia, Bosnia-Herzegovina, Macedonia, and Montenegro in the south (per capita income of $1,403 in 1997). The Serbs, although poorer, represented a majority of the population. In addition, the war and the killings were instigated by democratically elected demagogues—Franjo Tudjman in Croatia and Slobodan Milosevic in Serbia—who campaigned on platforms of Croatian and Serbian nationalism. Thus, Chua concludes, opportunistic politicians were able to seize on economic inequalities to gain power. What is missing from Chua's account of the ethnic violence in Yugoslavia, however, and what was missing from virtually all of the media accounts, was the prior economic devastation of Yugoslavia wrought by global financial institutions.

Almost universally, political leaders offered explanations of the genocide that distanced it from its economic roots. Former U.S. ambassador to Yugoslavia Robert Zimmermann said that the plight of the Balkans is the outcome of an "aggressive nationalism." Others attributed the violence to a clash of political personalities—"Tudjman and Milosevic are tearing Bosnia-Herzegovina to pieces." Others spoke of "ancient hatreds." What almost no one mentioned was the devastating impact on the people of the neoliberal reforms imposed on the country by international financial institutions. The social and political impact of economic restructuring in Yugoslavia, writes economist Michel Chossudovsky (1996),

> has been carefully erased from our social consciousness and collective understanding of "what actually happened." Cultural, ethnic and religious divisions are highlighted, presented dogmatically as the sole cause of the crisis when in reality they are the consequence of a much deeper process of economic and political fracturing.

Neoliberal reforms—privatization, monetary revaluation, bank reform, and so on—were initiated in Yugoslavia in 1980. The result was a reduction in economic growth to 2.8 percent during the years 1980–1987, and to –10.6 percent by 1990. By 1989, 248 firms were steered into bankruptcy and some 89,400 workers laid off. New IMF and World Bank reforms and structural adjustment were adopted in 1990 by which time the GDP was –7.5 percent, declining another 15 percent in 1991. After these reforms were adopted, another 889 enterprises with a workforce of 525,000 workers (out of a total workforce of 2.7 million) were forced into bankruptcy. The largest concentration of layoffs was in Serbia and Bosnia-Herzegovina, Macedonia, and Kosovo. Of the remaining 7,531 enterprises, the World Bank classified another 2,435 employing some 1.3 million workers as "loss making," adding those workers to the 600,000 already laid off. The shedding of surplus workers continued right through the civil war (Chossudovsky 1996).

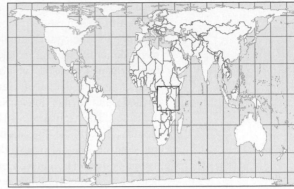

Rwanda

In retrospect, says Chossudovsky, it is worth recalling that prior to the beginning of economic reforms, and since the end of World War II and up until 1980, the growth of the GDP in Yugoslavia averaged 6.1 percent a year, there was free medical care with one doctor per 550 people, the literacy rate was 91 percent, and life expectancy was seventy-two years.

In sum, gross economic inequalities among ethnic groups are, indeed, the source of collective violence. But the evidence suggests that ethnic differences and economic inequalities, in themselves, are not enough to ferment violence. After all, Christian and Muslim Serbs had lived peacefully together for centuries, as had other ethnic groups who later found themselves battling each other. The problem emerges when economic differences that may exist between groups are exaggerated out of proportion by the expansion of neoliberal policies. Significant in this regard is the most notorious genocide of the 1990s, the slaughter of some 800,000 Tutsis in Rwanda.

GENOCIDE IN RWANDA Perhaps there is no better case than Rwanda of state killing in which colonial history and global economic integration combined to produce genocide. It is also a case where the causes of the killing were carefully obscured by Western governmental and journalistic sources, and blamed instead on the victims and "ancient tribal hatreds."

A country the size of Belgium, with a population of 7 million people (overpopulated according to most reports, but Belgium supports more than 10 million people), Rwanda experienced in 1994 one of the worst genocides of the twentieth century. Some 800,000 people, mostly but not exclusively Tutsis, were slaughtered by the Hutu-run state. Contrary to media and many government reports, the genocide was the result of Rwanda's political and economic position in the capitalist world system. It involved such global factors as its colonial history, the price of coffee, World Bank and International Monetary Fund policies, the global interests of Western nations (particularly France), the interests of international aid agencies, and Western attitudes toward Africa (Shalom 1996).

Archaeological evidence suggests that the area that is now Rwanda was first inhabited by Twa-speaking hunters and gatherers who dominated the area until around A.D. 1000. Hutu speakers then began to settle in the area, setting up farms and a clan-based system of monarchies that dominated the Twa. Around the sixteenth century, new immigrants from the Horn of Africa, the cattle-raising Tutsi, arrived and set up their own monarchy in Rwanda, establishing a system in which the Hutu were tied economically as "clients" to Tutsi "patrons." In reality, it was rarely possible based on physical characteristics to tell who was Hutu and who was Tutsi. *Tutsi* became a term applied to lineages that controlled wealth in the form of cattle, whereas Hutu were those without wealth and who were not tied to powerful people. The political system was not unlike that which existed in many other parts of Africa and which still exists today in some countries. The Hutu maintained their own chiefs, intermarriage was not uncommon, and many Hutu could attain power and influence virtually equal to that of Tutsi chiefs. In fact, a poor Tutsi could slide into becoming a Hutu, and a wealthy Hutu lineage could become Tutsi (Maybury-Lewis 1997:101). When the Germans assumed control of the area after the Berlin Conference of 1884, they applied their racist ideology and assumed that the generally taller, lighter-skinned Tutsis were the more "natural" rulers, whereas the Hutus were destined to serve them. Consequently, the Germans increased Tutsi influence.

After the defeat of Germany in World War I, Belgium took over colonial control of Rwanda and further intensified the split between Tutsi and Hutu by institutionalizing racist doctrines. They replaced all Hutu chiefs with Tutsis and issued identity cards that noted ethnic identity, making the division between Hutu and Tutsi far more rigid than it had been before colonial control. They also gave the Tutsi elite the responsibility to collect taxes and administer the justice system. The Tutsi chiefs used this new power granted them by Belgian rule to gain Hutu land. However, excluding the wealth and status of Tutsi chiefs, the average financial situation of Hutus and Tutsis was about the same.

Both groups were subject to the harsh colonial rule of Belgium in which forced labor was common, taxes were increased, and the beating of peasants by Belgian colonists became standard practice. Furthermore, the colonial rulers transformed the economy, requiring peasants to shift their activities from subsistence or food crops to export crops, such as coffee. Coffee production had the effect of extending the amount of arable land because it required volcanic soil that was not productive for other, particularly food, crops. As we shall see, this had far-reaching consequences and would contribute to the conditions that precipitated the genocide.

In the 1950s, the Tutsis began to campaign for independence from their colonial rulers. Because Belgians believed the Hutu would be easier to control, they shifted their support to them and began to replace Tutsi chiefs with Hutu. In 1959, when clashes between Hutu and Tutsi broke out, the Belgians allowed Hutus to burn down Tutsi houses. Belgium then allowed the Hutu elite to engineer a coup, and independence was granted to Rwanda on July 1, 1962. It is unclear how many Tutsis were killed in the actions preceding independence, but estimates vary from 10,000 to 100,000. In addition, 120,000 to 500,000 Tutsis fled the country to neighboring countries such as Burundi and Zaire, from which Tutsi guerrillas engineered raids into Rwanda. Within Rwanda, the Hutu rulers established ethnic quotas limiting Tutsi access to education and government employment.

In 1973 a military coup d'état brought to power Juvenal Habyarimana, who promised to establish "national unity." To this end he installed one-party political rule of the National Revolutionary Movement for Development (MRND) and made Rwanda a one-party state. Although the government or party was clearly totalitarian in nature, foreign powers appreciated the fact that Habyarimana "ran a tight ship," even requiring all Rwandans to participate in collective labor on Saturday. In fact, Habyarimana achieved many needed reforms: The civil service was modernized, clean water was made available to virtually everyone, per capita income rose, and money flowed in from Western donors. However, some projects, often imposed by multilateral organizations, were fiascoes and probably contributed to Hutu–Tutsi enmity. For example, in 1974 the World Bank financed a project to establish cattle ranches over an area of 51,000 hectares. The bank hired a Belgian anthropologist, René Lemarchand, to appraise the project; he warned that the Hutu were using the project to establish a system of patronage and spoils that served to reduce the size of Tutsi herds and grazing areas and to increase Tutsi economic and political dependence on the Hutu. He also said the project was aggravating Hutu–Tutsi conflicts, but Lemarchand's warnings were ignored (Rich 1994:93).

Soon, whatever progress Rwanda was making to climb out of the pit of its colonial past was undermined by the collapse of the value of its export commodities—tin and, more importantly, coffee. Until 1989, when coffee prices collapsed, coffee was, after oil, the second most traded commodity in the world. In 1989, negotiations over the extension of the International Coffee Agreement, a multinational attempt to regulate the price paid to coffee producers, collapsed when the United States, under pressure from large trading companies, withdrew, preferring to let market forces determine coffee prices. This resulted in coffee producers glutting the market with coffee and forcing coffee prices to their lowest level since the 1930s. Although this did little to affect coffee buyers and sellers in wealthy countries, it was devastating to the producing countries, such as Rwanda, and to the small-farm owners who produced the coffee.

If you are a coffee consumer, especially one who likes the new, premium, fresh-roasted varieties, you will pay between eight and ten dollars per pound. Of that, fifty to seventy cents represents the world market price, of which thirty to fifty cents goes to the farmer who produced the coffee. The remainder goes to mid-level buyers, exporters, importers, and the processing plants that sell and market the coffee. For Rwanda, the consequences of the collapse of coffee prices meant a 50 percent drop in export earnings between 1989 and 1991. Furthermore, because the soil in which coffee was grown is useless for most other crops (except coca, the source of cocaine), farmers could not shift production to other crops.

The sudden drop in income for small-farm owners resulted in widespread famine because farmers no longer had income with which to purchase food. The consequence for the Rwandan state elite was just as devastating; the money required to maintain the position of the rulers had come from coffee, tin, and foreign aid. With the first two gone, foreign aid became even more critical, so the Rwandan elite needed more than ever to maintain state power in order to maintain access to that aid.

Maintaining access to aid, however, particularly from multilateral organizations, required agreeing to financial reforms imposed by those organizations. In September 1990, the IMF imposed a structural adjustment program on Rwanda that devalued the Rwandan franc and further impoverished the already devastated Rwandan farmers and workers. The prices of fuel and consumer necessities were increased, and the austerity program imposed by the IMF led to a collapse in the education and health system. Severe child "malnutrition" increased dramatically, and malaria cases increased 21 percent largely because of the unavailability of antimalarial drugs in the health centers. In 1992, the IMF imposed another devaluation, further raising the prices of essentials to Rwandans. Peasants uprooted 300,000 coffee trees in an attempt to grow food crops, partly to raise money, but the market for local food crops was undermined by cheap food imports and food aid from the wealthy countries.

While the economy was collapsing, the Rwandan Patriotic Front (RPF), a group of Tutsi refugees from Uganda, invaded the country to overthrow the Habyarimana regime. Thus, the state was confronted with crises from two directions: economic collapse precipitated by the fall in coffee prices and military attacks from Tutsis who had been forced out of the country by ethnic rivalries fueled by colonial rulers. Fortunately, the Habyarimana regime was able to parley the invasion by the RPF into more foreign aid. The French, anxious to maintain their influence in Africa, began providing weapons and support to the Rwandan government, and the army grew from 5,000 to 40,000 from October 1990 to mid-1992. A French military officer took command of a counterinsurgency operation. Habyarimana used the RPF's actions to arrest 10,000 political opponents and permitted the massacre of some 350 Tutsis in the countryside.

In spite of increased state oppression and the French-supported buildup of the armed forces, in January, 50,000 Rwandans marched in a pro-democracy demonstration in Kigali, the country's capital. Hutu extremists in Habyarimana's government argued to crush the opposition on a massive scale, but instead Habyarimana introduced democratic reform and allowed the political opposition to assume government posts, including that of prime minister. However, he also authorized the establishment of death squads within the military—the *Interahamwe* ("those who attack together") and the *Impuzamugambi* ("those with a single purpose")—who were trained, armed, and indoctrinated in racial hatred toward Tutsis. These were the groups that would control most of the killing that was to follow.

By this time, the coming crisis was becoming evident; human rights groups were warning about the existence of the death squads, and members of Habyarimana's inner circle set up a new radio station—a potent source of power in a country that is 60 percent illiterate—using it to denounce attempts to forge a peace agreement between the government and the RPF and inciting racial hatred. Acts of violence against Tutsis increased after the president of neighboring Burundi was killed in an attempted coup by Tutsi army officers. Hutus were incited to kill Tutsis, and the RPF responded by killing Hutus: Some 50,000 peasants were reportedly killed, slightly more Tutsis than Hutus. As Habyarimana continued to negotiate with the opposition under international pressure to reach a settlement, his plane (a gift from President Mitterrand of France) was shot down, killing him and everyone on board. Within an hour of Habyarimana's death, roadblocks were put up throughout Kigali as militia and death squads proceeded to kill moderate Hutus, including the prime minister, whose names were on prepared lists. Then the death squads went after every Tutsi they could find, inciting virtually everyone in the civil service to join in the killing. The Hutu extremists set up an interim government committed to genocide. Yet, even when it was clear to most people that the genocide was orchestrated by an authoritarian state, journalists as well as UN secretary general Boutros Boutros-Ghali would characterize the slaughter as "Hutus killing Tutsis and Tutsis killing Hutus." Building on Western stereotypes of savage Africans, Mayor Ed Koch of New York City characterized the genocide as "tribal warfare involving those without the veneer of Western civilization."

As long as the killing could be characterized as inter-ethnic violence, the core states, whose actions had created the situation for the killings and whose economic policies precipitated the violence, could distance themselves from the conflict. U.S. and European leaders, in fact, went to great lengths *not* to use the word *genocide,* for to call it genocide may have required military intervention as agreed on in the United Nations Genocide Convention of 1948. It wasn't until months later, after some 800,000 Tutsis had been killed, that government leaders in the West began to acknowledge the genocide.

The slaughter did not end until the RPF finally defeated the government's armies and took control of the country. But the dying didn't stop. The fleeing Hutu elite used radio broadcasts to incite fear in the Hutu populace that to remain in the country meant certain retaliation from Tutsi survivors and the victorious RPF. Consequently, millions of Hutus fled the country, gathering in refugee camps in neighboring countries and becoming a country in exile for the Hutu extremists who fled with them, using their control over the fleeing army to maintain control of the Hutus in refugee camps. The press and media coverage of the refugees also served as a fund-raising bonanza for foreign aid organizations, although some 80,000 Hutus died in cholera epidemics in the camps. It was not until 1996 that Hutu refugees began to return to Rwanda and to the government of reconciliation established by the RPF.

Skeletal remains are strewn on the grounds of the Catholic mission on May 5, 1994, in Rukara, Rwanda. Hundreds of Tutsis were killed at the mission in one of the worst massacres of the Rwandan violence. (Scott Peterson/Getty Images News/Getty Images.)

In sum, the Rwandan disaster was hardly a simple matter of tribal warfare or ancient hatreds. It was the case of an ex-colonial, core-supported state threatened with core-initiated economic collapse and internal and external dissension resorting to genocide to remove the opposition that included, in this case, both Tutsis and moderate Hutus.

CONCLUSION

At the beginning of the chapter, we observed that one of the casualties of the expansion of the culture of capitalism is cultural diversity. There are a number of reasons indigenous peoples fared poorly with the expansion of capitalism. These included profound cultural incompatibilities between indigenous peoples and the culture of capitalism and the need of the nation-state to ensure political authority and control over economic resources desired by corporations or the nation-state itself. We also observed that the very features that make indigenous peoples excellent custodians of the environment make them susceptible, as are responsible corporations, to takeover and destruction. According to John Bodley (1990:138–139), a careful examination of the conditions of indigenous peoples before and after their incorporation into the world market economy

> [l]eads to the conclusion that their standard of living is lowered, not raised, by economic progress—and often to a dramatic decline. This is perhaps the most outstanding and inescapable fact to emerge from the years of research that anthropologists have devoted to the study of culture change and modernization.

Furthermore, we concluded that conflict between groups within nation-states, often characterized as ethnic violence, has more to do with the economic consequences of the expansion of consumer capitalism and the actions of the nation-state. The protagonists in these conflicts are not as much Sinhalese and Tamils, Hutu and Tutsi, Serbs and Croats, as they are those who have ready access to the market and those who don't. As multilateral institutions change the rules of the market to accommodate the need for capital accumulation, lives are disrupted and conditions created that fuel hatred and violence. In some cases, disadvantaged groups direct their resentment at those who may have little to do with their oppression. But in other cases, as we will see in Part III, the protest takes the form of one sort of rebellion or another.

PART THREE

Resistance and Rebellion: Introduction

People resist exploitation. They resist it as actively as they can, as passively as they must.

—IMMANUEL WALLERSTEIN, *Antisystemic Movements*

One of the consequences of the expansion of the culture of capitalism is the redefinition of space. Some people are free to move around the globe as never before; in the interests of "free trade," countries have dissolved spatial barriers; with modern travel and communication technology, there is no place in the world that can't be accessed almost instantaneously. Capital, of course, is particularly mobile, as billions of dollars speed around the globe daily, moving in and out of countries at will. But not everyone can move, and herein lies a number of problems. First, by dissolving spatial barriers and creating global citizens, the market removes ties and obligations to specific localities and communities. In his autobiography, Albert J. Dunlap (or "Chainsaw Al" as he was known in corporate circles) said, "The company belongs to people who invest in it—not to its employees, suppliers, nor the locality in which it is situated."

Dunlap made a name for himself as a CEO by drastically reducing the labor force of corporations he headed: As CEO of Scott Paper, he dismissed 11,200 people, or 20 percent of the workforce. At Sunbeam, he fired half of its 12,000 employees. These cost-cutting moves delighted investors as stock prices rose but devastated the lives and communities of laid-off employees. But by identifying investors as those to whom the corporate managers owed their allegiance, Dunlap acknowledged that capital was more important than people or communities and highlighted the disconnection of markets from local places and obligations—not only from employees, but also from the younger, the weaker, and the unborn generations—and the need to contribute to daily life and the continuity of the community. "Shedding the responsibility for the consequences," writes Zygmunt Bauman (1998:9), "is the most coveted and cherished gain which the new mobility brings to free-floating, locally unbound capital."

A second problem with the new "globalized space" is that it creates two kinds of citizens: those free to move about in this new space, and those who are unable to move—that is, while compressing space and allowing mobility for some, the market condemns others to remain local. Zygmunt Bauman (1998:92–93) calls these new categories of people "tourists" and "vagabonds." Tourists, he says, move "at their heart's desire."

Like capital, they can abandon a site when new opportunities or experiences beckon elsewhere. Vagabonds, such as labor migrants, on the other hand, know they can't stay in one place too long, regardless of how much they want to, knowing also that wherever they want to go, they will be unwelcome. Tourists move because they find the world "irresistibly attractive," while vagabonds are forced to move because they find the world within their reach unbearably inhospitable. The vagabond, while forced to move, is relegated to society's margins.

The material symbols of the division include the invisible barriers that separate rich from poor—tourist from vagabond—in urban centers all over the world. They exist in tourist areas where the rich arrive and leave at will, while those who work on the margins—the maids, servants, waiters, taxi drivers, and store clerks—or those unfortunate enough not to work at all are rooted in place. They exist in the annulment of entry visas for shoppers and the reinforcement of immigration controls and identity checks for everyone else.

For the inhabitants of the world of global businessmen, consumers, culture managers, or academics, state borders are dismantled as they are for the world's commodities, capital, and finances. But for the inhabitants of the other world, says Bauman (1998:89),

> the walls built of immigration controls, of residence laws and of "clean streets" and "zero tolerance" policies grow taller; the moats separating them from the sites of their desires and of dreamed-of redemption grow deeper, while all bridges, at the first attempt to cross them, prove to be drawbridges.

This division of the world between those who can participate as consumer/laborer/capitalist and those who cannot, between tourist and vagabond, creates a problem for everyone. The problem for the rich is what to do with all those superfluous people. There are various solutions. One is to imprison them. In the United States, 2 percent of the population is under the control of the penal law system. In 1979 there were 230 prisoners per 100,000 people; in 1997 there were 649 per 100,000; and by 2008 there were 2.2 million, or 1 for every 100 adults. In some areas, such as the Anacostia area where most of Washington's poorest residents live, half the male residents age sixteen to thirty-five are currently awaiting trial, in prison, or on probation. And in all wealthy countries, the prison population is growing. The remaining poor the rich try to keep at a distance with gated communities or stricter immigration laws; discipline with identity checks; or imprison, as it were in faraway ghettos and shantytowns, allowing them out only when needed to labor in one or another of the assembly plants constructed by capital, which is free to move where it can enjoy the greatest return.

For the vagabonds, the choices are yet more stark. With the spread of a culture in which a person's only option is to be a consumer/laborer/capitalist, no space remains to be anything else. The expansion of markets systematically destroyed numerous indigenous ways of living by convincing their members that they were "backward," or more frequently, simply leaving them no choice. We seem to be doing the same with other "civilizations." After the 2003 invasion of Iraq by the United States, a U.S. sergeant in Iraq, the cradle of civilization itself, remarked that "we're not trying to offload Texas here. . . . We want them to do it their way." Asked, then, what his mission was, he thought for a moment and added, "We're just trying to get them to evolve, to open their eyes. That's the mission" (Cohen 2003).

Finally, there is a third problem that emerges with the new notion of space: the invasion by those free to move into the territory of those rooted in place. The invaders may be real people as when, in "gentrification," developers evict the poor to build expensive housing for the wealthy; or the invasion may be of capital only, as corporate-run factory farms take over land occupied by peasant farmers. Regardless, another characteristic of a globalized world is an increase in "contested space," areas claimed, either literally or symbolically, by different individuals or groups.

The freedom of capital from local obligations, the divide between tourists and vagabonds, and the increase in contested space increase the potential for conflict and increase the resistance of those abandoned by capital, rooted in place, and whose space has been appropriated. Peasants, for example, who lost their land try to resist their dependence on sporadic wage labor; others resist colonial domination and the margins into which they were pushed by colonizers; laborers resist exploitation; while others resist the destruction of their environment or seek to defend a threatened culture through religion or religious violence. As Philippe Bourgois (1995) suggests in his study of drug use on the Upper East Side of New York City, and as Paul Willis (1981) documents in his study of English working-class kids, crime and drug use can be seen as a form of symbolic resistance to the marginalization and displacement of the poor.

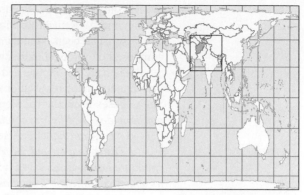

Most protest is local—that is, it is directed at a specific group for a specific purpose. Peasants revolt against their landlords, workers against their employers, and environmentalists against specific government policies or corporate practices. A problem, however, is that while the protest is local, the roots of the conflicts are global, and there are no global mechanisms for resolving these disputes. There is no universally recognized world court and no legal entity called "the market." One consequence is the increasing appeal to violence to settle disputes, often in the form of "terrorism." The use of violence to resolve disputes is hardly a new phenomenon as centuries of warfare attest. But even most wars were fought between legal entities called *states,* and there could be agreements regarding what was permissible and what was not. Perhaps this is why civil wars were so bloody; there was no recognized limit on the violence and destruction that one side could inflict on the other. And, of course, there is no Geneva Convention of terrorism.

Afghanistan

The labeling of violent protest as "terrorism" creates some problems itself. Ever since the attacks on the World Trade Center and the Pentagon on September 11, 2001, government and media are quick to label virtually any form of violent resistance "terrorism." By doing so, however, they obscure significant differences between acts of political violence and hide the economic and global roots of the problems. Therefore, before we examine different forms of protest, it will be useful to first examine what exactly "terrorism" means, and how, as a label for violent protest, it represents another use of language that obscures more than it reveals.

A PRIMER ON TERRORISM

On March 21, 1983, U.S. president Ronald Reagan issued a proclamation declaring that date Afghanistan Day. "The tragedy of Afghanistan," Reagan said, "continues as the valiant and courageous Afghan freedom fighters persevere in standing up against the brutal power of the Soviet invasion and occupation." Among the "freedom fighters" supported by the United States was Abdullah Azzam, cofounder of the *Makab al Khidmatlil Mujahidin al Arab* (MAK), which ultimately housed, trained, and financed the anti-Soviet Afghan Jihad in 1984. Azzam was also the founder of *al Qaeda al-Sulbah* (the Solid Base) and the mentor of Osama bin Laden (see Coll 2004; Cooley 2002; Gunaratna 2003).

The United States supplied money and weapons to the *mujahideen,* as the Muslim fighters were called, through the Pakistani Secret Service. They were instrumental in driving the Soviet Union (which had invaded Afghanistan in 1979) from the country. The United States supplied the means for many of those same Muslim fighters to travel to Bosnia in 1992 to aid the Bosnian Muslims who were being victimized by Bosnian Serbs.

Mahmood Mamdani (2004) suggests, in fact, that contemporary terrorism in general is a consequence of policy decisions by the United States, as well as other core nations, to support "proxy wars" in which extra-state groups are supplied with financial support, weapons, and intelligence in order to undermine states viewed as hostile to Western interests. Thus, not only did the United States and other Western nations support the *mujahideen* in Afghanistan against the Russians, but they also supported the contras in Nicaragua against the socialist government of the country, Renamo in Mozambique, and Unita in Angola against Marxist–Leninist states. The result has been, Mamdani suggests, the creation of privatized, stateless resistance forces composed of uprooted individuals with few ties to countries or families.

The fact that groups and individuals, who would later be labeled "terrorist" and would be instrumental in the devastation of September 11, 2001, were supported and nurtured by the United States raises a number of significant questions. First and most relevant is, *What is terrorism, and how does it differ from other forms of collective violence? Is one person's terrorist another person's freedom fighter?* A second question is, *What has changed? How do the attacks on the World Trade Center and the Pentagon differ, if at all, from the thousands of other violent acts committed around the world by small groups against both state and civilian targets? Is al Qaeda, for example, different from those thousands of groups going back for centuries that used violence to try to attain political goals?* And, finally, *What does it mean to conduct a "war" on terrorism?*

The declaration of a war on terrorism by the United States, Britain, and their allies was largely a consequence of the attacks of September 11. Intentionally or not and whatever its rhetorical advantages, the term *war on terrorism* contains some major assumptions that significantly obscure the nature of contemporary political violence.

Edmund Burke first used the term *terror* in the late eighteenth century in reference to the French Revolution and to violence calculated to induce widespread fear and achieve political goals. It gained its current meaning after the bombing of the U.S. marine barracks in Beirut in 1983 and was associated in both U.S. and Israeli political discourse with anti-state forms of violence that were so criminal that any method of enforcement and retaliation was viewed as acceptable and above criticism (see Falk 2003). With the help of the media, notes Richard Falk (2003:xviii–xix), nation-states have won the battle of definitions, exempting their own violence against civilians from being labeled "terrorism" and being referred to instead as "use of force," "retaliation," "self-defense," and "security measures."

But, as we mentioned, calling virtually all non-state political violence "terrorism" obscures the roots and the nature of the violence.

Terrorist acts can be carried out both by nonstate groups and by states. The photo on the left shows damage to a civil guard barracks after a car bomb exploded in the northern Spanish city of Burgos on July 29, 2009. The bomb slightly injured around 50 people in an attack authorities blamed on the Basque separatist group ETA. In the photo at the right, a crowd gathers on a road in El Salvador next to the body of a National University student, lying face down with hands bound, allegedly killed by state-sponsored death squads. (Left: CESAR MANSO/AFP/Getty Images. Right: Hinterlang/Image Works/Image Works/Time Life Pictures/Getty Images.)

First, it is necessary to appreciate that what we have labeled as terrorism is a technique, not an ideology or a state policy (see Steele 2003). Violent protest goes back thousands of years and is unlikely to be stopped, particularly given the billions of people in the world who have been marginalized in the global economy. What the United States did in Afghanistan is often supported by nation-states as a tool of international diplomacy. The United States, for one, has supported non-state violence repeatedly over the past fifty years as part of its contest with the Soviet Union.

Second, as a technique, terrorism has its own strategy (see Merari 1993; Pape 2003). It is a form of asymmetrical warfare that characterizes situations where one side in the conflict has overwhelming military dominance over the other. Since the weaker side has no chance to militarily defeat the other, it seeks to use violence for political gains. In some ways, as a U.S. Army lieutenant colonel put it concerning insurgent attacks in Baghdad in 2003, "terrorism is Grand Theater" (Danner 2003). Recent targets—the World Trade Center, the Pentagon, and the Oklahoma Federal Building—are selected for their symbolic significance and are intended to reveal the vulnerabilities of the nation-state, demonstrate that the nation-state is incapable of protecting its citizens, draw attention to the grievances of the attackers, and claim for the attackers the legitimacy of the use of violence. If instead of bombing the Oklahoma Federal Building in 1995, Timothy McVeigh had machine-gunned the victims as they emerged from work, it would hardly have had the same effect (see Juergensmeyer 2000:123).

Third, there is no specific ideology common to the use of political violence. It has been used in the name of both right-wing and left-wing ideologies and associated with religious beliefs, ethnic grievances, environmental issues, animal rights, and issues such as abortion (see Merari 1993).

Fourth, most political violence is local, directed at specific nation-states or their agents, and is afforded a certain legitimacy by international and national laws. The Geneva Convention, for example, recognizes the rights of citizens to resist foreign occupation, and the right of citizens to bear arms and to violently resist a tyrannical state is embedded in the Second Amendment of the U.S. Constitution (Ahmad 2003).

The recent movie theater shootings in Aurora, Colorado, are an example of domestic terrorism.   (UPI/Gary C. Caskey/Newscom.)

However, political violence of the twenty-first century does seem to have changed. It has, in effect, been "globalized." Global terror networks such as al Qaeda seek to destroy the whole foundation of the emerging global compact. "Megaterrorism," as Richard Falk refers to it (2003:39), differs from earlier forms of political violence by its magnitude, scope, and ideology, seeking to transform the world order, not simply challenge the power of a single nation-state. Al Qaeda, for example, has its origins in the global conflict that existed between the United States and the Soviet Union. It claims as part of its goal the defeat of the United States and the unification of Muslims all over the world. It is global in its reach, its cellular structure resembling the structure of international drug cartels. With active members from virtually every part of the world, al Qaeda represents what John Gray (2003:76) calls "a global multinational." Al Qaeda's organization, as those of various so-called terrorist groups, is also intertwined with global crime, particularly the trade in illegal drugs and international credit card fraud from which it draws a significant portion of its income (see Gray 2003:91).

Nevertheless, there is a sense in which al Qaeda and other terrorist groups resemble traditional resistance movements. The target, generally, is a specific nation-state, particularly the United States. Since 1968, the United States has headed the list of countries whose property and citizens were most frequently the target of political violence. In the 1990s, 40 percent of all acts labeled as terrorism were against American citizens and facilities (see Juergensmeyer 2000:178–179).

Different reasons are given for hatred of America: support of what is seen as corrupt or secular governments, the spread of American culture, globalization, and the expanded power of corporations.

Amy Chua (2003:231) sees the attacks on the United States as an expression of "demagogue-fueled" mass resentment of a global, market-dominant minority. This expression, she says,

> varies enormously in intensity, ranging from benign grumbling by French bureau-crats about bad films and bad food to strategic alliances between Russia and China to terrorism. Like the ethnic cleansing of Tutsi in Rwanda, the suicidal mass murder of three thousand innocents on American soil was the ultimate expression of group hatred. The attack on America was an act of revenge directly analogous to the bloody confiscations of white land in Zimbabwe, or the anti-Chinese riots and looting in Indonesia—fueled by the same feelings of envy, grievance, inferiority, powerless-ness, and humiliation.

Al Qaeda also resembles the secret societies that go back hundreds of years and that emerge as a consequence of oppression and exploitation (Hobsbawm 1959). Peter Schneider and Jane Schneider (2002), for example, draw a parallel between the Mafia and al Qaeda. The Mafia arose in Italy in the nineteenth century as a consequence of market reforms—enclosure of com-mon lands and abolishment of feudal arrangements that forced thousands of peasants off their land, many of whom comprised the mass nineteenth-century migration to other countries such as the United States. Some of the displaced took to banditry, attacking and kidnapping landowners, while those same landowners employed others as a bulwark against bandits. The Mafia emerged out of these arrangements, gaining power as protectors of the rich and influential. The Mafia was generally tolerated by various Italian governments until the Fascists took over Italy in the 1930s, but they reemerged after World War II.

Similar to groups such as al Qaeda or the Nicaraguan contras, the Mafia was used by the nation-state, first in countering peasant protest—sometimes murdering peasant leaders with impunity—and then by the ruling Christian Democratic Party in their battle with the Communist Party of Italy, then the largest Communist party in Europe. The government allowed mafiosi to penetrate Italy's land reform administration and urban produce markets, and looked the other way as the Mafia began to control the world heroin trade in the 1970s. Through its support of the Christian Democrats (and threats to withhold Marshall Fund money if the Communists won), the United States indirectly supported these arrangements between the Italian ruling party and the Mafia.

But in the 1980s, a group of mafiosi from the Italian town of Corleone, dissatisfied with being left out of real estate, construction, and drug deals, launched an offensive in which they kidnapped wealthy persons and those allied with competing mafiosi groups. In the 1990s, they began attacking public figures. Through savage bombings, they killed two of the most important anti-mafiosi prosecutors in Italy and set off bombs at artistic monuments.

The Schneiders relate how the outbreak of violence led to a government crackdown. To attack the Mafia, the government traced the movement of funds and turned some 200 mafiosi (out of some 5,000) into "justice collaborators." They also challenged political figures or government employees who had collaborated with the Mafia (identifying them as "pieces of the state") and demanded their removal. The result was a significant weakening of Mafia control and its gradual destruction. However, the Schneiders note that conditions that supported Mafia activity—poverty and unemployment—threaten to revive it. Graffiti claiming "Viva la mafia" has reappeared in poor neighborhoods.

The Schneiders compare the emergence of the Mafia, its relationship to the state, and the measures taken to eliminate them with the emergence of al Qaeda and the "war on terrorism." In Italy, the action against the Mafia was referred to as a "struggle," rejecting the notion of war and emphasizing international intelligence gathering, police action, and prosecution in international tribunals.

By using the metaphor of war, the United States and its allies justify the use of instruments of war—armed aggression against states, torture and interrogation, assassinations, bombings, and so on—the kinds of actions more likely to elicit a violent response and to create the kind of "failed" states in which global terrorism thrives. In addition, with no government to admit defeat, no territory to occupy, there is no reliable way to have confidence that the threat giving rise to the war has ended and no way to validate the disappearance of the threat (Falk 2003:8).

In the next three chapters, we examine the various forms of protest and resistance against market externalities. Using the now-common rhetoric, many of these would be labeled "terrorism." However, by doing so, we would seriously misunderstand the conditions from which these protests arise, and, consequently, misjudge the steps necessary to address them.

Peasant Protest, Rebellion, and Resistance

> *The bourgeoisie cannot exist without constantly revolutionizing the instruments of production, and thereby the relations of production, and with them the whole relations of society.*
>
> —KARL MARX AND FREDERICK ENGELS,
> *Manifesto of the Communist Party*

> *The cruelties of property and privilege are always more ferocious than the revenges of poverty and oppression.*
>
> —C. L. R. JAMES, *The Black Jacobins*

On January 1, 1994, the Zapatista Army of Liberation (EZLN) announced its existence by briefly occupying highland towns in the state of Chiapas in Mexico. In its declaration of war against the government, the Zapatistas claimed to represent the indigenous people of Mexico. It is unlikely that the Zapatistas, a group of poorly armed peasant farmers, had any hope of fighting and winning a revolution against a Mexican military equipped with modern weapons supplied largely by the United States, but they did threaten a guerrilla war in one of the most inaccessible areas of the country.

In this chapter we focus on peasant protest. Small-scale agriculturists have been among the groups most affected by the expansion of capitalism. As agriculture becomes more mechanized and landholdings concentrated in the hands of a few, more peasants have been driven off the land and forced to seek wage labor on the larger farms or in urban areas. Many resist this change in their living conditions. The question is, *How are we to understand the actions of peasant farmers who wish to resist or take up arms against a heavily armed and obviously superior opponent? Can they hope to win?*

History, of course, is full of successful and unsuccessful peasant revolutions. Eric Wolf (1969) examined successful peasant-inspired revolutions in Mexico, Russia, China, Algeria, and Vietnam. China, Russia, and England were the scene of thousands of peasant uprisings from the twelfth century onward. Yet, in the vast majority of such rebellions, the rebels gain little. And we rarely see the more subtle forms of everyday resistance that serves to protect peasant interests and prevent excessive exploitation. For example, in many societies, peasants could protest simply by moving to a new landholding or abandoning farming.

Peasant societies have long been a major focus of anthropological study. It was societies of small-scale agriculturists that generally preceded the emergence of industrialization around the world, and peasant societies today are still being modified by globalization of the capitalist economy. Billions try to survive by growing their own food, and the balance of their lives is often precarious. We can get an idea of how peasant farms work by looking at a typical medieval German farm. A forty-acre farm in Northeast Germany in 1400 produced 10,200 pounds of grain crops. Of this, 3,400 pounds were set aside for seed, and 2,800 pounds went to feed working livestock. This is referred to as the *replacement fund,* the output needed to continue the cycle of agricultural production. Of the remaining 4,000 pounds, 2,700 pounds were paid to the lord who held domain over the land. This constituted the *fund of rent.* Thus, of the 10,200 pounds produced, only 1,300 pounds of grain remained to sustain the farmer's family. With an average-sized family, that amounted to only 1,600 calories per day (Wolf 1967:9). Consequently, the family needed to seek other food sources, perhaps a garden or livestock kept for food. In addition, some of what is produced often goes into what Eric Wolf called a *ceremonial fund,* produce that is shared, generally at ritual occasions, with others in the community. The ceremonial fund may be used to give dinners or feasts or to contribute to community-wide celebrations.

Although there is wide variation in the structure of peasant societies, the division of produce on medieval German farms into replacement funds, ceremonial funds, and funds of rent gives us a good idea of what is required of the farm's produce. It also demonstrates the centrality of land to peasant life; obviously, what is produced depends largely on the amount and quality of land available for production. For this reason, virtually all peasant protest focuses in some way on the struggle over land. How the protest is conducted, the form of protest, and whether it involves collective and/or violent action depend on a number of factors.

Let's examine three twentieth-century cases of peasant protest, all focusing on land and changes in the peasants' relationship to it. In a case of contemporary peasant protest in Malaysia, we examine nonviolent resistance and the ways poor peasants try to deal with the impact on their lives of the green revolution. We examine a case of violent rebellion in Kenya inspired largely by British colonial policies during the first half of the twentieth century. Finally, in a case of peasant protest in Chiapas, we can appreciate how the globalization of the world economy can affect the lives of peasant farmers and precipitate a revolution. In all three cases, the protest was clearly related to global factors: The protest of Malaysian peasants was a consequence of the spread of high-technology agriculture, the Mau Mau revolt in Kenya a result of British imperialist expansion of the late nineteenth century, and the protest in Chiapas a direct consequence of the globalization of the modern economy.

MALAYSIA AND THE WEAPONS OF THE WEAK

In his study of the plight of poor Malaysian peasants, James Scott (1985) made the point that we have for too long focused on violent forms of protest and have neglected to study everyday resistance to oppression or simply excessive demands. *How do the relatively powerless resist oppression of the relatively powerful?* Because open revolt and resistance can be foolhardy, people find more subtle ways of resistance. We can see this in our everyday behavior. Anthropologists who have studied the culture of grade school and college classrooms have noted the different ways in which students resist classroom discipline. For example, they may slump in the chairs designed to force their bodies into positions of upright compliance, refuse to participate, talk to other students, or read or sleep in class. These forms of resistance are in response to what they perceive as attempts at cultural domination (Alpert 1991).

Subtle and nonconfrontational forms of protest are common in situations where those with little power want to register their resistance to what is forced on them. In the context of peasant society, Scott (1985:29) referred to these kinds of actions as the "weapons of the weak."

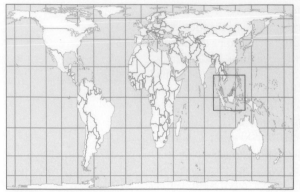

Malaysia

This resistance stops short of any kind of collective defiance; it is more likely to consist of such things as foot dragging, dissimulation, false compliance, pilfering, feigned ignorance, slander, arson, and sabotage. These actions, similar to those of the slouching, nonattentive student, require no planning or collective effort and avoid direct conflict with authority. But, said Scott, it is important to understand these weapons of the weak if we are to understand peasant resistance and begin to understand under what conditions these forms of resistance give way to outright rebellion.

Malaysian Peasants and the Green Revolution

Until the Asian economic collapse of 1997–1998, Malaysia of the 1990s was an excellent case of a country doing well economically. Its revenues from tropical hardwoods, oil, tin, rubber, and palm oil led to an annual economic growth rate of 3.9 percent from 1960 to 1976 and a per capita income twice as high as any other Southeast Asian country. But as in most Asian countries, the income is highly maldistributed, with agricultural incomes declining and many peasants finding their livelihoods threatened. Ironically, one of the reasons for the growing inequality of income involved agricultural changes wrought by the green revolution. In 1966, Malaysia, with the help of the World Bank, began the Mudra irrigation project on the Kedah Plain. It involved building two large dams that increased irrigation, permitting peasants to plant and harvest twice each year rather than once. Double-cropping of rice was extended to 260,000 acres. By 1974, the project was declared an unqualified success by the World Bank; it more than doubled production, reduced unemployment, and raised the rate of return on investments from 10 percent to 18 percent. There is little doubt that collectively the Malay peasantry is better off than before, and little doubt that if one wishes to be a rice farmer in Southeast Asia, the Kedah Plain is the place to be.

Scott said the changes in villages since the new prosperity are striking: There are new shops, roads, motorcycles, and mosques, and corrugated tin and plank siding has replaced attap roofs and siding. Peasants with the smallest plots can grow enough rice to feed their families. Infant mortality and malnutrition were cut by half. With securer incomes, fewer peasants lost their land and ownership stabilized. Thus, there was much good news following the green revolution in Malaysia.

But there is bad news as well, largely in the growing inequities in land access and income. The rich in the village (most still poor by greater Malaysia's standards) were getting richer and the poor poorer. *What does it mean to be poor and held in little regard by others in a peasant village?* One of the poorest villagers in Sedaka was Razak. His home was so decrepit that he avoided asking people inside. His children were poorly fed, and one died while Scott resided in the village. Others in the village avoided and ridiculed Razak, and Scott was regaled with the stories of Razak's unabashed begging, his fraudulent dealings (e.g., selling a pile of wood to two people), and his seeming lack of concern with village gossip about him.

The plight of poor villagers such as Razak was worsening because the green revolution was eroding traditional ties of dependence between rich and poor. In the past, landowning peasants could not farm all their land, so they rented it to land-poor tenants who worked the land for a rent. Although the rents may have been exploitative, they were negotiated after a harvest; after a bad harvest, the rents could be negotiated downward, and after a good harvest, rents would be higher.

In addition, traditionally the landowners needed the labor of the poorer farmers for plowing, transplanting the young rice plants, gathering the rice, and thrashing rice grains from the stalks. Although the wages were low, land-poor villagers could count on the income to supplement whatever they could grow themselves.

Finally, the land-rich and the land-poor farmers were bound together by gift giving and ceremonial exchange, with the rich expected to give gifts and charity to the poor. There were traditionally three forms of ritual giving in Sedaka: the Islamic *zakat,* alms that are given voluntarily; sharing of wealth by the rich with the poor, to cleanse the poor of envy, hatred, and resentment; and *derma* gifts and ritual feasts. Gift giving was a reciprocal arrangement: The recipient was obliged to return the gift at some later date. Because the poor were not expected to return charity, they repaid the rich with loyalty and an obligation to help with the labor of planting and harvesting.

In the past, then, the well-to-do villagers had justified their superior positions by claiming they benefited the poor; they rented land to them, paid them for their labor, and distributed gifts and gave feasts for the whole village. In effect, they legitimized their superior position by citing their services to the poor and claimed in return the poor's gratitude, respect, and deference. These traditional arrangements of dependency were disrupted by the agricultural changes that occurred in Sedaka, which operated virtually to make poor peasants superfluous.

First, the introduction of double-cropping and increased yield made the land more valuable. One effect of this was the change in the conditions of land rental and tenancy. Because land was more valuable, people from outside the community offered to rent it at higher prices than local land-poor peasants could pay. Moreover, because the land was more profitable, many richer peasants chose to farm it themselves rather than renting it, or they might give it to family members. To make matters worse, rent began to be paid in advance, not after the harvest, and there was no longer rent adjustment in the event of a poor harvest. As a result, the poor peasants of Sedaka found their access to land much reduced after the introduction of double-cropping.

Second, with the increase in the value of land, rich farmers were able to take advantage of new technologies, specifically mechanical harvesters and broadcast sowing. The harvesters, which could bring in the rice harvest quicker and with little or no increase in cost compared with human labor, greatly reduced the number of jobs available to poor farmers and their family members.

Third, in addition to the loss of land and labor, the poor found that traditional gift giving and charity of the richer members of the community declined. The motivation for gift giving was likely always the need of the rich to cement the obligations of the poor so the rich could call on them for labor when it was needed. With mechanical harvesters available to do most of the work, farmers were no longer dependent on local labor. Thus, in the course of a few years, the poor peasants of Sedaka saw their opportunities for land, jobs, and charity dramatically decreased. The social and economic ties that bound different levels of the community to each other began to unravel, and bonds of exploitation that tied the poor to the rich were freed; however, as Scott (1985:77) noted, "this is the freedom of the unemployed, the redundant."

The wealthier farmers, of course, were simply playing the economic game as it is played throughout the world. They took advantage of the increased value of land by raising rents, saving money and time with the use of mechanical harvesters, and redistributing less of their profit to others in the form of charity, gift giving, and ritual feasting. The problem is that their new behavior violated the old norms of the society, in which they were expected to rent land at prices people could afford; hire the poor to plant, harvest, and thresh the rice; and give charity, gifts, and feasts. These norms were once the basis of their authority. One of the accusations of the poor that rich must defend against is that they are failing to live up to their traditional obligations (Scott 1985:184).

In sum, advances in agricultural production wrought by the double-cropping of rice, made possible by the green revolution and the World Bank, increased the gap between rich and poor and, more importantly, weakened the social and economic ties between the various economic classes of the village. One solution available to poor peasants was flight; they could simply leave the village and migrate to another village or, more likely, to the urban centers to search for jobs. But for those unable to flee, there were few choices.

The question is, *What could the poor do to alleviate their condition? Was it possible to gain back what was lost?*

Fighting Back

The first question we might ask is, *What is resistance?* Scott (1985:290) defined it as

> any act(s) by member(s) of a subordinate class that is or are intended to either mitigate or deny claims (for example, rents, taxes, prestige) made on that class by superordinate classes (for example, landlords, large farmers, the state) or to advance its own claims (for example, work, land, charity, respect) vis-à-vis those superordinate classes.

Traditionally, peasants have found various ways to express their sense of being exploited or to resist directly what they see as excessive demands placed on them by landlords, the state, or others. As Scott (1985:300) pointed out, much of the folk culture of peasant societies legitimates resistance. Peasant folklore, for example, is full of stories of evasiveness and cunning, represented in Malaysia by the figure of *Sang Kancil,* a mouse deer figure—a small, weak being who survives and triumphs over more powerful figures using only wits and cunning. In the United States there is the figure of Br'er Rabbit. The myth and folklore of virtually every peasant society has a Robin Hood figure, a local hero who defends the peasant from the elite or represents the peasant who is willing and able to fight back. As Eric J. Hobsbawm (1959) pointed out, the bandit is almost always someone who is wrongly accused and convicted of a crime who then attempts to shield the peasants from their oppressors. In these ways, peasant culture underwrites and legitimizes resistance.

As James C. Scott (1985:301) indicated, however, the goals of peasant resistance are generally modest:

> The goal of most resistance is not necessarily to overthrow a system of oppression or domination, but, rather, to survive. The usual goal of peasants, as Hobsbawm has so aptly put it, is "working the system to their minimum disadvantage."

One of the ways the poor of Sedaka worked the system to their "minimum disadvantage" was through gossip, or character assault. But the gossip was of a particular sort, essentially an accusation against the rich that they were not living up to the rules of behavior the rich themselves had previously used to justify and legitimate their social position. It attempted to emphasize the apparent hypocrisy of the rich, much as American civil rights advocates of the 1950s and 1960s highlighted the ethical contradictions of racial segregation in a supposedly free society, or as Solidarity members in Poland of the 1970s used the existence of worker repression in a supposedly worker state.

Poor peasants in Sedaka used Islamic law and traditional relations between rich and poor to put pressure on the rich to live up to their obligations to those less fortunate. For example, Haj Broom was notorious as a miser who, some people say, acquired his land and wealth through shady business dealings. For the poor of Sedaka, his name was synonymous with greed and arrogance, and the low esteem in which he was privately (never publicly) held served as a warning to other wealthy farmers of behaviors to avoid. Put another way, gossip represented an appeal by the poor to previously held norms of tenancy, generosity, charity, employment, and feasts taken for granted before double-cropping (Scott 1985:282). Gossip chipped away at the reputations of wealthy farmers much as theft chipped away at their wealth. Gossip is also a relatively safe vehicle of protest because its author is generally unknown. The rich responded to these attacks by blaming the poor for their own plight, often using Razak as their example of the poor. Gossip, said Scott (1985:22–23), functions like propaganda and embodies whole stories. The mention of Razak's name by the rich conjured up visions of grasping and dishonest poor; the mention of Haj Broom by the poor incited visions of the "greedy, penny-pinching rich." The former represented to the rich where the poor were heading, as the latter represented to the poor the increasing violation of village standards by the rich.

In addition to gossip and an appeal to tradition, there were other ways the poor of Sedaka resisted their condition, such as theft. Although not as common as it once was, when rustlers stole water buffalo, theft was relatively common. Stolen items included water bottles left out to be filled by the government water truck, bicycles, motorcycles, fruit from trees, and, fairly commonly, sacks of rice left out in the fields. Most of the theft was believed to be done by the local poor, and the victims were almost without exception the wealthier members of the community.

There is some evidence that the poor viewed such theft, especially of rice, as a substitute for the charity that was less forthcoming than in the past. And although the losses were not great for wealthier farmers, the gain by the poor was, for them, substantial. The wealthy farmers reacted to theft with a combination of fear and anger, yet no rice theft has ever been reported to the local police. And people didn't report a theft from a neighbor even if they knew the identity of the thief, for fear of having their own rice stolen in retaliation. Another act of resistance was the killing of livestock of the rich by the poor, especially when the livestock posed a nuisance—for example, when they pecked open a rice sack and ate the rice.

Sabotage was a weapon of the poor used in Sedaka, specifically against the mechanical harvesters that were taking their jobs. Combine parts were smashed, sand and dirt were put in gas tanks, and trees were felled to block their progress. The owners of the combines, generally Chinese businessmen from urban areas, occasionally posted watchmen to guard the harvesters when they were left in the fields, but in one incident a watchman was forced to climb down while protesters set the harvester afire. Most of the protest in Sedaka was the acts of individuals, but there was some collective action, mostly by the women of the village. Women in Sedaka worked in crews that were hired by farmers to plant and transplant rice seedlings, something the combines could not do. Although the women would not openly tell a farmer that they would not be available to transplant if he used a combine to harvest, they could "let it be known," as they said, that they were upset at the loss of work. If they did "strike," they would simply tell the offending farmer they had other work that had to be completed before they could get to his fields. In this way, the women avoided any open confrontation that might result in their loss of jobs while putting pressure on farmers to abandon the mechanical combines. The farmers retaliated by threatening to bring in outside laborers to transplant (and some in fact did), and the threatened boycott collapsed. Farmers in other villages faced similar strikes that created a worker shortage, and women from Sedaka would go there to transplant fields. This "strike-breaking" behavior undermined the larger effort but made a point to the women's immediate bosses.

Thus, the people of Sedaka attempted to register their protest to the changes that affected their lives. *Were their protests effective?* To some extent they were. Some farmers hired people rather than use machines, even though they might have gotten their crops in quicker with the harvester; other farmers continued to lease their land to the poor when they could probably have gotten more money by renting it to outsiders or by farming it themselves. And some farmers still gave ritual feasts, thus honoring the traditional norms of the village rather than seeking to maximize their monetary gains.

Obstacles to Resistance

Although their income was declining in the face of agricultural change, there was little the peasants of Sedaka could do other than make use of the weapons of the weak. There were obstacles to more open resistance, not the least of which was a fear of losing what little was left. The rich were still powerful enough that gossip about them had to be done behind their backs. Moreover, the rich still had enough control over labor to maintain a viable threat. Thus, when the women "let it be known" that they wouldn't harvest unless wages were raised, the richer farmers in turn "let it be known" that they would bring in outsiders.

Furthermore, the change wrought by the green revolution was relatively slow. Changes in land tenure and technique did not hit all the poor and did not hit at once. For example, landlords gradually began to collect rents before rather than after the harvest, the complete change taking several seasons. Had it been done by one landlord to many tenants, there might have been open protest. The loss of tenancies to landlords who wanted to rent to outsiders, to farm themselves, or to give to children happened gradually, as did the raising of rents. The only thing that happened quickly was the use of combines to harvest, but that was an ambiguous change and many middle-class peasants took advantage of the speed, as did even a few of the poor. Even they were torn between getting the crops in fast and the loss of some wage labor for themselves or their children.

Moreover, the changes did not involve more exploitation of the poor; it meant cutting off relations with them. Thus, wages weren't reduced; they were done away with altogether. The poor were removed from the productive process rather than being directly exploited. In fact, it removed points of conflict: There was no longer a need to haggle over the end of harvest rent or over wages for harvesting or transplanting. And once the struggle in the realm of production is severed, so is the conflict in the realm of ritual. As Scott (1985:243) suggested, if the rich had increased their profits by demanding more from their tenants, rather than simply dismissing them, the protest would have been far more dramatic. The sites where class conflict had histori-cally occurred had been bulldozed. The plight of the Malaysian peasants, Scott (1985:243) said, is analogous to that of the recently fired American factory worker who remarked, "The only thing worse than being exploited is not being exploited."

Finally, in addition to normal constraints against openly protesting or resisting, such as the fear of losing work, tenancy, and charity, there is the routine repression of arrest and persecu-tion. Although the situation in Malaysia is not nearly as bad as in neighboring Indonesia, where killings, arrests, and repression from paramilitary units are more routine, there is in Malaysia still the real threat of arrests and persecution initiated by local political leaders.

Protest and Change

One of the great strengths of the modern capitalist economy is its adaptability, its ability to seek out sources of capital accumulation—that is, ways to make profit. However, although this may strengthen national economies and provide better lives for some, it can also disrupt the lives of others. We see this in the United States as thousands of people are thrown out of work by fac-tory closings as corporations take advantage of cheaper labor in other countries. Whereas this provides jobs for others and lower-priced goods for American consumers, it creates hardship for those whose jobs have been replaced. We see the same thing happening to the poor villagers of Sedaka. Capitalist agriculture may grow more rice and make greater profits for some landowners and farmers, but it also undermines the economic base of others. Whether their lives or the lives of their children will be improved as a result is, of course, another question. It is the disruptions of the short term that the poor are attempting to resist. Thus, from the perspective of the poor, although they might have been exploited under the traditional system of land tenancy, labor, and charity, now they have been cut adrift into uncertainty.

The precapitalist norms of the village emphasized relations between rich and poor that involved what might be called a "politics of reputation." The rich employed the poor, rented their land to them, gave them charity and gifts; in return, the poor supplied their labor and their respect. It was a system in which the rich benefited more than the poor and which they had a major hand in constructing. But this is the very system the rich have had to violate to take advantage of new opportunities. Put another way, it is the capitalization of agriculture that has revolutionized life in Sedaka; the poor, rather than being revolutionary in their resis-tance, find themselves trying to resist a revolutionary social and economic order. Again, as Scott (1985:346) said,

> it has been capitalism that has historically transformed societies and broken apart existing relations of production. Even a casual glance at the record will show that capitalist development continually requires the violation of the previous "social contract" which in most cases it had earlier helped to create and sustain....The

history of capitalism could, in fact, be written along just such lines. The enclosures, the introduction of agricultural machinery, the invention of the factory system, the use of steam power, the development of the assembly line, and today the computer revolution and robotics have all had massive material and social consequences that undermined previous understandings about work, equity, security, obligation, and rights.

In the case of Sedaka, we see peasant farmers trying not to change a system but rather to defend and maintain a social order that, although exploitative, nevertheless looked better than what the green revolution ushered in. Whether they are correct is another matter. It may be that as they lose access to land and labor, they will find something better. But the point is that their efforts at resistance were largely conservative, an attempt to preserve or return to previous forms of dependence. They accused the rich not of making excessive profits but of violating the very behaviors that the rich previously used to exploit the poor.

KIKUYU AND THE MAU MAU REBELLION

The everyday resistance of Malaysian peasants to their worsening economic situation was largely individual resistance, and it was generally nonviolent. But peasant protest sometimes involves collective action and sometimes results in violent conflict. We need to ask, *At what point does resistance take on a more collective form, and what are the conditions that result in peasant protest turning violent? Furthermore, what is the reaction to protest?* The case of the Kikuyu in Kenya is instructive.

From 1952 to 1956, the British struggled to repress a rebellion by mostly Kikuyu peasant farmers. By the end of the revolt, the British had taken the lives of more than 11,000 rebels and had forcibly detained nearly 100,000 people, while 200 Europeans and some 2,000 Africans loyal to the British were killed by the rebels. The Mau Mau rebellion was only one of hundreds that took place as Europeans attempted to assert colonial control over peoples of Africa, Asia, and the Americas, but it serves as a good example of the conditions under which a group is willing and able to go from passive resistance to active and even violent resistance. The Mau Mau rebellion also reveals the psychology of oppressors as they struggle to understand why they are objects of protest. Finally, it is important because it has been considered the first great African liberation movement and, according to Robert B. Edgerton (1989), was probably the most serious crisis of Britain's African colonies.

The British in East Africa

Toward the end of the nineteenth century, most of East Africa became an economic battleground between Germany and England, each attempting to control the resources of the area. To avoid conflict, the two countries met in Berlin in 1884 to carve up much of East Africa among themselves. Kenya was to be included among Great Britain's "sphere of influence." Their efforts to control the economic life of East Africa were, of course, often resisted by Africans, sometimes violently. But British military actions, often ruthless, soon subdued most resistance (Edgerton 1989:4). Kenyans not only had to deal with the British invasion, but they were also decimated by plagues of locusts, prolonged drought, cattle disease, and an epidemic of smallpox. Contemporary estimates of the number of Kenyan deaths during that period range from 50 percent to 95 percent of the population. When, at the encouragement of the British, white settlers arrived in 1902 to claim land, much of the territory seemed to them to be empty.

The Kikuyu, the largest cultural group in Kenya, reacted to the invasion by attacking settlers, prompting further British military expeditions and more Kikuyu deaths. In their rage in early September 1902, the Kikuyu seized a white settler, pegged him to the ground, and wedged his mouth open with a stick; then an entire village urinated into his mouth until he

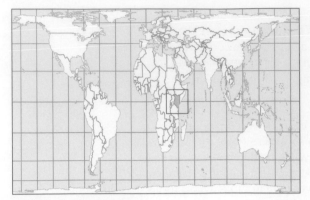

Kenya

drowned (Edgerton 1989:5). They cut off his genitals, disemboweled him, and defecated on his body. The British reacted by surrounding the village at night and massacring everyone, including old men and women, sparing only the children who had hidden in the forest.

The Kikuyu in many ways had the most to lose from the British occupation. They subsisted on a combination of horticulture and raising livestock on communally owned land, and they were governed by a council of elders soon to be replaced by the British with appointed chiefs. Consequently, the Kikuyu continued fighting the British, using spears and poisoned arrows. Their courage greatly impressed British officers, but by 1904, the resistance had ended. Other groups in Kenya, such as the Luo, Kamba, and Nandi, fought the British but with no more success than the Kikuyu. The cattle-herding Maasi, considered the most imposing warriors in Africa, fought alongside the British against the Kikuyu.

British officials made little effort to hide their intent to seize African land, confine the Africans to reserves, and use them as cheap labor. There was some protest registered in England to British actions and intents in East Africa. Sir William Harcourt (Edgerton 1989:3), a past professor of international law, exclaimed that "every act of force you commit against a native within a sphere of influence is an unlawful assault; every acre of land you take is robbery; every native you kill is murder."

Settlement continued, however, and advertisements appeared in British newspapers at home and in British colonies describing the economic virtues of Kenyan settlements. Many of the settlers were South African, others came directly from Britain, traveling by ship to Mombassa, then taking the newly built Uganda Railroad to Nairobi, where they went by oxcart with their belongings to the farmland they had claimed. Many of the settlers were offspring of wealthy British lords sent to Kenya to make their fortunes, some receiving title to more than 100,000 acres. Even people of limited means, such as the father of British writer and aviatrix Beryl Markham, were able to save enough by working for the wealthy to buy a 1,000-acre farm. The often elaborate lifestyles of the white elite, especially in a part of the highlands called "Happy Valley," consisted of well-publicized drinking and drug parties, polo matches, and sexual escapades. A standard joke in Britain at the time was, "Are you married or are you from Kenya?" (Edgerton 1989:17).

To succeed, however, settlers both rich and poor needed African labor. The Africans were not anxious to work for wages, and those who did hardly displayed the work ethic and discipline for which the settlers had hoped. The Kikuyu soon learned the value of money and would walk 300 miles to Mombassa to work, but the settlers were not willing to pay the wages available in Mombassa.

To solve the problem of getting the Africans to work for settlers, the government introduced a hut and poll tax that forced Africans to work for wages to pay the taxes; at the same time, they prohibited them from growing cash crops, such as coffee, sisal, and maize. Each African was also forced to carry a pass (*kipande*) that bore their name, tribal affiliation, fingerprints, work history, and, later, photograph. The *kipande* had to be worn around the neck in a metal container (Edgerton 1989:15). Any white could virtually ruin an African's prospect for employment by writing such descriptions as "lazy" or "arrogant" on a pass.

To administer their colonial holdings, the British developed a system that became known as *indirect rule.* They assumed, wrongly, that every African group must have a ruling chief, so they appointed someone from each group to the position of paramount chief who served as an intermediary between colonial administrators and the group. The Kikuyu, for example, had no paramount chief. The major ruling body among the Kikuyu was the *ciama,* or council of elderly and respected people, who dealt with all aspects of life from settling disputes to circumcision (required for both boys and girls), marriage, and other rituals. They had the power to levy fines on wrongdoers and force them to pay compensation to victims, usually the sacrifice of a goat that would be eaten by the members of the council. The British practice of appointing paramount chiefs created a ruling elite with special access to the wealth and privilege that the colonial government had the power to bestow. Thus, the power of the chiefs originated in and depended on the armed might of the British. They used this authority to extort money from whoever they could, whenever they could, appropriating livestock, demanding land, and ordering women to have sex with them. If anyone protested the chief's behavior, he or she was killed. A chief could cane a person who did not remove his hat and bow to him or arrest someone who coughed while he was speaking at a meeting. The British also selected and trained Africans to staff, under white officers, the police and their African army. These people also became part of an African elite generally loyal to the British.

The Mau Mau rebellion began in 1952, led largely by peasant agriculturists evicted from lands that they had worked, along with a disenfranchised urban group and others restricted to reserves that were soon unable to hold the growing African population. Probably the biggest role was played by peasants who had lived in the White Highlands, an area of fertile agricultural land on which British settlers were given farms.

The White Highlands

To take advantage of their domination of Kenya, the British seized land held by Kikuyu in some of the most fertile areas of the country, such as the White Highlands, and distributed it to British settlers. The settlers were required to pay the sum of three rupees (approximately one dollar) per acre to the Kikuyu owners. Because the settlers required laborers to work the land for them and because the peasants required income to pay the newly imposed taxes, the people from whom the land was forcibly purchased were urged to remain in the Highlands and work for the new settlers. In exchange for three to five months of labor per year, each family was given six to seven acres (much of which had been theirs) on which to grow their own crops and graze their cattle and sheep (Kanogo 1987). They were also given a small wage, rarely exceeding fourteen shillings (about fourteen American cents at the time) per month. By way of comparison, the poll tax was twenty shillings, and a cheap shirt cost four shillings.

At first the Kikuyu who remained in the White Highlands working for the settlers adapted quickly to their situation. The squatters, as they were called, were free to raise crops, cattle, and sheep and to support family members, many of whom did not work for the settlers. If a settler tried to limit the amount of land a squatter worked or to evict relatives who were not workers, the squatter was free to move to the land of another settler. The labor demands were relatively meager and could be met by a man's wife, children, or relatives. Moreover, the squatters could favorably compare their lives with those of other Africans working on farms for wages only.

More important for the Kikuyu, their livestock herds—cattle, goats, and sheep—thrived. Cattle and goats were particularly important for the Kikuyu. They represented wealth and were used in all kinds of ceremonial and economic exchanges. They served as brideswealth, presentations made by a groom's family to the bride's family at marriage. They were important in ritual observances and constituted a financial reserve that could be sold for cash to pay taxes or school fees or purchase consumer goods.

The squatter arrangement also worked for many of the European settlers. Although many were wealthy, a large number had little capital to pay workers but could acquire land cheaply enough to exchange for the labor they needed. In addition, many settlers allowed Africans to work land in exchange for cash or a portion of the produce, thus securing crops that they themselves might be having trouble growing. Thus, within twenty years of the British takeover of the White Highlands, many Kikuyu had been converted from landowning peasants to squatters working the same land in exchange for their labor and, occasionally, a portion of their produce. The squatters were able to sell their surplus produce and build up sizable herds of cattle and sheep.

But the settlers were not content with this arrangement; they wanted to limit squatter cultivation and livestock raising to what the squatters needed for subsistence. In effect, the settlers wanted to reduce the Kikuyu to dependent laborers by removing the peasant option. Thus, the period from 1920 to 1950 was marked by repeated attempts by the settlers to reduce the amount of land and livestock available to Kikuyu squatters. For example, by 1920, the settlers had convinced the colonial government to pass legislation requiring squatters to work for Europeans 180 days per year and allowing settlers to call on the labor of women and children during times of peak labor demand. In 1930 the government, at the settlers' urging, initiated what the Kikuyu called *kifagio,* or "sweeping away"—where squatter stock was reduced from an average of several hundred head for each laborer to about five per family with no corresponding increase in wages. The losses in wealth to the squatters were considerable; some squatters had accumulated as many as 1,000 goats.

In 1937 the colonial government passed legislation that, in effect, gave the settlers the authority to reduce or eliminate squatter livestock and regulate the number of working days required of each squatter. The settlers reacted to this new authority by increasing the number of working days to 240 and then 270 per year. They passed regulations regarding the number of livestock that squatters were legally able to keep; these regulations eliminated all cattle and goats, allowing each family to keep only fifteen to twenty sheep. The settlers enacted these regulations without increasing wages (which remained at about fourteen shillings per month) and against the advice of the colonial government (Kanogo 1987:63).

In addition to reducing the land and livestock held by squatters, there were other forms of squatter oppression. A settler might graze his animals on the African's fields or simply destroy the crop, or might evict the squatter before he could harvest his crop, the settler keeping the crop for himself. Thus, as the squatters struggled to remain economically viable and relatively independent, the settlers did all they could to turn them into dependent wage laborers.

The Kikuyu resisted the constant modifications of their relationship to the land and livestock and, consequently, to each other in ways peasants had always resisted oppression. They failed to show up for work, settled illegally on unused land, tried to organize strikes, killed or maimed settlers' livestock, or fled to the forests, reserves, or cities. But the campaign to drive the Kikuyu off the land was highly successful. By 1948, 3,000 Europeans owned more arable land in the highlands than was available to the more than 1 million Kikuyu on their reserves.

The Roots of the Rebellion

Organized political resistance to British colonization of Kenya began in 1922, when a Kikuyu named Harry Thuku organized the Young Kikuyu Association to protest the poll tax and *kipande* identity containers and preached that the British had stolen Kikuyu land. He was quickly arrested, and a crowd that included the future first president of Kenya, Jomo Kenyatta, surrounded the jail. When a woman named Mary Nyanjira raised her dress over her head and insulted the manhood of the guards facing the crowd, they opened fire, killing her and 25 to 250 people, depending on whose accounts you believe. It was reported that Europeans dining on a verandah opposite the jail also fired into the fleeing crowd. Thuku was never put on trial, but he was exiled for nine years.

In 1925 the Kikuyu Central Association (KCA) was formed, and Jomo Kenyatta became its general secretary. Kenyatta was sent by the KCA to England to be educated because they saw him as a future leader. He traveled to Russia, became a skilled orator in English, married an Englishwoman (in spite of a pledge to the KCA that he would never marry a European), studied anthropology under noted anthropologist Bronislaw Malinowski, and wrote a competent, if idealized, ethnography of the Kikuyu called *Facing Mount Kenya* (1962). He is pictured on the cover holding a spear.

Realizing that a successful movement would need to involve more than only the Kikuyu, Kenyatta organized the Kenyan African Union (KAU). To assure the loyalty of members and to establish a sense of solidarity and purpose, he used a traditional Kikuyu device, an oath. Oaths among the Kikuyu were common and used to prove one's innocence in legal cases, to pledge loyalty before going to war, to show devotion during religious services, or to prove they had not impregnated a particular woman. The Kikuyu believed that violating an oath, like lying after swearing on a Bible, could kill you; the KAU oath (Edgerton 1989:48) stated simply,

> If you ever argue when you are called
> If you ever disobey your leader,
> If called upon in the night and you fail to come
> May this oath kill you

Seemingly typical of colonial regimes, the British either did not recognize or refused to admit that their African subjects wanted to drive them out. Even on the eve of the Mau Mau revolt in 1952, the retiring British governor of Kenya, Sir Phillip Mitchell, announced that all was well in Kenya.

But all was not well. First, the peasant squatters were continually being squeezed by the settlers. The colonial government had tried to help by opening a resettlement area called *Olegurone* for Kikuyu who were evicted from the highlands and who had settled on Maasi land, sometimes marrying with Maasi. But the government insisted that the land was owned by the government and could only be used, not owned, by the Kikuyu. Furthermore, the government dictated inheritance patterns of anyone on the land, allowing a man to pass along his right as tenant only to the eldest son of the eldest wife, instead of dividing the land among children as Kikuyu had done traditionally. They also set strict rules over what could be planted, where it could be planted, and how it was to be farmed. When most Kikuyu refused to accept British directives on the control of land and agricultural activities, they were evicted and sent back to the reserves.

But the reserves were another flash point for revolt. Ignored and virtually never entered by settlers, the reserves had become overpopulated, and the resultant overplanting had eroded most of the land. Hunger was widespread, which the British should have realized because they rejected 90 percent of Kikuyu recruits for the British army at the start of World War II because of malnutrition. When the government introduced modern agricultural methods to the reserves, they never bothered to consult with the Kikuyu. One of the colonial government's pet projects was terracing the land to prevent erosion. This project required the chiefs to round up laborers, mainly women, to do the work. The Kikuyu did not understand the need for terracing, and many assumed the work was being done to prepare it for British settlers.

As a result of the situation on the reserves, thousands of landless Africans fled to the cities in search of jobs. Few found them, and the cities became home to thousands of unemployed people. In Nairobi, the fortunate few who found shelter were living fourteen to a room, four to a bed; the less fortunate slept under buses, cars, or wherever they could find shelter. In Nairobi many Kikuyu organized themselves into gangs that roamed the streets, robbing non-Kikuyu Africans and Asians. The most powerful Kikuyu gang, called the Forty Group because most of its members were circumcised and initiated in 1940, controlled prostitution. But they also had decided that all Europeans had to be driven out of Kenya, and some took a secret oath to obey orders and kill if asked. One prominent gang leader was Fred Kubai, who would play a major role in the development of Mau Mau and later claim it was his brainchild (Edgerton 1989:35).

In addition to the poverty and the loss of land, the Kikuyu were split between those who benefited from and those who suffered under colonial rule. In fact, in many ways the coming rebellion resembled a Kikuyu civil war, with the rebels directing much of their rage against those who remained loyal to the British and continued to profit from the patronage they received.

Finally, another reason for protest was the color bar and racism. The British, especially the settlers, considered Africans to be one step removed from savagery, saved only by the thin veneer of civilization brought to them by the British. Settlers considered Africans to have the intelligence of twelve-year-olds, claimed they did not feel pain as Europeans did, and even believed Africans could will themselves to die. Although beating and killing of Africans by whites was not uncommon, it was not until 1959, after the rebellion, that a white was convicted of killing an African, and even that conviction shocked and outraged the white community.

The Rebellion

The Africans resisted these conditions as best they could. For example, women refused to work on new agricultural projects imposed by the colonial government; the labor unions in the cities called strikes; and more and more people began to take the Mau Mau oath. The oaths became more demanding over the years and were accompanied by an elaborate ceremony. For example:

> "If I am called out at night by the Mau Mau, even if it is to kill Europeans, Government servant or Chiefs, I must go; if I do not go I must die. If I am called out to do damage to the property of Europeans, Government Servants of Chiefs I must do it or I must die. If I hear of any member of Mau Mau who is in trouble with the Government I must help him or I will be killed. I must not pay money when I go to Church as the money is not for God but for Europeans. If I tell the secret of Mau Mau oath to anyone, I will be killed." (Hudson-Koster 2010:103)

The ceremony was patterned after the Kikuyu male initiation ceremony; it involved slaughtering a male goat of one solid color, if possible, and collecting its blood in a gourd bowl and cutting out its chest. Those who took the oath were cut seven times and their blood mixed with that of the goat. (This cutting was later stopped because the scars were conclusive evidence to colonial authorities that a person had taken the oath.) The initiate was asked, "What are you?" After answering, "I am Kikuyu," a cross standing for Kikuyu and Mumbi, the mythical parents of the Kikuyu people, was made on the initiate's forehead with the blood. Then the initiate ate the goat's meat, which was dipped into the blood seven times; afterward, they were taken into a hut and lectured about the oath and the "movement" (Edgerton 1989:53).

Later, when the violence was about to begin, the rituals became more elaborate and the oath included promises to kill whites and steal their guns and valuables and to kill anyone opposed to the movement. The British found out about the oath and reacted with horror.

The British government knew of Mau Mau but thought it was a religious movement. But, as we shall see, the oath obsessed Kenyan whites, and they believed, or wanted to believe, that it was responsible for the entire rebellion.

As the rebellion was about to occur, as thousands of Kikuyu were fleeing the reserves for the Kenyan forests that were to become the rebel base, and as hundreds of thousands of Kikuyu were taking the Mau Mau oath, Jomo Kenyatta was kept ignorant about the Mau Mau plans. The militants in the KAU, which included most of the Mau Mau leaders, did not trust Kenyatta; they knew he was opposed to violence and that the British had sworn to arrest him if he did not publicly denounce Mau Mau. Yet whites in Kenya never doubted that Kenyatta was the "evil genius" behind Mau Mau, its "puppet master," as writer Elspeth Huxley called him (Edgerton 1989:55).

Members of the movement did not call it Mau Mau, and there is no agreement on where the term originated. They called themselves "the movement," "the African government," or other native names, but the term "Land and Freedom Army" became the most common and survived the end of the rebellion. The British probably maintained the term "Mau Mau" because it conjured up images of a secret society and hid the fact that it was a rational political organization fighting for land and freedom. The British government and the police did everything they could to make sure Mau Mau was depicted to the world media as a group of criminals leading an irrational attack against the forces of law and order.

But the rebellion had been carefully planned. The central planning committee consisted of twelve members. Another group of thirty members directed the taking of oaths and shielded the central committee from the police. The committee was in charge of recruiting government employees who could provide information on British plans, setting up networks for food and provisions for the rebels in the forests, and acquiring weapons. This proved particularly difficult. The British had long banned Africans from owning guns, and those owned by whites were locked in "gun safes" when not in use. One method of obtaining guns was to attack police officers, steal their weapons, and dismember and hide their bodies. This worked so well that the British thought that the missing police officers had simply gone home, until they discovered the dismembered foot and boot of one victim. Later the rebels secured arms by raiding police stations and army posts of the government's African soldiers. Rarely did they attack the well-armed British soldiers sent in to quell the rebellion.

Kikuyu women were to play a major role in the revolt. Women had already organized district committees to fight for land and become active in political processes. Although Kikuyu women traditionally never administered oaths, women became oath givers before and during the rebellion (Presley 1992:129). It was largely women who organized and ran the networks that supplied the rebels in the forests with food, medicine, guns, ammunition, and information. And whereas only about 5 percent of the rebel forces in the forest were women, many took active roles in military actions.

"State of Emergency"

Isolated attacks against whites and Africans loyal to the British began in September 1952, but the act that precipitated the British declaration of a "state of emergency" was the assassination in October 1952 of Senior Chief Waruhiu when he left the native court where he presided. The sixty-two-year-old chief was with two friends in his Hudson sedan when it was stopped by three men wearing police uniforms; one approached and asked if Senior Chief Waruhiu was in the car; and when the chief identified himself, the man shot him in the mouth and three times in the body, leaving the two friends and the driver unharmed. One of the first government acts after the emergency was declared was to arrest Jomo Kenyatta, certain he was the mastermind and believing his arrest would end the rebellion.

The leaders of the movement targeted Kikuyu such as Chief Waruhiu who had cooperated with and, in some cases, benefited greatly from collaboration with the British. They also targeted settlers, causing outrage when they killed Roger Ruck; his wife, Esme, a doctor; and their six-year-old son, Michael. Kenyan and international newspapers gave great attention to the details of the killings, and Kenyans were particularly horrified when the man who confessed turned out to be one of Ruck's Kikuyu servants who had cared for Michael. International press reports about rebel attacks on settlers and Kikuyu loyal to the government appeared under headlines about "helpless" or "heroic" whites being slaughtered by "fanatical," "bestial," "degraded," or "satanic" gangsters or terrorists. Unreported were the stories of Kikuyu captives who were stripped of their clothing and possessions and machine-gunned to death as white officers looked on (Edgerton 1989:80).

By 1953, 30,000 young men and women were assembled in the forest, with the active army consisting of 3,000 men. There was little coordination to Mau Mau operations; rebel actions consisted largely of hit-and-run attacks, often on symbolic targets such as the Royal Sagana Lodge where Queen Elizabeth had stayed the previous year on her visit to Kenya. The rebels did not have sufficient weapons to mount a concerted attack on well-armed British positions. Few of the leaders had any education; perhaps as a caricature of British titles, they gave themselves such names as General China, General Russia, and General Hitler. Dedan Kimathi, the leader of the rebels in the forest whose capture virtually ended the rebellion, called himself Field Marshall Sir Dedan Kimathi, later adding the title of prime minister. Most of the rebels were young men and women who joined the rebellion in the forest with the enthusiastic belief that they would drive the British out of Kenya and receive land on which to farm.

By the end of 1953, 3,064 of the Mau Mau had been killed and 1,000 captured; almost 100,000 Mau Mau supporters had been arrested and 64,000 brought to trial. Nevertheless, the fight did not go well for the British army. They were ill prepared for forest warfare; they made noise, shot at phantoms, feared attacks from elephants and rhinoceros, and fared poorly in the high altitude of the mountain forests. Soon the British soldiers sent to fight were patrolling the periphery of the forests while African soldiers, recruited after the emergency was declared, fought in the forest for the "Home Guard."

Mau Mau activity spread to neighboring Uganda and Tanganyika, and Mau Mau agitating in Nairobi was widespread. Theft of money and guns increased, and Kikuyu gangs forbade Africans in the cities to engage in such European practices as smoking European tobacco, drinking European beer, wearing hats, and riding city buses. They set up courts and were essentially running the city.

To end resistance in Nairobi, the British surrounded the city and went through it section by section, rounding up Kikuyu and others and sending them to detention camps or reserves. When 3,000 women and 6,000 children were rounded up to be sent back to the reserve on trains, the women threw the food given them at railway staff and out of windows while singing Mau Mau songs. Thereafter, the British put screens on the train windows to "protect the railway staff."

Finally, British power wore down the rebels. They had destroyed the urban base and cut off most communication with the reserves by building a fifty-mile-long ditch between the forests and the reserve with sympathetic Kikuyu. The ditch was ten feet deep and sixteen feet wide in places, filled with barbed wire and sharpened bamboo stakes. It was dug by forced Kikuyu labor—women, children, and the elderly working from 6:00 A.M. to 6:00 P.M. under orders of loyalist chiefs. The British bombed the forests, often with nineteen-pound bombs from small Pipers and Cessnas; before the emergency was over, they had dropped 50,000 tons of bombs on the forests and fired 2 million rounds of ammunition on strafing runs. Finally, the British relocated 1 million Kikuyu from their scattered homesteads into villages surrounded with barbed wire, where thousands died from hunger and disease. Dedan Kimathi's capture in October 1956 marked the end of the organized resistance.

The Mau Mau rebellion shook the British, but more interesting was the reaction to Mau Mau violence. There is no question that the rebels committed atrocities, especially against Africans loyal to the British. But if the atrocities committed by the rebels were awful, those committed by the settlers and the African police were far worse. Prisoners were routinely tortured and suspects killed with impunity. Settlers advocated killing all Kikuyu and even using an atomic bomb. Trials were rigged. When Kenyatta was tried on the charge of being the Mau Mau leader, the British judge, carefully selected by the governor of the colony, guaranteed a conviction in exchange for a payment of £20,000 on which he could retire to England. He received it. When the sole witness against Kenyatta admitted afterward that he had been bribed with the promise of an English university education, he was promptly arrested for perjury. Settlers openly "hunted" Kikuyu, others bragging that they had killed hundreds. Edgerton provided a particularly graphic account concerning two Kikuyu boys who were stopped by settlers reacting to a report of Mau Mau activity in the area. Unable to tell the settlers what they wanted to know, the boys were tied by the ankles to back of a Land Rover and dragged until their faces had been torn off. The men left them in the road and returned home, laughing, to drink brandy. Police came upon one group of Kikuyu and killed them all, later discovering they were loyalist Kikuyu who had huddled together for protection against the rebels. But the most gruesome charges were to come later because of atrocities committed against Kikuyu held in detention camps.

The Oath and the Detention Camps

At the beginning of this discussion, we asked how those against whom protest is directed react. Obviously, the British and the settlers reacted brutally. Edgerton (1989:242) compared their reaction to that of the terrible vengeance wrought by white slaveholders in response to slave revolts. White Kenyans, he said, always feared a violent uprising but masked their fear with assurances that Africans were loyal, docile, and cowardly. When this illusion was shattered, they felt betrayed and tried to regain their pride, as well as their wealth and privilege, by reacting with torture, massacre, and mutilation—all to try to demonstrate the futility of protest.

So difficult was it for the British government and the settlers to understand the revolt that they attributed it almost entirely to the Mau Mau oath. They could understand no other reason why loyal retainers might be compelled to take up violence, why "decent, trusted servants" could turn into what they assumed were inhuman monsters. So fearful were they of the oath that of the first 1,015 Mau Mau who were hanged during the state of emergency, 222 were found guilty of no crime except administering oaths (Edgerton 1989:174). Thus, ignoring their expropriation of Kikuyu land, their racism, and the legislation that required Africans to carry identification cards, ignoring the conditions on the reserve, the poverty, and the destitution in the cities, and the destruction of Kikuyu livestock, they assumed that if they could wipe out the effects of the oath, they could once more convert the savages into loyal workers and retainers.

Suspected Mau Mau rebels detained by the British army in 1953. By the end of the rebellion, the British had arrested almost 100,000 Kikuyu. (Bettmann/Corbis.)

Statements such as this echo the European witch trials of the fifteenth through seventeenth centuries, when it was believed that only by getting a witch to confess could he or she be cured.

Following the advice of British psychiatrists in Kenya, the British assumed the way to resolve African protest was to reeducate Kikuyu, and the place to do so was the detention camps. By 1959, 80,000 suspected Mau Mau, Mau Mau sympathizers, or simply oath takers were imprisoned and subjected to everything from Christian schooling to beatings, mutilation, and torture. Although the horrendous conditions in the camps—starvation rations, electric shock, torture, castration, rape, and so forth—were reported, little was done until eleven men were killed in a savage attack by prison guards resulting from a plan initiated by a senior superintendent of prisons.

Because the British believed the oath prevented Mau Mau from working for Europeans, the superintendent reasoned that if he could force Mau Mau leaders to work, their violation of the oath would release them from its hold. In 1959 he had an officer in charge of one camp at Holamarch 85 men into the fields surrounded by 111 African guards to force them to work. Despite their willingness to work, the prisoners were attacked again and again by the guards until eleven were beaten to death. The officer in charge later claimed they died from drinking polluted water, not knowing that an autopsy was in progress and that the results would be made public. The outcry, especially in England, over indisputable proof of the conditions in the detention camps caused a political scandal that led to canceling the emergency and releasing all detainees; it also set in motion a process that would lead to Kenyan independence four years later. What the deaths of more than 11,000 Mau Mau rebels could not accomplish was accomplished by the deaths of the eleven detainees.

Independence

At the time of the Mau Mau rebellion, colonial rule was being threatened elsewhere in Africa. The French were involved in a long and costly rebellion in Algeria, Ghana had achieved independence in 1960, and Belgium was leaving the Congo. White settlers in Kenya still thought independence and black rule were at least a decade or two off. But in Great Britain, the government, weakened by economic decline and in no condition to defend the colonies, developed a plan to turn Kenya into a parliamentary democracy and give Africans full participation in the government. Kenyatta was released from detention and soon became the head of the Kenyan African National Union (KANU). The British permitted elections and suffrage, and in a ceremony on December 12, 1963, with Jomo Kenyatta and Prince Phillip representing the royal family standing side by side, the British flag was lowered and the new Kenyan flag raised.

Whites began to leave. Those who remained did so largely because they couldn't sell their land. But Kenyatta did everything he could to allay their fears, proclaiming a doctrine of "forgive and forget" for both Africans and whites and trying to steer a course through the fear of civil war among Africans of different ethnic groups, such as the one that had erupted in the Congo. We must remember that the European agreements that had carved up Africa into states paid little attention to cultural and ethnic boundaries, and ethnic groups had little opportunity or need to form political alliances or accommodations under repressive colonial rule. Thus, Kenyatta had to mold diverse ethnic groups—Luo, Kikuyu, Lao, Kanga, and Maasi—into one government modeled after European states. Think of a country, such as Canada, that has been trying for hundreds of years with mixed success to accommodate only two linguistic groups—English and French—and you get an idea of the problems of African states with far greater cultural and linguistic divisions.

Kenyatta granted political office to one person who had tried to kill him while they were both in prison and appointed judges who had been responsible for his detention. But he also largely ignored the sacrifices of the Mau Mau rebels and the allegiance of loyalists to the British. For example, Ian Henderson, a Kikuyu-speaking police officer who had interrogated and tortured General China in 1954 after his capture, was retained as an officer in the Kenya police. General China was denied a commission in the Kenyan army, being forced instead to enlist as a private and to endure basic training under the command of British officers who had been retained to train the army. In fact, those Africans who fought with the British against the Mau Mau fared far better than those who had fought against the British. Mau Mau veterans claimed they deserved free land and recognition for their sacrifices and even formed a political party to advance their demands, but to little effect. For this, Kenyatta was severely criticized. He was also attacked for the wealth that he, his family, and his backers accumulated, earning them the nickname "the Royal Family."

Bitter stories surfaced, such as that of Wanjohi Mung'au, who was imprisoned for ten years by the colonial government. After his release, he attempted to organize Mau Mau veterans into cooperatives to force Europeans off their land; he was imprisoned by Kenyatta's government for another seven years. Solomon Memia (Edgerton 1989:234), a Mau Mau veteran living in the Nairobi slums, said,

> I regret to state that those of us who fought for freedom were never given a chance to participate in the present government. The majority of ex-freedom fighters are among those who live here in these shanties, because they have nowhere else to go. We weren't given jobs because it was alleged we were uneducated. The young who were in school during the freedom struggle are the ones who have the say in our government, and they are not concerned with our affairs.

Yet Kenya ultimately thrived; many whites stayed, and many American whites joined them. Tourism boomed, and the economy did relatively well. But most Kenyans remain poor, and with the population now five times what it was when the British arrived, land is scarce.

By 1988, a vast gap had opened between the African elite and the bulk of the Kenyan population. Here is Edgerton's (1989:231) summary:

> The Kenya elite live luxuriously in the same neighborhoods that were once reserved for whites. They drive expensive cars, vacation in Europe, and send their children to private schools, and have their needs taken care of by servants. Their life-style resembles those of the wealthy whites who used to live in the same large houses, except that they hire more guards, have embedded more broken glass on top of the walls that surround their estates, and spend more money on electronic security systems. There are many more desperately poor people in Nairobi today than ever before, and they often burglarize and sometimes kill the wealthy "Black Europeans" (or "Benzi," as they are often called after the Mercedes-Benz cars they often drive). There are even more poor people in rural areas, many of whom remain landless. Only about 25 percent of Kenya's land is arable, and the fertile land that was once plentiful enough for six million people must now support four times that number. But the vast "white highlands" that were once a symbol of injustice and dispossession, are now almost entirely in African hands. Wealthy Africans are the new targets of discontent.

THE REBELLION IN CHIAPAS

We saw in the cases of Malaysia and Kenya how global economic developments—the green revolution in the case of Malaysia and nineteenth-century British imperial expansion in the case of Kenya—created conditions that spurred peasant protest. In the case of the Zapatistas, the revolt is clearly related to globalization of the economy. Not coincidentally, January 1, 1994, the day the Zapatistas declared their revolt, was also the day that marked Mexico's entrance into the North American Free Trade Agreement (NAFTA), a free trade treaty between Mexico, the United States, and Canada that would gradually phase out protective tariffs in all three countries. That the events were not unrelated in the eyes of the Zapatistas was made clear by the masked Zapatista leader Sub-Commandant Marcos when he said, "NAFTA was the death certificate of the indigenous peoples of Mexico."

On the left is Emiliano Zapata, Mexican revolutionary leader, from whom the present-day Zapatistas took their name. On the right is the leader of the present Zapatista rebellion in Chiapas, Sub-Commandante Marcos, and one of his officers.   (Left: Bettmann/Corbis. Right: Pablo Virgen/EPA/Newscom.)

The Zapatista army was named for Emiliano Zapata, one of the heroes of the Mexican Revolution of 1910. Zapata led the army of the state of Morelos against the sugar plantation owners in an attempt to gain land for landless peasants. Prior to 1860, most land in Mexico was owned collectively by village communities, but legislation passed under the leadership of Mexico's first president, Benito Juarez, gave individuals title to village land. The legislation was intended to free indigenous peoples and peasants from the domain of their community and give them control of their own property. But the right to own also included the right to sell, and over the course of the next fifty years, 2 million acres of communally held land was absorbed into large haciendas or landholdings. In many cases it was pawned to meet living expenses and the expenses of sponsoring religious feasts, from which people gained respect and prestige (Wolf 1969:17).

The succeeding government of Porfiro Díaz, which ruled Mexico from 1876 to 1910, sold huge tracts of state land, mostly to American corporations to attract foreign capital. The result of these changes in land ownership was that by 1910, the year the Mexican Revolution began, the vast majority of the Mexican population was landless. For example, in 1910, in the northern state of Chihuahua, where rebel leader Pancho Villa operated with his revolutionary army, seventeen persons owned two-fifths of the state, whereas 95.5 percent of family heads owned no land at all (Wolf 1969:33).

The Mexican Revolution of 1910 was fought to regain the land that was lost, and the government installed by the victorious rebel armies quickly wrote into the Constitution of 1917 a law (Article 27) that provided for the redistribution of land held by the state and private owners to landless peasants. The major provision for redistribution required at least twenty people to present a petition to the government for contiguous landholdings (*eijidos*) that they would receive collectively, with the stipulations that they work the land and that they could not sell or mortgage it. Thus, the Constitution of 1917 reestablished, in part, the collective ownership of land that the government had done away with in the mid-nineteenth century.

Part of the paradox of the Zapatista rebellion of 1994 was that it occurred in a country whose constitution included a provision for land redistribution. To understand this apparent contradiction, it is necessary to know a little more about Chiapas, the Mayan Indian population, the globalization of the world's economy, and the Mexican government's altering in 1992 of Article 27 of the Constitution.

Poverty and Inequality in Chiapas

Chiapas is the southernmost state in Mexico, bordering Guatemala to the south and the Pacific Ocean to the west. It is the poorest state in Mexico, with the highest malnutrition and illiteracy rates; 28 percent of the population consist of Mayan Indians. The Mayans are the second-largest indigenous group in the Western Hemisphere, second in number only to the Quechua-speaking descendants of the Inca.

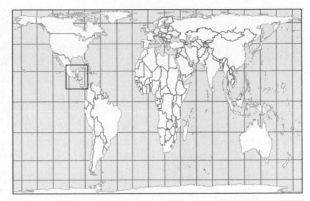

Chiapas is a highly stratified society, with a few wealthy landowners at the top; a small middle tier consisting of merchants, small-scale farmers, coffee growers, government bureaucrats, and political leaders; and a large poor population of small-scale landholders, wage laborers, artisans, and the unemployed. In 1994 almost 20 percent of the population had no income, and another 40 percent had an income less than the minimum wage.

Chiapas region of Mexico

The societies of Chiapas were always stratified to some degree. Mayan society had its elite, and when the Spanish conquered Mexico, they maintained a two-tier society that remains in place today, with themselves and later their Ladino descendants on top and the indigenous people at the bottom. This division is particularly evident in the tropical forests of Chiapas, the area from which the Zapatistas have drawn most of their active support.

While Zapata and Pancho Villa were fighting at the beginning of the twentieth century for land for peasants in the north, ranchers in Chiapas created private armies, the *mapaches* ("raccoons," so called because of their habit of raiding fresh corn from Indian corn fields), to suppress any movement for land reform on the part of the Indians of Chiapas. These ranchers controlled huge landholdings and terrorized the local population, hanging virtually the entire male population (500 people) in one local church during the Mexican Revolution to demonstrate their power. *Mapache* officers received landholdings in exchange for their services. In 1916 the federal army moved into Chiapas to initiate land reform, but those officers and soldiers who did not take land themselves were driven back by the *mapaches,* whose acts are still celebrated by Chiapas ranchers. In 1916, 8,000 private landholders owned 3 million hectares (7.4 million acres), virtually all of the good land in the state; by 1993, the number of private landholders was reduced to 6,000, whereas the Indian population had grown ten times to 2 million (Nigh 1994:9).

As in the case of Malaysia and Kenya, the Zapatista protest concerned relationships within local communities and the divisions of power and wealth. There is in Chiapas a clear economic and political hierarchy, even in Mayan communities, with those at the top supporting the government and the ruling political party, the Partido Revolucionario Institucional (PRI), and those at the bottom supporting, or at least sympathizing with, the Zapatistas. Villages, towns, and cities in Chiapas are generally governed by political bosses (*caciques*) whose authority comes from their position in the ruling party. The *caciques* generally control such sources of wealth as soft drink and beer distributorships and trucking and communication services. These divisions within Mayan communities were clearly evident after the Zapatista began their rebellion and the army moved in to occupy the area. Representatives of human rights organizations reported seeing homes flying white flags, signaling the occupants' support for the army, whereas many homes without flags were empty. In addition, some Mayans formed local vigilante groups that, along with the private armies of the ranchers, the *guardias blancas* ("white guards"), attacked and harassed Zapatista supporters and sympathizers. Thus, as with Malaysian villages and Kikuyu settlements and reserves, there was a clear division between the well-to-do and the poor and, as in the case of the Mau Mau rebellion, community members who sympathized with the rebels and those loyal to the government. The question is, *How did this inequality develop?*

The Zapatista base is largely in eastern Chiapas, in the foothills of the central highlands and the Lancandon rain forest that borders Guatemala. Until the 1950s, the rain forest was largely unoccupied. The Chol and Cholti Maya who inhabited the area in the sixteenth and seventeenth centuries were either killed by military and missionary expeditions or relocated to work on Spanish haciendas (Nations 1994:31). In the 1950s, the government encouraged settlement in the rain forest by Tzeltal and Tzotzil Mayans from the overpopulated central highlands. There the Mayan colonists competed with loggers and ranchers for land. A pattern developed whereby loggers would build roads into the rain forests, take whatever timber they wanted, and be followed by Mayans practicing slash-and-burn agriculture. However, because of poor planning and limited support from the government, along with the lack of relevant agricultural skills by the new settlers, the soil was soon denuded, and Mayan settlers found it necessary to move to other areas of the forest where the same cycle was repeated (Earle 1994:28).

Furthermore, the government never issued clear land titles to the Mayan farmers, paving the way for cattle ranchers to graze their stock on the cleared forest. As a result of this pattern, two-thirds of the Selva Lancandona has been cleared, leaving only the Montes Azules Biosphere Reserve with its original vegetation. In addition, the area's population increased from 6,000 in 1960 to more than 300,000 in 1994. Although some of the Mayans in the rain forest have received title to land (and the leaders of their communities quickly declared their loyalty to the government), the vast majority have not and have continually been harassed by the *guardiasblancas* to move off the land. Another category of Zapatista supporters are Protestant converts who were evicted from their villages in the 1970s and 1980s. They were expelled ostensibly because they undermined the traditional religious practices of the largely Catholic population, but most were forced to move because they challenged the traditional political system of local bosses, refused to pay taxes to support traditional religious ceremonies, and refused to consume liquor or beer, an important source of income for town officials (Gossen 1994:19).

In addition to the Mayans who moved into the area in the 1950s and 1960s and the religious and political refugees, there are others whom the government encouraged to settle in the rain forests to serve as buffers against the Mayans from Guatemala, who were streaming across the border to escape the Guatemalan army.

Economic inequality was aggravated by the economic boom of the 1960s and 1970s in Mexico. During that time, Mexico borrowed heavily from world financial organizations to invest in energy. Much of the investment went for oil exploration and drilling and hydroelectric projects in Chiapas. Although Chiapas supplies fully 50 percent of Mexico's electricity, almost 35 percent of Chiapas homes have no electricity. The jobs and wealth that came into Chiapas in the 1960s and 1970s were not equally distributed, and one consequence was increased village conflict. Furthermore, as some members of the population were earning large sums working on government projects, others were losing their land to cattle and dairy ranchers and to the flooding created by the hydroelectric dams. June Nash (1994), who did fieldwork in a Chiapas village in the 1960s, reported that some poor peasants assumed that the rich had accumulated their wealth through the use of witchcraft, whereas others believed the wealth was given to the rich by cave dwellers in exchange for their souls. She also reports that interpersonal conflicts that took the form of witchcraft accusations or expressions of envy—the evil eye—were settled by homicide.

The rebels, therefore, likely consisted of representatives of different Mayan groups, some religious and political victims of more prosperous Mayans, along with some Ladinos. The question is, *Why did they join in or support the revolt?*

The Rebellion and the Global Economy

One of the major reasons for the plight of poor Chiapas peasants is the decline in support for small-scale agriculture in Mexico. The debate over whether Mexico needed peasant agriculture at all increased in 1982 when the debt crisis (Mexico had a $96 million foreign debt) forced Mexico to adopt an austerity budget in exchange for a restructuring of the debt. One of the measures adopted that affected Chiapas peasants was the removal of the subsidy for fertilizer (Collier 1994:16). Cooperatives were formed, and the Indians began to agitate for political and economic reform. They were met by brutal repression from the *guardiasblancas*. Next, believing the world coffee market had stabilized, Mexico ended coffee price supports for farmers. Coffee production was the major cash crop of Chiapas peasants. As soon as Mexico cut its price support, the world market price for coffee plunged, further damaging the livelihood of peasants in the Chiapas lowlands and throwing many into bankruptcy (Nations 1994:33).

Then, in the clearest sign of the government's withdrawal of support for small-scale agriculture, they modified Article 27 of the Mexican Constitution so that if landholders agreed, *ejido* land could be sold. In addition, the government let it be known that there was no more land to redistribute. This ended the land redistribution program, leaving Chiapas peasants without land or without title to land on which they were squatting.

Finally, NAFTA was negotiated and approved. Free trade in itself might not have damaged the economic prospects of Chiapas's peasants. They might have done well with their agricultural, forest, and handicraft products, but it was clear there was little or no support from the government. Furthermore, with NAFTA signed and with dreams of an increase in American beef imports, ranchers in Chiapas began talking openly of expanding their cattle production, which clearly would have required taking over additional peasant land. This meant increased confrontations with the *guardiasblancas*. In fact, many peasants had reportedly begun arming themselves before the revolt to protect themselves from the ranchers' private armies.

As James D. Nations (1994:33) put it, it is little wonder, therefore, that some Chiapas farmers began to feel they were victims of a conspiracy, with no market for their crops and no land to grow them on anyway:

> It is not difficult to imagine a Tzeltal or Tojolbal farmer sizing up his choices: he can move to San Cristobal de las Casas and sell popsicles from a pushcart, he can work for a cattleman punching cows, or he can rebel against a situation that seems to have him trapped. That hundreds of farmers chose to rebel should come as no surprise.

The Revolt and the Reactions of the Mexican Government

James C. Scott (1985) pointed out that poor farmers in Malaysia were protesting not so much their traditional position in their villages but rather the worsening of that position as a consequence of technological change. The Kikuyu in Kenya were not protesting the initial seizing of land by the British; they had adapted quite well as squatters. Their protest was against the constant worsening of their economic position as British settlers tried to increase their economic domination. The rebellion occurred only after the settlers destroyed African livestock and evicted people en masse from their farms. Likewise, the peasants in Chiapas had adapted to voluntarily or involuntarily leaving their villages in search of land in the rain forests of the Chiapas lowlands. Resistance occurred only after a series of changes by the Mexican government, culminating in the altering of Article 27 and NAFTA, as the government was forced to adapt to changes in the global economy.

The Chiapas rebellion reveals another feature of resistance that we saw in Sedaka and Kenya: the attempt of those resisting oppression to use the past ideals and rhetoric of their oppressors against them. In Chiapas, the Zapatistas used the rhetoric and principles that gave the Mexican government and the ruling political party, the PRI, its original legitimacy, much as the peasants in Malaysia fight the rich with the ideology that the rich once used to justify their legitimacy in the traditional social order. The Zapatistas made it clear that the government betrayed the very principles that gave it legitimacy in the beginning, even going so far as to negate the very laws and rationale that the Mexican Revolution was fought for and reinstituting the land alienation that created the conditions for the Mexican revolution to begin with.

Two aspects of the government's reaction are worth noting. First, they seem to have been relatively restrained in their reaction, in part, no doubt, because of the Zapatistas' skilled handling of the media and the Internet, whose supporters maintained the Web site (www.ezln.org)

to report the Zapatistas' version of events. With the revolt making international headlines and the Zapatistas compared with Mexican heroes of the revolution, the government could not move to crush the rebellion militarily. Given the effectiveness of the Guatemalan genocide against its Mayan population, the Mexican army, at least as well equipped as the Guatemalan military, certainly could have done, and may still do, the same. The Zapatistas also made skilled use of the Internet to distribute its communiqués and report moves of the Mexican military and the *guardiasblancas*. The second interesting feature of the revolt is the reaction of the world's financial community. One of the fears created by the Zapatista rebellion is that it would undermine investor confidence in the Mexican government, and investors would either pull their money out of Mexico, causing a further collapse of the Mexican economy, or dissuade them from putting money into the Mexican economy. These concerns were clearly voiced by an advisor to the Chase Bank; Riordan Roett, in an internal memo, advised that if the Mexican government was to retain investor confidence, it must "eliminate the Zapatistas" (Silverstein and Cockburn 1995). Whether by coincidence or not, within three weeks of the memo's circulation, the Mexican military moved offensively against the Zapatistas.

James D. Nations (1994) suggested that there are some real problems for the Mexican government, problems that any government faces if confronted by peasant resistance. First, if the government does react with financial aid, it may become simply more political patronage and reach only those loyal to the PRI. Second, if the media—which has served to limit the violence of the government response and prevent it from mounting a genocidal campaign as in Guatemala—loses interest, massive repression may result. Some 50,000 Guatemalan refugees still in Chiapas may become targets of violence. Third, the factions have been arming themselves. Arms sales have increased, and groups are forming to defend traditional rights and powers, reminiscent of the death squads formed by eastern Chiapas ranchers. This factional conflict exploded on December 22, 1997, with the massacre of forty-five unarmed Indian sympathizers of the Zapatistas, including four pregnant women and eighteen children. The killers were apparently pro-government gunmen armed with AK-47 combat rifles distributed by a local PRI official (Preston 1998). Finally, the government must find some way to provide additional income and employment, but to do so by increasing the land under cultivation would mean taking land from cattlemen or from the Mayan farmers in the rain forest. Whether or not the Mexican government can remedy the situation remains to be seen. The response up until now has been a virtual military occupation of the area. However, the root causes of the Zapatista revolt—the global expansion of capitalist agriculture, the expansion of trading agreements, and the general marginal role of small-scale agriculturists—will likely remain, leading to the question of the future role of peasants in the world economy.

The Future of Peasants

According to Duncan Earle (1994:27), the central dilemma of peasants in the expanding capitalist world is whether small-scale agriculture has any place in the modern world. Michael Kearney (1996:3) concludes that "peasants are mostly gone and that global conditions do not favor the perpetuation of those who remain." The option is the American system, where 2 percent of the population supplies food for the other 98 percent. Duncan made the point that peasant farmers do and can make profits; that peasant farming is a far more sustainable form of production; and that it does not degrade the rain forest, especially if it is based on coffee production that substitutes coffee plants for bushes under the rain forest canopy. But even coffee production is changing to a factory-type model, in which it is grown in vast open fields devoid of tree cover.

Another development is the demand in core countries for what are termed *nontraditional commodities* (NTCs), items that have not been produced traditionally in peripheral countries but for which there is a demand in core countries. Thus, in Gambia, people produce flowers, a range of Asian vegetables, and eggplants to sell to European and Asian buyers. But even with these commodities, the market is highly concentrated in a few hands, and wages are low (about eleven cents a day in 1994); however, large producers do contract out to small-scale farmers (Little and Dolan 2000).

Overall, however, the Mexican government and other governments around the world have taken actions that indicate that their answer is no, there is no place for peasants, and that the major question is whether it is best for peasants to move into the cities already burdened with millions living in squatter settlements or to have them in the countryside as laborers.

CONCLUSION

One of the main questions often asked about global problems is, *What can we do about them?* Protest is one answer, and the kinds of actions that people took in Malaysia, Kenya, and Mexico provide three illustrations.

These three examples of peasant protest and rebellion reveal some of the factors that produce discontent in peasant populations. Peasant protest, however, will likely disappear as the need and opportunity for small-scale farmers disappears. It would take a major overhaul of the world economy to reverse the concentration of agricultural wealth that exists today. However, there remain other sources of discontent, much of it coming from those people or their descendants who were the peasant farmers of past generations.

11 Anti-Systemic Protest

To sum up then: direct action represents a certain ideal—in its purist form, probably unattainable. It is a form of action in which means and ends become effectively indistinguishable; a way of acting engaging with the world to bring about change, in which the form of the action—or at least, the organization of the action—is itself a model for the change one wishes to bring about. At its most basic, it reflects a very simple anarchist insight: that one cannot create a free society through military discipline, a democratic society by giving orders, or a happy one through joyless self-sacrifice. At its most elaborate, the structure of one's own act becomes a kind of micro-utopia, a concrete model for one's vision of a free society.

—DAVID GRAEBER, *Direct Action*

That man over there says that women need to be helped into carriages, and lifted over ditches, and have to have the best place everywhere. Nobody helps me into carriages, or over mudpuddles, or gives me any best place! And ain't I a woman? Look at me! Look at my arm! I have ploughed and planted and gathered into barns, and no man could head me! And ain't I a woman? I could work as much and eat as much as a man—when I could get it—and bear the lash as well! And ain't I a woman? I have born thirteen children, and seen most of them sold into slavery, and when I cried out with my mother's grief, none but Jesus heard me! And ain't I a woman?... If the first woman God ever made was strong enough to turn the world upside down all alone, these women together ought to be able to turn it back, and get it right side up again.

—SOJOURNER TRUTH (CITED SILVERBLATT), *Women in States*

The rebellions of peasants in Malaysia, Kenya, and Mexico resemble the peasant rebellions of centuries ago against landlords, nobles, elites, or whoever controlled their land and whose demands became excessive or who threatened peasant survival. The major difference between the revolts we examined and those of centuries ago is that the conditions that today's peasants protest clearly are a consequence of the globalization of the capitalist economy and the resulting social and economic transformations. *But what of other forms of protest, such as workers' organizations and strikes; national liberation; civil rights; and feminist, militia, environmental, and fundamentalist religious movements? Is there any relationship among the diverse groups of people involved in these protests, and is there a way to conceptualize them as a whole? That is, can we place these movements in any sort of global perspective?*

There is a school of thought in anthropology, sociology, history, geography, and political science that attributes these protests to the expansion of the capitalist world system. For that reason, they term these *anti-systemic protests* (Amin 1990).

Capitalism requires constant change—new modes of production, new organizations of labor, the expansion of markets, new technology, and the like. It requires a society of perpetual growth. On the one hand, this allows a capitalist economy enormous adaptability and flexibility. It allows business to take advantage of new technologies; create new products and jobs; pursue new markets; experiment with new forms of financing; and abandon unprofitable products, forms of labor, or markets. On the other hand, this flexibility often has far-reaching negative effects on patterns of social and political relations.

The invention and development of the automobile revolutionized American society; it created millions of jobs and new industries and provided salaries for people to buy homes, appliances, and more automobiles. But the revolution wrought by the new technology also created pollution, dependence on petroleum, and industries that, in search of profit, open and close plants, first creating jobs and prosperity and then leaving unemployment and depression. Other innovations, such as the computer, revolutionized the workplace, possibly improved efficiency, created new modes of communication, and made vast stores of information available at a finger's touch. But the computer also made thousands of management jobs obsolete, just as agricultural changes made millions of peasants obsolete. While marveling over a technological innovation, we often neglect to consider those whose livelihoods are endangered. In our fascination with the benefits of the automobile, we rarely remember those whose livings depended on horse-drawn transportation.

One can argue, as many have, that in the long run these innovations will benefit everyone. We can, as some economists do, demonstrate that in the long run business fluctuations eventually balance out. But the ups and downs of the economist's growth chart are experienced by people as alternative phases of prosperity and crisis (Guttmann 1994:14). The economy may seek equilibrium in the long run, but people do not live in the long run; having a job and an income is an everyday concern.

In this chapter, we examine the protests of those who claim that the culture of capitalism has had a detrimental effect on their lives or on the lives of others. These protests can be seen as emerging from what world system theorists identify as the two world revolutions, which occurred in 1848 and 1968. We will look at labor protest associated with the revolution of 1848, feminist protest whose origins can also be said to lie in 1848, and the Occupy Wall Street protests that have spread around the world in the last few years.

PROTEST AS ANTI-SYSTEMIC: THE TWO WORLD REVOLUTIONS

Immanuel Wallerstein (1990) suggested that the first world revolution occurred in 1848, when workers, peasants, and others staged rebellions in eleven European countries. The series of revolts that began in France were all put down within a few months, but they succeeded in setting an agenda for protest that ultimately led to most of the reforms called for by protesters.

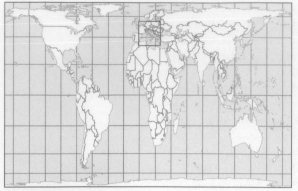

Italy

The second world revolution occurred in 1968, when workers, students, peasants, and others in the United States, France, Italy, Czechoslovakia, Japan, and Mexico participated in popular uprisings. These movements also failed to gain the immediate objectives of the protesters, but they, too, set the agenda for reforms—civil rights, gay rights, women's rights, indigenous rights, and environmental reform, among others—that have defined the goals of social movements since.

The Revolution of 1848

The revolution of 1848 began in France when on February 24, workers declared a new republic based on universal suffrage; within a month it had spread to Southwest Germany, Bavaria, Berlin, and most of Italy. Within weeks, the governments of most of continental Europe had been overthrown; the revolution even incited a rebellion in Brazil, and another revolution a year later in Colombia (Hobsbawm 1975:10). Within a year and a half, however, the revolution was defeated and, except in France, previous regimes restored to power. But although workers failed to gain their immediate objectives, the revolution of 1848 defined two sets of social movements: worker movements protesting the oppression of laborers originating in Industrial Revolution and movements of national liberation motivated by a desire of peripheral countries to gain freedom from imperialism and colonial oppression. Both types of movements were modeled after the French Revolution of 1789 and its call for "liberty, equality, and fraternity." The year 1848 did not, of course, mark the beginning of such movements; organized worker protests against the abuses of industrialization go back at least to the seventeenth century in Europe, and the movements for national liberation include the American Revolution and the successful revolt against the French by Haitian slaves in 1802. But by 1848, the general guidelines and issues involved in the protests were clearly formulated.

WORKER MOVEMENTS   The revolution of 1848 marked the first occurrence of a proletariat-based political group trying to achieve political power. Although they failed, said Wallerstein (1990), the revolution began an intense debate among labor rights advocates over the best way of improving the situation of the growing number of industrial workers. One option was to organize unions and gain the right to strike. The problem was that the nation-states of Europe and the Americas outlawed worker unions and made strikes a criminal offense. Another option was to fight for the right to vote and form political parties to represent workers' rights. If suffrage—the right to vote—was extended to more of the electorate, and the workers comprised a majority of the population, then they could simply assume power through the ballot box. Others argued that the governing elite would never let itself be voted out of power and that violent revolution was the only solution. The result was that two competing strategies emerged in Europe and the United States to improve the conditions of workers—one led by social democratic parties seeking political power through the vote, the other by communist organizations advocating revolution.

By 1945, unions and labor-led political parties attained power in the United States, England, France, and much of Western Europe, resulting in a vast improvement in the conditions of the working class. Most core countries recognized the rights of workers to strike and bargain collectively and developed programs of social insurance (e.g., social security programs, unemployment programs, workers' compensation programs, health programs, and education programs), and extended the vote to ethnic minorities and women. From the mid-nineteenth to the mid-twentieth century, the number of people in poverty in the United States and Western Europe decreased dramatically. By 1949, most American and Western European workers enjoyed a level of prosperity that few would have dreamed of in 1848.

At the same time, workers in revolutionary states, including Russia and most of Eastern Europe, achieved their goals under communist regimes, and although they were not as prosperous as their Western counterparts, they probably enjoyed greater guarantees of basic needs (e.g., jobs, food, and shelter). Thus, within a century, workers enjoyed benefits fought for in the revolution of 1848.

NATIONALIST ANTI-SYSTEMIC MOVEMENTS As working-class movements in Europe and the United States were struggling to improve people's lives, national liberation movements were occurring on the periphery. Whereas the social democratic and communist movements in the core were led by the industrial proletariat, the nationalist movements in the periphery were initiated by the middle class and intelligentsia reaching out to other anticapitalist segments of their populations. Thus, virtually all the countries of Latin America gained their independence in the nineteenth century. The countries of Asia and Africa under European colonial rule gained their independence after World War II. By 1968, with the exception of the continuing struggle in Vietnam and continued colonial domination in a few African states, colonial powers had been forced to abandon politically their nineteenth- and early twentieth-century empires and ostensibly hand over power to indigenous elites.

The enormous world economic growth that followed World War II created an illusion. In the West, people thought they had found the solutions to the problems of economic depression and unemployment and that their

Citizens and workers in Paris, France, barricade the streets during the revolution of 1848. (Bettmann/Corbis.)

world had entered a period of perpetual prosperity and growth; world hunger would be erased, infectious diseases would be eradicated, and class conflict would be a thing of the past. In the communist countries, people believed they had discovered the economic formula for economic security; Russian premier Nikita Khrushchev would boast that by 1980 the U.S.S.R. would have overtaken and surpassed the United States in providing for its citizens. In the Third World, the leaders of national liberation movements, such as the one we examined in Kenya, felt that their mixtures of socialism and capitalism would enable them to develop economically and begin to achieve the prosperity of the West. In sum, as Samir Amin (1990:96) suggested, in the period after 1945 in a majority of countries, the ostensible objectives of the anti-systemic movements of the nineteenth century had come to pass as workers' or other popular movements gained control of major nation-states (Wallerstein 1990:33).

According to Wallerstein, each of the movements that emerged out of the revolution of 1848 can take credit for one fundamental reform. The social democrats of the West claimed to have transformed the core states into welfare states with social insurance and an increase in real wages, a compromise Wallerstein called "Fordism." Conservative forces acceded to these reforms because they subdued protest without endangering capital accumulation; furthermore, they made good economic sense. However, conservative forces still sought to whittle away at the welfare state and the reforms embedded in them. In the communist countries, the socialization of the means of production was the great reform, along with social insurance and welfare but at a lower level than in the West, albeit with a higher degree of security and employment. The great achievement of the national liberation movements was not an increase in wages or social security or the socialization of the means of production, but the increased participation of indigenous people in government and the creation of an indigenous elite, such as those in Kenya, Mexico, and Malaysia.

Yet 1968 would see the beginning of another world revolution, this time against states that were controlled by or contained representation of the very groups that had initiated the revolution of 1848. The labor-oriented Democratic Party was in power in the United States; the Labor Party ruled in Britain; socialists controlled France and Italy; and Eastern European countries, at least in theory, were ruled by the workers through national communist parties. The question is, *Why, when so many of the objectives of the first world revolution were realized, did another revolution occur?*

The Revolution of 1968

The revolution of 1968 was marked in the United States by student protests over Vietnam, demonstrations at the Democratic National Convention in Chicago, and campus demonstrations that led to the killing of students at Jackson State and Kent State Universities by state militia. In France, workers and students barricaded the streets of Paris; similar demonstrations occurred in Japan, Mexico, and elsewhere.

From a world system perspective, 1968 was as much a turning point as 1848. The "old" movements had attained state power or at least a voice in the state, so that the popular uprisings in 1968—in the United States, France, Italy, Czechoslovakia, Japan, and Mexico—were not so much uprisings against the existing world system as they were protests against the "old" anti-systemic movements in power in the world system. The 1968 revolution was triggered by the conviction that the old movements had not fulfilled their objectives, that is, they had become "part of the problem." However, the 1968 revolution also represented a protest by groups who felt they were not sharing in the system (Wallerstein 1990:27).

In the United States, people protested against the government's attempt to brutally suppress the nationalistic objectives of the Vietnamese peoples; in Russia and Eastern Europe, people

Demonstrators outside the Democratic National Convention in Chicago in 1968 are attacked by police. (CSU Archives/ Everett Collection/ Newscom.)

learned about the brutalities of Stalin and witnessed the repression of freedom movements in Hungary and Czechoslovakia; in the periphery, the dream of economic development turned into a nightmare of poverty, government repression, and corruption. These developments combined to leave those who had failed to gain relief with no place to turn. Thus, in the midst of a continuing and unpopular war in Vietnam and a growing "counterculture" protesting consumerism and the growing gap in wealth between the core and the periphery, the dissidents could turn to neither the social democrats nor the communists to express their discontent. Instead, new social movements were created that focused on "identity issues," such as civil rights, women's rights, gay rights, indigenous people's rights, and handicapped rights (Wallerstein 1990:41). For a time, there was a sense of mutual solidarity among these movements expressed in the idea of a "rainbow coalition."

Whereas in the West the theme was the forgotten people—minorities, women, and gays—in the East the struggle was directed against the bureaucrats of the communist states, a protest that would culminate in what some claim was the world revolution of 1989 that toppled the communist regimes of Eastern Europe (Wagar 1991:102). In the periphery, it was not that social and economic reforms failed to help half the people or that reforms created as many privileged people as they removed. Rather, it was that those in power promoted, or at least acquiesced in adopting, economic reforms and practices that resulted in continuing (often worsening) economic conditions, neocolonial subordination, and the emergence of a new elite.

Thus, the anti-systemic movements born in 1848 faced the new anti-systemic movements born in 1968. Yet, as Immanuel Wallerstein (1990:45) suggested,

> [w]hen all is said and done, all these movements (as movements) emerged out of a rejection of the injustices of the existing world-system, the capitalist world-economy. Each in its own way was seeking to fulfill the slogan of the French revolution: more liberty, more equality, more fraternity.

A range of anti-systemic movements emerged out of the two world revolutions. Our assumption is that each of these we examine in this chapter represents protest against various features of the culture of capitalism. This is not to suggest that all the movements conceptualized their protest in that way; often they did not. Members of the militia movements in the United States, for example, do not focus on capitalism in their protests; their targets include the United Nations, Jews, blacks, the World Trade Organization, and other agencies or groups that they blame for their economic distress. Yet on closer analysis, it is clearly the globalization of trade, the loss of manufacturing jobs to overseas assembly plants, and the decline of small-scale farmers and ranchers that caused them economic harm (see Beeman 1997; Junas 1995).

THE PROTESTS OF LABOR: COAL MINERS IN NINETEENTH-CENTURY PENNSYLVANIA

In his book *St. Clair,* Anthony F. C. Wallace (1987) offered an intimate glimpse of life in the nineteenth-century Pennsylvania coal town of St. Clair, the conditions that led to labor protest, and the efforts of mine owners and operators to suppress it. For various reasons, coal mining was not economically viable in much of Pennsylvania, yet mine operators persisted in their efforts to make profits, scrimping on safety and workers' wages and then blaming the workers for their lack of success. As we shall see, the workers responded with a labor protest that was met with systematic repression.

The Coal Industry and the Worker's Life

In the 1820s and 1830s, investors from Philadelphia and New York turned their attention to the coal fields of Pennsylvania, investing heavily in land they thought would yield high profits in coal. The landowners generally did not run the mining operations themselves but rented or leased the land to coal mine operators. The operators expected to make a profit because of the need for coal to provide warmth in homes and fuel for the furnaces of what they hoped would be a thriving U.S. iron industry. Labor for the mines came from new immigrants from England, Germany, Ireland, and Wales.

Coal mining in the anthracite region of southeastern Pennsylvania entailed digging shafts underground to locate the veins of coal, building tracks or hoists in the shafts to haul coal and transport men and equipment to and from the surface, and constructing pumps to drain the water in the shafts. Aboveground was a series of conveyer devices called *breakers* that broke the large pieces of coal into desired sizes and loaded the coal onto railroad cars or canal barges for shipment to its destination. Each mine in southeastern Pennsylvania, where St. Clair is located, employed 200 to 300 persons. Work organization, as it is in most industries, was hierarchical and divided between those who worked belowground in the mines and those who worked aboveground. The lowest-level workers in the mines were boys eight to twelve years of age who worked the ventilation doors that controlled airflow in the mine as men, mules, and equipment passed back and forth. Next were the teenage boys who drove the mules that pulled the carts filled with coal. Next in the underground hierarchy were the miners' helpers, and next were the contract miners, who were paid according to the amount of coal they loaded. Toward the top of the worker's hierarchy were the craftsmen—masons, carpenters, blacksmiths, and pumpmen—who worked underground. In charge of this group were the mine boss and the fire boss, whose main duty was to inspect the mine each morning to ensure that it was safe from methane gas produced by the coal, rock falls, and flooding.

Aboveground, the bottom of the hierarchy consisted of the slatepickers, who picked debris out of the coal before it was loaded for shipment and who might be as young as four years of age, and other unskilled workers doing a variety of loading chores. Higher up in the aboveground hierarchy were the highly skilled workers, such as engineers, machinists, carpenters, and teamsters.

The workforce in the mine was also divided by ethnic group; the top jobs were held by migrants from areas with a coal mining tradition—England, Wales, and Germany. At the bottom were migrants from Ireland who had little or no mining experience. The place of the Irish at the bottom of the hierarchy was also a consequence of their reputation for rowdiness, drunkenness, and unsafe conduct in the mines.

Mining grew significantly in the St. Clair area from the 1840s through the 1870s, despite the fact that few people were making any money and many were losing a great deal. The costs to operators of mining a ton of coal seemed to vary from $1.56 to $3.16. These figures did not include township taxes, canal or railroad shipping costs, commissions to sales agents, or depreciation on property or interest on loans. Railroad shipping costs varied, climbing or falling from an average of about $1.60 per ton. In sum, the actual cost of mining a ton of coal must have been at least $3.16 to $4.16, although, given the absence of accounting methods, it is unlikely mine operators knew their full production costs. However, depending on the competition, the time of year, the supply, and other factors, the price of coal to customers averaged only about $2.75 per ton. Moreover, there were frequent interruptions to mining operations caused by accidents, breakdowns, overproduction, and flooding.

Wallace suggested that one reason people continued to mine despite losing money was the inadequacy of their accounting procedures: By the time they realized they were losing money, it was too late to do anything about it. Wallace (1987:25) estimated that 95 percent of all collieries failed from 1820 to 1875, and the median survival time of a company was less than one year.

Why was coal mining unprofitable in St. Clair and the surrounding area? Apparently there were two reasons: the geology of the area and the frequent work stoppages caused by accidents.

Veins of coal are stratified deposits of decomposed organic materials transformed underground by pressure and heat into masses of carbon-rich materials. Movements of the Earth's crust sometimes bring these veins to the surface, forming vertical or diagonal deposits. The size and directions of these deposits determine how easy or difficult they are to mine. Those veins brought to the surface are obviously the easiest to mine, and these deposits were the first to be exploited. Other deposits can be reached only by digging underground. For these, the ease of mining depends on the size of the vein and the depth to which one has to dig to reach it. The problem in the St. Clair area was that the nature of the coal deposits required a lot of digging to reach veins that were often small or of poor quality.

Apparently, coal mine operators could have avoided their losses if they had taken seriously the reports of geologists who concluded that mining in the area would not be profitable. But the landowners and the mine operators chose to ignore those reports, believing instead those who attacked the scientists' findings and claimed that the investments that had already been made could prove profitable.

The second reason the mines failed to make money—the frequency of work stoppages because of accidents—was related to the first. Given the small profit margin to be made mining coal in the anthracite district, mine operators had to save money on operations, and one way they did that was by scrimping on safety. Coal mining is dangerous. In addition to cave-ins, flooding caused by pump failures, and the risks of working around the conveyor belts of the breakers, there was the constant danger of explosions. Coal produces methane gas, and when the amount of methane reaches a 5 percent to 12 percent mixture with oxygen, any flame or spark will ignite it. Because miners of the period carried open-flame lamps attached to their helmets, the possibility of explosion was immense.

One way to prevent the critical buildup of methane was to construct ventilation systems that ensured constant airflow through the shafts. Such systems were costly, however, and because the profit margins were so small, most mine operators invested a minimum in such systems. Moreover, there were no state or federal safety standards that the mine operators had to follow. The costs of neglecting safety were high to both miners and mine operators: Miners lost lives and limbs in accidents and explosions, and operators lost money in the destruction of equipment. The mine owners failed to recognize or admit that the geology of the coal fields made it uneconomical to mine: They blamed their economic failure not on the geology or their business practices, but on the federal government for not putting a high enough tariff on British iron being imported into the country. Coal mining profits were closely tied to the rise and fall of the American iron industry; if the iron industry did not expand, the coal industry could not grow. But British iron was cheaper, and perhaps better, than American iron. If British iron was made more expensive by high import tariffs, both the American iron industry and the coal industry would expand and profit.

Accidents and work stoppages, however, could not be blamed on the British or the government. Mine operators and owners, instead of recognizing their own culpability, blamed careless workers. When Wallace reviewed accident reports for the period, he found that in almost every case, the accident was blamed on miners' negligence. This not only absolved the mine owner of blame for the economic losses, but it also relieved the mine operator of any financial liability for the accident.

The accident and death rates as a result of inadequate ventilation and lack of emergency tunnels to allow miners to escape from explosions or cave-ins were appalling. It is difficult to get reliable figures on injuries and deaths in the mines from 1850 to 1880. After examining fatality rates from 1870 to 1884, Wallace estimated that fatality rates varied from 2.3 percent to 6.8 percent of the workforce per year—and this was after the passage in Pennsylvania in 1869 of a mine safety law. We do know that the numbers killed in Pennsylvania mines were far higher than in Great Britain; there was one fatality for every 33,433 tons mined in Pennsylvania as opposed to one fatality per 103,000 tons in Great Britain.

Before the passage of the mine safety law in 1869, no one kept consistent records, but by using reports in the *Miner's Journal* (the major publication for the mining industry), Wallace concluded that each year, 6 percent of people employed in mining, including those who worked aboveground, were killed; another 6 percent were crippled for life; and yet another 6 percent were seriously injured. Thus, a mining employee had less than an even chance of surviving for twelve years, and he could expect to be killed or crippled for life in six (Wallace 1987:253). Because mine operators continued to see the accidents as caused by careless miners and because the courts absolved them of any responsibility for death or accidents, there was little need for them to change their practices.

Given the difficulty of making a profit in coal mining, mine operators cut costs on safety and minimized the pay of miners. It was a buyer's market for labor. The transformation of agriculture in Europe, as we saw in Chapter 2, created millions of landless peasants, whereas the fluctuations in demand for such products as textiles, iron, and coal resulted in great economic insecurity for those dependent on jobs for their livelihood.

Mine managers made $1.95 per day, foreman $1.25 per day, blacksmiths $1.08 per day, and miners $1.16 per day if they worked twenty-four days in the four-week pay period (or about $28 per month). Contract miners were a different category and were paid by the wagonload or by the yard if they were cutting tunnels. But out of this the contract miner had to pay his helpers and other expenses, such as lamps and wicks. Helpers generally earned $0.85 to $0.95 per day, which meant the contract miner had to earn about $50 per month simply to earn as much as he paid his helper.

The income was above subsistence level for the time, but that assumed no work stoppages, no illness, and no layoffs—all three of which were likely at some point. In some respects, this was compensated for by the fact that most households had more than one wage earner; a household with one worker might make $150 to $200 per year. Some households took in boarders, and some women worked as seamstresses, cooks, and maids.

Food was cheap; corn was fifty cents per bushel, eggs eleven cents per dozen, flour five dollars per barrel, butter eighteen cents per pound, bacon seven cents per pound, beef eight cents per pound. Housing was also cheap. Thus, a laborer with a wife and two children who earned an average of $20 per month could subsist and even save a little; families with more than two children would have required income from other family members, but children could be put to work by the time they were eight or nine. The problem was that work was often not steady—strikes, floods, and accidents frequently closed down the mines or disabled the miners.

Furthermore, working in the mines took a devastating toll on the miner's health. Coal mining produced methane gas and tiny particles of coal dust that worked their way into the lungs. The rates of disability and death as a result of "miner's asthma," or black lung disease, were extremely high. As one mine inspector (Wallace 1987:257) of the time wrote,

> [a]fter six years' labor in a badly ventilated mine—that is a mine where a man with a good constitution may from habit be able to work everyday for several years—the lungs begin to change to a bluish color. After twelve years they are densely black, not a vestige of natural color remaining, and are little better than carbon itself. The miner dies at thirty-five of coal miner's consumption.

Worker Resistance and Protest

How could the laborers protect their interests, and formally or informally protest the dangers they faced in the mines and the economic insecurity brought about by low wages, layoffs, and work stoppages?

Miners protested their low wages and dangerous work conditions in various ways; there were spontaneous work stoppages, acts of sabotage against the mines, demonstrations and marches, and probably work slowdowns. Many of these acts were met with force from the police or state militia. The first regional strike occurred in 1858, when lower coal prices resulted in wage cuts. Miners closed down the mines and marched through the streets banging drums and waving flags. The sheriff called out the militia, and men were arrested on riot charges.

The first effective strike occurred in 1868, when the Pennsylvania legislature passed a law making eight hours a legal workday, although it also meant a cut in wages. Miners began a strike, demanding that the eight-hour day be instituted with no cut in wages, resulting, in effect, in a 20 percent pay raise. The dispute was settled after the miners closed down the mines, with workers obtaining a 10 percent wage increase. Although unions were illegal, the miners formed the Workingmen's Benevolent Association of St. Clair in 1868, the forerunner of the United Mine Workers of America. Although the mine owners and operators refused to recognize the association as the bargaining agent for mine workers, it was effective in lobbying for safety legislation and improved living conditions, as well as in organizing strikes.

Also central to Irish protest against discrimination, both on the job and off, were the Molly Maguires. The term *Molly Maguires* originated in the south of Ireland and was applied to groups of peasants who organized to retaliate against landlords, magistrates, and others guilty of injustices to poor, Irish families. The name was suggested by the practice of young men who disguised themselves by blackening their faces with burnt cork and dressing in women's clothing. In these disguises they beat or killed gamekeepers, servers of eviction notices, cottage wrecking crews, or others responsible for oppressing Irish families. It was Benjamin Bannan, in his *Miner's Journal,* who began to articulate the idea of Irish Catholics and the Molly Maguires in the role of conspirators, calling it a secret Roman Catholic organization that aims to control the political process and the Democratic Party.

To what extent the Molly Maguires were a formal secret society or an imagined conspiracy is a moot question. There is no question, however, that Irish Catholics organized to protect themselves and to retaliate, sometimes with violence, against discrimination or what they perceived as injustice. Organizations such as the Molly Maguires are not uncommon in social situations in which there is little effective public order or among groups that view the state authorities as hostile to them. These groups become institutionalized systems of law outside the official law, a parallel government outside the official government. Eric Hobsbawm (1959:6) referred to such groups as *mafia,* seeing them as a form of organized rebellion against hostile groups or public authorities.

In the struggle between Irish mine workers and the mine owners and operators, the main importance of the Molly Maguires was that they became the focus of the owners' and operators' attempts to destroy the miners' association and to link it, as well as other worker organizations, with an international conspiracy. In many ways, the Molly Maguires represented to the mine owners what the Mau Mau oath represented to the British in Kenya. It also represented attempts by nation-states or capitalist enterprises to associate social protest with activities defined as illegal and to label such protest as criminal or terrorist activity.

Whether there was a secret society operating in the coal fields of Pennsylvania, or the name Molly Maguires was applied to any group seeking retributive justice is unclear. It is clear that there were individuals who did not hesitate to use violence on those who they felt inflicted injustice on the Irish or whose injustice went unpunished by the courts. Furthermore, labor violence was real enough: There were attacks on strikebreakers, sabotage at the mines, and physical attacks on mine operators or their agents, and the workers' association often used the language of violence. In addition, many believed that the parent organization of the Molly Maguires was the Ancient Order of Hibernians, an Irish Catholic benevolent association modeled after fraternal organizations, such as the Knights of Columbus, from which Irish were excluded.

In September 1875, there was an epidemic of murders and attempted murders; the victims had been guilty of attacks on Irish or of firing or blacklisting Irish workers. As Wallace (1987:374) said, those who were called Molly Maguires acted on "the demand for retributive justice in an atmosphere of ethnic discrimination by the authorities and bitter resentment by those who felt that they had systematically been denied their rights."

The punishments dealt out by the Molly Maguires were carefully weighted according to the crime. Capital offenses included killing an Irishman and being acquitted by the court, trying to kill an Irishman and not being arrested, and depriving an Irishman of his livelihood. Verbally threatening an Irishman called for a severe beating. The victims were always selected because they were the ones who committed the injury and were never attacked as random targets; women and children were never targeted, even if they were witnesses (Wallace 1987:359). Defense funds were established for Mollies, as Irishmen believed, with some justification, that they were being discriminated against and could not expect justice from the courts or police.

Thus, workers had various means to protest their treatment by mine owners and operators, other miners, and state or local authorities. They ranged from informal and spontaneous acts, to formal labor organizing, to organized violence, much of which originated in ethnic discrimination, as it did in labor protest. But labor and ethnic discrimination were tied together by the mine owners and operators in their attempts to destroy the workers' organizations.

Destroying Worker Resistance

Mine owners and operators were vehemently opposed to any legislation that either increased safety in the mines or recognized workers' rights to collective bargaining. Additional safety measures, they argued, would make the mines uneconomical, and collective bargaining would give the workers too great a say in mine operation. The Pennsylvania legislature did pass safety legislation in 1869, but only five months later a mine explosion at Avondale, Pennsylvania, killed 108 people, most of whom were asphyxiated by gases while waiting to be rescued because there was no escape tunnel.

The owners also tried to destroy the Ancient Order of Hibernians, claiming it was simply a front for the Molly Maguires. But the ultimate goal of the mine operators was to destroy the union and other miner organizations. The leader of the attack was John Gowen, an ex-coal operator and attorney for the Philadelphia and Reading Coal and Iron Company, which by 1885 came to dominate the anthracite coal district.

Gowen's strategy was to portray the Workingmen's Benevolent Association and the Ancient Order of Hibernians as extensions of the Molly Maguires, in effect scapegoating worker organizations for real or imagined offenses of the Molly Maguires. First, he hired the Pinkerton Detective Agency to infiltrate the Workingmen's Benevolent Association to uncover connections between it and the Ancient Order of Hibernians and the Molly Maguires. The operative could find no evidence of any connection between the union and any secret organization.

Gowen then hired another agent to infiltrate the Ancient Order of Hibernians. The agent reported only that many people were leaving the organization because of the attempt to connect it to the Molly Maguires. In fact, the smear campaign against the order was so effective that some Irish clergy had condemned it, even threatening to excommunicate any Catholic who remained a member.

Gowen finally got his chance to destroy the order in a case of attempted murder of a Welshman, M. "Bully Bill" Thomas. Thomas, a prizefighter, was involved in a melee between the Welsh and Irish fire companies, both of which arrived to put out the same fire; shots were fired, a man was killed, and a young Irishman named Daniel Dougherty was charged with murder. Dougherty was acquitted, and this time the avengers were Welshmen, not Irish. Bully Bill Thomas and others made an attempt on Dougherty's life, and local members of the Ancient Order of Hibernians planned a retaliation. Thomas was attacked and shot but survived; based on his complaint and evidence from the Pinkerton agent, arrests were made. Gowen put the Ancient Order of Hibernians and the Workingmen's Benevolent Association on trial, painting them in such sinister terms that being a member was tantamount to having a bad reputation. A succession of trials resulted in the hanging of twenty men convicted of conspiracy to murder. The trial, in effect, succeeded in scapegoating the miners and their organizations for the economic failure of the coal fields.

In fact, according to Wallace (1987), there was little or no connection between the Workingmen's Benevolent Association and the Ancient Order of Hibernians, although there is little doubt that the Molly Maguires served as a mechanism for Irish Catholics to achieve retributive justice in a hostile world. More interestingly, the reaction of Gowen and others is reminiscent of the reaction of the British to the Mau Mau, refusing to recognize any real oppression and blaming instead oath taking and secret ritual. The end result was to discredit an already broken union and fix the blame for the problems of the coal trade on forces outside the trade, such as the absence of protective tariffs on British iron and the workers themselves.

Wallace's story of St. Clair also provides some insights into the origin of labor conflict, a story being repeated today in industries all over the world. In St. Clair we found a marginally profitable industry trying to squeeze a profit by lowering wages and scrimping on safety measures, creating conditions ripe for labor protest. Today we find marginally profitable, highly competitive industries, such as textiles, electronics, and toys, cutting labor costs by moving into countries whose lack of labor legislation mirrors the labor situation in Pennsylvania in the nineteenth century. Workers in these countries face the same problems of low wages and unsafe working conditions that workers in the Pennsylvania coal fields of the nineteenth century faced. These conditions have led to attempts to organize, attempts generally met with legal repression or violence by industry owners or managers and the state.

In their 2006 Report (International Confederation of Free Trade Unions 2003), the International Confederation of Free Trade Unions reported that worldwide 115 trade unionists were murdered for defending workers' rights in 2005, while more than 1,600 were subjected to violent assaults and some 9,000 arrested. Nearly 10,000 workers were sacked for their trade union involvement, and almost 1,700 detained. In Colombia more than seventy unionists were assassinated, while a further 260 received death threats; in Ecuador, forty-four workers at one plantation were sacked simply for setting up a trade union, as were twenty-three employees of a telecommunications company in the Philippines. Diosdado Fortuna, a leader of the Nestlé workers' union, was shot dead by two unidentified gunmen. He had been heading a strike at Nestlé Philippines when he was gunned down on leaving the picket line for home. In Burma, where there are no trade union rights, ten union organizers received jail sentences of up to twenty-five years, one dying in prison five months later.

GLOBAL FEMINIST RESISTANCE

In September 1995, representatives from nongovernmental organizations all over the world gathered in Beijing, China, at the Fourth World Conference on Women to develop what conference participants called "strategic sisterhood," an international organization to unite the causes of women in the periphery with those in the core. The model for present-day protests about the rights of women can be traced to the world revolution of 1848. In that year, 400 participants gathered in Seneca Falls, New York, to plan their strategy to fight for the abolition of slavery. At the meeting, Elizabeth Cady Stanton, one of the leading social activists of the nineteenth century, introduced a resolution that women be given the right to vote. Such an idea was radical even in that setting, and it passed only after Frederick Douglass, the most prominent African American of the nineteenth century, supported the resolution. The resolution was greeted with contempt by most Americans: One newspaper called it an insurrection; another accused the women of being Amazons. And although black men were given the right to vote in 1869, women, with the exception of those in a few Western states such as Wyoming, Colorado, Idaho, and Utah, were not allowed to vote until 1920. Although it took more than seventy years, the right for women to vote was one of the changes that emerged out of the revolutionary mood of 1848.

Although the modern feminist movement has helped raise the status of women, at least in the West, women remain among the most economically, politically, and socially marginalized members of global society. As Martha Ward noted in *A World Full of Women* (1996:221), the major occupations of women worldwide are "street-selling, factory assembly lines, piecework, cash-cropping and commercial agriculture, prostitution or sex work, and service in domestic settings, like maids who change the sheets on hotel beds."

At the same time that women produce 75 percent to 90 percent of food crops in the world, they are responsible for the running of households. According to the United Nations, in no country in the world do men come anywhere close to women in the amount of time spent doing housework. Furthermore, despite the efforts of feminist movements, women in the core still suffer disproportionately, leading to what sociologists refer to as the "feminization of poverty," where two out of every three poor adults are women. The informal slogan of the Decade of Women became "Women do two-thirds of the world's work, receive 10 percent of the world's income and own 1 percent of the means of production" (Ward 1996:224).

These conditions have incited feminist protest in virtually every country of the world. In India, dowry—the money and gifts a bride brought with her to her husband's household—became an object of protest in the 1970s when a young woman was killed by her in-laws because her parents could not meet the in-laws' increasing demands for dowry. Apparently, this was not uncommon; there were other reports of in-laws dowsing daughters-in-law with kerosene and setting them on fire. These were often classed by authorities as suicide and passed off as family affairs of no concern to the state (Kumar 1995). In Bangladesh, women organized to gain access to employment and fair wages and to revise inheritance laws that favored men (Jahan 1995). In the Philippines, women organized to gain labor rights after the imposition in 1972 of martial law by President Ferdinand Marcos, a movement that contributed to the election of Corazon Aquino as the first woman president of the Philippines. In South Africa, women have organized to protest sexual abuse, economic inequality, and the exclusion of women from public policy decision making (Kemp et al. 1995). In Kenya, women's groups have proliferated to support the entry of women into business, community projects, and revolving loan programs (Oduol and Kabira 1995).

The women's movements that proliferated in the 1970s have had significant effects in some areas. In Peru, for example, it would have been unusual twenty years ago to see, as one can now, a woman conducting the national symphony orchestra, working in politics, or running a business. Twenty years ago, Peruvian women's lives centered on their family and the home (Blondet 1995).

In spite of some gains, however, the economic position of women in global society remains, as a whole, marginal to that of men. For example, women represent about 60 percent of the billion or so people earning one dollar or less per day. We need to ask, *What are the factors that contribute to the inferior position of women in the world, and what are some of the strategies that can be employed to improve their position?*

Women in New Delhi march to protest high food prices in 1973.
(Bettmann/Corbis.)

Gender Relations in the Culture of Capitalism

Eleanor Leacock, who has studied the role of women in capitalism around the world, concluded that some women hold some measure of influence and power (1986:107). But the degree of power varies with the gender system of their culture; the status of the race, religious group, or class to which they belong; the political system under which they live; and their personal attributes and life histories. Leacock agreed with Karl Marx and Friedrich Engels that capitalism is patriarchal and paternalistic, that is, the mode of production that creates a hierarchy of labor and a family structure that relegates women to domestic work inevitably leads to the oppression of women. The question is, *What evidence is there that the marginalization of women and the protest that it inspires, particularly in the periphery, are a consequence of the expansion of the culture of capitalism?*

Four developments that accompanied the expansion of the culture of capitalism helped define its system of gender relations: the loss of control by women over valuable and productive resources, the transformation of extended families into male-dominated nuclear families, the expansion of industry into the periphery, and the imposition on peripheral countries by multilateral institutions of structural adjustment programs. Let's examine each of these developments.

In the eighteenth and nineteenth centuries, capitalist expansion altered two sets of social relations in societies into which it spread. First, capitalism resulted in the loss of control by most members of societies of the means of production, making them dependent for survival on the sale of their labor. Second, capitalism undermined large, extended family groups, isolating people into individual or nuclear families, each a separate economic unit ruled over by male household heads. In these developments, said Leacock (1983:268), lie the origins of the modern suppression of women. For example, women among the Cherokee and Iroquois in North America were equals or near equals of men. Women generally controlled the production of food crops and played a major role in public decision making; among the Iroquois, women chose the political leaders and could decide themselves to terminate a marriage. Colonists initiated changes by negotiating or trading only with men and by introducing a European model economy to replace horticulture and hunting. This undermined the authority of extended kin groups, in which women played a major role, thus creating a society based on male-dominated agriculture. Among the Montagnais-Naskapi of Labrador, cooking, cleaning, and housework did not become institutionalized as women's work until women became dependent on fur-trapping husbands and individual households of husbands, wives, and children replaced family lodges. In this way, said Leacock (1986:117), women's productive activities and decision-making authority shifted from the larger kin groups and the fields to the household domain, whereas their social status was redefined as subservient to and dependent on male household heads.

Missionaries further undermined women's authority—especially in societies where women had important ritual responsibilities—by refusing to deal with women and by using their power to undermine traditional family arrangements. The missionaries believed the patriarchal nuclear family was ordained by God and taught that a woman's role was to provide loving care for husband and children. As a result, women's unpaid household labor became, for all practical purposes, a gift to plantation or mine owners, manufacturers, or traders who realized their profit from the work of husbands and sons (Leacock 1983:271).

In her survey of Africa, Ester Boserup (1970:277) noted much the same process: The economic and social policies of British, German, Dutch, Portuguese, and French colonizers undercut the traditional role of women as farmers, merchants, and participants in the political process of families by undermining the power of extended families or clans, taking away women's rights to land, and relegating women to the household or low-paying wage labor. In Chapter 6, we saw the consequences of this in the case of the famine in Malawi.

Karen Sacks (1979) summarized these changes in Africa by contrasting the roles of "sisters" with the roles of "wives." "Sisterhood," Sacks argued, is shorthand for a relationship in which women have access to valuable resources (land, livestock, and money) based on their

320 Part III • Resistance and Rebellion

membership in the extended kin group of brothers and sisters. Sisterhood connotes autonomy, adulthood, and the possibilities of gender equality. Wife or "wifehood," however, connotes a relationship of dependency. According to Sacks, the development of nation-states in the culture of capitalism undermined women's status by dismantling the larger, family-based institutions on which "sister" relations rested, turning women into dependent wives.

The works of such writers as Leacock, Boserup, and Sacks raise an interesting issue (see Silverblatt 1988). Modernization theorists who argue about the benefits, and sometimes the inevitability, of modernization generally point to the decline of the extended family and the emergence of the nuclear family as the basic unit of society as a major example of progress. Most feminist theorists propose that the nuclear family is partly responsible for the inferior position of women. Because we propose that this change has little to do with "modernization" and more to do with the emergence and expansion of the culture of capitalism, we need to ask, *Why was the extended family not compatible with other elements of capitalist culture?*

We examined in Chapter 1 the reason the nuclear family promoted consumption by requiring each small unit to purchase and consume commodities that in extended family units could easily be shared. In Chapter 9, we examined why communal property held by extended families is problematic to the economic and legal relations in capitalism. But there are other reasons why small nuclear family units are preferred in the culture of capitalism. For example, the extended family, as a political entity, conflicts with the needs of the nation-state to educate and control its citizens. Members of large extended families are more difficult to control than are members of small, isolated, nuclear families. In addition, the demands for a flexible and mobile labor supply make the extended family impractical. It is far better for capitalism to reduce people's social and emotional ties to others, to make it easier for them to relocate to where labor is needed. *If we assume that it is the preferred family unit in the culture of capitalism, how does the nuclear family lend itself to the relegation of women to an inferior position?*

First, the emergence of the nuclear family tended to release men from the ties to the extended family and make them more autonomous, giving them greater control over resources and over the members of their households. In societies where women retain close ties to their families, such control is rarely present. Furthermore, recognition of the male as head of the household conveys to male household head's control of those resources.

Second, the nuclear family and the patrilocality of the workforce serve to separate adult women from their peers, therefore reducing the potential for the social support of other women and for building class consciousness among women. The classic example, of course, is the nuclear family with a mother who does not work outside the home (Tétreault 1994:10). In some cases, as in Japan and China, the young bride is brought into the patriarchal home and virtually isolated from outside society.

A third feature of the nuclear family that supports the subservient position of women is the prevalent form of marriage. The nuclear family is traditionally composed of a larger, older, better-educated, richer, more sexually experienced, and generally legally favored man who is married to a smaller, younger, less-well-educated, propertyless, inexperienced, and socially less-well-protected woman. Although this form of marriage is not restricted to the culture of capitalism, its historic prevalence in European cultures and its spread through economic colonization and missionary activity to the periphery certainly helped sustain or create households of dominant men and subservient women (Tétreault 1994:9–10).

In addition to removing from women access to the means of production and making the male-dominated nuclear family the main social unit of society, the expansion of industrial production from the core to the periphery served to marginalize women economically. Beginning in the 1960s and 1970s, the growth of assembly plants in countries such as Mexico, Haiti, Guatemala, and Indonesia depended on a disproportionately female workforce in low-paying jobs. Although some have argued that such work expanded women's economic options, the fact remains that, as global capital spread, women worked harder, either in and from their homes or in assembly plants. Yet the work is economically marginal, temporary, or low paying. Globally, two-thirds of all part-time workers and 60 percent of all temporary workers are women. Furthermore, while working for pennies an hour, women remained responsible for all or most of the household labor necessary to sustain their families (Eisenstein 1997).

The global economic trends of the 1990s have further undermined women. Nation-states have been forced by the International Monetary Fund and the World Bank to terminate social services intended to alleviate the conditions of people living in poverty, a disproportionate number of whom are women and children (Basu 1995:6). Thus, the withdrawal or reduction by the state of its support of workplace legislation, social service programs, job programs, health programs, and education programs disproportionately affects the position of women in society (Eisenstein 1997).

In sum, feminist protest arises from conditions that relegate women to the private or domestic sphere, that offer only low-paying jobs, and that undermine public policies geared to protect women and children from the widespread poverty that exists in the periphery. The question is, *What are some of the ways people can resist the marginalization and subjugation of women globally?*

Strategies of Protest

Clearly, to the extent that the inferior status of women is linked to the nature of the economy, family, and the nation-state, it becomes difficult, if not impossible, to change. For this reason, some have suggested that the revolutionary overthrow of capitalist nation-states is the only solution to female oppression. Historically, this may help explain the prominent role of women in revolutionary programs. We saw in Chapter 10 the prominent role played by women in the protests of peasants in Malaysia, the Mau Mau revolt in Kenya, and the revolt in Chiapas. Women were given prominent places, at least initially, in the communist revolutions in Russia, China, and Cuba. Yet it is arguable how much these revolutions improved the status of women.

After the Chinese government's victory in 1949, one of its first acts was to establish the All-China Women's Federation to further the status of women. The communist government banned the Chinese custom of foot binding of women, built a system of universal health care, and dramatically improved women's health. Yet today some of the worst cases of female labor exploitation are found in China. In an incident reminiscent of the notorious 1911 Triangle Shirtwaist Factory fire in New York City that killed 145 garment workers and prompted new labor legislation, a fire in November 1993 killed eighty-four female workers in a toy factory in Shenzhen in South China. They were prevented from escaping through doors and windows that had been barred to prevent stealing. Furthermore, the Chinese government repeatedly cracks down on the formation of independent labor unions whose work, although not specifically aimed at improving the condition of women, would greatly benefit women laborers.

After the socialist revolution of 1959 in Cuba, Fidel Castro's government moved to better integrate women into the public spheres of government and labor. In 1960 the government formed the Federation of Cuban Women (FMC) to consolidate existing women's institutions in support of the revolution and to integrate women into the workforce. Whereas only 13.7 percent of the potential female workforce was active in 1953, by 1990, 45 percent of working-age women were employed. Yet in spite of such apparent gains, "motherhood" remains at the heart of the official view of women in Cuba; child care and domestic duties remain at the core of the female role, and Cuban women continue to bear the brunt of domestic labor—housework and child care (Lutjens 1994).

Although the goals of socialist revolutions to improve the status of women clearly did not live up to their promise, the fall of communism in Eastern Europe has worsened the condition of women. Seventy-three percent of Russia's unemployed are women, half of whom have college educations. The overwhelming numbers of peddlers on the streets of Moscow are old women and young mothers. Without the protection of the socialist nation-state, the traditional view of women as housewives has reemerged. Gennady Melikyan, Russia's labor minister, made this clear when he said, "Why should we employ women when men are unemployed? It's better that men work and women take care of children and do the housework" (Eisenstein 1997).

In Western countries, women's movements have focused on affirmative action, reproductive rights, and greater access of women to education. At the Fourth World Conference on Women in Beijing, there was a strong movement for women in the periphery to begin to adopt the strategies employed by feminists in the core. Yet many women and women's groups in the periphery are wary of Western forms of feminist protest. Many women's groups in the periphery or the ex-communist countries of Eastern Europe see attempts to export Western feminism as a new form of colonialism or imperialism. In Muslim countries, in particular, many women reject what they see as the "man-hating" feminism of Western women's movements.

Anthropologists such as Aihwa Ong (1997) have warned against the tendency of Western feminists to impose their value system of individual autonomy on women's movements in peripheral countries. Ong noted that male leaders in Asian countries, such as China, Indonesia, and Malaysia, have argued that women's rights are not simply about individual rights but about culture, community, and the nation-state. These leaders counter accusations that men are exploiting female labor in assembly plants by arguing for the community's right to develop economically and for the obligation of all members of the community or nation to contribute to that development in any way they can; they argue that the right to develop is also a "human right." Asian leaders claim that the family, state, or nation is the primary unit of advancement, not the individual. The problem, said Ong, is, how can women's movements in the periphery counter these arguments that in their cultural context are so persuasive?

Insufficient attention has been given to cultural and religious differences between core and peripheral countries regarding the role of women and the place of political protest (Ong 1997). Feminists must be sensitive to "othering," wherein Westerners gain their sense of being liberated by defining others, particularly women from the periphery, as being backward and oppressed. For example, when delegates at the conference from Catholic and Muslim countries argued for a strategy that recognized a "separate but equal" status for women, they were accused of being traditional and marginalized by Western representatives.

Ong (1997) suggested that it would be more fruitful for women's movements in the core to be more receptive to an exchange of ideas and to consider the idea that strategies for improving the status of women must recognize cultural differences and the nature of power relations in different societies. We must, said Ong, "analyze the ways women and men in different societies struggle over cultural meanings that structure their lives." To illustrate, Ong related the story of the Sisters in Islam, a group of Western-educated feminists who are trying to change gender relations in Malaysia, not by employing Western feminist methods but within the context of their own culture through the reinterpretation of Islamic texts. Islam, particularly Islamic fundamentalism, has been targeted by Western feminists and human rights advocates as being particularly oppressive toward females. Islam permits polygyny, restricts the inheritance rights of females to half that of males, restricts the movements of women, and, in extreme cases, denies women educations or any positions outside the home.

Sisters in Islam, instead of condemning Islamic belief, argue that women should be afforded the same access to religious education as men, and with this education they should enter into debate with the almost-exclusively male Muslim clerics about the meaning of sacred texts such as the Qur'an and their interpretation of the role of women in society. Using newspaper columns to reach out to the public, the Sisters in Islam argue that the interpretation of the sacred texts must put Qur'anic recommendations in historical context. For example, male clerics justify Islam's approval of polygyny by claiming the Qur'an justified polygyny because the male sex drive made them "adulterous by nature." The Sisters in Islam counter this interpretation by pointing out that the Qur'an does not give men a blanket right to more than one wife; the sanctioning of polygyny in the Qur'an must be understood in the historical context in which the death of men through wars left women and children without male support. Allah thus sanctioned polygyny, they argue, not because of any intrinsic difference in the sex drive of men and women, but because it helped alleviate the problem of war orphans and widows by allowing widows to remarry men who already had a wife or wives.

The Sisters in Islam also argue against the stringent dress codes that male clerics say are demanded by the Qur'an. Citing verses of the sacred texts, the Sisters in Islam argue that "[c] oercion is contrary to the spirit of the Qur'an which states that there is no compulsion in [Islamic] religion" (Ong 1997) and that it is wrong to try to enforce faith through authority. The proper way to protect women, they say, is through decent and respectful treatment. Coercive dress policy, "in fact, runs counter to Islam's emancipatory emphasis upon reason [and] freedom as the basis of human morality" (Ong 1997).

Groups such as the Sisters in Islam have produced results. One Malaysian official (Ong 1997:89), who is now chair of the UN Commission for Human Rights, noted that

> Malaysia used to be a male-dominated society.... In the old days, there was no talk of women's rights, but through the gradual process of politicization, women...are able to assert themselves. Compared with ten years ago, there is much more publicity, consciousness, and more sensitivity on questions of women's rights.

Malaysia is still a male-dominated society, but by entering into a dialogue with Muslim clerics on their own terms, the Sisters in Islam have produced what Ong called a kind of "feminist communitarianism" that combines the liberal right to question authority, certainly recognized in the Qur'an, with the cultural norms of their own community. These kinds of movements, said Ong, should not be dismissed by Western feminists; rather, the idea of women's rights makes sense only in the context of specific cultural communities.

Direct Action and Occupy Wall Street

On December 17, 2010, a twenty-six-year-old Tunisian street vendor, Mohammed Bouazizi, set himself on fire to protest the continued extortion, harassment, and confiscation by corrupt police of his wares. Photos and videos of Bouazizi's self-immolation went viral on Facebook, resulting in street demonstrations in Tunisia and the January 14th ouster of Tunisian president Ben Ali. It also fomented what became known as the "Arab Spring." Antigovernment protests erupted in Algeria, Lebanon, Jordan, Oman, Egypt, and Saudi Arabia. By January 2011, 250,000 people had flocked into Cairo's Tahrir Square, leading to the eventual overthrow of President Hosni Mubarak. By February protestors in Wisconsin were demonstrating against the state legislatures' passage of a bill curbing the collective bargaining rights of state workers. In May, marchers gathered in Spain to protest wide unemployment and budget austerity measures that cut welfare and pension benefits. They were met with violence by the police, and put out a call on Facebook for support, soon gathering hundreds of thousands of supporters. *Los Indignados*, as they became known, set up camps in Spanish cities, giving the occupiers another name, *Las Acampadas* ("camp-outs").

In June in New York City, a group called New Yorkers Against Budget Cuts (NYBC) protesting Mayor Michael Bloomberg's budget proposal to layoff over 4,000 city workers, set up an encampment outside City Hall. They called their camp "Bloombergville" after the so-called "Hoovervilles," shantytowns built by the homeless at the onset of the 1930s depression and named after then President Herbert Hoover. At about the same time, independent journalist David Degraw and a group called Anonymous (which had supported his Web site after it was hacked by persons unknown), put out a call for Operation Empire State Rebellion for Flag Day, June 14th, to organize protests against banks and urging people to close accounts. And finally, *Adbusters*, a magazine in British Columbia, sent out on its Web site (http://www.adbusters.org/campaigns/occupywallstreet) a call asking, "Are you ready for a Tahrir moment," and calling for demonstrations on Wall Street on September 17, 2011, to demand a presidential commission to end the influence of money on representatives in Washington.

Occupy Wall Street protests. (Rachel Ceretto/ZUMAPRESS/ Newscom.)

In August over a hundred activists, inspired by the Bloombergville occupation, met in lower Manhattan at Bowling Green in front of the statue of the bull on Wall Street to plan the September 17th occupation. The group threatened to dissolve to a conventional rally when a few people, including anthropologist David Graeber, went around recruiting likely looking members for what was called a "general assembly" (GA), a consensus-based group central to what is called "direct action." They formed into working groups to deal with such practical concerns as food, medicine, Internet facilitation, tactics, and media and the arts, and scheduled weekly meetings. The Tactical Committee searched lower Manhattan for a suitable place to camp, settling on the Chase Manhattan Plaza. However, on noon of January 17th, they discovered that the police, apparently getting advance information, had it barricaded. They decided then to move the action to nearby Zucotti Park. It was chosen because it was a privately owned, public space created in exchange for favorable zoning modifications for the owner and by agreement had to be unfenced and kept open twenty-four hours a day. Furthermore, the police could not evict them without a request form the property owner.

The occupation of Zucotti Park began on September 17th, with the slogan "We are the 99%," referring to growing inequality in the United State in which the top 1 percent owned almost 40 percent of the wealth. The protesters issued Principles of Solidarity (OWS 2012:22):

• Engaging in direct and transparent participatory democracy
• Exercising personal and collective responsibility
• Recognizing individuals' inherent privilege and the influence it has on all interactions
• Empowering one another against all forms of oppression

- Redefining how labor is valued
- The sanctity of individual privacy
- The belief that education is a human right
- Endeavoring to practice and support wide application of open source

As more people showed up amid doubts that anything would come of the occupation, the Food and Working Group scouted around for local mom-and-pop restaurant that could provide food for occupiers. They discovered Liberato's Pizza on Ceder Street, whose name was consistent with the movement. They twitted calls for pizza orders; within hours the restaurant was deluged with callers from around the world ordering food on their credit cards for the occupiers.

What perhaps most galvanized the movement and brought it national and international attention was the pepper spraying, on September 24th, of peaceful demonstrators by a New York Police inspector and the posting of the incident on the YouTube. Immediately the video went viral, condemnation of the police and sympathy for the protesters grew, and the message of the Occupy movement became, along with the pepper spraying, a major topic of conversation on media news and talk shows. The population of Zucotti Park (or Liberty Square, as it had been named) doubled overnight. By September 27th, the *Newark Star Ledger* carried an editorial that said, "The nation should listen to this small Wall Street Encampment" (Newark Star Ledger 2011).

People began asking who were the 1 percent? Were they greedy or rotten? Was it right to hate them? Were the doctors or celebrities in the group as evil as the bank executives? How did they get so rich—doing good things or bringing the economy to near-ruin by excessive risk-taking with other people's money (Gitlin 2012)?

After the initial demonstration, Occupy actions sprang up around the world. By December 8, 2011, 143 towns and cities in California, about 30 percent of the total, had Occupy sites posted on Facebook, and the term *income inequality* was turning up six times more frequently in media stories than before the demonstration (Gitlin 2012).

The movement branched out to support actions by other groups such as unions or people who were threatened with evictions as a consequence of the subprime mortgage collapse and the recession that began in 2007.

But while Occupy Wall Street galvanized attention to economic inequalities and other issues, it has also been criticized for not having a single message or a concrete set of demands. At the initial occupation there were signs calling for the abolishment of the Federal Reserve, others urging the reinstatement of the Glass-Steagall Act forbidding savings institutions from engaging in securities trading, and still others called for the complete overthrow of capitalism, the abolition of all hierarchies in American government and society, and the reformation of campaign contribution laws in the United States (OWS 2012:61). One pungent sign stated, "*I'll believe Corporations are People when Texas Executes One,*" and another, "*Corporations are Not People, and Money is Not Speech.*"

Anarchism and Direct Action

But to understand the lack of a clear set of demands, one needs to understand the philosophy and goals of direct action and its anarchistic roots.

David Graeber, in his book *Direct Action: An Ethnography*, describes direct action, and anarchism itself, as a way of engaging the world to bring about change in which the form of action, or its organization, is a model for the change one wishes to bring about. As he puts it (2009:210),

> it reflects very simple anarchist insight that one cannot create a free society through military discipline, a democratic society by giving orders, or a happy one through joyless self-sacrifice. At its most elaborate, the structure of one's own act becomes a kind of micro-utopia, a concrete model for one's vision of free society.

Direct action answers the question of "What's the alternative?" by modeling an organizational structure that is truly democratic, and then engaging in actions that create for the activist participant a space, albeit temporary, in which autonomy is experienced. The action itself is not directed at the state, nor is it necessarily a gesture of defiance. Instead, "one proceeds…as if the state does not exist, acting as if one is already free" (2009:203). If toxic waste is being dumped in a poor community, one does not ask authorities to do something about it; one acts to stop it. A labor strike is a direct action, albeit in some cases a legal one. During the civil rights protests of the 1960s, black students who sat at segregated lunch counters, or took seats in the front of buses reserved for whites only, were engaging in direct action.

Part of the logic of anarchist thought is that if one makes demands on the state, one is legitimating state power. Thus the anarchist does not solicit the state; rather, one proceeds as if the state does not exist (Graeber 2009:203).

Direct action methods, then, emerge from the desire to model a truly democratic society and to legitimate the anarchist idea that people engaging each other as equals and with mutual respect, do not need governments to control their actions. In fact, traditionally anarchists make the point that governments rarely engage in people's everyday lives. Instead people forge relations, interactions, and even contracts and obligations, with each other completely absent of any government influence (see, e.g., Kropotkin 2007). Responding to the critique that anarchism is naïve and utopian, Russian anarchist Peter Kropotkin responded that "What was naive and utopian was to believe that one could give someone arbitrary power over others and trust them to exercise it responsibly" (Graeber 2009:352–353).

Anarchists are absorbed with questions such as, what is direct action? What kind of tactics are beyond the pale and what sort of solidarity do we owe to those who employ them? Or what is the most democratic way to conduct a meeting? At what point does organization stop being empowering and become stifling and bureaucratic?

Drawing from Quaker philosophy and belief, the anarchist tradition, and methods developed by the Zapatistas in Chiapas, Mexico, direct action advocates follow a system of organization that attempts to recognize the legitimacy of every member of the group. For example, the General Assembly (GA), the preferred mode of governance, has no leader. Every member has the right to participate, and a single person, simply by folding her or his arms over her or his chest, can "block" a proposed action. To ensure that discussion is not dominated by white males, the GA practices "stacking," alternating speakers by gender or minority status. Because NYC police forbid the use of electronic voice amplifiers, such as bullhorns, groups developed the technique of the "human microphone," (the "people mic"), in which those within hearing distance of a speaker would repeat their sentences for those behind them, sometimes, with large crowds, in as many as three waves. To facilitate actions, "spokes councils," consisting of a representative of each working group, meet to discuss courses of actions or to solve problems that emerge. To ensure that no one comes to dominate the discussion each working group sends a different representative to each successive meeting. To facilitate discussion, participants adopted hand signals ("twinkling") from the American Sign Language gesture for applause; wiggling fingers up was approval, down was disapproval. Curling one's hand into a C shape means a need for clarification. Thus gatherings are what Graeber (2009:287) calls "pure zones of social experiment" where people can treat each other as they feel they should treat one another and create the kind of social world that they want to bring about.

Direct action advocates acknowledge that these procedures are sometimes slow, sometimes frustrating, and not without conflict. Since GAs are open to anyone, they sometimes dissolve into wide disagreement. Advocates acknowledge that in the GAs in Zucotti Park, schisms developed between the white, largely middle-class white participants, and minority homeless participants, and between males and females. And with no formal leadership, groups often split away from each other and tend not to be long-lived. Yet, in spite of these difficulties, actions are planned and initiated successfully.

As Graeber (2009:421) describes it, the planning of an action, the action itself, and the response of authorities ritually represent for activists and onlookers a version of a less oppressive society while revealing the arbitrary state power that it is trying to replace. Thus, the inevitable violent actions of the police—attacks on peaceful protesters and innocent bystanders, on medics, along with the arbitrary infliction of pain and humiliation—confront the protestors with the reality of state power with all the pretense of benevolence stripped away. If arrested, says Graeber, and consequently under the power of the state, "one would seem to encounter both its brutality and its stupidity in unadulterated form."

How to deal with the police is a constant topic for planners. Police, Graeber points out, are essentially unaccountable for their actions, which is why they sometimes react brutally. While many protesters are arrested during actions, very few ever come to trial. Consequently, as long as they don't do permanent damage, the police are free to beat, detain, pepper-spray, and maltreat demonstrators without fear of being held accountable in court. Generally, battles with the police involve determining who gets to define the terms of engagement. The typical protest narrative places the police in the role of maintaining order; yet invariably in all the protests described by Graeber, the police start the violence, as they did on Wall Street. The standard story of the World Trade Organization (WTO) protest in Seattle in 1999, for example, is that some protesters began breaking windows and the police reacted with tear gas to disperse the crowd. In fact, the violence began when Secretary of State Madeline Albright called the governor to demand the police clear the peaceful protestors blocking the entrance to the conference. It was only after the violent actions of the police did any window breaking take place, a fact known to all media representatives at the time. Yet the narrative of police violence being only a reaction to violent behavior by the protesters persists.

Another problem for activists is how to treat the media. Do they ignore them, as some argue, since they will never report things accurately, or do you try to get them, somehow, to report events accurately? Almost never will the media report the reason for a protest; rather they describe an action only in terms of security.

Graeber argues that it would be almost impossible for an American journalist in the mainstream media to report events accurately; the standard narrative is that the police are there to maintain order and the idea that the police themselves would provoke violence is simply not acceptable. When police use provocateurs to incite violence, as FBI documents going back to the Civil Rights marches of the 1960s revealed, it is rarely reported. During a globalization protest in Barcelona, a local reporter hired by AP saw police start fights among themselves to draw in protesters as an excuse to wade into the crowd. This made the news, but was not given prominence. The most notorious example of a failure to cover police actions to foment violence was the filming during protests in Genoa of police dressed as protestors leaving a police station at the time of those protests. Hearing about the video, the police targeted anyone with a camera and raided the independent media center and confiscated every bit of film that they could find. But the video did exist and was shown on Italian TV, although never mentioned in the U.S. press.

The issue of violence has been a constant concern. Direct action advocates, consistent with their Quaker origins, eschew violence, although there are demonstrators who advocate the destruction of corporate property. While direct action advocates often try to stop such actions, they don't always succeed. In addition, in the United States, Graeber suggests, nonviolent tactics advocated by Mohandas Gandhi and Martin Luther King don't always work. The idea of nonviolence is to provoke police or law enforcement authorities into brutal actions to reveal to the public, to whom one is directing an action, the brutality of the state. In the United States, however, what often happens is that the public is persuaded through the media that violent and brutal tactics against nonviolent protesters is legitimate. When students protesting the destruction of old-growth forests in California tied themselves to equipment or trees and refused to unlock themselves, the police began systematically using Q-tips to rub pepper spray into their eyes. With the media filming the action, the police described to reporters what was being done so that it appeared to be a clinical operation. It was in fact torture, and not unlike what was done to prisoners in Iraq and Guantanamo, but the public was convinced that the police had to do this to maintain order (and access to first-growth forests by Pacific Lumber).

For protesters, one reaction to this media problem is to create their own media. While years ago, if an action was not reported somewhere, it simply disappeared and might not as well have happened. But with blogs, the Internet, and the emergence of independent media, that is not now likely to happen.

CONCLUSION

We suggested in this chapter that rebellion and protest that seems endemic to the culture of capitalism is largely anti-systemic, consisting of responses of groups who at some time were socially or economically marginalized or who have suffered disproportionately in the expansion of capitalism into the periphery. However, it is important to note that in only a few cases is protest directed explicitly at the culture of capitalism itself. Rather, protesters select as objects of their protest groups or individuals who they hold specifically responsible. We saw in the case of the protests of poor Malaysian peasants that the object of their ire was peasants who were richer than themselves, rather than the green revolution or the institutions such as the World Bank that ultimately were responsible for their distress. Likewise, laborers in the coal mines of Pennsylvania blamed mine operators, many of whom made virtually no profit from their efforts, rather than the system that drove them and the mine operators to try to accumulate capital in a failing industry. In other words, rarely do social protest movements specifically attack the system that is the source of their distress; instead they focus on real or symbolic figures who, for them, embody their oppression.

This was, in part, the strategy of the Occupy Wall Street movement. Concerns varied—growing economic inequality, the government bailout of banks, campaign finance and corruption in the electoral process in the United States, and so on. Protestors choose Wall Street to symbolize those concerns. The question remains, of course, how effective the protest can be? In spite of years of organization, the environmental movement may have slowed the rate of environmental destruction, but has not stopped it. In spite of protest against economic inequality, the latter continues to grow, and in the United States, is as high as it was eighty years ago. In spite of the civil rights movement, blacks in America are losing their jobs at a higher rate than any other group (see, e.g., Robbins 2012). In spite of global movements to ease the plight of indebted countries, they still stagger under levels of debt that make it impossible for them to respond to the basic needs of their citizens. We'll examine in Chapter 13 why these problems seem intractable, and offer some ways of dealing with them.

12

Religion and Anti-Systemic Protest

> *Religious distress is at the same time the expression of real distress and the protest against real distress. Religion is the sigh of the oppressed creature, the heart of a heartless world, just as it is the spirit of spiritless conditions.*
>
> —KARL MARX, *Critique of Hegel's "Philosophy of Right"*

> *If one's goal is not harmony but the empowerment that comes with using violence, it is in one's interest to be in a state of war. In such cases war is not only the context for violence, but also the excuse for it. War provides a reason to be violent. This is true even if the worldly issues at heart in the dispute do not seem to warrant such a ferocious position.*
>
> —MARK JUERGENSMEYER, *Terror in the Mind of God*

The rebellions and movements that we examined in Chapters 10 and 11 each sought, in their own way, to reform what participants saw as the excesses of capitalism. Few of these movements, however, offered a radical cultural alternative; that is, although they decried the constant economic and social change, the uneven distribution of wealth, the exploitation and marginalization of selected groups, or the environmental damage fostered by the culture of capitalism, none actively sought to replace it with another. Peasants seek land, not the overthrow of the society that displaces them; laborers seek higher wages and better working conditions within the culture of capitalism from which, in their other roles as consumers and capitalists, they benefit; women and minorities seek improved status within the existing society; indigenous groups struggle to be left alone; and environmental protesters, with the exception of those who offer a largely undefined spiritual alternative, seek only greater environmental safeguards.

Communism was often depicted as a major challenger to capitalism, yet communism and its authors—Lenin, Stalin, and Mao—never rejected the larger nineteenth-century culture of industrial capitalism. They sought largely to modify the nation-state to give workers greater influence and to obtain a more equitable distribution of wealth within a system of production, distribution, and consumption that differed little, if at all, from that of capitalism. They simply wanted to replace private capitalism with state capitalism. Even Marx and Engels did not call for overthrow of the industrial order; their solution was to seize the nation-state and raise the power of labor above or at least equal to the power of capital (the power of people over the power of money). The views of Marx and Engels (similar to those of many early nineteenth-century industrialists) were utopian; they called for the end of private property, recognition of the equality of women, dismantling of the patriarchal nuclear family, discarding of organized religion, and, most of all, the end of class distinctions. But the only groups to attempt to follow that or a similar agenda were the small utopian or intentional communities that proliferated in the first half of the nineteenth century, such as New Harmony, the Oneida Community, and Amana, and later, following the political unrest of 1968, Twin Oaks and the many small communal groups that thrived in late 1960s and early 1970s, some of which survive today (Erasmus 1972; Kanter 1972; Oved 1988).

Although the peasant, labor, feminist, indigenous, and environmental protests and rebellions did not seek to change the basic tenets of the culture of capitalism, there were and are movements to overthrow and replace it. Most of these are religious in character; through some spiritual agency these groups seek either the removal or destruction of what they believe is an immoral culture, a withdrawal from it, or the forceful or voluntary adoption of a new way of life.

Religion has always had a revolutionary element; most religions began as a rebellion against one or another established order. Christianity began as a Jewish protest against behaviors and beliefs that the protesters felt were violations of God's word. The gospels of the New Testament are clearly revolutionary in intent, whereas the Old Testament documents the struggles of people against what they believed was illegitimate authority.

Yet the fact that religion is often the source of anti-systemic protest should not obscure the role of religion in legitimizing some of the basic premises of the culture of capitalism. Certainly, there was a good deal of cooperation between the church and the state in the early expansion of the world system. Missionaries accompanied the conquerors and explorers and helped pacify populations, convert them to one or another brand of Christianity, and transform them into willing laborers for the global economy. Missionaries served as a capitalist vanguard introducing their converts to Western concepts of time, space, and the person embedded in the culture of capitalism. As Jean Comaroff (1985:27) observed,

> [t]he mission was an essential medium of, and forerunner to, colonial articulation; it was the significant agent of ideological innovation, a first instance in the confrontation between the local system and the global forces of international capitalism. The coherent cultural scheme of the mission—its concepts of civilization, person, property, work, and time—was made up of categories which anticipated and laid the ground for the process of proletarianization.

In his classic work *The Protestant Ethic and the Spirit of Capitalism,* Max Weber (1958) suggested that the Protestant Reformation provided an ideological basis for capitalism as well as a motivation for making a profit by equating material success with personal salvation and a sign of God's blessing. Historians have seen in religion of the nineteenth century a replacement for the moral restraints that had been provided by family and community but destroyed by the explosive growth of cities and the mobility of labor. Anthony F. C. Wallace (1987), for example, pointed out how Irish immigrants in Pennsylvania confronted in the local Catholic Church a replacement for behavioral restraints that had been provided by extended families in Ireland, a moral restraint very much welcomed by mine owners, business people, and others. Paul E. Johnson (1978) traced the religious revival in the United States in the 1830s and 1840s to the need for religion to replace the moral guidelines and social constraints that had been provided in small rural communities by the family but absent in the newly industrialized cities of the Northeast. As we saw in Chapter 1, most religious leaders in the early twentieth century had little difficulty accommodating to the shift from an ideology of self-denial to one of self-fulfillment and indulgence. Nevertheless, although religion has served to buttress the assumptions of the culture of capitalism, it has served in some forms also to resist them.

The goal of this chapter is to ask the questions, *To what extent have religious movements been expressions of anti-systemic sentiments? That is, how have religious movements served as a means of protest against the expansion, both in the core and in the periphery, of the culture of capitalism? And why does religious protests sometimes manifest itself in spectacular violence?* To answer these questions we first examine some religious movements in the periphery, and then turn our attention to the large-scale protests that have emerged from the world's major religions.

INDIGENOUS RELIGIOUS MOVEMENTS AS ANTI-SYSTEMIC PROTEST

Central in anthropology to the idea of religious change is Anthony F. C. Wallace's concept of revitalization movement. Wallace (1966:30) suggested that religious beliefs and practices start from situations of social and cultural stress as a "conscious, organized effort by members of a society to construct a more satisfying culture." All religion, he said, originates in a revitalization process. Thus the origins of all the major religions lay in reactions to social and/or cultural systems that the founders found unsatisfying. Consequently anthropologists, historians, and sociologists have documented hundreds of instances of religious movements around the world that originated in protest over people's conditions and have used the idea of revitalization to conceptualize everything from Melanesian cargo cults to the militia movements in the United States (Beeman 1997).

As useful, however, as the concept of revitalization has been in furthering our understanding of religious change and protest, it has a basic weakness. As applied to religious movements of the past 200 years, it has failed to consider the fact that virtually all such movements have been reactions to a single phenomenon—the development and expansion of industrial or consumer capitalism. Generally, revitalization movements, such as the cargo cults of Melanesia and New Guinea; the Ghost Dance among the Native Americans of the American Plains; and large-scale religious movements that have emerged from Islam, Christianity, Judaism, and others, have been as much anti-systemic protest as they have been revitalization. That is, the attempt to construct a more "satisfying culture," as Wallace aptly put it, has generally been a protest to the negative effects of capitalist expansion. For this reason, it may be more fruitful to view these movements as expressions of anti-systemic protest rather than solely attempts at revitalization.

To illustrate, let's examine three religious movements of peoples in the periphery—the Ghost Dance, the cargo cults, and the Zionism movement in South Africa. Each was an expression of protest against economic and social conditions emerging from capitalist expansion but with important differences: They varied in the degree to which they used the trappings of core religions as opposed to indigenous belief and ritual. Furthermore, they varied in the extent to which they expressed overt hostility to the nation-state and, consequently, the extent to which they prompted oppressive and violent retaliation.

The Ghost Dance

In 1889 a missionary-educated Paiute Indian named Wovoka had a vision (Mooney 1965). He had been taken up to heaven where, he said, he met God; he also met Indians who had died and who were in heaven living their traditional life. God, he said, instructed him to return to Earth and tell people that they must live in peace with whites and with each other. He was also given instructions for a ritual dance that, if performed for five days and five nights, would reunite people on Earth with friends and relatives in the other world. Converts carried Wovoka's message from Nevada to indigenous groups throughout the United States and Canada, where it was often embellished in various ways. In some versions whites and Native Americans would live in harmony; in others the world would be destroyed and only indigenous people brought back to life. In other versions the buffalo would return, and people would live as they had before the invasion of European peoples.

The message of the Ghost Dance, as it became known, was carried by representatives who had traveled to meet with Wovoka. They spread his message to groups throughout the American Plains and beyond to peoples seeking a revival of a way of life disrupted by capitalist expansion. The message of the Ghost Dance was particularly attractive to groups such as the Lakota who had been systematically deprived through treaty and deceit of most of their land and confined to reservations where they were dependent on government provisions that were often not delivered. However, the Ghost Dance, which held the promise to the Lakota of a revival of their traditional culture, ended in one of the great military tragedies in American history.

Alarmed that the Ghost Dance might presage an open rebellion by the Lakota, an Indian agent assigned to one of the Lakota reservations called in the military. Frightened that they might be attacked, some of the Lakota fled; they were pursued by the Seventh Cavalry, George Armstrong Custer's old command that had been defeated by a combined force of Lakota and Cheyenne in 1876. The army caught up to the Lakota at a place called Wounded Knee and with cannon and rifles surrounded them. A surrender was arranged. As soldiers rummaged through Lakota shelters searching for guns, a shot was fired. The army responded by pouring cannon and rifle shot into the encampment, killing hundreds of men, women, and children, some of whom had sought shelter from the barrage hundreds of yards away.

In many ways, the Ghost Dance is a prototype of a form of religious resistance that parallels the "weapons of the weak" discussed in Chapter 10. They are religious movements that serve, if only symbolically, to protest economic, social, or political oppression. When they result in violence, it is almost always violence initiated by the nation-state or their representatives, either against whole groups, as in the massacre at Wounded Knee, or against leaders of the movements who the agents of the nation-state fear are leading or are capable of leading a general revolt. It was probably not a coincidence that days before Wounded Knee, the Lakota spiritual leader Sitting Bull was assassinated by Lakota police as they tried to arrest him.

The Cargo Cults

Among the most dramatic of the indigenous religious protests were the cargo cults of Melanesia and New Guinea. These movements arose in the late nineteenth century and early twentieth century as core nations sought to exploit the resources in the Pacific Islands. Cargo cults generally began when a prophet announced the imminence of a cataclysm that would destroy the world, at which point the ancestors, God, or some other liberating power would appear and deliver the cargo—commodities possessed by Europeans—and bring a reign of eternal bliss. People prepared themselves to receive the cargo by building storehouses, jetties, and plane runways, sometimes abandoning their gardens, destroying their livestock, eating all their food, or throwing away their money. Cargo cults represent a paradoxical response to capitalist expansion. On the one hand, they evidence themselves in a passionate desire to possess the commodities thought to be in abundance in the dominant culture; on the other hand, they tend to reject the power and influence of the Westerners who bring the cargo.

The story of European exploitation and the effects on indigenous peoples of the Pacific closely followed the patterns we examined in Chapter 9. Cargo cults were a response to the excesses of colonial exploitation and were documented by Peter Worsley (1968) in his classic analysis *The Trumpets Shall Sound.*

Capitalist expansion came to Fiji in the eighteenth century, for example, as Europeans sought sandalwood to supply the Chinese market with material for joss sticks and incense for religious services. By 1813 the supply of trees on Fiji was exhausted.

By the 1860s there was a large influx of European settlers to Fiji, which resulted in a vastly increased alienation of land from Fijians as well as increased lawlessness in the European community, which local governments were unable to control. There was also an increase in the need for native laborers to supply the growing coconut plantations. Colonial powers countered the reluctance of indigenous peoples to work on the plantations by introducing tax laws, forcing them to work to earn cash when they could have easily subsisted on their own produce. Treatment of native laborers, as in other areas, was harsh. In New Guinea colonial governments sanctioned various forms of punishment, such as flogging or hanging by the wrists, for laborers whose efforts did not satisfy labor supervisors. Equally harsh were the economic dislocations, ill understood by indigenous peoples, that were part of the global economy. Prices for coconuts, oil, and other cash crops rose and fell with the vagaries of the market, creating either new demands for labor or widespread unemployment.

Missionary activity was also a major factor in the development of the cargo cults. Missionaries played a major part in the colonial process in the South Pacific, comprising 15 percent of the European population in most areas. The missionaries divided up territories among themselves, often leading natives to question why rivalries existed between the different denominations. Religion was one area of European life that the natives did not reject. In fact, religion was thought by those participating in the cargo cults to be the source of the magical power that created the goods. Native peoples had no knowledge of the material reality of European society and the production process that created commodities, and the Europeans they knew apparently did not work for the goods they possessed; with their missionary education the natives concluded that secret magical power was the key to European wealth, power they wished to obtain (Worsley 1968).

It was in response to these conditions that the cargo cults flourished. A good example was the "Vailala madness" first reported in New Guinea in 1919. The most obvious manifestation of the Vailala madness was the trancelike state or possession into which adherents fell. The movement occurred in an environment of colonial exploitation; oil had been discovered and plantations were being built. Most followers had been indentured laborers, often in conditions of severe discipline and illness. In June 1910, for example, in the Lakekamu gold fields, 225 of 1,100 workers died of dysentery and other causes.

The originator of Vailala madness was said to be an old man named Evara, who fell into a trance when he disappeared for four days. He said that a sorcerer had "ripped up his belly." He prophesied the coming of a steamer carrying spirits of dead ancestors who would bring the cargo with them. Rifles were among the expected goods. Cargo would be contained in crates, each identified according to the village to which it would be delivered. The spirits, said Evara, revealed that all the flour, rice, tobacco, and other trade belonged to Papuans, not whites, and that the whites would be driven away (Worsley 1968:81).

The hostility to whites in Papua New Guinea was not surprising. One plantation manager used his whip to silence the lamentations of some "boys" mourning for a dead friend; another said, "I want the nigger to work for me so I can make my pile and leave this so-and-so country" (Worsley 1968:82). Although the movement evidenced hostility to whites, people believed also that the ancestors would be white. Some whites were actually followed around by natives who believed the whites were their deceased relatives.

Ceremony and ritual accompanied the movement. People had visions of heaven in which food was abundant and people wore long, flowing robes. Many claimed to receive messages from Jesus Christ or God. Villagers set up tables and decorated them with flowers in beer bottles, bowls of rice, betel, and coconut husks; relatives of the dead who were thought to be returning sat around these tables feasting, while other villagers sat silently, their backs to the tables, awaiting the arrival of the cargo. Temples were built that resembled mission churches, and a flagpole was erected that was thought to be the medium through which people could communicate with the dead ancestors. There was a strict moral code that encouraged the giving of feasts for the ancestors, abandoning adultery and theft, and observing the Sabbath. There was also the idea that all native paraphernalia should be destroyed and gardens should be abandoned.

The movement lasted twelve years before it ceased spreading; by the time it ended, in the 1930s, people claimed the prophesies had been fulfilled—that they had seen the steamers,

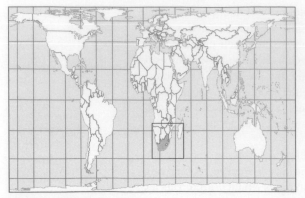

South Africa

that messages had been received from flagpoles, and that tracks of the dead were seen on beaches. Furthermore, the cargo had been delivered as more and more people gained access to the European commodities they so much desired.

Zionism in South Africa

Both the Ghost Dance and cargo cult movements were influenced to some extent by missionary activity. This should not be surprising. The message of the Bible, particularly the Gospels, must have contained an appealing message to participants in the movements: The equality of all under God, the favored divine status of the weak, the common stewardship over God's earthly domain are all messages designed to appeal to an oppressed people. Furthermore, if indigenous religious movements derived, at least in part, from missionary teachings, participants in the movement might expect them to be sanctioned by political authorities. Missionary activity was tolerated by European and American colonizers; indeed, it was welcomed, but only to the extent that it contributed to the maintenance of a disciplined and submissive population. Thus, the degree of the protest and resistance contained in indigenous religious movements had to be carefully measured against the likelihood of government retaliation.

One of the most repressive nation-states to emerge out of the culture of capitalism was the apartheid government of South Africa, whose military power made open rebellion by Africans virtually impossible. In that setting religious protest was often the only way to express resistance. Let's examine one such movement, the Full Witness Apostolic Church in Zion described by Jean Comaroff (1985) in her work on the Tshidi of South Africa, *Body of Power, Spirit of Resistance.*

The Tshidi are representative of many of the peoples of South Africa who lived primarily by a combination of agriculture and herding. The takeover of South Africa by the British resulted in African people being confined to theoretically self-governing protectorates or homelands. Agricultural and livestock production declined not only because of such factors as cattle disease and drought but also because agricultural labor was being drained by the demand for labor in the diamond mines, gold fields, factories, and white farms.

The result for people such as the Tshidi was the underdevelopment of their rural base and the emergence of a system in which they were dependent on the sale of their labor for their survival. By 1970 more than half the women were employed outside the home for extended periods and more than three-quarters of the men were working away from home for at least nine months each year. Labor on the farms was left to the remaining women and children, who were prevented by South African law from accompanying their husbands and fathers to industrial centers. Furthermore, the passage of blacks between the town and countryside was carefully regulated by the apartheid government; movement outside the homelands required a pass, strict curfews were imposed, and the African population was carefully watched by uniformed police and bureaucrats. Thus, the Tshidi came to realize their state of oppression in the brutal mine compounds and in the degrading rituals of apartheid.

Suppression of African resistance has long been a feature of the South African landscape. Only in the past few years has the degree of violence—assassinations, kidnapping, and torture—used by the white South African government to suppress dissent become public. Consequently, resistance needed to be more subtle. People could not directly challenge the mechanisms of political, social, and economic domination of the apartheid South African government; instead, they contested the logic of the system on which it is based and of which they are a part. Resistance was to be symbolic.

To appreciate this kind of resistance we might think back to the means of resistance used by Malaysian peasants, the weapons of the weak, as James C. Scott (1985) called them. Or we might consider symbols of resistance and independence used by American youth—the clothing, music, and other activities used to contest the discipline imposed by schools, parents, and the larger community. The Tshidi used as their vehicle a religious movement imported from the core, the Full Witness Apostolic Church in Zion. Comaroff sees the Zionist movement as a means by which Tshidi members protested their marginality to and the effects of the capitalist world system. The protest is expressed in dress, ritual, and ideology.

The Christian Catholic Apostolic Church of Zion (CCACZ) was founded in 1847 by a Scotsman, Alexander Dowie, who came to North America in 1888. In 1899 he built his Zion City on 6,500 acres on Lake Michigan, forty-two miles north of Chicago. Within a year the "city" boasted a population of several thousand, a bank, a brickyard, stores, small factories, schools, and a printing press.

Zion City was to be a haven from the sinful environment represented by the city of Chicago. The majority of its members were clerics, self-employed artisans, struggling small-scale businesspeople—mostly poor and working class. This was a population marginal to nineteenth-century capitalism who rejected much of the emerging capitalist culture, which they found alienating (Comaroff 1985:179). Zionists conceptualized the alienation they felt as an uncoupling of man and God; they expressed it in metaphors of sickness and health, which replaced the established doctrines of damnation and salvation. Through the metaphor of healing, Zionists sought to cast out disease and the influence of Satan by reintegrating body, soul, and spirit. As Zionism was exported to the periphery, it seemed to draw together everything that the experience of colonialization and wage labor had driven away, offering the possibility of rebuilding a holistic community from which the culture of capitalism could be resisted.

The first representative of the CCACZ to South Africa arrived in Johannesburg in 1904, largely at the invitation of a Dutch Reformed missionary. Zionism was introduced to the Tshidi by returning migrant laborers or lone itinerant prophets searching for a local following. At that time most Tshidi had converted to Methodism, the dominant colonial religion in the area, although black and white churches were carefully separated; but by the 1970s the CCACZ had made considerable inroads. According to Comaroff (1985), 4,750 people were still members of the orthodox churches, but at least 3,750 had converted to Zionism, whereas another 1,000 were members of other independent churches.

The Full Witness Apostolic Church in Zion was founded in 1956 by Bishop N, a Zulu contract worker in the Johannesburg mines. The church itself is a 240-square-foot mud brick

The flowing white robes worn by members of the Zionist Church in South Africa contrast sharply with the drab khaki, back, or tight-fitting uniforms required of workers. (Julio Etchart.)

structure. Followers dress distinctively in white robes, green tunics, and white head scarfs with red, black, and white yarn cords that are never removed.

Typical Sunday services begin with a meal; when all have eaten, the bishop's senior wife signals the start of hymn singing, clapping, and drumming. Church members dance and the men sink to their knees facing east, the direction of the rising sun. The spirit seizes several women and people begin to testify. The testimony contains themes of oppression, often contrasting the outside world (wage labor, the city, and strangers) with the inside world (home and the congregation). Central to the act of testifying is the idea of healing (Comaroff 1985:210).

The Full Witness Apostolic Church in Zion represents what anthropologists refer to as a "cult of affliction," a community of sufferers, a solitary band of "wounded healers," whose bodies reflect their oppressed social state. Indeed, many converts, Comaroff noted, come to the church with real organic distress. The ritual of testimony involves a healing process that dramatizes the difference between the corruption of the outside world and the healing spirit of the congregation.

The Zionist church also serves to ritually cleanse the commodities that Tshidi must purchase, at the same time rejecting the culture in which they originate. Members bring all their purchased commodities, such as foodstuffs, shoes, and blankets, and place them on a table located in the center of the church; during the service they are sprinkled with holy water. Thus, the cargo of the rejected system is not itself repudiated; rather it is reformed and cleansed through a ritual act. As Comaroff (1985:218–219) said, "as alienated products are given a new social and spiritual identity, the experience of alienation is reversed."

In the same way that Zionists rework commodities through ritual, they also rework the body in dress. Members of the church clothe themselves in a combination of Protestant and indigenous garb to re-create an order that rejects the one prevailing in their lives. Their white robes, flowing hair, and colored tunics contrast sharply with the drab, often threadbare clothing worn by the majority of rural Tshidi, clearly communicating their "otherness," dress that combines the biblical appearance of the world of the Christian mission with hints of a pre-colonial Tshidi past. These clothes also contrast in color and form with the drab khaki or black, tight-fitting uniforms of the military, mine, mission, or domestic service.

Comaroff noted that dissenting movements in the periphery seem to adopt these "side alleys" of Western culture, such as faith healing and occultism. But despite often diverse origins, these symbolic orders share an opposition to the culture of capitalism and seek to subvert the structures of colonial societies. The Zionist Church, like other small-scale religious movements, serves as a refuge and emblem for those who are marginalized by the expansion of capitalist culture. As Comaroff (1985:254) said,

> Zionism is part of a second global culture; a culture lying in the shadow of the first, whose distinct but similar symbolic orders are the imaginative constructions of the resistant periphery of the world system.

THE GLOBAL CHALLENGE OF ANTI-SYSTEMIC RELIGIOUS PROTEST

Religious movements such as the Zionist protest, of which there are probably thousands in the world, cannot hope to challenge the domination of global capitalism. Instead, they offer a respite from the hopelessness and alienation felt by those at the economic periphery of capitalist culture. The rituals, services, and gatherings represent periods of withdrawal from the system during which members can collectively regain their integrity and identity. They are not unlike the various utopian or alternative communities that flourished after the revolutions of 1848 and 1968, which sought to create alternative worlds within tightly bound, sometimes physically isolated, communities that gain public attention only when their members commit an illegal or seemingly irrational act.

Far more prominent are the large-scale religious protests represented by "fundamentalist movements" that have gained public attention in the past four decades. Rather than small-scale, isolated instances of religious protest, these movements are offshoots of the world's major religions, contain millions of participants, and have serious designs on the control of the nation-state. The cultures represented by these movements remain the only legitimate challengers to the global domination of capitalist culture.

In many ways these movements are difficult to characterize. They are called fundamentalist movements by the media, government analysts, and many religious scholars, but the designation has been criticized by some as containing derogatory connotations. Mark Juergensmeyer (1993;1996) suggested calling them "nationalist religious movements." However, that implies that the movements are primarily political in nature, whereas they seem to be protesting a much greater range of cultural features. For that reason, perhaps *anti-systemic* is a more accurate phrase, although we will retain the term *fundamentalism,* largely because of its widespread use.

To explore the extent to which large-scale religious protests represent anti-systemic movements, we will examine the rise of Islamic fundamentalism in the Middle East and the role of Protestant fundamentalism in the United States. Each fundamentalism arose out of discontents with specific features of the industrial revolution and modern life, and each claims to provide a formula for transforming modern culture and society. Although each of the movements is rooted in a particular cultural tradition, and often in local conditions, they share some features in common.

1. Contrary to impressions left by the mass media that these are recent movements, most had their origins in the nineteenth century, as a reaction to the secularization of religion in modern life or as a reaction to the expansion of the world economy and/or domination by colonial powers.
2. Each is historically oriented and interprets contemporary global events (the debt crisis, war and ethnic strife, and disease) as divine portents that validate their central doctrines. Furthermore, each attributes what it perceives as the relative decline or lack of prominence of its country in global affairs to a loss or lack of faith in whatever religious principles it espouses.
3. Each contemporary fundamentalism has designs on state power and has, in one form or another, adopted contemporary political structures (e.g., political parties, youth organizations, and modern communication techniques) to attain that end. In some cases they seek control over established nation-states, whereas in others they wish to establish their own, independent states.
4. All insist that although converting others to their worldview is a central goal, believers should keep themselves separate from nonbelievers.
5. Each makes and has a strong appeal to young people, particularly college students, and has developed organizations to reach them.
6. Although each has attempted to reach its goals by socially approved methods, each has a militant segment, such as Hizbullah in Lebanon, Operation Rescue in the United States, and Gush Emunim in Israel, that challenges the power of the secular state by disobeying secular law with violent and/or nonviolent means in what they claim is a call to a higher law.
7. Most religious fundamentalisms stress the importance of the family in social life, claiming that the family as an institution has been undermined by the secular nation-state. Some place a striking emphasis on the duty of women to embody tradition, with the home being for men a sanctified retreat from the world of work, where they can relax and assert their authority.
8. Although none of the fundamentalisms, with the exception of Islam, has a well-developed economic agenda to replace the corporate libertarianism of capitalism, they do have in common certain criticisms of it. They feel that capitalism has replaced the fraternal

atmosphere of the premodern economy with ruthless economic competition and bitter competition over public resources (Kuran 1993:290–291). They all believe that the economic problems of today are caused by moral degeneration. Modern economics, they say, sees human wants and consequently human demands as unbounded; the supply can never catch up with demand. Most fundamentalisms reject this amoral approach, seeing human wants not as unbounded but as a problem of modern civilization's ability to control individual acquisitiveness. Individuals can be persuaded against pursuing an immoral lifestyle (Kuran 1993:295). Islam, however, does offer an alternative financial system, Islamic banking and finance, which in itself has anti-systemic elements (see, e.g., Maurer 2005:37), and which we will examine in the next chapter.

9. The redistribution of wealth is a common theme in religious fundamentalisms, although not all deal with it in the same way. All encourage the wealthy to aid the poor, but none insists on full equality. Islamic fundamentalists encourage the state to enforce traditional Qur'anic rules on a religious tax whose proceeds go to help the poor. Christian fundamentalists are generally opposed to economic redistribution, advocating instead the end to transfer programs, arguing that obeying God's commands will alleviate poverty and inequality.

Islamic Fundamentalism

Islamic fundamentalism gained international prominence with the Iranian revolution, Iran's transformation into an Islamic state, and the return from state-imposed exile of the Ayatollah Khomeini in 1979. The media has paid much attention to the fundamentalist resurgence, as have the leaders of nation-states with sizable Muslim populations. There has also been much media attention to so-called Islamic terrorist organizations, attention that has often bordered on bigotry. Thus, when the Oklahoma Federal Building was blown up by American militia sympathizers in 1995, the media first reported the presence of "Middle Eastern–looking" men in the area of the blast. There has also been a tendency in the Western media to assume that the beliefs, goals, and organizational methods of Islamic fundamentalists are everywhere the same, thus ignoring important local differences.

The general thrust of Islamic fundamentalist belief is that Muslims have strayed from the moral life that the Qur'an dictates and that true Muslims must return to a life of piety and faith. Fundamentalists believe that the early success of Islamic civilization was because of their faith and that the decline of Islamic influence over the past centuries is a result of their straying from that faith. If Muslims can return to their previous religious idealism, they can eliminate the social, political, economic, and moral problems afflicting the Muslim people and create an ethical order on Earth (Sachedina 1991:406).

Muslims attribute the decline of Islamic piety to the influence of the West on their societies in general, and on colonial and economic domination and the rise of Western secular influence in particular. Islamic fundamentalists are not opposed to modernization; rather, they argue that the Qur'an could provide the foundation for appropriate social institutions and social ethics in a modern, technical age. Islamic fundamentalists see a conflict between the religion that God ordained and the historical development of the world He controls. Consequently they have tried to prevent further erosion in what they see as the true faith, at the same time resisting what they see as alien domination in any form over Muslim societies.

Islamic fundamentalists in different countries attribute the ills of their country—poverty, loss of influence, and conflict—to a straying from true Muslim belief and behavior and to some degree blame the West, or modernization in general, for their political, economic, and social problems. In Egypt, for example, fundamentalists believe that their defeat at the hand of Israel in the Six Days' War in 1968 was a sign from God that they had strayed from the true faith. National good fortune, however, is attributed to maintenance of the faith; the discovery of offshore oil in Malaysia, for example, was attributed by Muslims to their faith.

Although Islamic fundamentalists in different countries share certain beliefs and goals, there are significant differences among them. In Egypt, for example, fundamentalists believe that creating an Islamic society will help people compensate for the loss of family relationships incurred as people find it necessary to leave villages and become more independent of their families. For that reason, suggested Andrea B. Rugh (1993), the most militant are the young people, especially those who, despite having college educations, can find no jobs and consequently see in Islam a non-Western alternative. The dominant feature of Islamic fundamentalism in Malaysia is the *dakwah* movement. The *dakwah* is a small religious group or commune that separates itself from the larger society to lead lives that members believe are based on Muslim law as given in the Qur'an. Manning Nash noted that *dakwah* is a youth movement of largely university-educated men and women. Members of *dakwah* express discontent with what they see as the modern, urban, pluralistic, and secular world. They see it as sensual, corrupt, neurotic, and trivial (Nash 1991:695). They read Islamic literature, carefully evaluating their behavior according to passages from the Qur'an. Women wear ankle-length dresses and, in public, the *chador* or a version of it. Members of the *dakwah* try to maintain small businesses or stalls or bake items to sell locally. Another unique feature of Islamic fundamentalism in Malaysia is its ethnic character and its appeal to Malays as opposed to other ethnic groups, such as Indians and Chinese. To some extent, it is a nationalist protest against the influence of Indians and Chinese who gained economic prominence in Malaysia during the British colonial period. It also relies heavily on anti-Western, antimodern rhetoric. The West, wrote Nash (1991:731),

> [i]s seen primarily as the threatening "other," personified variously by the United States and Western Europe—a chaotic power, lacking in discipline, in morality, and indeed in simple human decency. Thus, for most dakwah organizations, the West remains the princip[a]l enemy, an aggressor who through its educational systems and its mastery of science has been successful in implanting atheism, materialism, and moral decadence in the heart of Malaysian Islam.

Islamic Fundamentalism in Iran

The Islamic revolution in Iran has all the characteristics of an anti-systemic movement. Iran was controlled by core states—Russia, Great Britain, and the United States—for more than a century. The secular government of the shah was put in power by an American CIA-engineered coup in 1953 against an elected government and the country was rapidly industrializing, led by the sale of its plentiful oil supplies to core nations. The Islamic revolutionary government quickly acted to reverse what they saw as the imposition of a foreign culture on their own. It's important, therefore, to understand the social and historical background of this revolution.

Iran was the center of the Ottoman Empire that began to rise to prominence in the Middle East in the sixteenth century. As the Ottoman polity began to break up in the nineteenth century, both England and Russia inflicted military defeats on Iran and gained concessions to exploit various resources such as tobacco. But the tobacco concessions so angered merchants and the Islamic religious leaders, the *ulama,* that they forced the government to rescind the concession to the British. A leader in this revolt was Jamal al-Din al-Afghani, who preached against Western imperialism and became one of the central figures in Islamic resurgence at the turn of the twentieth century in both Iran and Egypt. Thus, the protest against Western influence hardly began with the overthrow of the shah in 1979; it extends well back into the nineteenth century.

The British gained economic control over Iran when the Russians withdrew after the Bolshevik Revolution in 1917. Because of the weakness of the Iranian central government there were various revolts, the most serious being the Jangali revolt of 1917–1921 led by Kuchik Khan—referred to by one English writer as the Robin Hood of the Caspian Marshes—who financed their revolt by stealing from wealthy landlords (Munson 1988). Reza Khan defeated the Jangali by gaining the support of the merchants and the army. Reza wanted to establish a republic but the *ulama* objected, so Reza had himself declared shah and established the Pahlavi dynasty. With the support of the British, he rapidly secularized the country, clearly trying to Westernize it; he forced men to wear European clothes, including brimmed hats, and forbade women from wearing the *chador* or veil, analogous to requiring European women to go bare breasted. Public protests followed. More importantly, trade and commerce under the shah was monopolized by Europeans.

The gradual withdrawal of the British from Iran after World War II allowed the *ulama* to regain some of their authority and led to the democratic election in 1951 of Mohammad Mosaddeq as prime minister. One of Mosaddeq's first acts was to nationalize the Anglo-Iranian Oil Company. He also banned a militant religious group, the *Fada'iyan-e Islam,* led by Ayatollah Kashani. These two acts ultimately led to his downfall in a coup arranged by the American CIA to install the son of Reza Khan as shah. After the coup, the shah banned the parties that had helped put him in power and began the period of American domination of Iran and continued the Westernization of the country. When the shah announced that women would be allowed to vote, there was a religious protest in Qum, the religious center of Iran, to which the shah responded by attacking the seminary. With the help of the CIA, the shah set up a security apparatus, SAVAK, to suppress domestic opposition.

The revolution of 1979 that overthrew the shah and brought Ayatollah Khomeini to power represented a joining together of the *ulamas,* the merchants, and the intellectuals in reaction to the shah's policies, the repressions, and the killings. The stage was set for the return of Khomeini on February 1, 1979, aboard a jet from France.

We can see in this history the interplay between, on the one hand, British and American attempts to control political events in Iran and, consequently, the vast Iranian oil fields and, on the other hand, Islamic leaders who objected largely to the secularization of Iran that seemingly arose from British and then American influences. But the fundamentalist revolution in Iran was neither sudden nor surprising. There were many factors involved in the revolution, including the poverty of the majority of Iranian peasants, the violent repression of dissent led by SAVAK, and the economic excesses of the leaders who took great pains to flaunt the wealth gained by oil sales to the West. It also marked the continued resistance by many Iranians to the assimilation of their country into the culture of capitalism.

Protestant Fundamentalism in North America

Protestant fundamentalism has gained almost as high a profile in the United States as Islamic fundamentalism has in Arab and Southeast Asian countries. Although it is difficult to estimate precisely how many people in the United States are fundamentalists, it is clear that many people share the same beliefs. For example, 72 percent of Americans say the Bible is the word of God and 39 percent say the Bible is literally true. Two-thirds say that Jesus Christ rose from the dead, and 44 percent are creationists who agree that God created the world in pretty much its present form within the last 10,000 years (Ammerman 1991).

Protestant fundamentalism clearly has gained a strong voice in the political process in the United States, demanding that political candidates adhere to certain fundamentalist principles, including support for the banning of abortion, support for school prayer, and support for laws controlling what can appear in the mass media.

FOUNDATIONS OF PROTESTANT FUNDAMENTALISM   There are three basic tenets held by people who consider themselves to be Protestant fundamentalists. First, they are evangelicals, that is they begin with the fact that they are saved. Not all evangelicals are fundamentalists, but this is one point on which evangelicals and fundamentalists agree. Second, they believe in the inerrancy of the Bible; they believe the Bible to be true, even when it says things they don't like. Furthermore, they believe it provides an accurate view of history and science, as well as God-given moral guidelines. Theologians may argue about what different passages mean, but through prayer and study the truth evident in the Bible will be revealed. Third, they believe in premillenialism, the doctrine of rapture. Fundamentalists, like other Christians, believe in the end times, a point in history when the present world ends and the thousand-year reign of Christ on Earth begins. But fundamentalists also believe that prior to that, Jesus Christ will appear and to the blare of heavenly trumpets lift his bride, the (true) church, up to heaven. This is the rapture. Then begins the tribulation, a seven-year period when all unfulfilled Bible prophesies are fulfilled, when God, Satan, Christ, and anti-Christ meet in the final battle of Armageddon in Israel, and when Christ returns with his army of believers to begin his millennial reign on earth. Christians have no role in the playing out of these events, and nothing that anyone can do will change the date of the rapture; that date was set by God at the beginning of time (Harding 1991:61). However, it is possible, through careful observation of world events, to predict the coming of the rapture.

There are some variations in Protestant fundamentalist belief and practice, but the essentials are relatively consistent. The question is, *What was the stimulus for the rise of Protestant fundamentalism, and how can we account for its recent resurgence?*

THE EMERGENCE OF FUNDAMENTALISM IN NORTH AMERICA Fundamentalist belief began to form in the mid-nineteenth century, largely in reaction to the modernization and secularization of Protestant churches and as a response to the challenge to religion of nineteenth-century science, technology, and culture. Darwin's theory of evolution was one of the most threatening scientific developments, but others, such as sociologist Émile Durkheim's ideas about the power of social forces to shape individual behavior, Sigmund Freud's theories of sexuality, and the works of anthropologist Franz Boas that attacked ethnocentrism and absolutism, struck at some of the basic beliefs and the truth of the Bible. Fundamentalists were particularly offended when biblical scholars turned a scientific eye to the scriptures, claiming the Bible is neither unique nor the "word of God" and comparing biblical stories with the myths of other societies.

But it was not only the work of academics who threatened the inerrancy of the Bible that triggered a fundamentalist reaction; there was also the change in American culture itself. There were new attitudes and values that accompanied the shift from a primarily agrarian society to an urban industrial society. From the end of the Civil War to the beginning of the twentieth century the industrial workforce quadrupled, and inventions such as the telegraph, electricity, and telephones were transforming the country. It was to science and technology that people began to look for improvements in their lives.

In addition, immigration and urbanization were changing where people lived and with whom they lived and worked. All of these changes prompted religious reactions. Some of those who were religiously inclined joined the Social Gospel movement, which sought to alleviate the ills caused by urban crowding and poverty; others became Adventists or Jehovah's Witnesses, carrying on the early nineteenth-century prophesies of William Miller and Charles Russell that the world was about to end. Or people became possessed by the Holy Spirit and joined Pentecostal movements. Those who were fundamentalists, however, differed in that they rejected any compromise with those who no longer saw the Bible as the word of God (Ammerman 1991:14).

Inerrancy of the Bible became the centerpiece of the fundamentalist movement in the early twentieth century. Theologians attacked the works of German scholars who claimed the Bible was an historic document composed by many authors. Fundamentalists argued that if the Bible claimed to be divinely inspired then, because it was the word of God, it must be inspired. Those trying to show that the Bible was in error, fundamentalists said, had to "prove" that a disputed fact was in the original texts—those unsullied by copying and transmission—and that it really meant what the critic said it meant and was really in conflict with a proven fact of science. Given such a standard, it was virtually impossible to prove the Bible wrong.

After World War I fundamentalists interpreted Germany's defeat as punishment for the work of German scholars trying to examine the Bible scientifically and for the acceptance of

The Scopes trial in Tennessee in 1925 was turned into a battle between religion and science, pitting Clarence Darrow (on the left) in the defense of John T. Scopes against William Jennings Bryan (on the right) defending the validity of the Tennessee law prohibiting the teaching of evolution.   (Bettmann/Corbis.)

Darwin's theory of evolution, whereas they saw the League of Nations as the world government that they believed would appear just prior to the tribulation. Thus, as Christian fundamentalists do today, they interpreted world events in terms of their religious beliefs.

Early twentieth-century fundamentalists focused their early protests on schools and the teaching of Darwin's theory of evolution. There is some misunderstanding about fundamentalist objections to Darwin's theory of evolution. Most theologians had little problem accommodating Darwin's theory to religious doctrine (see Robbins and Cohen 2009). The problems were created by two implications of Darwin's theories. The first was that if evolution operated through random beneficial variations and the destruction of the weak, then, by implication, the God of Darwin acted randomly and cruelly. Darwin could not accept that and became an agnostic (Larson 1997:17). The second implication was that the social world operated on the same principles as the natural world and that these principles (e.g., natural selection) could be used, as many were, to justify laissez-faire capitalism, imperialism, and militarism. Furthermore, the application of Darwin's theories to the workings of society legitimated the then very popular doctrine of eugenics, the idea that the state should enact laws to ensure that only the "fittest" bred. This, of course, further imposed human will on a divinely guided universe.

The protest over the teaching of evolution in American schools may never have received the prominence it did had not William Jennings Bryan volunteered to prosecute John Scopes, a Tennessee High school teacher charged under Tennessee law with illegally teaching the theory of evolution (see Robbins 2009). Bryan was a major American figure, three-time presidential candidate, advisor to presidents, crusader for women's rights, and defender of the Bible. To counter Bryan, the American Civil Liberties Union sent a team of lawyers headed by Clarence Darrow to defend Scopes. Darrow, in his way, was as imposing a public figure as Bryan, and probably the most famous lawyer of his time. He had also worked for Bryan in his presidential campaigns and shared much of his social philosophy.

The Scopes trial has been depicted in theater, movies, and literature as a battle between science and rationality on the one side, and religion and superstition on the other. Lost in that depiction of the struggle was a genuine anti-systemic sentiment, particularly on the part of Bryan. Bryan had voiced his objections to Darwin as early as 1904. In one speech he said,

> The Darwinian theory represents man as reaching his present perfection by the operation of the law of hate—the merciless law by which the strong crowd out and kill off the weak. (Larson 1997:39)

For Bryan, who had built his career denouncing the excesses of capitalism and militarism, this was unacceptable.

Darrow, however, succeeded in turning the case into a science versus religion contest, forcing Bryan to defend a literal interpretation of the Bible, and the issue of using the theory of evolution to interpret social history and human behavior never received a hearing. Bryan won the case; Scopes was convicted. But the public ridicule of fundamentalist arguments of the inerrancy of the Bible resulted in American public opinion largely supporting Scopes.

After the Scopes trial and the public reaction to it, Protestant fundamentalists were convinced that American culture had come under the sway of what later came to be called "secular humanism," a godless view of the world that substituted human action and wisdom for divine action and guidance. Because they could not transform society, they turned to saving individual souls. Most fundamentalist churches broke away from their parent churches and formed their own organizations, such as the American Council of Christian Churches founded in 1941 by Carl McIntire. Fundamentalists joined missionary organizations, and there was enormous growth in Bible colleges and institutes as well as expansion into publishing and radio and television broadcasting. Charles Fuller's *Old Fashioned Revival Hour,* which appeared in 1934, became one of the most popular programs on radio, followed on television by the enormously popular *Oral Roberts* and *Rex Humbard*.

There was also a growth in political radicalism; Gerald Winrod wrote in his journal of seeing the end times, a Jewish anti-Christ, and a Jewish conspiracy to rule the world. In the 1950s, fundamentalists took up the banner of anticommunism, with Carl McIntire arguing that the Revised Standard Version of the Bible was a communist plot, and that Jews and blacks constituted the main threat to white Christian civilization. But it was the revolution of 1968, the civil rights movement, the feminist movement, and the antiwar movement with its slogan "question authority" that seemed to provide evidence for fundamentalists that society was disintegrating and the rapture must be near.

Burned-out hippies and disenchanted liberals, along with other seekers who had failed in the 1968 revolution to transform society, began to join fundamentalist churches. As one hippie-turned-fundamentalist said (Ammerman 1991:39),

[o]ne person tells you to do one thing, and the next person tells you to do the opposite. "Get a job, get a haircut." Or "Turn on, tune in, drop out." Or "Support the President," and someone else says "Impeach Nixon" or "Stop the War," or whatever it is, you know. It makes you crazy. What do you do? It's typical of the world. You're in confusion. In the Lord the Word shows you what to do, and you can rest in it. You don't have to be gray.

Fundamentalists were also concerned about America's role in the world; in spite of their condemnation of what was happening to American culture, America was still the fundamentalists' "city on a hill"; moreover, America's military strength and economic influence provided the entree into other countries for fundamentalist missionizing; there was a fear that "the light of the gospel might go out because it would have no great chosen nation to carry it" (Ammerman 1991:40).

Finally, there were a series of changes that seemed to be challenging fundamentalists to come out of their political isolation. Among them was the Equal Rights Amendment (ERA) to the Constitution; fundamentalists feared it would prevent women from fulfilling their biblical role as submissive wives. They saw laws promoted by governmental and private social agencies that sought to define the limits of a parent's right to punish their children as an attack on parental authority as it was defined in the Bible. They saw the extension of the civil rights movement to homosexuals, whose lives seemed to fundamentalists grossly immoral, as a direct attack on biblical injunction. They fought against the prevention of prayer in school. And, finally, they saw behind *Roe v. Wade* and the legalization of abortion all the forces that were trying to destroy the family and Christian morality.

The defense against the scientific attack on the inerrancy of the Bible did not go away; it resurfaced in the doctrine of scientific creationism, the use of the tools and language of science to prove that the world was indeed created in 4004 B.C. But where the inerrancy of the Bible was the major issue 100 years ago, today the focus of fundamentalist interest is the protection of the traditional family—a legally married man and woman with their children preferably supported by the husband's work—as the basic unit of society (Ammerman 1991:45). From this flows the fundamentalist opposition to gay and lesbian rights, the ERA, and laws designed to protect abused wives and children. And at the centerpiece of this agenda is the opposition to abortion.

With these agendas, and the active participation of Protestant fundamentalists in politics, there has been a resurgence of fundamentalist influence in American life. One of the clearest indications of this is the enormous growth in church schools and home schooling. From 1965 to 1983 enrollment in evangelical schools rose sixfold, and the number of schools approached 10,000. As many as 100,000 fundamentalist children were being taught at home. This pattern is evident also at the college level. For example, enrollment in the ninety-eight evangelical colleges in the United States represented by the Council for Christian Colleges and Universities increased almost 50 percent from 1990 through 2000, as opposed to about 10 percent of all other colleges and universities in the United States (Council for Christian Colleges and Universities 2001).

Some of these positions have served to unite fundamentalists with other groups with whom they have, at one time or another, been vehemently opposed: their opposition to abortion with Catholics, their opposition to pornography with the feminist movement, their opposition to the ERA with Mormons, and their support of Israel with Jews. But it has also created splits with those who decried such alliances.

VARIATIONS IN DOCTRINE   There are also new variations of Protestant fundamentalist belief, most markedly the Christian reconstructionists, probably the most clearly anti-systemic fundamentalist group. Christian reconstructionists seek to replace the "modern bureaucratic state" with a Christian state modeled after the Bible; their ideal is the seventeenth-century Puritans of Massachusetts. They argue that people must submit to the rule of God and follow a doctrine they call "theonomy."

The economics of Christian fundamentalists are more complex and varied than generally supposed (Iannaccone 1993; Kuran 1993). Most people associate Christian fundamentalists with support of the free market economy, opposition to government redistribution programs, defense of private property, and opposition to any form of socialism. Yet little is made of economics in the writings of most Christian fundamentalists, and many fundamentalist colleges or universities do not even have economics departments. Jerry Fallwell was the most outspoken of the Christian fundamentalist leaders when it comes to the defense of the free market, but the Christian recon-structionists are the only group to systematize a conservative economic agenda, arguing that the Bible dictates that private property should be regulated only by the family and the religious community, not by the state. The Bible, they say, imposes a flat tax of 10 percent and argues against any kind of centrally planned economy. Metallic currency is the only kind permitted, and income redistribution violates the eighth commandant, "Thou shalt not steal," and is simply institutionalized theft.

There is also an evangelical left that argues that the Bible teaches that God is on the side of the poor. Best represented by the writings of Jim Wallis (*Agenda for Biblical People,* 1984), they draw attention to the vast disparities in wealth that exist in the modern world and argue that "overconsumption is theft from the poor," that the wealth of the core comes only at the expense of the poor of the nonindustrial world. The biblical solution, they argue, is redistribu-tion. Christians should consume less, they say, and contribute more to the poor. Influenced by the secular left, the counterculture of the 1960s, and communitarian Christian groups such as the Amish, Mennonites, and Hutterites, said Laurence R. Iannaccone (1993:350), the evangelical left argues that

> [t]he system which creates and sustains much of the hunger, underdevelopment, and other social ills in the world today is capitalism. Capitalism is by its very nature a system which promotes individualism, competition, and profit-making with little or no regard for social costs. Its puts profits and private gain before social service and human needs. As such it is an unjust system and should be replaced.

"TERROR IN THE MIND OF GOD"

Religion, as we mentioned previously, has always had a revolutionary dimension. Most (if not all) religious movements began at a moment of dissatisfaction, if not despair, and sought to reorder or revitalize a world that its members found wanting. In addition, virtually all the major religions of the world contain texts detailing violent battles between the forces of good and the forces of evil. They all have what Mark Juergensmeyer (2000:158) refers to as "shadowy foes," "thems," "strangers," and such who dwell in the

> shady edges of known civilizations…. They represent what was chaotic and uncer-
> tain about the world, including those things that defied categorization altogether.

The Book of Revelation of the New Testament with its description of the forces of Satan and the ultimate battle between good and evil provides one of the best (and most violent) metaphors of war and redemption in Western literature.

Characterizing one's enemies as "Satanic," as Elaine Pagels (1995:xix) points out in her book *The Origin of Satan,* lends a moral and religious meaning to conflict in which "we" are God's people, and "they" are God's enemies—an interpretation which, as Pagels notes, has been extraordinarily successful in justifying hatred and mass slaughter.

Therefore, it should not be surprising that religion is used by some as a justification for violent acts. The juxtaposition of religion and violence has become more common since the attacks on the World Trade Center and the Pentagon on September 11, 2001, and has focused added attention on radical religious groups. Attempts to understand the motivations and rationales of religious violence, however, have tended to underestimate the deep religious convictions of religious group members. It would be a mistake to dismiss them as "cultic," or "irrational," or "alienated." Followers of these movements believe that the religious forms they follow are the ones with the deep historical roots; they are the "true" Christianity, the "true" Judaism, the "true" Islam, and so on.

In addition, it would be a mistake to neglect the political aspects of religious violence. Religion provides a framework for viewing events and interpreting experience. When followers of Christianity, Judaism, Sikhism, Buddhism, or Islam commit violent acts in the name of God or some spiritual mission, they are acting in response to some social, political, or economic grievance. When Reverend Michael Bray set fire to abortion clinics in the name of a heavenly mandate, he was convinced that the U.S. government was undermining individual freedoms and moral values; his acts were directed at the nation-state as much as at the clinics themselves. Osama bin Laden sought the establishment of an Islamic state, but clearly his acts were as much political as they were religious. The Israeli occupation of Palestinian territories, the stationing of U.S. troops in Saudi Arabia, and the U.S. support for oppressive governments in the Middle East were as much reasons for his acts as anything religious (see Guardian-Observer 2002).

It is common for the media to see so-called "suicide bombing" as motivated solely by religious (usually Islamic) "fanaticism." Yet, as Robert A. Pape (2003) notes in his study of suicide bombers, of the 188 incidents he documented from 1980 to 2002, seventy-five were instigated by the Tamil Tigers in Sri Lanka, a Marxist-Leninist group whose members adamantly oppose any religion. Thus, whether religion provides the motivation for political violence or is simply an additional justification for it remains an open question.

Regardless, however, given the deep religious convictions common to many members of all societies, it would be a mistake to underestimate the power of believers of projecting social, political, and economic grievances onto a religious or spiritual frame. The questions we need to ask are, *How do people explain their use of religion as a justification for violent acts, and how do we explain the conditions under which such justification occurs?*

Some Examples of Religious Violence

THE MILITANTS OF PROTESTANT FUNDAMENTALISM   The militant groups of Protestant fundamentalism include Operation Rescue and the Army of God, both dedicated to, among other things, halting abortion. Randall Terry began Operation Rescue in Binghamton, New York, in 1988. Its goal was to protest legal abortion by barricading abortion clinics, blocking women's access to clinics, confronting women entering and leaving the clinics, and harassing them verbally and physically, even following them or tracing their license plate numbers and calling them at home. Operation Rescue picketed clinics and the homes of clinic physicians, sent threatening letters, and made threatening phone calls. By 1990, Operation Rescue reported that 35,000 of their protesters had been arrested, whereas another 16,000 risked arrests in what the group called "rescues" (Ginsburg 1993).

The ultimate goal, however, was more than simply stopping abortion. Rather, they intended to use the opposition to abortion, in the words of evangelical Protestant leader Francis Schaeffer (Ginsburg 1993:558), "as a way for evangelicals to challenge the entire legitimacy of the secular modern state, withholding allegiance until the nation returns to its religious roots in matters like public prayer and religious education." As Faye Ginsburg (1993:558) noted, the opposition to abortion is the means protesters use to return America to "traditional Christian values."

Operation Rescue was not the first group to use violence to protest abortion. The Right to Life movement goes back to the 1973 Supreme Court ruling in *Roe v. Wade* that recognized a woman's right to abortion. Some groups had already adopted confrontational tactics of blocking the entrances to clinics and harassing abortion providers. The National Abortion Federation keeps a record of "violent incidents" against abortion providers that includes invasions of clinics, vandalism, murders, death threats, bomb threats, bombings, assaults, arson attempts, arson, and kidnapping attempts. From 1977, through April 2009, the National Abortion Federation (ND) has recorded 6,143 incidents of violence, including 8 murders, 17 attempted murders, 41 bombings, 175 cases of arson, 1,400 cases of vandalism, and 179 assault and battery cases (see National Abortion Federation 2009).

The state's official reaction to the violence has been ambiguous. In an influential antiabortion essay in 1983, President Ronald Reagan, an opponent of abortion, said the increase in attacks on abortion clinics did not constitute terrorism because they were not carried out by an organized group; he did reverse himself in 1985, speaking out against these "violent anarchistic activities."

The painting by François Dubois, "An Eyewitness Account of the Saint Bartholomew's Day Massacre," depicting the 1572 killings in France of Protestants by French soldiers and Catholic clergy. The attacks spread throughout the country resulting in the deaths of hundreds of thousands of people.   (The Print Collector/Alamy.)

It is clear that Randall Terry's agenda is to refashion what he sees as a godless society according to the beliefs and values of his version of Christian fundamentalism. Thus, as Ginsburg (1993:579) said, it is a mistake to look at Operation Rescue only in the context of the abortion debate; rather, its intent is to impose on American society its version of Christian culture: "For 'rescuers,' fighting abortion is simply a first step in reversing America's 'moral decline,' much as opposition to the teaching of evolution was considered a way to fight secularization in the 1920s."

A more militant Christian fundamentalist group is the Army of God. Its doctrine was outlined in an underground manual, *Army of God,* whose authorship is attributed to the Reverend Michael Bray (see Juergensmeyer 2000:21). Regardless of whether Bray was the author, he clearly sympathizes with its sentiments. Bray was convicted in 1985 of setting fire to seven abortion clinics on some of which were found the initials AOG. He is also the author of the book *A Time to Kill,* which defends his own actions as well as the killing of abortion providers. He was also a friend and defender of the Reverend Paul Hill who was convicted and executed for killing Dr. John Britton and his bodyguard, retired Air Force lieutenant colonel James Herman Barrett.

According to Bray, Americans live in a state of "hidden warfare," comparable to that of Nazi Germany, and a dramatic event, such as an economic collapse, would reveal the demonic role of the government, at which point the people would take up arms in a revolutionary struggle and establish a new moral order based on biblical law. Until then, Bray believes, he and others must have the moral courage to resist, particularly by defending unborn babies and killing those who threaten them. Bray justifies his acts by drawing on the work of theologians, such as Reinhold Niebuhr, who, trying to come to grips with when it is permissible to use force, argued that force could be used moderately in the cause of justice.

Jessica Stern (2003:150) asked one young member of the Army of God how he became involved with the group. "I am a Christian," he said, "and therefore opposed to abortion. Unborn babies are dying by the millions, and I feel compelled to help." For members of the group, killing abortion providers is "justifiable homicide."

The organization even has developed an operational strategy designed to escape electronic detection by U.S. law enforcement officials. They call it "swarming," in which many, semi-independent networks converge rapidly and stealthily on chosen targets. One member described his vision of a swarming operation:

> So we have the Army of God, which in the future will organize and coalesce like those of Europe who had centuries of underground work, and there will be skilled assassins and skilled saboteurs after the abortion industry, which is not only the abortionists but also the people on top of them, including Supreme Court judges. Now Paul Hill has called for the Supreme Court judges to be killed and also for chemical and biological weapons, and we support this call, at least I do. (Stern 2003:151–152)

TERROR IN THE HOLY LAND   Perhaps there is no better example of violence over contested space than Israel and the Palestinian territories, an area sacred to three of the world's major religions—Judaism, Christianity, and Islam. And perhaps there is no greater symbol of this contestation than the Qubbat as-Sakhra, housing the al-Aqsa mosque that encloses the Dome of the Rock. The mosque was built by the Caliph Abd al-Malik and completed in A.D. 691. The rock at the center of the structure is one of the holiest places in Islam. According to tradition, the Prophet Muhammad ascended to heaven from the rock at the end of his Night Journey. In the Jewish tradition this is the Foundation Stone, the symbolic foundation on which the world was created, and the place where Abraham was preparing to sacrifice his son Isaac when an angel of God told him to stop. It is also the site of the *Beit Yahweh* (Temple of Jerusalem) destroyed by the Romans in A.D. 70 and the holiest place of worship in Judaism.

The contest for control over the Holy Land is, of course, centuries old, but it is the Arab–Israeli conflict of today that has more recently fueled religious violence. For that reason it is

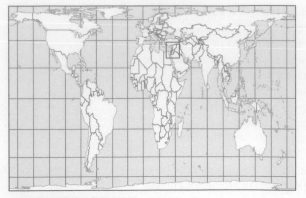

Israel and the Palestinian Territories of Gaza and the West Bank

necessary to understand something of the history of the conflict (see Cohn-Sherbok and el-Alami 2002; Smith 2000).

Very briefly then, in the nineteenth century the often virulent anti-Semitism in Europe persuaded many Jews of the need for a Jewish homeland in Israeli, the biblical origin of Judaism. From this emerged the Zionist movement that began to raise money from wealthy patrons (e.g., the Rothschild's) to fund Jewish settlements in Palestine. In the middle of the nineteenth century there were already some 10,000 non-Zionist Jews in Palestine, but by 1914, with the influx of Zionists, there were some 90,000 compared with some 500,000 Arab Palestinians. At that point Palestine was part of the Ottoman Empire controlled by Turkey. But after World War I and the defeat of Germany and her allies—including Turkey—the Ottoman Empire was disbanded and Palestine was assigned as a protectorate to Great Britain. With European Jews lobbying for a Jewish homeland, the British Cabinet, in consultation with Zionist leaders, issued a letter in 1917 from Arthur James Lord Balfour to Lord Rothschild making known their intent to establish a Jewish homeland in Palestine. The interpretation of the Balfour Declaration became a center of dispute for the next forty years.

With the defeat of the Germans and the Turks in 1918, the remaining population of Palestine consisted of 66,000 Jews, 512,000 Muslims, and 61,000 Christians. Arab hostility to the influx of Jewish immigrants, however, led to riots in 1920 and 1921 when as many as forty-seven Jews were killed. Jewish immigration increased in the 1920s and 1930s as Russia permitted more Jews to leave and as many Jews fled Germany in the face of Nazi persecution. The increased conflict between Jews and Palestinians led to the formation of armed Jewish groups, such as *Haganah,* the first Jewish defense force. A more militant group, the *Irgun* (*Irgun Tsvai-Leumi or* "National-Military Organization"), was regarded by the British as a terrorist organization. Jewish protest against both the Palestinians and the British increased in the late 1930s and the British hung a Jew for attacking an Arab bus. The *Irgun* responded by exploding land mines in Haifa, killing seventy-four people. In 1937 the British issued a white paper (the Peel Commission) suggesting a partition of the Palestinian protectorate into Jewish and Arab sections, and then they issued another in 1939 that recommended the protectorate be declared an independent Palestinian state but with the rights of Jews protected. This satisfied neither the Palestinians nor the Jews.

The beginning of World War II added complications to British-run Palestine because neither the Jews, intent on establishing a Jewish state on their ancestral homeland, nor the Arab Palestinians, intent on establishing an independent Palestinian state, recognized the legitimacy of British rule. After the war, during which the Jews allied themselves with the British and the Arabs with the Germans, and after the full extent of the Nazi Holocaust was known, the British insisted on implementing the 1939 white paper declaring an independent Palestine, resulting in an armed uprising by the Jews against the British, fanned in part by messages over the illegal Voice of Israel radio station. The *Haganah* blew up the Palestinian railway system and the *Irgun* bombed the King David Hotel, the site of British offices, killing close to 100 people. In 1948, the *Irgun* and another Jewish group, the *Lehi,* massacred men, women, and children in the village of Deir Yassin, and entire Palestinian villages fled (Cohn-Sherbok and el-Alami 2002). Following these incidents, the British withdrew their mandate, and David Ben-Gurion, the first prime minister of Israel, declared the independence of the state of Israel, which was quickly recognized by both the United States and the Soviet Union. At this time, the United Nations called for a partition of Palestine into Arab (the West Bank) and Jewish sections at which point combined Arab forces invaded Israel and within three months were turned back by Israeli forces.

Beginning in 1948 there were intermittent hostilities between Israel and its Arab neighbors (wars in 1957, 1967, and 1973), and, as a consequence of the wars, Israel occupied areas that had been Palestinian land, and proceeded to establish Jewish settlements in violation of various UN resolutions. Militant Palestinian groups, such as the Palestine Liberation Organization (PLO), Black September, Hamas, and Palestine Islamic Jihad, emerged in response to Israeli exploitation and oppression of the Arab population and with their own nationalistic aspirations. Black September claimed responsibility for the kidnapping and killing of Israeli athletes at the 1972 Olympics in Munich, Germany, whereas Hamas and Islamic Jihad have taken responsibility for hundreds of attacks on Israeli civilians and military targets. Israel responded with increasingly violent repression, particularly after the Palestinian uprising (*intifada*) in 1987.

In 1993, both sides were brought together in Oslo, Norway, and the Israeli prime minister Yitzhak Rabin signed a peace treaty with Yaser Arafat, head of the PLO, to end hostilities. The Oslo Accord recognized the Palestinian authority as a governing group and gave it civil authority in Palestinian-occupied areas (the West Bank and the Gaza Strip). But radicals on both sides refused to accept the agreement, and, in November 1995, Rabin was assassinated by a right-wing Jew, Yigal Amir, who defended himself by saying, "I acted on God's order and I have no regrets." As the Oslo Accord stalled and as Israeli settlements on the West Bank grew, violence on both sides increased. When the accord collapsed in 2000 with the election of the Likud Party, a second Arab *Intifada* began. In 2002 and 2003 Palestinian attacks increased as Israel allowed more and more Jewish settlers into what had been Palestinian territory, increased military operations within occupied territory, and began the building of a wall intended to separate the Jewish and Palestinian populations while Israeli politicians spoke openly of the "ethnic cleansing" of the Palestinian population.

Religion clearly plays a major role in the conflict, in spite of the obvious political and economic factors, not the least of which is the annexation of Palestinian land and territory by Israel. Jewish settlers, regardless of where they come from, justify their taking of land held by Palestinians for decades by reference to the Old Testament creation of the land of Israel. Palestinians justify their resistance by reference to the Qur'an, as well as by UN resolutions that condemn the Israeli takeover.

In 1990, a Jewish messianic group known as the Temple Mount Faithful announced their intent to lay a 4.5 ton cornerstone at the site of the ancient Temple of Jerusalem and the Haram al-Sharif. Palestinians reacted to the threat to the Haram al-Sharif with massive riots. One member of the Temple Mount Faithful, Yoel Lerner, a Brooklyn-born, MIT-trained mathematician, was imprisoned for a plan to blow up the dome of the rock to make room for the rebuilding of the Temple of Jerusalem (Stern 2003:86). For Lerner, no one has the moral right to give up any territory that comprised the ancient state of Israel. Furthermore, the rebuilding of the temple is necessary for people to practice their religion; the Torah, he says, has 613 commandments and 240 of these require worship at the temple. Thus, for almost two millennia, says Lerner, Jews have not been able to practice their religion. The assassination of Rabin, says Lerner, was completely justified because by signing the Oslo Accord, Rabin was stealing Jewish property. "The land is a sacred thing," he says, trying to justify Amir's decision to kill Rabin (Stern 2003:91). As Jessica Stern (2003:92) put it:

> The biblical promise of Eretz Israel, The Land of Israel, to God's chosen people, makes the concept of land a key component of religious doctrine to fundamentalist Jews, who believe that possession of the land of Israel is part and parcel of the Jews' covenant with God. Accordingly, relinquishing or dividing any part of the land promised by God to the children of Israel would constitute a breach of the Covenant.

Lerner was also a follower of Rabbi Meir Kahane who was assassinated in New York City in 1990 by a Muslim. Kahane was radically anti-Arab and founded the Jewish Defense League and the organizations Kach and Kahane Chai, both of which were declared terrorist organizations by the Israeli Cabinet in 1994. One of its members, Dr. Baruch Goldstein, a Brooklyn-born

Jewish fundamentalist, walked into a mosque in Hebron in 1994 and massacred more than thirty Palestinians as they prayed. Goldstein remains a hero to right-wing Israelis.

While Jews commit violence in the name of reestablishing the Jewish ancestral homeland, Palestinians kill in the name of Islam and the establishment of an independent Palestinian state. One of the groups prominent in the Palestinian resistance is Hamas. In 1999, Mark Juergensmeyer interviewed Abdul Aziz Rantisi, who, after the Israeli assassination in March 2004 of Hamas founder Sheik Ahmed Yassin, was selected as the leader of Hamas, and, later that same year, targeted and killed by Israeli airstrikes. Juergensmeyer asked Rantisi the meaning and significance of suicide bombings. Rantisi explained that it is called "self-chosen martyrdom" because that doesn't carry the connotation of impulsive or deranged individuals. In response to the question of why Hamas targeted innocent civilians and bystanders, Rantisi replied that the bombings were moral lessons. "We want to do the same thing to Israel as they have done to us," he said. It was necessary, he added, for the Israeli people to actually experience the violence before they could understand what the Palestinians had gone through (Juergensmeyer 2000:74).

As Jewish fundamentalists justify their violence and the seizing of Palestinian land by reference to Judaism, Islamic fundamentalists justify their violence as a defense of Islam. Egyptian writer Abd al-Salam Faraj, whose writings have great influence among Islamic fundamentalists, argued that the Qur'anic concept of *jihad,* or "struggle," was meant to be taken literally and not allegorically. Muslims, wrote Faraj, have neglected their sacred duty of targeting for jihad enemies of Islam as well as apostates within the Muslim community. A true soldier of Islam, he argued, is permitted to use any means to achieve a just goal (Juergensmeyer 2000:81). These ideas, and similar ones by other writers, circulate in Islamic universities and among Muslim clergy. Thus, the contest in Israel between Arabs and Jews is placed in the larger context of defending the integrity of Islam.

ARMAGEDDON IN A TOKYO SUBWAY On March 20, 1995, five members of the Aum Shinrikyo movement, all with scientific training, walked into the Tokyo subway and with sharp-ended umbrellas, punctured plastic bags filled with deadly sarin gas killing twelve people and injuring more than 5,500, some permanently. When Mark Juergensmeyer spoke to members, they explained that Aum Shinrikyo represented for them a critique of Japanese religion and of the hierarchical Japanese social system that did not exemplify principles of justice, fairness, and freedom (Juergensmeyer 2000:105). The movement was founded by Shoko Asahara in the belief that a world catastrophe would occur, a World War III or "Armageddon," in which the forces of good and evil will confront each other, but members of Aum Shinrikyo would survive. The question is, *How does one find justification for killing in Buddhism?* Juergensmeyer points out that Buddhism, similar to other religions, has a tradition of conquest and empire, generally in the name of routing infidels. In the case of Asahara, he found justification for his act in Tibetan Buddhism.

Instead of focusing on the effect that killing has on the killer's moral purity, this doctrine focuses on the one who is killed and the merit that comes after death. As Juergensmeyer (2000:114) explains it,

> The concept of *phoa*—that consciousness can be transferred from the living to the dead to elevate their spiritual merit—was extended by Asahara to imply that in some cases people are better off dead than alive. According to Asahara's interpretation of this Tibetan principle, if the persons killed are scoundrels, or are enmeshed in social systems so evil that further existence in this life will result in even greater negative karmic debt, then those who kill are doing their victims a favor by enabling them to die early. Their early deaths would be a kind of mercy killing, allowing their souls to move to a higher plane than they would otherwise have been able to achieve. (Juergensmeyer 2000:114)

Understanding Religious Violence

As we mentioned, it is tempting to dismiss religious violence as the work of irrational fanatics or worse. But that would be overlooking the varied backgrounds and motives of people such as the Reverend Michael Bray, Dr. Baruch Goldstein, Shoko Asahara, Osama bin Laden, Timothy McVeigh, or Abdul Aziz Rantisi. In addition, in no case was the violence arbitrary. In all cases there were specific grievances that the violence was intended to address. The question then is, *Under what conditions do people seek to justify violence through religious means?*

Mark Juergensmeyer (2000:146) suggests that locating a struggle on a cosmic scale elevates its importance beyond local concerns and, instead, invokes legendary battles between good and evil. Michael Bray defended the need to kill and, if necessary, die over the issue of abortion. There is a great cosmic war going on, he said, a confrontation between good and evil, but it is unseen because the enemy has imposed control. Osama bin Laden justified violence by projecting the struggle as that between the forces of Islam and those trying to destroy it. The rhetoric of wars of good versus evil has even entered the U.S. political mainstream with terms such as *axis of evil*.

There is real power, suggests Juergensmeyer, in elevating a political conflict to a cosmic war. "To live in a state of war," says Juergensmeyer

> is to live in a world in which individuals know who they are, why they have suffered, by whose hand they have been humiliated, and at what expense they have persevered. The concept of war provides cosmology, history, and eschatology and offers the reins of political control. Perhaps most important, it holds out the hope of victory and the means to achieve it. In the images of cosmic war this victorious triumph is a grand moment of social and personal transformation, transcending all worldly limitations. One does not easily abandon such expectations. To be without such images of war is almost to be without hope itself. (2000:154–155)

The next questions are, *When does violence call for religious justification, or why do real-world struggles involve religion?* Juergensmeyer (2000) suggests three reasons: First, when the struggle is perceived as a defense of basic identity and dignity, religious justifications are needed. "To die as a suicide bomber," said Abdul Aziz Rantisi, "is better than to die daily in frustration and humiliation." Baruch Goldstein justified his killing of Muslims because he believed that Jews were being humiliated by the Israeli government's protection of Arab Muslims. At the point when members of religious movements see the struggle as a defense of entire cultures, rather than of individuals, the conflict becomes a cultural war with spiritual implications. The conflict in Northern Ireland between Protestants and Catholics, for example, became spiritualized when the Reverend Ian Paisley interpreted the Catholic demand for independence from Great Britain as an attack on Protestants, and the Palestinian struggle took on a religious aura after a significant number of sheiks and mullahs interpreted it as a defense of Islam. Second, suggests Juergensmeyer, the political confrontations adopt religious justifications when losing the struggle would be unthinkable. For Yoel Lerner, a failure to rebuild the Temple of Jerusalem would threaten the very foundations of the Jewish religion. Finally, if the struggle is blocked and cannot be won in real time, suggests Juergensmeyer (2000), it is more likely to be reconceived on a sacred plane where victory is in God's hands.

CONCLUSION

We began this chapter by asking to what extent religious movements have been expressions of anti-systemic sentiments and how they have served as a means of protest against the expansion, both in the core and in the periphery, of the culture of capitalism. It is clear, we believe, that in the case of small-scale religious protests, such as the Ghost Dance, the cargo cults, and the attraction of Western religious movements such as Zionism, participants are responding to the effects of the expansion of the culture of capitalism. It is less clear, however, in the case of the various fundamentalisms that have gained popularity in the latter part of the twentieth century whether they represent anti-systemic movements. These cultural movements oppose what they call *modernization, secular humanism,* or, in the periphery, *Westernization,* seemingly synonyms for capitalism. Yet they contain elements, particularly in their views of women, the family, and opposition to alternative lifestyles, that suggest that they are more reactions to the anti-systemic revolution of 1968 than protests to capitalism.

It may be fruitful to look at instances of religious protest, particularly its violent manifestations, as protest over the decline of social and political capital, an unraveling of social compacts and feelings of marginalization, and both symbolic and geographic isolation. The rhetoric of religious violence that we examined is certainly filled with images of contested spaces and cultures; it is no accident that the objects of terrorist violence are laden with symbolism of the market.

Regardless of the object of their protest, in seeking to transform capitalism by using the Qur'an, the Old Testament, the New Testament, the teachings of Buddha, or some other cultural alternative, fundamentalisms represent, with the exception of small-scale secular and religious movements, the only viable alternative to the culture of capitalism and, in the event of a global economic collapse, the only cultures prepared, politically and ideologically, to replace it.

Solving Global Problems: Some Options and Courses of Action

… the [financial] crisis also represents a moral failure; that of a system built on money values. At the heart of the moral failure is the worship of economic growth for its own sake, rather than as a way to achieve the "good life". As a result, economic efficiency— the means to economic growth—has been given absolute priority in our thinking and policy. The main moral compass we now have is a thin and degraded notion of economic welfare, measured in terms of quantity of goods. This moral lacuna explains uncritical acceptance of globalization and financial innovation, and the sanctification of those practices which give the pursuit of wealth priority over other human concerns.

—Robert Skidelsky, *Keynes: The Return of the Master*

… we can produce more than enough food to feed everybody, and there's definitely enough work for everybody in the world. But there is clearly not enough money to pay for it all. The scarcity is on our national currencies. In fact, the job of central banks is to create and maintain that currency scarcity. The direct consequence is that we have to fight with each other in order to survive.

—Bernard Lietaer, *Beyond Greed and Scarcity*

Nowadays, economic growth is heralded as the ultimate goal by so many governments. To an extent, this goal is forced upon society as it struggles to meet the interest charges on its debt. Whilst debt grows at compound interest towards infinity, in the physical world everything depreciates towards zero. I propose that the price we shall all pay for running this unwinnable race against compound interest is a polluted and depleted world.

—Tarek El Diwany, *The Problem with Interest*

THE CENTRAL DILEMMA OF GROWTH

In 2011, the George W. Bush Presidential Center launched what it calls "The 4% Project." The directors gathered together elite economists to plan how the United States could attain a 4 percent economic growth rate. As they note on the website, "The stakes are high. In 2010, U.S. GDP was $14.6 trillion. At a 4 percent growth rate, GDP would reach $26.5 trillion in 2025. But at a growth rate of 2.4 percent, GDP would reach only $21 trillion—a 25 percent gap in wealth in just 15 years!" (http://www.bushcenter.com/economic-growth/4percent-project).

The project, of course, reflects mainstream economic thinking that economic growth is the way to solve global problems. Growth will solve environmental problems, so this reasoning goes, reduce poverty, lead to advances in medicine that will save lives, and reduce conflict. Yet it gets more difficult to maintain this assumption when, in spite of a more than tenfold increase in economic activity over the past seventy years, environmental problems are getting more severe, inequality is growing, conflict over scarce resources is increasing, and environmental destruction is leading to the emergence of new and more lethal diseases.

Yet, it is clear of course that any diminution of growth creates its own problems of much the same sort—more environmental damage, greater inequality and joblessness, reduced access to health care, and, yes, increased conflict. It seems that the world is trapped in a "damned-if-we-do and damned-if-we-don't" scenario. To make the problem even more difficult, stopping growth will lead to almost immediate financial disaster, while continuing growth will result in long-term catastrophe. The question is, as Tim Jackson (2009) asked, *can we grow sustainably or slow or stop growth without crashing?*

To answer this question, we need to reconsider why we are faced with the need to grow or crash? Economists are not much help in this regard. The major textbooks on economic growth (see, e.g., Barro and Sala-i-Martin. 2004; Jones 2002) nowhere address the question of why economies must grow. Nor is the subject broached in the collection of papers in the *Handbook of Economic Growth* (Aghion and Durlauf 2006). Rather, neoliberal economists assume that the benefits of growth are self-evident. Language use reinforces this idea: "growth," after all, is synonymous with "development," "progress," "advance," "evolution," and "improvement," while its antonyms include "diminishment," "failure," "stagnation," and "underdevelopment." Economists do recognize that the wealthier a country becomes, the more difficult it is to accumulate more wealth. They call this the "convergence factor" (Jones 2002:63ff; Barro and Xavier Sala-i-Martin 2004:462–463) explaining that developing countries will "converge" to the growth rate of "advanced economies." But there are more logical reasons to why capital accumulation gets more and more difficult.

First, as Chris Martenson emphasizes in his book *The Crash Course: The Unsustainable Future of Our Economy, Energy, and Environment,* economic growth must be exponential. The difference between arithmetic and exponential growth is the difference between 1, 2, 3, 4, 5 and 1, 2, 4, 8, 16, 32, 64. You can also conceptualize it as "the rule of 70": take the percentage at which something is growing and divide it into 70 and you have the time it will take for something to double. Something growing at 5 percent a year will double in fourteen years; something growing at 8 percent a year (e.g., Chinese oil consumption) will double in nine years (Martenson 2011:23).

To take a real-life example, from 1990 to 1995 the lumber industry in the United States maintained a growth rate of about 3.5 percent by cutting down the equivalent of one and a half million more trees than they had in the previous five-year period. However, in order to maintain the same 3.5 percent growth rate from 2005 to 2010 they would have had to cut down the equivalent of two and a half million more trees (Howard 2007)—that is, one million more trees. Extrapolate those growth figures to water use, energy use, automobiles, fish stocks, etc., and the difficulty of sustaining exponential growth becomes more easily apparent.

Another reason why exponential growth is harder to maintain is that fewer people have to keep doing more. That is, population growth cannot keep up with economic growth (see Table 13.1). In 1940, the population of the United States was 132 million; GDP per capita was $767.47. Since then U.S. population has increased about one and a half times; but GDP, adjusted

TABLE 13.1 What Does It Mean to Perpetually Grow: U.S. GDP, Population, and Per Capita GDP, 1940–2010

Year	U.S. Nominal GDP (millions of dollars)	Real GDP (in 2005 dollars)	U.S. Population (in thousands)	U.S. Nominal GDP Per Capita (in current dollars)	Real GDP per Capita (in 2005 dollars)
1940	101,400	1,666,900	132,122	767.47	8,831.99
1950	293,700	2,006,000	151,684	1,936.26	13,224.86
1960	526,400	2,830,900	180,760	2,912.15	15,661.10
1970	1,038,300	4,269,900	205,089	5,062.68	20,819.74
1980	2,788,100	5,839,000	227,726	12,243.22	25,640.46
1990	5,800,500	8,033,900	250,181	23,185.21	32,112.35
2000	9,951,000	11,226,000	285,335	36,049.56	39,749.59
2010	14,526,500	13,088,000	310,106	46,843.66	42,204.92

Source: Louis Johnston and Samuel H. Williamson, 2011. "What Was the U.S. GDP Then?" *Measuring Worth*, http://www.measuringworth.org/usgdp/

for inflation, has increased by a factor of nine. Consequently, each person has had to do almost six times more to ensure that capital accumulation rose at the necessary rate. Consequently ways had to be found to produce the equivalent of more laborers (e.g., new technologies, adding to the workforce by requiring more workers per family, outsourcing manufacturing to countries with a surplus labor supply). Financial instruments, technologies, and rules (e.g., expansion of the money supply, going to fiat money, expanding credit) had to be developed or changed to allow individual investors to realize more return on their capital. And finally, ways had to be found for people to consume more or to find more people to consume (e.g., more aggressive advertising, loosening credit requirements, developing new technologies of persuasion such as TV).

The increasing difficulty of maintaining investor returns at any cost is evidenced by U.S. and global economic policy over the past forty years. After WW II the U.S. and global economy grew relatively rapidly, but began to slow down in the 1970s. Perhaps more importantly, the rate of inflation, that is the decreasing value of the dollar, increased. This meant that lenders were being repaid in dollars worth considerably less than the dollars they initially lent. From 1970 to 1980 average yearly inflation was almost 8 percent. Thus if you lent $100 in 1970, the $100 you were repaid in 1980 would only buy about $50 worth of stuff. This is good for borrowers, but not for lenders, because the money they received from borrowers was worth less than the money they lent. Because high inflation was accompanied by a slightly lower economic growth rate, the 1970s were characterized by what was called "stagflation."

This may sound like something that would only interest economists, but it led to changes in our economy that affected everyone. In order to adjust for slower growth, and the reduced rate of return on capital for investors, the following steps were taken, each of which, as we'll see, diminished our natural, political, and social capital or wealth.

First, taxes on the wealthy were reduced. Before 1980, the top tax bracket in the United States was 70 percent, where it had been since the 1930s and down from 90 percent in the early 1970s. It has since been reduced to between 30 percent and 40 percent (see Noah 2012:110). Furthermore, the profits on money earned through investments are taxed at about half the rate of income earned through wages. As we'll see, this greatly increased economic inequality as well as reduced financial support for the collective good (e.g., education, maintenance of infrastructure, environmental cleanup).

Second, labor's share of increased capital has been vastly reduced, such that in real wages, it has remained steady or even declined, while the share of profits going to investors has vastly increased (see Wolf 2010:125). One way that this was accomplished was by systematically destroying workers' unions. Union membership in the United States has declined from 21 million persons, or 31 percent of the workforce, to 15 million, or 12 percent of the workforce,

7 percent if you exclude government employees (Noah 2012:128). This, also, increased social inequality and reduced social mobility.

A third way to continue growing return on capital is to weaken monopoly laws, thus decreasing competition among corporations and keeping prices (and profit) relatively high. The so-called "merger-frenzy" of the 1980s and early 1990s is illustrative of the weakening monopoly laws in the United States. One result, as we'll see, was to give corporations and financial institutions greater political power and make them "too big to fail." It may not be an exaggeration to say that corporate entities virtually control governments all over the world.

Fourth, you can maintain the profitability of investments by keeping inflation low. Inflation reduces the value of currency over time by reducing what you can buy with it. It also cuts into the profits of investors, as we mentioned above, by reducing the value of money received compared to the money that was lent or invested. On the other hand, inflation is desirable for debtors because it makes it easier to repay debt. As we'll see, this results in more money flowing from the less rich to the more rich.

Fifth, you can loosen government regulations or enforcement on environmental laws, labor laws, advertising, illegal immigration, and capital flows. So-called free trade, for example, by changing the regulations on how goods, services, and capital can flow across national boundaries, allows more capital to be drawn from less economically sophisticated economies, as we discussed earlier (Chapter 5) in the case of Mexico and the United States. In the 1980s, U.S. regulations regarding advertising targeted to children were loosened, promoting a barrage of sophisticated ads targeting kids two years and older. Laws aimed at protecting the environment were either gutted or went unenforced (see Speth 2008), and international treaties aimed at controlling climate change went unratified by Australia and the United States. Restrictions on banks, such as the Glass-Steagall Act that limited speculative investing by commercial banks, were removed, thus exposing the economy to greater risk. Loosening or removing regulations may have accelerated economic growth, but it also accelerated the liquidation of natural, political, and social capital.

Sixth, tax dollars can be used to stimulate economic activity or to protect investment institutions, such as commercial and investment banks. In addition, military spending can be used as an economic stimulus by funneling money through the armaments and security industry. This, of course, means that there is a reduction in our collective efforts to fund education, physical infrastructure, environmental cleanup, and so on.

Finally, you can maintain the growth of return on capital by keeping interest rates low and easing credit. Thus people are able to borrow more in order to spend and consume, although to do so requires them to go into greater debt. This not only allows banks and investors to profit, it also, as we'll see, increases economic inequality. Increased borrowing also increases the risk of a financial crisis that impacts more heavily on the less rich and weakens the ability of governments to help those in need. Furthermore, the higher debt load increases the required rate of growth in order for lenders and investors to get their money back with greater value.

All of these steps, among others, can keep investor profits growing in spite of the inherent difficulty of maintaining the necessary rate of growth, although each, in some way as we've discussed in earlier chapters, exposes the majority of persons all over the globe to lower incomes, more hunger and poverty, greater environmental pollution, greater exposure to disease, and conflict. The problem, of course, is that, as exponential economic growth becomes harder and harder to maintain, the measures that decrease nonmonetary wealth in order to create more money must continually accelerate.

As we noted in the Introduction to Part I, and as we discussed in Chapter 3, the need for perpetual growth or capital/wealth accumulation has to do with the nature of our financial system. As long as money is issued as debt, the economy has to grow to furnish the interest on the debt; as long as capitalists invest money and expect to get more back, our economic system must function to produce more and more monetary wealth ad infinitum.

This is, of course, a socially constructed economic system; it is not the only way to produce and distribute wealth or to inject money into the economy. Our system began to emerge some 300 years ago and can be said to have originated when European rulers, and later the founders of the United States, in order to pay off debts accumulated in war, granted to private parties—banks—the right to issue currency and to maintain only a portion of the money deposited as a reserve—thus vastly increasing their ability to issue money as debt. People can argue, as many have, over the virtues of issuing money as debt and a privatized financial system, and point to their success at increasing monetary wealth and the standard of living of many. Regardless, it is clear also that by constructing an economy on debt and interest, we have constructed one that must perpetually grow exponentially. The result is that as we extract more and more resources from the earth in the form of food, lumber, oil, steel, and so on, the earth's ability to furnish these resources continually diminishes. And as monetary wealth grows, primary wealth—that is our environment, our political freedoms, and the quality of our social lives—continues to deteriorate.

We noted in the Introduction to Part I that we can conceptualize the working of our society and economy as a process of capital or wealth conversion. That is, we take primary wealth, such as trees, water, social relations, and political freedoms, and convert it into money (see Figure I.4). Before we examine how to escape the bully of perpetual growth, let's examine more closely the process of capital conversion. *What are the rules by which these conversions occur? How are we doling out natural, political, and social capital to bloat our economic accounts? And, how have the measures taken to ensure that investors realize a constant return on capital over the past thirty years affected our lives?*

The Depletion of Natural Capital/Wealth

Much like money in a bank, natural capital consists of those features of the natural world that human beings and all other living things draw on for their maintenance and survival. In the culture of capitalism, we draw on the environment for our food, shelter, travel, communication, and virtually every other activity. Clearly, the growth of GNP is dependent on the environment. Freshwater, for example, is part of our natural capital. Whenever we use water, we are withdrawing some of that capital. Because carefully regulating the industrial and agricultural use of water would hamper economic growth, there seems to be little doubt that we are running out of clean water. Globally, 10 percent of those withdrawals go to household usage, whereas some 90 percent is used by global industry and 65 percent for global agriculture and meat production. According to the United Nations, however, there are 1 billion people who lack access to fresh drinking water. Furthermore, in the interests of economic growth, industry expects to double its consumption of freshwater in the next twenty-five years, leaving about two-thirds of the world's population with a severe water shortage. In the United States alone, users are depleting the High Plains Ogallala aquifer, which stretches from Texas to South Dakota, eight times faster than nature can replenish it (Barlow 1999). Then there is the increase in fracking, or hydraulic fracturing, where millions of gallons of water, sand, and chemicals are injected, under high pressure, into a well in order to open fissures that allows natural gas to flow and be extracted. Fracking gets us more energy essential for economic growth, but it uses enormous amounts of water while, at the same time, injecting chemicals into the earth and possibly into our water supply. And we don't know what these chemicals are because a 2005 Energy Bill exempted natural gas drilling from the Safe Drinking Water Act thus exempting companies from disclosing the chemicals used during hydraulic fracturing, depriving the public of information needed for political action.

Every product or service that we consume—that is, everything on which we spend money—has at least four sets of costs: (1) the costs that manufacturers pay to get something produced and distributed, costs that are then reflected in the prices people pay. Costs not assumed directly by manufacturers or consumers—that is, not included in the retail price—include (2) environmental costs associated with the production of products, (3) environmental costs of the item's use, and (4) environmental costs of the product's disposal. Failure to regulate these costs means that we pass them on to those directly affected by the environmental costs or on to future generations. However, for the most part, our system of national accounts considers only one of these costs.

Computers provide a good example of the rules that allow us to externalize costs. Computer makers must spend money to purchase computer components or the raw materials to make them, purchase machines and pay the labor to design and make their products, pay interests on loans and dividends on stocks, and pay shippers—truckers, railroads, shipping companies, and so on—to distribute their product. These costs are generally reflected in the price of the computers, and all contribute to the GNP. However, there are a whole range of costs, many of them environmental, that are externalized—that is, passed on to the general public or to future generations. It begins with the silicon chip, the basic component in computers. There are 220 billion chips manufactured each year that contain highly corrosive hydrochloric acid; metals such as arsenic, cadmium, and lead; volatile solvents such as methyl chloroform, benzene, acetone, and trichloroethylene (TCE); and a number of supertoxic gases. A single batch of chips requires on average twenty-seven pounds of chemicals, nine pounds of hazardous waste, and 3,787 gallons of water requiring extensive chemical treatment. Silicon Valley in California has the largest number of Environmental Protection Agency's (EPA) Superfund sites (29), and researchers have detected more than hundred contaminants in the local drinking water. None of these environmental costs of cleaning up the waste or despoiling resources (or the health costs that may result, for that matter) are included in the price of the computer.

Also not included in the price consumers pay are disposal costs. In the year 2007, experts estimate that we had more than 500 million obsolete computers in the United States, many destined for landfills, incinerators, or hazardous waste sites in the periphery. "If everyone threw them out at once," one person said, "we would have a one mile high waste mountain of junked computers the size of a football field." Computers are not benign waste; those 500 million computers represent 1.2 billion pounds of lead, 2 million pounds of cadmium, 400,000 pounds of mercury, and 1.2 million pounds of hexavalent chromium, to name a few of the toxic substances from which they are made. Yet the cost of cleaning up these substances is not included in the cost or price and so must be assumed by the general public. Any legitimate accounting system would deduct that cost from what computer sales contribute to the economy or internalize the cost that is passed on to the consumer. Instead, we count computer sales as additions to the GNP and ignore the environmental costs. In other words, using our current rules for national accounting, there is no economic deficit involved in using up our natural capital. Yet, clearly that makes no sense from an economic or any other point of view. However, from the narrow perspective of consumers, capitalists, and laborers, it is beneficial to continue to externalize costs; it keeps production costs down, but consumption and wages up. Yet in the long run, of course, it encourages the continued conversion of natural capital into economic capital (money).

The Depletion of Political Capital/Wealth

In the 1991 *Human Development Report,* the United Nations issued its "freedom index," an attempt to measure the existence and effectiveness of democratic institutions among the countries of the world. Among the some thirty-nine items considered were freedom to travel, freedom of association, freedom of expression, various measures of freedom from arbitrary persecution, measures of political freedom, and measures of freedom of access to information. In that survey, countries were assigned a number from one to forty, forty being the highest level of freedom (see Table 13.2).

The Human Freedom Index, while dated (the data on which the ranking were made goes back to 1985), captures part of the essence of political capital. A society rich in political capital enables its members to have a say in decisions that affect their lives. Political capital is measured by the extent to which each person can signify by a vote or other means their satisfaction or dissatisfaction with the state of things. It can be measured by the degree of access people have to those responsible for decision making. At one extreme are those societies in which individuals have virtually no say in their own fate, such as with slavery. The other extreme is the society that operates on consensus in which each and every person can affect collective decision making.

TABLE 13.2   Human Freedom Index (based on conditions in 1985)

The Top Ten Countries with Highest Freedom Ranking	Points	The Ten Countries with Lowest Freedom Ranking	Points
Sweden	38	Zaire	5
Denmark	38	Pakistan	5
Netherlands	37	Bulgaria	4
Finland	36	South Africa	3
New Zealand	36	USSR	3
Austria	36	China	2
Norway	35	Ethiopia	2
France	35	Romania	1
West Germany	35	Libya	1
Belgium	35	Iraq	0

Source: Data from Michael Wolff, Peter Rutten, and Albert Bayers III, eds., 1992. *Where We Stand.* New York: Bantam Books.

Examples would be small-scale gathering and hunting societies or a small group of friends deciding on which movie to see. Things that detract from political capital but that may add to monetary capital are authoritarian regimes, the application of deadly force, the undermining of democratic institutions, and economic debt.

The question is, *How do authoritarian regimes promote economic growth?* There is no overall consensus. Studies done in the 1970s and 1980s indicated that authoritarian political regimes had higher rates of economic growth than did more democratic regimes. Other studies claim that the more democratic the regime, the higher the rate of economic growth (see, e.g., Scully 1995). Most recently, in a cross-cultural empirical study of determinants of economic growth, Robert J. Barro (1996:2) concluded that, at low levels of political rights, an expansion of [democratic] rights stimulates economic growth. However, once a moderate amount of democracy has been attained, a further expansion reduces growth.

The key question is, *Why should increased democratization inhibit economic growth?* Barro suggests that democratization retards growth because, as growth increases, citizens become more concerned with economic inequality and social justice and demand social programs and income redistribution, neither of which is conducive to the uninhibited accumulation of monetary capital. But the relationship was perhaps best expressed by a J. P. Morgan currency strategist commenting on the establishment of a democratic government in Indonesia in 1998: "Democracy," he said, "is a desirable form of government, but it's not necessarily the most efficient form of government" (Arnold 1999). What he meant, of course, is that authoritarian governments are better for business, and hence for economic growth, than democratic governments—that is, rules that encourage the centralization of power and the depletion of political capital also allow for greater accumulation of economic capital. Authoritarian governments are better able to suppress labor organizing, put down resistance to environmental destruction, confiscate property, control the media and the flow of information, offer generous tax benefits to investors, and cut back on social and education programs—all actions that encourage economic growth.

The rules now in existence in the global economy that permit the concentration of power in the hands of multinational corporations provide another example of how political capital can be converted into economic capital. Of the world's 100 largest economies, almost half are internal to corporations (see Table 13.3). The sales of Walmart are larger than the GDP of Nigeria, a country with a population of 162 million people. The combined sales of the world's top 200 corporations are equal to 28 percent of the total world GDP (Anderson and Cavanagh 2000).

TABLE 13.3 The Top 100 Global Financial Entities, 2006–2007

Rank	Country or Company	GDP/Revenue in Billions	Rank	Country or Company	GDP/Revenue in Billions
1	United States	12980	41	Algeria	253.4
2	China	10000	42	Hong Kong	253.1
3	Japan	4220	43	Switzerland	252.9
4	India	4042	44	Greece	251.7
5	Germany	2585	45	Czech Republic	221.4
6	United Kingdom	1903	46	Norway	207.3
7	France	1871	47	Portugal	203.1
8	Italy	1727	48	Chile	203
9	Russia	1723	49	Denmark	198.5
10	Brazil	1616	50	Romania	197.3
11	Korea, South	1180	51	General Motors	192.6
12	Canada	1165	52	Chevron	189.5
13	Mexico	1134	53	Nigeria	188.5
14	Spain	1070	54	DaimlerChrysler	186.1
15	Indonesia	935	55	Toyota Motor	185.8
16	Taiwan	668.3	56	Peru	181.8
17	Australia	666.3	57	Ford Motor	177.21
18	Turkey	627.2	58	Ireland	177.2
19	Iran	610.4	59	Venezuela	176.4
20	Argentina	599.1	60	Hungary	172.7
21	Thailand	585.9	61	Finland	171.7
22	South Africa	576.4	62	ConocoPhillips	166.7
23	Poland	542.6	63	Israel	166.3
24	Netherlands	512	64	General Electric	157.2
25	Philippines	443.1	65	Total	152.4
26	Pakistan	427.3	66	Morocco	147
27	Saudi Arabia	374	67	Kazakhstan	138.7
28	Colombia	366.7	68	Singapore	138.6
29	Ukraine	355.8	69	ING Group	138.2
30	Exxon Mobil	339.9	70	Citigroup	131.0
31	Bangladesh	330.8	71	AXA	129.8
32	Belgium	330.4	72	United Arab Emirates	129.4
33	Egypt	328.1	73	Allianz	121.4
34	Wal-Mart Stores	315.7	74	Volkswagen	118.4
35	Malaysia	308.8	75	Fortis	112.4
36	Royal Dutch Shell	306.7	76	Crédit Agricole	110.8
37	Sweden	285.1	77	American Intl. Group	108.9
38	Austria	279.5	78	New Zealand	106
39	BP	267.6	79	Assicurazioni Generali	101.4
40	Vietnam	258.6	80	Siemens	100.1

Rank	Country or Company	GDP/Revenue in Billions	Rank	Country or Company	GDP/Revenue in Billions
81	Sinopec	98.8	91	State Grid	87
82	Slovakia	96.3	92	Hewlett-Packard	86.7
83	Nippon Telegraph & Telephone	94.9	93	BNP Paribas	85.7
84	Carrefour	94.5	94	PDVSA	85.6
85	HSBC Holdings	93.5	95	UBS	84.7
86	ENI	92.6	96	Bank of America Corp.	84
87	Aviva	92.6	97	Hitachi	83.6
88	Intl. Business Machines	91.1	98	China National Petroleum	83.6
89	McKesson	88.0	99	Pemex	83.4
90	Honda Motor	87.5	100	Nissan Motor	83.3

Source: Data for the top 100 countries is available at Index Mundi at http://www.indexmundi.com/g/r.aspx?t=100&v=65 and the top 100 corporations at CNN Money at http://money.cnn.com/magazines/fortune/global500/2006/full_list/

To further economic growth, nation-states have allowed and encouraged corporations to accumulate enormous economic and political power. CEOs can assign or withdraw resources at will, open and close plants, change product lines, or lay off workers with no recourse by persons or communities that are affected. Corporations can dictate tax laws, environmental regulations, and labor rules. The culture of capitalism, in the interests of increasing GNP, has transferred planning functions from governments accountable to their citizens to corporations accountable only to their shareholders.

The monopolistic consolidation of power and money in fewer and fewer corporations continues virtually unabated. Half of the top 200 corporations represent only five economic sectors—trading, automobiles, banking, retailing, and electronics. In automobiles, the top five firms account for 60 percent of global sales; in electronics, the top five control more than half of global sales. The top five firms in the areas of air travel, aerospace, steel, oil, computers, chemicals, and media control more than 30 percent of all global sales (Anderson and Cavanagh 2000). The ten largest corporations in each sector control 86 percent of the telecommunications industry, 85 percent of the pesticides industry, 70 percent of the computer industry, 35 percent of pharmaceuticals, and 32 percent of commercial seed. In the interests of economic growth, we are moving rapidly toward ever greater consolidation of this unaccountable corporate power. Since 1992, the total value of corporate mergers has increased 50 percent a year in all but one, and most mergers are accompanied by massive layoffs.

The U.S. nation-state also permits the erosion of political capital through the rules that regulate (or fail to regulate) campaign financing. As corporations have gained more and more power, they are able to translate economic power to political power through massive donations to the country's elected representatives. Few politicians would disagree with the fact that, at the very least, money gains a hearing before our government officials, and that, in many cases, influences legislation. Market exchanges are surrounded by a lot of rules, rules concerning union organization, free trade, and the environment; these rules are then determined by a political process that is shaped by money donated to political candidates. In 2010, the Supreme Court of the United States in their ruling in the case of *Citizens United v. the Federal Election Commission* prohibited the government from restricting independent political expenditures by corporations and unions, although corporations and business donate from five to ten times more than unions (Chapin 2010). And research indicates that companies that give political donations and spend money lobbying legislators, enjoy higher profits and higher stock prices (Wolf 2011).

Globally over the past thirty years we can see the diminution of political capital and its conversion into economic capital in the nondemocratic regimes of the WTO and IMF, and in trading agreements such as the North American Free Trade Agreement (NAFTA) and the Free Trade Area of the Americas (FTAA). These agreements represent a transfer of power from largely democratically elected governments accountable to their citizens to nondemocratic institutions, controlled largely by multinational corporations and accountable to no one, except perhaps their stockholders. The panels empowered by these agreements can challenge environmental, health, labor, and social laws and regulations established by legislative bodies. These panels can, in secret and with no possibility for appeal, make decisions that may run counter to the wishes of the citizens of member countries. Thus, even if citizens in the United States wished to pass legislation to protect the environment or individual health, the WTO arbitrators could impose a severe economic penalty if the legislation was deemed to be a restriction of trade.

Debt, which contributes to the depletion of natural capital, also encourages the generation of rules that require indebted countries to sacrifice their autonomy and the political rights of their citizens to the nondemocratic regimes of the IMF and WTO. Thus, against the will of citizens, indebted nation-states are forced to cut necessary social programs, devalue currency, or permit the takeover of services or property by corporations or foreign investors.

The expansion of armament production and distribution poses an additional danger to political capital. The production of armaments generates enormous wealth. As we saw in Chapter 4, nation-states spend almost one and a half trillion dollars on weapons. Much of this wealth comes at the expense of political freedoms crushed by these weapons. American "security aid" has contributed at one time or another to the establishment and maintenance of dictatorial governments in Guatemala, Haiti, Chile, the Philippines, Indonesia, Iran, the Congo, Brazil, Argentina, and Nicaragua, to name only a few. Governments use these weapons primarily to maintain control over their citizens; they contribute to state terrorism and killing.

Increased protests of the sort we examined in the previous three chapters, and which are seen as threats to overall economic growth, elicit greater repression and denial of human rights by nation-states. Thus, the U.S. Patriot Act enacted after the attacks of 9/11, which may be seen by some as the necessary price for security, nevertheless increases the degree of government surveillance while diminishing individual rights.

And military expenditures represent a form of government economic stimulus that citizens generally support. Since 2002, the United States has spent over one trillion dollars on homeland security, most of which went to large corporations (Mueller and Stewart 2011). And the expenditures on U.S. military action in Iraq and Afghanistan is close to four trillion dollars (Costs of War 2012).

Perhaps more importantly, there has been a decline in rates of political participation in the United States. Theta Skocpol (2003) and her associates document the decline of civic participation in the United States, a decline that mirrors the decline in collectivities—groups of people necessary to enact civic action. People have withdrawn into class-based groups, rather than participating together in voluntary associations as they did up to half century ago. Skocpol (2003:254) concludes that

> critical aspects of the classic civic America we have lost need to be reinvented—including shared democratic values, a measure of fellowship across class lines, and opportunities for the many to participate in organized endeavors alongside the elite few.

There are other areas in which our political capital is converted to economic growth, such as the increased concentration of media sources in the hands of fewer and fewer people. The media is able to control what sorts of information we get and to whom we listen. In the United States, the media has the power to choose the political candidates and the range of political positions to which people are exposed.

A society in which people must believe that perpetual increase in consumption is a virtue, that perpetual capital accumulation is progress, that material possessions provide happiness, and that there is no such thing as enough, requires the development of highly sophisticated technologies of manipulation and control. Whether we call it marketing, public relations, or propaganda, we have secured the research, skills, and creativity of biologists, psychologists, engineers, anthropologists, artists, musicians, writers, educators, and others to explicitly develop instruments of persuasion. These instruments create the desires, tastes, and values most conducive to the patterns of consumption, labor, and profit required to ensure perpetual capital accumulation. In a society of perpetual growth we must assign to the most creative among us the job of manipulating and intensifying the wants of others.

Marketers, freed from governmental regulation, have devised methods to manipulate children to buy or "nag" their parents to buy more and more. Public relations have advanced to the point that politicians can brag that "we create our own reality." Political campaigns become "spin" competitions or "selling" campaigns. Technologies designed to help cure illness or repair broken bodies, such as magnetic resonance imaging devices, are used to increase the wants of children by studying the brain's reaction to specific marketing stimuli.

But perhaps the greatest danger in the erosion of political capital is that it may reach the point where so little is left that it becomes impossible to offer any resistance to its continued conversion into wealth.

The Depletion of Social Capital/Wealth

Perhaps the most insidious result of the need to maintain perpetual growth is on the quality of our social lives. Human beings are the most social of the primates. Whatever qualities define us as human beings, the ability to form and maintain social networks and relationships surely is as important as any other characteristic. Consequences of breakdowns in social relations include anxiety, stress, and, as we'll see, physical illness. However, our need to maintain the flow of capital to investors is clearly endangering our ability to relate meaningfully to one another.

The depletion of social capital has received more recent attention through the work of sociologist Robert D. Putnam (2000). Putnam's work documents what he considers the measurable decline in social capital in America, a decline captured in his book *Bowling Alone.* For Putnam (2000:19),

> social capital refers to connections among individuals—social networks and the norms of reciprocity and trustworthiness that arise from them. In that sense, social capital is closely related to what some have called "civic virtue."

Social capital allows people to acquire benefits through their memberships in social networks, to resolve problems, and make decisions collectively. Social capital bonds people together in groups, enhancing trust and the conviction that others will "do the right thing." Social capital is evidenced in what anthropologists call *generalized reciprocity,* the giving of things to others with only the understanding that at some time in the future something will be received in exchange.

Social capital can improve our lives by making people aware of how our fates are linked while building social networks that help people fulfill individual goals. In U.S. communities that are rich in social capital, persons serve in local organizations, attend public meetings, vote, spend time working on community projects, visit friends frequently, entertain at home, and feel that "most people can be trusted," or agree with the statement that "most people are honest."

In *Bowling Alone,* Putnam (2000:287) measures the evolution of social capital in America over the past century and concludes that "by virtually every conceivable measure, social capital has eroded steadily and sometimes dramatically over the past two generations."

Putnam attributes the decline of social capital to four factors. About half of the decline, he says, is a result of the slow, steady replacement of a long "civic generation" by a generation of their less involved children and grandchildren, and about one-quarter to the advent of electronic entertainment, particularly television. The rest of the decline he attributes to time and money pressures on two-career families and the increase of suburban sprawl that creates communities with no centers.

It is significant that most of the factors Putnam identifies as contributing to the decline of social capital also contribute to economic growth. We have converted social capital into economic capital by enacting rules and regulations that encourage suburban sprawl that, while reducing contact among people, creates new and larger homes, more expenditures on household items, and more road and bridge construction, while creating a dependence on automobiles and all the expenses and profits that they involve. Two-income families exchange time that might be spent in family activities for increased monetary exchanges and income, while television watching, which further reduces family interaction, exposes people to thousands of hours of advertisements and media images that create new consumer needs and offer happiness through goods. It is noteworthy perhaps that in an earlier study, Putnam (1996) named television as the main culprit in the decline of American social capital.

There are other ways, however, that we convert social capital into economic capital. To a great extent, the economic growth in core countries of the past fifty years has been produced by transferring social, capital-rich functions, such as child care, food preparation, health care, entertainment, and maintenance of physical security, from households or communities, where they did not count in GNP figures, to the market where they did count. Of course, this is not an entirely new phenomenon. The process began with the first act of trade, but its acceleration over the past few centuries has completely transformed our social environments. When families gathered to collect food or slaughter game or livestock, multiple social interactions ensued. In the modern economy, those interactions are replaced by a simple exchange of money at the grocery checkout counter.

But to better understand the price we pay or the social wealth we lose to maintain economic growth, let's look careful at only two items that affect how we relate to others—time and social equality.

Few would argue that our most valuable resource is time and, obviously, how we allocate our time is critical to how we relate to each other. How much time do we devote to interacting with friends and families and how much time must we devote to economic activities? The necessity for perpetual growth and the servicing of debt means that people spend less time with family; for example, the conflict between work and family is higher in the United States than elsewhere in the developed world. The typical American middle-income family worked, on average, 11 more hours a week in 2006 than it did in 1979 (Williams and Boushey 2010).

In societies in which individuals are not strapped for time, community members allocate a portion of their time to collective actions that serve the common good. We compensate for that by allocating a portion of our income to taxes, with which people are hired to perform necessary tasks for which we no longer have the time, such as maintaining infrastructure, teaching our children, caring for the elderly, delivering the mail, and defending borders. But as the need to work increases, instead of raising the share we contribute to these functions, we have, through a regressive tax code, reduced it, thus further impoverishing our community. By reducing the share we contribute to the common good, we maintain the illusion of growth. Investors are increasingly taking for themselves the resources that at one time would have been devoted to education, childcare, care of the elderly, community infrastructure, and so forth.

People all over the world are spending more time on their computers and cell phones than with their families or with real people. They are buying robots for companions in much the same way as children cradled their "Furbies" for friends (see Turkle 2011). Sherry Turkle, in her book *Alone Together: Why We Expect More from Our Technology and Less from Each Other*, describes how children, as well as adults, are absorbed with their technology, wedded to their messaging and tweeting. People disagree whether this is good or bad, but it clearly generates profits for technology companies and their investors and for advertisers who can selectively

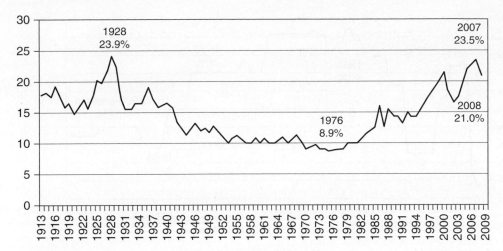

FIGURE 13.1   Top 1% Share of National Income, 1913–2008   *Source:* Thomas Piketty and Emmanuel Saez, "Income Inequality in the United States, 1913–1998," Quarterly Journal of Economics, 118(1), 2003. Updated at http://emlab.berkeley.edu/users/saez.

target people based on their Facebook profile and web travels. We have, essentially, commodified social relations, now paying for something that historically has been a free good.

The second indicator of a loss of social capital is economic inequality. From the 1930s to 1970s, the gap in incomes in the United States contracted. Since then it has once again increased to what it was in the 1920s. In 1928, the top 1 percent in income took in 24 percent of the total. By 1970, the top 1 percent took in nine percent. By 2007 it was back to 24 percent (see Noah 2012:11). (See Figure 13.1.)

Income gains over the past thirty years, largely because of the measures discussed above to maintain a constant return on capital, have gone largely to the very rich (see Figure 13.2).

Furthermore, economic mobility has dramatically decreased; only 6 percent of those born into the bottom 20 percent will make it to the top 20 percent. Individuals in the United States

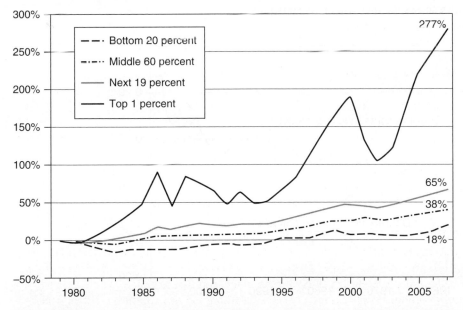

FIGURE 13.2   Percent Change in Real After-Tax Income, 1979–2007   *Source:* Congressional Budget Office.

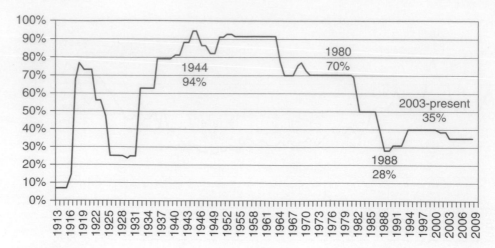

FIGURE 13.3 Top Marginal Tax Rate, 1913–2008 *Source:* Tax Policy Center.

have less of a chance of moving up the economic ladder than any other wealthy countries with the exception of Italy and the United Kingdom, and only slightly more than them (Noah 2012:35). About 62 percent of Americans (male and female) raised in the top fifth of incomes stay in the top two-fifths, and 65 percent born in the bottom fifth stay in the bottom two-fifths (DeParle 2012).

There are various reasons for the growing inequality, including some of the measures noted above to maintain return on capital. The lower tax rate on the wealthy (see Figure 13.3), the stagnating wages paid to workers, and the gutting of union membership, all contribute to the growing wealth gap. But the most important may be the expansion of debt. Debt, believed essential for economic growth, also concentrates wealth and power in the hands of a few and further accelerates social inequality. We have become a society and a world in which the great majority are indebted to a tiny minority, a world in which the ratio between the amount of interest gained from debt and the amount paid has increased dramatically (see, e.g., Kennedy and Kennedy 1995:26).

As we noted, one way that growth was maintained was to loosen borrowing requirements. Figure 13.4 charts the increase in household debt as the ratio between debt, assets, and income, and Figure 13.5 shows the increase in consumer debt.

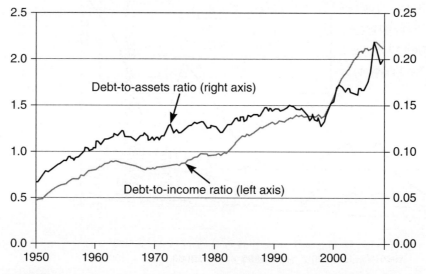

FIGURE 13.4 The Ratio Between Debt and Income/Assets: 1950–2010

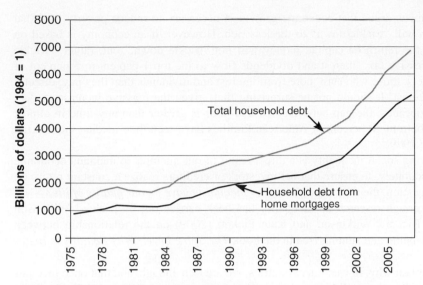

FIGURE 13.5   U.S. Household Debt, 1975–2007   *Source:* Matthew Ruben,
Forgive Us Our Trespasses? The Rise of Consumer Debt in Modern America,
February 2009, ProQuest Discovery Guide.

Since 1975, total household debt, adjusted for inflation, in the United States has grown by
a factor of 41/2.

The increase in debt is important because debt and social inequality are directly related.
To understand this we need to divide the population into net debtors and net creditors. Net debtors are those that pay out more in interest than they receive in interest and/or dividends. Net
creditors are those that receive more in interest and/or dividends than they pay out. If we were to
graph the difference we would get something like the following (Figure 13.6) distribution based
on a 1985 study in Germany (Kennedy and Kennedy 1997:26).

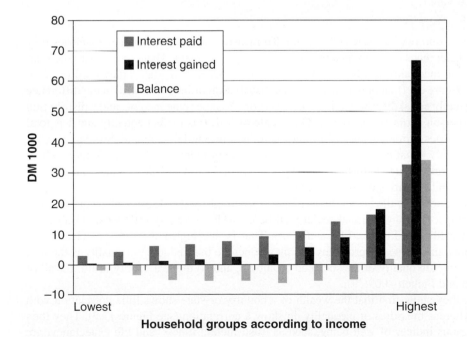

FIGURE 13.6   The New Social Order: A Society of Debtors and Creditors

Some economists argue that economic growth is necessary to reduce poverty, and that increases in wealth will "trickle down" to the less rich. However, if an economy is based on debt, interest, and the return on capital, money will not "trickle down," but, rather, "trickle up." Debt is a regressive tax. Interest and dividends flow to the top 1 percent to 5 percent of the population, that is, those who earn more from interest and dividends than they pay, directly or indirectly, in interest. It should not be surprising that, given the massive increase in debt over the past two decades, the gap between rich and poor is greater than any time in almost 100 years and the bottom 30 percent of American families have seen their median income fall by 29 percent since 1979.

In sum, growing social inequality is a direct result of our attempts to maintain economic growth, or more accurately, to ensure that net investors or creditors realize a constant return on capital. The next question, then, is, *what effect does inequality have on our quality of life?*

The most thorough research on inequality has been carried out by Richard Wilkinson (1996, 2005) and Richard Wilkinson and Kate Pickett (2009) on the relationship between inequality and well-being and summarized in the book *The Spirit Level: Why Equality is Better for Everyone.*

First, they explain why, in wealthier countries, we are rich enough, and that once incomes climb to about $20,000 a year, well-being stops increasing (see, e.g., McKibben 2007). However, social, psychological, and physical well-being, they claim, are most related to the degree of inequality in a society.

To examine the relationship between inequality and health, they first devised an Index of Health and Social Problems for each country and each U.S. state using the following measures:

- level of trust
- rates of mental illness (including alcohol and drug addiction)
- life expectancy and infant mortality
- rates of obesity
- children's educational performance
- teenage births
- homicides
- imprisonment rates
- degree of social mobility

They then used two measures of equality. To measure differences between countries they used income differences between the top and the bottom 20 percent. Then, to compare the relationship between inequality and health and well-being between U.S. states, they used the Gini index, a three-figure coefficient that measures the distribution of income based on the difference between a perfectly equal distribution in which everyone has the same income, and a distribution in which one person earns all the money. On a scale of 0–1, 0 is perfect equality and 1 is total inequality. Countries or regions then fall somewhere in between. For example, Sweden, a country with a relatively equal distribution of income, has a Gini index of 23, while Bolivia, where income is more concentrated at the top, has a Gini index of 58.2. The United States is highest of the major industrial countries with a Gini index of 48.6.

They conclude that the social environment, measured by the degrees of inequality, has a significant impact on physical and social well-being well above any differences in absolute measures of wealth (see Figures 13.7 and 13.8). That is, the higher the Index of Health and Social Problems, the worse the problems and they conclude that reducing inequality is the best way of improving the quality of the social environment, and so the real quality of life for all of us (Wilkinson and Pickett 2009:29).

In sum, they show first that the wealth of a country or state shows little correlation with well-being, whereas measures of inequality do show a correlation (see Figure 13.7). They then show how various indices of well-being, such as trust, mental illness, and life expectancy, are related to inequality (Figure 13.8).

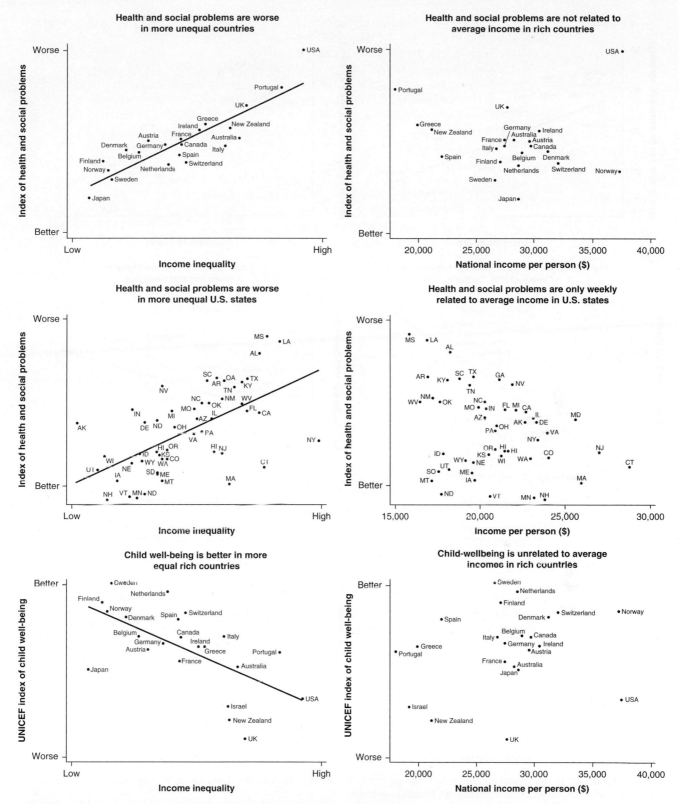

FIGURE 13.7   The Impact of Social Inequality on Physical and Social Wellbeing: By Countries and U.S. States   Source: *The Spirit Level*, Wilkinson & Pickett, Penguin 2009. See also http://www.equalitytrust.org.uk/resources/slides.

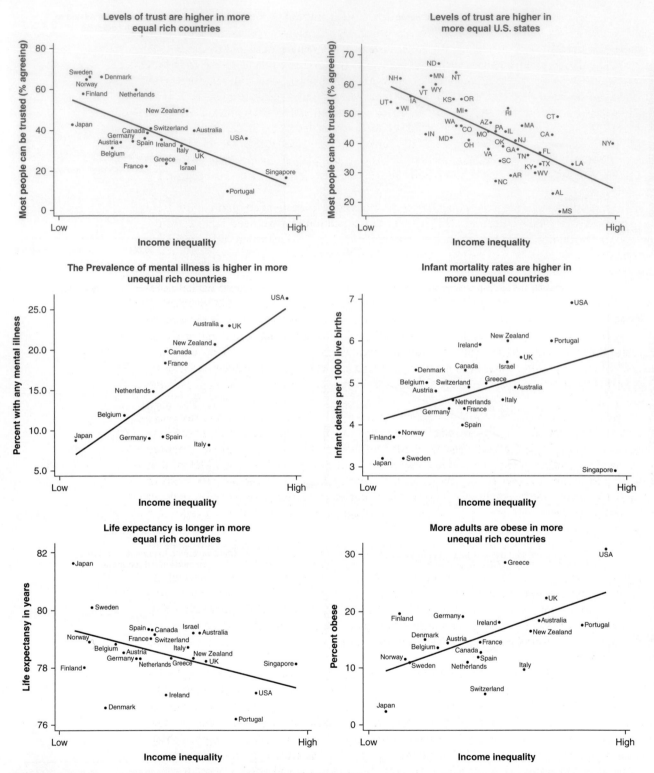

FIGURE 13.8 Other Relationships Between Inequality and Wellbeing   Source: *The Spirit Level*, Wilkinson & Pickett, Penguin 2009. See also http://www.equalitytrust.org.uk/resources/slides.

They next examine what features of inequality might influence the rate of health and social problems. That is, why are human beings sensitive to inequality? We know, for example, from studies over the past forty years, that stress levels, which can be measured by the amount of a central stress hormone called cortisol in the saliva or blood, are related to the frequency of physical and mental illness. Research also shows that stress levels vary with what are called "social evaluative threats." That is, when people perceive that others' evaluation of their social standing is negative, stress levels increase. We know, for example, that when minorities believe that their performance on tests is being evaluated, their scores decline, whereas if subjects are told that the test is relatively meaningless, they perform at the same level as others. We know also from psychological research that anxiety levels over the past fifty years have risen, such that by the late 1980s the average child in the United States was more anxious than psychiatric patients in the 1950s.

The results of the research on inequality have not gone unchallenged, particularly from conservative think tanks objecting primarily to the implication that we need more effective income redistribution measures (see, e.g., Snowdon 2010), critiques that Wilkinson and Pickett answer on the website *The Equality Trust* (http://www.equalitytrust.org.uk/resources/response-to-questions/).

In addition to demanding more time and inequality, the need for increased capital accumulation must also undermine group solidarities while requiring psychologically devastating individuation. Sharing and cooperation is not conducive to economic growth as it reduces the need to consume and reduces the amount of time spent consuming, laboring, and profiting. Capital-producing technologies, such as individualized digital devices, television, and video games, while increasing capital accumulation, promote a decline in face-to-face interactions. Perpetual growth requires that we devise methods to extract capital from even our most basic human activities.

National policies that undermine the formation and rights of labor unions may be necessary to increase corporate profits, but they destroy worker solidarity and cooperation while reducing wages as well as safety in the workplace. Of course, corporations themselves are likewise trapped in the need for endless growth, even if that requires exploitation of workers and withdrawal of support to communities in which they are located. The emergence of the corporate philosophy of "shareholder value" (and the subsequent decline in customer and community service) is a direct consequence of the requirements of corporations to maintain required growth rates and return capital to creditors (see Ho 2009).

Finally, the debt load of developing countries, debts that realistically can never be repaid, requires the increasing exploitation of land for industrial agriculture, forests for lumber products, and oil and other resources for energy. These developments, particularly in the developing world, force people off the land and forests where they might subsist into cities in search of wage labor. Consequently more than half the world's population now live in urban areas, with some 60 percent to 80 percent of those in developing countries (as opposed to 6 percent in the developed world) living in slums with their associated social and health problems.

The practice of religious faith is limited by the necessary increase in values that emphasize materialistic acquisition over spiritual development, sharing and giving. With the continually increasing need to consume, labor, and profit, there is little time or opportunity for traditional religious observance, let alone reflection, contemplation, or meditation. How can a Muslim, Jew, Hindu, Christian, or follower of any faith find the time to pray, to congregate for religious observances, or perform community services required by their faith? How can a Buddhist or a Quaker find time for silent sitting? How can a lover of nature find time for a walk in the woods? It would be hard to imagine Confucius, the Buddha, Jesus, or Mohammad or any of the great religious leaders of the past countenancing the lives their followers are required to lead for the sake of perpetual capital accumulation.

Things We Could Do

The question, of course, is, *How can we address the problems we have discussed in this book?* Some of these are hardly new, and predate our present economic system. But the need for our economy to perpetually grow in order to return wealth to investors has reached a point where any benefits of growth seem to be exceeded by the environmental, political, and social costs.

There is no shortage of recommendations by which we can stop and even reverse the damages that have been done. To save the environment, for example, Herman E. Daly (1990) recommends that we meet three conditions:

1. Rates of consumption of renewable resources must not exceed the rates at which the ecosystem is able to regenerate them.
2. Rates of consumption or irretrievable disposal of nonrenewable resources must not exceed the rate at which renewable substitutes are developed and phased into use.
3. Rates of pollution emission into the environment

To stop the decline of political capital, David Korten (1999) recommends ending the legal fiction of corporate personhood and excluding corporations from political participation. It is clearly not fair to allow corporations with billions of dollars in financial resources to lobby elected legislators in ways not open to individual citizens. We can reduce military spending and allocate that money to education, poverty alleviation, infrastructure, and health.

As we must do to rebuild natural and political capital, to rebuild social capital we must rebuild local communities. We can begin, suggests Korten (1998:57–58), by trying to determine how rich our own communities are in social capital. Ask yourselves the following questions about your community:

- Do people prefer to shop in small local shops run by merchants they know by name or in mega–shopping malls and large retail chain outlets? Do they favor the farmer's market or the supermarket?
- Are farms small, individually owned, and family operated? Or are they controlled by huge corporate enterprises and worked mainly by itinerant landless laborers?
- Are there local noncommercial print, radio, and television media where members of the community can express diverse ethnic, social, political, and cultural views where they will be heard by most of the community? Or is the majority of community news and needs filtered through commercially controlled media?
- Do people devote their free time to Little League baseball, community gardens, local theater, community choirs, community centers, and school boards—or to watching commercial TV?
- Are there credit cooperatives and local banks committed to supporting local enterprise or only branches of large urban banks engaged in channeling local deposits into their global financial operations?
- Do residents consider the area their permanent homes, or are working and professional people largely itinerant?
- Do most households feel secure in their basic sustenance, or do they depend for their survival on poorly paid temporary work?
- Are productive assets owned locally or by distant corporations?
- Are forests harvested selectively and sustainably by local firms to provide material for local industry? Or are local forests stripped bare every forty to sixty years by global corporations and the raw timber exported to distant lands?

The answers to these questions predict the sense of dignity, freedom, responsibility, prosperity, and security of individual people and the extent to which relationships are characterized by trust, caring, and cooperation.

The role of women, says Korten (1998:62–63), is critical in the rebuilding of social capital. Hence, there must be policies that create incentives to provide multiple economic, political, and social options for women.

Clearly money has become more important than a clean environment, a rewarding social life, and individual political freedoms. However, it is not government per se that is solely responsible for this development. Rather it is a financial system that has developed over the past three or four centuries in which money is created by debt and whose primary function is to make money with money. To be sure, government ceded these rights to private financial institutions as a way to eliminate debts accrued largely in war. But if governments ceded those rights, it can surely reclaim them in order to lift the burden imposed by debt and the need for perpetual growth.

At one time it may have been reasonable to issue money as debt. Theoretically such an arrangement reduces the possibility of excessive issues of currency and the monetary inflation that could ensue. Debt-based money is also a means of disciplining people to labor. However, debt-based money does not foster long-range thinking, does not motivate people to contribute to the common good, and is certainly not conducive to solving our environmental, social, and political problems.

To reclaim financial rights and protect a true market economy, governments must themselves issue currency, rather than leaving that right solely to banks. This is not a radical request. This was done by some American colonies and is done by countries today. While a modest interest could be charged, most issues of currency should be through grants. Existing debts must be modified; the current debt level of countries, governments, businesses, and financial institutions is unsustainable and must be renegotiated. Student loan obligations, specifically, must be modified. Limits on interest rates must be lowered, laws regarding bankruptcy must be loosened, and the debts of developing countries must be renegotiated or, in some cases, eliminated. In a world not ruled by capital, we would have recognized that most of these countries are owed more by developed countries than they owe to multilateral institutions and global financial institutions. Local communities should be encouraged to develop their own currencies and economies.

One of the biggest problems facing young people in the United States is student debt. It has almost tripled since 2004. Thus college students are graduating with an average of anywhere from $25,000 to $28,000 in debt. (ZUMA Wire Service/Alamy.)

While there are common sense solutions to the problem of the unsustainability of per-petual growth, the question is, *What would provide the impetus to action?* We are, after all, talking about a significant cultural change, not entirely unlike those promoted for the periphery by core governments and institutions, such as the World Bank. Most of the measures proposed have existed for some time, but clearly national priorities have not veered from the promotion of economic growth regardless of the consequences. Clearly then, as desirable as restoring non-monetary capital is, most of the measures would entail a threat, in one way or another, to our prime directive of perpetual economic growth. *That means that the initial task must be a reform of a financial system that drives us to consume more, labor more, earn more, and support a governmental system designed to further those ends.* Furthermore, to the extent that perpetual growth is driven by debt, we must come up with some way to devise a financial system not dependent on debt and the payment of interest. But is that possible?

Fortunately, there are, in fact, existing models for a reformed financial system. Islamic finance, for example, while centuries old in principle, emerged in the late 1960s and early 1970s in response to the rise of pan-Islamism and the oil boom. Islamic finance rests on the application of Islamic law, or *sharia,* which emphasizes justice and partnership. Financially that means that speculation (*gharar*) and charging of interest (*riba*) are banned, because they involve a fixed interest rate in an uncertain world. Relevant passages (see Maurer 2005:27) in the Qur'an that refer to a ban on interest (usury) include the following:

> God has laid his curse on usury and blessed almsgiving with increase. God bears no love for the impious and the sinful. (2:276)

or

> Believers, do not live on usury, doubling your wealth many times over. Have fear of God, that you may prosper. (3:310)

Generally Islamic financial contracts are constructed in such a way as to be profit-sharing transactions (*mudaraba*) or joint partnerships (*musharaka*). Rather than gaining interest, bank depositors share in the profits of the bank. For example, if I want to open a pizza parlor, I still approach the bank to get the money, but instead of *lending* me the money, the bank becomes my partner in the enterprise, and, in place of interest on the loan, shares in the profits. Unlike Western finance and a loan at interest where you are obligated to pay the extra amount whether or not your venture succeeds or fails, with Islamic finance that is not the case; the "lender," or more properly the partner, shares in whatever income accrues, as well as shares in the risk. The economy may, of course, grow, but only if the real economy (the pizza parlor) succeeds.

Home mortgages in Islamic banking are a little more complicated. In some cases the bank buys the house and the borrower buys it back at some future date, but at a higher price (*murabaha*), or the bank may "lease" the house to the buyer, who pays rent until some agreed-upon amount is reached and the title is passed to the renter (*ijara*). In the case of home mortgages, the amount of growth will depend on whether the end amount is equal to or greater than the amount on price inflation.[1]

There are some who claim that Islamic finance is simply a contrivance to get around the ban on interest by naming it something else (e.g., repurchase at a higher price). But it is clear that Islamic financial instruments are growing in number, with enormous potential for additional growth. In 2011 *sharia*-compliant assets amounted to a trillion dollars and are predicted to reach almost 2 trillion by 2015 (Pasha 2011). While that represents only about 1 percent of worldwide financial instruments, Muslims account for 20 percent of the world's population, thus posing the

---

[1]Of course, without the necessity of perpetual growth, patterns of price inflation may change.

potential for significant growth in interest-free financial transactions. And while Islamic finance may not be the only alternative financial system, it can serve as a model for others.

There are other alternative financial systems, most notably those based on alternative or local currencies, that are designed to avoid interest, keep money circulating, and keep it in local communities (see, e.g., Kennedy and Kennedy 1995; Hallsmith and Lietaer 2011). Or currencies can be issued for special purposes. Brazil introduced a system in which the Ministry of Education issued a currency, called a *Saber*, that could only be redeemed for tuition fees at participating colleges for the year printed on the Saber. The Sabers were issued to students in primary school who could use them to pay upper-level students to mentor them. At the end of the chain, the Sabers would go to a seventeen-year-old who could use them to pay part of their university tuition. The university could then exchange the Saber for conventional money through the Education Fund, but at a discount rate of 50 percent. The logic is that since the university expenses are fixed, the addition of one new student adds little to those expenses. Thus, instead of earning no tuition, the program utilizes excess university space and gives the colleges 50 percent (instead of nothing) of the individual's tuition. Thus, not only do more children go to college, but you encourage a form of learning (teaching others) that creates better students. Thus not only are they more likely to go to college, they are more likely to be prepared.

At the University of Missouri, Kansas City, they issue Buckaroos that represent community service. Thus for each hour of community service, a student gets one buckaroo. And a portion of student's tuition must be paid in Buckaroos.

But regardless of whether or not we adopt an Islamic model, or various local currency schemes, exiting from the treadmill of perpetual growth will require a dramatic alteration of the financial system and the creation of one that is not as heavily dependent on debt.

Since the wealthy profit from debt and the perpetual economic growth that it requires, it is unlikely that they would be willing to reform the financial system from which they gain. *How, in that case, can any meaningful reform ever occur?* Violent revolution is both morally wrong and impractical given the control of legitimate violence by the state. Education and persuasion through public discourse would, given the nature and control of the media by the wealthy, be difficult, at best. Change through the ballot box is extremely difficult given the extent to which money permeates politics in the United States. ("…the banks," according to one U.S. Senator, "are still the most powerful lobby on Capitol Hill. And they frankly own the place" (see Greenwald 2009; Grim 2009). So is there any nonviolent, citizen action that could promote economic reform?

We should note emphatically that the reform required is not anti-market. On the contrary, classic economists, such as Adam Smith, John Stuart Mill, John Maynard Keynes, and, more recently, Amartya Sen, did not envision perpetual economic growth as a goal. They saw economics providing the tools for economies to grow to a certain point, as organisms do in nature,[2] and then, when people could live "wisely, agreeably and well," in the words of Keynes, leveling off (see Jackson 2009:41–42; Skidalsky 2009:xvii). And empirically they were probably correct. All studies of national happiness, well-being, and general health show these measures increasing with per capital income until it reaches some $15,000 to $20,000 a year and then leveling off and even declining (see also Jackson 2009; Kasser 2002). The goal, therefore, of any reform movement, is to save the market economy from devouring itself, and not destroying or undermining it. But what are the means to do it?

THE DEBT STRIKE

There is one right that we maintain and that has the potential to promote changes that, in the long run, benefit everyone, and that is the right to withhold one's debt payments. People are told, of course, that repayment of debt is a moral obligation; but debt is not freely entered into.

---

[2]For an excellent illustration see http://www.impossiblehamster.org.

As our economy is presently constituted, without debt, there would be no money. Furthermore, if governments and municipalities can, without penalty, default on pension obligations or renounce obligations to protect children, the poor, and the elderly, surely people retain the right in the name of a just society to withhold our debt payments. If banks can arbitrarily change interest rates, surely withholding debt payments is equally just. How can debtors have a moral obligation to repay debts, when at least 30 members of the U.S. House of Representatives and 33 U.S. Senators, attempting to force budget cuts, voted in 2012 against the government repaying its debt obligations?[3]

A debt strike deprives creditors, a small minority of our society, of a source of their power and requires them to consider the harm that present arrangements inflict on all. *A debt strike must not constitute a refusal to pay debts*; rather it must be considered an act of civil disobedience to *withhold debt payments*, particularly on securitized debt (e.g., mortgages, automobiles, credit cards, and student loans), until action is taken to reform the presently unsustainable financial system. This would not be a strike against finance, per se; some means of moving money from where it is to where it is needed is necessary for a thriving economic system. However, a financial system founded on a privatized monetary system, debt and interest, and the resulting need for perpetual growth is clearly unsustainable.

The mechanics of a debt strike are relatively easy to institute. A date in the future, perhaps a year off, should be set, at which point, unless there is significant movement to reform the financial system, citizens will withhold their debt payments. Until that date, there will be a good faith effort, perhaps led by some existing legislative or citizen group, or by a citizen group formed for the purpose, to draw up a series of reforms, such as some of those outlined above. The effort must be global in scope. The requirement for perpetual growth is not one faced only by the United States; it is faced by every country that has adopted a Western-style financial system.

This group will need to decide what changes in the financial system or in the rules through which financial systems are created constitute significant progress. If such progress does not occur, debtors will begin to withhold debt payments.

There will, naturally, be some concern on the part of debtors that their withholding of payments will result in some negative consequence (e.g., foreclosure or repossession of assets, fines, lowered credit rating). However, it will require only a small minority (e.g., some 20 percent) to begin the strike to make it impossible for creditors (or the government or financial institutions) to effectively impose penalties. It is not illegal to miss a few debt payments. This would not be, as mentioned above, a refusal to pay debts, but rather an act of civil disobedience to effect change that will not only benefit all, but also save our economy from recurrent crises and collapse.

A debtor's strike is not without its dangers. If the strike succeeds and there is a refusal to implement financial reform, the economy will collapse in a credit crisis. A debt strike, in that regard, is no different than a labor strike. As in a labor strike, all parties have a vested interest in changing a situation that threatens the firm with collapse. However, without some form of financial reform, we remain in a world in which ephemeral economic gain can occur only by abandoning visions of free societies thriving in hospitable environments.

CONCLUSION

While the first step in rebuilding a sustainable and just market economy requires the reform of the financial system, in the end, it will also require a change in values. Every day we make choices that reduce, maintain, or add to our natural, political, or social capital. When we choose to purchase an item at a large-scale chain store, we may save money, but we may also take away business from local enterprises whose success supports our neighbors. By purchasing the item,

---

[3]http://www.senate.gov/legislative/LIS/roll_call_lists/roll_call_vote_cfm.cfm?congress=113&session=1&vote=00011; http://projects.washingtonpost.com/congress/113/house/1/votes/30/

we may tacitly support the exploitation of cheap labor and add to the economic power of multi-national corporations whose power can then be used to sway or control the policy decisions and legislation of local and national governments. By choosing to purchase an item or not purchase an item, we add, perhaps imperceptibly, to pollution and waste. Individual decisions themselves, of course, may have little impact. But when millions, following some cultural imperative, make the same choice, the results can be either destructive or constructive.

Meaningful change, therefore, will only occur when cumulative decisions and the rules that dictate those decisions change. However, it is hard to conceive of individuals altering these choices when their view of the world and of others is essentially materialistic. Over the past three centuries, we have evolved a cosmology that assumes that the creation of the universe was essentially accidental and that the evolution of life consisted of millions of random occurrences. Those of us (including the author) who reject any sort of divine or spiritual intervention in the creation of life have a difficult time attributing any special significance to living things or to other members of our species for that matter. But this view creates a dilemma because this view of the world is not one that would inspire anyone to want to save it.

In January of 1990, at a meeting in Moscow of the Global Forum of Spiritual and Parliamentary Leaders, a group of well-known scientists organized by Carl Sagan presented "An Open Letter to the Religious Community"[4] to encourage a common cause to save the Earth. The letter recognizes the awe and reverence that the authors have felt before the universe, and that our world ought to be held sacred. Consequently, we all need to safeguard our planetary home, and that requires, the authors write, a deeper understanding of science and technology if we are to understand and fix the problems we face. Thus, they say, there must be a role for both science and religion.

The letter led to a meeting in May of 1992 in Washington DC hosted by the then U.S. vice president Al Gore. The conference brought together scientists, including Sagan, Stephen Jay Gould, and Edward O. Wilson, and a few religious leaders with the goal of crafting a joint statement in support of environmental sustainability. Economist Herman Daly attended the conference and asked whether scientists were recruiting religious leaders to provide a moral imperative lacking in science while dismissing these religious leaders for their "distorted" view of reality. For science, the universe is largely random and meaningless; as Steven Weinberg (1999), winner of the Nobel Prize for physics, said, "The more the universe seems comprehensible, the more it also seems pointless."

Apparently, some religious leaders had the same thought as Daly and wondered how a change toward sustainability could take place without a conviction that the universe carries meaning or that it is the "unfolding of a promise." As theologian John F. Haught (quoted in Daly 1996:19) put it,

> A commonly held sense that the cosmos is a significant process, that it unfolds something analogous to what we humans call "purpose," is, I think an essential prerequisite of sustained global and intergenerational commitment to the earth's well being.

Stephen Jay Gould (1991:14) expressed this dilemma well when he said that

> we cannot win this battle to save species and environments without forging an emotional bond between ourselves and nature as well—for we will not fight to save what we do not love.

---

[4]The letter is available online at http://earthrenewal.org/Open_letter_to_the_religious_.htm.

But from where does this "love" come? Where is this spirituality supposed to originate? There is a disconnection in the idea that scientists can use love as a tool for saving what for them is an accidental and pointless universe. In the words of Daly (1996:21),

> There is something fundamentally silly about biologists teaching on Monday, Wednesday, and Friday that everything, including our sense of value and reason, is a mechanical product only of genetic chance and environmental necessity, with no purpose whatsoever, and then on Tuesday and Thursday trying to convince the public that they should love some accidental piece of this meaningless puzzle enough to fight and sacrifice to save it.

Environmentalists who utilize indigenous spirituality and a supposedly mystic tie to nature are guilty of also trying to appropriate religious values to lend legitimacy to sustainability. Like the scientists, they are trying to inculcate some sort of religious legitimization into an essentially materialist agenda.

Yet there seems also to be a realization that without some moral, religious, or spiritual imperative, the kinds of changes that are required to solve the questions we have addressed in this book cannot be addressed with any sort of urgency, if at all. In the history of social movements in America, only a few, such as the abolitionist movement and the civil rights movement, have succeeded in joining political and religious agendas in the cause of change. The efforts, however, highlight the question of whether there must be some philosophical or religious foundation to impel us to restore our waning natural, political, and social capital. Herman Daly (1996:201), I think, sums up the prospect for change well when he says that significant change will require

> [a] change of heart, a renewal of the mind, and a healthy dose of repentance. These are all religious terms, and that is no coincidence, because a change in the fundamental principles we live by is a change so deep that it is essentially religious whether we call it that or not.

REFERENCES

Abu-Lughod, Janet L. 1989. *Before European Hegemony: The World-System* A.D. *1250–1350*. New York: Oxford University Press.

Aghion, Philippe, and Steven N. Durlauf. 2006. *Handbook of Economic Growth*. Amsterdam: North–Holland.

Ahmad, Nik Nazmi Nik. 2003. The State Under Seige. *Asia Times*, December 25.

Allen, James (editor). 2000. *Without Sanctuary: Lynching Photography in America*. Santa Fe, NM: Twin Palms.

Alpert, Bracha. 1991. Student's Resistance in the Classroom. *Anthropology and Education Quarterly* 22:350–366.

Amin, Samir. 1990. The Social Movement in the Periphery: An End to National Liberation. In *Transforming the Revolution: Social Movements and the World-System*, edited by Samir Amin, Girovanni Arrighi, Andre Gunder Frank, and Immanuel Wallerstein. New York: Monthly Review Press.

Amin, Samir, Girovanni Arrighi, Andre Gunder Frank, and Immanuel Wallerstein. 1990. *Transforming the Revolution: Social Movements and the World-System*. New York: Monthly Review Press.

Ammerman, Nancy T. 1991. North American Protestant Fundamentalism. In *Fundamentalisms Observed*, edited by Martin E. Marty and R. Scott Appleby (Fundamentalism Project, volume 1). Chicago, IL: University of Chicago Press.

Anderson, Benedict R. O'G. 1991. *Imagined Communities: Reflections on the Origin and Spread of Nationalism*. New York: Verso.

Anderson, Sarah and John Cavanagh. 2000. *Top 200: The Rise of Global Corporate Power*. Corporate Watch, www.globalpolicy.org/socecon/tncs/top200.htm

Arnold, Wayne. 1999. Foreign Investors Express Concern about Indonesia's New President. *New York Times*, October 27.

Baker, Brenda J., and George Armelagos. 1988. The Origin and Antiquity of Syphilis. *Current Anthropology* 29:703–721.

Bales, Kevin. 1999. *Disposable People: New Slavery in the Global Economy*. Berkeley, CA: University of California Press.

Bamford, James. 2002. *Body of Secrets: Anatomy of the Ultra-Secret National Security Agency*. New York: Anchor Books.

Barlow, Maude. 1999. *Blue Gold: The Global Water Crisis and the Commodification of the World's Water Supply*. International Forum on Globalization, http://www.thirdworldtraveler.com/Water/Blue_Gold.html

Barnes, Barry. 1974. *Scientific Knowledge and Sociological Theory*. London: Routledge & Kegan Paul.

Barnes, Ethne. 2005. *Diseases and Human Evolution*. Albuquerque, NM: University of New Mexico Press.

Barro, Robert J. 1996. *Determinants of Economic Growth: A Cross-Country Empirical Study*. NBER Working Paper 5698. Cambridge, MA: National Bureau of Economic Research.

Barro, Robert J., and Xavier Sala-i-Martin. 2004. *Economic Growth*, 2nd ed. Cambridge, MA: The MIT Press.

Basu, Amrita. 1995. Introduction. In *The Challenge of Local Feminisms: Women's Movements in Global Perspective*, edited by Amrita Basu. Boulder, CO: Westview Press.

Basu, Indrajit. 2003. India's Growing Urge to Splurge. *Asia Times*, August 22.

Bauman, Zygmunt. 1998. *Globalization: The Human Consequences*. New York: Columbia University Press.

BBC. 2009. *Soap Operas Prompt India Divorce*, November 17, http://news.bbc.co.uk/2/hi/south_asia/8363859.stm

Beal, Merrill D. 1963. *I Will Fight No More Forever: Chief Joseph and the Nez Perce War*. Seattle, WA: University of Washington Press.

Beard, Charles (editor). 1959. *The Enduring Federalist*. New York: Frederick Ungar.

Beaud, Michel. 1983. *A History of Capitalism 1500–1980*. Translated by Tom Dickman and Anny Lefebvre. New York: Monthly Review Press.

Beder, Sharon. 2002. *Global Spin: The Corporate Assault on Environmentalism*. Devon, UK: Green Books.

Beeman, William O. 1997. Revitalization Drives American Militias In *Conformity and Conflict: Readings in Cultural Anthropology*, 9th ed., edited by James Spradley and David W. McCurdy. New York: Longman.

Belk, R. W. 1988. Possession and the Extended Self. *Journal of Consumer Research* 15:140–158.

Berthelsen, John. 2003. Asia's Consumer Revolution Deepens. *Asia Times*, November 26.

BGH Bulletin. 2000. *BHG Bulletin: News of Lawsuit Exposing Media Coverup of Suspected Dangers in Milk*, www.foxbghsuit.com/

Bidwai, Praful. 2003. Editorial. *Daily Star* (Bangladesh), November 7.

Binswanger, Hans. 1994. *Money and Magic: A Critique of the Modern Economy in the Light of Goethe's Faust*. Translated by J. E. Harrison. Chicago, IL: University of Chicago Press.

Bittman, Mark. 2008. Rethinking the Meat-Guzzler. *New York Times*, January 27, http://www.nytimes.com/2008/01/27/weekinreview/27bittman.html?ex=1202274000&en=8f4b924e4f931ff3&ei=5070&emc=eta1

Blankenburg, Stephanie, and José Gabriel Palma. 2009. Introduction: The Global Financial Crisis. *Cambridge Journal of Economics* 33:531–538.

Blondet, Cecilia. 1995. Out of the Kitchens and onto the Streets: Women's Activism in Peru. In *The Challenge of Local Feminisms: Women's Movements in Global Perspective*, edited by Amrita Basu. Boulder, CO: Westview Press.

Bodley, John H. 1990. *Victims of Progress*, 3rd ed. Mountain View, CA: Mayfield Publishing.

Bodman, Samuel. 2006. Energy Secretary on the Future of Oil and the Need for Alternatives. *Energy Bulletin*, U.S. Department of Energy, www.energybulletin.net/22364.html

Boserup, Ester. 1965. *The Conditions of Agricultural Growth*. Chicago, IL: Aldine Publishers.

Boserup, Ester. 1970. *Women's Role in Economic Development*. New York: St. Martin's Press.

Bourdieu, Pierre. 1986. The Forms of Capital. In *Handbook of Theory and Research for the Sociology of Education*, edited by John G. Richardson. New York: Greenwood Press.

Bourgois, Philippe. 1995. *In Search of Respect: Selling Crack in El Barrio*. Cambridge: University of Cambridge Press.

Boykoff, Jules, and Matthew Boykoff. 2004. Journalistic Balance as Global Warming Bias. *Fairness and Accuracy in Reporting*, www.fair.org/ index.php?page=1978

Braudel, Fernand. [1979] 1982. *Civilization and Capitalism 15th–18th Century: Vol. II, The Wheels of Commerce*. Translated by Siân Reynolds. New York: Harper & Row.

Brown, Ellen Hodgson. 2010. *The Web of Debt: The Shocking Truth About Our Money System and How We Can Break Free*. Baton Rouge, LA: Third Millennium Press

Bureau of Labor Statistics. 2012. *Foreign-Born Workers: Labor Force Characteristics*, http://www.bls.gov/news.release/pdf/forbrn.pdf

Business Week. 1997. Gen X Ads: Two for Me, None for You. August 11.

Calder, Lendol. 1999. *Financing the American Dream: A Cultural History of Consumer Credit*. Princeton, NJ: Princeton University Press.

Caldwell, John C. 1982. *Theory of Fertility Decline*. New York: Academic Press.

Carneiro, Robert. 1978. Political Expansion as an Expression of the Principle of Competitive Exclusion. In *Origins of the State*, edited by Ronald Cohn and Elman Service. Philadelphia, PA: Institute for the Study of Human Issues.

Carr, Marilyn, and Martha Alter Chen. 2001. Globalization and the Informal Economy: How Global Trade and Investment Impact on the Poor. *Women in Informal Employment: Globalizing and Organizing (WIEGO)*, http://www.ilo.org/wcmsp5/groups/public/@ed_emp/documents/publication/wcms_122053.pdf

Carrier, James G. 1995. *Gifts and Commodities: Exchange and Western Capitalism Since 1700*. London: Routledge.

Caufield, Catherine. 1996. *Masters of Illusion: The World Bank and the Poverty of Nations*. New York: Henry Holt.

Chapin, Laura. 2010. Supreme Court Ruling Empowers Corporations More Than Labor Unions. *U.S. News*, http://www.usnews.com/opinion/blogs/laura-chapin/2010/01/22/supreme-court-ruling-empowers-corporations-more-than-labor-unions

Chase, Allan. 1977. *The Legacy of Malthus: The Social Costs of the New Scientific Racism*. New York: Alfred A. Knopf.

Chen, Shaohua, and Martin Ravallion. 2000. How Have the World's Poorest Fared Since the Early 1980s? *World Bank Research Observer* 19(2):141–169. Oxford: Oxford University Press, http://ideas.repec.org/p/wbk/wbrwps/3341.html

Chossudovsky, Michel. 1996. *Dismantling Former Yugoslavia, Recolonizing Bosnia,* http://groundwork.ucsd.edu/bosnia.html

Chossudovsky, Michel. 1997. *The Globalisation of Poverty, Impacts of IMF and World Bank Reforms*. London: Zed Books.

Chossudovsky, Michel. n.d. *Global Falsehoods: How the World Bank and the UNDP Distort the Figures on Global Poverty*, http://www.adelinotorres.com/economia/TFF%20FEATURES2-%20Articles.htm

Chua, Amy. 2003. *World on Fire: How Exporting Free Market Democracy Breeds Ethnic Hatred and Global Instability*. New York: Doubleday.

Chua, Swee. 1999. Economic Growth, Liberalization, and the Environment: A Review of the Economic Evidence. *Annual Review of Energy and the Environment* 24:391–430.

CNN. 2001. Congress Looks to Shield Economy, September 15, http://archives.cnn.com/2001/US/09/15/rec.congress.terror/

Coale, Ansley. 1974. The History of Human Population. *Science* 231:40–51.

Cohen, Joel. 1995. Population Growth and the Earth's Carrying Capacity. *Science* 269:341–346.

Cohen, Lizabeth. 2003. *A Consumer's Republic: The Politics of Mass Consumption in Postwar America*. New York: Alfred A. Knopf.

Cohen, Mark. 1977. *The Food Crisis in Prehistory: Overpopulation and the Origins of Agriculture*. New Haven: Yale University Press.

Cohen, Mark. 1989. *Health and the Rise of Civilization*. New Haven: Yale University Press.

———. 1994. Demographic Expansion: Causes and Consequences. In *Companion Encyclopedia of Anthropology*, edited by Tim Ingold. New York: Routledge.

———. 1998. *The Culture of Intolerance*. New Haven: Yale University Press.

Cohen, Mitchell. 2002. How Bush Sr. Sold the Bombing of Iraq. *Counter Punch*, December 28.

Cohen, Roger. 2003. Iraq and Its Patron, Growing Apart. *New York Times*, December 21.

Cohen, Ronald, and Elman R. Service (editors). 1978. *Origins of the State: The Anthropology of Political Evolution*. Philadelphia, PA: Institute for the Study of Human Issues.

Cohn-Sherbok, Dan, and Dawoud el-Alami. 2002. *The Palestine-Israeli Conflict: A Beginners Guide*. Oxford: One World.

Coll, Steve. 2004. *Ghost Wars: The Secret History of the CIA, Afghanistan, and Bin Laden, from the Soviet Invasion to September 10, 2001*. New York: Penguin Press.

Colley, Linda. 1992. *Britons: Forging the Nation 1707–1837*. New Haven: Yale University Press.

Collier, George A., Jr. 1994. Roots of the Rebellion in Chiapas. *Cultural Survival Quarterly* 18:14–18.

Collins, Jane L. 2000. Tracing Social Relations in Commodity Chains: The Case of Grapes in Brazil. In *Commodities and Globalization: Anthropological Perspectives*, edited by Angelique Haugerud, M. Priscilla Stone, and Peter D. Little. New York: Rowman & Littlefield.

Comaroff, Jean. 1985. *Body of Power, Spirit of Resistance: The Culture and History of a South African People*. Chicago, IL: University of Chicago Press.

Connell, K. H. 1965. Land and Population in Ireland, 1780–1845. In *Population in History: Essays in Historical Demography*, edited by D. V. Glass and D. E. C. Eversley. Chicago, IL: Aldine Publishers.

Conrad, Joseph. [1902] 1972. *Heart of Darkness*. New York: W. W. Norton & Company.

Cook, Sherburne Friend, and Woodrow W. Borah. 1960. The Indian Population of Central Mexico, 1531–1610. *Ibero-Americana 44*. Berkeley, CA: University of California Press.

Cooley, John. 2002. *Unholy Wars: Afghanistan, America and International Terrorism*. London: Pluto Press.

Copeland, Nick, and Christine Labuski. 2013. *The World of Wal-Mart: Discounting the American Dream*. New York: Routledge

Cordell, Dennis. 1994. Extracting People from Precapitalist Production: French Equatorial Africa from the 1890s to the 1930s. In *African Population and Capitalism: Historical Perspectives*, edited by Dennis Cordell and Joel W. Gregor. Madison, WI: University of Wisconsin Press.

Costs of War. 2012. 236 Thousand Killed, $3-$4 trillion, http://costsofwar.org/

Council for Christian Colleges and Universities. 2001. *Enrollment Continues to Surge at Christian Colleges*, http://www.cccu.org/news/articles/2001/enrollment_continues_to_surge_at_christian_colleges

Courtwright, David T. 2001. *Forces of Habit: Drugs and the Making of the Modern World*. Cambridge: Harvard University Press.

Crosby, Alfred. 1976. *America's Forgotten Pandemic: The Influenza of 1918*. Cambridge: Cambridge University Press.

———. 1986. *Ecological Imperialism: The Biological Expansion of Europe, 900–1900*. Cambridge: Cambridge University Press.

Crotty, James. 2009. Structural Causes of the Global Financial Crisis: A Critical Assessment of the New Financial Architecture. *Cambridge Journal of Economics* 33:563–580.

Daly, Herman E. 1990. Towards Some Operational Principles of Sustainable Development. *Ecological Economics* 2:1–6.

———. 1996. *Beyond Growth: The Economics of Sustainable Development*. Boston, MA: Beacon Press.

Danner, Mark. 2003. Delusions in Baghdad. *New York Review of Books*, December 18.

Dargis, Manohla. 2009. The Camera Zooms in on Fashion's Empress. *New York Times*, August 28, http://movies.nytimes.com/2009/08/28/movies/28issue.html

Davis, Mike. 2006. *Planet of the Slums*. New York. Verso

De Vries, Jan, and Ad van der Woude. 1997. *The First Modern Economy: Success, Failure, and Perseverance of the Dutch Economy, 1500–1815*. Cambridge: Cambridge University Press.

DeParle, Jason. 2012. Harder for Americans to Rise From Lower Rungs, *New York Times*, January 4, http://www.nytimes.com/2012/01/05/us/harder-for-americans-to-rise-from-lower-rungs.html?pagewanted=all

Dettwyler, Katherine. A. 1994. *Dancing Skeletons: Life and Death in West Africa*. Prospect Heights, IL: Waveland Press.

Devore, Irven, and Richard Lee. 1968. *Man the Hunter*. Chicago, IL: Aldine Publishers.

Dobyns, Henry F. 1983. *Their Number Become Thinned: Native American Population Dynamics in Eastern North America*. Knoxville: University of Tennessee Press.

Drèze, Jean, and Amartya Sen. 1989. *Hunger and Public Action*. Oxford: Clarendon Press.

Driscoll, David D. 1992. *What Is the International Monetary Fund?* Washington, DC: International Monetary Fund.

Dubos, Rene. [1952] 1987. *The White Plague: Tuberculosis, Man, and Society*. New Brunswick, NJ: Rutgers University Press.

———. 1968. *Man, Medicine, and Environment*. New York: Mentot.

Durning, Allan. 1992. *How Much Is Enough: The Consumer Society and the Future of the Earth*. New York: W. W. Norton & Company.

Earle, Duncan. 1994. Indigenous Identity at the Margin: Zapatismo and Nationalism. *Cultural Survival Quarterly* 18:26–30.

Edgerton, Robert B. 1989. *Mau Mau: An African Crucible*. New York: The Free Press.

Ehrlich, Paul R. 1968. *The Population Bomb*. New York: Ballantine Books.

Eisenstein, Zillah. 1997. Stop Stomping on the Rest of Us: Retrieving Publicness from the Privatization of the Globe. In *Feminism and Globalization: The Impact of the Global Economy on Women and Feminist Theory*, edited by Alfred C. Aman, Jr. *Indiana Journal of Global Legal Studies,* Spring 1997 (special issue).

Emanuel, Kerry. 2007. Phaeton's Reins. *Boston Review*, January/February, http://bostonreview.net/BR32.1/emanuel.html

Ember, Carol R. 1983. The Relative Decline in Women's Contribution to Agriculture with Intensification. *American Anthropologist* 85:285–304.

Ensminger, Marion E. 1991. *Animal Science*. Danville, IL: Interstate Publishers.

Erasmus, Charles J. 1972. *In Search of the Common Good: Utopian Experiments Past and Future*. New York: The Free Press.

Esty, Daniel C., and Maria H. Ivanova. 2003. Toward a Global Environmental Mechanism. In *Worlds Apart: Globalization and the Environment*, edited by James Gustave Speth. Washington, DC: Island Press.

Evans-Pritchard, E. E. 1940. *The Nuer*. Oxford: Oxford University Press.

Ewald, Paul. 1993. The Evolution of Virulence. *Scientific American* 269:86–93.

Ewen, Stuart. 1996. *PR: A Social History of Spin*. New York: Basic Books.

Fabre, Guilhem. 2002. Criminal Prosperities, Financial Crisis and Money Laundering: The Case of Mexico in a Historical Perspective. In *Globalization, Drugs and Criminalization*. Final Research Report on Brazil, China, India and Mexico. UNESCO, http://unesdoc.unesco.org/images/0012/001276/127644e.pdf

Falk, Richard. 2003. *The Great Terror War*. New York: Olive Branch Press.

Farmer, Paul. 1992. *AIDS and Accusation: Haiti and the Geography of Blame*. Berkeley, CA: University of California Press.

———. 1999. *Infections and Inequality: The Modern Plagues*. Berkeley, CA: University of California Press.

Ferguson, Niall. 2008. *The Ascent of Money*. New York: Penguin Press.

Fernandez-Armesto, Felipe. 2002. *Near a Thousand Tables: A History of Food*. New York: Free Press.

Fernández-Kelly, María Patricia. 1983. *For We Are Sold, I and My People: Women and Industry in Mexico's Frontier*. Albany: State University of New York Press.

Fey, Harold, and D'Arcy McNickle. 1970. *Indians and Other Americans: Two Ways of Life Meet*. New York: Harper & Row.

Finkel, David. 2000. Few Drugs for the Neediest HIV Patients. *Washington Post,* November 2.

Fintan, O'Toole. 1998. The Masked Avenger. *New York Review of Books*, XLV, Number 131, p. 21.

Firth, Raymond. 1959. *Social Change in Tikopia: A Re-Study of a Polynesian Community After a Generation*. London: Allen & Unwin.

First Post. 2011. *How India is Set to Become a Big Player in Global Consumption*, http://www.firstpost.com/economy/how-india-is-getting-ready-to-become-a-big-player-in-global-consumption-126836.html

Fishman, Charles. 2003. The Wal-Mart You Don't Know. *Fast Company*, December Issue 77: 68, www.fastcompany.com/magazine/77/walmart.html

Fjellman, Stephen M. 1992. *Vinyl Leaves: Walt Disney World and America*. Boulder, CO: Westview Press.

Flannery, Kent V. 1972. The Cultural Evolution of Civilization. *Annual Review of Ecology and Systemics* 3:339–426.

———. 1973. *The Origins of Agriculture*. In Siegel, Beals, and Tyler, eds., *Annual Review of Anthropology* 2:271–310.

Foster, John Bellamy. 1993. "Let Them Eat Pollution": Capitalism and the World Environment. *Monthly Review* 44:10–20.

Frank, Andre Gunder. 1998. *ReOrient: Global Economy in the Asian Age*. Berkeley, CA: University of California Press.

Fratkin, Eliot. 1997a. Pastoralism: Governance and Development Issues. *Annual Review of Anthropology* 26:235–261.

———. 1997b. Maasa and Barabaig Herders Struggle for Land Rights in Kenya and Tanzania. *Cultural Survival Quarterly* 21:3.

Franklin, Benjamin. 1748 [2012]. *Advice to a Young Tradesman*. In *Benjamin Franklin: Selections from Autobiography, Poor Richard's Almanac, Advice to a Young Tradesman, the Whistle, Necessary Hints to Those That ... Prayers, Selected Letters*. Forgotten Books.

French, Hilary. 2000. *Vanishing Borders: Protecting the Planet in the Age of Globalization*. New York: W. W. Norton & Company.

Fried, Morton H. 1967. *The Evolution of Political Society: An Essay in Political Anthropology*. New York: Random House.

Gallagher, Kelly Sims. 2006. China *Shifts Gears: Automakers, Oil, Pollution, and Development*. Cambridge: MIT Press.

Gardner, Gary, and Brian Halweil. 2000. *Overfed and Underfed: The Global Epidemic of Malnutrition*. Worldwatch Paper 150. Washington, DC: Worldwatch Institute.

Garrett, Laurie. 1994. *The Coming Plague*. New York: Farrar, Strauss & Giroux.

———. 2005. The Next Pandemic. *Foreign Affairs* 84:3–23.

———. 2009. The Path of a Pandemic. *Newsweek*, May 2, http://www.newsweek.com/id/195692

Garson, Barbara. 2001. *Money Makes the World Go Around: One Investor Tracks Her Cash Through the Global Economy*, from Brooklyn to Bangkok and Back. New York: Penguin

Geffray, Christian. 2002. Social, Economic and Political Impacts of Drug Trafficking in the State of Rondonia, in the Brazilian Amazon. In *Globalization, Drugs and Criminalization*. Final Research Report on Brazil, China, India and Mexico. UNESCO, http://unesdoc.unesco.org/images/0012/001276/127644e.pdf

Gellner, Ernest. 1983. *Nations and Nationalism*. Ithaca, NY: Cornell University Press.

George, Alexander. 1991. *Western State Terrorism*. New York: Routledge.

Ginsburg, Faye. 1993. Saving America's Souls: Operation Rescue's Crusade against Abortion. In *Fundamentalisms and the State: Remaking Polities, Economies, and Militance*, edited by Martin E. Marty and R. Scott Appleby (Fundamentalism Project, volume 3). Chicago, IL: University of Chicago Press.

Gitlin, Todd. 2012. *Occupy Nation: The Roots, the Spirit, and the Promise of Occupy Wall Street*. It Books.

Glanz, James. 2007. Iraqi Factories, Aging and Shut, Now Give Hope. *New York Times*, January 18, http://www.nytimes.com/2007/01/18/world/middleeast/18factory.html

Gleick, James. 2000. *Faster: The Acceleration of Just about Everything*. New York: Vintage.

Global Footprint Network. 2008. *Ecological Footprint and Biocapacity, 2006,* http://www.footprintnetwork.org/en/index.php/GFN/page/ecological_footprint_atlas_2008/

Global Humanitarian Forum (GHF). 2009. The Anatomy of a Silent Crisis. *Human Impact Report: Climate Change. Global Humanitarian Forum.* Geneva, http://www.ghf-ge.org/human-impact-report.pdf

Goodenough, Ward. 1963. *Cooperation in Change.* New York: Wiley.

Gossen, Gary H. 1994. Comments on the Zapatista Movement. *Cultural Survival Quarterly* 18:19–21.

Gould, Peter. 1993. *The Slow Plague: A Geography of the AIDS Pandemic.* Cambridge: Blackwell.

Gould, Stephen Jay. 1991. Unenchanted Evening. *Natural History,* September.

Goulet, Denis. 1971. *The Cruel Choice: A New Concept in the Theory of Development.* New York: Atheneum.

Graeber, David. 2009. *Direct Action: An Ethnography.* Edinburgh: AK Press

———2001. *Toward an Anthropological Theory of Value: The False Coin of Our Own Dreams.* New York: Palgrave Macmillan.

———2011. *Debt: The First 5000 Years.* Brooklyn, NY: Melville House

Gray, John. 2003. *Al Qaeda and What It Means to Be Modern.* New York: The New Press.

Greenhouse, Steven. 2000. Foreign Workers at Highest Level in Seven Decades. *New York Times,* September 4.

Greenwald, Glenn. 2009. Top Senate Democrat: Bankers "Own" the U.S. Congress, http://www.salon.com/news/opinion/glenn_greenwald/2009/04/30/ownership

Grim, Ryan. 2009. Dick Durbin: The Banks Own the Place. *Huffington Post.* May 30, http://www.huffingtonpost.com/2009/04/29/dick-durbin-banks-frankly_n_193010.html. See also http://www.youtube.com/watch?v=CZbC_IqWEJY

Guardian-Observer. 2002. Full Text: Bin Laden's "Letter to America," http://observer.guardian.co.uk/worldview/story/0,11581,845725,00.html

Gunaratna, Rohan. 2003. *Inside Al Qaeda: Global Network of Terror.* New York: Berkley Books.

Guttmann, Myron. 1988. *Toward the Modern Economy: Early Industry in Europe, 1500–1800.* New York: Alfred A. Knopf.

Guttmann, Robert. 1994. How *Credit-Money Shapes the Economy: The United States in a Global System.* London: M. E. Sharpe.

Hallsmith, Gwendolyn, and Bernard Lietaer. 2011. *Creating Wealth: Growing Local Economies with Local Currencies.* Philadelphia, PA: New Society Publishers

Halweil, Brian, and Lisa Mastny. 2004. *State of the World, 2004: Special Focus, The Consumer Society.* Worldwatch Institute. New York: W. W. Norton & Company.

Handwerker, W. Penn. 1989. *Women's Power and Social Revolution: Fertility Transition in the West Indies* (Frontiers of Anthropology, volume 2). Newbury Park, CA: Sage.

Hanson, F. Allan. 1993. *Testing, Testing: Social Consequences of the Examined Life.* Berkeley, CA: University of California Press.

Hanson, Gordon H. 2009a. "The Economic Consequences of the International Migration of Labor," *Annual Review of Economics, Annual Reviews* 1(1):179–208, 05.

Hanson, Gordon H. 2009b. *The Economics and Policy of Illegal Immigration in the United States.* Cambridge, MA: National Bureau of Economic Research, http://irps.ucsd.edu/assets/037/11124.pdf

Harbaugh, William, Arik Levinson, and David Molloy Wilson. 2002. Reexamining the Empirical Evidence for an Environmental Kuznets Curve. *The Review of Economics and Statistics* 84:541–551.

Hardin, Garrett, and John Baden. 1977. *Managing the Commons.* New York: W. H. Freeman.

Hardin, Garrett. 1968. Tragedy of the Commons. *Science* 162:1243–1248.

Harding, Susan. 1991. Imagining the Last Days: The Politics of Apocalyptic Language. In *Accounting for Fundamentalisms,* edited by Martin E. Marty and R. Scott Appleby (Fundamentalism Project, volume 4). Chicago, IL: University of Chicago Press.

Harris, Marvin. 1971. *Culture, Man, and Nature.* New York: Crowell.

———. 1987. *The Sacred Cow and the Abominable Pig.* New York: Touchstone.

Harris, Marvin, and Eric B. Ross. 1987a. *Death, Sex, and Fertility. Population Regulation in Preindustrial and Developing Societies.* New York: Columbia University Press.

———. 1987b. *Food and Evolution: Toward a Theory of Human Food Habits.* Philadelphia, PA: Temple University Press.

Harris, Ron. 1989. Children Who Dress for Excess: Today's Youngsters Have Become Fixated with Fashion. The Right Look Isn't Enough—It Also Has to Be Expensive. *Los Angeles Times,* November 12.

Hart, Keith. 2000. *Money in an Unequal World: Keith Hart and His Memory Bank.* New York: Texere.

Hartmann, Thom. 2002. *Unequal Protection: The Rise of Corporate Dominance and the Theft of Human Rights.* New York: Rodale Press.

Hartwick, Elaine, and Richard Peet. 2003. Neoliberalism and Nature: The Case of the WTO. *American Academy of Political and Social Science* 590, November.

Hatton, Timothy J., and Jeffrey G. Williamson. 2008. *Global Migration and the World Economy.* Cambridge, MA: The MIT Press.

Haugerud, Angelique, M. Priscilla Stone, and Peter D. Little (editors). 2000. *Commodities and Globalization: Anthropological Perspectives.* New York: Rowman& Littlefield.

Harvey, David. 2007. A Brief History of Neoliberaism. Oxford University Press.

Henson, Scott. 2005. Grits for Breakfast Blog, June 30, http://gritsforbreakfast.blogspot.com/2005/06/illegal-drugs-14-of-world-ag-exports.html

Herman, Edward S., and Noam Chomsky. 2002. *Manufacturing Consent: The Political Economy of the Mass Media*. New York: Pantheon.

Ho, Karen. 2009. *Liquidated: An Ethnography of Wall Street*. Durham, NC: Duke University Press.

Hobsbawm, Eric J. 1959. *Primitive Rebels: Studies in Archaic Forms of Social Movement in the 19th and 20th Centuries*. New York: Frederick A. Praeger.

———. 1964. *Age of Revolution: Seventeen Eighty-Nine to Eighteen Forty-Eight*. New York: NAL/Dutton.

———. 1975. *The Age of Capital: 1848–1875*. New York: Charles Scribner's Sons.

———. 1990. *Nations and Nationalism Since 1780: Programme, Myth, Reality*. Cambridge: Cambridge University Press.

Hobsbawm, Eric J., and Terence Ranger. 1983. *Inventing Tradition*. Cambridge: Cambridge University Press.

Hodder, Kathryn. 1999. *Annual Survey of Violations of Trade Union Rights*. ICFTU International Confederation of Free Trade Unions, www.icftu.org

Hodges, Michael. 2009. *America's Total Debt Report*, http://grandfather-economic-report.com/debt-nat.htm

Howard, James L. 2007. *U.S. Timber Production, Trade, Consumption and Price Statistics 1965 to 2005*. Research Paper FPL-RP-637. United States Department of Agriculture, http://postcom.org/eco/sls.docs/USFS-US%20Timber%20Prod,%20Trade,%20Consumption.pdf (Checked 03/24/2012).

Howell, Nancy. 1979. *Demography of the Dobe! Kung*. New York: Academic Press.

Hudson, E. H. 1965. Treponematosis and Man's Social Evolution. *American Anthropologist* 76:885–901.

Hudson-Koster, Mickie. 2010, The Making of Mau Mau: The Power of the Oath. A Thesis Submitted in Partial Fulfillment of the Requirements for the Degree, Doctor of Philosophy. Rice University. http://scholarship.rice.edu/bitstream/handle/1911/62115/3421426.PDF?sequence=1

Iannaccone, Laurence R. 1993. The Economics of American Fundamentalists. In *Fundamentalisms and the State: Remaking Polities, Economies, and Militance*, edited by Martin E. Marty and R. Scott Appleby (Fundamentalism Project, volume 3). Chicago, IL: University of Chicago Press.

Ignatiev, Noel. 1995. *How the Irish Became White*. New York: Routledge.

Intergovernmental Panel on Climate Change (IPCC). 2007. *An Assessment on the Intergovernmental Panel on Climate Change*, http://www.ipcc.ch/pdf/assessment-report/ar4/syr/ar4_syr.pdf

International Bank for Reconstruction and Development (IBRD). 1950. *The Basis of a Development Program for Colombia*. Baltimore: Johns Hopkins University Press.

International Confederation of Free Trade Unions. 2003. *Annual Survey of Violations of Trade Union Rights*, www.icftu.org/

International Labor Organization. 2007. Global Employment Trends Brief, http://www.newunionism.net/library/internationalism/ILO%20-%20Global%20Employment%20Trends%20-%202007.pdf

Jackson, Tim. 2009. *Prosperity Without Growth: Economics for a Finite Planet*. London: Earthscan Publications.

Jahan, Roushan. 1995. Men in Seclusion, Women in Public: Rokeya's Dream and Women's Struggles in Bangladesh. In *The Challenge of Local Feminisms: Women's Movements in Global Perspective*, edited by Amrita Basu. Boulder, CO: Westview Press.

Jaimes, Annette M. (editor). 1992. Federal Indian Identification Policy: A Usurpation of Indigenous Sovereignty in North America. In *The State of Native America: Genocide, Colonization, and Resistance*. Boston, MA: South End Press.

James, C. L. R. 1963. *The Black Jacobins: Toussaint l' Ouverture and the San Domingo Revolution*, 2nd ed. New York: Random House.

Johnson, Chalmers. 2004. *The Sorrows of Empire: Militarism, Secrecy, and the End of the Republic*. New York: Henry Holt and Company.

Johnson, Paul E. 1978. *A Shopkeeper's Millennium: Society and Revivals in Rochester*. New York: Hill & Wang.

Jones, Charles. 2002. *Introduction to Economic Growth*. New York: W.W. Norton & Company

Jubilee. 2000. *Jubilee USA Network*, www.j2000usa.org/index.html

Juergensmeyer, Mark. 1993. *The New Cold War? Religious Nationalism Confronts the Secular State*. Berkeley, CA: University of California Press.

———. 1996. The Worldwide Rise of Religious Nationalism. *Journal of International Affairs* 50:1–20.

———. 2000. *Terror in the Mind of God: The Global Rise of Religious Violence*. Berkeley, CA: University of California Press.

Junas, Daniel. 1995. Rise of Citizen Militias: Angry White Guys with Guns. *Covert Action Quarterly* Spring:22–25.

Kanogo, Tabitha. 1987. *Squatters and the Roots of Mau Mau 1905–1963*. Athens: Ohio University Press.

Kanter, Rosabeth Moss. 1972. *Commitment and Community: Communes and Utopias in Sociological Perspective*. Cambridge: Harvard University Press.

Kasser, Tim. 2002. *The High Price of Materialism*. Cambridge, MA:The MIT Press.

Kaye, Jeffrey. 2010. *Moving Millions: How Coyote Capitalism Fuels Global Immigration*. John Wiley and Sons.

Kearney, Michael. 1991. Borders and Boundaries of State and Self at the End of Empire. *Journal of Historical Sociology* 4:58–74.

———. 1996. *Reconceptualizing the Peasantry: Anthropology in Global Perspective*. Boulder, CO: Westview Press.

Kemp, Amanda, Nozizwe Madlala, Asha Moodley, and Elaine Salo. 1995. The Dawn of a New Day: Redefining South African Feminism. In *The Challenge of Local Feminisms: Women's Movements in Global Perspective*, edited by Amrita Basu. Boulder, CO: Westview Press.

Kennedy, Margrit, and Declan Kennedy. 1995. *Interest and Inflation Free Money: Creating an Exchange Medium that*

Works for Everyone and Protects the Earth. Philadelphia, PA: New Society Publishers.

Kennedy, Paul. 1993. *Preparing for the Twenty-first Century.* New York: Random House.

Kenyatta, Jomo. 1962. *Facing Mount Kenya.* New York: Random House.

Kincheloe, Joe L. 1997. McDonald's, Power, and Children: Ronald McDonald (aka Ray Kroc) Does It All for You. In *Kinderculture: The Corporate Construction of Childhood,* edited by Shirley R. Steinberg and Joe L. Kincheloe. Boulder, CO: Westview Press.

Kindleberger, Charles P. 1978. *Manias, Panics and Crashes: A History of Financial Crisis,* 4th ed. John Wiley and Sons.

Klare, Michael 2001. *Resource Wars: The New Landscape of Global Conflict.* New York: Henry Hold & Co.

Klare, Michael T. 2004. *Blood and Oil: The Dangers and Consequences of America's Growing Dependency on Imported Petroleum.* New York: Henry Hold and Company.

Klein, Naomi. 2004. Baghdad Year Zero: Pillaging Iraq in Pursuit of a Neocon Utopia. *Harper's Magazine,* September, http://harpers.org/BaghdadYearZero.html

Kopytoff, Igor. 1988. The Cultural Biography of Things: Commoditization as Process. In *The Social Life of Things: Commodities in Cultural Perspective,* edited by Arjun Appadurai. Cambridge: Cambridge University Press.

Korten David. 1995. *When Corporations Rule the World.* Hartford, CT: Kumarian Press.

———. 1998. *Globalizing Civil Society: Reclaiming Our Right to Power.* New York: Seven Stories Press.

———. 1999. *The Post-Corporate World: Life after Capitalism.* West Hartford, CT: Kumarian Press and San Francisco: Berrett-Koehler Publishers.

Kowinski, William Severini. 1985. *The Malling of America: An Inside Look at the Great Consumer Paradise.* New York: William Morrow.

Kroeber, Alfred L. 1939. *Culture and Natural Areas of Native North America.* University of California Publications in American Archeology and Ethnology, volume 38. Berkeley, CA: University of California Press.

Kroll, Gary, and Richard H. Robbins. 2009. *Worlds in Motion: The Globalization and Environment Reader.* New York: AltaMira Press.

Kropotkin, Peter 2007. *Kropotkin's Revolutionary Pamphlets: A Collection of Writings by Peter Kropotkin,* edited by Roger N. Baldwin. New York: Dover

Kumar, Radha. 1995. From Chipko to Sati: The Contemporary Indian Women's Movement. In *The Challenge of Local Feminisms: Women's Movements in Global Perspective,* edited by Amrita Basu. Boulder, CO: Westview Press.

Kuper, Leo. 1990. The Genocidal State: An Overview. In *State Violence and Ethnicity,* edited by Pierre L. van den Berghe. Boulder, CO: University of Colorado Press.

Kuran, Timur. 1993. Fundamentalisms and the Economy. In *Fundamentalisms and the State: Remaking Polities,*

Economies, and Militance, edited by Martin E. Marty and R. Scott Appleby (Fundamentalism Project, volume 1). Chicago, IL: University of Chicago Press.

LaFeber, Walter. 1999. *Michael Jordan and the New Global Capitalism.* New York: W. W. Norton & Company.

Landes, David S. 1969. *The Unbound Prometheus: Technological Change and Industrial Development in Western Europe from 1750 to the Present.* Cambridge: Cambridge University Press.

———. 1998. *The Wealth and Poverty of Nations: Why Some Are So Rich and Some Are So Poor.* New York: W. W. Norton & Company.

Lappé, Marc. 1994. *Evolutionary Medicine: Rethinking the Origins of Disease.* San Francisco: Sierra Club Books.

Larson, Edward J. 1997. *Summer for the Gods: The Scopes Trial and America's Continuing Debate over Science and Religion.* New York: Basic Books.

Lasch, Christopher. 1977. *Haven in a Heartless World: The Family Besieged.* New York: Basic Books.

Layard, Richard. 2005. *Happiness: Lessons From a New Science.* New York: Penguin Press.

Le Bon, Gustave. [1895] 2002. *The Crowd: A Study of the Popular Mind.* Mineola, NY: Dover Publications.

Leach, William. 1993. *Land of Desire: Merchants, Power, and the Rise of a New American Culture.* New York: Pantheon.

Leacock, Eleanor. 1983. Interpreting the Origins of Gender Inequality: Conceptual and Historical Problems. *Dialectical Anthropology* 7:263–283.

———. 1986. Women, Power, and Authority. In *Visibility and Power: Essays on Women in Society and Development,* edited by Leela Dube, Eleanor Leacock, and Shirley Ardener. Delhi: Oxford University Press.

Lears, T. J. Jackson. 1983. From Salvation to Self-Realization: Advertising and the Therapeutic Roots of the Consumer Culture, 1880–1930. In *The Culture of Consumption: Critical Essays in American History, 1880–1930,* edited by Richard Wrightman Fox and T. J. Jackson Lears. New York: Pantheon.

Lee, Edmund. 2012. Global Ad Spending Rose 6.2% in Fourth Quarter, Nielsen Says. *Bloomberg,* http://www.bloomberg.com/news/2012-04-09/global-ad-spending-rose-6-2-in-fourth-quarter-nielsen-says.html (Checked 7/1/2012)

Levine, Robert. 1997. *A Geography of Time.* New York: Basic Books.

Lewellen, Ted C. 1992. *Political Anthropology: An Introduction,* 2nd ed. Westport, CT: Bergin & Garvey.

Lincoln, Bruce. 1989. *Discourse and the Construction of Society: Comparative Studies of Myth, Ritual, and Classification.* Oxford: Oxford University Press.

Little, Peter D., and Catherine S. Dolan. 2000. What It Means to Be Restructured: Nontraditional Commodities and Structural Adjustment in Sub-Saharan Africa. In *Commodities and Globalization: Anthropological Perspectives,* edited by Angelique Haugerud, M. Priscilla Stone, and Peter D. Little. New York: Rowman & Littlefield.

Livi-Bacci, Massimi. 1992. *A Concise History of World Population.* Cambridge: Blackwell.

Lohr, Steve. 2003. *Discount Nation: Is Walmart Good for America? New York Times*, December 7, http://query.nytimes.com/gst/abstract.html?res=F1071EF839590C748CDDAB0994DB404482

Low, Patrick. 1993. *Trading Free: The GATT and US Trade Policy.* New York: Twentieth Century Fund Press.

Lozano, W.S., V. Pinedo, J.A. Patz. 2006. The Effect of Deforestation on the Human-biting Rate of Anopheles Darlingi, the Primary Vector of Falciparum Malaria in the Peruvian Amazon. *American Journal of Tropical Medicine* 74(1):3–11

Lutjens, Sheryl L. 1994. Remaking the Public Sphere: Women and Revolution in Cuba. In *Women and Revolution in Africa, Asia, and the New World*, edited by Mary Ann Tétreault. Columbia: University of South Carolina Press.

MacMillan, Susan. 2012. New ILRI Study Maps Hotspots of Human-animal Infectious Diseases and Emerging Disease Outbreaks. *International Livestock Research Institute*, http://www.ilri.org/ilrinews/index.php/archives/9172

Maddison, Angus. 2003. *The World Economy: A Millennial Perspective.* Paris: Development Centre of the Organization for Economic Co-operation and Development.

Malthus, Thomas Robert. 1826. *Essay on the Principle of Population.* London: John Murray.

Mamdani, Mahmood. 1972. *The Myth of Population Control: Family, Caste, and Class in an Indian Village.* New York: Monthly Review Press.

———. 2004. *Good Muslim, Bad Muslim: America, the Cold War and the Roots of Terrorism.* New York: Pantheon.

Manning, Patrick. 1990. *Slavery and African Life: Occidental, Oriental, and African Slave Trades.* Cambridge: Cambridge University Press.

Manning, Richard. 2004. The Oil We Eat. *Harper's Magazine*, February, www.harpers.org/TheOilWeEat.html

Market Research Portal. 2006. *Teen Spending to Top $190 billion by 2006*, www.marketresearchworld.net/index.php?option=content&task=view&id=615&Itemid=

Martenson, Chris. 2011. *The Crash Course: The Unsustainable Future of Our Economy, Energy, and Environment.* Hoboken, NJ: John Wiley & Sons

Martin, Jack, and Eric A. Ruark. 2010. The Fiscal Burden of Illegal Immigrants on U.S. Taxpayers. FAIR: Federation for American Immigration Reform, http://www.fairus.org/site/DocServer/USCostStudy_2010.pdf?docID=4921

Marx, Karl, and Frederick Engels. [1848] 1941. *Manifesto of the Communist Party.* New York: International Publishers.

———. 1972. *Ireland and the Irish Question: A Collection of Writings.* New York: International Publishers.

Maurer, Bill. 2005. *Mutual Life, Limited: Islamic Banking, Alternative Currencies, Lateral Reason.* Princeton, NJ: Princeton University Press.

Maybury-Lewis, David. 1997. *Indigenous Peoples, Ethnic Groups, and the State.* Boston, MA: Allyn & Bacon.

McCracken, Grant. 1988. *Culture and Consumption: New Approaches to the Symbolic Character of Consumer Goods and Activities.* Bloomington: Indiana University Press.

McKibben, Bill. 2007. *Deep Economy: The Wealth of Communities and the Durable Future.* New York: Times Books

McNeal, James. 1999. *The Kids' Market: Myths and Realities.* Ithaca, NY: Paramount Market.

McNeil, Donald, Jr. 2000. Drug Companies and the Third World: A Case Study of Neglect. *New York Times*, May 21.

Mead, Margaret. 1961. *New Lives for Old.* New York: New American Library.

Meade, J. E. 1967. Population Explosion, the Standard of Living, and Social Conflict. *The Economic Journal* 77:233–255.

Meggitt, Mervyn. 1962. *Desert People: A Study of the Aalbiri Aborigines of Central Australia.* London: Angus & Robertson.

Merari, Ariel. 1993. Terrorism as a Strategy of Insurgency. *Terrorism and Political Violence* 5:213–251.

Miller, Michael B. 1994. *Bon Marche: The Bourgeoise Culture and the Department Store 1869–1920.* Princeton, NJ: Princeton University Press.

Mintz, Sidney W. 1985. *Sweetness and Power: The Place of Sugar in World History.* New York: Viking.

Mishan, E. J. 1967. *The Costs of Economic Growth.* London: Staples Press

Mooney, James. 1965. *The Ghost-Dance Religion and the Sioux Outbreak of 1890.* Chicago, IL: University of Chicago Press.

Mueller, John, and Mark G. Stewart. 2011. *Terror, Security, and Money: Balancing the Risks, Benefits, and Costs of Homeland Security.* Oxford: Oxford University Press.

Mumford, Stephen D. 1996. *The Life and Death of NSSM: How the Destruction of Political Will Doomed a U.S. Population Policy*, http://www.population-security.org/28-APP2.html

Munson, Henry, Jr. 1988. *Islam and Revolution in the Middle East.* New Haven: Yale University Press.

Nag, Moni (editor). 1975. *Population and Social Organization.* The Hague: Mouton.

Nagengast, Carole. 1994. Violence, Terror, and the Crisis of the State. *Annual Review of Anthropology* 23:109–136.

Nash, George. 1988. *The Life of Herbert Hoover: The Humanitarian (1914–1917).* New York: W. W. Norton & Company.

Nash, June. 1994. Global Integration and Subsistence Insecurity. *American Anthropologist* 96:7–30.

Nash, Manning. 1991. Islamic Resurgence in Malaysia and Indonesia. In *Fundamentalisms Observed*, edited by Martin E. Marty and R. Scott Appleby (Fundamentalism Project, volume 1). Chicago, IL: University of Chicago Press.

National Abortion Federation. 2009. *NAF Violence and Disruption Statistics*, http://www.prochoice.org/pubs_research/publications/downloads/about_abortion/violence_stats.pdf

Nations, James D. 1994. The Ecology of the Zapatista Revolt. *Cultural Survival Quarterly* 18:31–33.

Needleman, Jacob. 1991. *Money and the Meaning of Life.* New York: Doubleday.

Newark Star Ledger. 2011. *Occupy Wall Street Demonstrators Send Message: Where Are the Jobs?* http://blog.nj.com/njv_editorial_page/2011/09/occupy_wall_street_demonstrato.html

Newman, Lucile F. (editor). 1990. *Hunger in History.* Oxford: Basil Blackwell.

Ng, Erica. 2010. China's Ad Spending Hits $120 Bil. *Adweek,* http://www.adweek.com/news/television/chinas-ad-spending-hits-120-bil-101570 (Checked 7/1/2012)

Nigh, Ronald.1995. Animal Agriculture for the Reforestation of Degraded Tropical Rainforests. *Culture and Agriculture* 51–52:2–5.

Noah, Timothy. 2012: *The Great Divergence: America's Growing Inequality Crisis and What We Can Do About It.* New York: Bloomsbury Press

Noriega, Jorge. 1992. American Indian Education in the United States. In *The State of Native America: Genocide, Colonization, and Resistance,* edited by M. Annette Jaimes. Boston, MA: South End Press.

NORML (National Organization for the Reform of Marijuana Laws). 2000. *United States Marijuana Arrests,* http://norml.org/index.cfm?Group_ID=7042

North, Douglass, and Robert Paul Thomas. 1976. *The Rise of the Western World: A New Economic History.* Cambridge: Cambridge University Press.

Nye, Joseph. 2003. *The Paradox of American Power: Why the World's Only Superpower Can't Go It Alone.* Oxford: Oxford University Press.

O'Brien, Jay. 1994. Differential High Fertility and Demographic Transitions: Peripheral Capitalism in Sudan. In *African Population and Capitalism: Historical Perspectives,* edited by Dennis Cordell and Joel W. Gregor. Madison, WI: University of Wisconsin Press.

Oduol, Wilhelmina, and Wanjiku Mukabi Kabira. 1995. The Mother of Warriors and Her Daughters: The Women's Movement in Kenya. In *The Challenge of Local Feminisms: Women's Movements in Global Perspective,* edited by Amrita Basu. Boulder, CO: Westview Press.

Office of National Drug Control Policy. 2007. *Drug Facts: Marijuana,* www.whitehousedrugpolicy.gov/drugfact/marijuana/index.html

Ong, Aihwa. 1987. *Spirits of Resistance and Capitalistic Discipline: Factory Women in Malaysia.* Albany: State University of New York Press.

———. 1990. Japanese Factories, Malay Workers: Class and Sexual Metaphors in West Malaysia. In *Power and Difference: Gender in Island Southeast Asia,* edited by Jane Atkinson and S. Errington. Palo Alto, CA: Stanford University Press.

———. 1997. Strategic Sisterhood or Sisters in Solidarity? Questions of Communitarianism and Citizenship in Asia. In *Feminism and Globalization: The Impact of the Global Economy on Women and Feminist Theory,* edited by Alfred C. Aman, Jr. *Indiana Journal of Global Legal Studies,* Spring (special issue).

Open Secrets. n.d. *WalMart Stores,* http://www.opensecrets.org/pacs/lookup2.php?strID=C00093054&cycle=2008

Oreskes, Naomi. 2004. The Scientific Consensus on Climate Change. *Science* 306:1686

Oved, Yaacov. 1988. *Two Hundred Years of American Communes.* New Brunswick, NJ: Transaction.

OWS Writers for the 99%. 2012. *Occupying Wall Street: The Inside Story of an Action that Changed America.*

Paddock, William, and Paul Paddock. 1967. *Famine—1975.* Boston, MA: Little, Brown.

Pagels, Elaine. 1995. *The Origin of Satan.* New York: Vintage Books.

Pape, Robert A. 2003. The Strategic Logic of Suicide Terrorism. *The American Political Science Review* 97:343–361.

Parenti, Christian. 2011. *Tropic of Chaos: Climate Change and the New Geoography of Violence.* Nation Books.

Pasha, Shaheen. 2011. Western Debt Spurs Growth of Islamic Finance. Reuters News Service, November 30, http://www.reuters.com/article/2011/11/30/us-finance-islamic-idUSTRE7AT1DS20111130

Pera, Lee, and Deborah McLaren. 1999. *Globalization, Tourism, and Indigenous Peoples: What You Should Know about the World's Largest "Industry."* Rethinking Tourism Project, www.planeta.com/ecotravel/resources/rtp/rtp.html.

Perryman Group. 2008. *An Essential Resource: An Analysis of the Economic Impact of Undocumented Workers on Business Activity in the US with Estimated Effects by State and Industry.* Perryman Group, http://americansforimmigrationreform.com/files/Impact_of_the_Undocumented_Workforce.pdf

Pimentel, David, and Marcia Pimentel. 1979. *Food, Energy and Society.* New York: Wiley.

Pimentel, David, O. Bailey, P. Kim, E. Mullaney, J. Calabrese, L. Walman, E. Nelson, and X. Yao. 1999. *Will Limits of the Earth's Resources Control Human Numbers? Environment, Development, and Sustainability* 1:19–39.

Platt, Anne E. 1996. *Infecting Ourselves: How Environmental and Social Disruption Trigger Disease.* Washington, DC: Worldwatch Institute.

Polanyi, Karl. [1944] 1957. *The Great Transformation.* Boston, MA: Beacon Press.

Polgar, Steven. 1972. Population History and Population Policies from an Anthropological Perspective. *Current Anthropology* 13:203–211.

Polgar, Steven. 1975. Birth Planning: Between Neglect and Coercion. In *Population and Social Organization,* edited by Moni Nag. The Hague: Mouton.

Pollan, Michael. 2002. Power Steer. *New York Times Magazine,* March 31.

Population Reference Bureau. 2009. *World Population Data Sheet,* http://www.prb.org/pdf09/09wpds_eng.pdf

Posey, Darrell A. 1996. Protecting Indigenous Peoples' Rights to Biodiversity. *Environment* 38:6–13.

Power, Samantha. 2002. *"A Problem from Hell": America and the Age of Genocide*. New York: Perennial Books.

Presley, Cora Ann. 1992. *Kikuyu Women, the Mau Mau Rebellion, and Social Change in Kenya*. Boulder, CO: Westview Press.

Preston, Julia. 1998. Feuding Villages Bring Mexican Region to Brink of War. *New York Times*, February 2, www.nytimes.com.

Putnam, Robert D. 1996. The Strange Disappearance of Civic America. *The American Prospect* no. 24, Winter.

———. 2000. *Bowling Alone: The Collapse and Revival of American Community*. New York: Simon & Shuster.

Ramos, Alcida Rita. 1995. *Sanumá Memories: Yanomami Ethnography in Times of Crisis*. Madison, WI: University of Wisconsin Press.

Reed, Richard. 1997. *Forest Dwellers, Forest Protectors: Indigenous Models for International Development*. Boston, MA: Allyn & Bacon.

Regan, Tom. 2002. When Contemplating War, Beware of Babies in Incubators. *Christian Science Monitor*, September 6.

Reinhart, Carmen M., and Kenneth S. Rogoff. 2009. *This Time is Different: Eight Centuries of Financial Folly*. Princeton, NJ: Princeton University Press.

Restad, Penne L. 1995. *Christmas in America: A History*. Oxford: Oxford University Press.

Rich, Bruce. 1994. *Mortgaging the Earth*. Boston, MA: Beacon Press.

Rideout, Victoria J., Donald F. Roberts and Ulla G. Foehr. 2010. Generation M: Media in the Lives of 8-18 Year-Olds. Washington, DC: The Kaiser Family Foundation, http://www.kff.org/entmedia/upload/8010.pdf (Checked 7/1/2012)

Rifkin, Jeremy. 1992. *Beyond Beef: The Rise and Fall of the Cattle Culture*. New York: Dutton.

Robbins, Jim. 2012. The Ecology of Disease. *New York Times*, July 14, http://www.nytimes.com/2012/07/15/sunday-review/the-ecology-of-disease.html?pagewanted=all

Robbins, Richard. 2005. Technology in History: United States and Western Europe. In *Science, Technology, and Society: An Encyclopedia*, edited by Sal Restivo. Oxford: Oxford University Press.

———. 2008. *Cultural Anthropology: A Problem-Based Approach*, 5th ed. Belmont, CA: Wadsworth Publishing.

———. 2009. William Jennings Bryan and the Trial of John T. Scopes. In *Darwin and the Bible: The Cultural Confrontation*, edited by Richard Robbins and Mark Cohen. Boston, MA: Penguin Academics.

———. 2012. Neoliberalism, Race and Racism. In *Encyclopedia of Race and Racism*, 2nd ed., edited by Patrick Mason. Cengage Publishers.

Robbins, Richard, and Mark Cohen. 2009. *Darwin and the Bible: The Cultural Confrontation*. Boston, MA: Penguin Academics.

Romero, Simon. 2012. Slum Dwellers Are Defying Brazil's Grand Design for Olympics. *New York Times*, March 4, http://www.nytimes.com/2012/03/05/world/americas/brazil-faces-obstacles-in-preparations-for-rio-olympics.html?pagewanted=all

Rosenberg, Matt. 2012. *Maquiladoras in Mexico*. About.com, http://geography.about.com/od/urbaneconomicgeography/a/maquiladoras.htm

Rosenberg, Nathan. 1982. *Inside the Black Box: Technology and Economics*. Cambridge: Cambridge University Press.

Ross, Eric. 1980. *Beyond the Myths of Culture: Essays in Cultural Materialism*. New York: Academic Press.

Rowbotham, Michael. 1998. *The Grip of Death: A Study of Modern Money, Debt Slavery and Destructive Economics*. Charlbury, Oxfordshire: Jon Carpenter.

Roysdon, Keith. 2006. Shoppers and Experts Say This Season Will See Big Money Spent on Gifts. *The Star Press*, www.thestarpress.com/apps/pbcs.dll/article?AID=/20061112/NEWS01/611120360

Rugh, Andrea B. 1993. Reshaping Personal Relations in Egypt. In *Fundamentalisms and Society: Reclaiming the Sciences, the Family, and Education*, edited by Martin E. Marty and R. Scott Appleby (Fundamentalism Project, volume 2). Chicago, IL: University of Chicago Press.

Rummel, R. J. 1994. *Death by Government*. New Brunswick, NJ: Transaction.

Ruskin, Gary. 1999. Why They Whine: How Corporations Prey on Our Children. *Mothering Magazine*, www.mothering.com/SpecialArticles/Issue97/whine.htm

Ryan, John C., and Alan Thein Durning. 1997. *Stuff: The Secret Lives of Everyday Things*. NEW Report No. 4, January. Seattle, WA: Northwest Environmental Watch.

Sachedina, Abdulaziz A. 1991. Activist Shi'ism in Iran, Iraq, and Lebanon. In *Fundamentalisms Observed*, edited by Martin E. Marty and R. Scott Appleby (Fundamentalism Project, volume 1). Chicago, IL: University of Chicago Press.

Sachs, Wolfgang. 1999. *Planet Dialectics: Explorations in Environment and Development*. New York: Zed Books.

Sacks, Karen. 1979. *Sisters and Wives: The Past and Future of Sexual Equality*. Westport, CT: Greenwood.

Sale, Kirkpatrick. 1991. *The Conquest of Paradise: Christopher Columbus and the Columbian Legacy*. New York: Alfred A. Knopf.

Sanderson, Stephen K. 1995. *Social Transformation: A General Theory of Historical Development*. Cambridge: Blackwell.

Scheper-Hughes, Nancy. 1992. *Death Without Weeping: The Violence of Everyday Life in Brazil*. Berkeley, CA: University of California Press.

Schlosser, Eric. 2003. *Reefer Madness: Sex, Drugs, and Cheap Labor in the American Black Market*. Boston, MA: Houghton Mifflin Company.

Schmidt, Leigh Eric. 1995. *Consumer Rites: The Buying and Selling of American Holidays*. Princeton, NJ: Princeton University Press.

Schneider, Jane, and Peter Schneider. 2002. The Mafia and al-Qaeda: Violent and Secrctive Organizations in Comparative and Historical Perspective. *American Anthropologist* 104:776–782.

Schneider, Jane. 1989. Rumpelstilskin's Bargain: Folklore and the Merchant Capitalist Intensification of Linen Manufacture in Early Modern Europe. In *Cloth and Human Experience*, edited by Annette B. Weiner and Jane Schneider. Washington, DC: Smithsonian Institute Press.

Schor, Juliet. 1999. *The Overspent American: Why We Want What We Don't Need.* New York: Harper Perennial.

Schusky, Ernest L. 1989. *Culture and Agriculture: An Ecological Introduction to Traditional and Modern Farming Systems.* New York: Bergin & Garvey.

Scott, James C. 1985. *Weapons of the Weak: Everyday Forms of Peasant Resistance.* New Haven: Yale University Press.

———. 1998. *Seeing Like a State: How Human Schemes to Improve the Human Condition Have Failed.* New Haven and London: Yale University Press.

Scully, Gerald W. 1995. *Multiculturalism and Economic Growth.* National Study for Policy Analysis, Policy Report Number 196, http://www.heartland.org/policybot/results/17237/Multiculturalism_and_Economic_Growth.html

Sen, Amartya. 1990. Food Entitlements and Economic Chains. In *Hunger in History*, edited by Lucile F. Newman. Oxford: Basil Blackwell.

Service, Elman R. 1975. *Origins of the State and Civilization: The Process of Cultural Evolution.* New York: W. W. Norton & Company.

Shalom, Stephen R. 1996. The Rwanda Genocide: The Nightmare That Happcncd. *Z Magazine*, April, www.lbbs.org/zmag/article/april96shalom.htm

Sherman, Irwin W. 2006. *The Power of Plagues.* New York: AMS Press.

Shiva, Vandana. 2000. Poverty and Globalization. *BBC Reith Lectures,* http://news.bbc.co.uk/hi/english/static/events/reith_2000/lecture5.stm

Siegfried, André. 1928. The Gulf Between. *The Atlantic Monthly*, March, pp. 289–296.

Silverblatt, Irene. 1988. Women in States. *Annual Review of Anthropology* 17:427–460.

Silverstein, Ken, and Alexander Cockburn. 1995. Major U.S. Bank Urges Zapatista Wipe-Out: "A Litmus Test for Mexico's Stability." *Counterpunch* 2(3), February 1. http://www.unz.org/Pub/Counterpunch-1995feb01-00001?View=PDFPages

Sinclair, Upton. [1906] 1971. *The Jungle.* Cambridge: R. Bentley.

Sisci, Francesco. 2002. Risky Business: Exporting the American Dream. *Asia Times*, March 15.

Skaggs, Jimmy M. 1976. *Prime Cut.* College Station, TX: Texas A&M University Press.

Skidelsky, Robert. 2009. *Keynes: The Return of the Master.* New York: Public Affairs

Skocpol, Theda. 2003. *Diminished Democracy: From Membership to Management in American Civic Life.* Norman, OK: University of Oklahoma Press.

Sluka, Jeffery A. (editor). 2000. *Death Squad: The Anthropology of State Terror.* Philadelphia, PA: University of Pennsylvania Press.

Smith, Adam. 1776 [1994]. *The Wealth of Nations*, edited by Edwin Cannan. New York: Modern Library.

Smith, Charles D. 2000. *Palestine and the Arab-Israeli Conflict.* New York: St. Martin's Press.

Smith, Dan, and Janani Vivekananda. 2007. *A Climate of Conflict: The Links Between Climate Change, Peace and War.* London: International Alert Publication.

Snowdon, Christopher. 2010. *The Spirit Level Delusion.* London: Democracy Institute.

Speth, James Gustave. 2008. *The Bridge at the End of the World: Capitalism, the Environment and Crossing from Crisis to Sustainability.* New Haven: Yale University Press.

Steel, Billy. 2006. Billy's Money Laundering Information, www.laundryman.u-net.com/page2_wisml.html

Steele, Jonathan. 2003. A War That Can Never Be Won. *The Guardian*, November 22.

Stern, Jessica. 2003. *Terror in the Name of God: Why Religious Militants Kill.* Ncw York: HarperCollins.

Stiffarm, Lenore A., and Phil Lane, Jr. 1992. The Demography of Native North America: A Question of American Indian Survival. In *The State of Native America: Genocide, Colonialism, and Resistance*, edited by Anncttc Jaimes. Boston, MA: South End Press.

Stone, Lawrence. 1976. *The Family, Sex, and Marriage in England 1500–1800.* New York: Harper & Row.

Strauss, Samuel. 1924. Things are in the Saddle. *The Atlantic Monthly*, November, 577–588.

———. 1927. Rich Men and Key Men. *The Atlantic Monthly*, December, 721–729.

Sutherland, Daniel. 1989. *The Expansion of Everyday Life: 1860–1876.* New York: Harper & Row.

Tambiah, Stanley J. 1996. *Leveling Crowds: Ethnonationalistic Conflicts and Collective Violence in South Asia.* Berkclcy, CA: University of California Press.

Tardieu, Vincent. 1999. The Economics of Disease Remedies. *Le Monde Diplomatique*, September.

Taussig, Michael. 1977. The Genesis of Capitalism amongst a South American Peasantry: Devil's Labor and the Baptism of Money. *Comparative Studies in Society and History* 19:130–155.

———. 1987. *Shamanism, Colonialism, and the Wild Man: A Study in Terror and Healing.* Chicago, IL: University of Chicago Press.

Tétreault, Mary Ann (editor). 1994. Women and Revolution: A Framework for Analysis. In *Women and Revolution in Africa, Asia, and the New World.* Columbia: University of South Carolina Press.

Tett, Gillian. 2009. *Fool's Gold: How the Bold Dream of a Small Tribe at J.P. Morgan was Corrupted by Wall Street Greed and Unleashed a Catastrophe.* New York: Free Press.

Thomas, Landon, Jr. 2009. Dubai Debt Woes Raise Fear of Wider Problem. *New York Times*, November 28, http://www.nytimes.com/2009/11/28/business/global/28dubai.html

Thompson, E. P. 1967. Time, Work-Discipline and Industrial Capitalism. *Past and Present* 38:56–97.

Thoreau, Henry David. [1854] 1957. *Walden*. Boston, MA: Houghton Mifflin.

Thornton, John. 1992. *Africa and Africans in the Making of the Atlantic World, 1400–1680*. Cambridge: Cambridge University Press.

Trocki, Carl A. 1999. *Opium, Empire and the Global Political Economy*. London: Routledge.

Tsing, Anna Lowenhaupt. 1993. *In the Realm of the Diamond Queen: Marginality in an Out-of-the-Way Place*. Princeton, NJ: Princeton University Press.

Tucker, Catherine M. 2011. *Coffee Culture: Local Experiences, Global Connections*. New York: Routledge.

Turkle, Sherry. 2011. Alone Together: Why We Expect More from our Technology and Less from Each Other. New York: Basic Books.

Twitchell, James B. 2002. *Living It Up: Our Love Affair with Luxury*. New York: Colombia University Press.

———. 2004. A (Mild) Defense of Luxury. In *Talking Points on Global Issues: A Reader*, edited by Richard H. Robbins. Boston, MA: Allyn and Bacon Publishers, pp. 9–17.

Tynan, Dan. 2010. Are Custom Ads Getting Just a Bit Too Personal? *PC World*, http://www.pcworld.com/article/209348/are_custom_ads_getting_just_a_bit_too_personal.html (Checked 7/1/2012)

U.S. Bureau of the Census. 1990. *Statistical Abstract of the United States*, 110th ed. Washington, DC: U.S. Government Printing Office.

———. 1993. *Statistical Abstract of the United States*, 113th ed. Washington, DC: U.S. Government Printing Office.

———. 1994. *Statistical Abstract of the United States*, 114th ed. Washington, DC: U.S. Government Printing Office.

———. 2000. *Agricultural Fact Book 2000*. Office of Communications, U.S. Department of Agriculture, www.usda.gov/news/pubs/fbook00/factbook2000.pdf

UN-HABITAT. 2003. *The Challenge of Slum: Global Report on Human Settlements 2003,* London: Earthscan Publications, http://www.unhabitat.org/downloads/docs/GRHS.2003.0.pdf

UNAIDS. 2009. *AIDS Epidemic Update*, http://www.unaids.org/en/dataanalysis/knowyourepidemic/epidemiologypublications/2009aidsepidemicupdate/

United Nations. 2004. *World Population to 2300*. United Nations Department of Economic and Social Affairs, Population Division, http://www.un.org/esa/population/publications/longrange2/WorldPop2300final.pdf

United Nations. 2005. *World Drug Report,* http://www.unodc.org/unodc/en/data-and-analysis/WDR-2005.html

———. 2009. *Human Development, Report 2009*. Overcoming Barriers:

United Nations Population Fund (UNPF). 2000. *The State of the World's Population, 2000: Lives Together, Worlds Apart: Men and Women in a Time of Change*, www.unfpa.org/swp/swpmain.htm

UNODC. 2006. *World Drug Report*, http://www.unodc.org/unodc/en/data-and-analysis/WDR-2006.html

USDA. 2009. *Expenditures on Children by Families, 2008*. Miscellaneous Publication Number 1528–2008, http://www.cnpp.usda.gov/Publications/CRC/crc2008.pdf

van den Berghe, Pierre. 1992. The Modern State: Nation-Builder or Nation-Killer? *International Journal of Group Tensions* 22:191–208.

Vaughn, Megan. 1987. *The Story of an African Famine: Gender and Famine in Twentieth-Century Malawi*. Cambridge: Cambridge University Press.

Wackernagel, Mathis, and William E. Rees. 1996. *Our Ecological Footprint: Reducing Human Impact on the Earth*. Gabriola Island, BC: New Society.

Wagar, W. Warren. 1991. *The Next Three Futures: Paradigms of Things to Come*. New York: Greenwood Press.

Waits, William. 1992. *The Modern Christmas in America: A Cultural History of Gift-Giving*. New York: New York University Press.

Wallace, Anthony F. C. 1966. *Religion: An Anthropological View*. New York: Random House.

———. 1987. *St. Clair: A Nineteenth-Century Coal Town's Experience with a Disaster Prone Industry*. New York: Alfred A. Knopf.

Wallace, Ernest, and E. Adamson Hoebel. 1952. *The Comanches: Lords of the South Plains*. Norman, OK: University of Oklahoma Press.

Wallace, Mike. 1985. Mickey Mouse History: Portraying the Past at Disney World. *Radical History Review* 32:35–57.

Wallerstein, Immanuel. 1989. *The Modern World-System III: The Second Era of Great Expansion of the Capitalist World-Economy, 1730–1840s*. New York: Academic Press.

———. 1990. Antisystemic Movements: History and Dilemmas. In *Transforming the Revolution: Social Movements and the World-System*, edited by Samir Amin, Girovanni Arrighi, Andre Gunder Frank, and Immanuel Wallerstein. New York: Monthly Press.

———. 1997. Ecology and Capitalist Costs of Production: No Exit. Keynote Address at PEWS XXI, *The Global Environment and the World-System*, University of California, Santa Cruz, April 3–5, http://fbc.binghamton.edu/iwecol.htm

Wallis, Jim. 1984. *Agenda for Biblical People*. San Francisco: Harper San Francisco.

Ward, Martha C. 1996. *A World Full of Women*. Boston, MA: Allyn & Bacon.

Warner, Jessica. 2002. *Craze: Gin and Debauchery in an Age of Reason*. New York: Four Walls Eight Windows.

Watson, James L. 2000. China's Big Mac Attack. *Foreign Affairs*, May/June 79(3): 120–134.

Weatherford, Jack. 1988. *Indian Givers: How the Indians of the Americas Transformed the World.* New York: Fawcett Columbine.

Weber, Eugen. 1976. *Peasants into Frenchmen: The Modernization of Rural France, 1870–1914.* Stanford, CA: Stanford University Press.

Weber, Max. 1947. *The Theory of Social and Economic Organization.* Translated by A. M. Henderson and Talcott Parsons, edited by Talcott Parsons. Glencoe, IL: The Free Press.

———. 1958. *The Protestant Ethic and the Spirit of Capitalism.* Translated by Talcott Parsons. New York: Scribner.

Weinberg, Steven. 1999. No to Cosmic Design. Presentation at the Cosmic Questions Conference, April 15, unpublished text.

Weisbrot, Mark, Robert Naiman, and Joyce Kim. 2000. *The Emperor Has No Growth: Declining Economic Growth Rates in the Era of Globalization.* Center for Economic and Policy Research, Briefing Paper, www.cepr.net/images/IMF/the_emperor_has_no_growth.htm

White House Conference on Child Health and Protection. 1931. *The Home and the Child: Housing, Furnishing, Management, Income, and Clothing.* New York: Arno Press.

Wilhite, Harold. 2008. *Consumption and the Transformation of Everyday Life: A View from South India.* New York: Palgrave Macmillan.

Wilkinson, Richard G. 1996. *Unhealthy Societies: The Afflictions of Inequality.* London: Routledge.

———. 2005. *The Impact of Inequality: How to Make Sick Societies Healthier.* New York: The New Press.

Wilkinson, Richard, and Kate Pickett. 2009. *The Spirit Level: Why Equality is Better for Everyone.* New York: Bloombury Press.

Williams, Joan C. and Heather Boushey. 2010. *The Three Faces of Work-Family Conflict: The Poor, the Professionals, and the Missing Middle,* http://www.americanprogress.org/issues/2010/01/three_faces_report.html

Williams, Jonathan (editor). 1997. *Money: A History.* New York: St. Martins Press.

Willis, Paul. [1977] 1981. *Learning to Labor: How Working Class Kids Get Working Class Jobs.* New York: Columbia University Press.

Wilson, Edmund. [1931] 1961. *The Shores of Light ("An Appeal to Progressives").* New York: Vintage Books.

Wittfogel, Karl A. 1957. *Oriental Despotism.* New Haven: Yale University Press.

Wolf, Amy. 2011. *Campaign Spending's Clear Winners: Corporations,* http://news.vanderbilt.edu/2011/03/campaign-spending-winner/

Wolf, Eric. 1967. *Peasants.* Engelwood Cliffs, NJ: Prentice-Hall.

———. 1969. *Peasant Wars of the Twentieth Century.* New York: Harper & Row.

———. 1982. *Europe and the People without History.* Berkeley, CA: University of California Press.

Wolff, Michael, Peter Rutten, and Albert Bayers III (editors). 1992. *Where We Stand.* New York: Bantam Books.

Wolff, Richard. 2010. *Capitalism Hits the Fan: The Global Economic Meltdown and What to Do About It.* Ithaca, NY: Olive Branch Press.

Woolf, Virginia. 1950. *The Captain's Death Bed and Other Essays.* New York: Harcourt.

World Bank. 2009. World Development Indicators—Last Updated, November 11, http://datafinder.worldbank.org/life-expectancy-at-birth

The World Commission on Environment and Development. 1987. *Our Common Future.* Oxford: Oxford University Press.

———. 2002. *The Tobacco Atlas.* Judith Mackay and Michael Eriksen, http://www.who int/tobacco/media/en/title.pdf

Worsley, Peter. 1968. *The Trumpets Shall Sound: A Study of "Cargo" Cults in Melanesia,* 2nd ed. New York: Schocken Books.

York, Geoffrey. 1999. A Deadly Strain of TB Races Toward the West. *Toronto Globe and Mail,* March 24.

Zakaria, Fareed. 2003. *The Future of Freedom. Illiberal Democracy at Home and Abroad.* New York: W. W. Norton & Company.

Zogby. 2006. U.S. Troops in Iraq: 72% Say End War in 2006, February 28, http://www.informationclearinghouse.info/article12103.htm

Zollo, Peter. 1999. *Wise Up to Teens: Insights into Marketing and Advertising to Teenagers,* 2nd ed. Ithaca, NY: New Strategist Publications.

NAME INDEX

PLACE AND CULTURE INDEX

SUBJECT INDEX